## THE ACTA AND THE PLURILATERAL ENFORCEMENT AGENDA

The Anti-Counterfeiting Trade Agreement (ACTA) is the most important effort undertaken to lay down a plurilateral legal framework for the enforcement of intellectual property rights. With the view to learn more about the origins of this treaty, the process leading to its conclusion and its implications for lawmaking in this field, *The ACTA and the Plurilateral Enforcement Agenda: Genesis and Aftermath* analyses in great depth both the context and the content of the agreements. In order to attain this objective, a large and diverse group of experts – renowned scholars, policy makers and civil society actors – who represent different perspectives on the necessary balance between intellectual property enforcement and other economic and social interests have been gathered together. This book is the most comprehensive analysis of ACTA, and of its relation with ongoing initiatives to improve enforcement of intellectual property and norms pertaining to a range of international legal regimes, conducted so far.

Pedro Roffe is Senior Associate at the International Centre for Trade and Sustainable Development, where he contributes to the work of the Programme on Technology, Innovation and Intellectual Property and Development. He often advises governments, international organizations and private entities. In his work he has paid particular attention to international negotiations and has advised governments on strategies and policies on international aspects of transfer of technology, intellectual property and foreign direct investment. In his various capacities, he has published articles and books and has been responsible for a number of collective publications.

Xavier Seuba is Senior Research Associate and Lecturer at Centre d'Études Internationales de la Propriété Intellectuelle at the University of Strasbourg and at Pompeu Fabra University, Barcelona. He has advised governments and international organizations in the context of trade negotiations and the adoption of policies and laws relating to intellectual property and pharmaceutical products. The books, articles and papers that he has authored, coordinated or edited deal with a range of topics falling within the areas of public international law and intellectual property law.

# The ACTA and the Plurilateral Enforcement Agenda

## GENESIS AND AFTERMATH

Edited by

**PEDRO ROFFE**
International Centre for Trade and Sustainable Development

**XAVIER SEUBA**
Centre d' Études Internationales de la Propriété Intellectuelle

CAMBRIDGE
UNIVERSITY PRESS

**CAMBRIDGE**
**UNIVERSITY PRESS**

32 Avenue of the Americas, New York NY 10013-2473, USA

Cambridge University Press is part of the University of Cambridge.

It furthers the University's mission by disseminating knowledge in the pursuit of education, learning and research at the highest international levels of excellence.

www.cambridge.org
Information on this title: www.cambridge.org/9781107070127



First published 2015

*A catalogue record for this publication is available from the British Library*

*Library of Congress Cataloguing in Publication data*
The ACTA and the plurilateral enforcement agenda : genesis and aftermath / edited by Pedro Roffe, International Centre for Trade and Sustainable Development; Xavier Seuba, Université de Strasbourg.
pages cm
Includes bibliographical references and index.
ISBN 978-1-107-07012-7 (hardback)
1. Anti-Counterfeiting Trade Agreement (2011 October 1) 2. Product counterfeiting--Law and legislation. 3. Industrial property (International law) I. Roffe, Pedro, editor. II. Seuba, Xavier, 1977– editor.
K1577.5.A38A28 2014
345′.02668–dc23 2014016490

ISBN 978-1-107-07012-7 Hardback
ISBN 978-1-107-67862-0 Paperback

# Contents

*List of Contributors* — *page* ix

*Foreword* — xiii
*by Ricardo Meléndez-Ortiz*

*Acknowledgments* — xix

*Acronyms* — xxi

**Introduction: ACTA and the International Debate on Intellectual Property Enforcement** — 1
*Pedro Roffe and Xavier Seuba*

PART I. THE FINAL ACT: ITS MAIN FEATURES AND CONTENTS

1. **An Overview of the Agreement: Contents and Features** — 31
*Frederick M. Abbott*

2. **ACTA Initial Provisions and General Definitions** — 46
*Xavier Seuba*

3. **ACTA General Obligations with Respect to Enforcement** — 66
*Xavier Seuba*

4. **Provisions on Civil Enforcement – Section 2 of ACTA** — 80
*Anselm Kamperman Sanders*

5. **Legal Framework for Enforcement: Border Measures** — 88
*Henning Grosse Ruse-Khan*

6. ACTA and Beyond: Towards a Differentiated Approach to Criminal Enforcement of Intellectual Property Rights at the Global Level 100
*Christophe Geiger*

7. ACTA's Digital Chapter: Remaining Concerns and What Can Be Done 115
*Rita Matulionyte*

8. The ACTA Committee 143
*Peter K. Yu*

PART II. DOMESTIC LEGISLATIVE CHALLENGES

9. ACTA's Constitutional Problem in the United States 157
*Sean Flynn*

10. Trick or Treaty? The Australian Debate over the Anti-Counterfeiting Trade Agreement 169
*Matthew Rimmer*

11. A Brazilian Perspective: *Res Inter Alios Acta* 202
*Denis Borges Barbosa*

12. Lessons to Be Drawn from the ACTA Process: An African Perspective 211
*Andrew Rens*

PART III. IMPACT ON RELATED PROCESSES

13. Three Steps Taken toward a Reinterpreted Three-Step Test: The Impact of ACTA and SOPA on TPP 225
*Jonathan Band*

14. ACTA and the Future of Access to Knowledge in the Digital Environment: US Enforcement Trends as a Global Predictor 236
*Annemarie Bridy*

15. ACTA, East African Enforcement Legislation and Generic Medicines: A Comparison 244
*Christoph Spennemann*

16. The EU and Its IP Policies: ACTA and Third Countries 259
*Anselm Kamperman Sanders*

PART IV. VIEWS FROM STAKEHOLDERS: LESSONS

17. Lessons Learned from the ACTA Process: An Industry Perspective 273
*Candice Li*

18. Lessons Learned from the ACTA Process: The View of Creators 281
*Adriana Moscoso del Prado*

19. ACTA, a View from the Eye of the Storm 291
*Marietje Schaake*

20. ACTA, the EU, and Economic, Social, and Cultural Rights in the Digital Environment 299
*Ante Wessels*

PART V. WHAT LIES AHEAD ACTA

21. Assessing the Implications of ACTA for the European Union: Legitimate Aim but Wrong Means 313
*Christophe Geiger*

22. ACTA: Anatomy of a Failed Agreement 329
*Bryan Mercurio*

23. What Was Left Out of ACTA 338
*Kimberlee Weatherall*

24. Slaying the ACTA Myths 345
*Michael Geist*

25. Developing Countries and the Contestation of ACTA at the TRIPS Council 357
*Ahmed Abdel-Latif*

26. ACTA: What Lessons for Future Plurilateral Trade Agreements? 376
*Ricardo Meléndez-Ortiz and Ahmed Abdel-Latif*

*Annex I: Anti-Counterfeiting Trade Agreement* 391

*References* 415

*Index* 441

# Contributors

**Frederick M. Abbott** is Edward Ball Eminent Scholar Professor of International Law, Florida State University College of Law.

**Ahmed Abdel-Latif** is Senior Programme Manager for Innovation, Technology and Intellectual Property at the International Centre for Trade and Sustainable Development.

**Jonathan Band** established his law firm, policybandwidth, in 2005, which focuses on copyright policy matters. He is also an adjunct professor at the Georgetown University Law Center.

**Denis Borges Barbosa,** LLB (UERJ), LLM in Business Law (UGF), LLM (Columbia U.), JSD in International Law (UERJ), is Permanent Professor of the master and doctoral programs of the Institute of Economy of the Federal University of Rio de Janeiro, the Intellectual Property and Innovation Academy of the Brazilian Patent and Trademark Office and the Graduate Program on Intellectual Property of the Catholic University of Rio de Janeiro.

**Annemarie Bridy**, JD, PhD, is Associate Professor of Law at the University of Idaho College of Law.

**Sean Flynn** teaches courses on the intersection of intellectual property, trade law and human rights and is the Associate Director of the Program on Information Justice and Intellectual Property at the American University Washington College of Law.

**Christophe Geiger** is Associate Professor, Director General and Director of the Research Department of the Centre for International Intellectual Property Studies at the University of Strasbourg (France).

**Michael Geist** is a law professor at the University of Ottawa where he holds the Canada Research Chair in Internet and E-commerce Law.

**Henning Grosse Ruse-Khan** is Senior Research Fellow at the Max Planck Institute for Intellectual Property and Competition Law and Associate Fellow at the Centre for International Sustainable Development Law (McGill University, Montreal).

**Anselm Kamperman Sanders** is Professor of Intellectual Property Law at Maastricht University.

**Candice Li** is the External Relations Manager, Anticounterfeiting, for the International Trademark Association.

**Rita Matulionyte**, Dr. iur. (Munich and Freiburg), LLM. IP (Munich), is Lecturer at Newcastle Law School.

**Ricardo Meléndez-Ortiz** is the cofounder and Chief Executive of the International Centre for Trade and Sustainable Development.

**Bryan Mercurio** is Professor of Law and Associate Dean (Research) at the Chinese University of Hong Kong.

**Adriana Moscoso del Prado** is a lawyer, specializing in copyright. She is also a legal adviser at the General Society of Authors and Composers in Spain and General Secretary of Instituto de Derecho de Autor.

**Andrew Rens** is a Senior Lecturing Fellow at Duke University Law School where he is also an SJD candidate.

**Matthew Rimmer**, BA/LLB ANU, Phd UNSW, is an Australian Research Council Future Fellow, an associate professor at the Australian National University College of Law and an associate director of the Australian Centre for Intellectual Property in Agriculture.

**Pedro Roffe** is Senior Associate, International Centre for Trade and Sustainable Development, where he contributes to the work of the Programme on Technology, Innovation and Intellectual Property and Development.

**Marietje Schaake** is a Member of the European Parliament with the Alliance of Liberals and Democrats for Europe.

**Xavier Seuba** is Senior Research Associate and Lecturer at Centre d'Études Internationales de la Propriété Intellectuelle, Université de Strasbourg.

**Christoph Spennemann**, LLM, works as Legal Expert in the Intellectual Property Unit of the United Nations Conference on Trade and Development.

**Kimberlee Weatherall** is an Associate Professor of intellectual property law at the Sydney Law School, University of Sydney.

**Ante Wessels** is an analyst with the Foundation for a Free Information Infrastructure and the Vrijschrift Foundation.

**Peter K. Yu** holds the Kern Family Chair in Intellectual Property Law and is the founding director of the Intellectual Property Law Center at Drake University Law School.

# Foreword

*Ricardo Meléndez-Ortiz*

Intellectual property policies have existed for decades and in some instances for centuries. Until recently, however, they have been largely the domain of specialists, practitioners and producers of intellectual property rights (IPRs), and thus relatively insulated from the kind of debate common in most areas of public policy. IPRs are principally conceived as a tool to encourage innovation, but as firms perceive their intangible assets as crucial to the protection of their global competitiveness, their intellectual property (IP) interests have increasingly shifted towards stronger protection, to the detriment of any sustainable balance between private and societal interests.

It is against this background that the current debate on the enforcement of IPRs has emerged. Although the achievement of more effective IPR enforcement was already one of the main driving forces behind the conclusion of the Agreement on Trade-Related Aspects of Intellectual Property Rights (TRIPS), it increasingly appears that TRIPS – while being an important milestone – did not represent a conclusive and satisfactory response to what is perceived as a significant rise in levels of counterfeiting and piracy. In this context, recent years have witnessed an unprecedented proliferation of initiatives relating to enforcement of IPRs. Perhaps the most conspicuous and exposed attempt has been the proposed move towards the Anti-Counterfeiting Trade Agreement (ACTA).

A number of countries and civil society groups opposed to ACTA have resisted such a move on the basis that tinkering with rules on enforcing IPRs can have profound effects on the regulation of knowledge goods and flows in our knowledge-based economies. As issues of competitiveness, innovation, access to knowledge, technological development and, more importantly, sustainable development are at stake, ACTA is too large an issue to avoid analysis. The plurilateral agreement, aimed at providing the means for the enforcement of IPRs, has been the subject of much controversy as the appeal of IPRs risks losing some of its shine if these rights cannot be enforced.

In light of the current limited amount of in-depth empirical study attributed to ACTA, resulting in the amplification of distinctly polarised perspectives, this book attempts to contribute to the fostering of a more informed and constructive discussion. With the view to learn more about the origins of ACTA, the process leading to the conclusion of the agreement and its implications for lawmaking in this field, the International Centre for Trade and Sustainable Development (ICTSD) has convened a diverse group of experts to draw lessons from what ACTA represents as a normative IP experiment. This book represents a compilation of different perspectives and approaches to legislation on enforcement issues as well as different standpoints on the necessary balance that should prevail in conceiving normative approaches in this area. Participants in this project include academics, policy makers and civil society actors, and, consequently, the corresponding styles of the book chapters differ, reflecting the respective profile of each author. It is these different styles and perspectives which add immense value to this unique compilation of papers around the "ACTA" phenomenon.

To ensure consistent treatment of the different issues and with a view to depict the most comprehensive portrait of ACTA, its origins, process, outcome and consequences, the book begins with a conceptual introduction to the plurilateral enforcement agenda before splitting into five distinct parts: (I) The Final Act: Its Main Features and Contents; (II) Domestic Legislative Challenges; (III) Impact on Related Processes; (IV) Views from Stakeholders: Lessons; and (V) What Lies Ahead ACTA.

Part I opens with an overview of ACTA followed by a comprehensive and detailed analysis of the agreement. It is noted that although ACTA attempts to build on the TRIPS Agreement, much has been transplanted, including the unanswered questions left over from TRIPS. In their critique of the agreement some note that although ACTA provides a framework for the enforcement of IPRs, it fails to ensure the presence of explicit checks and balances. ACTA's inability to fully reconcile itself with TRIPS also provides a source of discomfort for many who cite their concerns over the implementation of the agreement. Authors within this part note that provisions on the criminal enforcement of ACTA are problematic and extend to the increasingly digital medium in which much trade is carried out.

Part II of the volume highlights some of the domestic challenges faced by different countries (United States, Australia, Brazil and Africa) concerning the implementation of ACTA. The secretive nature of negotiations is picked up on by authors in this part, and many recognise that there was very little by way of consultation with civil society groups, leading to the talks being characterised by a "country club" approach. In light of this model for setting international standards, there is a concern raised among the authors that the evolution of the ACTA agreement has somewhat damaged the image of the efforts put on the enforcement of IPRs and highlighted the political nature of the discussions instead. A note of hope is sounded from some quarters, however. As initiatives similar to ACTA are spreading, albeit in a regional or other limited context, the movement of IP into the arena of trade has itself created a norm whereby enforcement is no longer considered unusual.

As the trade of third parties to the ACTA agreement will be effected by the treaty, ACTA clearly has the ability to effect multilateral trade and inform future IP law negotiations. Part III identifies these touch points where ACTA and its associated processes have had an impact on other IP negotiations across the globe. Perhaps unsurprisingly ACTA has already influenced the negotiations of the Trans-Pacific Partnership agreement, with some hoping that it will contain language on copyright exceptions, for example, which will lead to more balanced copyright regimes. The need for policy coherence is emphasised within this section and is especially brought to light when ACTA is compared to East African enforcement legislation at the IP, trade and public health nexus. In making suggestions as to where future gains concerning IP law at a bilateral level may be made, this section also makes a valuable contribution to where we can pick up valuable evidence to inform future decisions.

On the subject of lesson leaning, Part IV contains views on ACTA from a range of stakeholders and spectators. Some within this section view ACTA as an extremely important step in the fight against piracy and counterfeiting, despite the firmly held opinion of others that the process has been a failure with regards to both international policy making and IPR protection. Suggested causes for this failure range from a lack of leadership from politicians to the deliberate spread of misinformation by activists. On balance, however, it is more generally agreed, at least within this part, that better attempts to provide fair and impartial information on IP agreements and their effects are required.

The final part of this volume seeks to analyse the broader sociopolitical context behind ACTA in order to gain useful insights into how the agreement's evolution can further inform future negotiations concerning IP freedoms and rights within the realm of trade. It is clear that ACTA tells us about the dynamics of IP lawmaking at the present time, and there are lessons to be learnt from the defeat of ACTA – largely that IP law needs to be fair and be seen as fair for both sides. In addition, a different negotiating approach is required to ensure that the credibility of related institutions is not undermined. The ACTA text as it stands, and with its rejection by a number of countries, means that some nations may be better off. However, there are still calls within this volume for alternatives to protect against losses incurred as a result of the trade of counterfeit goods. Against strong criticism from some in this book, optimism still shines through. It may still be possible to achieve the necessary protection of IPRs at a multilateral level with the recognition that this may involve compromise. The ACTA process has resulted in a lost opportunity.

An overarching question raised in this book and the distinctive contributions made by several scholars, policy makers and stakeholders relate to the role of plurilateral agreements in addressing new and emerging challenges raised by the globalization of trade in intangible goods and services.

Plurilateral attempts in multilateral forums such as the World Trade Organization (WTO) have been the exception and not the rule. Their relevance and contextual place in the organisation have been controversial. They are seen by some as a practical solution to experiment with new disciplines in the absence of consensus and precisely as a way forward to overcome the stalemate in the current trade round instead of leaving these matters to be dealt with in bilateral or regional free trade agreements. There are, however, views that consider that this type of arrangement erodes the multilateral trading system and the legitimacy of one of its fundamental principles – that of the most favoured nation.

Throughout this book there is a discernable concern that ACTA parties are trying to avoid the established fora for IP agreements, namely the World Intellectual Property Organization or the WTO – and thereby threatening the established multilateral framework. ACTA, in this respect, would be part of a 'forum-shifting' strategy which seeks to promote offensive interests in IP outside the scope of specialised organisations. It is also the concern of many that for ACTA to be meaningful, a critical mass of countries, specifically a significant number of developing countries at whom, in many respects, the principles and norms of ACTA are targeted, must participate. ACTA parties have refuted such criticisms, arguing that ACTA would complement existing international IP agreements and fora rather than undermine them.

In any case, the ACTA experiment constitutes in this respect an important lesson for future negotiations of this sort. There is no doubt that much more reflection is required on how plurilateral agreements could truly advance the trade agenda in an inclusive manner. This book makes an important contribution to this reflection.

A central tenet of ICTSD's Program on Innovation, Technology and Intellectual Property, launched in July 2001, has been that in a knowledge-based economy, a better understanding of innovation and IP-related issues is imperative for informed policy making in virtually all areas of development. Our focus has been on ensuring a proper balance between the different interests at stake in designing appropriate IP regimes that are supportive of sustainable development objectives and compliant with international commitments. An additional central objective has been to facilitate the emergence of a critical mass of well-informed stakeholders in developing countries – including decision makers and negotiators as well as actors in the private sector and civil society – able to define their own sustainable human development objectives in the field of innovation and IP and effectively advance them at the national and global levels.

This book, and its respective parts, is the result of recent work undertaken by ICTSD and is characterised by the continuous search for an objective and evidence-based analysis of the different issues at stake. At ICTSD we strive for the development of an IP system that is responsive to the needs of sustainable development whilst acknowledging and remaining open to a range of diverse opinions. The participatory nature of this volume, involving a wide variety of stakeholders with divergent views and perspectives, reflects the priorities of ICTSD and has been an enriching experience. The feedback received so far is equally as encouraging, and we are determined to continue our efforts to generate knowledge and enhance understanding of the extraordinarily complex interface between IP policy, innovation, trade and sustainable development in general. This book is unique in that it brings together diverse of voices on enforcement issues that today occupy a central space in international economic debates as we have witnessed with the recent experience of ACTA.

I sincerely hope that you find this volume a useful contribution to efforts aimed at improving our understanding of the changing IP debate in order to move it in a constructive way which results in concrete actions and solutions.

# Acknowledgments

This book has been produced as part of the efforts of the International Centre for Trade and Sustainable Development (ICTSD) to promote the use and management of knowledge and technology to strive for a more sustainable and development-oriented intellectual property (IP) regime. Under the guidance of Ricardo Meléndez-Ortiz, ICTSD's chief executive, the Programme on Innovation, Technology and Intellectual Property is responsible for the preparation and successful culmination of the varied chapters which make up this book. Gratitude is expressed to the ICTSD staff members instrumental in bringing the book to completion, including Christophe Bellmann, Deborah Vorhies, Ahmed Abdel-Latif, Pedro Roffe, Anja Halle, Daniella Allam, Marco Valenza and Chris Ruck. Pedro Roffe and Xavier Seuba are the principal editors of the book.

The editors would particularly like to extend their thanks to the authors of the various chapters of the book for their dedication and superb work.

Finally, the ICTSD wishes to gratefully acknowledge the continual support of its core and thematic donors.

# Acronyms

| | |
|---|---|
| A2K | Access to Knowledge |
| ACP | African Caribbean and Pacific Countries |
| ACTA | Anti-Counterfeiting Trade Agreement |
| APEC | Asia-Pacific Economic Co-operation |
| AUSFTA | Australia-US Free Trade Agreement |
| BASCAP | Business Action to Stop Counterfeiting and Piracy |
| BRICS | Brazil, Russia, India, China, South Africa |
| BTIAS | Broad-based Trade and Investment Agreements |
| CARICOM | Caribbean Community |
| CAS | Copyright Alert System |
| CCIA | Computer & Communications Industry Association |
| CETA | EU-Canada Comprehensive Economic and Trade Agreement |
| DFAT | Department of Foreign Affairs and Trade (Australia) |
| DMCA | Digital Millennium Copyright Act |
| EAC | East African Community |
| ECHR | European Convention on Human Rights |
| ECJ | European Court of Justice |
| EDRi | European Digital Rights |
| EFF | Electronic Frontier Foundation |
| EGA | Environmental Goods Agreement |
| EPP | European People's Party |
| EU | European Union |
| FDI | Foreign Direct Investment |
| FFII | Foundation for a Free Information Infrastructure |
| FOIA | Freedom of Information Act |
| FTA | Free trade agreement |
| FTAA | Free Trade Area of the Americas |

| | |
|---|---|
| GATT | General Agreement on Tariffs and Trade |
| GDP | Gross domestic product |
| GI | Geographical indication |
| GIZ | German International Cooperation Agency |
| GPA | Government Procurement Agreement |
| ICANN | Internet Corporation for Assigned Names and Numbers |
| ICESCR | International Covenant on Economic, Social, and Cultural Rights (UN) |
| ICTSD | International Centre for Trade and Sustainable Development |
| IFPI | International Federation of the Phonographic Industry |
| IIPA | International Intellectual Property Alliance |
| INN | International non-proprietary name |
| INTA | Committee on International Trade of the European Parliament |
| INTA | International Trademark Association |
| INTERPOL | International Criminal Police Organization |
| IP | Intellectual property |
| IPFI | International Federation of the Phonographic Industries |
| IPR | Intellectual property right |
| ISP | Internet service provider |
| ITA | Information Technology Agreement |
| JSCOT | Joint Standing Committee on Treaties (Australia) |
| KAM | Kenya Association of Manufacturers |
| KEI | Knowledge Ecology International |
| LCA | Library Copyright Alliance |
| LDC | Least Developed Country |
| MAI | Multilateral Agreement on Investment |
| MEP | Member of the European Parliament |
| MERCOSUR | Southern Common Market |
| MFN | Most favoured nation |
| NASA | National Aeronautics and Space Administration (United States) |
| NGO | Non-governmental organisation |
| OECD | Organisation for Economic Co-operation and Development |
| OSP | Online service provider |
| P2P | Peer-to-peer |
| PGR | Procuraduría General de la República (Attorney General's Office, Mexico) |
| PhRMA | Pharmaceutical Research and Manufacturers of America |
| PIPA | Protect Intellectual Property Act |
| PTA | Preferential Trade Agreement |
| RMI | Rights management information |

| | |
|---|---|
| RTA | Regional Trade Agreement |
| SFFC | Spurious/falsely labelled/falsified/counterfeit (medicines) |
| SMEs | Small and medium enterprises |
| SOPA | Stop Online Piracy Act |
| TAFTA | Transatlantic Free Trade Area |
| TFEU | Treaty on the Functioning of the European Union |
| TiSA | Trade in Services Agreement |
| TPM | Technical protection measure |
| TPP | Transpacific Partnership Agreement |
| TPSEP/P4 | Trans-Pacific Strategic Economic Partnership Agreement |
| TRIPS | Agreement on Trade-Related Aspects of Intellectual Property Rights |
| TTIP | Transatlantic Trade and Investment Partnership |
| UAE | United Arab Emirates |
| UGC | User-generated content |
| UNESCO | United Nations Educational, Scientific and Cultural Organization |
| UPU | Universal Postal Union |
| US | United States |
| USC | United States Code |
| USTR | United States Trade Representative |
| WCIT | World Conference on International Telecommunications |
| WCO | World Customs Organization |
| WHO | World Health Organization |
| WIPO | World Intellectual Property Organization |
| WPPT | WIPO Performances and Phonograms Treaty |
| WTC | WIPO Copyright Treaty |
| WTO | World Trade Organization |

# Introduction

## *ACTA and the International Debate on Intellectual Property Enforcement*

*Pedro Roffe and Xavier Seuba*

### FRAMING THE ENFORCEMENT DEBATE

The intellectual property enforcement debate is probably less about the goals than the methods used to achieve those goals. In effect, while it seems irrefutable that "the attractiveness of intellectual property rights risks being seriously undermined if they cannot be enforced in an appropriate manner,"[1] given that "without effective enforcement, intellectual property rights are nothing but empty shells,"[2] views diverge widely when the discussion focuses on the legal mechanisms, human resources and financial means that should be deployed.

Disagreement may start even before deciding on how to react to intellectual property infringements, because data concerning the magnitude of the problem and the consequences of infringing activities differ widely.[3] For some, the economic and social impacts are profound[4] and are not only limited to innovation and

The introduction represents a reflection by the editors, drawing particularly on the various chapters that integrate this volume, on the genesis and aftermath of the negotiations to establish a first ever treaty on IP enforcement. The authors, being personally responsible for this work, thank the various contributors to the book for their lucid and incisive contributions to a better understanding of ACTA. Authors wish to thank particularly comments made to an earlier version by Jonathan Band, Michel Geist and Elena Dan.

[1] Geiger, Chapter 21 in this volume.

[2] R. M. Hilty, 'Economic, Legal and Social Impacts of Counterfeiting', in C. Geiger (Ed.), *Criminal Enforcement of Intellectual Property: A Handbook of Contemporary Research*, Cheltenham: Edward Elgar, 2012, p. 11.

[3] *See* C. Fink, 'Enforcing Intellectual Property Rights: An Economic Perspective', in ICTSD, *The Global Debate on the Enforcement of Intellectual Property Rights and Developing Countries*, Geneva: ICTSD, 2008; C. Fink, *Enforcing Intellectual Property Rights: An Economic Perspective*, Advisory Committee on Enforcement, WIPO/ACE/5/6, August 26, 2009, www.wipo.int/edocs/mdocs/enforcement/en/wipo_ace_5/wipo_ace_5_6.pdf (accessed March 2013).

[4] *See*, e.g., Li and Moscoso, Chapters 17 and 18 in this volume, respectively.

creativity,[5] since in some cases they amount to an unacceptable global-scale problem possibly linked to organised crime[6] and even to terrorism and drug trafficking.[7] Others, by contrast, think that statistics on counterfeiting are exaggerated,[8] and the problem is not pressing enough when compared to other issues both within the intellectual property arena and more broadly with respect to law and order enforcement in general. There are also those, probably the majority, who assume that there is a problem, but are cautious about expressing conclusive views on the specifics of its economic and social impacts.

While the debate on the lack of respect for intellectual property is fuelled by astonishing figures,[9] the data and statistics often result from controversial methodologies and tend to be supplied by partisan sources. The often quoted maxim – intellectual property rights are private rights and, as such, should be privately enforced – has had a side effect: in general, private actors have been precisely those quantifying the problem.[10] This is probably why, until recent times, there were hardly any public institutions estimating and monitoring the global extent and relevance of infringement activities. Now, the World Intellectual Property Organization and

5 See Explanatory Memorandum of the Amended Proposal for a Directive of the European Parliament and of the Council on criminal measures aimed at ensuring the enforcement of intellectual property rights of 26 April 2006, COM(2006) 168 final, 2.

6 In the failed EU Intellectual Property Rights Enforcement Directive (IPRED2), the preamble affirmed that "infringements of intellectual property in general, are a constantly growing phenomenon which nowadays has an international dimension, since they are a serious threat to national economies and governments. (...) In addition to the economic and social consequences, counterfeiting and piracy also pose problems for consumer protection, particularly when health and safety are at stake. Increasing use of the Internet enables pirated products to be distributed instantly around the globe. Finally, this phenomenon appears to be increasingly linked to organised crime. Combating this phenomenon is therefore of vital importance for the Community. Counterfeiting and pirating have become lucrative activities in the same way as other large-scale criminal activities such as drug trafficking (...)." *See Amended proposal for a DIRECTIVE OF THE EUROPEAN PARLIAMENT AND OF THE COUNCIL on criminal measures aimed at ensuring the enforcement of intellectual property rights (presented by the Commission)*, Brussels, 26.4.2006, COM(2006) 168 final, 2005/0127 (COD), http://register.consilium.europa.eu/pdf/en/06/st08/st08866.en06.pdf (accessed March 2013). *See also* M. R. Roudaut, "From Sweatshops to Organized Crime: The New Face of Counterfeiting", in C. Geiger (ed.), *Criminal Enforcement of Intellectual Property, op. cit.*, p. 184.

7 The International Anti-Counterfeiting Coalition affirms that "[t]he profits from counterfeiting have been linked to funding organized crime, drug trafficking and terrorist activity". *See* IACC, "About counterfeiting", https://www.iacc.org/about-counterfeiting/ (accessed May 2013).

8 D. Chow, "Counterfeiting as an Externality Imposed by Multinational Companies on Developing Countries", *Virginia Journal of International Law*, vol. 51, no 4, 2011, p. 785.

9 See in particular the figures quoted in OECD, "The economic impact of counterfeiting and piracy", Paris, OECD Publishing, 2008, updated in 2009: OECD, "Magnitude of counterfeiting and piracy of tangible products: an update", November 2009, 1.

10 For instance, the International Federation of the Phonographic Industry affirmed in 2012 that "[t]he overall impact of digital piracy has been to contribute substantially to the dramatic erosion in industry revenues in recent years. Despite the surge by more than 1000 per cent in the digital music market

the European Observatory on Infringements on Intellectual Property could start correcting this apparent deficit.[11] But for many years the plausible lack of interest and action on the part of the global community with regard to intellectual property enforcement norms has propelled those affected by activities associated with infringement to become more vociferous, not only in the quantitative aspect but also qualitatively speaking. The use of alarming terms such as "piracy" or "theft," even in normative texts,[12] to allude to all sorts of infringement[13] is a clear manifestation of this semiotic burden.[14]

In this context, it has been difficult for observers to arrive at an objective assessment of the exact prevalence of the problem. In fact, governmental sources have recognised, for instance, that the socio-economic impact of counterfeiting cannot be scientifically determined for lack of reliable data.[15] The tendency to exaggerate figures has reduced the credibility of some sources and, concomitantly, may have downplayed the extent of infringement. Obviously, others also may have had an interest in minimising the problem, even denying its existence. The lack of reliable data and the polarisation of the debate may scare off non-partisan stakeholders and complicate the management of the problem. There is indeed a methodological aspect difficult to solve, which ultimately relates to the valorisation of intellectual property rights. To assess the dimension of infringement activities, it is necessary to agree on how to value the distinct categories of intellectual property. This

from 2004 to 2010 to an estimated value of US$4.6 billion, global recorded music revenues declined by 31 per cent over the same period." IFPI, Digital Music Report 2011, "Music at the touch of a button", 2011, p. 14

11 See in the same sense Moscoso, Chapter 18 in this volume. In September 2013, the European Observatory on Infringements on Intellectual Property released its first impact study, jointly with the European Patent Office, which affirms to be "the first to quantify the overall contribution made by IPR-intensive industries to the EU economy, in terms of output, employment, wages and trade, taking into account the major IP rights (patents, trade marks, designs, copyrights, geographical indications)", which, "despite the conservative approach, reflected in the rigorous methodology applied", *See* OHIM-EPO, *Intellectual property rights intensive industries: contribution to economic performance and employment in the European Union', Industry-Level Analysis Report*, September 2013, available at: http://oami.europa.eu/ows/rw/resource/documents/observatory/IPR/joint_report_Epo_ohim.pdf (accessed October 2013). The methodology was earlier described in this document: http://oami.europa.eu/ows/rw/resource/documents/observatory/meetings/meeting_27–09–2012/02_ip%20impact%20study-%20pptx.pdf (accessed March 2013).

12 Take, for instance, the case of the *Preventing Real Online Threats to Economic Creativity and Theft of Intellectual Property Act* of 2011, S.968, 112h Cong. (PROTECT IP Act of 2011, commonly referred to as PIPA).

13 *See* Alliance Against IP Theft, *Comments on the European Commission's proposal for a Directive on criminal measures* (October 2005), http://www.eurim.org.uk/activities/ipr/0510crimsanc-AAIPT.pdf

14 As noted by Loughlan, "words like 'theft', 'thief', 'stealing', 'burglar's tools' and occasionally even 'robbery' [are] increasingly employed to describe the unauthorised use of intellectual property"; P. Loughlan, "'You Wouldn't Steal a Car': IP and the Language of Theft", *EIPR*, 2007, p. 401.

15 United States Government Accountability Office, *Observations on Efforts to Quantify the Economic Effects of Counterfeit and Pirated Goods*, April 2010, p. 37.

valorisation cannot be constrained to the already difficult commercial valorisation, but has to be enlarged to include its welfare implications and, ultimately, the social value of intellectual property. All this implies entering into the intricate areas of, for instance, the ecological and health impact of the protected technologies, as well as consumers and competitors' views and interest in enforcement issues.

Treaties dealing with enforcement such as the Anti-Counterfeiting Trade Agreement (ACTA) continue to be adopted based on general perceptions of their necessity and relevance to trade negotiations. In the context of ACTA, society at large and particularly those in a position to adopt decisions were suddenly flooded with contradictory and distorted information. Confronted almost for the first time with the responsibility of decision making in an area as obscure as intellectual property enforcement, they were under pressure to act by those linking counterfeiting to harmful effects on public health or activities such as terrorism or drug trafficking. At the other end of the spectrum were those who associated ACTA with serious concerns over fundamental rights. The non-informed citizen and the non-expert politician had to make judgements and formulate perceptions in the context of this polarised scenario.

## THE MAIN ACTORS AND THEIR INVOLVEMENT IN THE ACTA DEBATE

As any other international covenant, ACTA is a treaty which binds states. Both in its promotion and progression, however, the agreement was subject to intense scrutiny from non-state actors. This was the case particularly for industry, civil society and academic stakeholders who rose to an almost unprecedented prominence in the genesis and fate of the treaty. In many respects the influence exerted by non-state actors reminds us of the origins of the TRIPS negotiations,[16] or even the OECD Multilateral Investment Agreement. However, contrary to ACTA, in the case of the TRIPS agreement, the industrial sector monopolised the scene.

It is widely acknowledged that major industrial groups – whose business models depend on a strong system of enforcement – played a key role in persuading governments of the necessity of a new international instrument to control, and possibly eradicate, intellectual property infringements. As Andrew Rens[17] and Marietje Schaake[18] explain, the information and privileged access to ACTA negotiations provided to a select group of companies and industrial associations, even while the negotiations were secret, proves their powerful and influential position. In the late 1980s and early 1990s, Susan Strange pointed to the acquisition by companies of roles and quotas of

[16] See references below to the works of P. Ryan, S. K. Sell and A. C. Cutler, V. Haufler, and T. Porter.
[17] *See* Rens, Chapter 12 in this volume.
[18] *See* Schaake, Chapter 19 in this volume.

authority in the international political economy that had traditionally been the realm of states.[19] These early views have undergone a very rich evolution, both within and external to the academic domain. In the late 1990s, the notion of private international authorities emerged. This concept tried to reflect both the capacity of private actors to collaborate and privately manage, among themselves, topics of common interest, as well as their public interaction and influence on institutional and normative issues.[20] The role and relevance of private international actors in the area of intellectual property has been thoroughly addressed, among others, by Susan K. Sell, who framed the adoption of TRIPS in this context.[21] Today, no debate in this area is complete without recognition of the fact that companies belonging to a wide range of sectors promote and trigger the adoption of specific intellectual property norms.

With regard to the involvement of private corporations, the most noticeable feature in ACTA was not the lobbying carried out by traditional demanding stakeholders, but the fact that the negotiations became a battleground between (mainly copyright-dependent) content provider firms on the one hand and technology firms (service and platform providers) on the other. The former had privileged access to the negotiators and draft texts, while the latter tried to influence ACTA as outsiders, mixing their concerns with those of non-profit civil society groups or those governments which were not invited to join the negotiations. Important Internet service providers and communication companies demanded to have a voice in the negotiations and resisted the privileged position of IP right holders. While it can hardly be said that the two sides wielded equal influence, the final outcome seems to reflect different winners than those originally expected.

19 J. Stopford and S. Strange, *Rival States, Rival Firms: Competition for World Market Shares*, Cambridge: Cambridge University Press, 1991; S. Strange, "Big Business and the State", *Millennium Journal of International Studies*, vol. 20, no 2, 1991, pp. 245–250; S. Strange, "States, Firms and Diplomacy", *International Affairs*, vol. 68, no 1, 1992, pp. 1–15; S. Strange, *The Retreat of the State*, Cambridge: Cambridge University Press, 1996; S. Strange, "Territory, State, Authority and Economy: A New Realist Ontology of Global Political Economy", in R. Cox (ed.), *The New Realism. Perspectives on Multilateralism and World Order*, Tokyo; New York; Paris: Macmillan / United Nations University Press, 1997, pp. 3–19.

20 A. Claire Cutler, V. Haufler and T. Porter (eds.), *Private Authority and International Affairs*, Albany: New York State University Press, 1999; "transnational companies exercising not only power but also authority in processes of self-regulation and co-regulation", in the words of J. Ibanez, "Transnational Private Authorities and the Erosion of Democracy", in I. Filibi, N. Cornago and J. O. Frosini (eds.), *Democracy with(out) Nations? Old and New Foundations for Political Communities in a Changing World*, Universidad del País Vasco Servicio Editorial, 2011, p. 204.

21 *See* Michael P. Ryan, *Knowledge Diplomacy: Global Competition and The Politics of Intellectual Property*, Washington, DC: The Brookings Institutions, 1988; S. K. Sell, "Multinational Corporations as Agents of Change: The Globalization of Intellectual Property Rights", in A. C. Cutler, V. Haufler and T. Porter (eds.), *Private Authority and International Affairs*, Albany: State University of New York Press, 1999, pp. 169–198; S. K. Sell, *Private Power, Public Law: The Globalization of Intellectual Property Rights*, Cambridge: Cambridge University Press, 2003.

Further, the ACTA negotiations and the ultimate fate of the treaty cannot be fully understood without underlining the role of NGOs. As Frederick Abbott observed, many of the most troubling provisions envisaged in early drafts did not materialise owing to a "pushback from NGOs, academics and developing country governments."[22] The civil society movement against ACTA was, in fact, not an accidental phenomenon. As Marietje Schaake explained, there was a borderless network of people fighting against other conflicting intellectual property initiatives.[23] In the United States this was the case of the Stop Online Piracy Act (SOPA) and the Protect Intellectual Property Act (PIPA). In the international context, intellectual property enforcement provisions laid out in preferential trade agreements had already been targeted as problematic. In fact, "[t]he anti-ACTA movement is part of a broader backlash against secretive intellectual property agreements,"[24] and probably stemmed from the generalised discontent[25] and social distrust provoked by features of the recent evolution of intellectual property.[26]

In the course of the past decade, a very active and well-informed global network of NGOs has gained considerable influence.[27] Intellectual property interfaces with public interests constitute a new area of intense activism, joining other traditional topics such as women's rights, environment or development.[28] There is, however, considerable diversity regarding the role and legitimacy of the organisations involved in different fora and negotiations. This variety is accompanied by the heterogeneity that exists within the non-profit civil society community. Some NGOs, in close partnership with academia, have emerged as specialists, often advocating smart solutions to specific problems. In addition, a number of popular NGOs of a more general nature have also become interested in the interface between IP and basic freedoms. In the context of ACTA, the fundamental contribution of the second group was founded on its ability to reach out to the general public. In this sense, the ACTA process amounted to a paradigm shift characterised by collaboration among very

[22] Abbott, Chapter 1 in this volume.

[23] Schaake, op. cit.

[24] Geist, Chapter 24 in this volume.

[25] *See*, among others, A. B. Jaffe and J. Lerner, *Innovation and Its Discontents: How Our Broken Patent System is Endangering Innovation and Progress, and What to Do About It*, Princeton: Princeton University Press, 2004.

[26] See, e.g., work by Barbosa and Rens, Chapters 11 and 12 in this volume, respectively.

[27] In the area of health, for instance, the genealogy of the proposed negotiations for the conclusion of an international treaty on R&D reveals its NGO origin. With regards to free trade agreements, diverse coalitions of numerous NGOs have been following, assessing and proposing amendments to the IP chapters of each agreement. In WIPO, initiatives such as the Development Agenda or the Treaty on limitations and exceptions for visually impaired persons–persons with print disabilities cannot be fully understood without the participation of some NGOs.

[28] M. E. Keck and K. Sikkink, *Activists Beyond Borders: Advocacy Networks in International Politics*, Ithaca: Cornell University Press, 1998.

diverse NGOs, somewhat evoking the campaign that in the mid-1990s frustrated the adoption of the OECD Multilateral Investment Agreement.

The global relevance intellectual property acquired among the members of the internationally linked NGO network also has national determinants. In this context, it is interesting to highlight the reflection Schaake made with regard to the reasons behind the protests against the agreement in Poland. She saw those as a manifestation of the links between ACTA and "the relatively high prices Eastern Europeans pay for legal access to culture online (lower wages but same price for media as in Western Europe) as well as the recent memory of the secret police monitoring people and their communications in the Soviet era."[29]

Private economic actors and civil society organisations are not the only entities to have had a relevant role in the discussions leading to the conclusion of ACTA. Scholars and technical experts have also become relevant actors, both stimulating the debate and forcefully expressing their views.[30] Declarations such as the Opinion of European Academics on Anti-Counterfeiting Trade Agreement[31] or open fora such as the Congress on Public Interest Analysis of the Intellectual Property Enforcement Agenda, held in 2010 in the American University College of Law,[32] played an important role in the debate. In this particular regard, it is interesting to note that in parallel to the emergence of a global network of highly specialised NGOs and think tanks, together with the emergence of international private authorities, there is also a global community of experts that influences the adoption of norms. This network of experts has achieved, and not only in the context of ACTA, an authority and influence similar to that Peter Haas identified in the early 1990s with regard to global communities of experts sharing some basic

[29] *See*, Schaake, op. cit.

[30] See, among others, the various contributions to this book. *See also* D. Matthews, 'The Rise and Fall of the Anti-Counterfeiting Trade Agreement (ACTA): Lessons for the European Union', Queen Mary University of London, School of Law Legal Studies Research Paper No. 127/2012, and M. A. Carrier, "SOPA, PIPA, ACTA, TPP: An Alphabet Soup of Innovation-Stifling Copyright Legislation and Agreements", *Northwestern Journal of Technology and Intellectual Property*, vol. 11, no 2, 2013, http://scholarlycommons.law.northwestern.edu/njtip/vol11/iss2/1 (accessed May 2013).

[31] Opinion of European Academics on Anti-Counterfeiting Trade Agreement, http://www.iri.uni-hannover.de/tl_files/pdf/ACTA_opinion_200111_2.pdf; this opinion even prompted a reply by the EU Commission. *See* Comments on the "Opinion of European Academics on Anti-Counterfeiting Trade Agreement", 27 April 2011, http://trade.ec.europa.eu/doclib/docs/2011/april/tradoc_147853.pdf (accessed May 2013).

[32] In addition to the network that emerged, the meeting resulted in the adoption of a text that "reflects the conclusions reached at a meeting of over 90 academics, practitioners and public interest organizations from six continents gathered at American University Washington College of Law, June 16–18, 2010". *Text of Urgent ACTA Communique: International Experts Find that Pending Anti-Counterfeiting Trade Agreement Threatens Public Interests*, 23 June 2010, American University Washington College of Law, http://www.wcl.american.edu/pijip/go/acta-communique

methodologies, principles and beliefs.[33] In spite of sharing some of the positions of civil society groups and private economic actors,[34] the role of academic networks has become complementary and distinct, and its influence continues to be exerted in other negotiations and fora.

It is also important to recall that, as many of the scholars argue, "ACTA appears [to be] primarily addressed to non-signatory third countries which will be later invited to 'join the club', either by ratifying the Agreement a *posteriori* or by concluding bilateral agreements."[35] The fact that ACTA is a treaty conceived to be applied not only by its members but also by third countries that did not participate in its drafting is the reason why governments not part of the "country club" sought to have their say in the negotiations. Indeed, the position of developing countries towards ACTA rapidly evolved from caution to open defiance and hostility.[36]

In multilateral fora, mainly the WTO and WIPO, developing countries and emerging economies expressed their preoccupation and framed this concern in the context of the wider campaign of strengthening intellectual property enforcement. Ahmed Abdel-Latif points at the role that these countries had in the TRIPS Council. Indeed, the use of the Council as a platform for contestation is remarkable and unprecedented, since developing and emerging country concerns about "TRIPS-plus" obligations had never been articulated so forcefully from the point of view of their systemic implications on multilateral trade-related intellectual property rules.[37] In fact, from a substantive point of view, as noted by Kampermann Sanders, "[p]aradoxically ACTA has prompted the tabling on the agenda of the issue of enforcement in the TRIPS Council for the first time."[38]

In the wider context of the multilateral trade system, both the ACTA negotiations and the final text offer valuable lessons for the design and negotiation of plurilateral trade agreements. Ricardo Meléndez-Ortiz and Ahmed Abdel-Latif reflect on the broad parameters that should guide negotiations of plurilateral agreements, including a persuasive narrative, trust and transparency, inclusiveness and empirical evidence, and introduce the complex question of the legal relationship of plurilateral agreements with the multilateral trade system. As the authors illustrate, debates exclusively focused on the Vienna Convention on the Law of the Treaties and the

33 P. M. Haas, "Introduction: Epistemic Communities and International Policy Coordination", *International Organization*, vol. 46, no 1, 1992.

34 In this same line, Matulionyte states that the initial provisions had been strongly watered down "due to strong criticisms expressed by both civil groups and academics during the period of negotiations". Matulionyte, Chapter 7 in this volume

35 Geiger, op. cit.

36 Abdel-Latif, Chapter 25 in this volume.

37 Ibid.

38 Sanders, Chapter 16 in this volume.

limits set forth therein to *inter se* agreements hardly reflect the complexity and the fundamentally political nature of the debate regarding plurilateral agreements.

## SECRECY, TRANSPARENCY AND LEGITIMACY

The lack of transparency provoked widespread criticism, and will probably remain throughout time as ACTA's distinguishing feature. Many scholars and other actors touch upon not just this lack of transparency but also the initial silence on the very existence of the negotiations. The opaqueness surrounding ACTA fuelled opposition to the undertaking and generated an understandable suspicion among governments and economic actors excluded from the discussions, as well as members of civil society at large.

For a number of reasons, the secrecy regarding almost every aspect of ACTA[39] has probably been the worst ally to those wishing it to be a success comparable to that of TRIPS.[40]

First, trying to maintain secret a treaty dealing with the digital environment is not only doomed to failure but also fails to acknowledge the very nature of the Internet and the major transformation that it has made in the way society perceives transparency in public affairs.

Second, not disclosing what happens in a room is obviously the best way to stimulate speculation on, precisely, what happens in that room. If the non-disclosure, moreover, affects fundamental rights and important economic interests, the outcome seems obvious. In this sense, it has been rightly pointed out that secrecy was one of the factors behind "the widespread dissemination of misleading and false information."[41]

Third, the lack of information and participation reduces the legitimacy of the treaty when this attribute increasingly depends on something that exceeds the formal legitimacy of the source. In effect, intellectual property has become a clear example of the need to open channels of participation to a wide range of stakeholders, not only governments and select actors. This would allow an improvement in the quality of the outcome as well as the level of adherence to the treaty of those who are likely to be ruled by its norms.

ACTA provides a helpful example to reflect on the present methodology for the negotiation of intellectual property norms in the context of trade agreements. One

39 Secrecy maintained until pressure was untenable: only when the European Parliament demanded in March 2010 full information about ACTA, the first official version was released. *See* European Parliament resolution of 10 March 2010 on the transparency and state of play of the ACTA negotiations, P7_TA(2010)0058).

40 Geiger, op. cit.

41 Mercurio, Chapter 22 in this volume.

of the crucial questions refers to whether it is necessary, as trade diplomats frequently state, that negotiations should take place behind closed doors.

The frequently held argument surrounding the requirement to keep discussions secret is that parties need to put forward proposals freely, knowing that these are part of a broader deal. In other words, negotiations should be confidential to allow "each party to feel comfortable to make concessions and/or to try options before finally settling for an agreement."[42] As such, trade diplomats are reluctant to anticipate conclusions, since the final outcome will necessarily be different. Although this argument is increasingly disputed by civil society and parliamentarians,[43] and has proved counterproductive in the context of ACTA, the European Court of Justice has upheld the EU Commission's position with regard to the confidentiality of the ACTA negotiations. For the Court, secrecy is important "to allow mutual trust between negotiators and the development of a free and effective discussion," because "any form of negotiation necessarily entails a number of tactical considerations of the negotiators, and the necessary cooperation between the parties depends to a large extent on the existence of a climate of mutual trust."[44]

In our view, the position of the EU Commission and the arguments of the European Court may have their origins in a conception of intellectual property akin to that of tariff negotiations, where hundreds of tariffs are negotiated in the context of a haggling or bargaining exercise. In that situation, parties sometimes exaggerate or try to feign interest in issues that are not really their priority. They assume, however, that this is part of a process to achieve what they really want, given that the other parties behave in the same way. Moreover, the nature of tangible goods makes this sort of negotiation plausible.

Although intellectual property has a totally different nature and rationale, discussions leading to the adoption of IP norms in the context of trade negotiations have assumed considerations and attitudes proper to tariff deals. Negotiations taking place in WIPO are more transparent than those in other contexts, and the same

[42] K. de Gucht, EU DG Trade Commissioner, quoted in his response to EU parliamentarians. *See* ICTSD, "EU Parliament Criticises Secrecy of ACTA Negotiations in Landslide Vote", *Bridges Weekly Trade News Digest*, vol. 14, no 10, March 2010.

[43] See the questions posed by the EU Parliamentarians Sophia in 't Veld (ALDE), Cecilia Wikström (ALDE), Michael Cashman (S&D) on the "Confidentiality agreements concluded prior to international negotiations" in 13 January 2013: http://www.europarl.europa.eu/sides/getDoc.do?pubRef=-//EP//TEXT+WQ+E-2013–000254+0+DOC+XML+V0//EN (accessed March 2013).

[44] Case T-301/10, Judgment of the General court (Second Chamber), 19 March 2013, Par. 119. In a decision dated 7 June 2013, the Court of Justice of the European Union dismissed an action for annulment of a decision of the European Commission (EC), refusing the applicant in the case (Corporate Europe Observatory) full access to several documents relating to the negotiations on the Free Trade Agreement between the EU and the Republic of India. *See* http://curia.europa.eu/juris/document/document.jsf?text=&docid=138132&pageIndex=0&doclang=EN&mode=req&dir=&occ=first&part=1&cid=665977 (accessed May 2013).

can be said with regard to past negotiations on multilateral IP agreements. The content of intellectual property negotiations falls into the realm of industrial and public policy, including its relation with fundamental rights. This is why ACTA's process has shown "the need for a fundamentally different approach to negotiating international agreements. The EU should embrace new forms of multi-stakeholder involvement, especially when working on agreements and laws that impact people's fundamental rights."[45]

ACTA, as well as negotiations taking place in the context of free trade agreements, calls for an attitude change when adopting international norms on intellectual property. In our view, these negotiations should be approached from the broad perspective of public policy rather than that of traditional trade negotiations. Thus, the bargaining approach should be replaced by a different perspective, focused on the construction of sound and nationally adjusted IP regimes that build, among others, on the objective of TRIPS to "contribute to the promotion of technological innovation and to the transfer and dissemination of technology, to the mutual advantage of producers and users of technological knowledge and in a manner conducive to social and economic welfare, and to a balance of rights and obligations."[46] Another important matter, common to all kinds of negotiations, is what the European Court calls "mutual trust" and legitimate "tactical considerations."

A valid question, however, remains: Is it still possible to conclude new intellectual property covenants in the currently polarised multilateral framework? Or is it easier to agree on new IP commitments in the context of trade agreements? To answer this question, Kampermann Sanders suggests focusing attention on the legislative constituencies: "Even more interesting will be the upcoming negotiations in the context of an EU-US Transatlantic Agreement, with which both parties aim to blast their way out of the economic crisis. With intellectual property relegated to one of the topics in a wider negotiating package, parliaments may be far less critical if the overall deal promises economic growth and more jobs."[47]

On a distinct set of issues, the North American, European and Australian internal experiences with regard to the process of the negotiation and approval of ACTA, described by Sean Flynn, Marietje Schaake and Matthew Rimmer, reveal the importance of the parliamentary control of IP treaties. Not only are transparency and legitimacy better safeguarded with the participation of a legislative body; its participation is also crucial because of the interests and fundamental rights affected by the new international obligations undertaken.

[45] Schaake, op. cit.

[46] *See* TRIPS agreement Part I – General Provisions and Basic Principles, Article. 7, available online at http://www.wto.org/english/tratop_e/trips_e/t_agm2_e.htm

[47] Sanders, op. cit.

The frustration among stakeholders in the United States[48] as well as in Australia[49] over the lack of recognition of the need of congressional supervision and approval of ACTA found a sharply contrasting scenario in the European Union. In effect, not only did the Parliament vote decisively; it also held several informative meetings and technical discussions before the vote. A concomitant effect of the lack of participation of the United States legislature was that the worldwide community of actors interested in ACTA focused its attention on the European Parliament.[50] This not only attracted an unprecedented level of interest but can also be seen as an indication of the new role and pre-eminence of the Parliament when negotiating treaties perceived to affect fundamental rights.

## THE LIMITS OF TRANSPLANTATION

### *The Phenomenon*

For a long time, transplantation of the law has been a useful stratagem to legislate on matters that have transnational features. Indeed, the phenomenon of legal transplantation has flourished and has become a fertile technique to adopt new norms or amend existing ones in the area of intellectual property.[51]

The views on the benefits of transposing the law of one country to another have been heterogeneous, and frequently opposed. On one extreme, in the 1970s Professor Watson considered that importing a rule or a system of law from another country was either a neutral or even a positive phenomenon, and that transplantation simply happens because it is a "good idea."[52] In contrast, Kahn-Freund held that although legal transplantation is not impossible, it is certainly problematic given the lack of relation of the transplanted norm to the local context.[53] While these are obviously simplifications of their thoughts, they nevertheless represent fairly well the poles of the discussion.

Transplantation of intellectual property law has become common practice, and its implementation happens through a range of channels. Among the most

48 Flynn, Chapter 9 in this volume.

49 Rimmer, Chapter 10 in this volume.

50 Schaake, op. cit.

51 *See*, for instance, R. C. Dreyfuss, "TRIPS-Round II: Should Users Strike Back?", *University of Chicago Law Review*, vol. 71, 2004, p. 21; and P. Yu, "Currents and Crosscurrents in the International Intellectual Property Regime", *Loyola of Los Angeles Law Review*, vol. 38, 2004, p. 396.

52 A. Watson, *Legal Transplants: An Approach to Comparative Law*, Edinburgh: Scottish Academic Press, 1974; P. Legrand, "The Impossibility of 'Legal Transplants'", *Maastricht Journal of European and Comparative Law*, vol. 4, 1997, p. 111.

53 *See*, for instance, O. Kahn-Freund, "On Uses and Misuses of Comparative Law", *Modern Law Review*, vol. 37, no 1, 1974, p. 1.

fertile means of transplantation are the accession procedures to regional integration schemes, the negotiation and conclusion of free trade agreements, the mimesis occurring between intellectual property offices and the conclusion of multilateral treaties on IP.

ACTA resembles a patchwork of transplanted norms that have their origin in certain national and international legal orders. Select pieces of US and EU law, as well as extracts from TRIPS, have been woven together to make up an ambiguous treaty on enforcement. This has been done in a way that is very similar to other recent transplantation experiences, such as free trade agreements.

## *Competitive Transplantation*

One of the characteristics of transplantation is its competitive nature, in the sense that those promoting exportation try to win the race over other countries also wishing to export their tradition and culture. The first country capable of transferring its own regulation will generally block the adoption of related proposals, drafted by competing commercial powers. Hence, from the point of view of those exporting their norms, transplantation may have both a defensive and an offensive role since it enables both the preservation and expansion of their national views and underlying principles on IP.

The exportation of law from Europe and the United States has become routine in free trade agreements, and it is also an important feature of ACTA. The European Union, for instance, failed in its attempt to transplant its entire regime on enforcement at the border,[54] but achieved the objective of negotiating a regime that did not directly conflict with the controversial European border enforcement system, particularly with regard to the control of products in transit. From this angle, and absent a decision in the World Trade Organization concerning the legality of the European system, ACTA backs the European Union's view that its regime does not contradict international law. It should also be noted that some provisions of the EU Information Society Directive are incorporated in the final version of ACTA.[55]

In this context, Kimberlee Weatherall discusses the extent to which the United States managed to realise its initial aspirations.[56] The United States originally had expectations of introducing its digital copyright regulations in ACTA, particularly with respect to rules against "hacking" technological protection measures, making Internet intermediaries an actual "police," as well as extensive rules criminalising even non-commercial copyright infringements. According to the author, the United States largely failed on this score, although some traces of the original proposals did make it into the text of the agreement. In this regard, the United States has

54 Grosse Ruse-Khan, Chapter 5 in this volume.

55 For instance, article 27.6 of ACTA.

56 Weatherall, Chapter 23 in this volume.

been considerably more successful with equivalent provisions in several free trade agreements. Moreover, US law – and in many respects the TRIPS *aquis* – is present in other provisions of the agreement. For instance, as Frederick M. Abbott shows, in deference to US law (28 USC §1498), ACTA Article 8.2 provides that remedies against government use may be limited to the payment of remuneration.[57]

TRIPS provisions have also been the object of transplantation, and many of them are part, or partially present, in ACTA.[58] This occurrence is in some cases verbatim, that is, ACTA articles exactly reproduce the parallel TRIPS provision. ACTA Article 6, which lays down the general obligations with regard to enforcement, is a good example of this kind of transplantation. On other occasions, transplantation becomes somewhat innovative because it incorporates the legislation by reference, according to which ACTA entirely embraces the referenced provisions. As noted, this is the case, for instance, for TRIPS objectives and principles, since ACTA Article 2.3 simply provides that TRIPS articles 7 and 8 apply *mutatis mutandis* to ACTA.[59]

## *Unbalanced Transplantation: Exploring Possible Responses*

Another important feature of the agreement is the frequently unbalanced transplantation of exported norms. Exporting countries have developed comprehensive and complex national legal regimes to promote innovation, reward authors, foster competition and ensure intellectual property enforcement. However, it has become a frequent practice in negotiations of international treaties to attempt to transpose sections found in national laws that mostly reflect the interests of some industrial sectors to the detriment of other IP stakeholders. Although exceptions do exist,[60] several scholars emphasise that ACTA is a prime example of an unbalanced transposition of legal norms. A number of authors point to different examples in areas such as injunctions and precautionary measures.[61]

57 Abbott, op. cit.

58 See the section on "Unbalanced transplantation: exploring possible responses" in this chapter.

59 *See* Seuba, Chapter 3 in this volume.

60 There is at least one case where the partial transplantation has resulted in the treaty going further – in the sense of offering more guarantees for alleged infringers – than the original legislation did. This case concerns the proportionality principle. In TRIPS this principle is mentioned in article 46 (on "other remedies") and refers to actions adopted in judicial proceedings and regarding the destruction of infringing goods or its disposal outside the channels of commerce, and it is also mentioned in article 47, which affects the right of information. In ACTA, by contrast, by virtue of article 6, the principle of proportionality applies to civil, criminal and administrative enforcement, and to the specific provisions enshrined regarding digital enforcement. Thus, all authorities related to intellectual property enforcement, and not only the judiciary, are requested to assess the alleged infringement and its consequences, and discretionally decide whether or not to proceed in light of the foreseeable impact on balance.

61 *See* the section in this chapter devoted to the relation between human rights and ACTA, as well Professor Sanders, who points out that "ACTA does not explicitly provide for the possibility of

In some cases, the challenges do not result from lack of balance, vagueness or even silence of the exported norms. Occasionally, imported norms bring inbuilt problems that can become more acute in their new context. For instance, the transplantation of some TRIPS provisions into ACTA has implied importing old uncertainties and unsettled questions into the new agreement. Indeed – particularly with regard to the initial provisions, definitions and general principles – the norms imported from TRIPS are almost as controversial as they are important. Their real meaning, scope and implications are still open to speculation and debate. These uncertainties are exacerbated in ACTA, since not all the links made in TRIPS to related norms within that agreement have been incorporated into ACTA.

Problems that result from a lack of balance and vagueness of the exported norms refer mostly to issues related to access to public goods, the protection of fundamental rights and coherence within the system. There are, in our view, several ways to address these questions.

When the negative impact affects fundamental rights, ACTA itself could provide a first answer. In line with the interpretation offered later in the chapter, ACTA Article 1 would enable fundamental rights norms to take precedence over conflicting obligations in the agreement.

When attention is focused on the impact of unbalanced norms on the entire system and its coherence, a comprehensive approach is needed. Complementing the norms with additional legislation and interpreting the adopted compromises pursuant to basic principles and fundamental rights is a way to tackle important imbalances.

Responding to the lack of important procedural and substantive safeguards in ACTA requires a proper identification of the unbalanced provisions. Once this has taken place, it will be possible to consider possible checks and balances that can be introduced at national level to complement the already existing text or obligations. Nothing impedes ACTA members from legislating in a sense not expressly forbidden in the agreement. If the needs are known and the normative answer is not prohibited, members may just implement it.

There are numerous sources of inspiration that can be used to reconstruct the system by introducing the missing balance, including the law of other ACTA members, relevant international commitments[62] or national and international jurisprudence. Indeed, A. K. Sanders recalls that "ACTA needs to be studied in the broader IP context provided for international and national norms."[63] There is no legal limit to drafting adequate text other than the limits set forth in ACTA.

applying pecuniary compensation as an alternative to injunction, as is customary in EU Member States." Sanders, Chapter 4 in this volume.

62 As A. K. Sanders states, "what may first appear to be gaps in ACTA may actually be filled by the TRIPS Agreement." Sanders, Chapter 4 in this volume.

63 Ibid.

Legislation will be also necessary in the case of a number of norms that purport to protect fundamental rights. While some ACTA provisions have been concisely drafted, and this facilitates its direct transposition, the references to basic interests and rights remain very general. In this regard, Rita Matulionyte underlines the need for "more specific guidelines on how these rights should be effectively ensured."[64] Whether with the assistance of guidelines such as these, or having recourse to other relevant legal instruments or (as Kimberlee Weatherall suggests) developing autonomous responses, ACTA makes it necessary to devise an important legislative agenda.[65]

The area of digital enforcement is a clear target of that agenda. In principle, ACTA seems to oblige parties to apply conventional enforcement measures to the digital environment. It commands, in effect, the application of its civil and criminal chapters to infringements occurring online. However, in response to the possible problems arising from that lack of differentiation, Matulinoyte recommends "to take the implicit flexibility of Article 27.1 into account and draft Internet-tailored enforcement rules, which would reflect the specific nature and needs of Internet environment."[66]

The important principles set forth in the initial provisions of ACTA (Articles 1–5) and the general obligations concerning enforcement (Article 6) could also be useful in introducing some balance. Article 6, for instance, mandates respect for fundamental due process principles. Invoking fairness and equity, it lays out an overarching proportionality principle. This can be useful in the daily interpretation of the agreement, as well as in the interpretation of national implementing legislation. In case of doubt, or when the apparent interpretation is contrary to the principles established in the initial provisions and in Article 6, these provisions will come into play. Moreover, and probably more importantly, they also have a legislative function since, as stated with regard to ACTA Article 6, it "allows Parties to maintain and apply additional procedural safeguards."[67]

There are, however, clear limits to interpretation. First, vague principles can become meaningless in presence of clearly worded provisions. Moreover, while balanced interpretations may provide an adequate legal response, they are generally non-binding. Additionally, the abundance of one-sided provisions and ambiguous clauses suggest that the initial provisions, and Article 6 in particular, seem to have a quasi-legislative function. The fact that a number of clauses are called to systematically adjust the content of most of the provisions confirms an important gap in the agreement, anticipating a great deal of speculation and debate on the specific interpretation of ACTA.

[64] Matulionyte, op. cit.
[65] Weatherall, op. cit.
[66] Matulionyte, op. cit.
[67] Sanders, op. cit.

### *The Underlying Question*

In the final chapters of this volume Kimberlee Weatherall and Brian Mercurio draw different conclusions from the same facts. Both share the view that ACTA in itself is a weak agreement, plagued with ambiguous provisions, which rarely exceed the international framework for IP enforcement, not to mention the constraints posed on the main drafters of the agreement. The authors also agree that this ambiguity would not have been the outcome any of the central parties wished for. They point to the insistence of the EU and the United States on the exportation of their own legislations as one of the causes of ACTA's failure. Both think that some of the rules proposed by the United States could not be agreed in ACTA because they were inconsistent with EU law, while some European proposals could not be included because they were contrary to US law.

However, while they share the diagnosis, the authors differ in their prognosis. For Mercurio, the key to achieving an efficient enforcement regime is the negotiation of a *real* international treaty, meaning an agreement that contains clear enforcement norms reached through an authentic compromise, and hence harmonisation and lawmaking.[68] By contrast, Weatherall favours further diversity. After pointing out that ACTA was watered down in the areas where the US and the EU legislation diverged, she concludes: "This suggests developing local models in other important countries – such as India, Brazil, China, and others – as a strategy to counter the attempt to 'multilateralise' any harmful ACTA or other IP provisions."[69]

## WHAT ABOUT THE VALUE-ADDED OF ACTA?

### *TRIPS as the Point of Departure*

To assess the real value of ACTA, it might be helpful to raise first the question on whether, if it became the global common standard on enforcement, the treaty would imply a major change to the present normative landscape.

A comparison between the agreement's initial drafts and the more moderate final version makes it tempting to hold that ACTA is, in fact, both ambiguous and ambitious. Most of the controversial provisions contained in the early drafts disappeared, or were attenuated, in the final text. This is the case, for instance, concerning the incorporation of patents in the border measures section, the implementation of graduated response systems for combating file sharing, and the obligations of third parties to control infringing activities occurring on the Internet. However, a focus on whether or not the final Act has improved initial versions misses the central

[68] Mercurio, op. cit.

[69] *See* Weatherall, op. cit.

question: Does ACTA, as finally concluded, imply major changes to the present normative landscape?

A second approach would be to compare ACTA's final text with the legislation of the states behind the adoption of the agreement. The treaty could indeed be relevant if parties agreed to move forward and create new enforcement standards. However, from this perspective ACTA appears to offer little substance. Although it has been proved that in some instances the agreement does imply changing the legislation of the countries that promoted it, the treaty remains in general a "codification of the status quo among the negotiating parties"[70] and does not alter in a significant way the law of the central negotiating parties. While there are situations where the agreement might induce interpretations that could imply changes in domestic law, ACTA does not prescribe one interpretation over another. And although there could be cases of more acute tensions,[71] in our opinion they are not representative of the general implications of the agreement.

A third approach to assessing whether ACTA implies a major shift from the present legal framework can be drawn from a comparison between the treaty and free trade agreements (FTAs). The latter, particularly in the last decade, have incorporated stringent IP enforcement standards. They have also created committees or organs with the competence to monitor the FTAs' implementation. This parallelism with ACTA makes these agreements a clear source of comparison. From this perspective, the conclusion is that ACTA contains less demanding obligations than those enshrined in commercial treaties promoted either by the United States or the EU. It may, however, be misleading to dismiss the real relevance of ACTA due to the fact that the number of countries having concluded these agreements is, globally speaking, still relatively low. By contrast, ACTA could be relevant to third countries that could, without entering into a free trade agreement, become obliged by it.[72]

The preceding observations suggest that any genuine comparison of ACTA should be done on the basis of a more comprehensive and globally binding parameter, characteristics only met by the TRIPS Agreement. On the one hand, TRIPS is *the* international treaty, near universal in character, and binding nearly 160 WTO member states. Its comprehensive enforcement provisions were unprecedented at

[70] Mercurio, op. cit.

[71] For instance, Sanders underlines a delicate case regarding damages: "The criteria for damages in ACTA (i.e., the value of the goods or services concerned measured by market or retail price) do, for example, not appear to fully match the criterion of 'appropriateness of the damage to the actual prejudice suffered' as expressed in Article 13 of Directive 2004/48/EC of the European Parliament and of the Council of 29 April 2004 on the enforcement of intellectual property rights (hereafter the EU IPR Enforcement Directive). As such, where EU Member States continue to apply the IPR Enforcement Directive's criterion they may potentially be in violation of the ACTA requirement to have their judges consider such, non-traditional forms of measuring damages." Sanders, op. cit.

[72] *See* Barbosa, Chapter 11 in this volume.

the time TRIPS was adopted. Indeed, TRIPS Part III still is the most inclusive multilateral legal framework on IP enforcement.

If TRIPS – and not earlier ACTA drafts, its proponents' legislation or IP chapters in FTAs – is the primary parameter to be taken into account, the agreement becomes an ambitious compromise. From the normative, institutional and systemic angles, the treaty is, in comparison to TRIPS, an important legal instrument. In its daily operation, the three dimensions mentioned would function together, hence the suggested triple approach – normative, institutional and systemic – provides the most rational basis for analysing the real implications of the agreement.

### *TRIPS and ACTA from a Normative Point of View*

From a normative perspective, ACTA does not represent a major departure from TRIPS, although it offers some novel features. This is particularly the case of ACTA Chapters I and II, which deal with initial provisions, general definitions and the legal framework for enforcement. Other chapters of the agreement address questions that are relevant from either an institutional or a systemic point of view.

Most of the provisions in ACTA Chapters I and II restate what TRIPS already provides. The most noticeable difference has to do with imbalance: where TRIPS sets forth procedural guarantees and limitations to right holders, ACTA remains silent at best. In this context, Weatherall points to the rules on the search and seizure of alleged infringing goods, and the fact that the right of the alleged infringer to be heard and to be given notice enshrined in TRIPS is not explicitly present in ACTA.[73] While omissions constitute one of the treaty's disconcerting features, this apparent gap can be dealt with either through appropriate implementing legislation or an appropriate interpretation of the agreement.[74] With respect to the normative differences between TRIPS and ACTA, those based on different substantive content – and not only on silence or ambiguity – are to be found in all sections of Chapter II, that is, civil, criminal, border and digital enforcement. As the TRIPS Agreement has no specific provisions on digital enforcement,[75] the comparison has to be made with respect to the other three sections of ACTA Chapter II.

Mercurio identifies several ACTA provisions that go beyond TRIPS. For instance, ACTA Article 8 establishes that injunctions apply to imports and exports, whereas

[73] For the relations between ACTA and TRIPS, *see* Seuba, Chapter 3 in this volume.

[74] See the second section of this chapter.

[75] Matulionyte, op. cit. Very importantly, ACTA "sets elaborated civil and criminal enforcement mechanisms for Internet IP infringements for the first time by reference to other chapters within ACTA." In effect, article 27 prescribes "that the civil and criminal chapters shall be applied in their entirety to infringements occurring online."

TRIPS Article 44.1 only applies to imports. This is also the case for ACTA Article 9, which sets up a more prescriptive regime for the calculation of damages than TRIPS Article 24.1. There are also fundamental differences in the perspective adopted with regard to several situations. For instance, ACTA advances the moment of action when it refers to "alleged infringer" instead of just "infringer" (as is the case in TRIPS), or "suspected goods" instead of "infringing goods."[76] In a similar fashion, a number of ACTA provisions have a mandatory character whereas in TRIPS they are merely optional.

Furthermore, the border measures sections of TRIPS and ACTA diverge in important respects. Henning Grosse Ruse-Khan focuses attention on the fact that, in contrast to TRIPS, ACTA's border measures section does not solely mention counterfeit and pirated goods as its mandatory target but also applies to goods infringing any other IP category, except patents and data protection. This would create an avenue for impeding the transit of confusingly similar trademarked goods, a measure that would particularly affect pharmaceutical goods sharing an international nonproprietary name (INN) in their trademark.[77] The importance and implications of similar legislation in Africa has been considered by Christophe Spennemann in his analysis of the East African enforcement legislation.[78]

For many authors, the most troubling provisions in ACTA are those on criminal measures. Christophe Geiger is of the view that the treaty's provisions in this area are probably its most problematic feature, fundamentally because of the difficulties that stem from the perspective of due process and the principle of legality.[79] There is also a noticeable difference in some of the definitions contained in ACTA Chapter I, namely those on "counterfeit trademark goods" and "pirated copyright goods." Whereas in TRIPS the infringing nature is evaluated in accordance with the law of the country of importation, in ACTA the relevant law is that of the country in which the procedures are invoked.[80]

### *The Institutional Departures from TRIPS*

Another area where ACTA and TRIPS differ significantly concerns the institutional framework. In this case, the debate revolves around the institutional structure created by ACTA and the potentially far-reaching powers of the ACTA Committee. The institutional dimension also brings into consideration a second question, the

[76] Compare articles 11 of ACTA versus article 47 of TRIPS, and article 25 of ACTA against article 49 of TRIPS.

[77] *See* H. Grosse Ruse-Khan, op. cit.

[78] Spennemann, Chapter 15 in this volume.

[79] See the human rights section later in this chapter.

[80] *See* Seuba, op. cit.

forum-shifting phenomenon or technique. Indeed, forum shifting is of the utmost relevance in the context of ACTA given that it not only explains its existence but also permits predicting its eventual fate.

Regarding the ACTA Committee, Peter Yu explains that the setup of this organ represents the most far-reaching and daring aspect of the agreement owing to the important competences (some compulsory, some optional) assigned to the committee. In effect, and regardless of the fact that the committee is not a dispute settlement body, its competences are dynamic, comprehensive and, above all, allow ACTA to develop into a much more IP-demanding and self-evolving forum.[81]

The creation of the ACTA Committee is part of the wider phenomenon of forum shifting. ACTA negotiations lasted three years and occurred outside existing multilateral bodies. Its creators decided to sidestep well-established fora with almost universal participation, because a number of governments had been unsuccessful in their efforts to increase the level of attention devoted to enforcement in those bodies. A majority of countries reject the need for a new international treaty on enforcement. In fact, many countries believe that intellectual property enforcement already receives the attention it deserves at the international level, and that the ongoing cooperation of activities in the legislative, technical, judicial and quasi-judicial[82] domains suffice for that purpose.

It was this lack of interest in undertaking forceful enforcement measures –sometimes perceived by the IP-demanding actors as obstruction to efforts to improve enforcement[83] – that moved a number of countries to promote a new international covenant. In the words of Sean Flynn, those countries "regime-shifted" into a new lawmaking forum.[84] This move has become so common in international intellectual property lawmaking that it gave rise to the "regime-shifting" terminology and its rationale almost a decade ago.[85]

[81] Yu, Chapter 8 in this volume.

[82] *China – Measures affecting the protection and enforcement of intellectual property rights*, Report of the Panel, January 26, 2009, WT/DS362/R.

[83] "It is necessary to stress that attempts by the European Union and other supporters of an effective IPR system to constructively address enforcement problems in multilateral fora (World Trade Organisation, World Intellectual Property Organisation, World Customs Organisation) have been opposed by countries like Brazil and India, often supported by China, Argentina and others. This has prevented some of these institutions from addressing pressing IPR enforcement issues that could suitably be resolved multilaterally." Commission Staff Working Document, IPR Enforcement Report 2009, Brussels, SEC(2009) 1360, p. 4, available at: http://trade.ec.europa.eu/doclib/docs/2009/october/tradoc_145204.pdf (accessed 13 February 2013).

[84] Flynn, op. cit.

[85] *See* the seminal article, L. Helfer, "Regime-Shifting: The TRIPS Agreement and the New Dynamics of Intellectual Property Policymaking", *Yale Journal of International Law*, vol. 29, no 1, 2004.

Another term related to forum shifting is the "country club" approach,[86] that is, those interested in the adoption of a certain regulation just negotiate among themselves and exclude others. Numerous authors underline in their respective chapters of this book the detrimental effects of this negotiating strategy and the concomitant weakening of the existing multilateral legal framework.[87] Moreover, and at least in the case of ACTA, some authors rightly point out the negative reputational effects of the country club approach.[88]

## *The Systemic Shift*

ACTA represents a major systemic shift compared to TRIPS. Whereas the latter represented a compromise subject to specific boundaries, ACTA – also an imperfect compromise – gives more the impression of a "framework" agreement announcing the direction of a future IP enforcement agenda. The assumption that TRIPS was a stable reference has obviously proved to be ephemeral, considering that new bilateral trade agreements demanding IP commitments beyond those agreed in TRIPS emerged almost contemporaneously. In contrast, ACTA is widely seen as a mere instrument to continue through diverse means strengthening IP enforcement internationally.

ACTA is not, however, a precise road map, probably because even the specific destination is still disputed by those proposing the agreement. This is a central issue in our view, since there is a general perception that ACTA (or its failure) constitute just a springboard for new initiatives to expand an overreaching enforcement agenda. The fact that ACTA has in-built mechanisms to move in that direction, and the previous experience regarding the multiple sources of influence to shape third countries' laws, is what really perturbs most analysts and third countries.

The challenges arising from ACTA have to do not only with the present text but also with its divergent readings and potential follow-up implementation that could be encouraged by interested actors.[89] Indeed, there is a general understanding that ACTA contains the main predominant common denominators in the major central countries and that its main threat lies in its potential maximalist implementation. The suspicion is that 'ACTA-plus' implementation will be promoted through a range of means.[90] In this regard Peter Yu highlights the potential role that the ACTA

86 Yu, op. cit.

87 Geiger, Weatherall, Yu, Barbosa, Rimmer, Sanders, all in this volume.

88 Weatherall, op. cit.

89 ACTA provisions worded in a non-binding manner "can nevertheless reflect an intention to induce the parties to introduce those provisions into their national law." Geiger, op. cit. See also the Opinion of European Academics on the Anti-Counterfeiting Trade Agreement (ACTA).

90 Geiger suggests that ACTA provisions drafted in a non-binding manner "can nevertheless reflect an intention to induce the parties to introduce those provisions into their national law." Geiger, op. cit.

Committee and the agreement's advocates will play in undertaking this task. This is even more important considering the general consensus that ACTA was drafted with third countries in mind, including China, which did not even participate in the negotiations.[91]

There are, however, more optimistic visions. Jonathan Band, for instance, has pointed out that in the case of the United States, the harsh criticisms of the holder-friendly stance and one-sided rules contained in ACTA have caused a change of attitude on the part of the US Trade Representative. Band holds that the United States now supports the need for an appropriate balance in providing exceptions and limitations in the area of copyright in the Trans-Pacific Partnership Agreement (TPP), something that could be achieved through exporting to the TPP exceptions comparable to those found in the United States.

Be that as it may, the majority of views reveal anxiety with regard to the direction suggested by ACTA on the future of the intellectual property enforcement agenda. This is the result of both the *demandeurs*' perceived expectations and ACTA's in-built ratchet up enforcement mechanisms.

Michel Geist and Rita Matulionyte identify the permissive provisions contained in ACTA as ideal tools to further increase the levels of enforcement. According to Geist, "there will be considerable pressure to reinterpret these provisions as mandatory rather than permissive," while "the experience with other treaties, such as the WIPO Internet treaties, indicates that flexible, permissive language is gradually transformed into mandatory, best-practice language."[92] Matulionyte expands on this issue by sustaining that "the importance of non-binding (or 'may') provisions should not be underestimated. When ACTA is used as a negotiating basis in bilateral negotiations with non-negotiating states, these provisions could easily be turned into 'shall' clauses as experience shows."[93]

Together with this permissiveness, the lack of clarity of the treaty's provisions has also been identified as a source of potential "ACTA-plus" implementation. Between description and irony, Matulionyte states for instance that "[w]hat exactly Article 27.2 obliges parties to do is a difficult question to answer." By contrast, it is easy to foresee that regardless of the obscurity of this provision, there will be elaborate proposals for its implementation. This is precisely why a number of authors agree that the main source of the problem in ACTA is "the vague and uncertain nature of some provisions and the lack of clear limits."[94]

91 Sanders, op. cit.
92 Geist, op. cit.
93 Matulionyte, op. cit.
94 Geiger, op. cit.

Vagueness and uncertainty could give rise to diverse modes of implementation, including schemes that could be in conflict with fundamental rights. This is the case, according to Annemarie Bridy, of ACTA provisions on civil enforcement by seizure and cooperative efforts, which would presumably be carried out mirroring the US implementation of similar provisions. This is a cause for concern and criticism from the human rights and access-to-knowledge angle.[95]

Silence, lack of clarity and omissions are potential avenues to continue ratcheting up enforcement. Kamperman Sanders cautions against the consequences of these omissions with respect to implementation: "The fact that ACTA omits any reference to such safeguards and limitations presents a real danger in the context of national implementation."[96]

Finally, from the point of view of ACTA's potential evolution, its effects will also expand to other agreements and situations in principle unrelated to it. As mentioned, the forum-shifting trend permits the partial prediction of the future of ACTA and international enforcement norms. In effect, as Peter Yu suggests, some of the potential uses and intentions of ACTA will be its incorporation in third countries by explicit or implied reference through FTAs, as well as its use as a standard to judge other countries in the context of unilateral evaluations, such as those regularly performed by the United States in the context of Section 301 of its Trade Act.[97] In the same line of reasoning, Kamperman alludes to the "unstated ambition of the ACTA states to influence not only future multilateral negotiations, but to equally use ACTA as a template for regional and bilateral agreements."[98]

## HUMAN RIGHTS

Subsequent ACTA drafts have been thoroughly scrutinised from the perspective of fundamental and human rights by legal experts, NGOs and public institutions. This has also been the case with regard to the final text, albeit with less intensity. The attention paid to ACTA's impact on fundamental rights was unprecedented in the context of negotiations for an intellectual property treaty. This level of attention must be contextualised, in our view, within the growing attention being paid to the intersection between intellectual property rights and human rights.

Human rights analyses of ACTA have focused on the agreement's potential impact on welfare and its intended effects on private life and the "alleged infringer" position in legal proceedings. With regard to the treaty's impact on welfare, it was

95 See discussion later in the chapter.
96 *See* Sanders, Chapter 4 of this volume.
97 *See* Yu, op. cit.
98 Sanders, op. cit.

advanced that cultural and social rights could be threatened by ACTA's prospective restraint on trade, competition and access in areas such as food, culture and health. Moreover, the initially proposed draconian provisions affecting privacy and the parties' position in judicial or administrative infringement procedures were seen as alarming threats to civil rights.

From the point of view of cultural and social rights, the facet of ACTA that received most attention during its negotiation was that of border measures. In this regard, ACTA was almost contemporaneous with cases of seizures of patented goods transiting through Europe. The controversial seizures and the EU's initial proposal to include in ACTA provisions resembling those already existing in the Union raised awareness and concern in the global health community. As Henning Grosse Ruse-Khan explains, and Christophe Spennemann identifies in the case of East African countries, the final text still presents some potential avenues that may complicate the free flow of generic products while in transit.[99]

In addition to the direct restriction of access caused by specific ACTA interpretations, there is also another phenomenon of great relevance in terms of welfare. The 'chilling effect' on competition caused by new enforcement obligations – particularly those of an unbalanced nature – is an important, albeit difficult to quantify, outcome of ACTA and other treaties like it. Some enforcement provisions have been drafted in a way that may deter totally legal activities. In this regard, the eventual consequences of an adverse ruling, or just the costs of litigation, may be severe enough to discourage individuals, businesses or governments from undertaking perfectly legal activities. In the case of patents, such chilling effects can result from enforcement measures linked to disputable questions, such as those related to the interpretation of the patentability criteria. This, in turn, may result in a reduction of competition, thus leading to a lower supply of goods and higher prices.

Most of the preoccupations arising from the intersection between ACTA and fundamental rights rise from its impact on civil rights, mainly with regard to fair trial standards and privacy guarantees. While the concern over ACTA's impact on due process is almost general and affects provisions contained all through the agreement, the impact of ACTA on privacy is most noticeable in the digital enforcement section.

For Candice Li and Brian Mercurio, the digital environment section is key to understanding many of the controversies around fundamental rights, as well as the section's perceived general impact and ultimately its fate. Although the lengthy Article 27, which is the sole provision on the digital environment, states that procedures shall be implemented in a manner that preserves fundamental principles such as freedom of expression, fair process and privacy, the impression is left that

99 *See* Ruse-Khan, op. cit., and Spenneman, op. cit.

this sweeping statement will not be enough to counterbalance the specificity of the potentially deleterious mandates set forth in Article 27.

The criminal enforcement section has also been considered awkward. With regard to its impact on civil rights, ACTA's vague definition of "commercial scale" – described as "commercial activities for direct or indirect economic or commercial advantage" – leads Christophe Geiger to conclude that the provision still has "a very uncertain scope making this definition highly problematic with regard to the principle of legal certainty and legality of criminal offenses."[100] As he further explains, "the provisions on criminal enforcement are certainly one of the most problematic aspects of the agreement, if not *the* most problematic."[101]

From the point of view of due process and fair trial standards, the absence of procedural guarantees is what makes ACTA so troublesome. Many have highlighted the lack of reference to the right to be heard, as provided in TRIPS Article 41, or the lack of reference to the possibility of judicial review of final administrative decisions as major gaps in the agreement.[102] Analyses on specific provisions have also sought to demonstrate that the missing checks and balances reveal important problems from the angle of due process. This is the case, for instance, of provisional measures where problems may result from the lack of reference to the right to be informed without delay, the right to a review or the right to have the measures revoked in case proceedings are not instituted within a reasonable period.

Implementation is a central preoccupation in most of the analyses that touch on fundamental rights. Annemarie Bridy underlines two cases where specific – and predictable – implementation may undermine the right to transmit and receive information over the Internet, as well as due process guarantees. According to Bridy, provisions on "cooperative efforts" in the digital environment section, and those on seizure in the section on civil enforcement, can create problems if they are implemented as in the United States. This preoccupation stems from the potential privatisation of online copyright enforcement pursuant to business agreements that become binding for Internet users. With regard to civil seizure, its implementation may "undermine due process of law"[103] if it implies allowing the government to seize and retain suspect domain names on weak evidence of criminal infringement. Rita Matulionyte also contends that, "If private online enforcement mechanisms like these are created, guaranteeing fundamental rights, such as the protection of personal data, becomes even more complicated."[104]

[100] Geiger, op. cit.
[101] Ibid.
[102] Abbott, op. cit.
[103] Bridy, Chapter 14 in this volume.
[104] Matulionyte, op. cit.

Despite these conflictive areas, it is important to remember that, at least formally, ACTA Article 1 can be read as recognising the pre-eminence of fundamental rights.[105] It seems, however, that the conflict clause set forth therein is unlikely to be applied. First, international public law favours interpretation over conflict, and ACTA interpretations avoiding conflict with human rights norms shall prevail. In fact, as the final text stands, almost all provisions validate interpretations that would not pose conflicts from the human rights point of view. But even if this were not the case, any impact on human rights would probably be caused by norms interpreting and implementing ACTA in the national legal order. That is, the most likely conflict would take place between a national norm implementing ACTA and human rights treaties or national legislation. This is why the centre of attention should mainly be national implementation of ACTA and national norms on the incorporation and hierarchy of international law.

## WHAT LIES AHEAD?

ACTA's future as a meaningful international treaty is uncertain. Its rejection by the European Parliament could have been the final blow. In fact, for many of the commentators ACTA is a "failed agreement, and represents a failure of international lawmaking."[106] Having said that, there is a perception that ACTA is not over.

ACTA is an international treaty with an open process of ratification, and future accessions are actively sought. Both in general and with respect to particular countries, the United States has declared that it is working to bring ACTA into force.[107] Moreover, the United States uses ACTA to examine other signatory and non-signatory countries enforcement laws and practices. Along these lines, the United States recently urged Canada to "meet its Anti-Counterfeit Trade Agreement (ACTA) obligations by providing its customs officials with ex officio authority to stop the transit of counterfeit and pirated goods throughout its territory."[108] And third, ACTA is also the basis of several relevant ongoing initiatives in the area of IP enforcement.

Preferential trade agreements may possibly take over ACTA's legacy. The Transpacific Partnership (TPP) Agreement is presently the most important candidate

[105] Seuba, Chapter 2 in this volume.

[106] Mercurio, op. cit.

[107] In its 2013 301 report, the USTR declares that it "is working with Japan and other negotiating parties to bring ACTA into force" (and alludes to one of the negotiating countries), and "looks forward to the Mexican Senate's ratification of the Anti-Counterfeiting Trade Agreement."

[108] R. Kirk, USTR, 2013 Trade Policy Agenda and 2012 Annual Report of the President of the United States on the Trade Agreements Program, 2013, p. 140, http://www.ustr.gov/sites/default/files/Chapter%20III%20-%20Bilateral%20and%20Regional%20Negotiations%20and%20Agreements.pdf (accessed March 2013).

for the transposition of ACTA provisions. Leaked drafts of the TPP intellectual property chapter incorporate many clauses that were raised, discussed and eventually rejected during the ACTA negotiations. They could be viewed as one of the legacies or even the pursuit of the new enforcement agenda proclaimed by ACTA. Similarly, the EU's association agreements under negotiation restate ACTA's content and, in some cases, even surpass it.

Unilateral, bilateral and regional pursuits of the ACTA agenda confirm the preoccupation of a majority of authors contributing to this book. For many, ACTA was not problematic just because of its content, but because it was embedded into a context of unbalanced strengthening of IP protection. ACTA would simply be an additional step further, relevant largely because of its comprehensive content and multilateral aspirations. However, a valid question after ACTA is whether it is possible to continue with this trend.

Several decisive factors for change are identified in the chapters of this book, among them social pressure on the part of active consumers. Civil society and legislatures have joined trade diplomats and corporations in the debate, and the demand for transparent and consistent proposals is louder than ever. The new scenario points to the need for changing, both in the way that negotiations are conducted and the ultimate assumptions that justify international legislation in this area.

The new and still uncertain balance of power in international relations announces an era of stiffer resistance from the more powerful countries. The fact that emerging economies with both offensive and defensive positions on intellectual property are becoming more visible and active in international lawmaking is likely to engender different alliances and attempts to balance the content of new international norms.

At the same time, ACTA is a reflection of some of the most notorious characteristics of recent intellectual property initiatives, namely ambiguity and imbalance. It can be argued that these result in rules of low quality. Contradictory as it may seem, stiffer reaction on the part of emerging economies may well imply new proposals. Accurate identification of ACTA's gaps and problems may be a good point of departure for better and more balanced enforcement legislation. In fact, the likelihood that similar enforcement initiatives, modelled on ACTA, will be carried out in the future appears slim and uncertain.

Finally, attention to social, economic and psychological aspects of intellectual property protection is crucial for the success of global legislative initiatives. This calls for adjustment to national circumstances and social values of institutions closely linked to public interest and social sensitivities. The perception of fairness is key to ensuring a sense of ownership in agreements setting up new enforcement mechanisms, without which these agreements would probably lack not only legitimacy but also practical effect.

PART I

# The Final Act: Its Main Features and Contents

# 1

# An Overview of the Agreement

## *Contents and Features*

*Frederick M. Abbott*

### INTRODUCTION

The Anti-Counterfeiting Trade Agreement (ACTA) is a signed international agreement that is pending ratification and entry into force.[1] Signature and initial membership are limited to the group of countries which participated in its negotiation, and others that may be agreed to by consensus. The negotiating participants are the member states of the European Union (EU) as well as Australia, Canada, Japan, South Korea, Mexico, Morocco, New Zealand, Singapore, Switzerland and the United States.

Negotiation of ACTA provoked controversy from the outset. Proponents characterised it as an exercise needed to address an ongoing threat to the interests of intellectual property right (IPR) owners, as well as to defend the public against risks posed by goods coming from unreliable sources. Opponents portrayed ACTA negotiations as driven by IPR holder groups intent on moving their high-protection agenda away from multilateral institutions towards a more hospitable forum. In the multilateral organisations, a range of interested groups participate in negotiations, and the results should appropriately balance legitimate interests (if common ground can be found). The ACTA negotiating forum, by way of contrast, was predisposed to favour particular IPR holder objectives.

The initially proposed ACTA texts threatened to create an international trade and technology transfer environment, including in digital space, with serious obstacles to access for important public goods, including medicines and information. Proposed criminalisation measures were unbalanced. Ultimately, a number of the most troublesome elements of the initial proposals were dropped, alleviating some of the most pressing worries. However, the signed ACTA text still contains problematic elements, as discussed later in this chapter.

[1] Pursuant to Article 40, the agreement will enter into force thirty days following deposit of the sixth instrument of ratification, acceptance, or approval.

This relatively concise overview of ACTA is intended to inform the reader regarding its basic structure and rules. The reader is urged to consult other chapters for discussion of negotiating history, critical review of specific sections and the institutional concerns raised.

ACTA is made up of a preamble and five chapters. The first two chapters are divided into sections.

## THE PREAMBLE

The preamble sets out the premises and objectives of the parties. The initial premise is that "effective enforcement of intellectual property rights is critical to sustaining economic growth across all industries." A second set of premises emphasises that the "proliferation of counterfeit and pirated goods, as well as services that distribute infringing material" undermines legitimate trade and "sustainable development of the world economy," causes significant losses for right holders and, in some cases, provides a source of revenue for organised crime and otherwise poses risks to the public.

The initial premise foreshadows that substantive coverage of ACTA is not limited to goods traditionally included within the definitions of counterfeit trademark and copyright pirated goods, but rather extends across the range of goods and services that are addressed by IPRs under the WTO's Agreement on Trade-Related Aspects of Intellectual Property Rights (TRIPS Agreement). In that regard, ACTA negotiators may have indulged in deceptive labelling. By way of illustration, goods that infringe patents do not fall within the customary definition of counterfeit goods, nor do goods that use a geographical indication (GI) even when produced outside the source-identified region. They are, however, within the scope of ACTA. The second set of premises – that counterfeiting has a measurable and/or significant impact on global economic growth, and/or is hostile to sustainable development – is debatable. There is very little reliable data on the extent of counterfeiting and its impact on economic well-being. Sustainable development for countries at the lower end of the GDP scale may require inward transfers of technology that can be hampered by overprotective IP enforcement rules. Whether ACTA would promote sustainable development is not easily assessed.

The objectives of ACTA are stated to complement the TRIPS Agreement, including by ensuring that IPRs do not themselves become barriers to legitimate trade. The objectives include addressing infringement taking place in the digital environment, in a manner that balances the interests of rights holders, service providers and users. The signed text of ACTA scales back initially proposed IP rights holder controls that would have imposed liability on Internet service providers for failing to adequately monitor digital content. The preamble suggests promoting cooperation between service providers and rights holders to address infringement in the digital environment.

The preamble expressly "recognize[s] the principles set forth in the Doha Declaration on the TRIPS Agreement and Public Health." In light of the substantive provisions of ACTA, it is open to question whether it is consistent with those principles. For example, the signed text of ACTA mandates criminal liability for the use of trademarks in packaging and labelling that may take place as an ordinary incident of legitimate parallel trading. It also recognises (but does not mandate) the possibility of civil trademark infringement liability based on passage of generic medicines in transit through ports and airports. The European Court of Justice (ECJ) has recently rejected IP infringement based on mere transit.

## CHAPTER I, INITIAL PROVISIONS AND GENERAL DEFINITIONS

### *Section 1: Initial Provisions*

Article 1 provides that nothing in ACTA derogates "from any obligation of a Party with respect to any other Party under existing agreements, including the TRIPS Agreement." ACTA parties are typically party to various World Intellectual Property Organization (WIPO) agreements (e.g., the Paris and Berne Conventions, the WIPO Copyright and Performances and Phonograms Treaties), and this subjects ACTA commitments to a substantial range of potentially superior multilateral obligations. In addition, pre-existing bilateral and/or regional agreements in force appear to take priority over conflicting ACTA commitments.

It is important that ACTA parties remain subject to their TRIPS Agreement obligations because ACTA notably fails to include a significant number of due process protections found in the TRIPS Agreement.

It is a drafting curiosity, at the least, that ACTA Article 1 refers to preserving the obligations of the parties to each other, rather than more generally referring to obligations under existing agreements. The ACTA language seems to imply that only governments are beneficiaries of due process protections. Nonetheless, ACTA does not expressly attempt to alleviate parties of their protective TRIPS obligations.

ACTA Article 2 authorises parties to adopt more extensive enforcement of IPRs than is required by the agreement, leaving them free to determine the appropriate method of implementing commitments within their own legal systems and practice. It also incorporates the objectives and principles of Part I of the TRIPS Agreement, and in particular Articles 7 and 8, *mutatis mutandis*. Developing countries traditionally have placed considerable stock in maintaining the balance articulated in TRIPS Articles 7 and 8. They expressed concerns about the direction of the ACTA in the

WTO TRIPS Council, particularly its potential for shifting the balance between rights holders and consumers.

ACTA Article 3.2 provides that parties are not obligated to apply measures "where a right in intellectual property is not protected under its laws and regulations." In other words, ACTA does not require any party to create new substantive IPRs. This means, for example, that the United States does not need to adopt new protections for GIs so as to implement more extensive protection for EU GIs. It is curious that the European Commission stressed the importance of securing stronger protection for GIs as an objective in ACTA negotiations, while results in this regard are ambiguous at best.

ACTA Article 4 provides that parties are not required to disclose information contrary to their laws or the protection of privacy rights, or confidential information which would impede law enforcement or prejudice legitimate commercial interests. Further, when a party receives information, it is expected to refrain from disclosing it for a purpose other than for which it was provided, absent consent of the provider. The extent to which privacy is protected will depend on the legal framework in force in specific national/regional jurisdictions. Standards in this regard vary substantially among ACTA countries.

### *Section 2: General Definitions*

Section 2 contains only Article 5 on General Definitions. It includes definitions of counterfeit trademarked goods and pirated copyright goods that are substantially identical to the respective definitions in the TRIPS Agreement, footnote 14. It defines in-transit goods to include customs transit and transhipment. Perhaps most important, it provides that intellectual property refers to all categories of IP that are the subject of Sections 1 through 7 of Part II of the TRIPS Agreement, thus making clear that ACTA has a substantially broader subject matter scope than addressing "counterfeiting" as traditionally understood. As discussed later in the chapter, ACTA distinguishes the treatment of the forms of IP in various ways, that is, the forms of IP are not treated equally.

## CHAPTER II, LEGAL FRAMEWORK FOR ENFORCEMENT OF IPRS

### *Section 1: General Obligations*

The general obligations of the parties to make available effective enforcement procedures are in some respects similar to the obligations of WTO members under the TRIPS Agreement, although they differ in material ways. For example, the TRIPS Agreement (Article 41.3) requires that a decision on the merits will be based only on evidence in respect of which parties were offered the opportunity to be heard, but there is no such obligation in ACTA. TRIPS Agreement Article 41.4 requires the availability of judicial review of final administrative decisions, whereas ACTA does not. The TRIPS Agreement (Article 42) requires that defendants have a right to written notice which is timely and includes sufficient detail, and the opportunity to present all relevant evidence. There is no such obligation under ACTA.

### *Section 2: Civil Enforcement*

This section obligates parties to make available civil judicial procedures for the enforcement of "any intellectual property right," but footnote 3 allows each party to "exclude patents and protection of undisclosed information from the scope of this Section." When administrative procedures on the merits are substituted for judicial procedures, they are to conform with the principles of the Section (ACTA, Article 7). The footnoted right of exclusion was necessary because ACTA provisions on civil enforcement are inconsistent with patent law and practice in the United States, and this would raise considerable problems in securing congressional approval. Yet, the executive branch in the United States has so far maintained its intention to forgo the constitutionally required congressional approval processes for ACTA. It is unclear why the executive branch thought it could not unconstitutionally amend patent law as well.

Parties are to make available injunctions to prevent infringing goods from entering into the channels of commerce, and this should be extended to third parties over whom judicial authorities exercise jurisdiction. In deference to 28 USC § 1498 of the US (which prevents injunctions from being issued against government use of patents), Article 8.2 of ACTA provides that remedies against government use may be limited only to the payment of remuneration. Article 44.2 of the TRIPS Agreement includes a similar option for limiting injunctions with respect to government use of licenses, also in deference to US law and practice in this area.

Article 9 addresses damages, and generally provides that judicial authorities will have the power to order infringers to pay damages to right holders. Notably, Article 9.1 provides that judicial authorities shall have the power to consider any legitimate measure of value submitted by the right holder, "which may include lost profits, the value of the infringed goods or services measured by the market price, or the suggested retail price." Although the award of damages based on such measures is not mandatory, the use of suggested retail prices as the standard for damages is particularly troublesome. Such prices are not representative of payments to manufacturers by wholesalers and distributors, and in any case are likely to be artificial even from the retail sale standpoint. Article 9.3 requires the availability of pre-established damages, presumptions and additional damages at least for infringement of copyright and related rights, and for cases of trademark counterfeiting. Either judicial authorities or right holders will have the right to elect pre-established or presumptive damages (Article 9.4). In trademark and copyright cases, judicial authorities will have the power to order payment of court costs and attorneys' fees as provided under their law (Article 9.5). The importance of establishing higher benchmarks for damages based on infringement should not be underestimated in terms of potential for chilling legitimate business activities, particularly for small and medium-size enterprises that may not have the resources to engage in protracted litigation with larger market participants.

Article 10 provides that at least for pirated copyright and counterfeit trademarked goods, judicial authorities shall have the right to order the destruction of the goods without compensation, and to order the destruction or disposal outside channels of commerce of materials and implements that were used predominantly to manufacture or create the pirated/counterfeit goods. While copyright and trademark owners have legitimate interests in effective measures against producers of pirated copyright and counterfeit trademarked goods, remedies that extend to destruction of manufacturing equipment may also be a threat to producers of goods important to social welfare, such as authentic generic drugs. Caution must be exercised in crafting and applying such remedies.

Article 11 concerns provision of information and the authority of judges to order the infringer to provide relevant information to the judge or right holder. It is qualified by reference to protections under national laws regarding personal data, privilege and related matters. It extends to information regarding identification of third persons involved in production or distribution.

Article 12 stipulates that judicial authorities must have the power to order provisional measures against an accused infringer or a third party within its jurisdiction to prevent goods from entering the stream of commerce, and to preserve evidence. As with the TRIPS Agreement, judicial authorities shall have the power to adopt provisional measures outside the presence of the parties (i.e., *inaudita altera parte*). However, unlike TRIPS Agreement Article 50.4, there is no corresponding right of the accused infringer to have a hearing to review the grant of provisional measures. Further, unlike TRIPS Agreement Article 50.6, there is no provision requiring that a provisional measure cease to have effect if proceedings on the merits are not commenced within a reasonable period of time. This is a circumstance in which it is critical for the protection of accused infringers that TRIPS Agreement obligations (limiting government authority) remain effective within ACTA parties. Without the obligation found in the TRIPS Agreement, goods might be retained indefinitely by customs authorities, or at least until an accused infringer is able to obtain relief by petitioning the courts (and bearing the expense of doing that). Under ACTA, authorities shall have the right to order an applicant for provisional measures (i.e., right holder) to provide security, and judicial authorities shall have the right to provide an accused infringer with appropriate compensation in the event of a finding of non-infringement.

### *Section 3: Border Measures*

Two footnotes (3 and 4) generally qualify the scope of obligations under Section 3 on border measures. It does not require application among countries that have dismantled substantially all border measures in a customs union (e.g., the EU), and parties may elect not to apply the measures to parallel import goods (i.e., "goods put on the market in another country by or with the consent of the right holder").[2] A third footnote (6), contains an essential limitation on the scope of Section 3, providing that "[t]he Parties agree that patents and protection of undisclosed information do not fall within the scope of this Section."

Article 13 generally sets out the scope of border measures, providing that they should be applied by the parties "in a manner that does not discriminate unjustifiably between intellectual property rights." During negotiations the parties differed concerning the potential scope of coverage of ACTA, and the provision on non-discrimination may represent an attempt to take into account the interests of the EU in securing adequate treatment of GIs. However, this is not a particularly robust formulation, leaving the parties with considerable leeway in deciding what may or may not be discriminatory application. Note that Article 13 of ACTA uses the term "discriminate" that was interpreted by a WTO panel in the *Canada – Patent Protection of Pharmaceutical Products* case to be "a normative term, pejorative in connotation, referring to results of the unjustified imposition of differentially disadvantageous treatment."[3] Article 13 does not require that forms of IP be treated in the same way, but that differential treatment be justifiable.

Article 14.1 provides that the parties shall include "goods of a commercial nature sent in small consignments" among the products covered. This presumably was intended to include individual shipments of pharmaceutical products (e.g., purchased from Internet pharmacies) across borders, and would cover the shipment of individual counterfeit trademarked products (e.g., handbags). Article 14.2 allows the parties to exclude "small quantities of goods of a non-commercial nature contained in travellers' personal luggage." This presumably is intended to cover the holiday travel "take-home" of individual counterfeit watches, handbags, and so forth. It is

[2] The formulation for exhaustion uses the "consent" basis, as compared with the "lawfully placed on the market" basis, which itself entails a selection among policies. For example, a good placed on the market under a prior user right or on the basis of a compulsory license would not benefit from the provision.

[3] Report of the Panel, WT/DS114/R, 17 March 2000, at para. 7.94.

foreseeable that ACTA parties may be called upon by private right holders to block cross-border purchases of pharmaceutical products by individuals seeking to take advantage of substantial differences in pricing, such as exist between Canada and the United States.

Article 15 authorizes competent authorities to request a right holder to supply relevant information to assist it in taking border measures, and for the right holder to supply such information.

Article 16 is the core substantive provision of the Section. It requires parties to adopt and maintain procedures for import and export shipments under which customs authorities may act ex officio to suspend the release of "suspect goods" and, "where appropriate," allow right holders to request such suspension. It allows, but does not mandate, that parties maintain procedures regarding "suspect in-transit goods" or other circumstances under customs' control, allowing ex officio action to suspend release of suspect goods, and right holders to request such action. In other words, there is a mandatory general obligation to provide for border enforcement measures with respect to imports and exports, and an acknowledgment of a right to apply measures to goods in transit. The acknowledgment as to in-transit goods is problematic on various accounts, inter alia because (1) it is not limited to goods suspected of disguising an intent to enter the local stream of commerce (i.e., false transit); (2) it is inconsistent with principles of territoriality regulating IPRs (as per the ECJ in the *Philips/Nokia* decision[4]); and (3) it does not define suspect goods. Article 16 addresses one of the most difficult areas of IP law requiring a balance between maintaining competitive markets and freedom of trade, on one side, and protecting the interests of IP owners, on the other. By acknowledging the possibility of seizing goods in transit based on allegations of trademark, copyright and other non-patent (or data exclusivity) infringement, the text of the signed ACTA is contrary to customary principles of IP territoriality and independence. It threatens to create an unhealthy balance.

Article 17 regulates requests by right holders with respect to border measures, in particular the rights to request suspension under Article 16. Article 17.1 provides that competent authorities shall require the right holder "to provide adequate evidence to satisfy the competent authorities that, under the law of the Party providing the procedures, there is *prima facie* an infringement..." Article 17.2 requires that parties make provision for applications for suspension, which may cover multiple shipments. Article 17.4 allows the authorities to deny applications where an applicant has abused procedures or for due cause. What will constitute adequate prima facie evidence of infringement is central to determining

[4] *Philips Electronics v. Lucheng Meijing Industrial/Nokia v. HMCRC*, combined cases C-446/09; C-495/09, European Court of Justice, decided 1 December 2011.

the ultimate impact of an agreement such as ACTA on legitimate trade. Once customs authorities have acted to detain goods, the interests of the shipper/consignor are impaired because of expense and delay almost inevitably incurred in the process of securing release. The decision by negotiators of the TRIPS Agreement to limit the circumstances in which mandatory application of IP border measures is required (i.e., for copyright pirated and trademark counterfeit goods) takes account of the potential problems in delegating the assessment of IP-related evidence to customs authorities.

Article 18 concerns "security or equivalent assurance." It does not require that security be provided, but permits security to be provided by posting of a bond conditioned to protect the accused infringer from loss or damage if goods are found to be not infringing. Only in exceptional cases, or pursuant to judicial order, may an accused infringer post security to obtain possession of suspect goods. This provision tilts in favour of IP right holders because the posting of a bond may require only a limited use of capital, with the same possibility not reciprocally available to shippers/consignors.

Article 19 is a curiously worded provision, providing that "each Party shall adopt or maintain procedures by which its competent authorities *may determine*, within a reasonable period after the initiation of the procedures described in Article 16 (Border Measures), whether the suspect goods infringe an intellectual property right" (emphasis added). In light of the fact that ACTA does not establish a time frame for requiring the initiation of judicial proceedings, the follow-on fact that competent authorities are not required to make a legal determination as to whether goods are infringing (or to otherwise release them) suggests that indefinite suspension without a determination is permissible. Surely the parties could not have intended that, but it is unclear what they might have intended. Article 19 is one of the most problematic provisions of ACTA because, whether intentionally or not, it appears to give customs authorities the right to detain goods indefinitely, without obligating the initiation of substantive proceedings. This is a circumstance in which the contemporaneous applicability of the TRIPS Agreement (here Article 55, establishing mandatory limits on the duration of suspension absent initiation of proceedings on the merits) is essential.

Article 20 provides that competent authorities should have the power to order the destruction of goods when an infringement has been determined, and generally ensuring that goods are disposed of outside ordinary channels of commerce. Article 20.3 allows the imposition of administrative penalties following a determination of infringement. Article 21 provides that fees (e.g., for storage or destruction) will not unreasonably deter use of the border measure provisions. The potential for multiple layers of damages (i.e., damages assessed by a court and damages assessed as an administrative penalty) raises concern.

Article 22 empowers competent authorities to provide information to right holders, including concerning specific shipments, and providing the identity and contact information for persons involved in the shipment, subject to laws pertaining to privacy or confidentiality. Note that large business enterprises are commonly invoking the need to protect confidential commercial information against use by competitors as grounds for withholding information from investigating authorities and judicial bodies. Whether customs authorities will protect the confidential commercial information of legitimate traders is uncertain.

### *Section 4: Criminal Enforcement*

Provisions on criminal enforcement constitute a substantial part of ACTA. Article 23.1, on Criminal Offences, incorporates the TRIPS Agreement requirement that criminal procedures and penalties be made available at least in cases of wilful trademark counterfeiting and copyright piracy (though ACTA adds "related rights" to copyright, thereby covering matters such as performers' rights). ACTA defines commercial scale to "include at least those carried out as commercial activities for direct or indirect economic or commercial advantage." In this regard, ACTA effectively overrules the WTO panel in the *China – Enforcement* case brought by the United States.[5] In that decision, commercial scale was defined to mean activities conducted as a business, and also to have achieved some threshold level of scope such as to be material within the relevant context. ACTA refers only to "economic or commercial advantage," which could encompass *de minimis* activity.

Article 23.2 extends the criminalization elements to wilful importation and domestic use of labels or packaging to which a mark has been applied without authorisation, and which is intended to be used in the course of trade on goods or services for which the trademark is registered. This provision might be invoked by holders of trademarks against "parallel importers" or, more generally, against generic pharmaceutical producers who refer to their products as generic versions of trademarked products. As illustration, parallel traders within the EU routinely repackage and relabel pharmaceutical products to include additional languages, information regarding repackaged quantities, and so forth, and they use the trademark of the original manufacturer "without authorisation." Understood literally, ACTA could attach criminal liability to this conduct. Such use of ACTA rules would go beyond traditional trademark protection concepts, yet there is reason to expect that

[5] *China – Measures Affecting the Protection and Enforcement of Intellectual Property Rights*, Report of the Panel, WT/DS362/R, 26 Jan. 2009 (China – Enforcement).

trademark holders will attempt to use them in this way. These rules did not appear in ACTA inadvertently.

Article 23.4 requires that criminal liability be extended to aiding and abetting. The extent to which such a rule might cause problems for legitimate trading activity depends on how it is applied.

For the foregoing matters, Article 24 requires that penalties will include imprisonment and monetary fines sufficient to provide a deterrent to future acts of infringement.

Article 25 requires that parties authorise the seizure of suspect counterfeit trademark and copyright pirated goods, as well as any materials and implements used in the commission of an offence, and the assets derived from, or obtained directly or indirectly through, the alleged infringing activity. The broad requirement regarding seizure of assets obtained from the alleged infringing activity goes beyond the requirements of the TRIPS Agreement. Article 25.3 requires parties to make provision for the forfeiture or destruction of goods, and that any goods not destroyed be disposed of outside the channels of commerce. Article 25.4 extends the potential for forfeiture or destruction to materials and implements predominantly used in the creation of the counterfeit goods, as well as provides for the forfeiture or destruction of assets without compensation. Article 25.5 extends the potential for seizure and forfeiture of assets beyond the assets used in the commission of the counterfeiting, to other assets of corresponding value. This goes substantially further than the requirements of Article 61 of the TRIPS Agreement, which extend only to goods used in the commission of the offence. Article 26 provides that competent authorities may pursue criminal actions ex officio.

### *Section 5: Enforcement of Intellectual Property Rights in the Digital Environment*

Article 27 of ACTA broadly requires parties to make available effective enforcement procedures against acts of infringement taking place in the digital environment, including infringement of copyright or related rights over digital networks, while preserving "fundamental principles such as freedom of expression, fair process, and privacy." Article 27.4 permits (but does not mandate) that competent authorities of a party have the authority to order an online service provider to disclose information to right holders concerning the identity of subscribers alleged to be infringing. Article 27.5 mandates adequate legal protection and effective legal remedies against circumvention of technological measures used by authors, performers and producers of phonograms to protect their works. It specifically requires, in Article 27.6, that protection be provided against unauthorised circumvention carried out knowingly or with reasonable grounds to know, and offering a device to the public, including computer programmes, as a means to circumvent. It requires protection against manufacture, importation or distribution of devices or products, including computer programmes, or provision of services that are primarily designed for the purpose of circumventing an effective technological measure or that has limited commercial significance other than circumvention.

Article 27.7 addresses electronic rights management information, requiring protection against knowingly (or with respect to civil remedies, having reasonable grounds to know) inducing, enabling, facilitating or concealing an infringement of copyright or related rights by removing or altering rights management information, or distributing importing, broadcasting, communicating or making available to the public works from which rights management information has been removed or altered. Article 27.8 recognises that parties may adopt or maintain "appropriate limitations or exceptions" to the protective measures set out with respect to circumvention of technological measures or altering of rights management information.

The provisions of ACTA regarding enforcement of rights in the digital environment are more extensive than those set forth in the multilaterally negotiated WIPO Copyright Treaty (WCT) and WIPO Performances and Phonograms Treaty (WPPT), such as by mandating the unlawfulness of the manufacturer of a device, including a computer programme, that "has only a limited commercially significant purpose other than circumventing an effective technological measure" (Article 27.6 (b.ii)). Although this provision has potentially significant implications for activities such as legitimate file sharing, it was negotiated by a relatively small group of countries without the participation of important stakeholder groups. One of the concerns of those questioning the legitimacy of ACTA is that such a provision subsequently will be put forward as a model representing an international norm, yet was designed in a less than participatory environment.

## CHAPTER III, ENFORCEMENT PRACTICES

There are five articles (28–32) in Chapter III dealing with enforcement practices, each of which involves a "soft" commitment. These include encouraging the development of expertise regarding IPRs, collecting and analysing statistical data, promoting internal coordination among enforcement agencies, promoting informal advisory groups, consulting with relevant stakeholders regarding border risks, sharing information among competent authorities of different parties, and permitting authorities of an importing party to share information with the authorities of an exporting party to deter future infringements. There is a provision on promoting transparency of laws and regulations, and encouraging promotion of public awareness of the importance of IPRs. Destruction of goods should be carried out consistently with environmental laws.

## CHAPTER IV, INTERNATIONAL COOPERATION

There are three articles (33–35) in Chapter IV dealing with international cooperation. As with Chapter III, all of the commitments in Chapter IV are "soft." Parties are encouraged to cooperate regardless of the origin of goods or the nationality of the right holder, and to cooperate among enforcement agencies, including criminal enforcement agencies, subject to national and international rules, and enforcement priorities. Parties are encouraged to share information, such as statistical data and on legislative and regulatory measures, as well as "other information as appropriate and mutually agreed." Parties agree that, on request, they will endeavour to provide technical assistance to other parties (and to prospective parties), including on how to develop and implement national legislation and train enforcement authorities regarding IPRs. Parties may undertake such activities in conjunction with the private sector or international organisations.

The issues of who is providing technical assistance and training, what kind of training and support is being provided, and based on whose interests are currently being discussed at WIPO and in other multilateral fora. ACTA negotiations were not public or inclusive, and it is not clear how international cooperation based on ACTA would be carried out. This is representative of concerns with the potential establishment of a new limited-membership organisation that may substantially affect legitimate traders and users of technology.

## CHAPTER V, INSTITUTIONAL ARRANGEMENTS

Article 36 establishes the "ACTA Committee" on which each party is represented. The mandatory activities of the ACTA Committee are to review implementation and operation of the agreement, consider matters concerning its development and proposed amendments, decide upon terms of accession, as well as to "consider any other matter that may affect the implementation and operation of this agreement." The ACTA Committee may decide to establish other committees or working groups, seek advice from NGOs, make recommendations regarding implementation of the agreement, share information with third parties on reducing IPRs infringements, and take other actions.

The ACTA Committee will act by consensus, unless it decides otherwise by consensus. It will adopt rules and procedures, which may be amended. During a transitional five-year period, "signatories" to the agreement will participate in decision making on the same basis as parties. The Committee, which will not supervise specific IP cases, will meet at least once a year.

Article 37 provides that the parties will establish contact points to facilitate communications.

Article 38 provides for consultations between parties regarding matters affecting implementation of the agreement, but it does not establish any form of binding dispute resolution procedure, and does not preclude recourse to WTO dispute settlement.

One of the most serious concerns raised in ACTA negotiations was the lack of transparency and absence of participation by a broad base of interested groups. There is long-term concern with the establishment of a new plurilateral institutional structure that will develop rules, and recommend or mandate implementation, with limited country and interested group participation. It should not be surprising that groups with diverse interests in the EU, the United States and elsewhere are not enthusiastic about this potential new model for the development and implementation of international IP and trade rules.

## CHAPTER VI, FINAL PROVISIONS

Chapter VI includes six articles (39–45). Participants in the negotiations and others agreed to by consensus may sign the agreement up until 1 May 2013. Six ratifications/acceptances are required for entry into force. Parties may withdraw following written notification. A party may propose amendments to ACTA, and the Committee will decide whether to present those to the parties for acceptance. Amendments will be effective only after all of the parties have ratified or accepted. Following the initial period for signature, accession is open to all WTO members, but "the Committee shall decide upon the terms of accession for each applicant." In other words, there will be a process for accession along the lines of the WTO accession process where terms and conditions for each applicant are negotiated. The English, French and Spanish versions of ACTA are equally authentic. The government of Japan is the depositary of the agreement.

## OBSERVATIONS

ACTA is a very different agreement than the one initially contemplated and proposed by IPR holder groups. The ambition to dramatically scale up penalties for civil and criminal IPRs infringement, including by application at the border, was not fully realised as a consequence of pushback from NGOs, academics and developing country governments. However, this is not to suggest that ACTA rules reflect an appropriate balance between the interests of society at large and IPR holders.

The terms of ACTA are moving toward an environment in which right holders will have more substantial powers to intervene against traders in goods and technologies, and will place greater authority and discretion in the hands of customs and criminal authorities, as compared with judicial authorities.

Yet, ACTA must also be considered within a broader context. While public and governmental resistance to the agreement may have induced a somewhat more favourable balance in its terms, other international negotiations have moved forward prior to and contemporaneous with ACTA. Bilateral and regional agreements, particularly those negotiated by the United States and the EU, include IP and regulatory chapters with rules more protective of IPR holders than those in ACTA. By way of illustration, investment protection chapters have already generated private-to-government alternative dispute resolution challenges to judicial and legislative actions, such as the challenge to Australia's tobacco plain packaging legislation, alleged to constitute an unlawful "taking" of IPR holder property. Right holder interest groups have pursued a multipronged strategy that is not reliant on favourable results in one particular forum.

It is uncertain at this time whether ACTA will enter into force. If it does, as outlined above, implementation of some of its rules may prove problematic to legitimate traders, technology transfer, and access to information and public goods. The larger long-term question is whether ACTA will create a new plurilateral forum where rules lacking appropriate balance are made and transposed to national legal systems. The executive branch in the United States has already signalled that constitutionally mandated approval processes are not its concern. The combination of a limited group of countries and actors making rules, and refusing to subject those rules to parliamentary control, is the real long-term worry.

# 2

# ACTA Initial Provisions and General Definitions

*Xavier Seuba*

## INTRODUCTION

The proposed "new international standard for intellectual property enforcement,"[1] the Anti-Counterfeiting Trade Agreement (ACTA),[2] includes six chapters, the first of which contains the initial provisions (Section 1) and definitions (Section 2).

ACTA Chapter I addresses fundamental aspects and shapes the scope and the interpretation of the entire treaty. Moreover, most of the ACTA "provisions committed to balanced enforcement procedures"[3] are found in this chapter,[4] something which, added to its horizontal impact, explains its decisive role. In this last regard, given the overall orientation of the agreement, which is perceived as largely favouring right holders, some of the provisions of Chapter I could play an important balancing function.

Despite their importance, the implications of the six articles that make up this chapter are not always clear. Some of the provisions merely transplant twin provisions of the World Trade Organization (WTO) Agreement on Trade-Related Aspects

This chapter has benefited by comments of Pedro Roffe. All errors remain mine.

1 M. E. Kaminski, "An Overview and the Evolution of the Anti-Counterfeiting Trade Agreement", *Albany Law Journal of Science and Technology*, vol. 21, no 3, 2011, p. 387.

2 Anti-Counterfeiting Trade Agreement, opened for signature May 1, 2011, available at http://trade.ec.europa.eu/doclib/docs/2011/may/tradoc_147937.pdf (accessed October 2012).

3 Although stated in general terms, this affirmation expressed in the "Opinion of European Academics" probably refers to the initial provisions of the agreement as well as to article 6. *See Opinion of European Academics on Anti-Counterfeiting Trade Agreement, (b)* http://www.iri.uni-hannover.de/acta-1668.html (accessed October 2012).

4 C. Geiger, "Anti-Counterfeiting Trade Agreement: A Comprehensive Assessment from a European Perspective", EU DG for External Policies, *Workshop. The Anti-Counterfeiting Trade Agreement (ACTA)*, EXPO/B/INTA/FWC/2009-01/Lot7/25, 2012, p. 47. *See* online at http://www.europarl.europa.eu/committees/fr/studiesdownload.html?languageDocument=EN&file=73311 (accessed October 2012).

of Intellectual Property Rights (TRIPS)[5] and, together with them, old doubts and unsettled questions. Worth noting is also that the context of the transposed norms is now different, hence the interpretation of very similar articles in TRIPS and ACTA could diverge.[6] Potential difficulties are aggravated by the fact that not all the links originally made by the norms transplanted from TRIPS have been incorporated into the ACTA text. Added to this, the general wording that usually characterises this type of provisions and chapters permits diverging readings. Finally, Chapter I is not limited to general principles and guidance, and it also contains some important "TRIPS plus" provisions as well as some fundamental safeguards.

## ACTA SECTION 1: INITIAL PROVISIONS

### *Article 1: Relation to Other Agreements*

ACTA Article 1 states that nothing in the agreement "shall derogate from any obligation of a Party with respect to any other Party under existing agreements, including the TRIPS Agreement." This important conflict clause of subordination[7] raises significant issues, such as which agreements ACTA does not derogate from, what happens with provisions enshrining rights but not obligations and what to do with eventual conflicts between agreements concluded between ACTA members and non-ACTA members.

The first question – which agreements ACTA does not derogate from – seems simple. In accordance with the plain meaning of the words, the reference made to *other* agreements implies *all* international agreements. There is no mention of any limitation to treaties pertaining to the field of trade or intellectual property, and a restriction of this sort cannot be merely presumed. Other articles contained in ACTA confirm the reading favouring the widest scope of the reference to "agreements."[8]

5 Agreement on Trade-Related Aspects of Intellectual Property Rights, Apr. 15, 1994, Marrakesh Agreement Establishing the World Trade Organization, Annex 1C, *Legal Instruments Results of the Uruguay Round*, 33 *I.L.M.* 1197 (1994).

6 *See* Vienna Convention on the Law of Treaties, article 31.1, May 23, 1969, 1155 *U.N.T.S.* 331. This author, however, favours exporting as well interpretations delivered in the context of TRIPS. See *infra* comments on article 1 and complementarity.

7 It falls within the third category of conflict clauses that the International Law Commission distinguished in 2006: "clauses in subsequent treaty providing that it 'shall not affect' the earlier treaty." A category that may be understood as the evolution of those other clauses was identified in 1951 by Aufricht: clauses contained in the later treaty declaring that "it is not at variance with the letter or spirit of an earlier treaty." *See* ILC, *Fragmentation of International Law: Difficulties arising from the Diversification and Expansion of International Law, Report of the Study Group of the International Law Commission*, 13 Apr. 2006, A/CN.4/L.682, at par. 268.

8 Article 4.1(a), for instance, alludes to the right to not disclose information when this would be contrary to "international agreements to which it is Party."

The second question concerns the interpretation to be given to the reference found in Article 1 to the obligation to respect previous obligations, but not previous rights. For some, the reference to "obligations" would preclude demanding the fulfilment of previously existing norms enshrining "rights." This affirmation departs from a reading focused on the substantive content of norms enshrined in intellectual property treaties, and the point of view of states, competitors and consumers. From that point of view, rules enshrining rights include, inter alia, norms allowing some margin of manoeuvre, rules placing limits to intellectual property protection and norms that permit reacting against abuse of intellectual property rights. In contrast, norms ordering that an intellectual property right be granted, the application of national treatment or the provision of the legal means for interested parties to react against an infringement, would be "obligations." Since ACTA would only preserve "obligations," it would make it difficult to preserve a balanced intellectual property legal system.[9] Although this is a plausible interpretation, and it is true that other intellectual property treaties do clarify that both rights and obligations contained in other treaties will be preserved,[10] a different understanding is merited.

Article 1 establishes that nothing in ACTA "shall derogate from any obligation of *a Party* with respect to *any other Party*."[11] The reference made concerns inter-state relations. This means, for instance, that eventual rights of competitors, who are private parties, would not be affected by the abovementioned reading. More importantly, most intellectual property treaties contain an article which states something along the lines of "Members shall give effect to the provisions of this Treaty,"[12] an obvious restatement of the customary *pacta sunt servanda*. That is, the main inter-state obligation enshrined is the obligation to fulfil the treaty, which includes the respect of both rights and obligations of private parties. Hence, the reference found in Article 1 to the obligation to respect previous obligations includes this "umbrella" inter-state obligation, which entails by reference rights of right holders, users and competitors.[13]

9 M. Kaminski, op. cit., p. 395.

10 Article 196 of the Agreement between the European Union, Peru and Colombia states, for instance, that "The Parties reaffirm the rights and obligations under the TRIPS Agreement." *See* in Trade Agreement between the European Union and Colombia and Peru, EU/CO/PE/en 1, in http://trade.ec.europa.eu/doclib/press/index.cfm?id=691 (accessed October 2012).

11 Emphasis added.

12 *See*, for instance, Agreement on Trade-Related Aspects of Intellectual Property op. cit.; or ECONOMIC PARTNERSHIP AGREEMENT between the CARIFORUM States and the European Community and its Member States, article 138.4, *Official Journal of the European Union*, 30.10.2008, L 289/I/3.

13 A different reading, which also preserves both rights and obligations, sustains that "the principle of harmonious interpretation and systemic integration, which acts as a general presumption against conflict in the interpretation of treaties, would seem to require that the TRIPS safeguards continue to bind the Parties insofar as there is no attempt to disclaim or remove those standards in the text." K. Weatherall,

The third question refers to the limitation of the declared respect to previous covenants. In effect, the claimed respect is qualified because it only applies in treaty relations *between* the parties to ACTA.[14] That is, the conflict clause declaring respect for other international treaties is limited to the treaty relations between ACTA Members, whereas the relations between treaties subscribed by ACTA parties and third parties are not included.[15] Therefore, ACTA Members escape, in principle, from the uncertain outcomes resulting from the application of those rudimentary rules, as well as from the particularities derived from the application of those rules to integral or interdependent obligations eventually affected by ACTA.

In this last regard, and probably surprisingly, the conflict clause contained in ACTA can be read as an incentive to become a member of the ACTA club. In effect, if an explicit treaty guarantee of no supersession was sought, becoming a member of ACTA would be the only way of guaranteeing it. Hence, the country club approach used to negotiate and manage ACTA[16] would have in this provision an unexpected normative parallel and reflection, since the conflict clause contained therein creates an incentive to become a member of this, initially, selective club.

The only treaty expressly mentioned in Article 1 is TRIPS. This reference is in line with a previous one in the preamble, which states that ACTA complements TRIPS. Therefore, the complementary nature and the preference given to TRIPS formally characterise the relationship between both agreements.[17] But the complementarity need not end in the text of TRIPS. The obligations contained in this

"Politics, Compromise, Text and the Failures of the Anti-Counterfeiting Trade Agreement", *Sydney Law Review*, vol. 33, no 2, 2011, p. 258, http://sydney.edu.au/law/slr/slr_33/slr33_2/Weatherall.pdf. Another possibility for the preservation of limitations and exceptions is found in article 3.1. According to this article, the Agreement is without prejudice to provisions in the Parties' laws governing, inter alia, the scope of intellectual property rights, which encompasses exceptions and limitations. O. Vrins, "The impact of ACTA on the EU acquis and civil liberties", EU DG for External Policies, *Workshop. The Anti-Counterfeiting Trade Agreement (ACTA)*, EXPO/B/INTA/FWC/2009–01/Lot7/25, 2012, p. 121. *See* online at http://www.europarl.europa.eu/committees/fr/studiesdownload.html?languageDocument=EN&file=73311 (accessed October 2012).

14 Article 1 alludes to "obligation of a Party with respect to any other Party."

15 Article 30 of the Vienna Convention, op. cit., codifies the customary rule on *lex posterior*, while the principle of *lex specialis* also applies to the relations between international treaties.

16 According to Gervais, "The approach is neither regional nor truly multilateral; it is a 'club approach' in which like-minded jurisdictions define enforcement 'membership' rules and then invite other countries to join, presumably via other trade agreements." D. Gervais, "China-Measures Affecting the Protection and Enforcement of Intellectual Property Rights", *American Journal of International Law*, vol. 103, 2009, p. 555; *see also* P. Yu, "ACTA and Its Complex Politics", *The WIPO Journal*, vol. 3., no 1, 2011, p. 2.

17 See *infra* comments on ACTA articles 2.3 and 6, which make clear that at least the other way around the complementarity will be certain: numerous safeguards for competitors and consumers will be necessarily found in TRIPS.

treaty have been fine-tuned by WTO case law[18] and other agreements among the parties concerning TRIPS.[19] The jurisprudence and agreements can be also brought into consideration when interpreting ACTA and ruling on eventual interrelations between both treaties.

The reference to the no supersession of TRIPS obligations in ACTA Article 1 can be read as a conflict clause of subordination legally enforcing the reading of TRIPS as an agreement establishing ceilings.[20] That is, in absence of a clause such as this, the potential ceilings that TRIPS lays down can be broken while honouring the normal consequences of breaching an international obligation, that is, international responsibility of states. The WTO system has specific norms of adjudication, which allow dispute settlement organs to determine the state's responsibility with regard to TRIPS infringements. However, ACTA confirms those ceilings as *watertight*. It gives them full impact, that of nullifying those provisions in ACTA that could contravene TRIPS obligations. This means that states invoking TRIPS as a limit to the content of ACTA could invoke ACTA as well, or even invoke solely ACTA Article 1.

## *Article 2: Nature and Scope of Obligations*

ACTA Article 2 announces important principles with regard to the obligations undertaken, the implementation of the provisions of the agreement and the resource implications deriving from enforcement compromises. It also transplants the TRIPS objectives and principles to ACTA.

### Article 2.1

Article 2.1 first phrase – "Each party shall give effect to the provisions of this treaty" – codifies the *pacta sunt servanda* principle and echoes the first phrase of TRIPS Article 1. As in the case of TRIPS, there is no specific indication of how ACTA obligations must be fulfilled. In this regard, although in principle both the

[18] See all disputes concerning TRIPS in www.wto.org/english/tratop_e/dispu_e/dispu_agreements_index_e.htm (accessed November 2012).

[19] In the sense meant by Vienna Convention on the Law of Treaties article 31.2(a), op. cit.

[20] WTO Director General, Pascal Lamy, noted that while TRIPS does not preclude its members from introducing additional measures to protect IP rights, such protection cannot contravene TRIPS provisions. *See* Letter from Pascal Lamy, Dir.-Gen., World Trade Org., to EU Parliament Members (May 4, 2010), available at http://keionline.org/sites/default/files/WTO-Lamy_Answer-to-MEP-letter.pdf (accessed October 2012). For a doctrinal elaboration of the TRIPS as a treaty establishing ceilings *see* P. Yu, "TRIPS and Its Discontents", *Marquette University Intellectual Property Law Review*, vol. 10, 2006, p. 402; A. Kur and H. Grosse Ruse-Khan, *Enough Is Enough: The Notion of Binding Ceilings in International Intellectual Property Protection*, Max Planck Institute for Intellectual Property, Competition & Tax Law Research Paper Series No. 09–01, 2008, available at http://papers.ssrn.com/sol3/papers.cfm?abstract_id=1326429 (accessed October 2012).

direct invocation of the agreement and its domestic reception would be acceptable, the content of its provisions favours adopting or amending national laws as required.[21]

Next, the second phrase sets an obligation also present in TRIPS and other important international IP treaties: parties may implement more extensive protection provided that it does not contravene the agreement.[22] On the one hand, this reminds parties that the agreement contains minimum standards of protection. On the other hand, it allows members to enact more extensive protection provided that it does not contradict the treaty establishing the minimum standards of protection. The nature of TRIPS as a covenant establishing both the floor and the ceiling has been highlighted.[23] The specific relevance of its enforcement provisions in that context was noticed a decade ago, when it was sustained that TRIPS enforcement norms had been framed as mandatory standards that did not allow further strengthening.[24] Nevertheless, provisions in free trade agreements (FTAs) and ACTA itself oblige to either think otherwise or to conclude that this is an easily circumvented prohibition. The abundance of open terms, permissive provisions and ambiguous wording[25] facilitate readings that avoid clear conflicts with mandatory provisions foreseen elsewhere.

ACTA Article 2.1 also recognises the freedom to determine the appropriate method of implementing the provisions of the treaty within the national legal system and practice.[26] On the one hand, this permits members to bring into the analysis the possibility to choose between the direct application and the domestic incorporation of the treaty obligations.[27] On the other hand, the freedom to determine the appropriate

[21] While some of the promoters of ACTA, particularly the EU and the US, have repeatedly stated that the agreement does not imply any amendment of their respective IP law, most scholars have observed differences between ACTA and the law's of said promoters. For instance, in the case of the EU, *see* the conclusion in the *Opinion of European Academics on Anti-Counterfeiting Trade Agreement*, op. cit.

[22] *See* Agreement on Trade-Related Aspects of Intellectual Property Rights, op. cit.; Paris Convention for the Protection of Industrial Property, article 19, Mar. 20, 1883, (as last revised at Stockholm, July 14, 1967), 21 *U.S.T.* 1583, 828 *U.N.T.S.* 305; International Convention for the Protection of Performers, Producers of Phonograms and Broadcasting Organizations, article 22, Rome, 26 October 1961, (1992) *ATS* 29 / 496 *U.N.T.S.* 43; Berne Convention for the Protection of Literary and Artistic Works, article 5(1), Sept. 9, 1886, *as amended on* Sept. 28, 1979, 25 *U.S.T.* 1341, 1161 *U.N.T.S.* 30.

[23] *See* A. Kur, H. Grosse Ruse-Khan, op. cit.

[24] N. Pires de Carvalho, *The TRIPS Regime of Patent Rights*, The Hague: Kluwer Law International, 2002, p. 32.

[25] See, for the case of ACTA, *infra* and this book's chapter on article 6.

[26] A permission also foreseen in TRIPS and invoked by the WTO Appellate Body: parties can "determine the appropriate method of implementing the provisions of this Agreement in the context of their domestic legal systems." WTO Appellate Body, *India – Patent Protection for Pharmaceutical and Agricultural Chemical Products*, WT/DS5OIAB/R, § VI (Dec 19, 1997).

[27] See supra with regards the first phrase of article 2.1.

method of implementation does not allow the adoption of a lower standard, as WTO case law shows,[28] nor does it exclude the implementation from being scrutinised.[29] This last possibility may become controversial in ACTA, since it lacks the dispute settlement system that guarantees neutrality and balance as in the case of TRIPS disputes.[30] This is the reason why some states could judge themselves whether or not another state is complying with ACTA.[31] In any case, as rightly pointed out by the WTO panel in the report *China-Measures Affecting the Protection and Enforcement of Intellectual Property Rights*, this deference to national implementation is particularly important in the area of enforcement, were "differences among Members' respective legal systems and practices tend to be more important."[32]

**Article 2.2**

ACTA Article 2.2 states that "[n]othing in this Agreement creates any obligation with respect to the distribution of resources as between enforcement of intellectual property rights and enforcement of law in general." The provision parallels one found in TRIPS Article 41.5, which is commonly agreed to be a concession to developing countries.[33] Deference to national choices with regard to resource allocation can be also found in the chapter dealing with international cooperation.[34]

The real impact of this provision is not immediately clear. The panel report on the *China – Intellectual Property Rights* case seems to give meaningful impact to TRIPS Article 41.5 as a justification for non-compliance,[35] and some developing

[28] Panel Report, *China-Measures Affecting the Protection and Enforcement of Intellectual Property Rights*, Annex B-4, 33, WT/DS362/R (Jan. 26, 2009), at 7.513. Even stronger, it "does not permit differences in domestic legal systems and practices to justify any derogation from the basic obligation to give effect to the provisions on enforcement." Panel Report, *China-Measures Affecting the Protection and Enforcement of Intellectual Property Rights*, op. cit., at 7.513. In a related fashion, *see* Appellate Body Report, *India – Patent Protection for Pharmaceutical and agricultural Chemical Products*, op. cit.

[29] UNCTAD–ICTSD, *Resource Book on TRIPS and Development*, New York: Cambridge University Press, 2005, p. 28.

[30] As Professor J. H. Reichman stated, with regards the *India-mailbox case*, "The Appellate Body also manifested considerable deference to local law, if good faith efforts to implement the TRIPS Agreement were being made." J. H. Reichman, "The TRIPS Agreement Comes of Age: Conflict or Cooperation with the Developing Countries?" *Case Western Reserve Journal of international Law*, vol. 32, 2000, p. 446.

[31] Unilateral monitoring systems, such as the USTR Section 301 mechanism, may find in ACTA a text to use as reference, something that, given the tone and ambiguity of ACTA, may be particularly conflictive.

[32] Panel Report, *China – Measures Affecting the Protection and Enforcement of Intellectual Property Rights*, op. cit., 7.513.

[33] UNCTAD–ICTSD, op. cit., p. 585; Correa, op. cit., p. 417.

[34] "Cooperation under this Chapter shall be (…) subject to the laws, policies, resource allocation, and law enforcement priorities of each Party." Art. 33.3.

[35] P. Yu, "TRIPS Enforcement and Developing Countries", *American University International Law Review*, vol. 26, no 3, 2011, p. 780.

countries have invoked this provision in the TRIPS Council.[36] For instance, the Chinese delegate to the TRIPS Council stated that "the TRIPS agreement was clear about resource allocation, and gave due consideration to the limited resources of developing country governments to enforce IPR laws relative to other laws which might call for more urgent priority. Article 41.5 was cognisant of the capacity constraints of members and therefore created no obligation with the respect to distribution of resources as between the enforcement of IPRs and the enforcement of law in general."

Judging by international jurisprudence, as well as enforcement demands and practices, TRIPS Article 41.5 does not appear to have been particularly relevant. Enforcement norms are expensive to implement. To fulfil this obligation and simultaneously make use of the right to not modify the distribution of resources seems difficult to harmonise.[37] That is even more the case in a treaty such as ACTA, which does not explicitly recognise that intellectual property rights are private rights: only through the reference made in Article 1 to the TRIPS Agreement can the private nature be brought into consideration in the context of ACTA.[38]

**Article 2.3**

ACTA Article 2.3 declares that the "objectives and principles set forth in Part I of the TRIPS Agreement, in particular Articles 7 and 8, shall apply, *mutatis mutandis*, to this Agreement." Therefore, this provision can play a remarkable role or, by contrast, be merely hortatory, something that in great measure depends on the views with regard TRIPS Articles 7 and 8.

What follows puts particular attention on the reference to "objectives" contained in ACTA Article 2.3, and the concomitant inclusion of TRIPS objectives. However, it is also worth noting the reference to "principles" and the apparent limitation to those principles announced in TRIPS Article 8. It has been rightly asked "whether there are other objectives and principles in Part I of TRIPS which might apply to ACTA."[39] Among the missing principles are the national treatment principle, the most favoured nation principle and the principle of exhaustion of rights.

[36] Council for Trade-Related Aspects of Intellectual Property Rights, *Minutes of Meeting Held in the Centre William Rappard on 8–9 June 2010*, IP/C/M/63, par. 266.

[37] X. Seuba, "Checks and Balances in the Intellectual Property Enforcement Field: Reconstructing EU Trade Agreements", in C. Geiger (ed.), *Constructing European Intellectual Property*, Cheltenham–Northampton: Edward Elgar, 2012, pp. 417–418.

[38] By contrast, the preamble of the TRIPS expressly recalls the private nature of intellectual property rights.

[39] M. Blakeney, *Intellectual Property Enforcement. A Commentary on the Anti-Counterfeiting Trade Agreement (ACTA)*, Cheltenham–Northampton: Edward Elgar, 2012, p. 107.

Entering into the analysis of the goals of ACTA, it is worth noting that only the preamble states that the ACTA is aimed at strengthening the enforcement of IP rights.[40] The dispositive part of the agreement, by contrast, only mentions that the objectives will be those of TRIPS, that is, "the promotion of technological innovation and the transfer and dissemination of technology, to the mutual advantage of producers and users of technological knowledge and in a manner conducive to social and economic welfare, and to a balance of rights and obligations." Nevertheless, when ACTA parties express their views on the objective of the agreement, the unanimous answer is that the agreement's goal is the effective enforcement of intellectual property rights.[41]

[40] Although there are several views as to which is the practical value of preambles, for many this part of treaties has merely an interpretative function.

[41] According to the EU, "The goal of the ACTA negotiations is to provide an international framework that improves the enforcement of intellectual property right (IPR) laws." European Commission DG Trade, *The Anti-Counterfeiting Trade Agreement (ACTA), Fact sheet*, updated November 2008, http://trade.ec.europa.eu/doclib/docs/2008/october/tradoc_140836.11.08.pdf. For the Japanese Ministry of Foreign Affairs, "The ACTA initiative aims to define effective procedures for enforcing existing intellectual property rights", MOFA, *Anti-Counterfeiting Trade Agreement (ACTA) FACT SHEET*, March 2010, http://www.mofa.go.jp/policy/economy/i_property/acta_factsheet.pdf. For Canada Ministry of Foreign Affairs, "The objective of the ACTA is to put in place international standards for enforcing intellectual property rights in order to fight more efficiently the growing problems of counterfeiting and piracy", Foreign Affairs and International trade Canada, *Anti-Counterfeiting Trade Agreement (ACTA)*, http://www.international.gc.ca/trade-agreements-accords-commerciaux/fo/intellect_property.aspx?view=d. According to New Zealand, ACTA's goal is to "more effectively combating the trade in counterfeit and pirated goods." Ministry of Foreign Affairs and Trade, *Anti-Counterfeiting Trade Agreement (ACTA) FACT SHEET*, http://www.mfat.govt.nz/downloads/trade-agreement/acta/acta-factsheet.pdf; for the USTR, concerning ACTA, "a core US objective was to create an agreement that fosters increased leadership in the international fight against counterfeiting and piracy." USTR, *ACTA, meeting the US objectives*, http://www.ustr.gov/about-us/press-office/fact-sheets/2011/september/acta-meeting-us-objectives. For Mexico, the aim is "to combat more efficiently the problem of counterfeiting and piracy of marks, patents and intellectual and artistic works", INPI, *México firma el Acuerdo Comercial Contra la Falsificación (ACTA), Comunicado de Prensa, IMPI-010/2012*, en http://www.impi.gob.mx/work/sites/IMPI/resources/LocalContent/3693/7/IMPI_010_2012.pdf. For Morroco, ACTA is "A vise à définir des standards internationaux en matière d'application des droits de propriété intellectuelle afin que le fléau croissant de la contrefaçon et du piratage puisse être combattu de manière plus efficace", *Communique: Le Maroc signe l'Accord Commercial Anti-Contrefaçon (ACTA) à Tokyo*, http://www.ompic.org.ma/ressources/upload/com_acta2011.pdf. For Australia's Department of Foreign Affairs and Trade, ACTA's goal is "to establish a new standard of intellectual property (IP) enforcement to combat the high levels of commercial-scale trade in counterfeit and pirated goods worldwide"; http://www.dfat.gov.au/ip/index.html#acta, http://www.dfat.gov.au/ip/index.html#acta. According to the Swiss Federal Institute of Intellectual Property, "The goal of ACTA is to agree between contracting Parties upon effective enforcement and customs measures for combating large-scale, commercially oriented counterfeiting and piracy. In short: improve enforcement measures and adapt them to today's needs." *Important Information about ACTA (Anti-Counterfeiting Trade Agreement)*, Swiss Federal Institute of Intellectual Property, https://www.ige.ch/fileadmin/user_upload/Juristische_Infos/e/ACTA_Infopaper_e.pdf

If the intention of ACTA drafters was to promote enforcement, it would have been useful to state it in the articles, not only in the preamble. The discrepancy between the enforcement objective announced in the preamble and the goals included via the reference to TRIPS could raise doubts with regard to the real role attributed to the goals and principles stated in TRIPS and transplanted into ACTA. Another reading, however, is that only when negotiations on the real substance of ACTA were well advanced was it deemed necessary to introduce some balancing provisions. In fact, the reference to the content of TRIPS Articles 7 and 8 was included only at the last moment, in July 2010.[42] In that sense, recourse to TRIPS Articles 7 and 8 was probably the best choice for a number of reasons. First, these articles reflect a consensual understanding on the instrumental function that IP fulfils. And second, enforcement should pursue not only an economic purpose but also the promotion of technological and creative innovation and its dissemination to the public,[43] and hence the objective stated in TRIPS Article 7, as the WIPO Development Agenda recommendation 45 underlines.

Leaving aside the ultimate goals parties intended to achieve, the fact remains that TRIPS Articles 7 and 8 are integral components of the normative part of ACTA. Thus, they should be the primary source for identifying the goals pursued. The preamble, by contrast, gives the *context* to determine the ordinary meaning of the terms of the treaty.[44]

One of the corollaries of the general rule of interpretation codified by the Vienna Convention on the Law of Treaties is that interpretation must give meaning and effect to all the terms of a treaty. As the WTO Appellate Body has recalled, the interpreter cannot adopt a reading that would result in reducing whole clauses or paragraphs of a treaty to redundancy or effectiveness.[45] With regard to the TRIPS goals and principles referenced in ACTA – whether or not they reflect all the goals of the agreement, and whether or not parties really intended to incorporate them in a meaningful way – they do form part of the agreement and must be interpreted in a meaningful way.

A distinct aspect is agreeing with what would be a "meaningful" application of Articles 7 and 8. The potential is indeed vast, and it has been explored in great depth

42 *See* http://www.publicknowledge.org/files/docs/ACTA_consolidatedtext.pdf (accessed February 2013).

43 *See* in favor *Opinion of European Academics on Anti-Counterfeiting Trade Agreement, (e)* http://www.iri.uni-hannover.de/acta-1668.html (accessed October 2012).

44 *See* Vienna Convention on the Law of Treaties article 31.2, op. cit.

45 Appellate Body Report, *United States – Standards for Reformulated and Conventional Gasoline ("US – Gasoline")*, WT/DS2/AB/R, adopted 20 May 1996, DSR 996:I, 3, at 21; Appellate Body Report, *Japan – Taxes on Alcoholic Beverages ("Japan – Alcoholic Beverages II")*, WT/DS8/AB/R, WT/DS10/AB/R, WT/DS11/AB/R, adopted 1 November 1996, DSR 1996:I, 97, at 106; Appellate Body Report, *United States –Section 211 Omnibus Appropriations Act of 1998*, WT/DS176/AB/R, adopted 2 January 2002, at 95.

by doctrine[46] and some WTO case law.[47] Moreover, these articles are repeatedly quoted in policy statements in multilateral fora,[48] mostly by developing countries[49] and in IP chapters of FTAs that either invoke[50] or reproduce them.[51] The potential of TRIPS Articles 7 and 8 is even more important in ACTA than in TRIPS. The reason is simple: in comparison to ACTA, TRIPS is a very balanced agreement. As it is addressed in greater detail in the analysis of ACTA Article 6, numerous provisions of the agreement are drafted in either permissive or ambiguous terms, or lack any mention to other rights and interests at stake. This is why provisions such as those contained in ACTA Articles 2.3 and 6 could become central in the implementation of the agreement.

There is no guarantee that this will be the case, and the practice with TRIPS invites caution. On the one hand, the use and practical implementation of these articles in the context of WTO dispute settlement have been far below their potential and expectations.[52] In fact, the practical impact of TRIPS Articles 7 and 8 has probably been more on the policy side than the strictly legal arena. On the other hand, the role that these articles should play in the context of ACTA would be so great that they would in fact play a quasi-legislative function.[53]

Altogether, this leads to the conclusion that the two underutilised provisions in the context of a friendly legal system would be called to play an even more important role regarding a treaty that has probably incorporated them without much fervour. Indeed, the negotiation history shows that the reference to TRIPS Articles

[46] *See* P. Yu, "The Objectives and Principles of the TRIPS Agreement", *Houston Law Review*, vol. 46, 2009–2010, pp. 979–1046; H. Grosse Ruse-Khan, "A Comparative Analysis of Policy Space in WTO Law", *Max Planck Institute for Intellectual Property, Competition & Tax Law Research Paper Series*, Paper no 08–02, 2008.

[47] WTO Dispute Settlement Panel, *Canada – Patent Protection of Pharmaceutical Products*, WT/DSll4/R, § 7.26 at 154 (March 17, 2000), stating that when interpreting Article 30 of the TRIPS Agreement on exceptions, the goals and limitations stated in Articles 7 and 8.1 must be borne in mind.

[48] *See* Recommendation 45 of the *WIPO Development Agenda*.

[49] Request for Consultations by India, *European Union and a Member State – Seizure of Generic Drugs in Transit*, WT/DS408/1 (May 19, 2010), p. 3, stating that "the provisions of the TRIPS Agreement referred to above must be interpreted and implemented in light of the objectives and principles set forth in Articles 7 and 8 of the TRIPS Agreement, the Doha Ministerial Declaration on the TRIPS Agreement and Public Health adopted on 14 November 2001 and in the light of Article 12(1) of the International Covenant on Economic, Social and Cultural Rights, which recognizes the right of all persons to the enjoyment of the highest attainable standard of physical and mental health."

[50] *See* article 139.2 of the EU-Cariforum Agreement, op. cit.

[51] *See* article 195 of the EU-Peru and Colombia Agreement, op. cit.

[52] *See* P. Yu, "TRIPS Enforcement and Developing Countries", op. cit., pp. 765–772; H. Grosse Ruse-Kahn, *The (non) use of treaty object and purpose in intellectual property disputes in the WTO*, Max Planck Institute for Intellectual Property and Competition Law Research paper no 11–15.

[53] See comments with regards article 6.

7 and 8 in ACTA was a compromise. In July 2010, Canada, Australia, New Zealand and Singapore proposed the incorporation of the entire text of TRIPS Articles 7 and 8. In contrast, the United States and Mexico objected to a mention of these articles, while the European Union proposed the inclusion in the preamble of ACTA of 'some principles' enshrined in TRIPS Articles 7 and 8. In October 2010, the proposal by Canada, Australia, New Zealand and Singapore was substituted by a reference to TRIPS Articles 7 and 8 in ACTA Article 2.3 without including the text.[54]

In summary, TRIPS Articles 7 and 8 are formally called to play an important function, and the only comparable experience so far is that of the TRIPS Agreement. Whatever the practical implementations of the objectives stated in ACTA Article 2.3 might be, its drafters included the underlying objective of the agreement – to guarantee effective enforcement of IP rights – in the preamble and not within the articles. On the one hand, in accordance with the Vienna Convention on the Law of Treaties, the preamble gives the context within which to find the ordinary meaning to be given to the terms, but it is technically disputable whether the objectives stated in preamble can take precedence over those stated in the main body of the agreement. On the other hand, the more important and practical question is whether the content of ACTA reflects more the objective declared in the preamble (effective enforcement) or rather those incorporated by reference in ACTA Article 2.3 (promotion of technological and creative innovation and its dissemination to the public). Although it is rational to sustain that the former promotes the latter,[55] if the correlation was so straightforward and did not depend on the specific content of the agreement, probably all WTO Members would have already joined ACTA.[56]

[54] *See* July 2010 text in http://www.publicknowledge.org/files/docs/ACTA_consolidatedtext.pdf (accessed February 2013).

[55] Regardless of the fact that, for some delegates to the WTO, enforcement and the substantive objectives pursued in the TRIPS are unconnected. This is what seems to be inferred from the statement of the European Delegate in a TRIPS Council session, who said that "it was important to understand that ACTA was an enforcement treaty, not a substantive treaty, and it would therefore never affect the balance achieved in the TRIPS Agreement between the rights of the right holders and the legitimate goal of disseminating innovations." *Minutes of Meeting of Council for Trade-Related Aspects of Intellectual Property Rights*, 8–9 June 2010, IP/C/M/63, 4 October 2010, par. 327.

[56] According to Musungu the success of IP enforcement in the context of broader societal interests and development-oriented concerns "lies in ensuring that the application of IP enforcement procedures produces better outcomes for innovation generally, for IP right holders and consumers and contributes to the overall social and economic welfare of society. Meeting this challenge is by no means an easy task." S. Musungu, *The contribution of, and costs to, right holders in enforcement, taking into account Recommendation 45 of the WIPO Development Agenda*, WIPO Committee on Enforcement, WIPO/ACE/5/10, September 28, 2009, par. 18.

## *Article 3*

Article 3 establishes the relationship between ACTA and standards concerning the availability and scope of intellectual property rights. This is a relationship based on the independence between norms on enforcement, which ACTA lays down, and norms on the acquisition and scope of IPRs, which are found in a party's law and other international obligations. This independence has led to an emphasis on ACTA's focus on intellectual property enforcement rather than substantive matters, an affirmation that in general seems correct.

ACTA and other contemporary enforcement-related initiatives invite reflection on the meaning of "enforcement" and its relation with substantive rights. More precisely, the strengthening of enforcement leads to consider whether new substantive rights favouring right holders are being laid down.

For instance, in the case of secondary liability, it is legitimate to wonder whether the imposition of an obligation on a third party to control and enforce an intellectual property right is an enlargement of the scope of the original right of the right holder. It is indeed an obligation created with the intention to enforce an intellectual property right, but it confers to the right holder a new legal expectation that the intellectual property category itself did not grant: to demand of a third – private – party the surveillance of its right.[57]

There are other interesting situations, such as the case of patents and border measures. The final exclusion of patents from the scope of ACTA's border measures section does not impede holding that the authority to control patented products in transit, pursuant to the law of the country of transit, is an expansion of the rights conferred by a patent.[58] Although this is not mandated in ACTA, it is indeed allowed under the agreement. While the addition of this new authority to prohibit (the power to impede the transit is added to the traditional powers granted to the patent holder to prohibit the making, using, offering for sale, selling or importing the patented product) was present in the earlier drafts of ACTA, it has its origin in European legislation and is present in association agreements promoted by the EU, always under the enforcement label.

Going back to the announcement made in Article 3.1, implicitly declaring that ACTA has nothing to do with substantive rights, it is useful to bear in mind that

[57] In this context, it is worth to take into account norms on third party liability, which for some imply an expansion of IP substantive rights. These norms and other rules related to, for instance, anti-circumvention measures have lead to state that ACTA "represents a shift in intellectual property law that extends beyond mere enforcement." *See* M. Geist, "The trouble with ACTA: an analysis of the Anti-Counterfeiting Trade Agreement", EU DG for External Policies, op. cit., pp. 35–36.

[58] X. Seuba, *The Limits of Intellectual Property Enforcement at the Border*, Geneva: ICTSD, 2010, pp. 18–21.

norms on enforcement lay down the mechanisms and the legal framework that will compel compliance with the rights conferred by each of the intellectual property categories. Enforcement provisions are not expected to grant new substantive rights, but rather to refer to other norms. In this sense, these provisions fulfil a characteristic that H. L. A. Hart conferred to "secondary norms," and more precisely to *rules of adjudication*. This category gathers the norms that regulate the procedure to be used in judging infringements, the identification of the corresponding sanctions and the decision on who is to judge. As can be deduced from the examples previously mentioned (secondary liability and the control of patented goods in transit), it is disputable that all norms currently framed under the "enforcement" label are in fact solely norms on enforcement. This could be part of what the Chinese delegate to the TRIPS Council had in mind when she stated that "elevating the enforcement level did create substantive obligations on Members and consequently had an impact on them."[59]

Article 3.2 states that ACTA "does not create any obligation on a Party to apply measures where a right in intellectual property is not protected under its laws and regulations." This provision must be put into relation with ACTA Articles 3.1 and 5(h). As stated earlier, Article 3.1 clarifies that ACTA does not affect aspects such as the acquisition and scope of IPRs. Hence, it is a treaty on IP enforcement. Article 3.2 complements this reading since it confirms that ACTA does not create new "right(s) in intellectual property." ACTA measures therefore will apply to IP categories that Members already recognise, and these categories will be at the very least those provided in TRIPS,[60] since being a member of the WTO is a requisite to become part of ACTA.[61]

## *Article 4*

Article 4 deals with privacy and disclosure of information. The first of its two sections establishes that ACTA does not require parties to release information, the disclosure of which would be contrary to its law, including laws protecting privacy rights, or international agreements. It also states that the agreement does not require the disclosure of confidential information when it would either impede law enforcement or otherwise be contrary to the public interest, or when it would prejudice the legitimate commercial interests of particular enterprises, public or private. The second section of Article 4 establishes an obligation for the party receiving the information

59 *Minutes of Meeting of Council for Trade-Related Aspects of Intellectual Property Rights*, op. cit., par. 332.

60 See *infra* analysis on article 5(h).

61 ACTA article 43 establishes that "any Member of the WTO may apply to accede to this Agreement."

in writing, constraining the use or revelation of the information to the purpose for which the information was provided.

Article 4 presents two broad characteristics. On the one hand, it deals with rights and obligations of the parties, and not those of private stakeholders. On the other hand, it is a cross-cutting provision, which applies to the entire agreement.

Article 4 applies both to the relations between the members of ACTA and to those between ACTA participants and private actors. It concerns obligations of states regarding the protection of privacy and undisclosed information by states. This obviously includes sharing of information among law enforcement officials, be they customs officials, the judiciary or police. It does not apply, by contrast, in the context of exclusively private relations. Hence, it is not a provision that could for instance be invoked by an Internet Service Provider to protect the privacy of Internet users by not providing the data to another private entity, such as a right holders organisation. This is the reason why provisions totally or partially addressing these private relations contain autonomous references to the precedence of local laws "governing privilege, the protection of confidentiality of information sources, or the processing of personal data"[62] or the implementation in a manner that "preserves fundamental principles such as freedom of expression, fair process, and privacy."[63]

As happens with the rest of Chapter I, Article 4 relates to several chapters of ACTA. This article has been presented as a "privacy provision potentially restricting the scope of enforcement cooperation."[64] Thus, it seems that Article 4 is particularly related to some provisions of Chapter III, as well as Chapter IV, which deals with "international cooperation." Any exchange of information under Chapter IV will be subject to the stipulations of Article 4.

There are some concerns with regard to the practice of data transfer itself. Although ACTA limits its explicit regulation to data transfers among public actors, and Article 4 is aimed at protecting privacy, both the convenience and the scope of the protection have been questioned. On the one hand, the European Data Protection Supervisor put into question the convenience of data transfers themselves,[65] and favoured a limited version of ACTA where the focus would have been placed in fighting the most serious IP infringements. This was clearly not the policy objective of ACTA's promoters. On the other hand, the European Data Protection Supervisor

62 ACTA Article 11.

63 ACTA Article 27.

64 M. Kaminski, op. cit., p. 395.

65 According to his view, "it appears that the principles of necessity and proportionality of the data transfers under ACTA would be more easily met if the agreement was expressly limited to fighting the most serious IPR infringement offences, instead of allowing for bulk data transfers relating to any suspicions of IPR infringements." European Data Protection Supervisor, *Opinion of the European Data Protection Supervisor on the current negotiations by the European Union of an Anti-Counterfeiting Trade Agreement*, art. 66.

presented the legal framework that should be respected in case data transfers took place, particularly when these transfers are made between EU members and third countries.[66] Based on the European *acquis* on data protection, the recommendations of the Data Protection Supervisor can be adopted by other countries since they endorse a higher standard of protection for privacy rights and they can avoid problems pointed elsewhere with regard to pressures to define broad terms contained in Article 4, such as "public interest."[67]

It has been rightly pointed out that "without an enforcement or auditing mechanism (…) it is unclear how countries could ensure that a recipient of information would adhere to this requirement in practice."[68] This observation refers to the condition announced in Article 4.2, to subject the use and disclosure of the information to the conditions laid down when releasing said information. Although this concern can be shared, and some of the proposals made by the European Data Supervisor would be affected by the same problem, it does not touch upon something that affects other provisions of the agreement in a different manner. That is, ACTA does not have a dispute settlement body, and the ACTA Committee was created with more general objectives than the surveillance of issues such as the conditions mentioned in Article 4.2. Hence, the principles of good faith and *pacta sunt servanda* that govern the fulfilment of most international obligations will equally apply, and will be the sole guarantee in this case.

## SECTION 2: GENERAL DEFINITIONS

### *Article 5*

Article 5 offers a number of general definitions of terms that later on appear scattered throughout the text of the agreement. This article is critical to understanding the meaning of some provisions and the reach of ACTA, since the placement of the definitions in the initial chapter affects the scope of the entire agreement.[69] In any case, and despite the fact that Article 5 contains a small dictionary of relevant

66 *Ibid.*, par. 69–80

67 *See* M. D. Papadopoulou, "ACTA and Copyright in the EU: A Love or Hate Relationship?" Paper presented at the Fourth International *Conference on Information Law and Ethics*, available at http://www.google.com/url?sa=t&rct=j&q=&esrc=s&source=web&cd=3&ved=0CDYQFjAC&url=http%3A%2F%2Fconferences.ionio.gr%2Ficil2011%2Fdownload.php%3Ff%3Dpapers%2F034-papadopoulou-full_text-en-v001.pdf&ei=EQ6iUMbKBOjQ0QWM-YD4CA&usg=AFQjCNG8qBcYvpn1D_21I_0EUt9hB2K7tw (accessed November 2012).

68 M. Kaminski, op. cit., p. 395.

69 For instance, moving the definition of counterfeiting from the border measures section – where it was in the ACTA drafts – to the section containing of initial provisions greatly impacts the reach of the definition, which is not limited to specific field but applies to the entire agreement. M. Kaminski, op. cit., p. 422.

(and sometimes disputed) intellectual property terms, it is necessary to state that not all the definitions contemplated in the agreement can be found in Article 5,[70] and not all those found in Article 5 apply to the entire agreement.[71] In fact, some terms defined in Article 5 have other definitions in specific provisions of the agreement as the case of "persons."[72]

Some of the definitions provided in Article 5 notably expand the scope of enforcement when compared to TRIPS. It is in this sense that the article on definitions has been considered one of the most significant points of departure from existing intellectual property law.[73] Although there are diverging views on this aspect, the departure is particularly noticeable in the case of the definitions of "counterfeit trademark goods" and "pirated copyright goods,"[74] which are included in Article 5(d) and 5(k). Whereas in TRIPS the infringing nature is assessed in accordance with the law of the country of importation (which could be applied by the country of transit), in ACTA the relevant law is the law of the country in which the procedures are invoked. Goods in transit, for instance, can be seized and judged in accordance with the law of the country of transit, regardless of the fact that they may not infringe the law of the country of exportation or the law of the country of importation.

Article 5(e) states that "country" is to be understood to have the same meaning as that set forth in the Explanatory Notes to the WTO Agreement. These notes provide that "the terms 'country' or 'countries' as used in this Agreement and the Multilateral Trade Agreements are to be understood to include any separate customs territory Member of the WTO."

Article 5(f) refers to the notion of "customs transit" and states that it "means the Customs procedure under which goods are transported under Customs control from one Customs office to another." It thus repeats the 1974 definition provided in the Kyoto Convention on the Simplification and Harmonization of Customs Procedures, of 1974.[75]

Article 5(g) states that "days means calendar days," a useful definition in the context of Articles 40, 41, 42 and 43, but not with regard to Article 22, on disclosure of

[70] An important case is the definition of "commercial scale," which is found in article 23 and solely affects section 4, on Criminal Enforcement.

[71] For instance, the definition of territory as the "customs territory and all free zones of a Party" only applies to Section 3, whereas the definition of "technological measures" only applies to article 27.

[72] As will be seen in the case of the definition of "persons."

[73] M. Kaminski, op. cit., p. 387.

[74] *See*, in the same sense, B. Mercurio, "Significance of the Anti-Counterfeiting Trade Agreement", *Journal of International Economic Law*, vol. 15, no 1, 2012, p. 369.

[75] Definition E4/F7, Annex E, CONVENTION INTERNATIONALE POUR LA SIMPLIFICATION ET L'HARMONISATION DES REGIMES DOUANIERS (amendée), Conseil de Coopération douanière, Organisation Mondiale des Douanes, in http://www.wcoomd.org/Kyoto_New/Content/content.html (accessed November 2012).

information, which provides in a footnote that "for the purposes of this Article, days means business days."

ACTA Article 5(h) does not provide for a definition of "intellectual property" but maintains the reach given to this term by TRIPS Article 1.2, which specifies that "intellectual property" refers to the "categories of intellectual property that are the subject of Sections 1 through 7 of the Part II." Although the scope of ACTA and TRIPS is apparently the same, the conclusion is rather different.

- In first instance, it is opportune to recall that TRIPS "categories" do not match with the headings of Sections 1 through 7, but with the categories that are the *subject* of those sections. This is, for instance, the case of *sui generis* plant variety protection. There are also categories currently protected in various countries that are not the subject of TRIPS or of ACTA, such as the protection of non-original databases.
- The reference to the "categories" that are the subject of TRIPS Sections 1 through 7 of Part II has some effects. Using the term 'intellectual property' throughout ACTA while excluding from the reach of some sections only certain IP categories[76] has the effect of enlarging the scope of protection when compared to TRIPS.[77]
- ACTA also widens the reach of enforcement when compared to some FTAs, which explicitly exclude from their enforcement section some forms of protection covered by ACTA.[78]
- More surprisingly, however, ACTA also reduces the scope of protection and does not include some forms effectively covered by TRIPS and some FTAs.[79] Regarding the categories covered in TRIPS but eventually not in ACTA, this

[76] This is explicitly the case of patents and protection of undisclosed information in the border measures section.

[77] For instance, while in ACTA patents and trade secrets are excluded from its border measures section, and the rest of categories are included, TRIPS only obliges to adopt border measures in the case of piracy and counterfeiting.

[78] The agreements between the EU and some countries do not include, among the categories covered by the enforcement section, the protection of undisclosed information. This is the case, for instance, of the agreement with Colombia and Peru, op. cit. *See* art. 234 referral to article 196, subparagraphs 5(a) to 5(i)); the agreement between the EU and Central America (art. 260.1, footnote 39, in EU–Central America association agreement, CENTR-AM/EU/en 1 http://trade.ec.europa.eu/doclib/press/index.cfm?id=689 (accessed October 2012)); and, particularly important in the context of ACTA, the agreement between the EU and South Korea (*See* art. 10.41 referral to art. 10.2.2(a) through (h) in Free Trade Agreement between the European Union and its Member States and the Republic of Korea, *Official Journal of the European Union*, 28.6.2011, L168/1).

[79] Utility models are covered, for instance, in the entire enforcement section of the EU-CARIFORUM agreement (op. cit. art. 148), and a provision on criminal enforcement refers also to utility models in the article 121 of the Agreement between Japan and Indonesia for Economic Partnership, http://www.mofa.go.jp/region/asia-paci/indonesia/epa0708/agreement.pdf (accessed October 2012).

> would be the case of "utility models" and "trade names," which are not the *subject of* Sections from 1 through 7 of Part II of TRIPS but are included in TRIPS by Article 2.1, which states that "in respect of Parts II, III and IV of this Agreement, Members *shall comply* with Articles 1 through 12, and Article 19, of the Paris Convention." Since ACTA refers exclusively to categories *subject of* Sections 1 through 7 of Part II, but does not mention the Paris Convention, it applies the reasoning of the Appellate Body in *Havana Club*, in this case to exclude some forms of protection. Hence, although TRIPS Part II applies to "trade names" and "utility models" because TRIPS Article 2.1 expressly commands the compliance with TRIPS Part II, these are not forms of protection *subject of* Sections 1 through 7 of Part II of the TRIPS. To hold otherwise would mean that ACTA incorporates the categories of IP which are the *subject of* Sections 1 through 7, as well as the categories that, by reference, are governed by those sections.

The definition of intellectual property contained in Article 5(h) must be, moreover, put into relation with Article 3.2, which states that nothing in the agreement creates an obligation on a party to apply measures where an IP right is not protected under its laws and regulations.[80] This means that, for instance, ACTA would not apply in countries such as the United States to the protection of geographical indications.

The ramifications of Article 5(h) are broad. For instance, it permits stating that the title of the agreement (ACTA) does not match with its content. The name is unsuitable because, first, ACTA is not a trade agreement but an intellectual property treaty, and hence the "trade agreement" reference in the name is misleading. The incorrectness also stems from the fact that ACTA deals not only with trademark infringements (whatever its scale and intention) but also with the enforcement of all intellectual property rights that are the subject of TRIPS Sections 1 through 7. Hence, it is not an "anti-counterfeiting" – meaning trademarks – agreement. Although it is not possible to know whether this name has been the unintended outcome of the negotiations, it presents an almost unbeatable emotional (anti-counterfeiting) and economic (trade) attractiveness.

Article 5(j) defines "in-transit goods" as goods under customs transit or transhipment. The definition of "customs transit" was given earlier in the chapter, while the definition of transhipment is provided in Article 5(n): "the Customs procedure under which goods are transferred under Customs control from the importing means of transport to the exporting means of transport within the area of one Customs office which is the office of both importation and exportation." It is exactly

[80] See *supra*.

the definition that can be found in the Kyoto Convention on the Simplification and Harmonization of Customs Procedures, of 1974.[81]

According to Article 5(k), "person" means "a natural person or a legal person." Some have criticised this definition because it may perhaps "heighten liability for companies challenged as direct infringers, such as search engines or peer-to-peer services."[82] Articles 5(k), 11 and 27 are the only ones where "person" appears without further specification.

The definitions include a specific notion of territory in Article 5(m), which applies for the purposes of the border measures section. Pursuant to this article, territory means the "customs territory and all free zones of a Party." Article V of the GATT, on "Freedom of transit," only mentions "territory" but does not provide a definition of it, something which has to be understood in the context of an agreement that provides a definition for territory, but only for "customs territory."[83] Whether free zones are included in the definition of territory has been debated. This is probably the reason why ACTA footnote 1 to Article 5(m) states that "the Parties acknowledge that free zone means a part of the territory of a Party where any goods introduced are generally regarded, insofar as import duties and taxes are concerned, as being outside the customs territory."

81 Definition E1/F1, in the Kyoto Convention on the Simplification and Harmonization of Customs Procedures, op. cit.

82 M. Kaminski, op. cit., p. 397.

83 And defines it as a "territory with respect to which separate tariffs and other regulations of commerce are maintained." General Agreement on Tariffs and Trade, Oct. 30, 1947, 61 Stat. A-11, Article XXIV.2, 55 *U.N.T.S.* 194.

# 3

# ACTA General Obligations with Respect to Enforcement

*Xavier Seuba*

## INTRODUCTION

The Anti-Counterfeiting Trade Agreement (ACTA)[1] is a plurilateral agreement that establishes new international standards for the enforcement of intellectual property rights. Most of its substantive provisions can be found in Chapter II, which opens with a section on general obligations, followed by sections on civil, administrative and criminal enforcement, and a more innovative section on enforcement in the digital environment.

Section 1 of Chapter II contains a single key provision: Article 6 on general obligations with respect to enforcement. It (1) announces the competing legal interests at stake, namely intellectual property enforcement, free trade and protection from abuse; (2) commands the respect of fundamental due process principles, invoking fairness and equity; (3) and lays down an overarching proportionality principle.

Given its content and location, Article 6 should play a decisive and horizontal interpretative function, but it is not the only point of reference when looking for provisions protecting very basic legal interests. In effect, it is closely related to some of the treaty's initial provisions,[2] which also stipulate that broad principles and fundamental rights will be taken into consideration when implementing and interpreting the agreement. In a similar way, some articles in other parts of the treaty reinforce the importance given to the protection of several human rights, such as the rights to privacy, fair process and freedom of expression.[3]

This chapter has benefited from comments by Pedro Roffe. All errors remain mine.

1 Anti-Counterfeiting Trade Agreement, opened for signature May 1, 2011, available at http://trade.ec.europa.eu/doclib/docs/2011/may/tradoc_147937.pdf (visited October 2012).

2 Section 1 of Chapter I. *See* in this same publication "ACTA Initial Provisions and General Definitions."

3 This is the case of ACTA Article 27.2, 27.3 and 27, 4, which call for the preservation of "fundamental principles such as freedom of expression, fair process, and privacy" when reacting against infringement of copyright or related rights over digital networks, the promotion of cooperative efforts within

## CONTENT OF ARTICLE 6

### *Article 6.1*

In Article 6.1, ACTA parties commit to making enforcement procedures available under their law so as to permit effective action against infringements of intellectual property rights covered by the agreement, including expeditious remedies to prevent infringements and remedies which constitute a deterrent to further infringements. Importantly, Article 6.1 establishes that these procedures must be applied in such a manner as to avoid the creation of barriers to legitimate trade and to provide for safeguards against their abuse. It largely replicates Article 41.1 of the World Trade Organization (WTO) Agreement on Trade-Related Aspects of Intellectual Property Rights (TRIPS).[4]

In the analysis of ACTA Chapter I it was suggested that the complementarity between ACTA and TRIPS extends beyond the text and embraces TRIPS case law and WTO decisions regarding TRIPS.[5] Consequently, it may be useful to look at the treatment that Article 41.1 has received in recent WTO case law.

In the context of the controversy that gave rise to the panel report *China – Measures Affecting the Protection and Enforcement of Intellectual Property Rights (China – Intellectual Property Rights)*, the United States alleged that no enforcement procedures were available in China. The reason was that, as it was accepted, Chinese copyright law denied protection to works that did not pass the review (meaning censorship) process.[6] One of the underlying arguments was that China could not deny enforcement of copyright protection merely because it did not recognise a copyright as it was obliged to do by virtue of Article 5.1 of the Bern Convention, which TRIPS Article 9.1 incorporates by reference.[7] Hence, "in the panel's view,

the business community to effectively address trademark and copyright or related rights infringement and ordering an online service provider to disclose to a right holder information sufficient to identify a subscriber whose account was allegedly used for infringement. The protection of privacy, in addition to the mentioned Articles, is also mentioned in Article 4 and Article 22.

4 Agreement on Trade-Related Aspects of Intellectual Property Rights, April 15, 1994, Marrakesh Agreement Establishing the World Trade Organization, Annex 1C, *Legal Instruments Results of the Uruguay Round*, 33 *I.L.M.* 1197 (1994).

5 *See* in this same publication chapter 2 on "ACTA Initial Provisions and General Definitions," comments on Article 1.

6 As the United States pointed out, Article 4.1 of the Copyright Law applies to (a) works never submitted for content review in China; (b) works awaiting the results of content review in China; (c) the unauthorized versions of works edited for distribution in China; and (d) works that have failed content review. Panel Report, *China-Measures Affecting the Protection and Enforcement of Intellectual Property Rights*, WT/DS362/R, 26 January 2009 (adopted 20 March 2009), at 7.84 (hereinafter *China – Intellectual Property Rights*).

7 "Within (TRIPS) Section 1, Article 9.1 incorporates Articles 1 through 21 of the Berne Convention (1971) and the Appendix thereto." *China – Intellectual Property Rights*, op. cit., at 7.173.

censorship regulations cannot eliminate rights that are inherent in a copyrighted work."[8] This argument touches upon the first part of ACTA Article 6.1, which commits parties to making enforcement procedures available for "intellectual property rights covered by the agreement." This means that in case a party does not protect a right which it is bound to protect, it is understood that no enforcement procedures are made available and, hence, ACTA Article 6.1 is infringed. Seen from a different perspective, this ruling shows that norms on enforcement belong to the group of secondary norms. More precisely, norms on enforcement are secondary norms on adjudication,[9] inextricably linked to the material breadth of substantive norms laying down rights and obligations.

Also with regard to TRIPS Article 41.1, the *China – Intellectual Property Rights* panel noted a second issue, which concerned the nature of the obligation to ensure that "enforcement procedures as specified in this Part are available under their law so as to permit effective action."[10] The wording of TRIPS Article 41.1 differs slightly from ACTA Article 6.1, since there is no restriction to the enforcement procedures "specified in this Part." Hence, to be loyal to the ACTA version, the previous quote should be reformulated to clarify the nature of the obligation "to ensure that enforcement procedures are available under their law so as to permit effective action." The question arose because of the argument put forward by China, claiming that authors had "'access' to enforcement process," regardless of the validity of their claims or the adequacy of their evidence.[11] The panel refuted that argument, affirming that enforcement procedures are far more extensive than access to process,[12] and pointed at Article 41.1 to state that enforcement procedures also include remedies such as injunctions, orders to pay damages, orders for the disposal or destruction of infringing goods, and provisional measures.[13] Hence, pursuant to ACTA Article 6.1, enforcement procedures include not only access to process but also specific remedies.

The obligation enshrined in Article 6.1 to avoid the creation of barriers to legitimate trade as a result of enforcement procedures has also been imported from TRIPS. In recent years, TRIPS provisions on border measures have taken centre stage given the evolution of the law and practice of some WTO members in that area. Most of the analysis has focused on the relationship between patented products and the customs regime of transit, both from the angle of free trade norms and

[8] P. Yu, "TRIPS Enforcement and Developing Countries", *American University International Law Review*, vol. 26, no 3, 2011, p. 742.

[9] *See* in this same publication chapter 2, "ACTA Initial Provisions and General Definitions," the section dealing with the meaning and implications of ACTA Article 3.

[10] *China – Intellectual Property Rights*, op. cit., at 7.177.

[11] *Ibid.*, at 7.178.

[12] *Ibid.*, at 7.179.

[13] *Ibid.*

intellectual property law. The underlying debate is to what extent intellectual property rights can legitimately become trade disruptive. With regard to the controversy between India, Brazil and the European Union, it has been held that European seizures of patented products in transit call into question the legitimacy of international trade of generic products.[14] This argument was raised by India, Brazil and other developing countries both in the consultation phase of the controversy[15] and later on in meetings of the TRIPS Council.[16]

The controversy was settled with the compromise by the European Union to amend its customs regulations and to adopt interim guidelines for its customs officials. The goal was to harmonise customs actions with the jurisprudence of the European Court of Justice with regard to transit, risk of diversion and patented products.[17] It remains unclear whether the amended framework will suffice to keep to that compromise, given that seizures of legal patented goods in transit are still possible.[18] In any case, a central aspect of the discussion was the "legitimacy" of the trade that was being disrupted. The fact that products in question were legal in both exporting and importing countries – coupled with the objectionable power conferred to patent holders to control products in transit in accordance with local law, the widespread use of generic medicines to achieve better and more affordable health care, and the human rights component of the access to medicines objective – created a scenario that made it difficult for the European Union to defend its seizures and the regulation backing them.[19] In this context, it is useful to recall that the WTO panel report *Canada – Patent Protection of Pharmaceutical Products* had already given a definition of "legitimate." According to the panel, the term "must be defined in the way that it is often used in legal discourse – as a normative claim calling for protection of interests that are 'justifiable' in the sense that they are supported by

[14] X. Seuba, *Free Trade of Pharmaceutical Products: The Limits of Intellectual Property Enforcement at the Border*, Geneva: ICTSD, issue paper no 27, 2010, p. 10.

[15] *Request for consultations by Brazil, European Union and a Member State – Seizure of Generic Drugs in Transit*, WT/DS409/4, May 19, 2010.

[16] Council for Trade-Related Aspects of Intellectual Property Rights, *Minutes of Meeting Held in the Centre William Rappard on 8–9 June 2010*, IP/C/M/63, par. 253.

[17] Press Release, *Government of India Ministry of Commerce and Industry, Indian EU Reach an Understanding on Issue of Seizure of Indian Generic Drugs in Transit* (July 28, 2011), available at http://pib.nic.in/newsite/erelease.aspx?relid=73554 (visited November 2012).

[18] B. K. Baker, *Settlement of India/EU WTO dispute re seizures of in-transit medicines: why the proposed EU border regulation isn't good enough*, School of Law Faculty Publications. Paper 37, 2012, http://hdl.handle.net/2047/d20001231 (visited November 2012).

[19] With regard to these elements and the legitimacy of the trade that was being disrupted, *see* H. Grosse Ruse-Khan, "A Trade Agreement Creating Barriers to International trade?: ACTA Border Measures and Goods in Transit", *American University International Law Review*, vol. 26, no 3, 2011, pp. 696–697.

relevant public policies or other social norms."[20] This definition can now be taken into account when invoking ACTA Article 6.1.

Finally, the reference made in Article 6.1 to the obligation to make available "expeditious remedies to prevent infringements and remedies which constitute a deterrent to further infringements" is a reminder that national measures will be examined. The freedom to determine the method of implementing the provisions under Article 2.1[21] is not related to the outcome, but to the method of implementation. A similar reference is found in TRIPS Article 46. In accordance with the latter, the cited WTO panel determined that measures indicated by China as adopted to comply with its enforcement obligations were not enough, since they did not create an "effective deterrent to infringement."[22]

### *Article 6.2*

ACTA Article 6.2 also repeats the requirement in TRIPS Article 41.2 that enforcement procedures must be fair and equitable, and provide for the rights of all participants subject to such procedures to be appropriately protected. These procedures must not be unnecessarily costly or complicated, or entail unreasonable time limits or unwarranted delays. As can be seen, this fundamental section incorporates basic fair trial and due process guarantees, and may play, again, a crucial function when implementing the rest of the provisions of Chapter II.

One of the concerns regarding intellectual property enforcement has to do with the costs associated with litigation,[23] as well as the tactics employed to delay procedures. It will thus be interesting to see how ACTA's requirement to put in place procedures that are not unnecessarily costly or entail unreasonable time limits is interpreted.[24] The possibilities are numerous, and they pertain both to the judiciary and policy spheres.[25] European case law can provide some guidance, since the European Enforcement Directive contains a similar provision. For instance, when dealing with an injunction requiring the installation of a contested filtering system,

[20] Panel Report, *Canada – Patent Protection of Pharmaceutical Products*, WT/DS/114/R, 17 March 2000 (adopted 7 April 2000), at 7.69.

[21] ACTA Article 2.1, TRIPS Article 1.1.

[22] *China – Intellectual Property Rights*, op. cit. at 7.373, 7.374, 7.375.

[23] As the editorial of WIPO Magazine asked, "To what extent does the situation prevent right holders from taking legal steps against infringement? Do high litigation costs fuel a perception, more generally, that the IP system only benefits wealthy or large companies equipped with expensive legal expertise?" H. Wollgast, "IP Litigation Costs – An Introduction", *WIPO Magazine*, February 2010, http://www.wipo.int/wipo_magazine/en/2010/01/Article_0001.html (visited November 2012).

[24] M. Blakeney, *Intellectual Property Enforcement. A Commentary on the Anti-Counterfeiting Trade Agreement (ACTA)*, Cheltenham–Northampton: Edward Elgar, 2012, p. 134.

[25] *See* H. Wollgast, op. cit.

the European Court of Justice held that "such an injunction would result in a serious infringement of the freedom of the ISP concerned to conduct its business since it would require that ISP to install a complicated, costly, permanent computer system at its own expense, which would also be contrary to the conditions laid down in Article 3.1 of Directive 2004/48, which requires that measures to ensure the respect of intellectual-property rights should not be unnecessarily complicated or costly."[26]

As will be shown, the reference to fairness and equity in Article 6.2 is particularly important to competitors and users, not just to right holders. The role that the twin provision plays in the TRIPS Agreement is probably not as important as that of Article 6.2 in the context of ACTA. The reason is found in the balance, or lack of balance, in-built in both agreements: in TRIPS, many of the enforcement provisions contain the specific rights and guarantees that protect competitors and consumers (alleged infringers), something that is frequently not the case in ACTA.

## *Article 6.3*

Article 6.3 obliges parties to take into account the need for proportionality between the seriousness of the infringement, the interests of third parties and the applicable measures, remedies and penalties. It lays down the basic principle of proportionality, which is called to play an important function in the specific implementation of enforcement procedures. As Roxane DeLaurell has noted, "the concept of proportionality stands as a proscription against unreasonable criminal prosecutions and an assertion that, in civil matters, intellectual property rights may not exceed the bounds of equity under any circumstance."[27]

In this case, the corresponding provision in TRIPS (Article 46, on "other remedies") has been taken out of its original context, which refers to actions adopted in judicial proceedings. In ACTA, the proportionality principle applies to civil, criminal and administrative enforcement, and to the specific provisions regarding digital enforcement. Thus, all authorities related to intellectual property enforcement, and not only the judiciary, are requested to assess the alleged infringement and its consequences, and discretionally decide whether or not to proceed in light of the foreseeable impact on balance.

The call for proportionality is common in the human rights field. It requires an assessment of the potential impact of some enforcement provisions on related rights. For instance, in the context of the European Convention on Human Rights, the

26 *Scarlet Extended SA v Société Belge des auteurs, compositeurs et éditeurs (SABAM)*, [2011] EUECJ C-70/10 (24 November 2011), par. 48 (hereinafter *Scarlet Extended SA*).

27 R. DeLaurell, "The Anti-Counterfeiting Trade Agreement of 2010: Two Problems and one unanswered question", *The Global Business Law Review*, vol. 2, 2011–2012, p. 185.

principle of proportionality applies to the right to property enshrined in Additional Protocol No. 1,[28] as well as to the rights to privacy and freedom of expression. These three are related to many provisions contained in ACTA, and their interpretation under the principle of proportionality should become central to assessing the agreement's provisions and their implementation. Intrusions on other rights, such as freedom of religion and freedom of association, or guarantees related to detention and criminal sanctions, should also be evaluated under the principle of proportionality, and could be of relevance with regard to ACTA. Nevertheless, there are other situations where the principle of proportionality does not apply, such as the case of torture or inhuman or degrading treatment, where in principle no ambiguity is tolerated.[29]

The principle of proportionality is also key in intellectual property litigation. In Promusicae,[30] Scarlet[31] and Netlog,[32] the European Court of Justice has stated that it is necessary to achieve a balance between different fundamental rights and that intellectual property is not an absolute right.[33] According to the Court, Community law requires that, when transposing directives,

> Member States take care to rely on an interpretation of them which allows a fair balance to be struck between the various fundamental rights protected by the Community legal order. Further, when implementing the measures transposing those directives, the authorities and courts of the Member States must not only interpret their national law in a manner consistent with those directives but also make sure that they do not rely on an interpretation of them which would be in conflict with those fundamental rights or with the other general principles of Community law, such as the principle of proportionality.[34]

## *Article 6.4*

Article 6.4 establishes that "no provision of this Chapter shall be construed to require a Party to make its officials subject to liability for acts undertaken in the performance

[28] *James and Others V. The United Kingdom*, Application no. 8793/79, 21 February 1986, par. 50.

[29] *Saadi c. Italia*, Application no 37201/06, 28 February 2008.

[30] *Productores de Música de España (Promusicae) v. Telefónica de España SAU*, Case C—275/06, 28 January 2008 (hereafter *Promusicae*).

[31] *Scarlet Extended SA*, op. cit.

[32] *Belgische Vereniging van Auteurs, Componisten en Uitgevers (SABAM) v Netlog NV*, Case C-360/10, 16 February 2012 (hereafter *Netlog*).

[33] According to the European Court of Justice, "The protection of the right to intellectual property is indeed enshrined in Article 17(2) of the Charter of Fundamental Rights of the European Union ('the Charter'). There is, however, nothing whatsoever in the wording of that provision or in the Court's case-law to suggest that that right is inviolable and must for that reason be absolutely protected", *Scarlet Extended SA*, op. cit. par. 43.

[34] *Promusicae*, op. cit., par. 70.

of their official duties." Again, TRIPS is also reflected in this provision,[35] but only partially: the TRIPS reference to "good faith" – meaning that only acts taken in good faith would be condoned – has been omitted. The limitation of that exemption to acts related to the administration of laws on intellectual property enforcement or protection has also been removed.

The first omission implies that in principle there will be no subjective examination of any kind, and all acts performed by public officials will be exempted just because they have been undertaken by public officials. In this case, TRIPS Article 48.2 is not invoked, and acts undertaken in bad faith would be exempted from liability. This absence can play a decisive role in the context of an agreement that permits actions adopted *ex officio* at a lower standard of proof than TRIPS.[36]

On the other hand, the lack of reference to the limitation of the exemption of liability for acts related to the administration of laws on intellectual property enforcement or protection could lead to the conclusion that the exclusion is unlimited. This, however, is in our view not the correct reading. Given the link established between the provisions of "this Chapter" and the exemption of responsibility ("no provision of this Chapter shall be construed to require a Party to make its officials subject to liability…"), it can be sustained that this immunity applies to acts conducted in the areas of civil, administrative, criminal and "digital" enforcement.

## AMBIGUITY, UNBALANCE AND PERMISSIVENESS AS TARGETS OF ARTICLE 6

Together with its horizontal and cross-cutting function, ACTA Article 6 has three additional applications. Firstly, it is useful in presence of open terms and doubtful meanings. Secondly, it is an important recourse when dealing with provisions conceived solely to defend right holders' interests without taking into consideration other relevant public and private interests. Finally, Article 6 can also prevent

35 TRIPS Article 48.2: "In respect of the administration of any law pertaining to the protection or enforcement of intellectual property rights, Members shall only exempt both public authorities and officials from liability to appropriate remedial measures where actions are taken or intended in good faith in the course of the administration of that law."

36 "TRIPS permits, but does not require, member countries to allow border authorities to act on their own initiative to suspend the release of goods; and TRIPS places restrictions on how these authorities may act. To seize goods on their own initiative, the authorities must have *prima facie* evidence that an IP right is being infringed. Under ACTA, however, there is no such evidentiary restriction; authorities may seize and retain 'suspect goods,' a considerably lower standard than requiring *prima facie* evidence before seizure. Authorities can seize goods they suspect, without any actual evidence, and certainly without evidence arising to a *prima facie* standard, are infringing." M. E. Kaminski, "An Overview and the Evolution of the Anti-Counterfeiting Trade Agreement", *Albany Law Journal of Science and Technology*, vol. 21, no 3, 2011, p. 405.

legislative interpretations excessively based on the permissive language characterising the treaty.

More specifically, the interpretative function of Article 6 will come into play in presence of ambiguous provisions in the agreement. A second situation where Article 6 has a role to play has to do with the lack of reference of rights and guarantees that can be deduced from its other provisions or from general principles of law. A third situation is that relating to provisions drafted in permissive terms. These provisions may lead parties to legislate and act intensively in the direction of more aggressive enforcement, which could result in an imbalanced strengthening of the position of intellectual property right holders, conflicting with other provisions of the agreement or general principles of law. Article 6 is crucial with regard to the three situations identified earlier in the chapter as they are relatively common under ACTA.

The "vague and uncertain nature of many provisions"[37] of the agreement has been widely acknowledged.[38] In fact, that language is probably part of the "constructive ambiguity" that characterised TRIPS[39] and now also characterises ACTA. This term has been used for the practice of deliberately choosing imprecise wording in order to reach agreement when views differ on the meaning and scope of the institutions regulated, or situations covered by the agreement. "Constructive ambiguity" opened the doors to interpretation, and "interpretation of ambiguous clauses in certain ways may be one means of clawing back much of what was lost in the negotiating battles."[40]

One among the many examples of provisions containing ambiguous or open terms that need further interpretation is ACTA Article 23.1, which mandates the application of criminal measures in cases of piracy and counterfeiting on a commercial scale. This provision, however, does not define "commercial scale." Hence, the aforementioned references to proportionality, equity and fairness should play a significant role when "constructively interpreting" it.

[37] C. Geiger, "Weakening Multilateralism in Intellectual Property Lawmaking: A European Perspective on ACTA", *The WIPO Journal*, vol. 3, no 2, 2012, p. 176.

[38] See, with regards the ambiguity, C. Geiger, "Anti-Counterfeiting Trade Agreement: A Comprehensive Assessment from a European Perspective", EU DG for External Policies, *Workshop. The Anti-Counterfeiting Trade Agreement (ACTA)*, EXPO/B/INTA/FWC/2009–01/Lot7/25, 2012, pp. 15, 55. http://www.europarl.europa.eu/committees/fr/studiesdownload.html?languageDocument=EN&file=73311 (visited November 2012).

[39] J. Wattal, "Intellectual Property Rights and Agriculture: Interests of Developing Countries", paper presented at *The Conference on Agriculture and the New Trade Agenda*, World Bank, Geneva, 1999, http://www.bvindecopi.gob.pe/colec/jwatal.pdf (visited May 2014).

[40] *Ibid.*

Another frequently mentioned aspect of ACTA is the unbalanced content of some its provisions,[41] added to the fact that the treaty "offers very few limitations and exceptions; all of them are either permissive or included as safeguard provisions."[42] Before commenting further on ACTA's "unbalanced content," it is worth noting that the lack of balance in the treaty does not necessarily imply an imbalanced national intellectual property enforcement framework. The obligation to honour previous intellectual property commitments[43] and the scope of protection granted under national intellectual property systems[44] must be added to the maxim *permissum videtur in omne, quod non prohibitum*, that is, everything that is not prohibited by ACTA is permissible if that treaty alone is taken into account.

Many of the agreement's provisions can be considered imbalanced if examined in isolation. The case of provisional measures offers a good example. When ACTA regulates such measures, it does not mention the right – recognised, for instance, in European enforcement legislation – for the alleged infringer to be "informed without delay after the execution of the measures at the latest" in case measures are adopted *inaudita parte*. Nor does it mention the right to a "review, including a right to be heard," which should be granted upon request of the defendant.[45] Neither does mention that provisional measures should be revoked if "the applicant does not institute, within a reasonable period, proceedings leading to a decision on the merits of the case," as established by European legislation on civil enforcement.[46] The missing guarantees are clearly related to essential components of due process norms. As mentioned before, the Article 6 reference to fair trial standards can be brought into consideration to "balance" the missing entitlements in the provision governing provisional measures. European law provides important guidance on how these conflicting interests can be appropriately balanced.[47]

Together with the ambiguous language and the partially drafted provisions, already mentioned, the permissive wording contained in ACTA may benefit from

[41] See, with regards the absence of balancing provisions, M. Geist, " The trouble with ACTA: an analysis of the Anti-Counterfeiting Trade Agreement", EU DG for External Policies, op. cit., p. 25

[42] P. Yu, "Six Secret (and Now Open) Fears of ACTA", *SMU Law Review*, vol. 64, 2011, p. 1059.

[43] See comments in this publication with regards Article 1.

[44] See comments in this publication with regards Article 3.

[45] Compare Article 9.4 of the EU Enforcement Directive with Article ACTA 12. Directive 2004/48/EC of the European Parliament and of the Council of 29 April 2004 on the enforcement of intellectual property rights, *Official Journal of the European Union* L157 of 30 April 2004 (hereafter Enforcement Directive).

[46] Compare Article 9.5 of the EU Enforcement Directive with Article ACTA 12.

[47] See this same exercise with regards to other remedies and European trade agreements in X. Seuba, "Checks and Balances in the Intellectual Property Enforcement Field: Reconstructing EU Trade Agreements", in C. Geiger (ed.), *Constructing European IP: Achievements and News Perspectives*, Cheltenham–Northampton: Edward Elgar, 2012, pp. 409–431.

the wording of Article 6 and the initial provisions chapter. In effect, ACTA contains numerous provisions drafted in permissive terms, some of them closely related to the protection of fundamental rights, such as the rights to privacy or freedom of expression. The assumption is that either the balancing provisions come into play or the permissive language will be "gradually transformed into mandatory, best-practice language."[48]

Another useful example can be found in the provision dealing with the right to information.[49] ACTA Article 22 is drafted in permissive terms and states that members *may* authorise the provision of relevant information to right holders.[50] In this context, it can be expected that the provision of information to right holders can become routine if other interests are not given due credit. This is where it becomes relevant to recall Article 6 references to safeguards against abuse (Art. 6.1), the protection of the rights of all participants (Art. 6.2) and the need to take into account the proportionality between the infringement and other legitimate interests at stake (Art. 6.3).

## WILL ARTICLE 6 DELIVER?

Article 6, even in its earlier versions, was conceived to "temper" the remedies provisions.[51] As discussed, given the content and overall direction of ACTA, Article 6 can play several important roles which could be summarised as the interpretation, balancing and restraining functions. Given the importance of its tempering role, it is necessary to ask whether the expectations placed on Article 6 can be met. This question can be best answered if the interpretation and balancing functions are examined separately.

With regard to the interpretative function, there are at least two reflections to be made, one involving the tools available for this exercise and the other concerning the lack of clarity with regard to the consequences of potential discrepancies.

ACTA, like many other contemporary agreements in the field of intellectual property, lacks official records on the positions of parties in the negotiations. The lack of transparency that characterised ACTA resulted in the absence of official

48 Geist, op. cit., p. 37.

49 Other examples of permissive language are found in Articles 9.3 on Damages, 10.3 on Other Remedies, 14.2 on Small Consignments and Personal Luggage, 16.2 on Border Measures and 23.3 on Criminal Offences.

50 It states that members "*may* authorize its competent authorities to provide a right holder with information about specific shipments of goods, including the description and quantity of the goods, to assist in the detection of infringing goods."

51 E. Ayoob, "Recent Development: The Anti-Counterfeiting Trade Agreement", *Cardozo Arts and Entertainment Law Journal*, vol. 28, 2010–2011, p. 184.

*travaux préparatoires* that could have been invaluable in the context of treaty interpretation.[52] This lack of records enhances the importance of balancing provisions such as Article 6 and the initial provisions contained in Chapter I. However, and quite paradoxically, the lack of official records makes it impossible to determine the precise and specific meaning that parties intended to give to Article 6.

In fact, in some cases reaching agreement on the specific implications of Article 6 is just not possible. This is, for instance, the case of the application of a fundamental principle, such as proportionality. Even in limited and relatively homogenous areas and legal orders, the results are not easily predictable. This is the case in Europe regarding copyright enforcement in the digital environment, in which regard it has been held that "interpretation of the meaning of proportionality is problematic and could hardly be seen to have established a common ground for the rules existing in each of the Member States."[53]

The fact that interpretation is particularly important in the context of ACTA is a sign of the freedom given to the treaty's implementation in the way that best responds to local needs and legal systems. While such freedom could be interpreted as showing respect for national sovereignty, this conclusion should be placed in a wider context in which ACTA is only one element of a broader picture. On the one hand, there are other ongoing initiatives in this ecosystem, such as trade agreements and trade supervision mechanisms that also condition the "policy space" available to states. On the other hand, since interpretation will become so important, it seems necessary to wonder who will become the interpreter and in what context interpretation will be conducted.

In the absence of a dispute settlement body, it is possible that parties will assess other members' compliance in accordance with their own views. This is, for instance, regularly done by the United States through the Special 301 mechanism, which oversees the US trading partners' implementation of free trade agreements.[54] A situation could thus arise where a country interprets ACTA's ambiguous provisions in a way that does not coincide with another country's views on the same provision. In that situation, the aforementioned "constructive ambiguity" would probably

[52] The Vienna Convention on the Law of Treaties Article 32 provides that the preparatory work of the treaty is a supplementary means of interpretation.

[53] M. M. Frabboni, "File-Sharing and the Role of Intermediaries in the Market Place: National, European Union and International Development", in I. A. Stamatoudi (ed.), *Copyright Enforcement and the Internet*, Kluwer Law International, 2010, p. 133.

[54] P. Roffe and L. M. Genovesi, *Propuesta de estrategia y plan de acción: implementación del Acuerdo de Promoción Comercial con los EEUU en el área de propiedad intelectual*, Washington, DC: Banco Interamericano de Desarrollo, Vicepresidencia de Sectores y Conocimiento, Sector de Integración y Comercio, Washington, DC, 2009, p. 12. http://idbdocs.iadb.org/wsdocs/getdocument.aspx?docnum=2054292 (visited October 2012).

give place to a more *realistic* scenario, where power relations and available domestic mechanisms would allow some parties to impose their views on the issues at stake.

Another fundamental question pertains to the balancing function addressed earlier in the chapter. The problem of the lack of references to some guarantees and balancing provisions[55] has been addressed by intensive evocation of ACTA Article 6. This has been the case, for instance, with regard to provisions on the right to information, injunctions, corrective measures and damages. In all these cases, Article 6 has been invoked to fulfil several functions: (1) to introduce safeguards that were missing in ACTA[56]; (2) to bring in alternative measures to those mentioned in the agreement[57]; (3) to act in a different manner to what could be initially deduced from ACTA[58]; or (4) to avoid the punitive reading that ACTA permits or favours.[59] These are indeed primary examples of the balancing functions attributed to Article 6.

The question, however, remains whether it is realistic to expect that Article 6 will effectively play this role. First of all, there is no certainty that "balanced" interpretations and implementation will be preferred, since ACTA does not contain any obligation to adopt such interpretations. But even if this was the intention, the cases where recourse to Article 6 would be necessary are so numerous that it is unlikely that all countries in each case would prefer a reinterpreted and balanced version of ACTA. Although Article 6 seems more tangible and easy to *realise* than TRIPS Articles 7 and 8, the discussions revolving around Article 6 could be similar to those regarding the provision on the distribution of resources (ACTA 2.3).[60]

Together with the concerns related to the systemic feasibility of balanced interpretations, there are two other specific concerns with regard to Article 6.

First, the Article 6.2 stipulation that parties should not set up excessively costly or time-consuming procedures can be meaningless in the context of daily intellectual property litigation. It has been argued that this provision alludes to the procedures themselves, not to their specific implementation.[61] Hence, neither the costs nor the delays caused by the other party are determining factors; only proving that the legal framework for enforcement itself is the origin of such consequences would permit

[55] See *supra* section 3.

[56] This is the case of due process and fair trail guarantees in the context of the right of information. O. Vrins, "The impact of ACTA on the EU acquis and civil liberties", EU DG for External Policies, op. cit., p. 99.

[57] *Ibid.*, p. 100.

[58] Not ordering the destruction of goods that seems to demand Article ACTA Article 10. *Ibid.*, p. 101.

[59] Article 9 can be read as ordering that compensatory damages and infringer's profit may be ordered cumulatively, something that, allegedly, invoking Article 6.3 would impede. *Ibid.*, p. 104.

[60] *See* in this book X. Seuba, "ACTA Initial Provisions and General Definitions", Section 1.

[61] ICTSD-UNCTAD, *Resource Book on TRIPS and Development*, New York: Cambridge University Press, 2005.

the application of Article 6.2. It therefore seems sound to sustain that present costs associated to intellectual property litigation[62] would remain the same.

Second, as pointed out when alluding to Article 6.3, in ACTA the quest for proportionality applies to decisions adopted not only by judicial authorities but also by administrative authorities. However, this could also be interpreted in the context of a trend to give the latter greater powers to adopt decisions previously restricted to the judiciary. It is moreover disputable that administrative authorities are entitled to conduct such an assessment of "proportionality" without contradicting due process and basic legal certainty standards.

## CONCLUSION

ACTA Article 6 establishes the general obligations with respect to enforcement that apply in Chapter II. The most important obligations include the respect for fundamental due process principles, such as fairness and equity, and the implementation of an overarching proportionality principle. Article 6 also identifies the competing legal interests at stake, namely intellectual property enforcement, free trade and protection from abuse. The references in Article 6 to fundamental principles and basic legal interests to be protected encapsulate part of the contemporary debate on the normative promotion of intellectual property enforcement and its relation to other legal interests.

Article 6 is one of the instruments that permit redressing the ambiguity, imbalance and permissiveness that characterise a number of the treaty's provisions. Thus, it has at least three important functions: interpretation, balance and restraint. Whether the signatory countries will make use of this important provision and implement it in full depends on many factors, which are likely to vary across sectors, fora and topics. It is possible, however, to find some parallelism with similar provisions contained in TRIPS, which – at least in theory – have a central role. This chapter argues, however, that the functions of Article 6 are so numerous and the expectations so high that only a more precise drafting of the agreement would avoid much of the foreseeable speculation and guarantee more predictable and balanced outcomes.

[62] See above section 2, when dealing with Article 6.2.

# 4

# Provisions on Civil Enforcement – Section 2 of ACTA

*Anselm Kamperman Sanders*

## INTRODUCTION

ACTA provisions on civil enforcement are contained in Section 2 of the agreement: Articles 7 to 12. They cover issues such as injunctions available for IP infringements, damages and other remedies, provisional measures, and information related to the infringement.

Intellectual property rights are typically privately enforceable. Civil enforcement provisions apply to all types of infringement,[1] whether between legitimate competitors in a dispute or between a right holder and an unidentified infringer. The civil enforcement section of ACTA is obviously subject to the general enforcement obligations outlined in the treaty's Article 6. This provision obliges the parties to provide for effective action against any infringement of intellectual property rights, including expeditious options to prevent infringements and remedies, which constitute a deterrent for further infringements.

There is also a safeguard clause in the sense that the provisions must be applied in a manner that avoids the creation of barriers to legitimate trade and provides safeguards against their abuse (this is a direct reference to the TRIPS Agreement's safeguard provisions).[2] Courts can treat intellectual property remedies as equitable relief,[3] and competition authority bodies can act against IP right holders with economic positions of market dominance in relation to unilateral abusive behaviour or

This contribution draws on a 2011 study entitled *The Anti-Counterfeiting Trade Agreement (ACTA): An Assessment*, which the author prepared with Moerland A., Pugatch M., Shabalala D., and Vergano P. for the INTA Committee of the European Parliament DG EXPO Policy Department, (European Parliament, Brussels), http://www.europarl.europa.eu/studies. The author is indebted to D. Shabalala, who has been kind enough to provide suggestions to improve the manuscript.

[1] Except that parties may exclude patents and undisclosed information from the ambit of Section 2 (Article 7–12)

[2] See Articles 7 and 8 of TRIPS.

[3] *See*, for example, *eBay Inc. v. MercExchange, L.L.C.*, 547 US 388 (2006).

concerted practices in the exercise of their IPRs that harm the interests of consumers or competition as a whole. In addition, goods can be used (produced or imported) under compulsory licenses when sanctioned by government.[4] What follows here, however, is an overview of the contents of ACTA Section 2, which deals with civil enforcement only.[5]

## AVAILABILITY OF CIVIL PROCEDURES

ACTA Article 7 obliges the parties to make available to right holders civil judicial procedures concerning the enforcement of any intellectual property right as specified in Section 2. In terms of the subject matter, footnote 1 indicates that patents and the protection of undisclosed information may be excluded from the scope of this section. Civil remedies resulting from administrative procedures on the merits of a case shall be dealt with in a substantially equivalent manner to those set forth in ACTA's section on civil procedures, that is, rules on injunctions, damages, other remedies, information related to infringement, and provisional measures. By contrast, TRIPS Article 50.8, which does not fall under the civil enforcement section, affirms that, "[t]o the extent that any provisional measure can be ordered as a result of administrative procedures, such procedures shall conform to principles equivalent in substance to those set forth in this Section." The ACTA formulation appears to be narrower as it restricts the measures covered to *administrative procedures on the merits of the case*, while in TRIPS reference is made to just *administrative procedures*. However, given that ACTA's rules on injunctions are somewhat more rights-friendly than those of TRIPS, the effect may be to broaden right holders' options while diminishing the defendant-friendly provisions that appear to have been the main concern addressed by TRIPS Article 50.8.

## INJUNCTIONS

According to ACTA Article 8.1, each party must ensure that for the purpose of the enforcement of intellectual property rights, its judicial authorities can issue a cease-and-desist order not just against infringers but also against third parties (related or otherwise) over whom the court has jurisdiction. The primary aim is to prevent the goods from entering channels of commerce through allowing authorities to act against third parties who may have bought the goods from the infringing party in good faith in order to engage in retail or distribution.

4 See TRIPS Article 31 and equally Article 8.2 ACTA.

5 See respective chapters in Part I of this book for the consideration of the whole of ACTA.

ACTA Article 8.2 – equivalent to TRIPS Article 44.2 – allows parties to make an exception for goods produced under a compulsory license, provided that payment of remuneration to the right holder is available in accordance with the conditions set out in Part II of the TRIPS Agreement. Thus, if a party so wishes, it may choose not to apply injunctions to goods produced under a compulsory license, if they are part of a dispute regarding the validity, status, or appropriateness of the issued license. However, the content of TRIPS Article 44.2 has never been tested, and it is unclear how it would work in either agreement. The ACTA provision is clearly meant to address concerns regarding the use of injunctions to prevent the entry of goods produced under compulsory licenses into ACTA party markets. This is, however, not a mandatory exception, and it is unclear how many parties would use the option, and whether by failing to do so they would be in compliance with their obligations under the Doha Declaration on the TRIPS Agreement and Public Health.[6]

ACTA requires parties to provide that, in civil judicial proceedings concerning the enforcement of intellectual property rights, their judicial authorities be empowered to issue an injunction against the infringer aimed at prohibiting the continuation of the infringement and, inter alia, an order directed to the infringer or (where appropriate) a third party to prevent infringing goods from entering the channels of commerce.[7] The agreement does not explicitly provide for the possibility of applying pecuniary compensation as an alternative to injunction, as is customary in EU member states.[8] While nothing in the treaty forbids the provision of authority for judicial officials to order pecuniary compensation as an alternative,[9] recourse to this option may be called into question by other ACTA parties.[10]

## DAMAGES

The section on damages is significantly more detailed than TRIPS Article 45 on damages, providing for quite detailed control over the considerations to be taken into account by judges. Under ACTA Article 9, parties must provide right holders

[6] Doha Declaration on the TRIPS Agreement and Public Health, adopted on 14 November 2001, at the Fourth WTO Ministerial Conference.

[7] See Article 11 Directive 2004/48/EC of the European Parliament and of the Council of 29 April 2004 on the enforcement of intellectual property rights (IPR Enforcement Directive), which provides for similar language. However, according to Article 12 of the same Directive, judicial authorities can offer an alternative order for pecuniary compensation at the request of the person liable to be subject to the injunction and under specific circumstances.

[8] *See* the 'Opinion of European Academics on Anti-Counterfeiting Trade Agreement', available at http://www.iri.uni-hannover.de/tl_files/pdf/ACTA_opinion_110211_DH2.pdf (accessed 24.10.2012).

[9] This is a point also made by the EU Commission. *See* European Commission, 'Commission Services Working Paper', 27 April 2011. Available at http://trade.ec.europa.eu/doclib/docs/2011/april/tradoc_147853.pdf (accessed 24 October 2012), p. 6.

[10] *Ibid.*

the ability to seek damages from the infringer who, knowingly or with reasonable grounds to know, engaged in infringing activity. This provision introduces a constructive knowledge standard in that an order for payment of damages may be imposed not only in case of a knowing infringement but also in case of an infringement due to negligence.[11] Thus those who could be considered to have reason to know they were or might be infringing would be liable for damages even if they did not intend to infringe. While it seems clear that so-called innocent infringers are not covered by this provision, the standard may encroach on the behaviour of competitors in knowledge-based markets who may be aware of a potential risk that a product may be considered an infringement (e.g. computer-related inventions), but who cannot be certain due to the nature of the right. This is particularly true for trademarks and patents where the existence of trademark confusion or scope of a patent cannot be fully determined except through litigation. Damages should provide adequate compensation for the injury suffered by the right holder as a result of an infringement. Judicial authorities are given considerable leeway in determining the amount of damages.

The focus is not on objective tests, but on any "legitimate" measure of value put forward by the right holder. ACTA requires parties to empower, in civil judicial proceedings, their authorities to order: (1) compensatory damages (i.e. damages intended to compensate for the injury caused to the right holder suffered due to the infringement)[12]; and (2) damages equivalent to the infringers' profits from the violations.

ACTA Article 9.1 requires that judicial authorities have the authority to consider these measures, including the following two approaches: (1) market price of infringing goods based on the concept that each infringing product constitutes a lost sale; and (2) suggested retail price, another proxy for the concept that each infringing product represents a lost sale. ACTA requires that these damages be foreseen at least in cases of copyright or related rights infringements and trademark counterfeiting.[13]

Two of the criteria for compensatory damages (i.e. the value of the infringed goods or services measured by the market price, or the suggested retail price)[14] may be novel to several legal systems, so judicial authorities may feel compelled to reject them. The criteria for such damages do not, for example, appear to fully match the criterion of "appropriateness of the damage to the actual prejudice suffered" as expressed in Article 13 of Directive 2004/48/EC of the European Parliament and the Council of 29 April 2004 on the enforcement of intellectual property rights

[11] Article 9.1 of ACTA.

[12] *See* Article 9.1 of ACTA.

[13] *See* Article 9.2 of ACTA.

[14] *See* Article 9.1 of ACTA. *See also* 'Opinion of the European Academics on Anti-Counterfeiting Trade Agreement', *supra*.

(hereafter the EU IPR Enforcement Directive). As such, where EU member states continue to apply the directive's criterion, they would potentially have been in violation of the ACTA requirement to have their judges consider such non-traditional forms of measuring damages.[15]

ACTA Article 9.2 requires the parties to provide that the court can order an accounting of profits in case of copyright or related rights infringement and trademark counterfeiting, and may introduce the presumption that these profits are equivalent to the damages referred to in the preceding paragraph. It is important to note that while this article is limited to counterfeiting per se for trademarks, it applies to any act of copyright infringement, even as between two legitimate business actors in a legitimate dispute regarding the scope of an exception or limitation to copyright, or the extent to which a derivative work draws on another. Thus, while this provision appears to limit the applicability only to copyright and trademark subject matter, it covers much more than "pirated copyright" as defined in ACTA Article 5(k). This is also true for the rest of Article 9. The justification for providing more expansive damages provisions for copyright beyond pirated copyright goods is unclear, especially given that the concerns regarding normal trademark infringement and legitimate commercial activity may also be extended to copyright.

ACTA Article 9.3 also foresees that judicial authorities can order the infringer of all copyright and related rights, as well as trademark counterfeiting, to pay to the right holder (1) pre-established damages, or (2) presumption-based damages reflecting the harm caused by the infringement, or (3) for "at least for copyright" additional damages.[16] These damages are to be ordered as an alternative to the compensatory damages and damages equivalent to the infringers' profits. However, this is only mandatory for cases of trademark counterfeiting and "copyright and related rights protecting works, phonograms and performances." Infringement of designs, patents, or geographical indications is not included here, although nothing prohibits states from extending the provision to cover that subject matter.[17]

## OTHER REMEDIES

Under ACTA Article 10, parties must ensure that, at least with respect to pirated copyright goods and counterfeit trademark goods, judicial authorities have the power to order the destruction of infringing goods. In relation to "materials and implements"

[15] In its response to the Opinion of the European Academics, the Commission does not directly address this point, which under the IPR Enforcement Directive is a requirement, not an option. *See* 'Commission Services Working Paper', 27 April 2011. Available at http://trade.ec.europa.eu/doclib/docs/2011/april/tradoc_147853.pdf (accessed 24 October 2012), p. 7.

[16] See Articles 9.2, 9.3, and 9.4 of ACTA.

[17] See Articles 9.3 and 9.4 of ACTA.

used predominantly in the manufacture and creation of the infringing goods, the treaty requires that judicial authorities be empowered to order their destruction or disposal outside of the channels of commerce.[18] ACTA also requires that judicial authorities be empowered to order the destruction of pirated copyright goods and counterfeit trademark goods without compensation, except in exceptional circumstances. In both cases, the emphasis is that this may be done without any compensation whatsoever. What is not specified, particularly with regard to "materials and implements," is whether materials owned by third parties are subject to the no-compensation rule. To the extent that a state wishes to limit this only to compensation to the infringer, it may be in violation of this provision.

## INFORMATION RELATED TO THE INFRINGEMENT

ACTA Article 11 reiterates the safeguard that there shall be no requirement to alter or prejudice existing law on privacy, privilege, and confidentiality, but that states must enable their authorities to order the alleged infringer to hand over information. It is important to note that this requires a "justified" request by the right holder. What would be justified is apparently left to the law of each party.

## PROVISIONAL MEASURES

Article 12 obliges the parties to empower judicial authorities to order effective provisional measures against infringers and third parties so as to prevent infringement of any intellectual property right and preserve evidence related to the alleged infringement. Provisional measures are applicable in all infringement actions, except those on the seizure of goods, which only apply to copyright or related rights infringements and trademark counterfeiting, although states are free to extend these beyond the stated subject matter.[19] Thus, according to Article 12.2, the right holder can request such measures *inaudita altera parte*, meaning that the defendant does not need to be notified, or present and able to oppose such a request. The request must state a danger of irreparable harm or risk of evidence being destroyed. Balanced with this ease of access for the right holder is the permission that a party can require sufficient

[18] See Article 10 of the EU IPR Enforcement Directive. Please note that, under the EU IPR Enforcement Directive, these remedies also apply to "materials and implements" principally used in the creation or manufacture of the infringing goods. However, the EU *acquis* provides for two other remedies, namely the recall and definitive removal of the products infringing IPRs from the channels of commerce. This may lead to concerns about compatibility, but as a requirement that courts be granted a particular power, there does not appear to be a limitation on the EU also empowering judicial authorities to apply other remedies, to the extent that these authorities are also empowered to do as ACTA requires.

[19] See Article 12.3 of ACTA.

evidence, beyond simple assertions, from right holders concerning irreparable harm and risk of evidence being destroyed. However, there appears to be no requirement for a defendant to request the cessation of provisional measures, or to oppose the request once goods and evidence have been impounded. Only through the right holder's failure to act can provisional measures be ended before the conclusion of infringement proceedings. However, it is required that authorities be able to order compensation be paid to the defendant.

ACTA does not provide for specific procedural safeguards that would apply in the event of the adoption of provisional measures *inaudita altera parte*. Article 6 does, however, provide that procedures enforcing the protection of intellectual property rights be applied "in such a manner as to [...] provide for safeguards against their abuse" and that "procedures adopted, maintained, or applied to implement the provisions of this chapter shall be fair and equitable, and shall provide for the rights of all participants subject to such procedures to be appropriately protected." Read in conjunction with TRIPS Article 50.6, ACTA parties are required to ensure that a defendant does have the opportunity to challenge the imposition of provisional measures within at most 31 calendar days.[20]

Such safeguards can be explicitly found in, for example, the EU IPR Enforcement Directive Article 9.4, which includes, inter alia, the obligation to inform parties without delay and the possibility for the defendant to request a review of the decision to apply provisional measures, at which the defendant then has the right to be heard. Equally, the EU directive requires that provisional measures be revoked if the applicant does not institute proceedings leading to a decision on the merits of the case within a reasonable period of time.[21]

It has been argued in the 'Opinion of the European Academics on Anti-Counterfeiting Trade Agreement' that the lack of specific procedural safeguards in ACTA in case of provisional measures *inaudita altera parte* may be inconsistent with EU law, or the so-called *acquis communaitaire*. It can, however, also be argued that ACTA Article 6 allows parties to maintain and apply additional procedural safeguards.

Under ACTA Article 12.3, suspect goods, as well as materials and implements relevant to the act of infringement, may be seized in cases of copyright or related rights infringement and trademark counterfeiting. Furthermore, the seizure of documentary evidence should be available, at least in case of trademark counterfeiting.

Article 12.4 provides mandatory safeguards in that the applicant of provisional measures must provide reasonable evidence with a sufficient degree of certainty to

[20] On the interplay between ACTA and TRIPS, see the three first chapters in this volume.

[21] Under the EU IPR Enforcement Directive, the reasonable period of time is to be determined by the judicial authority ordering the measures where the law permits it or, in the absence of such determination, within a period not exceeding twenty working days or thirty-one calendar days, whichever is the longer.

the authority that (1) the applicant's intellectual property right is being infringed, or (2) infringement is imminent. In order to prevent abuse, the applicant may be ordered to post security or provide assurances, the level of which should not be so onerous as to act as a deterrent in applying for provisional measures.

Finally, Article 12.5 deals with the situation in which the provisional measures are revoked or lapse as a result of an act or omission by the applicant. This usually occurs when the applicant fails to initiate proceedings on the merits of the case in time, with an the upper limit prescribed by TRIPS Article 50.6, that is, not exceeding twenty working days or thirty-one calendar days, whichever is the longer. The defendant must then be compensated for any injury caused by the provisional measures. There is a clear link between the security that may be demanded from the applicant of the provisional measures and the compensation for injury caused to the defendant in case of revocation or lapse of the measures.

## FINAL REMARKS

ACTA provides an elaborate framework for civil enforcement, which can be termed right holder–friendly, but does not always make explicit what the checks and balances are. The treaty is often permissive in terms of rights for right holders, but does not contain limitations or exceptions other than by general reference. This means that the treaty, this section included, cannot be appreciated independently from the broader IP context provided for international and national norms.

The most striking aspects of Section 2 of ACTA are that: (1) calculation of damages is not subject to the usual limitations of proportionality other than in the most general sense in ACTA Article 6; (2) there are inexplicable variations in the levels of treatment of pirated copyright content, normal copyright infringement, and trademark counterfeiting; (3) optional safeguards contained in the TRIPS Agreement may be restricted by ACTA, especially in case of provisional measures.

Parties can implement national legislation that complies with both ACTA and the TRIPS Agreement. However, while ACTA purports to build on the TRIPS Agreement, it does not, except in the most general terms (Article 1), establish a consistent and workable framework for reading the two agreements together. Thus what may first appear to be gaps in ACTA may actually be filled by the TRIPS Agreement, especially with respect to safeguards and limitations. The fact that ACTA omits any reference to such safeguards and limitations presents a real danger in the context of national implementation where parliaments may not be aware of the specific safeguards that apply to particular ACTA provisions. The safeguards contained in the TRIPS Agreement, to the extent that they are mandatory, are nevertheless in no way modified by ACTA.

# 5

# Legal Framework for Enforcement

## *Border Measures*

*Henning Grosse Ruse-Khan*

### INTRODUCTION

In addition to specific provisions dealing with civil and criminal enforcement, as well as enforcement in the digital environment, ACTA contains a section prescribing how states bound by the agreement must provide for measures of IP enforcement at the border. In section 3 of Chapter II, Articles 13 to 22 contain rules on the scope of border measures (Articles.13, 14 & 16), the initiation of proceedings by right holders or custom authorities (Articles.15–17) and a further procedure that deals with allegedly infringing goods (Articles.18–22). These rules must be viewed in the context of the enforcement provisions in the TRIPS Agreement, in particular Articles 51–60. In general, ACTA goes beyond TRIPS and requires states to adopt higher enforcement standards. At the same time, the new treaty narrows those TRIPS provisions that protect the interests of traders and owners of goods subject to border measures.[1] This chapter discusses some particularly controversial aspects of these "TRIPS-plus" standards for enforcing IPRs at the border. The focus is on whether ACTA mandates (or allows) the seizure of goods – such as generic medicines – in transit,[2] and what safeguards the final text of the agreement contains to avoid such seizures.

I thank Pedro Roffe and Xavier Seuba for their comments. All errors remain mine.

[1] For details, *see*, for example, the Opinion of European Academics on ACTA, published in the *Journal of Intellectual Property, Information Technology and E-Commerce Law* (JIPITEC) Vol. 2, 65 (2011).

[2] Transit seizures have become a contested issue in international trade and IP matters after certain medicines shipped from India to Brazil were detained in transit in the Netherlands on the basis of alleged patent infringements in the transit country. Subsequently, India and Brazil initiated proceedings under the WTO dispute settlement system arguing that these seizures violate WTO trade and IP obligations under the GATT and TRIPS; *European Union and a Member State – Seizure of Generic Drugs in Transit*, WT/DS409&408, available online at http://www.wto.org/english/tratop_e/dispu_e/cases_e/ds408_E.htm.

## SCOPE OF ACTA BORDER MEASURES

ACTA's provisions on border measures extend the existing minimum standards under TRIPS Article 51, which obliges WTO members to foresee border measures only against "importation of counterfeit trademark or pirated copyright goods." Together, ACTA Articles 13 & 16 determine the IP infringements and the trade activities for which parties to the agreement must foresee border measures in their national laws. These rules were amongst the most contentious issues during the treaty's negotiations.

### *Patent Infringements*

Earlier ACTA drafts would have obliged contracting parties to foresee border measures against goods "in transit" and in relation to any goods "suspected of infringing intellectual property rights."[3] The latter phrase was defined as "goods infringing any of the intellectual property rights covered by TRIPS" – hence in principle including patents. This provoked a lot of criticism: for most commentators, the crucial issue was the threat that border measures covering alleged patent infringement pose for the free transit of medicines. ACTA negotiators, including the EU as *demandeurs* of this provision, responded by declaring publicly that "patents will not be covered in the Section on Border Measures." In the final text, the matter has been addressed: footnote 6 to the Border Measures Section clarifies that "[t]he Parties agree that patents and protection of undisclosed information do not fall within the scope of this Section."[4] As a result, no ACTA party will be *obliged* to introduce or maintain a system of border measures which applies to suspected patent infringing goods. From the perspective of international trade and access to medicines, this is certainly an improvement on earlier drafts. As this chapter shows, however, it is by no means a sufficient factor to ensure that transit seizures of generic medicines do not occur.

At the same time, ACTA does not per se *prohibit* the contracting parties from foreseeing border measures against potentially patent-infringing imports: under Article 2.1 they can implement "more extensive protection and enforcement of intellectual property rights than is required by this Agreement, provided that such protection and enforcement does not *contravene* the provisions of this Agreement." As I have argued elsewhere, extending border measures to patent infringements does not contravene footnote 6 of ACTA's Border Measure section – but it may well contravene free

3 ACTA Draft – April 21, 2010, Art.2.X:1–2.

4 This constitutes a derogation from the general ACTA definition of the term "intellectual property" as comprising "all categories of intellectual property that are the subject of Sections 1 through 7 of Part II of the TRIPS Agreement"; *see* Chapter One, "Section 2: General Definitions," Art. 5 lit. (h).

trade safeguards included in ACTA's general obligations in Article 6.1.[5] This is an important point that will be discussed in more detail later in the chapter. Given the dynamics of international IP law and policy, one must reckon with the trend of a continuous increase in protection and enforcement standards. It is probably not too far-fetched to surmise that in the near to medium future, some countries might consider ACTA standards as insufficient and strive for "ACTA-plus" standards in their own laws and/or in international agreements. From this perspective, it is crucial to examine the agreement for any binding safeguards against additional IP enforcement standards.[6]

### *In-Transit Goods*

The second controversy regarding the scope of border measures under ACTA concerns the treatment of goods in transit. In Article 16, the negotiating parties have agreed that only with regard to "import and export shipments" application procedures for right holders and ex officio measures by custom authorities are mandatory for ACTA parties.[7] The second section of this provision states that "[a] Party *may* adopt or maintain procedures for suspect in-transit goods or in other situations where the goods are under Customs control."[8] Based on these provisions, ACTA does not contain an obligation for contracting parties to introduce or maintain border measures against any form of goods in transit. This again appears as a significant improvement on most of the earlier options on the table, especially from the perspective of international trade in generic medicines. Given that patents are completely excluded from ACTA's border measure section and measures against transits are not mandatory but merely optional, one has to ask whether ACTA still represents a real threat for generics in transit.

### *Other Forms of IP Infringements*

One reason why ACTA may still pose threats to international trade, in particular in generic medicines, is the fact that border measures apply not only to counterfeit trademark and pirated copyright goods but in principle to all kinds of goods suspected of any other infringement of IP rights – except patents and the protection of undisclosed information. The remaining types of IP infringements for which

5 *See* H. Grosse Ruse-Khan, "A Trade Agreement Creating Barriers to International Trade? ACTA Border Measures and Goods in Transit," *American University International Law Review* Vol. 26, No. 3 (2011), 645–726.

6 See discussion later in the chapter.

7 *See* ACTA – Dec. 3, 2010, Chapter Two – Section 3, Art.16.1 (a) and (b).

8 *See* ACTA – Dec. 3, 2010, Chapter Two – Section 3, Art.16.2 – emphasis added.

future ACTA parties must provide border enforcement procedures thus cover all forms of trademark infringements. Commentators have rightly pointed to the threat this poses for transiting generic medicines: by relying on the same or similar words identifying the active ingredient, the signs used to identify generics may often be to some extent similar or close to the trademarks of the original manufacturer.[9] While a generic producer may be expected to take into account the scope of trademark protection in the country of final destination, combining such a wide scope of border measures with their optional extension to goods in transit imposes another significant barrier to international trade. The generic producer would need to ensure that its brands remain at sufficient distance from all protected trademarks in all transit countries in order to ensure that the medicines are not seized in transit. This in turn will increase transaction costs and may prevent traders from using the most efficient transit routes. It thus adds further barriers to the global trade in generics and the cheap provision of medicines to populations in need.

Another troubling point is that customs authorities are not well placed to act against "confusingly similar trademark goods" in general. Findings of likelihood of confusion based on the degree of similarity of both the signs and the goods require a comprehensive legal analysis, which is much less straightforward than determining counterfeit goods.[10] Such an assessment is typically performed by courts or trademark offices, which have the necessary legal expertise, case law and experience to rely on. Imposing this task on customs is likely to result in a considerable increase in seizures and temporary detentions based on right holder allegations that transiting generics are confusingly similar. Until the generic producer or subsequent owner of the goods is able to show that no likelihood of confusion exists (or that the goods do not pose any threat of being diverted onto domestic markets),[11] the goods will be detained for the time being. Even though there are good chances that in-transit generics are subsequently found by a court not to infringe trademarks in the transit country, ACTA does not generally allow the goods to be released against provision of a security. In general, the goods will remain detained until a court has decided on the infringement issue. Given the duration of court proceedings, such detention periods will likely pose another considerable obstacle to international trade in generic medicines.

One option to address this threat posed by the enlarged scope for border measures under ACTA may be to exclude all brands based on international non-proprietary

9 Compare S. Flynn and B. Madhani, ACTA and Access to Medicines, PIJIP Research Paper no. 5, 2011.

10 Compare K. Weatherall, *ACTA – Australian Section by Section Analysis*, 30 April 2010, at 28, available online at http://works.bepress.com/cgi/viewcontent.cgi?article=1020&context=kimweatherall.

11 In countries where such a requirement is part of the substantive trademark law, it may provide grounds for releasing the goods owing to the absence of infringement.

names (INNs) from seizure. Such an exclusion could be foreseen in the domestic border measure rules of ACTA parties. As the following section indicates, such an exclusion is consistent with the flexibility provided in the agreement.

### *Options to Limit the Scope of Border Measures*

ACTA Article 13 might be applied to exclude those "ordinary" forms of trademark infringement whose allegation may lead to (temporary) detention of goods in transit until a court in the transit country has ruled on the matter. Subject to certain conditions, the provision allows ACTA parties to exclude IP infringements from the scope of domestic border enforcement systems. It appears primarily to serve as a compromise tool bridging the differences between the EU and United States over covering infringements of geographical indications (GIs) and other IPRs beyond the minimum standards contained in TRIPS Article 51. The provision contains several open and ambiguous terms and conditions[12] which in sum create a form of constructive ambiguity that allows disguising the remaining differences amongst the parties in the treaty text. Instead, each party will be able to justify its own understanding by relying on a favourable interpretation of one or more of these terms. While this constructive ambiguity may have been primarily created to allow the negotiating parties to retain the different approaches on including infringements of GIs, it may equally serve as an appropriate tool to exclude "ordinary" trademark infringements or at least any brands based on INNs from a national system of border measures.

The basic obligation, repeated in Article 13, is to provide "for effective border enforcement of intellectual property rights … in a manner that does not discriminate unjustifiably between intellectual property rights and that avoids the creation of barriers to legitimate trade." Here, access to medicines and international trade (in generic medicines and other goods) can serve as justifications to exclude "ordinary" trademark infringements, especially if the country has introduced border measures against goods in transit. The chapeau provision in ACTA Article 13 hence allows excluding those types of infringements from a domestic system of border measures that are particularly problematic for generic drugs in transit.[13] The general obligation to foresee such measures for ordinary trademark infringements as well is therefore waived as long as such exclusion can be justified on public health grounds. In sum, the scope of the ACTA border measures section allows parties to the treaty to prevent seizures of generics from occurring. However, countries must implement

[12] Such as not to "discriminate unjustifiably"; "as appropriate" and "legitimate trade" and "consistent with a parties domestic system of intellectual property rights protection."

[13] One could also argue that the exclusion of patent rights from the border measure section – as foreseen by footnote 6 – essentially discriminates between IP rights, unless, of course, one can justify such a differential treatment by reasonable policy grounds (such as public health).

the agreement with all these options in mind in order to take public health issues into account.

## ACTA SAFEGUARDS FOR PUBLIC HEALTH AND AGAINST TRADE BARRIERS

We now look at the relevant safeguards contained in ACTA. Do they mandate, or at least allow, an implementation that would prevent trade barriers, protect public health concerns and, in particular, safeguard against the reoccurring seizures of generics in transit?

### *Interpretation Based on Articles 7 and 8 TRIPS*

Under the title Nature and Scope of Obligations, ACTA Article 2.3 provides that "[t]he objectives and principles set forth in Part I of the TRIPS Agreement, in particular in Articles 7 and 8 shall apply, *mutatis mutandis*, to this Agreement." These TRIPS provisions are commonly understood as embodying the balancing objectives and public interests principles which guide interpretation and implementation of TRIPS.[14] In addition, in the ACTA preamble the negotiating parties recognise "the principles set out in the Doha Declaration on the TRIPS Agreement and Public Health, adopted on November 14, 2001, by the WTO at the Fourth WTO Ministerial Conference, held in Doha, Qatar."

Against the background of the interpretative role of TRIPS Articles 7 and 8,[15] the question arises whether the incorporation of these provisions by reference can have the same impact on ACTA treaty interpretation. A good way to analyse this is by way of an example of an ACTA provision that – if interpreted widely – may be relevant in the context of transit seizures. In this regards, the fourth sentence of ACTA Article 18 on "Security or Equivalent Assurance" states that "a Party may, only in *exceptional circumstances* or pursuant to a judicial order, permit a defendant to post a bond or other security to obtain possession of suspect goods."[16] The question then is what would constitute exceptional circumstances. Could this provision function as public health safeguard, which allows (against posting of a security) the release of generics in transit – for example, if the traders or recipients of the medicines can make a case for a good faith public health use of the drugs?

[14] Doha Declaration on TRIPS and Public Health, para. 5(a).

[15] For a general discussion on the role of Articles 7 and 8 in TRIPS, *see* H. Grosse Ruse-Khan, "A Comparative Analysis of Policy Space in WTO Law," *Max Planck Institute for Intellectual Property, Competition & Tax Law Research Paper Series* No. 08–02 (2008), available online at http://ssrn.com/abstract=1309526.

[16] *See* ACTA – Dec. 3, 2010 (emphasis added), Art.18.

On the one hand, the term "exceptional circumstances" is likely to be interpreted narrowly and hence would allow only for a marginal scope of application in general. On the other hand, an interpretation based on TRIPS Articles 7 and Article 8 may lead to different results: in the ACTA preamble, the negotiating parties have recognised the principles set out in the Doha Declaration on TRIPS and Public Health. That declaration's approach to TRIPS Articles 7 and 8 provides the strongest argument for an equivalent role of these provisions in ACTA. In paragraph 5a, the Doha Declaration indicates *how* an interpretation that gives due regard to TRIPS Articles 7 and Article 8 makes it possible to take public health concerns into account: in order to interpret and implement TRIPS "in a manner supportive of WTO Members' right to protect public health," those members recognised in the Doha Declaration that "[i]n applying the customary rules of interpretation of public international law, each provision of the TRIPS Agreement shall be read in the light of the object and purpose of the Agreement as expressed, in particular, in its objectives and principles."[17]

The recognition of these principles of treaty interpretation in the ACTA preamble must be understood as giving Articles 7 and 8 the same interpretative weight as WTO members agreed to in the Doha Declaration. The balancing objectives and public interest principles embodied in Articles 7 and 8 hence function as the main objectives of ACTA. This result further supports a wide, public health-oriented interpretation of the term "exceptional circumstances." The example therefore proves the point that ACTA interpretation can be guided equally by the same balancing objectives and public interest principles which should drive treaty interpretation in relation to the TRIPS Agreement. At the same time, one must emphasise that for most of the concrete ACTA obligations with concise treaty language, the ordinary meaning of the terms in their context will be the starting point and primary elements for interpretation. Provisions that contain open and ambiguous treaty terms – such as "legitimate trade" and "proportionality" in ACTA Article 6 – will be more apt for guidance from ACTA's object and purpose as embodied in the provisions of TRIPS Articles 7 and 8.

It remains to be seen whether ACTA parties or any international tribunals that may be charged with interpreting ACTA in the future are willing to adopt such approach. As I have argued elsewhere, WTO dispute settlement concerning TRIPS has so far shied away from giving any real effect to Article 7 and 8 – despite the fact that there is Appellate Body precedence for a more flexible, object- and purpose-based reading of WTO obligations.[18]

[17] *See* Doha Declaration, para 5(a).

[18] *See* H. Grosse Ruse-Khan, "The (Non) Use of Treaty Object and Purpose in Intellectual Property Disputes in the WTO," *Max Planck Institute for Intellectual Property & Competition Law Research Paper* No. 11–15 (September 28, 2011), available online at http://ssrn.com/abstract=1939859.

### *Obligation to Avoid the Creation of Barriers to Legitimate Trade*

ACTA contains a provision that may function as a safeguard against the use of IP enforcement procedures as barriers to trade and against abusive reliance on such procedures. Under the "General Obligations with Respect to Enforcement" in Article 6.1, parties are not only obliged to permit effective action against IP infringements but must equally ensure that enforcement procedures are applied "to avoid the creation of barriers to legitimate trade and to provide for safeguards against their abuse." The obligation finds its origin in TRIPS Article 41.1 and builds on similar language in the ACTA preamble and in Article13 on the scope of border measures. The provision contains a binding obligation, horizontally applicable to all enforcement measures under ACTA.

India's invocation of this rule in the WTO transit dispute[19] shows that it can be particularly relevant for border measures under ACTA and seizures of drugs (and other goods) in transit: the decisive question is when the detention and seizure of goods in transit amounts to a "barrier to legitimate trade." Such detentions and seizures arguably are creating "barriers" to international trade: by temporarily preventing the free movement of goods in transit via detentions in the transit country and even more by permanent seizures (and subsequent destructions) of goods in transit, these border measures inhibit the free movement of goods from the country of origin towards the country of destination.

Difficulties, however, arise when attempting to find an appropriate meaning for the term "legitimate trade": how to determine the legitimacy of the trade inhibited or prevented by the operation of IP enforcement procedures, in this case border measures against goods in transit? In order to address this question, it is useful to look first at the understanding of the identical term in the second sentence of TRIPS Article 41.1. In the WTO/TRIPS context, so far, no panel or Appellate Body report has addressed the interpretation on this issue. However, the term "legitimate" – as part of the phrase "legitimate interests" in TRIPS Article 30[20] – has been interpreted by a WTO panel. According to the panel report in *Canada – Pharmaceutical Products*, "'legitimate' must be defined in the way that it is often used in legal discourse – as

[19] *See* the WTO dispute initiated by India against the EU and the Netherlands: *European Union and a Member State – Seizure of Generic Drugs*, WT/DS408 (May 19, 2010).

[20] TRIPS Art. 30 deals with the ability of WTO Members to foresee exceptions to patent rights in their national laws. It states: "Members may provide limited exceptions to the exclusive rights conferred by a patent, provided that such exceptions do not unreasonably conflict with a normal exploitation of the patent and do not unreasonably prejudice the *legitimate* interests of the patent owner, taking account of the legitimate interests of third parties" (emphasis added).

a normative claim calling for protection of interests that are 'justifiable' in the sense that they are supported by relevant public policies or other social norms."[21]

Determining legitimacy thus requires a normative assessment of the relevant action, conduct or measure – based on justifiable public interests and policies. Such a normative approach finds support in the literature which views Article 41.1 as an expression of the need for balancing the interest of right holders, alleged infringers and the public interest: while the first sentence of the provision mirrors the interests of right holders, the second sentence takes account of the public interest in the availability of IPR-protected products.[22] For the term "legitimate trade" in TRIPS Article 41.1, this would mean that any trade for which a justifiable public policy or interest exists or which is supported by other social norms is legitimate. Hence trade in "fake" drugs (e.g. those containing no, or a wrong dosage of, active ingredients) may hardly be considered legitimate, whereas trade in generic drugs to facilitate cheaper access to medicines is justified in the interest of public health and therefore legitimate. Under such a normative assessment of the term "legitimate trade," the barriers to trade created by seizing and detaining generic drugs in transit are arguably barriers to legitimate trade and thus inconsistent with the second sentence of TRIPS Article 41.1.

If one applies these findings to the question of what constitutes legitimate trade under ACTA Article 6.1, any enforcement procedures that create barriers to trade for which a justifiable public policy exists or which is supported by other social norms would be considered as barriers to legitimate trade. The remaining question is what and whose public policy or social norms are relevant. Although ACTA itself does not contain a comprehensive set of normative values which could guide the understanding of legitimacy, the reference to TRIPS Articles 7 and 8 indicates that, inter alia, public health concerns have to be taken into account in the interpretation of ACTA provisions.[23] This finds further support in the fact that the ACTA preamble recognises "the principles set out in the Doha Declaration on the TRIPS Agreement and Public Health."[24] This confirms not only the normative understanding of legitimacy but also that public health concerns are relevant elements of social norms.

[21] *Canada – Patent Protection of Pharmaceutical Products* (WT/DS114/R), Panel Report (17 March 2000), para. 7.69.

[22] *See* ICTSD-UNCTAD, Resource Book on Trips and Development: an Authoritative and Practical Guide to the Trips Agreement 75 (2005), Chapter 30 at 3.1.1., available online at http://www.iprsonline.org/unctadictsd/docs/RB_4.30_update.pdf.

[23] *See* ACTA Art.2.3, which states: "The objectives and principles set forth in Part I of the TRIPS Agreement, in particular in Articles 7 and 8 shall apply, *mutatis mutandis*, to this Agreement" (emphasis in the original). On the role of TRIPS Articles 7 and 8 for the interpretation of ACTA provisions, see the first section in this chapter.

[24] Under paragraph 5(a) of the Doha Declaration, the importance of the object and purpose of a treaty, as embodied in TRIPS Articles 7 and 8, is highlighted as a principle of treaty interpretation, which guides the understanding of all TRIPS provisions. Recognising this principle in ACTA means that

A more difficult question is which countries' normative considerations and public policies are decisive – those of the country of production, transit or final destination. Here, the specific free trade rationale of ACTA Article 6.1 comes into play: if safeguarding free trade is indeed the rationale for the second sentence of ACTA Article 6.1, we must take the international and cross-border nature of trade into account. Hence, justifiable public interests and social norms may originate from *any* country directly affected by the trade. This would certainly include the country of origin and the country of destination. Whether the public policy concerns of the country of transit are equally relevant should depend on whether the traded goods have a substantial connection to the transit country. Similar to questions of the applicable law in private international law, a substantial connection test could ask whether, for example, the threat of trade diversion onto the domestic market or other factors establish a sufficient connection to the territory of the transit country, which justifies the application of that country's normative values to affect the determination of "legitimate trade."[25] This would mean that seizures of goods in transit amount to the creation of barriers to legitimate trade whenever the trade in these goods can be justified primarily by a public policy in the country of origin or the country of destination.

If this insight is applied to the understanding of legitimate trade advocated here, the general obligation in ACTA Article 6.1 prohibits seizures of goods in transit as a form of barriers to legitimate trade whenever the trade in these goods can be justified primarily by a public policy in the country of origin or the country of destination. Given that the transit and trade in generic drugs usually will be justified by public health concerns in the country of destination, any ACTA contracting party must ensure that its system of border measures does not create barriers to such trade. The best option to do so would be to exclude transit from the scope of the domestic border IP enforcement system altogether. If, however, a country chooses to extend border measures to transits, it must – by virtue of the general obligation under Article 6.1 – ensure that free transit of generics is not affected. This in turn can be done by addressing the main threat to generics in transit, namely by excluding border measures against "ordinary" forms of trademark infringements. Other mechanisms may also be an option, such as the applicable law approach in the Swiss border measure system, which requires that goods in transit are infringing

TRIPS Articles 7 and 8 – incorporated into ACTA by reference in Article 2.3 – equally guide the interpretation of all ACTA provisions. For further details, see the first section in this chapter.

25 Compare also S. Kumar, "Border Enforcement of Intellectual Property Rights against In-Transit Generic Pharmaceuticals," *European Intellectual Property Review* Vol. 32 No. 10, 506–519, at 513. The author considers generics in transit as legitimate trade when there is no threat of diversion onto the domestic market of the transit country.

not only under domestic Swiss IP law but also under the law of the country of destination.[26]

In sum, ACTA Article 6.1 prohibits parties from applying their border measures in a way that creates barriers to trade in generics. In particular, when these countries go beyond ACTA to extend border measures to goods in transit, they are under an international obligation to ensure that their domestic border enforcement systems allow the free transit of generics. Other ACTA provisions, such as those on civil enforcement regarding injunctive relief and damages, must also be implemented in a way that does not affect legitimate trade in generics.[27] Article 6.1 therefore functions as a horizontal safeguard against trade barriers and IP enforcement abuse that – interpreted in light of TRIPS Articles 7 and 8 – should be used to establish the balance that Article 7 calls for and to give effect to the public interests Article 8 regulates.

## CONCLUSIONS

ACTA does not mandate but certainly *does not prohibit* the extension of border measures against goods in transit and the detention of these goods for suspected infringements of, inter alia, trademarks and patents in the transit country. This can easily lead to seizures of transiting generics. Since the main elements that cause a threat to the international trade in generic drugs are all non-mandatory, ACTA parties have the option to avoid this threat. Under the general obligation to prevent IP enforcement procedures from creating barriers to legitimate trade, future ACTA parties are even prohibited from implementing ACTA in a way that inhibits international trade and transit in generic medicines. Such an understanding of the safeguard against trade barriers finds strong support in the incorporation of TRIPS Articles 7 and 8 – an example that these provisions can play a strong interpretative role in the understanding of ACTA norms.

Nevertheless, a balanced interpretation of ACTA, and the checks and balances in favour of defendants and third parties contained in the general obligation provisions, cannot do away with the asymmetry in relation to the comprehensive and concise ACTA provisions extending the remedies for right holders. This raises grave systemic concerns which place the burden for a "proportional" and "fair and

[26] A general explanation on the Swiss approach to border enforcement can be found at https://www.ige.ch/juristische-infos/rechtsgebiete/faelschung-und-piraterie/rechtslage-ab-1-juli-2008.html#c3941.

[27] In this manner, ACTA Article 6.1 can also be applied to address concerns over the impact other IP enforcement obligations, such as those concerning injunctions, may have on the transit of generic medicines. On such concerns, *see* Third World Network (TNW) Info Service on Intellectual Property Issues, Concerns raised over ACTA at TRIPS Council (1 November 2010), published in SUNS#7030.

equitable" enforcement system primarily on ACTA parties: in their implementation of the agreement, they must take these general obligations seriously and draft concrete defences and other safeguards for all affected by the new extended remedies. It remains to be seen whether the uncertainty inherent in the general obligations will prevent countries from doing so.

# 6

# ACTA and Beyond

## *Towards a Differentiated Approach to Criminal Enforcement of Intellectual Property Rights at the Global Level*

*Christophe Geiger*

### INTRODUCTION

The Anti-Counterfeiting Trade Agreement (ACTA) is a plurilateral agreement aimed at combating the proliferation of counterfeiting within the global economy. It reflects the current tendency towards enhancing the enforcement mechanisms of intellectual property rights at international level.[1] The agreement has caused significant opposition among the general public and within certain institutions of the European Union, in particular the European Parliament, which rejected ACTA with an overwhelming majority on 4 July 2012.[2] Impediments to its adoption have also started to emerge in other countries that participated in the negotiations, including,

[1] ACTA was signed on 1 October 2011 in Tokyo by the representatives of eight of the negotiating countries (Australia, Canada, Japan, the Republic of Korea, the Kingdom of Morocco, New Zealand, the Republic of Singapore and the United States of America) and on 26 January 2012 by the European Union and twenty-two of its member states (Austria, Belgium, Bulgaria, the Czech Republic, Denmark, Finland, France, Greece, Hungary, Ireland, Italy, Latvia, Lithuania, Luxembourg, Malta, Poland, Portugal, Romania, Slovenia, Spain, Sweden and the United Kingdom). The United Mexican States signed ACTA on 11 July 2012. Until today, only one of those countries, Japan, has ratified the Agreement (on 6 September 2012).

[2] European Parliament legislative resolution of 4 July 2012 on the draft Council decision on the conclusion of the Anti-Counterfeiting Trade Agreement between the European Union and its Member States, Australia, Canada, Japan, the Republic of Korea, the United Mexican States, the Kingdom of Morocco, New Zealand, the Republic of Singapore, the Swiss Confederation and the United States of America (12195/2011 – C7–0027/2012 – 2011/0167(NLE)), P7_TA-PROV(2012)0287.

for example, Switzerland,[3] which postponed its signature, and Australia,[4] which has suspended its ratification process.

There are several reasons for this (most probable) failure,[5] including its negotiation process, which took place outside any of the specialised multilateral fora such as the World Intellectual Property Organization (WIPO) or the World Trade Organization (WTO), and the secrecy that surrounded the agreement, which caused considerable concern and gave rise to widespread speculation on its content and objectives, leading to the development of considerable mistrust.[6] Anyhow, the main reason that made the European Parliament reject the treaty was the lack of clarity

3 *See* the communication press by the Federal Authorities of the Swiss Confederation of 9 May 2012, stating that "since negotiations were concluded, criticism of ACTA in various countries has strongly increased. The Federal Council takes these concerns seriously as they are related to basic freedoms and important rights. For this reason, Switzerland postpones its signature for the moment", available at: http://www.news.admin.ch/message/index.html?lang=fr&msg-id=44484 (last accessed July 2014). Nevertheless, the Swiss Confederation has not signed ACTA within the deadline agreed by the negotiating states, until 1 May 2013, and therefore, it has no longer the status of a negotiating party, *see* the Swiss Federal Institute of Intellectual Property, "Anti-Counterfeiting Trade Agreement", available at: https://www.ige.ch/en/legal-info/legal-areas/counterfeiting-piracy/acta.html (last accessed July 2014).

4 *See* the Report on ACTA by the Australian Parliament's Joint Standing Committee on Treaties issued on 27 June 2012 (Report 126, Treaty tabled on 21 November 2011, Anti-Counterfeiting Trade Agreement (Tokyo on 1 October 2011), the Parliament of the Commonwealth of Australia, Canberra, June 2012).

5 *See* L. Floridi, "ACTA – The Ethical Analysis of A Failure, and Its Lessons", ECIPE Occasional Paper, No. 4/2012; D. Matthews, "The Rise and Fall of the Anti-Counterfeiting Trade Agreement (ACTA): Lessons for the European Union", Queen Mary University of London, School of Law, Legal Studies Research Paper No. 127/2012.

6 On the impact of the lack of transparency in the negotiations on the perception of the Agreement in public opinion, *see* for a European perspective for example A. Metzger, "A Primer on ACTA, What Europeans Should Fear about the Anti-Counterfeiting Trade Agreement", JIPITEC 2010, 109. For an international perspective, *see* P. K. Yu, "Six Secret (and Now Open) Fears of ACTA", *SMU Law Review* 2011, Vol. 64, No. 3, 975; C. R. McManis, "The Proposed Anti-Counterfeiting Trade Agreement (ACTA): Two Tales of a Treaty", *Houston Law Review* 2009, Vol. 46, No. 4, 1235; M. Kaminski, "The Origins and Potential Impact of the Anti-Counterfeiting Trade Agreement (ACTA)", *Yale Journal of International Law* 2009, No. 24, 247; M. Geist, "ACTA's State of Play: Looking Beyond Transparency", *American University International Law Review* 2011, Vol. 26, No. 3, 543; T. Hoeren, "ACTA ad acta? Überlegungen zum urheberrechtlichen 'Shitstorm'", MMR 2012, 137; D. S. Levine, "Transparency Soup: ACTA Negotiating Process and 'Black Box' Lawmaking", *American University International Law Review* 2011, Vol. 26, No. 3, 813, according to whom "the lack of transparency placed leaked documents and hearsay at the center of public policy discussions, caused debates over both real and imagined issues, and brought about a general erosion of public knowledge and confidence in the ACTA process."

of its provisions on "individual criminalization, the definition of 'commercial scale', the role of internet service providers and the possible interruption of the transit of generic medicines."[7]

Therefore, the provisions on criminal enforcement are certainly one of the most problematic aspects of the agreement, if not *the* most problematic. In fact, ACTA reflects one of the continued tendencies in international lawmaking to enhance criminal enforcement of intellectual property rights.[8] The Agreement dedicates Section 4 to criminal enforcement, which includes provisions on "Criminal Offences," "Penalties," "Seizure, Forfeiture and Destruction" and on "*Ex Officio* Criminal Enforcement" (Article 23 to Article 26). Criminal enforcement procedures apply also to Article 27, which deals with the "Enforcement of Intellectual Property Rights in the Digital Environment."

This chapter is dedicated to the legal framework for criminal enforcement in ACTA, concentrating on the most problematic aspect: the definition of criminal offences in Article 23, which sets the standard and preconditions for the application of all the provisions that follow. It first shows why criminal enforcement of intellectual property is generally a very sensitive issue at the international and European levels, and then briefly tries to demonstrate why ACTA is not the right answer in this regard, since criminal enforcement provisions clearly need a differentiated approach, which is not reflected in the treaty as it stands.

## THE CRIMINAL ENFORCEMENT PROVISIONS, A DELICATE AND LONG-STANDING ISSUE

Criminal enforcement of intellectual property has always been a controversial issue.[9] This is mainly owing to the following two factors: harmonisation in the field of criminal law and the extent to which enforcement of intellectual property rights should be subject to criminal law.

7 European Parliament legislative resolution of 4 July 2012, *supra* note 2, 6. *See* in this sense D. Matthews, "The Rise and Fall of the Anti-Counterfeiting Trade Agreement (ACTA): Lessons for the European Union", *supra* note 5, 31: "The fact that 'commercial scale' was not defined clearly in Article 23.1 of ACTA contributed significantly to uncertainty and public anxiety, and led to further public mobilisation against ACTA since it was not made clear whether or not private acts by individuals would be excluded from its scope."

8 *See* in this sense M. Blakeney, "International Proposals for the Criminal Enforcement of Intellectual Property Rights: International Concern with Counterfeiting and Piracy", I.P.Q. 2009, 1.

9 On this question *see* Ch. Geiger (ed.), *Criminal Enforcement of Intellectual Property: A Handbook of Contemporary Research*, Cheltenham, UK / Northampton, MA, Edward Elgar, 2012.

### *The Challenges of International Harmonisation in the Field of Criminal Enforcement of IPRs*

At international level, the harmonisation of criminal enforcement is highly sensitive, because criminal provisions are closely linked to moral and cultural conceptions within a society.[10] Criminal law has always been a tool to protect the public interest, with harm to society being the justification for the existence of a criminal penalty.[11] Of course, these conceptions diverge greatly in different parts of the world: the reasons for sending someone to prison are different in the United States, France, China, Russia or Singapore. Moreover, traditions regarding criminal procedure vary significantly in different legal cultures: while a certain procedure might seem totally normal in a given state, it may appear rather exotic in another one.

Sovereignty issues are very strong in criminal law.[12] Therefore, it is not surprising that during the negotiation of the TRIPS Agreement, there were very important disagreements concerning the form of IP infringement that should be subject to criminal enforcement.[13] This resulted in a compromise, reducing the mandatory provision of criminal procedures and penalties to cases of wilful trademark counterfeiting or copyright piracy on a commercial scale.[14] It is clear from the negotiations history that member states were meant, in consistency with Article 1.1 of the agreement, to have considerable flexibility when deciding the manner to implement these criminal penalties in their national law.

Moreover, the concept of "commercial scale" was sufficiently vague to leave enough room for flexible interpretations.[15] Given this internationally sensitive issue,

[10] In this sense, *see* D. P. Harris, "The Honeymoon Is Over: The U.S.-China WTO Intellectual Property Complaint", *Fordham International Law Journal* 2008, Vol. 32, No. 1, 96–187, 146.

[11] *See*, for example, in the context of IP, A. Wechsler, "Criminal Enforcement of Intellectual Property Law: An Economic Approach", in Ch. Geiger (ed.), *Criminal Enforcement of Intellectual Property*, *supra* note 9, 150; G. Szott Moohr, "The Crime of Copyright Infringement: An Inquiry Based on Morality, Harm and Criminal Theory", *Boston University Law Review* 2003, No. 83, 731, 747; M. Bitton, "Rethinking the Anti-Counterfeiting Trade Agreement's Criminal Copyright Enforcement Measures", *Journal of Criminal Law and Criminology* 2012, Vol. 102, No. 1, 77.

[12] *See* in this sense T. Mylly, "Criminal Enforcement and European Union Law", in Ch. Geiger (ed.), *Criminal Enforcement of Intellectual Property*, *supra* note 9, 215: "Criminal law – together with the disposition of the police monopoly on the use of force – has traditionally been thought of as an area belonging to the core of national sovereignty and competence."

[13] On the history of the Uruguay round negotiations and the preparatory work to the TRIPS Agreement regarding criminal enforcement, *see* A. Adam, "What is 'Commercial Scale'? A Critical Analysis of the WTO Decision in WT/DS362/R", EIPR, 2011, 342, 346 *sq*.

[14] Article 61 of the TRIPS Agreement lays down that "Members shall provide for criminal procedures and penalties to be applied at least in cases of wilful trademark counterfeiting or copyright piracy on a commercial scale."

[15] *See* H. Grosse Ruse-Khan, "Criminal Enforcement and International IP Law", in Ch. Geiger (ed.), *Criminal Enforcement of Intellectual Property*, *supra* note 9, 174: "It is important to highlight the

it is also not surprising that the WTO panel,[16] when asked to give a more precise definition of the notion of commercial scale, remained very cautious and proposed a flexible approach, holding that its interpretation depended on the situation, namely the product and the market in question and also the extent of the infringement.[17] This flexibility was the price to pay in order to reach agreement on criminal enforcement provisions at international level. But the consequence was that the enforcement rules in the TRIPS Agreement were considered to be relatively weak, as has been rightly pointed out by many scholars like Jerome Reichman and David Lange, as well as Peter Yu, who has described the enforcement provisions as the "Achilles' heel" of the TRIPS Agreement.[18] This is precisely why stronger provisions on criminal enforcement were included in ACTA.

In fact, ACTA Article 23 defines acts carried out on a "commercial scale" as "commercial activities for direct or indirect economic or commercial advantage," which broadens the notion considerably and seems far less flexible than the market/product based interpretation of the WTO panel.[19] However, even if less flexible,

limited scope of Art. 61 TRIPS and its inherent flexibilities as well as those external ones which allow WTO Member States to implement criminal procedures tailored to domestic circumstances."

[16] WTO Panel Report, 26 January 2009, *China – Measures affecting the protection and enforcement of Intellectual Property*, WT/DS362/R. For a comment *see* R. Creemers, "The Effects of World Trade Organization Case DS362 on Audiovisual Media in China", EIPR, 2009, 568; H. Xue, "Enforcement for Development: Why Not an Agenda for the Developing World?" in X. Li and C. M. Correa (eds.), *Intellectual Property Enforcement, International Perspectives*, Cheltenham, UK / Northampton, MA, Edward Elgar, 2009, 133; and from the same author *see* "An Anatomical Study of the United States versus China at the World Trade Organisation on Intellectual Property Enforcement", EIPR, 2009, 292; D. Gervais, "China – Measures Affecting the Protection and Enforcement of Intellectual Property Rights", *American Journal of International Law* 2009, Vol. 103, 549; H. Grosse Ruse-Khan, "Criminal Enforcement and International IP Law", and P. K. Yu, "Shaping Chinese Criminal Enforcement Norms through the TRIPS Agreement", in Ch. Geiger (ed.), *Criminal Enforcement of Intellectual Property*, *supra* note 9, 171 and 286; P. K. Yu, "The U.S.- China Dispute over TRIPS Enforcement", preprinted in: Drake University Law School, Occasional Papers in Intellectual Property Law No. 5, 2010, and from the same author *see* "The TRIPS Enforcement Dispute", *Nebraska Law Review* 2011, Vol. 89, No. 4, 1046; A. Adam, *supra* note 13.

[17] According to A. Adam, *supra* note 13, 348, the term "commercial scale" is a flexible concept, but the notion remains vague after the decision. According to this author, "for the time being, it is not possible to establish a clear and precise standard of criminal enforcement measures based on Art. 61 of the TRIPS Agreement. Consequently, Art. 61 remains an uncertain bare minimum, which may or may not be satisfactory to some parties."

[18] *See* J. H. Reichman and D. Lange, "Bargaining Around the TRIPS Agreement: The Case for Ongoing Public-Private Initiatives to Facilitate Worldwide Intellectual Property Transactions", *Duke Journal of Comparative & International Law* 1998, Vol. 9, No. 1, 34 *sq.*; P. K. Yu, "TRIPS and Its Achilles' Heel", *Journal of Intellectual Property Law* 2011, Vol. 18, No. 2, 479.

[19] *See* in this sense H. Grosse Ruse-Khan, "Criminal Enforcement and International IP Law", in Ch. Geiger (ed.), *Criminal Enforcement of Intellectual Property*, *supra* note 9, 171 *sq*. The China – Measures affecting the protection and enforcement of intellectual property rights, Report of the Panel, 2009, *supra* note 16 referred to "counterfeiting or piracy carried on at the magnitude or extent of typical or usual commercial activity with respect to a given product in a given market", para. 7.577.

the scope of the provision remains uncertain. It is, for example, unclear what can be considered as an "indirect economic advantage," making this definition highly problematic with regard to the principle of legal certainty and legality of criminal offenses.[20]

### *The Delicate Issue of Criminal Enforcement of IPRs in the European Union*

The same delicate issue of sovereignty can be found in the EU. As a proof, the question whether the EU has competence to act in the field of criminal law has always been a debated and unclear issue.[21] It was mainly for this reason that provisions on criminal enforcement were taken out of the first enforcement Directive adopted in 2004.[22] In a subsequent decision of 2005, the European Court of Justice, in a case about environmental law, partially clarified that the Union had a limited competence in the field of criminal law if the application of effective, proportionate and dissuasive criminal penalties is *necessary to ensure the efficiency of important Community policies*.[23] This very limited competence of the EU regarding criminal law has been reiterated in the Lisbon Treaty. Article 83.2 of the Treaty on the Functioning of the European Union (TFEU) only provides for the possibility of adopting minimum rules concerning the definition of criminal offences and penalties when the harmonisation of the legislative provisions proves to be *essential* to ensure the effective implementation of the EU's policy.[24] The "essential" nature of

[20] In the EU, the Court of Justice has repeatedly stated that "the principle of the legality of criminal offences and penalties implies that Community rules must define clearly offences and the penalties which they attract." The CJEU further emphasised that the principles of legal certainty and legality of criminal offences and penalties are "satisfied where the individual can know from the wording of the relevant provision and, if need be, with the assistance of the courts' interpretation of it, what acts and omissions will make him criminally liable" (Case C-308/06, *International Association of Independent Tanker Owners (Intertanko) and Others v. Secretary of State for Transport*, 3 June 2008, [2008] ECR I-04057, para. 71).

[21] *See* on the question of competence the interesting article by A. Ramalho, "The European Union and ACTA – Or Making Omelettes without Eggs (Again)", IIC 2011, 97.

[22] *See* Directive 2004/48/EC of the European Parliament and of the Council of 29 April 2004 on the enforcement of intellectual property rights, OJEU L 157 of 30 April 2004 corrected in OJEU L 195 of 2 June 2004, 16. *See* in this sense the comment of T. Mylly, "Criminal Enforcement and European Union law", in Ch. Geiger (ed.), *Criminal Enforcement of Intellectual Property*, *supra* note 9, 213 *sq*.

[23] Case C-176/03, *Commission of the European Communities v. Council of the European Union*, 13 September 2005, [2005] ECR I-07879.

[24] Article 83 (2) TFEU: "If the approximation of criminal laws and regulations of the Member States proves essential to ensure the effective implementation of a Union policy in an area which has been subject to harmonisation measures, directives may establish minimum rules with regard to the definition of criminal offences and sanctions in the area concerned." On this provision, *see* S. Peers, "EU Criminal Law and the Treaty of Lisbon", *European Law Review* 2008, 517. See also the "Lisbon" – decision of the German Constitutional Court, 30 June 2009, 2 BvE 2/08, stating that "only if it is demonstrably established that a serious deficit as regards enforcement actually exists and that it can

criminal penalties is actually debated, because there already is a harmonised framework for civil penalties in the EU, which might be considered sufficient and better suited in many cases.[25] Indeed, some scholars have pointed out that criminal law provisions are rarely used in EU countries and play a very subordinate role in practice, especially in the field of patent law.[26] Therefore, the competence of the EU in the field of criminal enforcement of intellectual property remains doubtful. In its ruling No. 1/94, the European Court of Justice stated that the power to ratify the TRIPS Agreement was divided, that is, the treaty required ratification by both the EU *and* the member states.[27]

But that is not all: if the EU has exclusive competence with regard to common commercial policy, including "commercial aspects of intellectual property" (TFEU Article 207 TFEU), it remains unclear whether criminal enforcement provisions are necessarily "commercial aspects of IP." It has been argued that "aspects of IP that relate to commerce and trade might be those which concern, enable, or are the object of commercial transactions – licensing of IP or its securitization are pragmatic examples."[28]

After a long period of lack of clarity, the European Commission finally revealed that ACTA's section on criminal enforcement has been negotiated *on behalf* of the member states and that ACTA needs to be considered as a mixed agreement, for which the European Union's competence is shared, meaning that the member states would have to ratify the agreement as well. Apparently, most of the member states had not examined the precise impact of the agreement on their national legislation, specifically on the criminal component of their intellectual property

only be remedied by the threat of a sanction, this exceptional constituent element exists and the annex competence for legislation in criminal law may be deemed conferred" (para. 358 *sq.*).

[25] *See* R. M. Hilty, A. Kur and A. Peukert, "Statement of the Max Planck Institute for Intellectual Property, Competition and Tax Law on the Proposal for a Directive of the European Parliament and the Council on Criminal Measures Aimed at Ensuring the Enforcement of Intellectual Property Rights", IIC 2006, 970; A. Ramalho, *supra* note 21, 98. According to T. Mylly, "Criminal Enforcement and European Union Law", in Ch. Geiger (ed.), *Criminal Enforcement of Intellectual Property*, *supra* note 22, 226, "the *ultima ratio* nature of EU criminal law measures could well be tested under the principle of proportionality."

[26] *See* J. Gibson, "The Directive Proposal on Criminal Sanctions", 245 *sq.* and J. Schmidt-Szalewski, "The French Case: Comparison of the Past, Present and Future of Criminal Law", in Ch. Geiger (ed.), *Criminal Enforcement of Intellectual Property*, *supra* note 9, 343: "Statistics show that in 2001 judicial decisions ordering criminal sanctions of infringement accounted to 0,1% of the total number of the French criminal courts' decisions"; R. M. Hilty, A. Kur and A. Peukert, *supra* note 25, 972.

[27] Opinion 1/94 of the Court of 15 November 1994 on the Competence of the Community to conclude international agreements concerning services and the protection of intellectual property – Article 228 (6) of the EC Treaty, [1994] ECR I-05267, paras. 59–60.

[28] *See* A. Ramalho, *supra* note 21, 99. According to T. Mylly, "Criminal Enforcement and European Union law", in Ch. Geiger (ed.), *Criminal Enforcement of Intellectual Property*, *supra* note 22, 213 *sq.*, ACTA is likely to become a test case "of the Union's competence to criminalize IP infringements internally and externally."

law, in order to be able to commit themselves in full knowledge of the consequences.[29] While it is true that a large majority of the member states already provide for criminal penalties for infringement of IPRs in their national legislation and that these are sometimes even stricter than those provided for by the agreement, the criminal element of intellectual property has not been significantly harmonised and the approaches differ considerably across the member states.[30] No comparative study on the provisions on criminal enforcement of IPRs in the national legislations of the EU had been done before the adoption of ACTA. Therefore, a lot of the opposition to the treaty was induced by the pressure exerted by the general public on their governments at national level, mainly owing to the fear of criminalisation of individuals and end users, which led some governments to refuse to ratify the agreement.[31]

The heated debate sparked by European Commission's attempt to introduce a Directive proposal on criminal enforcement provides a good example of the controversial nature of a harmonised standard on the matter, and the proposal ultimately met with failure[32] and was withdrawn by the Commission in September 2010[33] for reasons similar to ACTA, therefore worth mentioning here.[34] One of the most controversial

29 The European Commission incidentally concedes that "a very limited number of Member States may need to adapt their own legislation related to criminal enforcement to comply with the commitments they undertook (ACTA is a mixed EU/Member States' competence Agreement). This has been confirmed in very clear terms by the two Opinions of the Legal Service of the European Parliament of 5 October 2011 and of 8 December 2011, answering respectively to questions by the INTA and JURI Committees." *10 Myths about ACTA*, text published on the DG Trade website, available at http://trade.ec.europa.eu/doclib/docs/2012/february/tradoc_149112.pdf (accessed 25 January 2013). For a comment relating to French law, *see* J.-C. Galloux, RTDcom January/March 2011, 83, who emphasises that whereas the provisions of ACTA do not a priori lead to an amendment of the framework laid down by the Community directives, "this is not the case for French law."

30 *See* on this point J. Gibson, "The Directive Proposal on Criminal Sanctions", *supra* note 26.

31 In June 2012, the Dutch government decided not to sign ACTA. Bulgaria, which has signed ACTA, was the first EU country that has stopped ratification process of the Agreement after the European Parliament rejected it. Other EU countries such as Poland and the Czech Republic suspended ratification of ACTA before the European Parliament rejected it.

32 Modified Proposal for a Directive of the European Parliament and the Council on Criminal Measures aimed at Ensuring the Enforcement of Intellectual Property Rights dated 26 April 2006, COM(2006) 168 final. For a criticism of this text, *see* R. M. Hilty, A. Kur and A. Peukert, *supra* note 25, 974, 970. *See* J. Gibson, "The Directive Proposal on Criminal Sanctions", *supra* note 26, 245, stating that "the harmonisation of criminal law and procedure is still in its infancy within the European Union law and so the relationship between the commercial framework of intellectual property and the criminal enforcement of its standards remains an unsettled and unsettling adolescence. The Proposal for a Directive on criminal measures aimed at ensuring the enforcement of intellectual property rights is at the vanguard of the extension of EU competence, some going as far as describing it a competency Trojan Horse."

33 OJEU, C 252, 18 September 2010, 9.

34 For a parallel, *see* R. D'Erme, Ch. Geiger, H. Grosse Ruse-Khan, C. Heinze, T. Jaeger, R. Matulionyte and A. Metzger, "The Impact of the Anti-Counterfeiting Trade Agreement on the Legal

provisions defined a criminal offence as "any deliberate infringement of an intellectual property right committed on a *commercial scale*, and the attempt at such an infringement, complicity and incitement to commit such an infringement" (Article 3, emphasis added). The European Parliament considered the condition set by this provision too broad and vague, and requested that acts "carried out by private users for personal and not-for-profit purposes"[35] should be expressly excluded in order to avoid any ambiguity. There were also other areas of disagreement, including whether the proposal should apply to all IPRs (as originally proposed) or only to certain IPRs (to exclude patents, for example).[36]

The proposal's failure is not surprising as the issue of criminal enforcement is dealt very differently in the national legislations of the member states. To start with, not all of them provide for criminal enforcement provisions.[37] And even when criminal enforcement is provided, there is no uniformity as to what infringements should be criminalised: All IPRs? Only trademarks and copyrights, not patents? And what should be the threshold, since criminal law is in general meant, in most legal systems, to be a measure of last resort?[38]

In addition, some fundamental rights issues remained unclear, including whether criminal enforcement provisions are mandatory with regard to the constitutional protection of property.[39] In the EU, the unclear wording of Article 17.2 of the European

Framework for IP Enforcement in the European Union", in Ch. Geiger (ed.), *Constructing European Intellectual Property: Achievements and New Perspectives*, EIPIN Series Vol. 1, 394, Cheltenham, UK / Northampton, MA, Edward Elgar, 2013.

35 Position of the European Parliament adopted at first reading on 25 April 2007 with a view to the adoption of Directive 2007/.../EC of the European Parliament and of the Council on criminal measures aimed at ensuring the enforcement of intellectual property rights (EP-PE_TC1-COD(2005)0127). The European Parliament also clarified that "the fair use of a protected work, including such use by reproduction in copies or audio or by any other means, for purposes such as criticism, comments, news reporting, teaching (including multiple copies for classroom use), scholarship or research, does not constitute a criminal offence."

36 *See* J. Gibson, "The Directive Proposal on Criminal Sanctions", *supra* note 26, 245 *sq*.

37 At least not for all IP rights. Patent law is sometimes excluded from criminal liability (this is, for example, the case in the United Kingdom). According to Hilty, patent law is a particularly problematic area regarding criminal sanctions; *see* "Economic, Legal and Social Impacts of Counterfeiting", in Ch. Geiger (ed.), *Criminal Enforcement of Intellectual Property*, *supra* note 9, 18. For a comparative approach of criminal enforcement provisions in France, the United Kingdom, Canada, the United States and China, *see* the chapters by J. Schmidt, G. Westkamp, D. Gervais and P. K. Yu in Ch. Geiger (ed.), *Criminal Enforcement of Intellectual Property*, *supra* note 9.

38 *See* R. M. Hilty, A. Kur and A. Peukert, *supra* note 25, 973; T. Mylly, "Criminal Enforcement and European Union Law", in Ch. Geiger (ed.), *Criminal Enforcement of Intellectual Property*, *supra* note 22, 246, stating that "the nature of criminal law as *ultima ratio*, a means of last resort, has been overlooked."

39 Asking also this question, *see* J. Griffiths, "Criminal Liability for Intellectual Property Infringement in Europe: The Role of Fundamental Rights", in Ch. Geiger (ed.), *Criminal Enforcement of Intellectual*

Charter of Fundamental Rights[40] ("intellectual property shall be protected") and some recitals of the failed Directive on criminal enforcement could be interpreted as such. On the other hand, some scholars have underlined that this provision might also need to be interpreted in a more balanced way, inducing a duty not to strengthen excessively the enforcement ties.[41] And what about issues of competing fundamental rights such as privacy, freedom of expression and due process?[42]

In the EU, the principle of proportionality is another argument that has been brought forward to demonstrate the lacking need for some harmonisation of criminal provisions of IP: civil enforcement mechanisms already exist, and are now harmonised in the EU since the implementation of the 2004 Directive in all member states. These provisions might be considered sufficient, especially with regard to the potential for misuse that can result from the threat of criminal penalties that can have detrimental effect on competition.[43] The issue of misuse was also raised by the European Parliament in the debate on the Directive proposal[44] and in the comment

*Property*, *supra* note 9, 191 *sq*. *See also* D. Gervais, "Criminal Enforcement in the US and Canada", in Ch. Geiger (ed.), *Criminal Enforcement of Intellectual Property*, *supra* note 9, 270, where the author notices that the "deeply held belief by many in the United States that intellectual property deserves state protection as (private) property and that, normatively, helping individual intellectual property owners enforce their rights using public resources is justified, because, in aggregate, it serves the public good."

40 Charter of Fundamental Rights of the European Union, 2010 OJEU C 83/02 of 30 March 2010.

41 On this provision *see* Ch. Geiger, "Intellectual Property Shall Be Protected!? Article 17.2 of the Charter of Fundamental Rights of the European Union: A Mysterious Provision with an Unclear Scope", EIPR, 2009, 113; J. Griffiths and L. McDonagh, "Fundamental Rights and European IP Law – The Case of Art. 17.2 of the EU Charter", in Ch. Geiger (ed.), *Constructing European Intellectual Property: Achievements and New Perspectives*, Cheltenham, UK / Northampton, MA: Edward Elgar, 2013, 75.

42 *See* more detailed on this issue in J. Griffiths, "Criminal Liability for Intellectual Property Infringement in Europe: The Role of Fundamental Rights", *supra* note 39, 191 *sq*.; D. Matthews, "The Rise and Fall of the Anti-Counterfeiting Trade Agreement (ACTA): Lessons for the European Union", *supra* note 5, 15. *See also* Chapter 3 in this volume, in which X. Seuba states that "the call for proportionality is usual in the human rights field. When put into relation with measures on enforcement, it requires the assessment of the potential impact of some enforcement provisions with several rights. For instance, in the context of the European Convention on Human Rights the principle of proportionality applies in relation to the right to property enshrined in Additional Protocol no 1, as well as to the rights to privacy and freedom of expression. The three of them are indeed related to many provisions contained in ACTA, and their interpretation under the principle of proportionality should become central to assess ACTA provisions and their implementation."

43 *See* in this sense R. M. Hilty, "Economic, Legal and Social Impacts of Counterfeiting", in Ch. Geiger (ed.), *Criminal Enforcement of Intellectual Property*, *supra* note 37, 18, stating that "enforcement tools should be moderate enough to allow free competition to increase the supply of available product and services. We should be even more moderate and careful when dealing with criminal law. In its essence, criminal law constitutes a 'dangerous weapon' that makes the harm of any enforcement measure even worse."

44 Article 7 of the European Parliament's Position of 25 April 2007, *supra* note 35, requires the prohibition of the misuse of criminal procedures and sanctions, especially when they are employed for the enforcement of the requirements of civil law.

of the Max Planck Institute for Intellectual Property and Competition Law,[45] but it was not addressed in the ACTA draft.

In summary, there are several reasons that make the provisions on criminal enforcement in ACTA problematic at international and EU levels. As we have seen, in the field of criminal enforcement, ACTA seems therefore not to be the right answer because it risks undermining the flexibility of the TRIPS Agreement. So what would be the right answer then? This, of course, cannot be presented in detail here. What is for certain, however, is that any international framework on criminal enforcement needs a differentiated approach.

## BEYOND ACTA: THE NEED FOR A DIFFERENTIATED APPROACH FOR CRIMINAL ENFORCEMENT OF INTELLECTUAL PROPERTY RIGHTS

As it has been shown, the approach adopted by the WTO panel with regard to the notion of "commercial scale" is rather a flexible one, since it considers that only counterfeiting activities "carried on at the magnitude or extent of typical or usual commercial activity with respect to a given product in a given market" deserve punishment.[46] One can therefore hope that this definition will allow for a case-by-case approach, taking into account normative considerations as well. Nevertheless, given that public interest objectives lie at the very heart of criminal law, one can wonder whether the notion of commercial scale – a mainly economic notion based on a market approach – is the right criterion for deciding what should be criminalised.[47] In fact, the economic impact is already addressed by means of civil enforcement.[48] Should it not be *something else* – such as the aggravated social harm of the infringement (which certainly cannot be measured in solely economic terms) – that

[45] *See* R. M. Hilty, A. Kur and A. Peukert, *supra* note 25, 975. Stressing the need for countermeasures against misuse of criminal sanctions, *see also* R. M. Hilty, "Economic, Legal and Social Impacts of Counterfeiting", and J. Gibson, "The Directive Proposal on Criminal Sanctions", in Ch. Geiger (ed.), *Criminal Enforcement of Intellectual Property*, *supra* note 9, 9 and 245 *sq*.

[46] China – Measures affecting the protection and enforcement of intellectual property rights, Report of the Panel, 2009, *supra* note 16, para. 7.577.

[47] *See* in this sense A. Wechsler, "Criminal Enforcement of Intellectual Property Law: An Economic Approach", in Ch. Geiger (ed.), *Criminal Enforcement of Intellectual Property, supra* note 11, 150: "The solution of policy questions in the realm of the criminal enforcement of IP law requires not only regard to economic evidence but appropriate consideration for moral, philosophical, sociological, and historical dimensions as Beccaria's statement of 1764 still holds true today: 'The true measure of crimes is the harm done to society'."

[48] As it has been stated by one scholar, "distinctions between criminal law and civil law usually emphasize the greater magnitude or scope of the wrongdoing addressed by the former over the latter. In particular, the justification for wrongdoing to be a matter of the state's interest is that the activity is egregious enough to affect or offend the entire community." *See* T. Hardy, "Criminal Copyright Infringement", *William & Mary Bill of Rights Journal* 2002, Vol. 11, 305–341, 311.

should determine whether a more severe criminal sanction, such as imprisonment, is warranted?[49] For example, is it really appropriate to treat equally someone who illegally downloads music files from the Internet and the activities of often mafia-like organisations that mass-produce counterfeit medicines involving major risks to public health?[50]

Very interestingly, the Max Planck Institute in its comment on the failed Directive proposal on criminal enforcement suggested to mark the priority under criminal law "to acts that are particularly dangerous from the viewpoint of public interest" and "to regulate specific forms of IP infringement falling into that category separately," imposing qualified penalties for those infringements that carry a health or safety risk, or activities carried out in the form of organised crime.[51] This approach is convincing. While it might be appropriate to decriminalise certain activities, there are others that deserve much stricter penalties in the light of their dramatic consequences in terms of innovation and, above all, because of the danger to consumers[52] that

[49] Calling for a nuanced approach, *see also* M. Bitton, "Rethinking the Anti-Counterfeiting Trade Agreement's Criminal Copyright Enforcement Measures", *supra* note 11, 73, stating that "the fact that intellectual property crimes may at times be morally ambiguous does not necessarily mean that criminal law should not be applied to such crimes. Rather, the use of criminal law has to take a nuanced approach in which the moral ambiguity surrounding certain infringing conduct is acknowledged." In this spirit, the European Court of Human Rights has stated that in order to make an act criminal offence, there has to be evidence to justify that "the act has been injurious to moral standard" in a given society or that there has been "any public demand for stricter enforcement of the law." *See Dudgeon v. the United Kingdom*, No. 7525/76, 22 October 1981, ECHR, para. 60.

[50] However, it has been argued that from a public health perspective, it is necessary to differentiate concerns about counterfeit goods that infringe trademarks and medicine suspected to infringe patents; *see* D. Matthews, "Counterfeiting and Public Health", in Ch. Geiger (ed.), *Criminal Enforcement of Intellectual Property*, *supra* note 9, 42. According to this scholar, "the most immediate concern for public health lies with falsified medicines which contain the wrong or insufficient active ingredients that may be a risk to human health," not necessarily from trademark violations, 58.

[51] *See* R. M. Hilty, A. Kur and A. Peukert, *supra* note 25, 975. On the issue of criminal enforcement and organised crime, *see* M. R. Roudaut, "From Sweatshops to Organized Crime: The New Face of Counterfeiting", in Ch. Geiger (ed.), *Criminal Enforcement of Intellectual Property*, *supra* note 9, 75.

[52] Although even there scholars express skepticism regarding the appropriateness of criminal provisions; *see*, for example, A. Ohly, "Counterfeiting and Consumer Protection", in Ch. Geiger (ed.), *Criminal Enforcement of Intellectual Property*, *supra* note 9, 40, stating that "the question remains whether consumer interests strengthen the case for strict enforcement of patents and copyright, in particular by criminal law." He concludes that "concerns about product safety and quality should not be put to the cause of strengthening the law of patent or copyright enforcement since the infringement provisions of both legal areas do not distinguish between counterfeiting and imitation." *See also* R. M. Hilty, "Economic, Legal and Social Impacts of Counterfeiting", in Ch. Geiger (ed.), *Criminal Enforcement of Intellectual Property*, *supra* note 37, 23, according to whom, "discussing safety, health and the like in the isolated context of IP laws turns out to be mere window dressing, since stronger IPRs protection

might result from the counterfeiting of certain products (in particular in the field of medicine).[53]

Another good argument for a new approach to criminal enforcement is based on the negative impact that undifferentiated repression can have on the perception of IP in the mind of citizens.[54] The seemingly never-ending battle against file sharing is a good example. One remembers the particularly strict decision by the first instance court in Stockholm dated 17 April 2009 on the Swedish file-sharing platform "The Pirate Bay," which sentenced four of its representatives to one year of imprisonment and awarded damages to the amount of 2.7 million Euros for assistance in making copyrighted material available, having provided the means for the main offence (illegal downloading).[55] This decision was welcomed by right holders, favouring the use of a rhetoric of "punishment" and "theft" when communicating on file sharing.[56] The results are obvious: the criminalisation of a major part of the Internet community led to no reduction in illegal

by no means *per se* serves the public interest – particularly consumer interests – but primarily helps those who benefit from such a system."

53 However, the fight against falsified medicines by means of criminal enforcement is also sometimes questioned. According to, for example C. Correa, "Anti-Counterfeiting: a Trojan Horse for Expanding Intellectual Property Protection in Developing Countries?" in: Ch. Geiger (ed.), *Criminal Enforcement of Intellectual Property*, *supra* note 9, 74, in "the case of medicines, the fight against sub-standard products should not be addressed through enhanced measures to enforces IPRs, but by strengthening the capacity of drug regulatory authorities with the necessary finance, human resources and equipment."

54 *See* Ch. Geiger, "Introduction", and R. M. Hilty, "Economic, Legal and Social Impacts of Counterfeiting", in Ch. Geiger (ed.), *Criminal Enforcement of Intellectual Property*, *supra* note 37, 1 and 9 *sq*.

55 Stockholm District Court, 17 April 2009, Case No. B 13301-06. For a comment, *see* J. Edström and H. Nilsson, "The Pirate Bay Verdict – Predictable, and Yet…", EIPR, 2009, 483. In a decision issued on 26 November 2010 (Case No. B 4041–09), the Swedish Court of Appeal confirmed the criminal liability of the defendants, decreased the original prison terms (with prison sentences now ranging from four to ten months), but increased the damages to 5 million Euros each. The Swedish Supreme Court (*Högstadomstolen*) refused to hear the appeal on 1 February 2012. *See also* the decision of the Supreme Court of Finland, 30 June 2010, KKO:2010:47, which upheld the earlier judgment of Turku Court of Appeal and confirmed criminal liability of the file-sharing service, Finreactor, for copyright infringement through the collaboration with the file sharers (it was held that the operator participated with the user in the illegal reproduction and distribution of the work to the public and therefore intentionally infringed copyright). For a comment, *see* P. Honsakasalo, "Criminal Proceedings against the Administrators of a BitTorrent Tracker: Finreactor KKO:2010:47", EIPR, 2010, 591.

56 One still remembers the advertising campaigns pursued by the record industry suggesting that young Internet users should be put behind bars for having visited a peer-to-peer site. For more generally on the rhetoric of theft, *see* P. L. Loughlan, "You Wouldn't Steal a Car…, Intellectual Property and the Language of Theft", EIPR, 2007, 401. With regard to criminal enforcement of IP law, *see* S. T. Green, "Plagiarism, Norms, and the Limits of Theft Law: Some Observations on the

downloading.[57] Moreover, the "Pirate Bay" site and others alike are still online, and "pirate parties" have mushroomed in many parts of Europe; the Swedish Pirate Party even managed to win two seats in the European Parliament after the decision was rendered.

As a conclusion, a differentiation in terms of criminal enforcement appears both inevitable and desirable to guarantee that, in the long run, the IP system will not be rejected by the vast majority[58] and will be able to apply more severe sanctions in the future to those infringements that are causing serious threats to society.[59] This may also be desirable from an economic point of view when the costs of combating counterfeiting in certain sectors through criminal sanctions outweigh the limited results.[60] Unfortunately, such a differentiated approach to criminal enforcement – taking into account not only economic but also ethical, historical and psychological aspects[61] – was not addressed in ACTA. It is therefore doubtful whether its implementation would spell progress for the IP system. Moreover, it is to be hoped that

Use of Criminal Sanctions in Enforcing Intellectual Property Rights", *Hastings Law Journal* 2002, 54, 167, 240.

57 The opposite might even have occurred. For more details on this issue, *see* Ch. Geiger, "Counterfeiting and the Music Industry: Towards a Criminalization of End Users? The French 'HADOPI' Example", and A. Peukert, "Why Do 'Good' People Disregard Copyright on the Internet?" in Ch. Geiger (ed.), *Criminal Enforcement of Intellectual Property*, *supra* note 9, 386 and 151 *sq*.

58 *See also* I. D. Manta, "The Puzzle of Criminal Sanctions for Intellectual Property Infringement", *Harvard Journal of Law and Technology* 2011, Vol. 24, No. 2, 157, stating that "there is a danger of overly harsh sanctions and individuals' loss of respect for copyright and criminal law generally if, given the widespread culture of file-sharing, the law is perceived as criminalizing 'everybody'." Moreover, at the European Union level its seems that the European Commission seeks to renew the consensus on the intellectual property rights enforcement more generally, but also in regard to criminal sanctions applied to individuals. In this sense, it adopted on 1 July 2014 two new communications: "Towards a renewed consensus on the enforcement of intellectual property rights: An EU Action Plan", COM(2014) 392/2 and "Trade, growth and intellectual property – Strategy for the protection and enforcement of intellectual property rights in third countries", COM(2014) 389 final. The EU Commissioner for Internal Market and Services Michel Barnier stated: "Rather than penalising the individual for infringing intellectual property rights, often unknowingly, the actions set out here pave the way towards a 'follow the money' approach, with the aim of depriving commercial-scale infringers of their revenue flows.", *see*, Press release, IP/14/760, 1 July 2014.

59 In this sense, during the TRIPS Agreement negotiations, India and Hong Kong suggested that only infringements that have harmed the interests of society or that pose a threat to society, and not merely those of a private party, should be criminalised. *See* A. Adam, *supra* note 13, 346.

60 *See* in this sense the case of the lost battle against music file sharing: 1. Ch. Geiger, 'The Rise of Criminal Enforcement of Intellectual Property Rights…and Its Failure in the Context of Copyright Infringements on the Internet', in: S. Frankel and D. Gervais (eds.), *The Evolution and Equilibrium of Copyright in the Digital Age*, Cambridge, Cambridge University Press, 2014, 113. For an economic perspective, *see* A. Wechsler, "Criminal Enforcement of Intellectual Property Law: An Economic Approach", in Ch. Geiger (ed.), *Criminal Enforcement of Intellectual Property*, *supra* note 11, 128.

61 For a historical, economical and psychological perspective on criminal enforcement, *see* the chapters by D. Lefranc, A. Wechsler and A. Peukert, in Ch. Geiger (ed.), *Criminal Enforcement of Intellectual Property*, *supra* note 9.

the lessons learned from ACTA with regard to criminal enforcement can influence the content of other treaties currently under negotiation, such as the Transpacific Partnership (TPP)[62] or the bilateral free trade agreement between the European Union and Canada.[63]

[62] The negotiating parties to the Agreement to the date are Brunei Darussalam, Chile, New Zealand, the Republic of Singapore, Australia, Canada, Malaysia, the United Mexican States, Peru, the United States of America, Vietnam and Japan. On this Agreement and for a criticism of its "TRIPS-Plus" and even "ACTA-plus" approach, *see* S. K. Sell, "TRIPS Was Never Enough: Vertical Forum Shifting, FTAS, ACTA, and TPP", *Journal of Intellectual Property Law* 2011, Vol. 18, 447. For a general comment on the treaty for example, *see* M. K. Lewis, "The Trans-Pacific Partnership: New Paradigm or Wolf in Sheep's Clothing?" *Boston College International and Comparative Law Review* 2011, vol. 34, and P. K. Yu, "The Alphabet Soup of Transborder Intellectual Property Enforcement", Drake University Legal Studies Research Paper Series, Research Paper 2012 No. 12–13. For a comment on a proposal for the intellectual property criminal enforcement chapter in TPP, *see* S. M. Flynn, B. K. Baker, M. Kaminski and J. Koo, "The U.S. Proposal for an Intellectual Property Chapter in the Trans-Pacific Partnership Agreement", *American University International Law Review* 2012, Vol. 28, No. 1, 193.

[63] Negotiations on the European Union and Canada Comprehensive Economic and Trade Agreement (CETA) were initiated in 2009. After the rejection of ACTA by the European Parliament in July 2012, fears started to emerge over the similarities between the criminal provisions negotiated under CETA and those contained in ACTA. Nevertheless, the European Commissioner for Trade, Karel de Gucht, stated in an interview on CETA that "since the negative vote of the European Parliament on ACTA, we have been changing the language obviously" (interview with viEUws, "Trade Commissioner De Gucht on CETA, the EU-Canada Trade Agreement", 30 October 2012). In this regard, one scholar noticed that in "the long-term significance of ACTA may well not have ended with Parliament's vote on 4 July 2012. Instead, the vote could well provide a stimulus for reconsideration of the scope and applicability of intellectual property enforcement provisions in bilateral or regional trade agreements of the EU." *See* D. Matthews, "The Rise and Fall of the Anti-Counterfeiting Trade Agreement (ACTA): Lessons for the European Union", *supra* note 5, 33. More generally on the issue of increased inclusion of enforcement provisions in FTAs, *see* X. Seuba, "Checks and Balances in the Intellectual Property Enforcement Field: Reconstructing EU Trade Agreements", in Ch. Geiger (ed.), *Constructing European Intellectual Property: Achievements and New Perspectives*, *supra* note 34, 409.

# 7

# ACTA's Digital Chapter

## *Remaining Concerns and What Can Be Done*

*Rita Matulionyte*

### INTRODUCTION

The Anti-Counterfeiting Trade Agreement (ACTA) is a new plurilateral treaty with the goal of "improving global standards for the enforcement of IPR [in order] to more effectively combat trade in counterfeit and pirated goods."[1] It was negotiated by Australia, Canada, the EU (and EU member states in their own national capacity), Japan, Korea, Mexico, Morocco, New Zealand, Singapore, Switzerland and the United States between 2008 and 2010, leading to the adoption of the final text on 3 December 2010.[2] It is currently undergoing internal ratification procedures in negotiating states. It is open for signature until 31 March 2013; six signatories are needed before it comes into force.[3]

During negotiation ACTA was criticized by different stakeholders on many grounds. First of all, the secret nature of negotiations was condemned by the online community, academics,[4] as well as by the institutions of the EU such as the European

This chapter was first published in the *Queen Mary Journal of Intellectual Property*, Vol. 1, No. 3, pp. 248–271. The editors extend their thanks to the *Queen Mary Journal* for authorizing its reproduction. Websites mentioned herein were last accessed on May 2011.

1 *See* EU official website on ACTA at http://ec.europa.eu/trade/creating-opportunities/trade-topics/intellectual-property/anti-counterfeiting/.

2 The final text is available on http://trade.ec.europa.eu/doclib/docs/2010/december/tradoc_147079.pdf.

3 Arts 39–40 ACTA; in the EU, the consent of the European Parliament is needed; it has expressed its preliminary approval, see European Parliament resolution on the Anti-Counterfeiting Trade Agreement of 24 November 2010 (P7_TA-PROV (2010) 0432); some EP Members, however, have requested for the ECJ opinion on the compatibility of ACTA with EU law: *see* http://en.act-on-acta.eu/Letter_to_President_of_the_European_Parliament_for_an_opinion_of_the_ECJ_on_ACTA.

4 E.g. D. S. Levine, 'Transparency Soup: The ACTA Negotiating Process and "Black Box" Lawmaking' (2011) American University International Law Review, at http://ssrn.com/abstract=1763483.

Parliament[5] and the European Data Protection Supervisor.[6] Secondly, critics argued that by negotiating the agreement plurilaterally, parties are trying to avoid the established fora for IP agreements (i.e. the World Intellectual Property Organization [WIPO] or the World Trade Organization [WTO]) and thereby threatening the established international institutional framework.[7] Thirdly, although ACTA is intended to be a special agreement made under the auspices of the Agreement on Trade-Related Aspects of Intellectual Property Rights (TRIPS) and thus not derogate from its obligations,[8] some have argued that it may still violate TRIPS.[9] Its legality in some of the negotiating states has been contested. For instance, in the EU, the European Commission has repeatedly made reassuring noises that it will not set any *acquis*-plus standards, but European academics have warned that ACTA may lack conformity with EU law and require additional action by the EU institutions.[10] Its legality under US law has also been disputed.[11] Various issues addressed by ACTA have been attacked by groups of academics as well as individuals worldwide,[12]

5 European Parliament resolution of 10 March 2010 on the transparency and state of play of the ACTA negotiations of 10 March 2010 (P7_TA (2010) 0058).

6 Opinion of the European Data Protection Supervisor on the current negotiations by the European Union of an Anti-Counterfeiting Trade Agreement (ACTA) (2010/C 147/01), OJ C 5.6.2010, p 1–13, at point 5.

7 S. Bannerman, 'WIPO and the ACTA Threat' (2010) PIJIP Research Paper Series, at http://digitalcommons.wcl.american.edu/research/4.

8 See Art. 1, ACTA.

9 D. B. Barbosa, 'Untoward restrictions to trade and abuses of Intellectual Property rights: a Brazilian perspective to the ACTA exercise' (2010), at http://papers.ssrn.com/sol3/papers.cfm?abstract_id=1628744, p 8 et seq. (argues that TRIPS sets not only minimum but also maximum standards).

10 *See* Opinion of European Academics on Anti-Counterfeiting Trade Agreement, reprinted in [2011] 2 JIPTEC 65–72; *see also* European Commission's comments of 27 April 2011 on the Opinion, at http://trade.ec.europa.eu/doclib/docs/2011/april/tradoc_147853.pdf.

11 W. New and K. Mara, 'Rightsholders' Anti-Counterfeiting Trade Pact Could Have Broad Reach', at http://www.ip-watch.org/weblog/2010/10/12/rights-holders%E2%80%99-anti-counterfeiting-trade-pact-could-have-broad-reach/?utm_source=weekly&utm_medium=email&utm_campaign=alerts.

12 American University Washington College of Law Urgent ACTA Communique of 23 June 2010, at http://www.wcl.american.edu/pijip/go/acta-communique; The Wellington Declaration on ACTA, at http://www.michaelgeist.ca/content/view/4947/125/; E. Katz and G. Hinze, 'The Impact of the Anti-Counterfeiting Trade Agreement on the Knowledge Economy' (2009) *Yale Journal of International Law*, at http://www.yjil.org/docs/pub/o-35-katz-hinze-ACTA-on-knowledge-economy.pdf; P. K. Yu, 'Six Secret (and Now Open) Fears of ACTA' (2011) 64 SMU Law Review, at http://ssrn.com/abstract=1624813; M. Blakeney, 'International Proposals for the Criminal Enforcement of Intellectual Property Rights: International Concern with Counterfeiting and Piracy' (2009) Queen Mary School of Law Legal Studies Research Paper No. 29, at http://ssrn.com/abstract=1476964; A. Metzger, 'A Primer on ACTA: What Europeans Should Fear about the Anti-Counterfeiting Trade Agreement, [2010] 1 JIPITEC 109, at http://www.jipitec.eu/issues/jipitec-1-2-2010/2612/JIPITEC%202%20-%20Metzger-Acta.pdf; K. Outterson, 'Import Safety Rules Should Not Hinder Legitimate Generic Drug Markets: The Anti-Counterfeiting Trade Agreement (ACTA)', in C. Coglianese, A. Finkel and D. Zaring (eds.), *Import Safety: Regulatory Governance in The Global Economy* (Philadelphia: The University of

probably the most important of which being privacy and restriction on freedom of expression on the Internet,[13] criminal liability[14] and border measures.[15] Last but not least, strong concerns were expressed by developing countries which did not join the negotiations, such as China, India and Brazil.[16] Arguably, ACTA will be extended to non-negotiating parties by being adopted as a new baseline in bilateral negotiations.[17]

One of the most important parts of ACTA is section 5 on "Enforcement of Intellectual Property Rights in a Digital Environment" (the "Digital Chapter").[18] In the early years of secret negotiations of ACTA, rumors were spread that, inter alia, it would set a three-strike rule at an international level, as adopted by some countries,[19] or a monitoring duty to online (or Internet) service providers (OSPs or ISPs), comparable to the one set by the US Digital Millennium Copyright Act (DMCA).[20] The Digital Chapter in the final text of ACTA, however, seems to be less threatening. According to Michael Geist, one of the main commentators on this chapter, "[t] aken together, the Internet chapter must be seen as failure by the US."[21] Negotiators had repeatedly denied that the controversial three-strike rule would reach the text of ACTA[22] and the first ACTA texts did not contain it (see discussion later in the chapter). Likewise a DMCA-type regime for ISPs was discussed in early drafts but was entirely eliminated in later negotiation stages. The protection of technical

Pennsylvania Press, 2009), at http://ssrn.com/abstract=1407250; K. L. Port, 'A Case Against the ACTA' (2011), at http://ssrn.com/abstract=1808180.

13 E.g. Barbosa, supra n 9, pp. 4–7.

14 Ch. Geiger, 'Of ACTA, 'Pirates' and Organized Criminality – How "Criminal" Should the Enforcement of Intellectual Property Be?' (2010) IIC 629; H. G. Ruse-Khan, 'From TRIPS to ACTA: Towards a New "Gold Standard" in Criminal IP Enforcement?' in Ch. Geiger (ed.), *Criminal Enforcement of Intellectual Property: A Blessing Or A Curse?* (London: Edward Elgar, forthcoming), at http://ssrn.com/abstract=1592104.

15 H. G. Ruse-Khan, 'A Trade Agreement Creating Barriers to International Trade? ACTA Border Measures and Goods in Transit' (2011) American University International Law Review, at http://ssrn.com/abstract=1706567.

16 'China Slams Nearly Completed ACTA, Questions its WTO Compatibility', at http://insidetrade.com.proxy.wcl.american.edu/201011022343572/WTO-Daily-News/Daily-News/china-slams-nearly-completed-acta-questions-its-wto-compatibility/menu-id-173.html.

17 W. New and K. Mara, *supra* n11 ("success of ACTA depends on whether we find other countries to join [...] That was one of the goals").

18 *See also* Commission Comments, *supra* n10, p. 18. ("The chapter on digital environment is one of the most important contributions of ACTA.")

19 *See* discussion later in the chapter.

20 M. Geist, 'ACTA Ultra-Lite: The US Cave on the Internet Chapter Complete', at http://www.michaelgeist.ca/content/view/5352/125/ ("When it first proposed the chapter, the US was seeking new intermediary liability requirements with three strikes and you're out used as an example of an appropriate policy as well as language that attempted to create a global DMCA.")

21 Ibid.

22 M. Ermert, 'ACTA Negotiators: Maximal Protection Proposals Unlikely In Final Text', at http://www.ip-watch.org/weblog/2010/02/18/acta-negotiators-maximal-protection-proposals-unlikely-in-final-text/.

protection measures (TPMs) has also been watered down by providing signatories with the flexibility to remain in keeping with WIPO standards.

So what concerns remain, and how can they be addressed? The following sections examine those issues by looking at each of the relevant provisions, namely the general provision (Article. 27.1); third-party liability (Article. 27.2); the provision on "cooperative efforts" (Article. 27.3); the right to information (Article. 27.4); and protection of technological protection measures (Articles. 27.5–27.8).

## GENERAL PROVISION

To start with, Article 27.1 of ACTA sets a general requirement:

> Each Party shall ensure that enforcement procedures, to the extent set forth in sections 2 (Civil Enforcement) and 4 (Criminal Enforcement), are available under its law so as to permit effective action against an act of infringement of intellectual property rights which takes place in the digital environment, including expeditious remedies to prevent infringement and remedies which constitute a deterrent to further infringements.

This provision appeared in the first drafts of ACTA and has remained largely unchanged. The negotiating parties only discussed its scope: whereas most of them suggested limiting it to copyright and related rights, the United States wanted to include trademarks, and the EU suggested covering all IPRs.[23] The most extensive formulation was finally adopted.

### *Liability Standards: Online = Offline?*

The first question is what importance this provision has. No international instrument has set a comprehensive enforcement framework for IP infringements occurring online up till now. TRIPS was negotiated at a time when the Internet was only starting to reach a mainstream audience, and it does not deal specifically with online infringements; it also is not clear how rights provided by TRIPS ought to be implemented in the online environment. In 1996, the WIPO Copyright Treaty and WIPO Performances and Phonograms Treaty (WIPO Internet Treaties)[24] established international substantive standards on copyright and related rights for the first time, but they contain just a general provision concerning enforcement of online rights.[25] In particular, the Treaties do not mention what form of liability (civil or

[23] See Art 27.1 ACTA (leaked) draft of 25 August 2010.

[24] Both adopted on 20 December 1996, Geneva.

[25] Art 14.1 WIPO Copyright Treaty ("Contracting Parties shall ensure that enforcement procedures are available under their law so as to permit effective action against any act of infringement of rights

criminal) arises or what sanctions are available, covering only rights implemented under the Treaties. Also, the Joint Recommendation Concerning Provisions on the Protection of Marks and Other Industrial Property Rights in Signs on the Internet[26] (2001 WIPO Recommendation) does not set liability forms or sanctions, but rather suggests limitations of liability and remedies in case of trademark (or of other signs) infringement that occurs over the Internet.[27]

Thus, ACTA sets elaborate civil and criminal enforcement mechanisms for Internet IP infringements for the first time by reference to other chapters within ACTA. Importantly, in Article 27.1, there is no explicit wording providing leeway for parties to adjust general enforcement measures (as are found in the chapters on civil and criminal enforcement) to the online environment. Rather, the provision seems to require that the civil and criminal chapters shall be applied in their entirety to infringements occurring online.[28] At the same time, online infringements are of different technological, social, economic and political nature compared with offline infringements. For instance, online technologies enable easier reproduction and dissemination of works than it is possible in offline environments; unauthorized activities online are pursued not only by commercial actors (which is mainly the case offline) but more often by consumers; such conduct as unauthorized file sharing is generally not condemned by society; a new "culture of sharing" is often welcomed. Strong IP enforcement online conflicts with other policies such as those on information society or data protection – thus policymakers are hesitant to apply the same enforcement standards as in offline environments. Despite these and other differences, ACTA seems to treat online infringements in the same way as ordinary (offline) infringements.

On the other hand, despite the absence of explicit wording, ACTA does not seem to prevent national legislators or courts from adjusting enforcement rules to online cases. All the offline provisions are subject to the general principles implemented upfront in the agreement (e.g. fair process, privacy, proportionality, etc.), which might give parties a basis to argue that they can draft provisions for online infringements differently. Also, general provisions (e.g. concerning damages or injunctions) have inbuilt discretion for judicial authorities in applying them to specific (online

covered by this Treaty, including expeditious remedies to prevent infringements and remedies which constitute a deterrent to further infringements"), identical to Article 23.2 WIPO Performances and Phonograms Treaty.

26 Adopted by the Assembly of the Paris Union for the Protection of Industrial Property the General Assembly of the WIPO on 24 September–3 October 2001, Geneva.

27 See Artt. 6–8; 3–15 2001 WIPO Recommendation.

28 See "Each Party shall ensure that enforcement procedures, *to the extent* set forth in ss 2 (Civil Enforcement) and 4 (Criminal Enforcement), are available under its law (…)" (emphasis added) – "to the extent" seems to imply that ss. 2 and 4 shall be transposed to online infringement cases in their entire scope.

or offline) cases. In addition, national practice has shown that courts find it difficult (and are unwilling) to apply general IP enforcement laws to IP infringements online until legislators adopt more specific Internet-tailored provisions.[29] Thus, parties are encouraged to take the implicit flexibility of Article 27.1 into account and draft Internet-tailored enforcement rules, which would reflect the specific nature and needs of the Internet environment.

### *Criminal Sanctions Against Private File Sharers?*

The next issue to be briefly addressed here is criminal liability for online infringements as established by Article 27.1 of ACTA. It should be noted that efforts within the EU to establish an IP criminal enforcement framework have failed, at least for now,[30] leaving the adoption of the Criminal Chapter in ACTA open to criticism as conflicting with the EU *acquis*.[31] Some commentators have also expressed a fear that this provision requires parties to provide for criminal liability for private Internet users.[32] Without going into a complex discussion on ACTA Criminal Chapter,[33] several general remarks can be made.

Article 23.1 of ACTA requires parties to provide for criminal procedures and penalties "at least in cases of willful trademark counterfeiting or copyright or related rights piracy on a commercial scale." The "commercial scale" definition was one of the hottest issues in the negotiations of ACTA. The parties arguably intended to depart from the flexible and context-orientated concept of "commercial scale" adopted by the WTO Panel[34] and suggested a much stricter approach

[29] E.g. some German courts were unwilling to allow to disclose users' identities under a general right to information available under former German Copyright Act, until a better Internet-tailored disclosure duty was adopted by the German Parliament in § 101 of the German Copyright Act (*Urheberrechtsgesetz* of 9 September 1965 (BGBl I S 1273), as last amended by Art 83 of the Law of 17 December 2008 (BGBl. I S 2586)).

[30] The proposed Criminal Enforcement Directive was harshly criticised by the European Parliament: see Position of the European Parliament adopted at first reading on 25 April 2007 with a view to the adoption of (draft) Directive 2007/.../EC of the European Parliament and of the Council on criminal measures aimed at ensuring the enforcement of intellectual property rights (EP-PE_TC1-COD (2005) 0127). Previous proposal was thus eventually withdrawn by the Commission, but the issue remains on Commission's agenda; *see* Action Plan Implementing the Stockholm Programme, 20.4.2010, COM (2010) 171, p 38.

[31] European Academics Opinion on ACTA, supra n 10, para. 6.

[32] *See* e.g. M. Morris, 'ACTA's Abandoned Third-Party Liability Provisions and What They Mean for the Future', p 8, [2010] PIJIP Research Paper No. 10, at http://digitalcommons.wcl.american.edu/research/10/.

[33] For a collection of papers on criminal enforcement of IP, *see* C. Geiger (ed.), *Criminal Enforcement of Intellectual Property: A Blessing or a Curse?* (London: Edward Elgar, forthcoming).

[34] *See* World Trade Organisation (2009), Panel Report, China – Measures Affecting the Protection and Enforcement of Intellectual Property Rights (China – IPRs), (WT/DS362/R), 26 January 2009.

in earlier ACTA drafts.[35] After strong criticism and intense discussions, the final ACTA text defines "commercial scale" as covering "at least … commercial activities for direct or indirect economic or commercial advantage."[36] Thus, at least two requirements in regard of commercial scale must be met: the activity shall be of "commercial" nature and "for direct or indirect economic or commercial advantage."

In regard to private Internet users, it is barely possible that their activities will be found to be on a "commercial scale." Starting with the second requirement ("for direct or indirect economic or commercial advantage"), it is not entirely clear whether it is satisfied whenever any sort of advantage is established, or rather whether it (instead of or additionally) requires proof that the person had an *intention* to acquire such a commercial or economic advantage.[37] If the first interpretation is applied, most file-sharing cases would easily seem to lead to at least an "indirect economic advantage" for users because they attain the files without paying a price which is otherwise due when legally acquiring a copy. If the second, more restrictive interpretation applies, users acting without intention of economic gain could avoid criminal liability.[38] Furthermore, the first requirement (demanding the activity to be of a "commercial" nature) is even more difficult to meet in cases dealing with private use. Even though the concept "commercial" may have different interpretations, generally infringement should take place in a course of some business activity. If "commerce" or "business" is construed narrowly, not just individual users but also website operators who do *not* pursue activities in the course of business (but, e.g. as a non-profit organization for social or cultural purposes) would arguably not be covered by a "commercial scale" requirement.

On the other hand, because the provision sets a minimum ("at least") standard, it allows parties to extend criminal liability to a broader range of activities. Also, in cases of dispute between signatories to ACTA, the general requirements of the "effective action" and "deterrent remedies" in Article 27.1 leave much space for interested parties to argue that criminal liability *should* be extended to online file sharing. For instance, one may argue that the phenomenon of online piracy, because of its ever-expanding extent and few possibilities to limit it, cannot be effectively controlled by civil measures, and thus deterrent criminal measures are necessary in order to

35 See H. G. Ruse-Khan, supra n14, p. 12 et seq.

36 Art 23.1, second sentence, ACTA; cf. recital 14 Directive 2004/48/EC ("Acts carried out on a commercial scale are those carried out for direct or indirect economic or commercial advantage …").

37 See "commercial activities *for* direct or indirect economic or commercial advantage."

38 *See* e.g. 'Anne Muir in first conviction for illegal music sharing', at http://www.bbc.co.uk/news/uk-scotland-glasgow-west-13351116 (the convicted fifty-eight-year-old nurse had arguably not used the network for any financial gain, but to build up her self-esteem after suffering from depression for a number of years).

ensure an "effective action."[39] It therefore remains to be seen how this provision is to be interpreted by ACTA parties. At the same time, parties could make use of the unclear content of the "commercial scale" requirement and adopt the interpretation – broad or narrow – which they found more suitable to meet local needs.

## OSP LIABILITY: INTERNATIONAL ONLINE POLICE STILL TO COME

Article 27.2 develops the content of Article 27.1 as follows:

> Further to paragraph 1, each Party's enforcement procedures shall apply to infringement of copyright or related rights over digital networks, which may include the unlawful use of means of widespread distribution for infringing purposes. These procedures shall be implemented in a manner that avoids the creation of barriers to legitimate activity, including electronic commerce, and, consistent with that Party's law, preserves fundamental principles such as freedom of expression, fair process, and privacy
>
> [fn 13: For instance, without prejudice to a Party's law, adopting or maintaining a regime providing for limitations on the liability of, or on the remedies available against, online service providers while preserving the legitimate interests of right holder].

The article reflects what is left of the extensive provisions on OSP liability contained in earlier ACTA drafts.[40] In earlier stages of negotiations, Parties discussed options that were essentially based on OSP limited liability provisions found in the US DMCA[41] and the EU E-Commerce Directive.[42] These draft provisions were heavily criticized. It was argued that the proposed broad definitions of OSPs would "dramatically expand third party liability both in the United States and around the world."[43] With regard to the United States, whereas the draft clauses overtook DMCA provisions intended to protect the interests of right holders, they did not contain provisions parallel to the immunity doctrine provided by the US Communications Decency Act 1996 or the substantially non-infringing use doctrine of *Betamax* case.[44] Furthermore, whereas in some negotiating states the measures

39 The enforcement of such provision against any member is little likely, since ACTA does not establish a dispute resolution mechanism comparable to the one available under WTO. Still, according to Art 36.3(c), the ACTA Committee may make recommendations on the implementation of ACTA.

40 See art 2.18.3 ACTA (official) Draft of April 2010.

41 17 US Code § 512.

42 Directive 2000/31/EC of the European Parliament and of the Council of 8 June 2000 on certain legal aspects of information society services, in particular electronic commerce, in the Internal Market ("Directive on electronic commerce"), *OJ L 178, 17.7.2000, p 1–16.*

43 Morris, supra n32, p. 5; see also Urgent ACTA *Communique*, supra n12.

44 *Sony Corp. of America v Universal City Studios, Inc.*, 464 US 417 (1984), see Morris, supra n32, p. 7.

against online infringements are being strengthened,[45] in other states some courts are more circumspect when recognizing liability of third parties in online infringement cases[46]; thus the setting of an international set of rules on this issue would mean the exporting of the higher protection standards of the United States and EU worldwide. Also, a very broad definition of intermediaries suggested in draft texts of ACTA could arguably include also those dealing with generic drugs and thus may restrict access to medicine.[47] These and other problems led the negotiating parties to abandon essentially all provisions related to OSP liability. The only remaining explicit reference to OSPs is the footnote 13 as cited at the beginning of this section. In the last rounds of negotiation, parties were discussing only the scope of the article, namely whether it should include copyright and related rights or also trademarks.[48] The final text has adopted a narrower wording.

What exactly Article 27.2 obliges parties to do is a difficult question to answer. It makes clear that enforcement procedures mentioned in Article 27.1 should apply to copyright and related rights. This however should have been obvious from Article 27.1 since these are the most frequent infringements online. Article 27.2 no longer mentions what enforcement procedures – civil or also criminal – should be ensured. The reference to Article 27.1, however, implies that both liability forms shall also be available for the infringements of copyright and related rights. Further, one could speculate what a non-binding reference on "unlawful use of means of widespread distribution for infringing purposes" should cover. It is likely to target websites which have a reputation of being largely used for unauthorized file exchange (e.g. Pirate Bay or Rapidshare). However, it is not clear whether websites which are used in a substantial manner for legal activities (e.g. YouTube, eBay) are also covered. Finally, regarding the enforcement measures to be implemented by the parties, limited liability regimes for OSPs are mentioned only in a footnote and only as a non-binding example.

45 For example, the United Kingdom has recently adopted the Digital Economy Act 2010 which requires OSPs to provide right holders with a copyright infringement list, block access to sites that allow substantial infringement and disconnect repeat infringers; see ss. 4, 7 and 11 Digital Economy Act 2010, c. 24. Its legality has been recently confirmed by courts, *see R (on the Application of British Telecommunications Plc & TalkTalk Telecom Group Plc) v The Secretary of State for Business, Innovation and Skills* [2011] EWHC 1021 (Admin).

46 E.g., *Roadshow Films Pty Ltd v iiNet Ltd* (2011) 89 IPR 1 (Australia) (ISP that does not suspend an infringer's account is not liable for future infringements unless certain conditions are met); *21 Bonnier Amigo Music Norway AS v Telenor Telecom Solutions AS* [2010] ECDR 2 (Norway) (the petition for preliminary injunction to terminate access to the Pirate Bay website was rejected since Telenor, an Internet access provider, had not acted in an illegal or unlawful manner); Appeal Court of Düsseldorf, 27.4.2010 – I-20 U 166/09 Rapidshare (A host provider Rapidshare is not liable for illegal content).

47 *See* B. K. Baker, 'ACTA: Risks of Third-Party Enforcement for Access to Medicines', PIJIP Research Paper Series paper No. 1, at http://digitalcommons.wcl.american.edu/research/1, p. 5.

48 See Art 2.18.2 ACTA draft of 6 October 2010.

Overall, the intention of parties to establish a multilateral limited liability regime for OSPs has failed, at least for now.[49] The only requirement which the provision seems to set is an obligation to take some (civil and criminal) measures against the infringements of copyright and related rights online. It leaves open for the parties to decide on the type and scope of measures they want to apply. On the other hand, the importance of non-binding (or "may") provisions should not be underestimated. When ACTA is used as a negotiating basis in bilateral negotiations with non-negotiating states, these provisions could easily be turned into "shall" clauses, as experience shows, and the texts of earlier ACTA drafts containing elaborated clauses on OSP liability could also return to the negotiating table.[50] Here, the second sentence of Article 27.2 may be of use. It explicitly requires the preservation of a list of public interests such as electronic commerce, freedom of expression, fair process and privacy. Regretfully, these interests are merely enumerated, and ACTA does not further elaborate what particular measures should be taken in order to guarantee their effective application in practice.[51]

Thus, the provision demonstrates the concerns of parties over extensive unauthorized online exchange of files and considers OSP liability as a way of coping with the problem. However, because of the highly controversial nature of the issue (meaning lack of political consensus), the parties did not manage to agree on any kind of binding rules. How far this vague provision will be used in further political processes remains to be seen. An international online police is therefore still in the future.

## "COOPERATIVE EFFORTS": TOWARDS A PRIVATELY ENFORCED THREE-STRIKE RULE?

Article 27.3 of ACTA incorporates a rule which some fear encourages, if not requires, a so called three-strike rule (or a "graduated response"):

> Each Party shall endeavor to promote cooperative efforts within the business community to effectively address trademark and copyright or related rights infringement while preserving legitimate competition and, consistent with that Party's law, preserving fundamental principles such as freedom of expression, fair process, and privacy.

[49] At the same time WIPO plans to hold further discussions on OSP liability; *see* 'WIPO Slowly Advances Industrial Design Treaty, Eyes ISP Liability For Trademarks', at http://www.ip-watch.org/weblog/2011/04/04/wipo-slowly-advances-industrial-design-treaty-eyes-ISP-liability-for-trademarks/.

[50] See further elaborate provisions on OSP liability implemented in § 18.10.30 of US–Korean FTA, at http://www.ustr.gov/sites/default/files/uploads/agreements/fta/korus/asset_upload_file273_12717.pdf.

[51] See further infra chapter 5.

Early leaked drafts of ACTA mentioned a three-strike rule in the footnotes.[52] At the same time, negotiating parties were repeatedly reassuring the critics that ACTA would not contain such a rule,[53] and the first official draft of April 2010 made no explicit reference to it. However, this article still contained a stronger and more specific wording than in the final text of ACTA. The April draft required parties to promote the development of mutually supportive relationships between OSPs and right holders, whereas the final ACTA text requires a mere "endeavor to promote" and refers to the general "business community." Also, the first official draft covered all IPRs (patent, industrial design, trademark and copyright or related rights) and encouraged establishing guidelines for the actions which should be taken in cases of infringement. In the final text this was watered down to trademarks, copyrights and related rights, and reference to the guidelines was removed. Also, earlier drafts did not contain any provision on fundamental principles as found in the final text. Interestingly, in the draft of 6 October 2010, parties were still discussing whether trademarks should be included in the provision at all,[54] but in the end opted for a broader definition which did include them.

Amendments followed because of concerns by numerous commentators. Some claimed that the wording found in the draft of April 2010, despite no explicit reference to the three-strike rule, "both accommodates and promotes the adoption of graduated response."[55] The "strategy of compelled voluntary collaboration comes directly from the playbook of the IFPI (International Federation of the Phonographic Industry), which advocates government-backed systems of OSP cooperation and asserts that government pressure is crucial to producing collective action by all OSPs."[56] The lack of substantial and procedural safeguards on protection of personal data was said to be lacking.[57] Strong concerns have been also expressed by some European Parliament Members,[58] the European Data Protection Supervisor[59] and the Article 29 Data Protection Working Party representing EU national data

[52] See fn29 of ACTA (leaked) Draft of 18 January 2010 (as one of the alternative policies, ISP is requested to terminate the accounts of repeated infringers); also European Union Directorate-General for Trade, ACTA Negotiations, 30 September 2009, ref. 588/09.

[53] Joint Statement on Anti-Counterfeiting Trade Agreement of 16 April 2010 IP/10/437.

[54] See Art 2.18.3 ACTA draft of 6 October 2010.

[55] A Bridy, 'ACTA and the Specter of Graduated Response', (2010) PIJIP Research Paper Series, paper No. 2, at http://digitalcommons.wcl.american.edu/research/2, pp. 1 and 3.

[56] Bridy, supra n56, p. 7.

[57] A. C. Silva, 'Enforcing Intellectual Property Rights by Diminishing Privacy: How the Anti-Counterfeiting Trade Agreement Jeopardizes the Right to Privacy', (2010) PIJIP Research Paper Series, paper No. 11, at http://digitalcommons.wcl.american.edu/research/11, p. 23.

[58] *See* Carl Schlyter's request on Article 29 Working Party assessment of ACTA, at http://en.act-on-acta.eu/11_October_request_for_an_Article_29_Working_Party_assessment_of_ACTA.

[59] Opinion of the European Data Protection Supervisor, supra n6, at points 15–62.

protection authorities.[60] The European Data Protection Supervisor highlighted (in a lengthy opinion) that a three-strike rule would conflict with EU laws on data protection and would be disproportionate.[61]

The current situation in negotiating states regarding this rule differs. Three-strike legislation has been passed in France,[62] New Zealand,[63] South Korea,[64] Taiwan[65] and the United Kingdom[66]; the Belgian parliament recently proposed a "lighter" version of it.[67] In the United States[68] and Ireland,[69] a similar mechanism has been created through private agreements. Germany and Spain have opposed this approach,[70] and recent suggestions on copyright reform in The Netherlands do not contain these kinds of measures.[71] The lack of agreement among the EU member states on this issue was seen, for example, during the negotiation of the Telecom Package.[72] The Telecom Package was a proposal by the European Commission to reform the EU's regulatory

60 Letter of Article 29 Data Protection Working Party of 15 July 2010 to Mr. Karel de Gucht D. (2010) 11185, at http://ec.europa.eu/justice/policies/privacy/docs/wpdocs/others/2010_07_15_letter_wp_commissioner_de_gucht_acta_en.pdf.

61 Ibid.

62 Law supporting the diffusion and protection of content on the Internet No. 2009–669 of 12 June 2009, also known as the HADOPI Act.

63 New Zealand Copyright Act 1994 was modified by the Copyright (New Technologies) Amendment Act 2008 (No 27, date of assent 11 April 2008), which introduced a three-strikes provision; currently Copyright (Infringing File Sharing) Amendment Bill (SOP No 230, release 13 April 2011) is pending before the Parliament.

64 Art. 133*bis* South Korean Copyright Act, modified in April 2009.

65 Art. 90*quinquies* Taiwanese Copyright Act, modified in May 2009.

66 ss 4, 7 and 11 Digital Economy Act 2010 (c. 24).

67 *Proposition de loi favorisant la protection de la création culturelle sur internet* (Proposal of Bill for Better Protection of Cultural Creations on the Internet), at http://merlin.obs.coe.int/redirect.php?id=13130.

68 Bridy, supra n55, p. 8 et seq.

69 Right holders' and Ericom agreement on the application of three-strike rules has been approved by court; *see* 'High Court Approves File Sharing Settlement – ISP Addresses not Personal Data', at http://www.irelandip.com/2010/05/articles/privacy-1/high-court-approves-file-sharing-settlement-isp-addresses-not-personal-data/, also Bridy, supra n55, pp. 11–12; at the same time the courts have denied the disconnection claims against Internet access providers not covered by the settlement; *see* 'Music labels lose downloads case', at http://www.irishtimes.com/newspaper/breaking/2010/1011/breaking32.html.

70 *See* J. Cheng, 'Germany Says 'Nein' to Three-Strikes Infringement Plan', at http://arstechnica.com/tech-policy/news/2009/02/germany-walks-away-from-three-strikes-internet-policy.ars; H. Llewellyn, '"Three-Strikes" Off Anti-Piracy Agenda in Spain', at http://www.billboard.com/biz/articles/news/1269047/three-strikes-off-anti-piracy-agenda-in-spain.

71 Kelvin van 't Klooster, 'Downloading … soon to be Illegal in the Netherlands?' (2011) 5:1 IRIS 34, at http://merlin.obs.coe.int/newsletter.php?year=2011&issue=5&iris_ref=2011+5+34.

72 Directive 2009/140/EC of the European Parliament and of the Council of 25 November 2009 amending Directives 2002/21/EC on a common regulatory framework for electronic communications networks and services, 2002/19/EC on access to, and interconnection of, electronic communications networks and associated facilities, and 2002/20/EC on the authorisation of electronic communications networks and services (Text with EEA relevance), *OJ L* 337, 18.12.2009, *p* 37–69.

framework for electronic communications networks and services with a view to completing the internal market for electronic communications. While negotiating it, as one of the issues, the European Parliament discussed the provision allowing disconnection of Internet users for illegally downloading copyrighted material (i.e. a three-strike rule). The final outcome of the discussions on the Telecom Package was that it does not preclude member states from implementing a three-strike rule, but it does require that due process is guaranteed.[73] To sum up the main arguments, the three-strike rule has been encouraged by some as an efficient enforcement measure; it was thus strongly welcomed by right holders.[74] At the same time it has been attacked as unreasonably violating data protection laws,[75] prejudicing legitimate interests of users[76] and as an unwise long-term solution by record companies.[77]

The final text of ACTA obviously does not contain an explicit obligation for parties to implement a three-strike rule in their national laws. However, it sets a rather abstract requirement to "endeavor to promote cooperative efforts within the business community." Parties are not obliged to reach any results, and thus the extent of efforts will largely depend on the political will of each party.[78] On the other hand, according to some commentators, this provision exactly upholds the interests of the right holders.[79] As mentioned earlier in the chapter, at least in the United States and Ireland, Internet access providers have already cooperated with right holders in enforcing similar three-strike rules. Because both parties might come to find such cooperation ever more advantageous,[80] these types of business arrangements are likely to become more common.[81] Such cooperation, however, has been criticized.[82]

73 Art 1.3(a) provides: "Measures taken by Member States regarding end-users access to, or use of, services and applications through electronic communications networks shall respect the fundamental rights and freedoms of natural persons, as guaranteed by the European Convention for the Protection of Human Rights and Fundamental Freedoms and general principles of Community law."

74 *See* e.g. Ch. W. Wan, 'Three Strikes Law: A Least Cost Solution to Rampant Online Piracy', 5/4 *Journal of Intellectual Property Law and Practice* 232 (2010).

75 See e.g. European Data Protection Supervisor, supra n6.

76 See e.g. Bridy, supra n55.

77 G. Zilkha, 'The RIAA's Troubling Solution to File-Sharing', XX/2 *Fordham Intellectual Property, Media and Entertainment Law Journal* 667 (2010).

78 The EU has been already undertaking such efforts; with the help of the European Commission, a group of stakeholders (right holders and intermediaries) signed on 4 May 2011 a Memorandum of Understanding on the Sale of Counterfeit Goods over the Internet, at http://ec.europa.eu/internal_market/iprenforcement/docs/memorandum_04052011_en.pdf.

79 See Silva, supra n57, p. 24 ("promoting self-regulation seems an adequate manner to deal with the continuous changes and challenges of the technological environment, and with the usual delay of legal solutions").

80 For example, Verizon agreed in 2005 to forward notices of infringement to its customers for Disney, in return for which it received the right to transmit Disney programming over its network; see Bridy, supra n55, p. 8.

81 Bridy, supra n55, p. 8 et seq.

82 See e.g. Zilkha, supra n77; Bridy, supra n55.

If private online enforcement mechanisms like these are created, guaranteeing fundamental rights, such as the protection of personal data, becomes even more complicated.[83] Such a privately established three-strike mechanism would arguably conflict with European data protection laws.[84] If the Internet connection could simply be terminated on the basis of a standard-form contract between the Internet access provider and a private user without proper judicial review, then due process as required under EU Telecommunication Package would not be insured. Also, the implementation of such private enforcement mechanisms excludes other members of society. The argument being that allowing and even encouraging the business community to settle their own enforcement practices could create even worse effects than could arise if rules were set by a legislator through a democratic process where all interests could be weighted and balanced.

The negotiating parties tried to address these concerns by adding the requirement that the cooperation between stakeholders should take place while "preserving legitimate competition and, consistent with that Party's law, preserving fundamental principles such as freedom of expression, fair process, and privacy." A similar safeguard is repeated three times in the Digital Chapter alone.[85] However, commentators have doubted whether such a general mention of fundamental principles is sufficient to ensure their effectiveness and have regretted that more specific provisions on the protection of basic rights have not been developed.[86] In reply, the Commission has stated that since these fundamental principles are regulated very differently in the laws of negotiating parties, it is neither feasible to harmonize them internationally nor suitable to do so in the treaty dealing with enforcement measures.[87] One could, however, regret that whereas parties have been undertaking forceful attempts to ever more harmonise and raise the enforcement standards, no harmonisation attempts are made in respect of other fundamental rights such as freedom of expression, privacy and fair process. And it is not a secret that many countries with less developed legal systems often transpose international obligations word for word. In such jurisdictions these safeguards are likely to remain as vague guidelines with little practical effect, if at all.

Thus, although ACTA itself does not set a three-strike rule, it orders parties to promote private agreements between stakeholders (right holders and intermediaries)

[83] Similar Silva, supra n57, p. 24 (indicates that the self-regulatory models adopted in Ireland and the United Kingdom disrespected consumers' rights).

[84] See opinion of European Data Protection Supervisor, supra n6 (argues that three-strike rule would violate European data protection laws and be non-proportionate).

[85] See articles 27.2, 27.3 and 27.4 ACTA.

[86] Similar the Opinion of European Academics on ACTA, supra n10, paras. 15 and 16 (albeit in relation to other Articles).

[87] Commission's comments on European Academics Opinion on ACTA, supra n10, p. 19.

enabling the enforcement of this rule. In practice, however, such agreements may lead to even worse results than those a three-strike rule established through a democratic legislative process may cause. The mere mention of fundamental principles is not sufficient to ensure that at least a minimum standard in protecting fundamental freedoms is achieved.

## DISCLOSURE OF SUBSCRIBERS' IDENTITIES

Article 27.4 of ACTA implements another measure that is important for the enforcement of IPRs online, namely the obligation for the OSPs to disclose subscriber's identities:

> A Party may provide, in accordance with its laws and regulations, its competent authorities with the authority to order an online service provider to disclose expeditiously to a right holder information sufficient to identify a subscriber whose account was allegedly used for infringement, where that right holder has filed a legally sufficient claim of trademark or copyright or related rights infringement, and where such information is being sought for the purpose of protecting or enforcing those rights. These procedures shall be implemented in a manner that avoids the creation of barriers to legitimate activity, including electronic commerce, and, consistent with that Party's law, preserves fundamental principles such as freedom of expression, fair process, and privacy.

In short, parties are allowed ("may") to provide its competent authorities with the power to order an OSP to disclose information identifying an alleged infringer to a right holder, whilst at the same time preserving certain enumerated interests and fundamental principles. The intention of the provision is to enable right holders to obtain information about individual subscribers (alleged infringers) against which they are willing to enforce their rights. Although non-binding in nature, this is one of the most elaborated provisions in the Digital Chapter,[88] which makes it much easier to transpose into national laws than the more general norms found in Articles 27.1–27.3. In addition, Article 27.4 of ACTA is a special provision in relation to a general right to information as stipulated in Article 11 of ACTA. The latter calls on parties to provide judicial authorities with the power, upon request from a right holder, to require an alleged infringer to provide relevant information. Since the general provisions of the civil enforcement chapter also apply in the digital environment, it will be mentioned here also.

The first drafts of ACTA provided a much more general rule allowing the obtaining of information from an OSP directly (i.e. without permission of a competent

[88] Only protection of technical protection measures is regulated in more detail; see infra.

authority) and without mentioning any fundamental principles at all.[89] During ACTA negotiations, such a provision was criticised as going beyond the national laws of the negotiating parties. It contained a broad definition of an "online service provider" which arguably exceeded even the definitions available under US and EU law. It provided a broad scope of the right to information because it was arguably not limited to copyrights, but covered all IPRs; furthermore, it extended not only to piracy and counterfeiting cases but to criminal and civil enforcement of IPRs in general.[90] After taking these and other problems into account, the requirements for obtaining such information were further specified and the obligation to protect fundamental principles including privacy and fair process added to the draft in the final stages of the negotiations.[91]

As a general matter, a right to information was implemented for the first time at the international level by Article 47 of TRIPS. This is reiterated in Article 11 of ACTA, which in addition sets a "TRIPS-plus" standard in several respects, turning optional TRIPS provisions into mandatory ones. It allows parties to extend the right of information against "alleged infringers," while TRIPS mentions only "infringers." ACTA proposes a more extensive (albeit non-binding) list of the categories of information that might be requested.[92] Last but not least, the proportionality requirement explicitly found in Article 47 of TRIPS has been omitted in Article 11 of ACTA.[93] Instead, ACTA stipulates that the right of information should be "without prejudice" to the party's law governing privilege, confidentiality of information sources and personal data.

In contrast, a right to obtain information about the individual subscribers' identity from OSPs has not been given at the international level up until now. Article 47 of TRIPS does not specifically cover the issue of OSPs; the issue did not exist at the time of TRIPS negotiations, and negotiators could not take into account the special problems right of information would cause in Internet-related cases. Although adhering to TRIPS requirements, numerous countries have also rejected the derivation of such a duty for OSPs from a general right to information, often because of data protection concerns.[94] In the EU, Article 8 of the Enforcement Directive[95]

89 Art 27.3*ter* ACTA (official) Draft of April 2010.

90 Silva, supra n 57, pp. 14–19.

91 See Art. 27.4 ACTA Draft of 6 October 2010.

92 Art. 11 ACTA, second sentence includes "third persons" that are not mentioned in TRIPS.

93 On the other hand, proportionality requirement is found as a general principle in Art 6.3 ACTA.

94 For example, this has been denied by German courts until the amendment of copyright law in 2008; *see* G. Spindler, in G. Spindler and Schuster (eds.), *Recht der Neuen Medien. Kommentar* (Beck: München 2008) 640; also Swiss Federal Supreme Court decision of 8 September 2010 1C_285/2009 *EDÖB v Logistep AG*, at http://jumpcgi.bger.ch/cgi-bin/JumpCGI?id=08.09.2010_1C_285/2009.

95 Corrigendum to Directive 2004/48/EC of the European Parliament and of the Council of 29 April 2004 on the enforcement of intellectual property rights (OJ L 157, 30.4.2004), OJ L 195, 02/06/2004 P. 0016–25.

sets a general right of information; however, it does not specifically address the OSPs' duty to communicate their subscriber's data. Article 15.2 of the E-Commerce Directive[96] allows member states to establish certain information obligations for OSPs. The European Court of Justice (ECJ) has clarified; however, that none of those Directives requires member states to set a duty to disclose subscribers' data in the context of civil proceedings, but neither do they prohibit such disclosures.[97] Still, some commentators,[98] as well as the European Commission,[99] do tend to imply such a special information duty from these directives. On an international scale, countries seem to fall into groups, with some allowing the disclosure of subscribers' identities (e.g. Germany,[100] Austria,[101] France,[102] Ireland,[103] Netherlands,[104] Norway,[105] Israel)[106] and others not allowing such practices or strictly limiting them (e.g. Switzerland,[107] the United Kingdom,[108] Italy,[109] Belgium,[110] Spain).[111]

96 Supra n42.

97 ECJ decision of 29 January 2008 C-275/06 *Productores de Música de España (Promusicae) v Telefónica de España SAU*; confirmed in ECJ decision of 19 February 2009 C-557/07 *LSG v Tele2*.

98 M. Walter, S. v Lewinski, *European Copyright Law: A Commentary* (Oxford: Oxford University Press, 2010) para. 13.8.33.

99 See Commission comments on the European Academics Opinion on ACTA, supra n10, para. 16.

100 § 101 German Copyright Act.

101 Section 87b(3) Austrian Copyright Act and s. 18.4 E-Commerce Act; however, this duty does not apply to temporary IP addresses; see Austrian Supreme Court decision of 14 July 2009 4 Ob 41/09x – *LSG v Tele2*.

102 Article L.331–21 of the Intellectual Property Code, also the French Supreme Court decision of 23 March 2010 No: 09–80787 – *Edonkey-Armata* (IP addresses are not automatically personal data).

103 *EMI Records & Ors v Eircom Ltd* [2010] IEHC 108 (2010) the High Court (Dublin) noted that the Eircom subscriber contract creates a pact not to use the Internet for illegal purposes, and that the processing of data (in this context) is lawful on the basis of several grounds.

104 District court decision of 8 July 2008 *Stichting BREIN NL v Euroaccess Enterprises LTD* (court ordered Euroaccess [hosting provider] to provide BREIN with a number of information on the legal entities and/or natural persons that are "manifestly acting unlawfully vis-à-vis the BREIN Foundation").

105 Norway Supreme Court decision of 18 June 2010 No. HR-2010–01060 – A *Metronome v Altibox* (court granted the exemption under privacy laws and ordered an access provider to disclose users identities).

106 Tel Aviv court decision of 7 January 2009 (court ordered Google to disclose the identities of users).

107 Swiss Federal Supreme Court decision of 8 September 2010 1C_285/2009 *EDÖB v Logistep* AG (court has held that the collection of IP addresses, on which basis identities can be identified [and criminal enforcement proceedings can be started] violates data protection laws).

108 The UK Digital Economy Act obliges OSPs to provide the lists of infringements, but without disclosing the identities of users; see s 124B UK Digital Economy Act 2010.

109 Court of Rome decision of 15 April 2010 *FAPAV v Italia Telecom* (The court refused to provide identities of, and block access to, users who infringe copyright).

110 Art 86*ter* § 3 of the Belgian Copyright Act sets only a general duty of information: it allows the judge to order the defendant to disclose all information in his possession, including the identification of the infringer, but only in the context of judicial proceedings for copyright infringement.

111 Commercial Court No. 5 of Madrid decision of 17 March 2008 – *Promusicae*.

of disclosure should not be misused for any purposes other than the enforcement of rights; the privacy of correspondence could be limited only as far as necessary for enforcement purposes.[123]

In conclusion, whereas the disclosure of subscribers' identities is optional under ACTA, its rather specific wording makes it easy and thus encourages its word-for-word implementation into national laws which do not yet have such a provision. Regretfully, the article is not entirely balanced; thus, when transposing it into national laws, the protection of other interests should be addressed in a more specific and elaborated manner.

## TECHNICAL PROTECTION MEASURES: FURTHER PROTECTION

Some of the most important provisions of the ACTA Digital Chapter are the elaborate Articles 27.5–27.8 on the protection of technical protection measures (TPMs) and rights management information (RMI):

> 5. Each Party shall provide adequate legal protection and effective legal remedies against the circumvention of effective technological measures … that are used by authors, performers or producers of phonograms in connection with the exercise of their rights in, and that restrict acts in respect of, their works, performances, and phonograms, which are not authorized by the authors, the performers or the producers of phonograms concerned or permitted by law.
> 6. In order to provide the adequate legal protection and effective legal remedies referred to in paragraph 5, each Party shall provide protection at least against:
>    (a) to the extent provided by its law:
>       (i) the unauthorized circumvention of an effective technological measure carried out knowingly or with reasonable grounds to know; and
>       (ii) the offering to the public by marketing of a device or product, including computer programs, or a service, as a means of circumventing an effective technological measure; and
>    (b) the manufacture, importation, or distribution of a device or product, including computer programs, or provision of a service that
>       (i) is primarily designed or produced for the purpose of circumventing an effective technological measure; or
>       (ii) has only a limited commercially significant purpose other than circumventing an effective technological measure ….

[123] cf. § 101.10 German Copyright Act.

7. To protect electronic rights management information … each Party shall provide adequate legal protection and effective legal remedies against any person knowingly performing without authority any of the following acts knowing, or with respect to civil remedies, having reasonable grounds to know, that it will induce, enable, facilitate, or conceal an infringement of any copyright or related rights: (a) to remove or alter any electronic rights management information; (b) to distribute, import for distribution, broadcast, communicate, or make available to the public copies of works, performances, or phonograms, knowing that electronic rights management information has been removed or altered without authority.
8. In providing adequate legal protection and effective legal remedies pursuant to the provisions of paragraphs 5 and 7, a Party may adopt or maintain appropriate limitations or exceptions to measures implementing the provisions of paragraphs 5, 6, and 7. The obligations set forth in paragraphs 5, 6, and 7 are without prejudice to the rights, limitations, exceptions, or defences to copyright or related rights infringement under a Party's law.

In short, Article 27.5 sets a general requirement to provide protection against circumvention of TPMs. Article 27.6 clarifies what specific conduct in respect of TPMs should at least be prohibited. Article 27.7 provides protection against unauthorized removal of RMI. Finally, Article 27.8 seeks to preserve parties' ability to maintain exceptions and limitations available under their laws or adopt new ones.

The following paragraphs will primarily focus only on the provisions related to TPMs since, in regard to RMIs, ACTA does not propose any significant changes in comparison with the existing international or EU provisions.

The first leaked ACTA drafts, as well as the first official ACTA version of April 2010, suggested a rather broad protection of TPMs. For instance, the April 2010 version explicitly required parties to grant protection for TPMs controlling not only illegal reproduction but also a mere access to content; it required that adequate legal protection against violation of TPMs is "independent of any infringement of copyrights and related rights." Parties were obliged to grant both civil and criminal remedies in case of violation. Exceptions and limitations to copyright could be maintained only "so long as they do not significantly impair the adequacy of legal protection or effectiveness of legal remedies for violations of those measures."[124] These points, and especially the absence of more elaborate provisions on the preservation of exceptions and limitations, have been strongly criticised by numerous commentators,[125] which led to certain narrowing of the protection in the final text of ACTA.

124 See e.g. Articles 4–7 ACTA (official) Draft of April 2010.
125 See e.g. Washington College of Law PIJIP, ACTA Section Analysis, at https://sites.google.com/site/iipenforcement/acta-section-analysis

The provisions on the protection of TPMs (and RMI) have been first implemented in the 1996 WIPO Internet Treaties[126] and later regulated in more detail in national (or regional) acts such as EU Information Society Directive[127] or the American DMCA.[128] However, not all parties to TRIPS have joined the WIPO Treaties[129]; even some ACTA negotiating parties do not belong to them (e.g. New Zealand). Also, recent case law has shown that the scope of protection of TPMs still differs significantly under national laws.[130] Thus, it is not surprising that ACTA negotiating parties have undertaken to harmonise the issue, and the European Commission sees the agreed-upon common definition of TPMs as one of the most important contributions by ACTA.[131] However, certain problematic aspects are worth mentioning.

### *Which TPMs Are Protected?*

The first question is whether ACTA grants protection to TPMs which control conduct not covered by exclusive rights.[132] It is agreed by most commentators that the WIPO Internet Treaties require the protection only of those TPMs that restrict conduct in respect of *protected* subject matter and prohibit only conduct which is covered by exclusive (or remuneration) rights; in other words, WIPO Treaties grant protection only in relation to acts of circumvention that result in a copyright infringement.[133] However, WIPO signatories were allowed to extend the protection to TPMs controlling conduct not covered by copyright law. The EU Information Society Directive does this in Article 6 which omits such wording of the WIPO Treaties as "in connection with the exercise of their rights" and "restrict acts (…) which are not (…) permitted by law" and thereby prohibits circumvention (and trafficking) of TPMs even if this conduct alone would not lead to the infringement of copyright or a related right. This has received strong criticism from some

[126] Correspondingly, Art 11 WIPO Copyright Treaty and Art 18 WIPO Performances and Phonograms Treaty.

[127] Arts. 6–7 Directive 2001/29/EC of the European Parliament and of the Council of 22 May 2001 on the harmonisation of certain aspects of copyright and related rights in the information society, *OJ L 167, 22/06/2001 P. 0010–0019*.

[128] 17 US Code §§ 1201–05.

[129] On November 2010, there were eighty-eight contracting parties to WCT; WPPT–86, TRIPS–153.

[130] For more, *see* L Guibault et al., *Study on the Implementation And Effect in Member States' Laws of Directive 2001/29/EC on the Harmonisation of Certain Aspects of Copyright and Related Rights in The Information Society*, report to the European Commission, DG Internal Market, February 2007, at http://www.ivir.nl/publications/guibault/Infosoc_report_2007.pdf, p. 69 et seq.

[131] Commission comments the Opinion of European Academics on ACTA, supra n110, para. 15.

[132] For example, conduct covered by exceptions or conduct in respect of subject matter which is not (anymore) protected by copyright.

[133] See Guibault et al., supra n130, p. 78; S. v Lewinski, *International Copyright Law and Policy* (Oxford: Oxford University Press, 2008).

commentators.[134] A similar extension of protection is found in the DMCA. However, Canadian and Swiss laws grant a more limited protection as suggested under the WIPO Treaties.[135] Accordingly, Switzerland and New Zealand at least have opposed to such extension of the protection.[136]

It is not entirely clear what scope of protection is required under the final text of ACTA. On the one hand, Article 27.5 reiterates the formulation found in WIPO Internet Treaties, which is construed as not requiring grant of protection to TPMs controlling conduct not covered under exclusive rights.[137] On the other hand, Article 27.6 of ACTA largely overtakes the respective provisions of the Information Society Directive which, as mentioned earlier in the chapter, grants more extensive protection. The relationship of the two articles is not entirely clear. If a more restrictive interpretation is applied, one could argue that Article 27.6 is a clarification of Article 27.5 (and not a special provision of it).[138] In that case, the limited scope of protection granted under the latter article should be extended to Article 27.6. This would mean that ACTA requires protection only in respect of those circumvention acts which lead to the infringement of exclusive rights. Such interpretation would mean that ACTA preserves the standard provided in the WIPO Treaties.[139] Alternatively, Article 27.6 ACTA may be read as requiring protection in relation to *any* circumvention acts, that is, disregarding (non)-infringing aspects, which would go beyond the obligations set by the WIPO Treaties.

A related question is whether ACTA covers TPMs controlling access to content (as distinguished from copy-controlling TPMs). Some commentators see access as not falling within the scope of copyright protection and thus argue that the WIPO Treaties do not require protection of measures controlling access to works;[140] this was also the position of Japan, which does not grant protection against access under its national laws.[141] Other commentators claim that access implicates reproduction

[134] Guibault et al., supra n130, pp. 100–101.

[135] Guibault et al., supra n130, pp. 94–95; Canadian Parliament has repeatedly rejected the proposed legislature (Bill C-30, C-31 and C-32) that implemented high TPM protection standards comparable to the ones available under the US DMCA.

[136] See comments to Art 2.18.5 ACTA (leaked) Draft of 18 January 2010.

[137] The main difference here is that WIPO Treaties refer to rights "under this Treaty (i.e. WCT and WPPT) or the Berne Convention," whereas ACTA omits this wording. This most likely means that the rights granted under national laws are meant instead and the latter may be more extensive than those set in the Treaties.

[138] See "In order to provide such adequate legal protection and effective legal remedies."

[139] However, because ACTA sets only minimum standards, it allows parties to have a more extensive protection of TPMs.

[140] T Heide, 'Copyright in the E.U. and United States: What "Access Right"' (2001) 23 EIPR 468, 470; K. J. Koelman, 'A Hard Nut to Crack: The Protection of Technological Measures' (2000) 22 EIPR 272, 277.

[141] See ACTA (leaked) Draft of 18 January 2010, p. 31; Guibault et al., supra n130, p. 86.

rights (as digital access leads at least to a RAM copy) and underpins the distribution and communication right.[142] For instance, the DMCA first of all protects access control measures and grants only a limited protection for copy control measures.[143] The definition of TPM as provided in footnote 14 of ACTA almost literally reiterates the wording of Article 6.3 of the EU Information Society Directive,[144] which generally covers access control mechanisms.

### *Exceptions and Limitations*

On the other hand, ACTA curtails the scope of protection to some extent: footnote 14 stipulates that the definition of TPMs shall be "without prejudice to the scope of copyright or related rights contained in a Party's law." Also, under Article 27.8, in the second sentence of ACTA, the protection granted to TPMs (and RMI) is "without prejudice to the rights, limitations, exceptions, or defenses to copyright or related rights infringement under Party's law." This reservation seems to allow countries not to include access control measures in the scope of protection if this would prejudice the scope of national copyright law. Further, apart from exceptions and limitations to exclusive rights, ACTA allows parties to "adopt or maintain appropriate limitations or exceptions to measures implementing paragraphs 5, 6 and 7."[145] This is especially relevant to the EU in regard to TPMs concerning software. They are not covered by the Information Society Directive and granted a much narrower protection under the Software Directive.[146] This limited protection for TPM applied to software has been recognised as very important.[147] Interestingly, Article 27.8 is one of few ACTA provisions which allows not only for the maintenance of existing limitations in national law but also for the *adoption* of new ones.

One of the remaining problems, also highlighted by most commentators, is that ACTA does not provide any efficient mechanism to ensure the adoption and enforcement of such exceptions and limitations.[148] Although detailed provisions on

[142] Guibault et al, supra n130, p. 76; Lewinski, supra n133, para. 17.97.

[143] See 17 USC § 1201(a) and (b).

[144] The main difference between the two is that ACTA protection covers only works, performances or phonograms, whereas the Directive encompasses any related right as well as *sui generis* rights.

[145] Art. 27.8, first sentence, ACTA.

[146] For example, Art. 7.1(c) of the Software Directive prohibits only trafficking of means of circumvention and not circumvention of a TPM itself and it covers only means the "sole purpose" of which is to circumvent a TPM (i.e. means with dual purposes are excluded); see Directive 2009/24/EC of the European Parliament and of the Council of 23 April 2009 on the legal protection of computer programs OJ L 111 5.5.2009 pp. 16–22.

[147] Attempts to extend the protection granted under Information Society Directive to TPMs related to software have failed; see Walter and Lewinski, supra n98, para. 5.7.31.

[148] PIJIP, ACTA Section Analysis, supra n 125.

the protection of TPMs have been transposed from US and EU law, the elaborate provisions regulating exceptions and limitations contained, for instance, in the US[149] or the EU[150] law have been entirely left out. It is thus questionable whether users will be able to make practical use of this reservation or whether it will remain a "dead law." National practice shows that it is difficult to enforce the exceptions even where some local enforcement mechanisms have been created.[151] This would be even more difficult where no such mechanisms exist at all.

The other issue is whether ACTA merely allows or, rather, *obliges* parties to maintain exceptions where TPMs are applied. ACTA initially provided for a "may" provision.[152] However, in the later draft, parties have moved for an ambiguous concept, "without prejudice [to exceptions and limitations]." It is questionable if it could be regarded as an obligation to parties not to prejudice exceptions and limitations even where the TPM is applied. If such an interpretation were adopted, both the EU and US would have to review their corresponding provisions which extend protection over circumventions acts which are essentially covered by national copyright exceptions or limitations.

### *Scope of Prohibited Acts*

Article 27.5 ACTA sets a general requirement to provide "adequate legal protection and effective legal remedies against *circumvention*." Article 27.6 ACTA specifies this requirement by prohibiting both the circumvention of TPMs and preparatory acts such as manufacture, importation and distribution of a device or product facilitating circumvention. The WIPO Treaties contained only a general requirement similar to the one found in Article 27.5 and left it to the parties to decide what particular acts should be prohibited – either only circumvention acts, only preparatory acts or both. The EU and the United States have chosen to prohibit both types of conduct in their national laws. Japan, in contrast, prohibits preparatory acts and only "circumvention as a business in response to a request by the public" (which in essence means provision of circumvention services).[153] Australia also initially prohibited only

149 17 USC § 1201(a)(1)(C); §1201(d), (f), (g).

150 Art. 6.4, Information Society Directive.

151 For example, the mechanism created under Art 6.4 of the Information Society Directive has been criticized by Guibault et al., supra n130, p. 79 et seq.; *Gowers Review of Intellectual Property* 73 (London, HM Treasury, 2006), at http://www.official-documents.gov.uk/document/other/0118404830/0118404830.pdf; Patricia Akester, 'The Impact of Digital Rights Management on Freedom of Expression – the First Empirical Assessment' (2010) 41/1 IIC; A *Metzger* and T Kreutzer, '*Richtlinie zum Urheberrecht in der Informationsgesellschaft1: Privatkopie trotz technischer Schutzmaßnahmen*' (2002) MMR 139.

152 See Art. 2.18.7 ACTA (official) Draft of April 2010.

153 Guibault et al., supra n130, p. 94; Japanese Government comments to Art 2.18.6 in ACTA Draft of 18 January 2010.

preparatory acts.[154] ACTA has thus adopted the strongest option and sets it as a new minimum ("at least") multilateral standard.[155]

It is questionable whether it is reasonable to strengthen the protection of TPMs. On the one hand, stakeholders probably still believe that problems created by technology can be best solved by another technology. Without going into extensive debate on the need of protection of TPMs, it could only be pointed out here that in practice TPMs are often used to purposes other than protecting exclusive rights. Early US case law has already shown that TPMs can be used not to prevent illegal use of protected subject matter, but rather for certain anticompetitive purposes (e.g., to create a market share, to partition the markets, etc.).[156] One example is Sony Play Station, which has been litigated in different jurisdictions with different results. It has been argued that by making counterfeit copies and competitors' video games unable to interact with its PS2 consoles, Sony has succeeded in "binding" its video games to its consoles, which are usually sold below cost to attract consumers. Also, the subdivision of the global market into three different geographical zones, each area being charged the price (Sony estimates) consumers are willing to pay, is a clear price discrimination strategy whereby Sony attempts to maximize its worldwide profits.[157] Some authors refer also to iTunes as an example in which, with the help of TPMs, a different price is charged in different countries within the EU.[158] Instead of addressing these problems, ACTA parties have opted for the strengthening of TPM protection.

## CONCLUSIONS

ACTA is one step further in a seemingly never-ending story of ever stronger IP enforcement. The Digital Chapter of ACTA is of particular importance within this story. Although its initial provisions have been strongly watered down because of

[154] However, under a Free Trade Agreement with the United States, it had to extend prohibition over circumvention act; see s 116A Australian Copyright Act of 1968.

[155] On the other hand, the protection granted under ACTA is slightly narrower than the protection granted under the Information Society Directive: e.g. the Directive contains a more extensive list of prohibited acts and a slightly more extensive list of prohibited means for circumvention.

[156] *See Lexmark International v Static Control Components*, 387 F 3d 522; [2004] USCA 03–5400 (provider of replacement toner cartridges), *Chamberlain Group v Skylink Technologies* 381 F 3d 1178 (provider of garage door opener) and a recent Apple and RealNetworks case discussed in Ch. Arlt, '*Marktabschottend wirkender Einsatz von DRM-Technik – Eine Untersuchung aus wettbewerbsrechtlichem Blickwinkel*' (2005) 12 GRUR, 1003, 1004.

[157] E Arezzo, 'Video Games and Consoles Between Copyright and Technical Protection Measures', (2009) 1 IIC 82, at 83–84.

[158] Gowers Review, supra n151, p. 73 (Box 4.8); Gowers, however, notes that there might be also other reasons for such price discrimination, e.g. different agreements with collecting societies.

strong criticisms expressed by both civil groups and academics during the period of negotiations, they still raise some concerns which should be acknowledged if ACTA is to be transposed into national laws and practice or used in further political processes.

Firstly, the formulation of Article 27.1 ACTA seems to subject digital infringements to the same enforcement standards as ordinary (offline) infringements. However, it is argued here that it implicitly provides parties with a flexibility to draft Internet-tailored enforcement provisions. Thus, parties are encouraged to not apply general enforcement rules, but to draft provisions that take into account the special economic, social, technological and political nature of online infringements. This is especially encouraged when searching for a proper (broad or narrow) construction of a "commercial scale" requirement in online criminal enforcement cases.

Secondly, the most feared three-strike rule has not found its way into the final text of ACTA. Instead, ACTA obliges parties to merely "endeavor to encourage" cooperation in the business community. However, experience in the United States and Ireland shows that private enforcement mechanisms agreed upon between Internet access providers and right holders may make it even more difficult to protect public interests such as privacy and fair process than could be expected from statutory enforcement mechanisms. It is thus argued here that if this enforcement mechanism were adopted at all, it would be better achieved through a legislative process where the interests of all involved parties are more properly taken into account.

Thirdly, ACTA parties managed to agree on a duty to disclose subscribers' identities. Although it remains optional, its rather precise formulation facilitates and encourages its literary transposition into national laws, especially by countries which still do not have any comparable provision. A problem, pertinent to the entire ACTA, also applies here, however: such fundamental rights as freedom of expression, fair process and privacy are merely mentioned. Thus, when transposing ACTA into national laws, more specific guidelines on how these rights should be effectively ensured should be formulated.

Fourthly, ACTA addresses in detail the protection of TPMs. It sets "WIPO (and TRIPS)-plus" standards, at least on prohibited acts. The definition of TPMs is not entirely clear, however, and thus parties are encouraged to carefully consider which construction – broad or narrow – should be accepted in national legislation or practice. Also, when transposing ACTA into national laws, safeguards (such as exceptions and limitations) need to be properly regulated in order to ensure an effective balance of interests. In addition, elaborate discussions on OSP limited liability rules during ACTA negotiations led to a failure. The non-binding mention of limited liability regimes to OSPs in a footnote to Article 27.2 hardly has any legal weight. We need to take care, unless early ACTA texts (containing detailed provisions on this issue) are brought back on the negotiation table in later (international or bilateral) political discussions.

All in all, ACTA's final text appears to be less problematic than it was feared to be. Should it come into force, however, we note that much work still needs to be done in order for its provisions to be transposed into national (regional) laws in a well-balanced manner.

# 8

# The ACTA Committee

*Peter K. Yu*

## INTRODUCTION

In discussing the Anti-Counterfeiting Trade Agreement (ACTA), most policymakers and commentators have focused on either the lack of transparency and accountability in the negotiation process or the problems raised by the TRIPS-plus standards included in the agreement. While these issues deserve our urgent attention, it is important not to ignore the institutional arrangements laid out in Chapter V of the agreement. In the long run, this chapter is likely to become the most far-reaching and dangerous of all the chapters in ACTA.

Behind only the chapter on substantive standards, Chapter V is the second-longest chapter in the agreement. Included in this chapter are provisions creating and governing a little institution called the "ACTA Committee." On its face, those provisions are boring, mundane and highly administrative. In reality, they govern matters ranging from membership to amendments to rules and procedures. Those provisions also help institutionalise ACTA as a freestanding, self-evolving forum. As a result, they have the potential to determine the future development of not only ACTA but also the international intellectual property system.

This chapter explains why the ACTA Committee could become such a powerful institution. It begins by providing an overview of the provisions governing the Committee. It then explains how the ACTA Committee provides a freestanding, self-evolving architecture to facilitate the ratcheting up of international intellectual property standards. The chapter concludes with a discussion of the Committee's ramifications for both developing countries and the international intellectual property system.

This chapter draws on research for earlier articles in the *SMU Law Review* and the *WIPO Journal*. The author is grateful to Erin Cassidy, Srikant Mikkilineni and Lindsey Purdy for excellent research and editorial assistance.  Kern Family Chair in Intellectual Property Law and Director, Intellectual Property Law Center, Drake University Law School.

## ACTA PROVISIONS

Article 36 is the primary provision governing the ACTA Committee. Article 36.1 states that the Committee will be established and that each party will be represented on it. Article 36.2 lays out the Committee's functions. It states that the Committee shall undertake the following tasks:

(a) review the implementation and operation of this Agreement;
(b) consider matters concerning the development of this Agreement;
(c) consider any proposed amendments to this Agreement in accordance with Article 42 (Amendments);
(d) decide, in accordance with paragraph 2 of Article 43 (Accession), upon the terms of accession to this Agreement of any Member of the WTO; and
(e) consider any other matter that may affect the implementation and operation of this Agreement.

Using the optional "may," Article 36.3 further empowers the ACTA Committee to

(a) establish *ad hoc* committees or working groups to assist the Committee in carrying out its responsibilities under [Article 36.2], or to assist a prospective Party upon its request in acceding to this Agreement in accordance with Article 43 (Accession);
(b) seek the advice of non-governmental persons or groups;
(c) make recommendations regarding the implementation and operation of this Agreement, including by endorsing best practice guidelines related thereto;
(d) share information and best practices with third parties on reducing intellectual property rights infringements, including techniques for identifying and monitoring piracy and counterfeiting; and
(e) take other actions in the exercise of its functions.

Pursuant to Article 36.5, the ACTA Committee will adopt rules and procedures following the entry into force of the agreement. In addition to "chairing and hosting meetings ... and the performance of organizational duties relevant to this Agreement and its operation," the rules and procedures "may ... address such matters as granting observer status ... and any other matter the Committee decides necessary for its proper operation." Article 36.5 allows the Committee to invite those signatories that are not yet parties to the agreement to participate in deliberations on rules and procedures. Article 36.6 further grants to the Committee the power to amend those rules and procedures.

Anticipated to convene at least once every year, the Committee will make decisions based on consensus, unless chosen otherwise. During the first five years following the entry into force of the agreement, the Committee will make decisions concerning the adoption of or amendment to rules and procedures based on the consensus of both the parties to the agreement and signatories that are not yet parties to that agreement. After that period, the Committee may make those decisions based on the consensus of only the parties to the agreement.

In addition to article 36, ACTA includes three additional provisions concerning the Committee. Article 38.3 allows parties that have undertaken consultations with each other on implementation matters to notify, upon mutual consent, the ACTA Committee of the result of their consultations. Although all ACTA parties can propose amendments to the Committee, Article 42.1 states specifically that the Committee "shall decide whether to present a proposed amendment to the Parties for ratification, acceptance, or approval." Finally, Article 43.2 grants to the Committee the power to "decide upon the terms of accession" for those WTO Members applying to join the agreement after the expiration of the specified accession period.

Taken together, these provisions reflect the compromises struck by the negotiating parties. During the negotiations, countries disagreed over not only the name but also the function of the ACTA Committee. As shown in the 18 January 2010 draft leaked through WikiLeaks, Canada, the lead drafter of Chapter V, proposed the establishment of an "oversight committee" (which was also referred to as the "ACTA Oversight Council" in the general definitions). Mexico preferred the term "steering committee" instead, as such a term would suggest a more moderate role.

In addition, as Michael Geist noted at the time of the negotiations, Canada proposed to use the Committee to "resolve disputes that may arise regarding its interpretation or application."[1] Meanwhile, "New Zealand would like it excluded altogether, Australia want[ed] the committee to merely facilitate the avoidance of disputes, and Japan want[ed] to discuss later." According to Professor Geist, there were also some discussions about whether an ACTA Secretariat should be set up:

> The country that serves as chair of the ACTA Oversight Committee would provide the secretariat. There is currently some disagreement on this issue. For example, Japan favours using an international organization to provide secretariat services, Korea wants to entrust the Secretariat to the WTO, and Morocco supports the creation of a permanent secretariat (i.e. not rotating with the committee chair).

In the end, the negotiating parties settled on the creation of the ACTA Committee, with no designated secretariat, no oversight function and no explicit power to resolve disputes. To alleviate concern, Article 36.11 also states explicitly that "the Committee shall not oversee or supervise domestic or international enforcement or criminal investigations of specific intellectual property cases." Article 36.12 further stipulates

[1] Geist, M. (2010), "Toward an ACTA Super-Structure: How ACTA May Replace WIPO". Available at http://www.michaelgeist.ca/content/view/4910/125/

that the Committee "shall strive to avoid unnecessary duplication between its activities and other international efforts regarding the enforcement of intellectual property rights."

These two provisions serve two important functions. On the one hand, they seek to alleviate the concerns of those negotiating parties that are reluctant to establish an elaborate structure within ACTA. On the other hand, they seek to allay fears among the non-negotiating parties and international intergovernmental organizations that ACTA will be used to replace the existing framework for setting international intellectual property norms.

Although Article 36.3(b) states that the Committee may "seek the advice of non-governmental persons or groups," it is unclear how welcome the Committee will be to input from civil society organizations, as opposed to the intellectual property industries. If the past secret negotiations provide any guide, the ACTA parties and the Committee are unlikely to be open, inclusive, democratic and transparent.[2] This is particularly true considering that Article 36.4 states explicitly that "[a]ll decisions of the Committee shall be taken by consensus," except decided otherwise. One also has to wonder whether the documents of the Committee, its ad hoc committees or working groups will be accessible to the public.

## A FREESTANDING, SELF-REINFORCING AGREEMENT

Through the creation of the ACTA Committee and the empowerment of this Committee to further establish ad hoc committees or working groups, ACTA introduces a new architecture that would help facilitate the future evolution and reinforcement of the agreement. While commentators have widely focused on the present text of ACTA, that agreement, once ratified, will likely continue to evolve following its own amendment process. That process could result in the development of standards exceeding what is already laid out in the present text.

In addition, the administrative and ancillary powers recognised in Articles 36.2 and 36.3 will enable ACTA to grow in strength and scope. They will allow the agreement to develop into a full-fledged freestanding intellectual property forum. Depending on the goals and organizational structures, the creation of ad hoc committees or working groups could result in the development of bodies similar to those working groups or task forces found in APEC, G-8, OECD and other regional or international fora. Meanwhile, the endorsement of best practice guidelines and the sharing of "information and best practices with third parties on reducing intellectual property rights infringements," as acknowledged in Articles 36.3(c) and 36.3(d),

[2] Levine, D. S. (2011), "Transparency Soup: The ACTA Negotiating Process and 'Black Box' Lawmaking". *American University International Law Review* 26(3): 811–837.

could shape the future development of international intellectual property enforcement norms.

From the standpoint of the ACTA negotiating parties and intellectual property right holders, the development of this self-evolving architecture is highly efficient. It will help strengthen the protection and enforcement of intellectual property rights without the substantive and procedural constraints in existing multilateral agreements. Because the ACTA parties include only like-minded countries, the negotiation process will also provide a more satisfying outcome than those found in existing international fora, such as WIPO and the WTO. Many a times, standards proposed by developed and like-minded countries at multilateral fora were eventually watered down to meet concession demands from developing countries.

By creating a new freestanding forum, countries could also discuss issues that are likely to face significant resistance at the multilateral level. To some extent, ACTA provides a "safe space" for negotiating new enforcement norms and strengthened protections without reopening the TRIPS Agreement and other international intellectual property treaties.[3] Such a safe space is important to those countries that consider the TRIPS Agreement inadequate and badly outdated. For many of these countries, the TRIPS Agreement, which was adopted in 1994 with protection levels locked at those set around 1991, failed to anticipate the latest developments concerning the digital environment and the increasingly sophisticated network of piracy and counterfeiting.[4]

By contrast, from the standpoint of developing countries and consumers in developed countries, the absence of constraints can be quite problematic. After all, many of these constraints – whether procedural or substantive – are important safeguards that ensure not only the balance in the international intellectual property system but also congruence between such protection and local needs, interests and conditions. Having been negotiated outside the multilateral process, ACTA ignores many of the important safeguards that the negotiators put into the TRIPS Agreement to promote the public interest and the objectives laid out in Article 7 of the latter agreement.[5]

In sum, the present text of ACTA, the agreement's amendment process and the creation of the ACTA Committee, its ad hoc committees and working groups have encouraged the parties and signatories to adopt a pick-and-choose approach, selecting

3 Helfer, L. R. (2004), "Regime Shifting: The TRIPs Agreement and New Dynamics of International Intellectual Property Lawmaking". *Yale Journal of International Law* 29(1): 1–83, 58.

4 Gervais, D. J. (2007), "The TRIPS Agreement and the Doha Round: History and Impact on Economic Development" in *Intellectual Property and Information Wealth: Issues and Practices in the Digital Age*, Vol. 4. Yu, P. K. ed. Praeger Publishers, Westport, CT, p. 43; Yu, P. K. (2011), "Six Secret (and Now Open) Fears of ACTA". *SMU Law Review* 64(3): 975–1094, 1073; Yu, P. K. (2011), "TRIPS and Its Achilles' Heel". *Journal of Intellectual Property Law* 18(2): 479–531, 502–503.

5 Yu, P. K. (2009), "The Objectives and Principles of the TRIPS Agreement". *Houston Law Review* 46(4): 979–1046, 1041–1042.

only those TRIPS provisions they prefer while abandoning those they reluctantly adopted out of compromise two decades ago. To a large extent, ACTA can be seen as a revision of the TRIPS Agreement without going through the carefully designed multilateral amendment process. It throws away the many hard-earned bargains developing countries have won through the TRIPS negotiation process.

## IMPLICATIONS FOR DEVELOPING COUNTRIES

Even more problematic for developing countries, the self-evolving architecture supported by the ACTA Committee will help facilitate the creation of ACTA as a free-standing intellectual property agreement that can be incorporated by reference into other international agreements. Indeed, it will be no surprise if future international agreements include a reference to ACTA, similar to how the TRIPS Agreement incorporates by reference selected provisions of the Berne Convention for the Protection of Literary and Artistic Works, the Paris Convention for the Protection of Industrial Property and the Washington Treaty on Intellectual Property in Respect of Integrated Circuits. Many U.S. free trade agreements already require signatories to ratify the Patent Cooperation Treaty and the WIPO Internet Treaties. The ACTA standards could also be incorporated into the templates for developing new bilateral or plurilateral trade or investment agreements.

In addition, the United States Trade Representative (USTR) is likely to take ACTA into consideration in the Section 301 process once the agreement enters into force. For instance, the USTR has repeatedly put Canada on the Section 301 Watch List, citing the country's failure to ratify the WIPO Internet Treaties, among other shortcomings.[6] Before China acceded to those treaties, the USTR also stated in the 2005 *National Trade Estimate Report on Foreign Trade Barriers* that "the United States considers the WIPO treaties to reflect many key international norms for providing copyright protection over the Internet."[7] That report further noted that "China's accession to the WIPO treaties is an increasingly important priority for the United States."

In all fairness to the early proponents of ACTA, a leaked discussion paper, presumably from the United States, did suggest that countries should consider including in ACTA "[s]pecial measures for developing countries in the initial phase."[8] Nevertheless, those measures did not make it to the final text. Nor could they be

6 Yu, P. K. (2011), "Six Secret (and Now Open) Fears of ACTA". *SMU Law Review* 64(3): 975–1094.

7 Office of the United States Trade Representative (2005), *2005 National Trade Estimate Report on Foreign Trade Barriers*. Washington, DC, p. 96.

8 Titled "Discussion Paper on a Possible Anti-Counterfeiting Trade Agreement," this leaked document is available at http://ipjustice.org/wp/wp-content/uploads/ACTA-discussion-paper-1.pdf.

found in the earlier consolidated draft released jointly by the negotiating parties in April 2010, shortly after the Wellington Round. Thus, those developing countries that choose to apply to join ACTA will have to adopt the high "TRIPS-plus" standards established solely by developed countries and their like-minded partners.

To be certain, countries are free to join ACTA on a voluntary basis. As the leaked discussion paper stated:

> In the initial phase, it is important to join a number of interested trading partners in setting out the parameters for an enforcement system that will function effectively in today's environment. As a second phase, other countries will have the option to join the agreement as part of an emerging consensus in favor of a strong IPR [intellectual property rights] enforcement standard.

Nevertheless, the optional nature of that two-step process is true only in theory. In reality, as Robin Gross rightly pointed out in the IP Justice White Paper, "few countries will have the muscle to refuse an 'invitation' to join."[9] This is particularly true when the carrot of trade benefits or development aid is dangling in front of them or when the United States is waving a threatening Section 301 stick.

Indeed, many developing countries, especially the smaller ones, would fear being left out. As Professor Geist observed at the time of the negotiations, these countries were confronted with "a stark choice – remain on the ACTA sidelines and face a future filled with pressure to implement its provisions or demand a seat at the table now."[10] Even today, more than three years after the agreement has been concluded, that stark choice continues to haunt these countries.

Some developing countries may also be tempted by the tangible benefits they could obtain through strengthening intellectual property protection and enforcement in the image of ACTA. These benefits range from technical assistance to conference and travel support and from the provision of latest equipment and technology to the ability to make internal demands for more enforcement personnel and a larger institutional budget.[11] In fact, many policymakers have focused their attention more on compliance with international standards than on promoting

9 Gross, R. (2008), "IP Justice White Paper on the Proposed Anti-Counterfeiting Trade Agreement (ACTA)". Available at http://ipjustice.org/wp/wp-content/uploads/IPJustice_ACTA-white-paper-mar2008.pdf, p. 2.

10 Geist, M. (2009), "The ACTA Threat to the Future of WIPO". Intellectual Property Watch, 14 April. Available at http://www.ip-watch.org/2009/04/14/the-acta-threat-to-the-future-of-wipo/.

11 Chow, D. C. K. (2000), "Counterfeiting in the People's Republic of China". *Washington University Law Quarterly* 78(1): 1–57, 30–31; Deere, C. (2009), *The Implementation Game: The TRIPS Agreement and the Global Politics of Intellectual Property Reform in Developing Countries*. Oxford University Press, Oxford, p. 200; Drahos, P. (2010), *The Global Governance of Knowledge: Patent Offices and Their Clients*. Cambridge University Press, Cambridge, p. 136; Mertha, A. C. (2005), *The Politics of Piracy: Intellectual Property in Contemporary China*. Cornell University Press, Ithaca, NY, p. 16.

innovation or developing an intellectual property system that suits their own needs, interests, conditions and priorities.[12]

In sum, by intentionally excluding the input and participation of developing countries, the ACTA parties will be able to set norms that have serious ramifications for these countries without the need to deal with their concession demands. Through the ACTA Committee, the contracting parties determine the terms under which developing countries accede to the agreement. As Robin Gross lamented in the IP Justice White Paper,

> ACTA takes a remarkably imperialistic worldview in that it attempts to regulate global IPR enforcement from the perspective of the world's wealthiest and to the detriment of the needs of developing nations and the global public interest. Developing countries are not permitted to participate in the negotiation of ACTA's terms, although they will be expected to abide by them.
>
> Through trade agreements like ACTA, IPR-exporting countries are able to impose policies that favor them onto the domestic legislation of IPR-importing countries. A clear example of neo-colonialism, ACTA will, at best, benefit a few private interests at the expense of the many.[13]

## IMPLICATIONS FOR THE INTERNATIONAL INTELLECTUAL PROPERTY SYSTEM

Apart from imposing high TRIPS-plus standards that do not correspond to the needs, interests, conditions and priorities of developing countries, ACTA and the freestanding, self-evolving architecture supported by the ACTA Committee could harm the international intellectual property system in three different ways. First, by embracing the "country club" approach to international norm setting, the ACTA negotiating parties have created great resentment among developing countries.[14] To make this approach even more unpalatable, countries that had been put on the USTR's Special 301 Watch List – such as Canada, South Korea and a few EU member states – were invited to join the negotiations. Meanwhile, the four biggest

[12] Deere, C. (2009), *The Implementation Game: The TRIPS Agreement and the Global Politics of Intellectual Property Reform in Developing Countries*. Oxford University Press, Oxford, p. 242; Maskus, K. E. and Reichman, J. H. (2005), "The Globalization of Private Knowledge Goods and the Privatization of Global Public Goods" in *International Public Goods and Transfer of Technology under a Globalized Intellectual Property Regime*, Maskus, K. E. and Reichman, J. H., eds. Cambridge University Press, Cambridge, p. 18.

[13] Gross, R. (2008), "IP Justice White Paper on the Proposed Anti-Counterfeiting Trade Agreement (ACTA)". Available at http://ipjustice.org/wp/wp-content/uploads/IPJustice_ACTA-white-papermar2008.pdf, pp. 8–9.

[14] Gervais, D. J. (2009), "China – Measures Affecting the Protection and Enforcement of Intellectual Property Rights". *American Journal of International Law* 103(3): 549–555, 555; IQsensato (2008), "The

middle-income countries – Brazil, Russia, India and China (the so-called BRIC countries) – and other similarly situated countries were all left out.[15]

Moreover, it is worth noting that all of the negotiating parties – except Morocco and Singapore – were members of the OECD. To some extent, ACTA has raised similar legitimacy questions as those confronting the now-failed Multilateral Agreement on Investment (MAI).[16] Using a two-phase approach, similar to the one outlined in the leaked discussion paper, MAI began in the OECD with the hope of extension to other non-OECD countries. One could also find striking resemblances between ACTA and the G-8 Financial Action Task Force.[17] Created in the G-7 to combat money laundering and later terrorist financing, that taskforce has now been extended to other OECD economies, as well as to a select group of non-OECD economies, such as Hong Kong and Singapore, and to regional organizations, such as the Gulf Cooperation Council (whose members include Bahrain, Kuwait, Oman, Qatar, Saudi Arabia and the United Arab Emirates).

The second line of harm concerns what commentators have widely described as "forum proliferation," "forum shifting," or "multiple forum capture."[18] To some extent, the creation of ACTA as a freestanding intellectual property forum resembles the earlier effort by developed countries to shift the intellectual property standard-setting forum from WIPO to GATT/WTO.[19] As Susan Sell observed, ACTA "would create an additional international intellectual property governance layer atop an already remarkably complex and increasingly incoherent intellectual property regime."[20]

Proposed Anti-Counterfeiting Trade Agreement (ACTA): Global Policy Implications". *In Focus*. 2 June", p. 4. Yu, P. K. (2011), "ACTA and Its Complex Politics". *WIPO Journal* 3(1): 1–16, 2–9.

15 Yu, P. K. (2013), "The Middle Intellectual Property Powers" in *Law and Development in Middle-Income Countries*, Ginsburg, T. and Peerenboom, R., eds. Cambridge University Press, Cambridge.

16 Muchlinski, P. T. (2000), "The Rise and Fall of the Multilateral Agreement on Investment: Where Now?" *International Lawyer* 34(3): 1033–1053; Salzman, J. (2000), "Labor Rights, Globalization and Institutions: The Role and Influence of the Organization for Economic Cooperation and Development". *Michigan Journal of International Law* 21(4): 769–848, 804–831.

17 Shams, H. M. (2004), "'Club Multilateralism' and Global Supranationalism: The Case of FATF" in *Multilateralism v. Unilateralism: Policy Choices in a Global Society*, Attanasio, J. B. and Norton, J. J., eds. British Institute of International and Comparative Law, London.

18 Braithwaite, J. and Drahos, P. (2000), *Global Business Regulation*. Cambridge University Press, Cambridge, pp. 564–571; Helfer, L. R. (2004), "Regime Shifting: The TRIPs Agreement and New Dynamics of International Intellectual Property Lawmaking". *Yale Journal of International Law* 29(1): 1–83; May, C. (2007), *The World Intellectual Property Organization: Resurgence and the Development Agenda*. Routledge, London, p. 66; Muñoz Tellez, V. (2009), "The Changing Global Governance of Intellectual Property Enforcement: A New Challenge for Developing Countries" in *Intellectual Property Enforcement: International Perspectives*, Li, X. and Correa, C. M., eds. Edward Elgar Publishing, Cheltenham, p. 9.

19 Yu, P. K. (2004), "Currents and Crosscurrents in the International Intellectual Property Regime". *Loyola of Los Angeles Law Review* 38(1): 323–443, 357–358.

20 Sell, S. K. (2010), "The Global IP Upward Ratchet, Anti-Counterfeiting and Piracy Enforcement Efforts: The State of Play". *PIJIP Research Paper no. 15*, American University Washington College of Law, p. 9.

This additional governance layer will further fragment that regime. Given the developing countries' lack of resources, expertise, leadership, negotiation sophistication and bargaining power, such fragmentation will make it particularly costly and difficult for them to negotiate and coordinate policies.[21] By facilitating the development of ACTA as a freestanding forum, the ACTA Committee therefore would help developed and like-minded countries counter and reduce the opposition from developing countries. Even if developed and like-minded countries do not succeed in inducing their developing counterparts to accept higher TRIPS-plus standards, ACTA would enable them to at least retain the status quo.

More problematic, the agreement's self-evolving, self-reinforcing architecture could lead to the creation of what Kal Raustiala described as "strategic inconsistencies." Occurring "when actors deliberately seek to create inconsistency via a new rule crafted in another forum in an effort to alter or put pressure on an earlier rule," these inconsistencies will pave the way for future changes in the international intellectual property system.[22]

In fact, the present text of ACTA is already inconsistent with Recommendation 45 of the adopted WIPO Development Agenda, which calls for WIPO "to approach intellectual property enforcement in the context of broader societal interests and especially development-oriented concerns." The process used to negotiate ACTA took into consideration neither the broader societal interests nor development-oriented concerns. That process was also inconsistent with the intention of the World Summit on the Information Society, and later the Internet Governance Forum, to promote a "multilateral, multi-stakeholder, democratic and transparent" policy dialogue on Internet governance.[23]

As if those inconsistencies were not troubling enough, ACTA threatens to undermine the goals of both the Doha Declaration on the TRIPS Agreement and Public Health and the proposed Article 31*bis* of the TRIPS Agreement. To be certain, the negotiating parties had paid lip service to the Doha Declaration, mentioning it in the last recital of the preamble. Upon close inspection, however, ACTA, in particular its provisions on border measures and civil and criminal infringement, threatens the much-needed access to essential medicines in developing countries.[24]

[21] Benvenisti, E. and Downs, G. W. (2007), "The Empire's New Clothes: Political Economy and the Fragmentation of International Law". *Stanford Law Review* 60(2): 595–631; Yu, P. K. (2009), "A Tale of Two Development Agendas". *Ohio Northern University Law Review* 35(2): 465–573, 555–556.

[22] Raustiala, K. (2007), "Density and Conflict in International Intellectual Property Law". *U.C. Davis Law Review* 40(3): 1021–1038, 1027–1028; Yu, P. K. (2007), "International Enclosure, the Regime Complex, and Intellectual Property Schizophrenia". *Michigan State Law Review* 2007(1): 1–33, 17.

[23] World Summit on the Information Society (2005), "Tunis Agenda for the Information Society". WSIS-05/TUNIS/DOC/6(Rev. 1)-E.

[24] Baker, B. K. (2011), "ACTA – Risks of Third-Party Enforcement for Access to Medicines". *American University International Law Review* 26(3): 579–599; Flynn, S. M. and Madhani, B. (2011), *ACTA and Access to Medicines*. Available at http://ssrn.com/abstract=1980865.

The final line of harm concerns the agreement's negative impact on traditional fora for setting international intellectual property norms, including both norms at WIPO and WTO. By facilitating the development of ACTA as a freestanding, self-evolving forum, the ACTA Committee undermines the stability of the international trading system and the preference for the multilateral process.[25] By alienating the trading partners of the ACTA negotiating parties, the agreement's "country club" arrangement has also made it more difficult for the international community to undertake future multilateral discussions.

Although the TRIPS Agreement, in the view of the ACTA negotiating parties, has yet to provide up-to-date protection to meet the needs of intellectual property right holders, both developed and developing countries have expended a tremendous amount of time, effort, resources and energy to create the TRIPS Agreement and the present international intellectual property enforcement regime. Because such creation entailed a considerable amount of coordination, negotiation and compromise, the costs of undermining such a well-built system are not to be ignored.

ACTA also has the potential to threaten the future development of WIPO, including all the important work it has done in the wake of the establishment of the Development Agenda.[26] It is indeed no surprise that Francis Gurry, the WIPO Director General, has expressed concern that the ACTA negotiating parties have "tak[en] matters into their own hands to seek solutions outside of the multilateral system to the detriment of inclusiveness of the present system."[27] Likewise, Professor Geist warned:

> ACTA is far more than a simple trade agreement. Rather, it envisions the establishment of a super-structure that replicates many of the responsibilities currently assumed by the World Intellectual Property Organization. Given the public acknowledgement by negotiating countries that ACTA is a direct response to perceived gridlock at WIPO, some might wonder whether ACTA is ultimately designed to replace WIPO as the primary source of international [intellectual property] law and policy making.[28]

In sum, by creating a new, freestanding and self-evolving forum for setting international intellectual property standards, ACTA would take away the opportunity

25 Atik, J. (2012), "ACTA and the Destabilization of TRIPS" in *Sustainable Technology Transfer: A Guide to Global Aid & Trade Development*, Lidgard, H. H., Atik, J. and Nguyen, T. T., eds. Kluwer Law International, Alphen aan den Rijn, p. 145.

26 Yu, P. K. (2009), "A Tale of Two Development Agendas". *Ohio Northern University Law Review* 35(2): 465–573, 515–522.

27 Saez, C. (2010), "ACTA a Sign of Weakness in Multilateral System, WIPO Head Says". Intellectual Property Watch. 30 June. Available at http://www.ip-watch.org/2010/06/30/acta-a-sign-of-weakness-in-multilateral-system-wipo-head-says/.

28 Geist, M. (2010), "Toward an ACTA Super-Structure: How ACTA May Replace WIPO". Available at http://www.michaelgeist.ca/content/view/4910/125/.

to strengthen enforcement norms in the current regimes – whether WTO or WIPO. The creation of multiple fora with overlapping jurisdictions has also created serious challenges for governments in the developing world. It is important to remember that not every country has sufficient resources and ability to undertake discussions in multiple fora. The more fora there are, the more difficult it will be for these countries to dedicate efforts to strengthening enforcement norms in a particular forum.

## CONCLUSION

Article 36 lays out the provisions governing the ACTA Committee. Although these provisions are seemingly mundane and highly administrative, they represent some of the most far-reaching and dangerous provisions in the agreement. First, the Committee's accession, amendment, administrative and ancillary powers enable ACTA to evolve into a much stronger intellectual property agreement than the one laid out in the present text. Second, the Committee's power to determine the terms of accession, coupled with the developed countries' ability to extend TRIPS-plus norms beyond the ACTA club, enables the ACTA parties to set norms for developing countries without their input and participation. Finally, by facilitating ACTA as a freestanding intellectual property agreement, the ACTA Committee undermines the stability of the international trading system and the preference for the multilateral process. The Committee also stifles further development of WIPO and the WTO, including the enforcement discussions at those fora.

PART II

# Domestic Legislative Challenges

# 9

# ACTA's Constitutional Problem in the United States

*Sean Flynn*

## INTRODUCTION

As explained elsewhere in this series, the Anti-Counterfeiting Trade Agreement (ACTA)[1] was negotiated under unprecedented secrecy for a multilateral process. In some countries, part of the justification for why the agreement should be seen as legitimate and lawful despite the lack of public process accompanying its formation resided in the fact that it would ultimately have to be approved by an elected legislature. The EU had long explained ACTA this way.[2] Indeed, soon after ACTA was finalised, it was presented to the European Parliament, which soundly rejected it.

Throughout the treaty's negotiation, US negotiators and officials held steadfast to an insistence that no congressional process would be needed for the agreement's ratification. This is despite the US Constitution giving the Senate the authority to advise and consent to treaties, and Congress the authority to make legislation on intellectual property laws. This chapter explains and criticises theories offered by US officials as to why ACTA does not need to obtain congressional approval. Ultimately, the audience for this information is not restricted to those in the United States being subject to a potentially unconstitutional international lawmaking process. Negotiators and citizens of other countries, including those involved in the ongoing Transpacific Partnership (TPP) Agreement negotiations, may benefit from a better understanding of the potential legal infirmities of the current US approach, which is bound to be

Thanks to Oona Hathaway, Amy Kapczynski, Peter Yu, Henning Grosse Ruse-Khan, David Levine and Chris Sprigman for many helpful comments and discussions. Parts of this chapter from a previous version were published as Sean M. Flynn, *ACTA's Constitutional Problem: The Treaty is Not a Treaty*, 26 AUILR 903 (2011), and in *American University, WCL Research Paper* No. 2012–04.

1 *See* Peter K. Yu, *Six Secret (and Now Open) Fears of ACTA*, 64 *SMU L. Rev.* at 4–15. *See also* Chapter 10 in this volume.

2 *See* Resolution of 10 March 2010 on the transparency and state of play of the ACTA negotiations, EUR. PARL. DOC. P7_TA(2010)0058 (2010) (resolving that the ACTA Treaty will not enter into force in the European Union until the European Parliament gives its consent).

raised elsewhere. The narrative serves as a warning to other countries where international agreements are currently subject to parliamentary approval but could likewise see proposals to remove that important check from the process.

## ACTA AS A SOLE EXECUTIVE AGREEMENT

During the ACTA negotiations, the United States Trade Representative's (USTR) first descriptions of the constitutional process that would be followed for its ratification under US law was that it could be entered as a "sole executive agreement" that did not require any congressional approval. USTR argued that the president could so act because the treaty's terms would be consistent with existing US law.[3]

The US Constitution explicitly defines one mechanism for the making of binding international treaties.[4] Article II section 2 gives the president the power to "make" treaties and provides that such agreements become part of the supreme law of the United States with a two-thirds vote of the Senate.[5] But other mechanisms for making binding international law have been interpreted to exist by virtue of other powers defined in the Constitution, including a narrow class of "sole executive agreements' that can be entered by the president alone by virtue of his independent constitutional authority.[6]

The key to the constitutionality of a sole executive agreement is that the subject matter of the treaty must reside in the sole executive province of the president. Such agreements have been found valid, for example, when made in performance of authority to act as Commander in Chief of the Army and Navy[7]; to receive ambassadors from, and thereby recognise, foreign nations[8]; and to issue pardons.[9] There

3 *See* Questions for Ambassador Ron Kirk. United States Senate Committee on Finance. Hearing on the 2011 Trade Agenda. March 9, 2011, available at http://keionline.org/sites/default/files/RonKirk_SFC_9Mar2011.pdf, accessed May 12, 2011.

4 *See* INS v. Chadha, 462 U.S. 919, 955 (1983) (discussing the Senate's treaty ratification power as one of a limited set of Constitutional unicameral actions that have the full force of law).

5 U.S. CONST. art. II, § 2.

6 *See* RESTATEMENT (THIRD) OF THE FOREIGN RELATIONS LAW OF THE UNITED STATES § 303(4) (1987) (stating that the president may enter a binding international agreement without congressional assent only for a "matter that falls within his independent powers under the Constitution"); *see also* Youngstown Sheet & Tube Co. v. Sawyer, 343 U.S. 579, 635 (1952) (admonishing that when the president acts pursuant to an "express or implied authorization of Congress, his authority is at its maximum," but "in absence of either a congressional grant or denial of authority, he can only rely upon his own independent powers").

7 U.S. CONST. art. II, § 2; *see* Oona A. Hathaway, *Presidential Power over International Law: Restoring the Balance*, 119 Yale L.J. (2009), at 151–152 (citing "defense" as the area of foreign policy with the most executive agreements).

8 U.S. CONST. art. II, § 3.

9 U.S. CONST. art. II, § 2; Bradford R. Clark, *Domesticating Sole Executive Agreements*, 93 Va. L. Rev. 1573, 1596 (2007) (describing the "vast majority" of sole executive agreements as "unobjectionable … means of exercising [the President's] independent statutory or constitutional powers").

are also a large number of (often mundane)[10] executive agreements grounded in the president's general power to "take Care that the Laws be faithfully executed."[11] In a small number of other borderline cases, such as settling foreign claims against the United States, the long historical practice of acquiescence by Congress has been used to justify sole executive action.[12] All such valid sole executive agreements, as long as performed within the bounds of constitutionally delegated power, "have as much legal validity and obligation as if they proceeded from the legislature."[13]

USTR's classification of ACTA as a sole executive agreement was highly unusual in that it did not fit any of the established categories for unilateral policy making by the executive. The final text of ACTA includes a substantial chapter defining a new international minimum "Legal Framework for Enforcement of Intellectual Property Rights."[14]

10 Oona A. Hathaway, *Presidential Power over International Law: Restoring the Balance*, 119 Yale L.J. 140, 149–150 (2009) (including, for example, "'energy-efficient labeling programs' [or] air transport agreement[s]" with a foreign country).

11 U.S. CONST. art. II, § 3; *see* Hathaway, *supra* at 154–155 n.29 (finding approximately 375 sole executive agreements between 1990 and 2000 on matters including "Agreed Minutes" and "Implementing Procedures").

12 CONG. RESEARCH SERV., *supra* at 90; Clark, *supra* at 1582, 1615, 1660 (noting that the practice of settling claims through executive agreements began more than 200 years ago).

13 United States v. Pink, 315 U.S. 203, 230 (1942) (citing THE FEDERALIST No. 64, (John Jay) (Independent Journal, 1788)) (describing the equal legal validity of "[a]ll Constitutional acts of power, whether in the executive or in the judicial department"); CONG. RESEARCH SERV., *supra* at 92 ("Sole executive agreements validly concluded pursuant to one or more of the President's independent powers under Article II of the Constitution may be accorded status as Supreme Law of the Land...."). *See* Am. Ins. Ass'n v. Garamendi, 539 U.S. 396, 413–17 (2003) (recognizing that an executive agreement may preempt otherwise permissible state laws given the concern for uniformity in dealing with foreign nations); CONG. RESEARCH SERV., *supra* at 95 (acknowledging that while a sole executive agreement within the president's constitutional authority has been held as valid federal law, "the question as to the effect of a Presidential agreement upon a prior conflicting act of Congress has apparently not yet been completely settled") (internal quotation and citation omitted); *see also* RESTATEMENT (THIRD) OF THE FOREIGN RELATIONS LAW OF THE UNITED STATES § 115 Reporter's Note 5 (1987) (explaining that constitutional acts, whether done by the executive, judicial or legislative branch, have the same legal status as federal law but could supersede one another depending on the circumstances). *But see* United States v. Guy W. Capps, Inc., 204 F. 2d 655, 659–60 (4th Cir. 1953), *aff'd on other grounds*, 348 U.S. 296 (1955) ("[W]hatever the power of the executive with respect to making executive trade agreements regulating foreign commerce in the absence of action by Congress, it is clear that the executive may not through entering into such an agreement avoid complying with a regulation prescribed by Congress.").

14 Anti-Counterfeiting Trade Agreement, December 3, 2010 6–17 [hereinafter ACTA Text – Dec. 3, 2010], available at http://trade.ec.europa.eu/doclib/docs/2010/december/tradoc_147079.pdf (containing eleven pages of text in Articles 6–27, which comprise "Chapter Two: Legal Framework for Enforcement of Intellectual Property Rights"). CF Youngstown Sheet & Tube Co. v. Sawyer, 343 U.S. 579, 587 (1952) ("In the framework of our Constitution, the President's power to see that the laws are faithfully executed refutes the idea that he is to be a lawmaker.").

A main argument of USTR for the use of the sole executive agreement model was that ACTA would not require a change to any existing US law. The factual premise of this argument was often debated. ACTA set up broad and abstract standards that could be interpreted in different ways in any ultimate adjudication under it. A study by the Congressional Research Service concluded that "[d]epending on how broadly or narrowly several passages from the ACTA draft text are interpreted, it appears that certain provisions of federal intellectual property law could be regarded as inconsistent with ACTA."[15] In any case, the consistency of an agreement with current US law has never been held to authorise a sole executive agreement on the matter where its subjects would normally fall within Congress's plenary powers. Intellectual property and the regulation of foreign trade are matters delegated to Congress under Article I Section 8 of the Constitution. They thus fall outside the scope of what can be entered through a sole executive agreement. The policy implications of such an interpretation are clear. If valid, ACTA as a sole executive agreement would subject the United States to international remedies for changing its law in a way inconsistent with the agreement – it thus binds Congress's policymaking options without its consent. The agreement is therefore making law – imposing new supra-constitutional constraints on it – without any input by the lawmaking arm of government.

These points were made repeatedly in a series of public letters and opinions of legal scholars.[16] USTR responded to the protests and criticisms through a "fact sheet" released on the occasion of the US signing of ACTA. The statement pointed to four agreements as precedents for entering international intellectual property agreements without congressional consent. Of these, only one – a pre-TRIPS IP agreement with Hungary – may not have been sent to Congress for post-signature ratification. The other three were actually ratified by the Senate.[17]

[15] CONGRESSIONAL RESEARCH SERVICE, POTENTIAL IMPLICATIONS FOR FEDERAL LAW RAISED BY THE OCTOBER 2010 DRAFT OF THE ANTI-COUNTERFEITING TRADE AGREEMENT (ACTA), October 29, 2010, available at http://www.techdirt.com/articles/20110421/16580813994/crs-report-withheld-ustr-confirms-that-acta-language-is-quite-questionable.shtml.

[16] *See Academics' Letter to President Obama*, PIJIP (Oct. 28, 2010) http://www.wcl.american.edu/pijip/go/academics10282010 (arguing that proposed terms in ACTA would be contrary to US law, threaten public interest concerns and may violate constitutional requirements for international law making); *Submission by 30 Professors to USTR*, INFOJUSTICE.ORG (Feb. 15, 2011) http://infojustice.org/wp-content/uploads/2011/02/ACTA-Comment-Thirty-Professors-USTR-2010-0014.pdf (docket #ustr-2010-0014) (same); *Law Professor Letter to Senate Finance Committee*, INFOJUSTICE.ORG (May 2012) http://infojustice.org/senatefinance-may2012 (urging Senate to demand Congressional ratification process for ACTA to comply with US Constitution). *See also* Jack Goldsmith and Lawrence Lessig, Anti-counterfeiting agreement raises constitutional concerns, *Washington Post* (March 26, 2010) http://www.washingtonpost.com/wp-dyn/content/article/2010/03/25/AR2010032502403.html; Oona A. Hathaway and Amy Kapczynski, Going It Alone: The Anti-Counterfeiting Trade Agreement as a Sole Executive Agreement, ASIL Insights, http://www.asil.org/insights110824.cfm

[17] *See* Sean Flynn, *USTR's Precedents do not justify ACTA as sole executive agreement*, http://infojustice.org/archives/5731

Soon after the signing of ACTA and the release of the fact sheet that accompanied it, Senator Ron Wyden, Chairman of the Senate Subcommittee on International Trade, Customs, and Global Competitiveness, weighed into the debate. In a letter to the president of the United States, citing the concerns of law professors, Wyden recounted:

> As you know, the executive branch lacks constitutional authority to enter binding international agreements on matters under Congress's plenary powers, including the Article I powers to regulate foreign commerce and protect intellectual property. Yet, through ACTA and without your clarification, the USTR looks to be claiming the authority to do just that.
>
> The USTR long asserts authority to enter ACTA as a 'sole executive agreement' with no congressional authorization or approval. In its latest explanation on this topic, the USTR stated:
>
> "ACTA is consistent with existing US law and does not require the enactment of implementing legislation. The United States may therefore enter into and carry out the requirements of the Agreement under existing legal authority, just as it has done with other trade agreements."
>
> This statement by the USTR confuses the issue by conflating two separate stages of the process required for binding the US to international agreements: entry and implementation. It may be possible for the US to implement ACTA or any other trade agreement, once validly entered, without legislation if the agreement requires no change in US law. But, regardless of whether the agreement requires changes in US law, a point that is contested with respect to ACTA, the executive branch lacks constitutional authority to enter a binding international agreement covering issues delegated by the Constitution to Congress' authority, absent congressional approval.[18]

Wyden's letter concluded with a request that the president "formally declare that ACTA does not create any international obligations for the US" or "provide the Congress, and the public, with a legal rationale for why ACTA should not be considered by the Congress, and work with us to ensure that we reach a common understanding of the proper way for the US to proceed with ACTA."[19]

Ambassador Ron Kirk, the US Trade Representative, responded to Senator Wyden on December 7, 2011.[20] The response largely avoided the issues raised by Senator Wyden, repeating the assertion that "US Negotiators were careful to ensure that ACTA is fully consistent with US law," and that "Congress will not need to enact

18 http://www.wyden.senate.gov/news/press-releases/wyden-to-president-isnt-congress-supposed-to-approve-international-trade-agreements

19 *Id.*

20 http://infojustice.org/wp-content/uploads/2012/01/Kirk-12072011.pdf

legislation in order for the United States to implement the agreement." The letter also cited a "longstanding practice" of entering intellectual property agreements without congressional authorisation or consent, citing agreements dating to 1994.

Dissatisfied with the response, Senator Wyden wrote again to the administration, this time to Department of State Legal Advisor Harold Koh.[21] Wyden's letter asked several specific legal questions, including:

> If ACTA is entered by the President without Congressional consent, what will be the nature of the agreement and its legal implications under US and international law?
>
> Would the US be in violation of the agreement if the Congress changed federal law in a way not consistent with the agreement, for example by ridding our law of statutory damages for online copyright infringement?
>
> What are the constitutional limits on the President binding the US to legislative minimum standard agreements over matters delegated to Congress under Article I Section 8 of the Constitution? Is the President free to bind the US to any international agreement he chooses merely because he deems them to be consistent with US law?

Koh's response affirmed that ACTA would bind Congress. He explained that, once in force, "subsequent changes in US law" could "put the United States in breach of its ACTA obligations," unless it convinced "the other parties that the ACTA should be amended" or "the United States could withdraw from the ACTA."[22]

After providing this cold comfort, the letter went on to shift the legal justification that the administration had been using for its avoidance of congressional authorisation. Koh's surprising response was that Congress had *already* approved it:

> Congress has passed legislation explicitly calling for the Executive Branch to work with other countries to enhance enforcement of intellectual property rights. For example, the Prioritizing Resources and Organization for Intellectual Property [PRO-IP] Act of 2008, Pub. L. No. 110–403, codified at 15 USC. 8113(a), calls for the Executive Branch to develop and implement a plan aimed at "eliminating (…) international counterfeiting and infringement networks" and to "work (…) with other countries to establish international standards and policies for the effective protection and enforcement of intellectual property rights." The ACTA helps to answer that legislative call.

The letter concluded by referring to ACTA as "part of a long line of trade agreements that were similarly concluded by successive Administrations."

[21] http://infojustice.org/wp-content/uploads/2012/01/Wyden-01052012.pdf.

[22] http://infojustice.org/wp-content/uploads/2012/03/84365507-State-Department-Response-to-Wyden-on-ACTA.pdf

## ACTA AS AN EX-ANTE CONGRESSIONAL-EXECUTIVE AGREEMENT

By relying on the "explicit call" of the PRO-IP Act, Koh was shifting the administration's description of ACTA from that of a sole executive agreement to a different class of lawful international agreements known as congressional-executive agreements. Such agreements, although they have not been approved through the treaty clause, are recognised as lawful international agreements by virtue of Congress's independent authority under Article I Section 8 of the Constitution to regulate foreign commerce.[23] In a congressional-executive agreement, Congress passes through both houses and the president signs legislation either delegating ex ante authority to enter into agreements or approving the agreement itself ex post.[24] Koh's argument was that Congress, through the PRO-IP Act, delegated authority to enter ACTA ex ante.

There is growing academic literature documenting and analysing the relatively recent shift in the United States, over the last twenty-five years, toward the use of congressional-executive agreements in international lawmaking.[25] Academics debate the extent to which Congress *should* delegate broad authority to the president to make law through congressional-executive agreements, particularly through the vague and open-ended delegations of ex ante authority.[26] It is generally accepted, however, that agreements made with ex ante congressional authorisation or ex post consent are lawful.[27] But they are only lawful because of the congressional action

[23] *See* John C. Yoo, *Laws as Treaties?: The Constitutionality of Congressional-Executive Agreements*, 99 Mich. L. Rev. 757, 768–771 (2001) (describing the historical debate over treaties infringing on statutory power).

[24] Bradford R. Clark, *Domesticating Sole Executive Agreements*, 93 VA. L. REV. 1573, 1596 (2007) (stating that "congressional-executive agreements (if enacted as 'Laws') qualify as 'the supreme Law of the Land'").

[25] *See, e.g.*, Curtis A. Bradley & Martin S. Flaherty, *Executive Power Essentialism and Foreign Affairs*, 102 MICH. L. REV. 545, 548 (2004); Oona A. Hathaway, *Presidential Power over International Law: Restoring the Balance*, 119 YALE L.J. 140, 149–150 (2009) (explaining that executive agreements now account for the great majority of international agreements entered into by the United States); Saikrishna B. Prakash & Michael D. Ramsey, *The Executive Power over Foreign Affairs*, 111 YALE L.J. 231, 252–256 (2001); Laurence H. Tribe, *Taking Text and Structure Seriously: Reflections on Free-Form Method in Constitutional Interpretation*, 108 HARV. L. REV. 1221, 1265–1269 (1995); Michael P. Van Alstine, *Executive Aggrandizement in Foreign Affairs Lawmaking*, 54 UCLA L. REV. 309, 337–359 (2006); Yoo, *supra* note 41, at 768–771 (2001).

[26] *Compare* Yoo, *supra* at 763 (supporting congressional-executive agreements as a means to "[preserve] Congress's constitutional powers over matters such as international commerce"), *with* Hathaway, *supra* at 146–147 (criticizing the growth of ex ante congressional-executive agreements because Congress grants broad executive authority to negotiate the agreements while reserving no further role for itself).

[27] *See* CONG. RESEARCH SERV. at 5 (stating that the constitutionality of congressional-executive agreements is considered "well established"). *But see* Tribe, *supra* at 1265–1270 (describing how congressional-executive agreements may violate the Treaty Clause).

validating them.[28] And thus, after Koh's letter, the inquiry into ACTA's constitutionality shifted to whether the PRO-IP Act language cited by Koh sufficiently authorised ACTA.[29]

Another group of law professors took on the task of analysing Koh's argument in a 16 May 2012 letter to members of the Senate Finance Committee (the Committee with primary jurisdiction for treaty ratifications). The letter concluded that Koh's argument that ACTA was authorised ex ante by the PRO-IP Act "fails on closer inspection." The letter explained:

> First, the plain language of Section 8113(a) of the PRO-IP Act does not authorize USTR to bind the US to any international agreement. Rather, the section merely describes the purposes of a "Joint Strategic Plan against counterfeiting and infringement," to be coordinated among multiple agencies by the Intellectual Property Enforcement Coordinator (IPEC). The purposes of the Plan include "working with other countries to establish international standards and policies for the enforcement of intellectual property rights." Nowhere in Section 8113 does the PRO-IP Act mention the negotiation of international agreements. Rather, subsection (f), which describes specific means for "enhancing enforcement efforts of foreign governments," requires only "programs to provide training and technical assistance to foreign governments for the purpose of enhancing the efforts of such governments to enforce laws against counterfeiting and infringement." Read in its context, the language cited by Koh as justifying ACTA does no more than require a multi-agency plan to provide technical assistance to foreign governments. Indeed, the cited passage is not addressed to USTR.
>
> Second, the PRO-IP Act cannot be an ex ante authorization for ACTA because it was not temporally ex ante. The ACTA negotiation began in 2007. PRO-IP was not passed until 2008, and was passed at a time Congress was being told that ACTA would be entered as a Sole-Executive Agreement – requiring no Congressional approval at all. The administration did not seek, and Congress has not given, ex ante authorization to bind the US to ACTA.

The law professors' letter asked the Senate Finance Committee to act affirmatively to cut off the administration's planned course of action and insist on a constitutional process for the ultimate ratification of the agreement. It asked the members to "secure from the Administration a public pledge to send ACTA to the Senate as a treaty, or to the Congress as an ex post Congressional-Executive Agreement," or "to pass legislation that would prevent the United States from binding itself to ACTA without express Congressional consent." Legislation to this effect was offered

[28] *See* Yoo, *supra* at 823 ("Not only are congressional-executive agreements acceptable, but in areas of Congress's Article I, Section 8 powers, they are – in a sense – constitutionally required.").

[29] *See* http://infojustice.org/archives/9072

by Senator Wyden.[30] But before any Congressional action took place, the EU Parliament rejected ACTA by a large margin, which halted any momentum toward its ratification in the United States as well.

## ACTA AS LAWMAKING "BETWEEN THE STOOLS"

Although the political storm around ACTA has dissipated in the wake of its rejection by Europe, State Legal Advisor Harold Koh addressed the controversy again in a recent lecture at Yale University. The lecture once more shifted the official legal justification for entry into ACTA without congressional approval back to the 'sole executive agreement' rationale. He no longer referred to the PRO-IP Act as giving "explicit" ex ante authorisation of ACTA. In an apparent admission that the agreement cannot be so justified, he returned an explanation of ACTA as a sole executive agreement:

> [W]e in the Legal Adviser's Office were surprised to find controversy surrounding the Executive's authority to enter into the Anti-Counterfeiting Trade Agreement, or ACTA, a multilateral agreement on enforcing intellectual property rights. [A] surprisingly large number of law professors questioned the Executive's legal authority even to enter the agreement. They said, "I don't see an express ex ante congressional authorization, so it can't fit into the congressional-executive agreement box, nor does this look like a traditional topic for a sole executive agreement. Since it falls between the stools, that must mean the US lacks any authority to enter the agreement!"
>
> But authority in this area sits not on isolated stools, but rather runs in a spectrum. Why was entering the agreement a legally available option? First, while Congress did not expressly pre-authorize this particular agreement, it did pass legislation calling on the Executive to "work (…) with other countries to establish international standards and policies for the effective protection and enforcement of intellectual property rights."
>
> Further, we and USTR determined that the agreement negotiated fit within the fabric of existing law; it was fully consistent with existing law and did not require any further legislation to implement.
>
> We also surveyed how the political branches have dealt with similar agreements in the past, and found that Congress' call for executive action to protect intellectual property rights arose against the background of a long series of agreements on the

30 A proposed bill introduced by Senator Wyden stated: "the President may not accept, or provide for the entry into force with respect to the United States of, any legally binding trade agreement that imposes obligations on the United States with respect to the enforcement of intellectual property rights, including the Anti-Counterfeiting Trade Agreement, without the formal and express approval of Congress." http://infojustice.org/wp-content/uploads/2012/03/Wyden-ACTA-Amendment.pdf

> specific question of intellectual property protection done in a similar fashion. What we saw in practice resembles a phenomenon I called in my book The National Security Constitution 'quasi-constitutional custom,' a widespread and consistent practice of executive branch activity that Congress, by its conduct, has essentially accepted. In this respect, the ACTA resembled the Algiers Accords that ended the Iranian Hostages crisis, whose constitutionality was broadly upheld by the Supreme Court 31 years ago in Dames & Moore v. Regan. There, the Supreme Court upheld the Algiers Accords by relying not on any particular express ex ante congressional authorization, but rather, on 'closely related' legislation enacted in the same area and a long history of Executive Branch practice of concluding claims settlement agreements. Although the Algiers Accords, like ACTA, did not fall neatly into any of these three 'boxes', the Supreme Court in Dames & Moore easily upheld the constitutionality of the Algiers Accords and found a "legislative intent to accord the President broad discretion" and, citing the Steel Seizure Case, noted that such legislation "may be considered to invite 'measures on independent presidential responsibility.'"

Koh's reliance on the "long history" of claims settlements by presidents returns to an attempt to justify ACTA as a valid sole executive agreement of the kind approved by the Supreme Court for the centuries-old practice of settling foreign claims. These settlements have indeed been justified by a long historical practice of acquiescence by Congress.[31] But the long history of congressional acquiescence in this area – reaching back to the early 1900s – is a lot longer than for international intellectual property agreements (the first of which was entered in the 1990s).[32] And they are very different in kind – historically they have been used to settle claims in which the United States receives foreign funds, and therefore do not directly implicate congressional spending authority.[33]

What Koh's statement suggests most clearly is that the question of ACTA's constitutionality must now be taken to a different forum. The administration is not backing down in the face of a relative onslaught of scholarly opinion against it. Although the question is a constitutional one, it is unlikely to be remedied by courts. A similar question was refused to be heard by courts with respect to US entry into the WTO through a congressional-executive agreement rather than an Article II treaty. That issue was deemed a "political question" that Congress could resolve through its legislative power and the courts had no jurisdiction to intervene.[34] Similar reasoning

[31] CONG. RESEARCH SERV., *supra* at 90; Clark, *supra* at 1582, 1615, 1660 (noting that the practice of settling claims through executive agreements began over 200 years ago).

[32] Oona Hathaway, *supra* at 171.

[33] Oona Hathaway, *supra* at 171 (noting that, historically, "sole executive agreements were used for claims settlements only when the United States or a U.S. citizen was the recipient of foreign funds").

[34] *Made in the USA Foundation v. United States*, 242 F.2d 1300 (11th Cir. 2001) (refusing to review whether NAFTA was unconstitutionally entered by executive agreement rather than through an Art. II treaty).

would likely apply in any court challenge here; it is within Congress's unique, and possibly sole, province to pass legislation forbidding the executive from binding the United States to international intellectual property agreements without its authorisation or consent.[35]

## A TREATY JUST THE SAME

One reason that congressional action is particularly needed in this case is that there is little in international law to stop the president from binding the United States to laws that Congress does not approve. International law determines the legal effect of international agreements. Although the president cannot make domestic law without Congress, he can unilaterally bind the United States under international law. Under international law, every nation-state has the capacity to conclude international agreements, and heads of state are presumptively authorised to represent a state for such purposes.[36] A country "may not invoke a violation of its internal law to vitiate its consent to be bound."[37]

As an international agreement between the negotiating parties, ACTA would bind all signatories to abide by its framework.[38] Parties to an international treaty with binding obligations must not derogate from its obligations and must perform them in good faith.[39] Accordingly, even though ACTA may not be enforceable domestically, it will nonetheless be a binding international agreement, and the parties, including the United States, must perform its obligations in good faith.

Currently, ACTA lacks a forum for enforcement or dispute resolution. But that hole in ACTA does not mean the agreement lacks binding effect. "Under international law, a state that has violated a legal obligation to another state is required to terminate the violation and, ordinarily, to make reparation, including in appropriate

35 *See* Wyden Amendment *supra*.

36 *See, e.g.*, Vienna Convention, Articles. 6, 7; RESTATEMENT (THIRD) OF THE FOREIGN RELATIONS LAW OF THE UNITED STATES § 311 (1987); Van Alstine, *supra* at n.62 ("Under international law, the president, except in extreme circumstances, has the authority to bind the United States even where he exceeds his domestic constitutional authority.").

37 RESTATEMENT (THIRD) OF THE FOREIGN RELATIONS LAW OF THE UNITED STATES § 311(3); *accord* Vienna Convention, art. 46 (noting that the violation of internal law must be "manifest" and concern a rule of "fundamental importance" to evade obligations under international law).

38 *See* ACTA Text – Dec. 3, 2010, art. 2 para 1 (stating that "[e]ach Party shall give effect to the provisions of this Agreement"); RESTATEMENT (THIRD) OF THE FOREIGN RELATIONS LAW OF THE UNITED STATES § 301(1) (defining "international agreement" as "an agreement between two or more states … that is intended to be legally binding and is governed by international law.").

39 *See* Vienna Convention, art. 26; RESTATEMENT (THIRD) OF THE FOREIGN RELATIONS LAW OF THE UNITED STATES § 321 (describing the doctrine of *pacta sunt servanda* ("agreements must be kept")). *Cf. See* Vienna Convention, *supra* art. 27 (stating that "[a] party may not invoke the provisions of its internal law as justification for its failure to perform a treaty."); RESTATEMENT (THIRD) OF THE FOREIGN RELATIONS LAW OF THE UNITED STATES § 321, cmt. a (explaining that "international obligations survive restrictions imposed by domestic law").

circumstances restitution or compensation for loss or injury."[40] In order to resolve disputes, "[a] state may bring a claim against another state for a violation of an international obligation (...) either through diplomatic channels" or an agreed procedure.[41] A party asserting that the United States is in breach of its international obligations under ACTA may resort to countermeasures under customary international law.[42] US courts may also use ACTA to interpret ambiguous commands in US domestic law.[43]

And thus, at bottom, the constitutional problem with ACTA is that it is a lawmaking process – creating binding law – that is being made in contravention of the US Constitution, which defines how binding law is to be made. Normally, compliance with the Constitution is how we define binding law. But here, international law operates as a higher set of principles and allows the president to violate the lawmaking law if he can get away with it. This is a bold move. And thus far, despite resistance, it has been successful. ACTA has not been submitted to Congress. Although the administration has not stated that it has deposited a ratification instrument joining the agreement, it still thinks it can.

This lesson should serve as a stark warning to citizens the world over. If the United States can try this and run around domestic process, others probably will too.

[40] RESTATEMENT (THIRD) OF THE FOREIGN RELATIONS LAW OF THE UNITED STATES § 901.

[41] *Id.* § 902(1).

[42] *See* G.A. Res. 56/83, arts. 12–15, U.N. Doc. A/Res/56/83 (Jan. 28, 2002).

[43] *See generally* Murray v. Schooner Charming Betsy, 6 U.S. (2 Cranch) 64 (1804) (acknowledging the modernizing world and recognizing that individuals are not only ruled by municipal laws or ordinances, but also by the "laws of nations"). The "Charming Betsy" convention of statutory interpretation holds that US courts should construe congressional statutes as consistent with US international obligations, whenever possible.

# 10

# Trick or Treaty?

## *The Australian Debate over the Anti-Counterfeiting Trade Agreement*

*Matthew Rimmer*

### INTRODUCTION

The secretive 2011 Anti-Counterfeiting Trade Agreement – known in short by the catchy acronym, ACTA – is a controversial trade pact designed to provide for stronger enforcement of intellectual property rights.[1] The preamble to the treaty reads like pulp fiction – it raises moral panics about piracy, counterfeiting, organised crime, and border security. The agreement contains provisions on civil remedies and criminal offences, copyright law and trademark law, the regulation of the digital environment, and border measures. Memorably, Susan Sell called the international treaty "a TRIPS Double-Plus Agreement"[2] because its obligations far exceed those of the World Trade Organization's TRIPS Agreement 1994,[3] and TRIPS-Plus Agreements, such as the Australia-United States Free Trade Agreement 2004.[4] The ACTA lacks the language of other international intellectual property agreements, which emphasise the need to balance the protection of intellectual property owners with the wider public interest in access to medicines, human development, and transfer of knowledge and technology.

In Australia, there was much controversy both about the form and the substance of ACTA.

[1] *Anti-Counterfeiting Trade Agreement* 2011, [2011] ATNIF 22, not yet in force.

[2] Susan Sell, 'The Global IP Upward Ratchet, Anti-Counterfeiting, and Piracy Enforcement Efforts: The State of Play' (Research Paper No 15, Program on Information Justice and Intellectual Property at Digital Commons @ American University Washington College of Law). Although Susan Sell made these comments in respect of draft versions of ACTA, the comments are still applicable, given the differences between TRIPS-Plus Agreements and ACTA.

[3] *Marrakesh Agreement Establishing the World Trade Organization*, opened for signature15 April 1994, 1867 UNTS 3, annex 1C (*Agreement on Trade-Related Aspects of Intellectual Property Rights*) (entered into force 1 January 1995).

[4] *Australia-United States Free Trade Agreement (AUSFTA)*, signed 18 May 2004 (entered into force 1 January 2005).

The Department of Foreign Affairs and Trade was a partisan supporter of ACTA. Nonetheless, there was criticism from a wide range of stakeholders about the treaty. After holding hearings and taking note of the position of the European Parliament and the controversy in the United States, the Joint Standing Committee on Treaties in the Australian Parliament recommended the deferral of ratification of ACTA.[5] This was striking – as representatives of all the main parties agreed on the recommendation. The Committee was concerned about the lack of transparency, due process, public participation and substantive analysis of the treaty. There were also reservations about the ambiguity of the treaty text, as well as its potential implications for the digital economy, innovation and competition, plain packaging of tobacco products, and access to essential medicines. The treaty has provoked much soul searching as to whether the *Trick or Treaty* reforms[6] on the international treaty-making process in Australia have been compromised or undermined.

Although ACTA stalled in the Australian parliament, the debate over it is yet to conclude. There have been concerns in Australia and elsewhere that ACTA will be revived as a "zombie agreement."[7] Indeed, in March 2013, the Canadian government introduced a bill to ensure compliance with ACTA.[8] Will it be also resurrected in Australia? Has it already been revived? There are three possibilities. First, the Australian government passes enhanced remedies with respect to piracy, counterfeiting and border measures in a separate piece of legislation – the Intellectual Property Laws Amendment (Raising the Bar) Act 2012 (Cth). Second, the Department of Foreign Affairs and Trade remains supportive of ACTA. It is possible, after further analysis, that the next Australian Parliament – to be elected in September 2013 – will ratify the treaty. Third, Australia is involved in the Trans-Pacific Partnership negotiations. The government has argued that ACTA should be a template for the Intellectual Property Chapter in the Trans-Pacific Partnership.[9] The United States Trade Representative would prefer a regime even stronger than ACTA.

[5] Joint Standing Committee on Treaties, *Report 126 – Treaty Tabled on 21 November 2011: Anti-Counterfeiting Trade Agreement 2011*, Canberra: Australian Parliament, June 2012, http://www.aph.gov.au/Parliamentary_Business/Committees/House_of_Representatives_Committees?url=jsct/21november2011/report.htm

[6] Senate Legal and Constitutional References Committee, *Trick or Treaty? The Commonwealth Power to Make and Implement Treaties*, November 1995, http://www.austlii.edu.au/au/other/dfat/reports/tortcon.html

[7] Activists are fond of Gothic metaphors to describe trade agreements. *See* Christian Engstrom, 'Introducing CETA – The ACTA Zombie', 12 July 2012, http://christianengstrom.wordpress.com/2012/07/12/introducing-ceta-the-acta-zombie/; and Lori Wallach, 'Can a "Dracula Strategy" Bring the Trans-Pacific Partnership into the Sunlight?' *Yes Magazine!* 21 November 2012, http://www.yesmagazine.org/new-economy/can-dracula-strategy-bring-trans-pacific-partnership-into-sunlight

[8] Michael Geist, 'Here Comes ACTA: Canadian Government Introduces Anti-Counterfeiting Trade Agreement', 1 March 2013, http://www.michaelgeist.ca/content/view/6796/125/

[9] The United States Trade Representative, *The Trans-Pacific Partnership*, http://www.ustr.gov/tpp and The Department of Foreign Affairs and Trade, *The Trans-Pacific Partnership Agreement Negotiations*, http://www.dfat.gov.au/fta/tpp/index.html

This chapter provides a portrait of the Australian debate over ACTA. It is the account of an interested participant in the policy proceedings.[10] This chapter first considers the deliberations and recommendations of the Joint Standing Committee on Treaties on ACTA. Second, there was a concern that ACTA had failed to provide appropriate safeguards with respect to civil liberties, human rights, consumer protection and privacy laws. Third, there was a concern about the lack of balance in the treaty's copyright measures; the definition of piracy is overbroad; the suite of civil remedies, criminal offences and border measures is excessive; and there is a lack of suitable protection for copyright exceptions, limitations and remedies. Fourth, there was a worry that the provisions on trademark law, intermediary liability and counterfeiting could have an adverse impact on consumer interests, competition policy and innovation in the digital economy. Fifth, there was significant debate about the impact of ACTA on pharmaceutical drugs, access to essential medicines and health care. Sixth, there was concern over the lobbying by tobacco industries for ACTA – particularly given Australia's leadership on tobacco control and the plain packaging of tobacco products. Seventh, there were concerns about the operation of border measures in ACTA. Eighth, the Joint Standing Committee on Treaties was concerned about the jurisdiction of the ACTA Committee and the treaty's protean nature. Finally, the chapter raises fundamental issues about the relationship between the executive and the Australian Parliament with respect to treaty making. There is a need to reconsider the efficacy of the *Trick or Treaty* reforms passed by the Australian parliament in the 1990s.

## THE JOINT STANDING COMMITTEE ON TREATIES

In early 2012, the Joint Standing Committee on Treaties held a number of hearings on ACTA.[11] The committee received twenty-five submissions from a range of stakeholders – including academics such as Kimberlee Weatherall, Luigi Palombi, Anna George and Hazel Moir; the Pirate Party Australia; the generic drugs manufacturer Alphapharm Pty Limited; copyright industry groups such as the Australian Copyright Council and the Australian Federation Against Copyright Theft; copyright collecting societies; and the Australian Digital Alliance, which represents libraries, universities

[10] This account builds on this research and policy work – Matthew Rimmer, 'A Submission to the Joint Standing Committee on Treaties on the *Anti-Counterfeiting Trade Agreement* 2011', February 2012, http://works.bepress.com/matthew_rimmer/109/; Matthew Rimmer, 'Appearance before the Inquiry into the *Anti-Counterfeiting Trade Agreement* 2011', Joint Standing Committee on Treaties, 23 March 2012; and Matthew Rimmer, 'Opening Pandora's Box: Secret Treaty Threatens Human Rights', *The Conversation*, 4 April 2012, https://theconversation.edu.au/opening-pandoras-box-secret-treaty-threatens-human-rights-6092

[11] The Joint Standing Committee on Treaties held hearings on 19 March 2012, 23 March 2012, and 7 May 2012 at Canberra at the Australian Parliament.

and technology developers such as Google. The Internet Industry Association and CHOICE – which represents Australian consumers – had participated in the larger public policy debate over ACTA.

In June 2012, the Australian Parliament's Joint Standing Committee on Treaties released its report on ACTA.[12] It recommended that

> [t]he Anti-Counterfeiting Trade Agreement not be ratified by Australia until the Standing Committee on Treaties has received and considered the independent and transparent assessment of the economic and social benefits and costs of the Agreement (…); Australian Law Reform Commission has reported on its Inquiry into *Copyright and the Digital Economy*; and the Australian Government has issued notices of clarification in relation to the terms of the Agreement as recommended in the other recommendations of this report.[13]

The committee further observed that "in considering its recommendation on whether or not to ratify the Anti-Counterfeiting Trade Agreement (ACTA), a future Joint Standing Committee on Treaties have regard to events related to ACTA in other relevant jurisdictions including the European Union and the United States of America."[14]

The chair of the Joint Standing Committee on Treaties, the Hon. Kelvin Thomson, discussed ACTA in the House of Representatives in the Australian Parliament.[15] Citing the controversy in the European Union, the United States and elsewhere over the treaty, the chair observed:

> The committee is concerned that, despite ACTA's intent, it exhibits a number of flaws, and the committee is not yet convinced that the agreement in its current form is in Australia's interest. We have asked for further analysis and clarification to be undertaken. This analysis includes the existing Australian Law Reform Commission Inquiry into *Copyright and the Digital Economy*.[16] The committee is concerned about the lack of clarity in the text, the exclusion of provisions protecting the rights of individuals, and ACTA's potential to shift the balance in the interpretation of copyright law, intellectual property law and patent law.[17]

[12] Joint Standing Committee on Treaties, *Report 126 – Treaty Tabled on 21 November 2011: Anti-Counterfeiting Trade Agreement 2011*, Canberra: Australian Parliament, June 2012, http://www.aph.gov.au/Parliamentary_Business/Committees/House_of_Representatives_Committees?url=jsct/21november2011/report.htm

[13] Ibid.

[14] Ibid.

[15] The Hon. Kelvin Thomson, 'Report 126: Treaty tabled on 21 November 2011 of the Joint Standing Committee of Treaties', the House of Representatives, Hansard, the Australian Parliament, 27 June 2012, 8172.

[16] Australian Law Reform Commission, Copyright and the Digital Economy, Sydney: Australian Law Reform Commission, 2014, http://www.alrc.gov.au/publications/copyright-report-122

[17] The Hon. Kelvin Thomson, 'Report 126: Treaty tabled on 21 November 2011 of the Joint Standing Committee of Treaties', the House of Representatives, Hansard, the Australian Parliament, 27 June 2012, 8172.

Considering the international reaction to ACTA, Thomson concluded: "Given all these events, it would be prudent for Australia to take the cautious approach that the committee has advocated."[18]

The Hon. Melissa Parke, the progressive Labor member for Fremantle, and a well-respected international and human rights lawyer and academic, discussed the treaty in the House of Representatives in the Federal Parliament.[19] Summarising criticism of ACTA, she observed:

> The committee's report rightly highlights the many worrying aspects of the agreement and of the National Interest Analysis that is being used to put the case for Australia's ratification of ACTA, including the absence of any economic cost-benefit analysis, the absence of justification for proposed new criminal penalties, the omission from ACTA of individual protections codified in the TRIPS Agreement and the vagueness of terms used in ACTA such as 'intellectual property,' 'piracy,' 'aiding and abetting' and 'commercial scale'.[20]

Parke concluded:

> Indeed, the list of frightening issues surrounding ACTA – in the way it was negotiated, in the content of the treaty itself and in the significant community and governmental opposition to the treaty around the world, particularly in Europe – indicated to me and to other members of the committee that Australia should be extremely wary about ratifying such an agreement in its present form.[21]

Senator Simon Birmingham, representing the Liberal Party and the State of South Australia, discussed how the report of the Joint Standing Committee of Treaties (JSCOT) on ACTA was exceptional.[22] He noted that "[i]t is noteworthy because it does not recommend ratification at this time but instead takes the unusual step for JSCOT in outlining a range of steps that the treaties committee believed should be taken prior to further consideration regarding potential ratification of the treaty."[23] Birmingham was of the view that the report "shows that the treaties committee is keen to ensure that its work in this parliament is work that enhances Australia's treaty-making process and that ensures appropriate scrutiny is applied to treaties

[18] Ibid.

[19] The Hon. Melissa Parke, 'Report 126: Treaty tabled on 21 November 2011 of the Joint Standing Committee of Treaties', the House of Representatives, Hansard, the Australian Parliament, 27 June 2012, 8174.

[20] Ibid. n.19

[21] Ibid.

[22] Senator Simon Birmingham, 'Report 126: Treaty tabled on 21 November 2011 of the Joint Standing Committee of Treaties', the House of Representatives, Hansard, the Australian Parliament, 27 June 2012, 4716.

[23] Ibid.

that Australia enters into."[24] He also noted that "some members of the committee are perhaps more hopeful that we will see a conclusion of ACTA than others."[25] He concluded that he would "certainly fall into the category of those who hope we will ultimately see something that provides a greater global strengthening of our copyright and IP laws, which can be done in harmony with other countries and provide greater protection for those who develop and should rightly have some ownership of their IP into the future."[26]

Senator Scott Ludlam, representing the Greens and the State of Western Australia, has been an eloquent critic of ACTA.[27] He was critical of the Department of Foreign Affairs and Trade's blind optimism about the treaty: "Australia risks being out there, effectively completely alone in its support for this flawed instrument."[28]

Ludlam made three points on the recommendations. First, he noted that there was a need for an independent and transparent assessment of the economic and social costs of the agreement. He observed: "For something such as this, it is not enough to simply proceed on some kind of blind ideological faith that all forms of trade agreement are uniformly good for all people in all countries, and that was the proposition that seemed to be advanced to JSCOT, with nothing to back it by way of formal or quantitative evidence."[29]

Second, he emphasised that the international treaty-making process should not override domestic law reform processes, such as the Australian Law Reform Commission's inquiry into copyright law and the digital economy: "We believe that the committee, before it opens up the question of whether ACTA actually should be ratified again, should have in its possession that important piece of work by the ALRC."[30]

Third, Ludlam proposed that the Australian government issue notices of clarification with regard to the terms of the agreement as recommended in other parts of the report: "They should just be upfront and let the Australian public know – in this instance through the committee – what exactly it is and who exactly it is who will be benefiting from this treaty should it pass."[31]

The Minister for Trade, Dr Craig Emerson, was disgruntled by the criticism of ACTA.[32] He argued that it was unwarranted, and insisted that ACTA required no

[24] Ibid.
[25] Ibid.
[26] Ibid.
[27] Senator Scott Ludlam, 'Report 126: Treaty tabled on 21 November 2011 of the Joint Standing Committee of Treaties', Senate, Hansard, the Australian Parliament, 27 June 2012, 4718.
[28] Ibid.
[29] Ibid.
[30] Ibid.
[31] Ibid.
[32] Peter Martin, 'Emerson Chasing Deals That Look Like Sellouts', *The Sydney Morning Herald*, 7 August 2012, http://www.smh.com.au/business/emerson-chasing-deals-that-look-like-sellouts-20120806-23q6h.html

legislative amendments. Nonetheless, he maintained that he was happy to accept the recommendation to conduct an independent and transparent analysis of ACTA prior to its ratification in Australia. He argued: "I am actually on the consumer's side here. I don't want people misled by mystifyingly complex computer-generated equilibrium models that are pre-determined to achieve a particular result."[33]

In November 2012, the Australian Government tabled its response to the report of the Joint Standing Committee on Treaties.[34] While the government agreed with a number of recommendations "in principle" and "in part," it did not by any means reject ACTA. The Government observed that it would "consider ratification of ACTA following the receipt of the analysis recommended at Recommendation 2, but would also consider any further, timely, recommendations of JSCOT as part of that consideration."[35] Indeed, even after much criticism, the government insisted that the treaty "allows considerable flexibility in its implementation" and that "Australia would retain considerable flexibility to modify its laws on copyright while still meeting its obligations under ACTA."[36] It would appear that the executive of the Gillard government remains enthusiastic about the treaty.

ACTA's fate in Australia will largely be determined by the composition of the future Australian Parliament. Much will depend on who forms the government – between the Australian Labor Party, the Conservative Coalition of the Liberal Party and the National Party, and the Australian Greens – and what their attitude is to free trade agreements, particularly those with intellectual property chapters. The Pirate Party Australia[37] and WikiLeaks founder Julian Assange[38] both campaigned on the issue of intellectual property and ACTA, but did not win a position in the Senate in September 2013.

## HUMAN RIGHTS

George Mina of the Department of Foreign Affairs and Trade asserted that ACTA would not violate human rights or civil liberties:

33 John Hilvert, 'Government Eyes Cost-Benefit Analyses for ACTA, TPP', *IT News*, 14 August 2012, http://www.itnews.com.au/News/311619,government-eyes-cost-benefit-analyses-for-acta-tpp.aspx

34 Australian Government, 'Response to the Joint Standing Committee on Treaties Response', November 2012, http://www.dfat.gov.au/ip/government-response-to-jscot-report-on-acta.html

35 Ibid.

36 Ibid.

37 Pirate Party Australia, 'Government Should Follow EU in Rejecting ACTA, says Pirate Party', 21 June 2012, http://pirateparty.org.au/2012/06/21/government-should-follow-eu-in-rejecting-acta-says-pirate-party/

38 ABC News, 'Julian Assange to Run For the Senate', *ABC News*, 19 March 2012, http://www.abc.net.au/news/2012-03-17/julian-assange-to-run-for-senate/3895958; Julian Assange, *The Unauthorised Autobiography*, Edinburgh: Canongate, 2012.

> ACTA will not infringe upon people's civil liberties. ACTA does not change, for instance, the balance struck between the rights of users and producers of IP inherent in Australian law or the balance inherent in the WTO TRIPS Agreement … ACTA will not impact on freedom on the internet. ACTA will not require internet services providers, or ISPs, to monitor the activities of individuals. ACTA will not lead to censorship of the internet. [39]

However, the Department of Foreign Affairs and Trade did not undertake any human rights assessment of ACTA.

ACTA Article 1 maintains: "Nothing in this Agreement shall derogate from any obligation of a Party with respect to any other Party under existing agreements."

There has been significant debate about the relationship between ACTA and human rights treaties. The agreement's preamble contains a number of rather anodyne statements about protecting fundamental freedoms and rights. However, the text of ACTA does not provide substantive protection for values such as human rights, privacy, consumer rights and access to justice and rule of law.

On the question of human rights, Amnesty International has branded ACTA a "Pandora's box" of potential human rights violations.[40] Amnesty International expressed the view that "the pact's content, process, and institutional structure impact in a number of ways on human rights – especially the rights to due process, privacy, freedom of information, freedom of expression, and access to essential medicines."[41] Widney Brown, Senior Director of International Law and Policy at Amnesty International, commented: "Worryingly, ACTA's text does not even contain references to safeguards like 'fundamental rights', 'fair use', or 'due process', which are universally understood and clearly defined in international law."[42] Parties to ACTA have no positive obligation to protect freedom of expression, consumer rights, fair process and privacy.

Australia is at a particular disadvantage to other jurisdictions because it offers comparatively weak individual protection of human rights, civil liberties and privacy rights. There is no express bill of rights under the Australian Constitution – merely a limited implied freedom of political communication.[43] Efforts to provide legislative protection of human rights under the Rudd and Gillard governments

[39] George Mina, 'Public Hearing', Hansard, Joint Standing Committee on Treaties, House of Representatives, 19 March 2012, 14.

[40] Amnesty International, 'EU Urged to Reject International Anti-Counterfeiting Pact', 10 February 2012, http://www.amnesty.org/en/news/eu-urged-reject-international-anti-counterfeiting-pact-2012-02-10

[41] Ibid.

[42] Ibid.

[43] See recent case law of the High Court of Australia on the implied freedom of political communication: *Attorney-General (SA)* v. *Corporation of the city of Adelaide* [2013] HCA 3 (27 February 2013); and *Monis* v. *The Queen* [2013] HCA 4 (27 February 2013).

have faltered.[44] The Australian Law Reform Commission, which undertook an extensive review of Australian privacy law and practice,[45] recommended that "federal legislation should provide for a statutory cause of action for a serious invasion of privacy."[46] At present, there is a lack of redress for intellectual property users and consumers who have suffered violations of privacy as a result of the conduct of intellectual property owners.

The Joint Standing Committee on Treaties made a number of comments in respect of copyright law. For instance, it recommended that "the Australian Government publishes the individual protections that will be read into the ACTA from the TRIPS Agreement and how the protections will apply in relation to the enforcement provisions contained in ACTA."[47]

In light of the treaty's clear human rights impacts, it would be appropriate for the new Parliamentary Joint Committee on Human Rights to consider ACTA and any attendant regulation, as required under the Human Rights (Parliamentary Scrutiny) Act 2011 (Cth).

## COPYRIGHT LAW AND THE DIGITAL ECONOMY

Peter Treyde of the Attorney-General's Department maintained that ACTA would benefit companies in the digital economy, including search engines like Google and social networks such as Facebook:

> It is the [United States] economy, with the framework that ACTA I guess supports, that has given rise to the Googles, the Facebooks and so forth. While there are many people who are concerned about freedoms being eroded, the other side of that balance is provided in creating the correct legal environment to support the establishment and growth of those industries. I think that is why we see it as being very important on a more regional level, because you will see that throughout the region and those same standards applying.[48]

This is a curious argument given that companies like Google and Facebook have often argued for the need for stronger copyright exceptions in the United States

[44] Australia's Human Rights Framework, http://www.ag.gov.au/Humanrightsandantidiscrimination/Australiashumanrightsframework/Pages/default.aspx

[45] Australian Law Reform Commission, *For Your Information: Australian Privacy Law and Practice*, Sydney: Australian Law Reform Commission, 2008, http://www.alrc.gov.au/publications/report-108

[46] Ibid.

[47] Joint Standing Committee on Treaties, *Report 126 – Treaty Tabled on 21 November 2011: Anti-Counterfeiting Trade Agreement 2011*, Canberra: Australian Parliament, June 2012, http://www.aph.gov.au/Parliamentary_Business/Committees/House_of_Representatives_Committees?url=jsct/21november2011/report.htm

[48] Joint Standing Committee on Treaties, 'Public Hearing', Hansard, House of Representatives, Monday 7 May 2012, 43.

and elsewhere in respect of the defence of fair use and safe harbours protection. The Department of Foreign Affairs and Trade also argued that strong obligations on copyright law under ACTA would be a boon to Australia's copyright industries.

The Joint Standing Committee on Treaties raised a number of concerns about the definition of piracy, the civil offences in respect of copyright law, the proportionality of criminal offences, and the interference with domestic inquiries into copyright exceptions and exceptions to technological protection measures.

First, the Joint Standing Committee on Treaties was concerned that ACTA had a broad, unwieldy definition of piracy.[49] The definition section is derived in part from a footnote to Article 51 of the TRIPS Agreement 1994. The ACTA clause defines "pirated copyright goods" as meaning

> any goods which are copies made without the consent of the right holder or person duly authorised by the right holder in the country of production and which are made directly or indirectly from an article where the making of that copy would have constituted an infringement of a copyright or a related right under the law of the country in which the procedures set forth in Chapter II (Legal Framework for Enforcement of Intellectual Property Rights) are invoked.

Australian courts have scorned the use of the term. In the "Panel" case, McHugh, Gummow and Hayne JJ of the High Court of Australia expressed deep reservations and concerns about the use of terms such as "piracy," "robbery" and "theft" to stigmatise the conduct of alleged infringers of intellectual property rights.[50]

Scholars have been concerned about the ill-defined nature of the term "piracy." In his scholarly historical monograph, *Piracy*, Adrian Johns traces the derivation and the various meanings of the term.[51] He comments on its slippery and mutable meaning: "To assume that piracy merely derives from legal doctrine is to get the history – and therefore the politics, and much else besides – back to front."[52] In the same vein, Andrew Rens comments: "The appearance of such a vague, yet central rhetorical term in a draft international instrument signals that the text is written entirely from the perspective of the interest group that uses the term, if not by that group itself."[53] William Patry has written about how copyright industries have used

[49] Joint Standing Committee on Treaties, *Report 126 – Treaty Tabled on 21 November 2011: Anti-Counterfeiting Trade Agreement 2011*, Canberra: Australian Parliament, June 2012, http://www.aph.gov.au/Parliamentary_Business/Committees/House_of_Representatives_Committees?url=jsct/21november2011/report.htm

[50] *Network Ten Pty Ltd* V. *Ten Channel Nine* [2004] HCA 14.

[51] Adrian Johns, *Piracy: The Intellectual Property Wars From Gutenberg to Gates*, Chicago and London: The University of Chicago Press, 2011.

[52] Ibid., 6.

[53] Andrew Rens, 'Collateral Damage – The Impact of ACTA and the Enforcement Agenda on the World's Poorest Peoples' (2011) 26(3) *American University Journal of International Law* 784–809. *See also* Spennemann, Chapter 15 in the current volume.

moral panics over "piracy" as a means to lobby in a self-interested fashion for corporate welfare measures in legislation and international treaties.[54] It is inappropriate to graft the political rhetoric of "piracy" to the text of an international intellectual property agreement such as ACTA.

Second, ACTA contains extensive obligations with regard to copyright law, which deal with civil remedies, criminal offences, border measures, enforcement of intellectual property rights in a digital environment, technological protection measures and electronic rights management information. David Quinn provides a good summary of the treaty's numerous, prescriptive obligations, as well as its best practice clauses.[55] The National Interest Analysis asserted, very controversially and without evidence, that such obligations "constitute best practice forms of IP enforcement."[56] There has also been concern that ACTA's language on injunctions is inconsistent with that of the TRIPS Agreement 1994. Article 8.1 of ACTA does not adopt the language in TRIPS Article 44.1 concerning innocent infringements.

Knowledge Ecology International (KEI) argues that "ACTA is an agreement to change current international rules for the enforcement of intellectual property rights."[57] KEI reiterated Professor Frederick Abbott's criticism that "suggested retail price" is an appropriate global norm in the calculation of damages.[58] It also observed that "by creating higher norms for damages from infringement, the ACTA makes it more risky for businesses and consumers to undertake activities are may or may not actually constitute infringement."[59] Finally, the group noted that "everyone must become more risk averse, even when the activity they are engaged in may ultimately be legal."[60]

Third, the Joint Standing Committee on Treaties was concerned about the proportionality of criminal offences relating to copyright law:

> The ACTA National Interest Analysis does not contain any empirical evidence that the criminal penalties contained in ACTA are proportionate. This makes it

54 William Patry, *Moral Panics and the Copyright Wars*, Oxford: Oxford University Press, 2009.

55 David M. Quinn, 'A Critical Look at the Anti-Counterfeiting Trade Agreement' (2011) 17 *Richmond Journal of Law and Technology* 1–25, http://jolt.richmond.edu/v17i4/article16.pdf

56 National Interest Analysis of the *Anti-Counterfeiting Trade Agreement* [2011] ATNIA 31, http://www.aph.gov.au/Parliamentary_Business/Committees/House_of_Representatives_Committees?url=jsct/21november2011/treaties/anti_counterfeiting_nia.pdf

57 James Love, 'What's Still Wrong with ACTA, and Why Governments Should Reject the Illegitimate Treaty', Knowledge Ecology International, 26 February 2012, http://keionline.org/node/1369

58 Frederick Abbott, 'Intellectual Property Provisions of Bilateral and Regional Trade Agreements in Light of U.S. Federal Law', February 2006. UNCTAD–ICTSD Project on IPRs and Sustainable Development. *See also* Abbott, Chapter 1 in this volume.

59 James Love, 'What's Still Wrong with ACTA, and Why Governments Should Reject the Illegitimate Treaty', Knowledge Ecology International, 26 February 2012, http://keionline.org/node/1369

60 Ibid.

> difficult for the Committee to make a judgement as to the veracity of criticisms of the proportionality of the criminal penalties.[61]

In written submissions and oral evidence, Kimberlee Weatherall provided an incisive analysis of the provisions on criminal offences in ACTA.[62] The JSCOT recommended that "in circumstances where a treaty includes the introduction of new criminal penalties, the treaty's National Interest Analysis justify the proposed new penalties."[63] It also recommended that the government clarify and publish the meaning of "aiding and abetting," as well as that of "commercial scale," as they apply to ACTA.[64]

Fourth, the Joint Standing Committee on Treaties was of the view that ACTA did not adequately address copyright exceptions and limitations:

> ACTA neglects to consider appropriate exceptions and limitations to IP rights to facilitate access to knowledge, culture, information and research; it also removes TRIPS safeguards on a number of IP remedies and provides no concrete protection for interests such as individual privacy or commercial confidentiality or the rights of defendants to legal action. Its emphasis on the rights holder risks creating an imbalance between appropriate protections for creators and the public interest in flexible and fair use of content.[65]

The JSCOT also emphasised that ACTA[66] should not be reconsidered until the Australian Law Reform Commission had handed down its report on *Copyright and the Digital Economy*.[67] The commission undertook a wide-ranging inquiry focused on Australia's copyright exceptions in 2012 and 2013. The Commission recommended that Australia should adopt a defence of fair use, like the United States.[68]

61 Joint Standing Committee on Treaties, *Report 126 – Treaty Tabled on 21 November 2011: Anti-Counterfeiting Trade Agreement 2011*, Canberra: Australian Parliament, June 2012, 29 http://www.aph.gov.au/Parliamentary_Business/Committees/House_of_Representatives_Committees?url=jsct/21november2011/report.htm

62 Kimberlee Weatherall, 'Submission to the Joint Standing Committee on Treaties on the *Anti-Counterfeiting Trade Agreement* 2011', February 2012, http://www.aph.gov.au/Parliamentary_Business/Committees/House_of_Representatives_Committees?url=jsct/21november2011/subs/sub3.pdf

63 Joint Standing Committee on Treaties, *Report 126 – Treaty Tabled on 21 November 2011: Anti-Counterfeiting Trade Agreement 2011*, Canberra: Australian Parliament, June 2012, http://www.aph.gov.au/Parliamentary_Business/Committees/House_of_Representatives_Committees?url=jsct/21november2011/report.htm

64 Ibid.

65 Ibid.

66 Ibid.

67 Australian Law Reform Commission, Copyright and the Digital Economy, Sydney: Australian Law Reform Commission, 2014, http://www.alrc.gov.au/publications/copyright-report-122

68 For a commentary, *see* Matthew Rimmer, 'A Fair Use Project for Australia: Copyright Law and Creative Freedom' (2010) 28 (3) *Copyright Reporter* 165–212 and Matthew Rimmer, 'The Fight for Fair Use in Australia: Copyright Law in an Age of Cloud Computing', Fair Use Week, Harvard Library, 28 February 2014, http://blogs.law.harvard.edu/copyrightosc/2014/02/28/fair-use-week-day-five-with-guest-expert-dr-matthew-rimmer/.

Fifth, concern was expressed during the inquiry that ACTA would undermine domestic reviews on technological protection measures as it prescribed extensive protection for so-called digital locks. Locking in standards in respect of para-copyright – technological protection measures and electronic rights management information – is also controversial.[69] Australia's position on technological protection measures is particularly messy given the undeniable tension that still remains between the ruling of the High Court of Australia in *Stevens v. Sony*[70] and the legislative measures introduced after the Australia–United States Free Trade Agreement 2004. The process for introducing new exceptions to technological protection measures has not been properly implemented. It would be inappropriate to adopt such heightened measures while the Attorney General's department is still reviewing exceptions to technological protection measures.[71]

## TRADEMARK LAW AND COUNTERFEITING

George Mina from the Department of Foreign Affairs and Trade argued that ACTA would benefit Australian companies in addressing trademark enforcement against counterfeiting.[72] He held that the treaty's intellectual property enforcement regime would support the "innovation economy" and "the knowledge economy":

> By setting out a new international framework for dealing with pirated and counterfeited products in world trade it supports the production of and trade in legitimate products protected by intellectual property rights. ACTA will support our iconic brands in overseas markets. Australian exports, such as Billabong surfwear or Penfolds Wines, depend on the protection of their brands in overseas markets. We want companies like these to thrive.[73]

Unfortunately, thus far there has been only passing analysis of the trademark dimensions of ACTA in both scholarly and policy circles in Australia. Meanwhile, a great

69 *Copyright Amendment (Digital Agenda) Act* 2000 (Cth); *Australia-United States Free Trade Agreement (AUSFTA)*, signed 18 May 2004 (entered into force 1 January 2005); *Stevens* v. *Kabushiki Kaisha Sony Computer Entertainment* [2005] HCA 58; *Copyright Amendment Act* 2006 (Cth); Circumventing an Access Control Technological Protection Measure – S 116AN of the *Copyright Act* 1968 (Cth); Manufacturing etc a Circumvention Device for a Technological Protection Measure – S 116AO of the *Copyright Act* 1968 (Cth); Providing a Circumvention Service for a Technological Protection Measure – S 116AP of the *Copyright Act* 1968 (Cth); and Remedies – S 116AQ of the *Copyright Act* 1968 (Cth).

70 *Stevens* v. *Kabushiki Kaisha Sony Computer Entertainment* [2005] HCA 58.

71 Attorney-General's Department, *Review of Technological Protection Measure Exceptions Under the Copyright Act 1968 (Cth)*, http://www.ag.gov.au/Consultationsreformsandreviews/Pages/ReviewofTechnologicalProtectionMeasureexceptionsmadeundertheCopyrightAct1968.aspx

72 Joint Standing Committee on Treaties, 'Public Hearing', Hansard, House of Representatives, 19 March 2012, 14.

73 Ibid.

deal of litigation has taken place of late in relation to trademark law, intermediary liability, counterfeiting and the digital economy.[74]

There has also been disquiet that ACTA favours trademark owners.[75] The agreement emphasises that "the proliferation of counterfeit and pirated goods, as well as of services that distribute infringing material, undermines legitimate trade and sustainable development of the world economy, causes significant financial losses for right holders and for legitimate businesses, and, in some cases, provides a source of revenue for organised crime and otherwise poses risks to the public."[76] ACTA was part of a push to expand secondary liability and limit safe harbours for intermediaries in the digital economy.

For instance, the International Trademark Association – one of the key proponents of ACTA – submitted to President Barack Obama: "ACTA can have a significant impact in fighting counterfeiting, a problem that exists globally and affects all national economies, and INTA supports the efforts by the United States and its negotiating partners who are working on this important initiative."[77]

First, counterfeiting is broadly and inclusively defined under ACTA.[78] The definition, again based on the TRIPS Agreement 1994, provides that:

> 'counterfeit trademark goods' means any goods, including packaging, bearing without authorization a trademark which is identical to the trademark validly registered in respect of such goods, or which cannot be distinguished in its essential aspects from such a trademark, and which thereby infringes the rights of the owner of the trademark in question under the law of the country in which the procedures set forth in Chapter II (Legal Framework for Enforcement of Intellectual Property Rights) are invoked.

According to Andrew Rens, "'Counterfeit' as used in the title and preamble has a vague but ominous meaning intended to homogenise a heterogeneous set of regulations and practices."[79] Indeed, the term "counterfeiting" is something of a free-

74 Matthew Rimmer, "Breakfast at Tiffany's': eBay Inc., Trademark Law, and Counterfeiting', (2011) 21 (1) *Journal of Law, Information, and Science* 128–166.

75 For an overview and commentary, *see* Michael Geist, 'ACTA's State of Play: Looking Beyond Transparency' (2011) 26(3) *American University Journal of International Law* 543–558.

76 *Anti-Counterfeiting Trade Agreement* 2011, [2011] ATNIF 22, not yet in force.

77 International Trademark Association, *Submission to President Barack Obama on the Anti-Counterfeiting Trade Agreement*, 23 March 2010, http://www.ustr.gov/webfm_send/1737

78 It is noticeable how far the concept of counterfeiting, as defined in ACTA, has drifted from its historical origins. In his elegant book, *The Forger's Shadow*, Nick Groom investigates the history and the derivation of the word "counterfeiting." *See* Nick Groom, *The Forger's Shadow: How Forgery Changed the Course of Literature*, Picador, 2003, 44.

79 Andrew Rens, 'Collateral Damage – The Impact of ACTA and the Enforcement Agenda on the World's Poorest Peoples' (2011) 26(3) *American University Journal of International Law* 784–809 at 798–799.

floating signifier in ACTA, which allows it to be constructed broadly by trademark owners. It should also be noted that "counterfeiting" has quite different connotations in other contexts, such as the debate over "counterfeit medicines," for instance, which is quite a separate discourse, as is the policy issue of "counterfeit currency."[80]

Second, the proposed international treaty contains obligations on border measures, as well as civil and criminal enforcement of trademark rights. The final agreement has some twenty-six references to trademarks. Initial drafts of the international treaty had a whole section devoted to online infringement. The final draft's Article 27.4 provides:

> A Party may provide, in accordance with its laws and regulations, its competent authorities with the authority to order an online service provider to disclose expeditiously to a right holder information sufficient to identify a subscriber whose account was allegedly used for infringement, where that right holder has filed a legally sufficient claim of trademark or copyright or related rights infringement, and where such information is being sought for the purpose of protecting or enforcing those rights. These procedures shall be implemented in a manner that avoids the creation of barriers to legitimate activity, including electronic commerce, and, consistent with that Party's law, preserves fundamental principles such as freedom of expression, fair process, and privacy.[81]

There have been concerns that the obligations could have an adverse impact on consumers' privacy, free speech, innovation, competition and the digital economy.

Third, ACTA fails to address the question of defences, exceptions and limitations under trade mark law. In the 2012 landmark case of *JT International SA v. Commonwealth of Australia*; *British American Tobacco Australasia Limited v. The Commonwealth*, French CJ emphasised that Australian trademark law and its exceptions should serve larger public purposes:

> There are and always have been purposive elements reflecting public policy considerations which inform the statutory creation of intellectual property rights. The public policy dimensions of trademark legislation and the contending interests which such dimensions accommodate were referred to in *Campomar Sociedad, Limitada* v *Nike International Ltd.*[82] The observation in that case that Australian trademarks law has 'manifested from time to time a varying accommodation of commercial and the consuming public's interests' has application with varying degrees of intensity to other intellectual property rights created by statute.[83]

80 Counterfeiting Currency, http://www.afp.gov.au/policing/counterfeit-currency.aspx

81 *Anti-Counterfeiting Trade Agreement* 2011, [2011] ATNIF 22, not yet in force.

82 *Campomar Sociedad, Limitada* v. *Nike International Ltd* (2000) 202 CLR 45.

83 *JT International SA* v. *Commonwealth of Australia British American Tobacco Australasia Limited* v. *The Commonwealth* [2012] HCA 43. For a commentary, *see* Matthew Rimmer, 'Cigarettes Will Kill

There is a need to revise Australian trademark law[84] so that it better recognises the interests of consumers.[85] One model would be an open, flexible defence of fair use in trademark law, as has already happened in the United States.[86] The US jurisprudence on the defence of fair use under trademark law arguably needs to be adopted by other jurisdictions, such as Australia, which have no such general defence for claims of trademark infringement, and instead rely on purpose-specific exceptions.[87]

Although it did not win support for ACTA from the Joint Standing Committee on Treaties, the Australian government nonetheless rushed through reforms on trademark enforcement in Schedule 6 of the Intellectual Property Laws Amendment (Raising the Bar) Act 2012 (Cth). The Minister for Innovation, Industry, Science and Research, Senator Kim Carr, emphasised in his second reading speech that the regime introduced a wide range of criminal and civil penalties in respect of trademark infringement, as well as border control measures. He stressed: "Criminal penalties play an important role in trademark enforcement, by deterring infringements and punishing infringers."[88] The minister also hoped that higher penalties would be "more effective in deterring infringement of trademark rights."[89] He also envisaged that the changes would "introduce some summary offences, but with lower fault elements and lower penalties."[90] In addition, Carr stressed that the amendments introduced a further remedy in civil actions for trademark infringement to allow a trademark owner to obtain "exemplary" damages, adding that "the aim of awarding additional damages is to increase the deterrence for infringers."[91]

You: The High Court of Australia and Plain Packaging of Tobacco Products', (2013) 1 *WIPO Magazine* 20–23, http://www.wipo.int/wipo_magazine/en/2013/01/article_0005.html

84 On trademark law theory, *see* Graeme Dinwoodie and Mark Janis (eds.), *Trademark Law and Theory: A Handbook of Contemporary Research*, Edward Elgar, 2008; and Lionel Bently, Jennifer Davis and Jane Ginsburg (eds.), *Trade Marks and Brands: An Interdisciplinary Critique*, Cambridge University Press, 2008.

85 There is some interesting work emerging on trademark law and consumers; *see* Rosemary Coombe, *The Cultural Life of Intellectual Properties*, Duke University Press, 1998; Laura Heyman, 'The Public's Domain in Trademark Law: A First Amendment Theory of the Consumer' (2009) 43 *Georgia Law Review* 651–715; Eduardo Penalver and Sonia Katyal, *Property Outlaws: How Squatters, Pirates, and Protestors Improve the Law of Ownership*, Yale University Press, 2010, and Stacy Dogan and Mark Lemley, 'Parody as Brand', Stanford Public Law Working Paper No. 2170498, 2 November 2012, http://ssrn.com/abstract=2170498

86 *See also* William McGeveran, 'Four Free Speech Goals for Trademark Law' (2008), 18 *Fordham Intellectual Property, Media & Entertainment Law Journal* 1205–1227.

87 The defences in Australian trademark law are fragmented and narrow – *see* for instance s 122 of the *Trade Marks Act 1995* (Cth).

88 Senator Kim Carr, 'Second Reading Speech on the *Intellectual Property Laws Amendment (Raising the Bar) Bill*', Hansard, Senate, the Australian Parliament, 22 June 2011, 3425, http://parlinfo.aph.gov.au/parlInfo/search/display/display.w3p;query=Id%3A%22chamber%2Fhansards%2F3114f036-d57a-4423-a536-f8c05c168c6e%2F0024%22

89 Ibid.

90 Ibid.

91 Ibid.

The Federal Government maintained that it was merely implementing the recommendations of the Advisory Council on Intellectual Property in relation to trademark enforcement.[92] However, there was no substantive debate at the committee stage over such amendments. There was concern that the government had, in effect, raised standards in respect of trademark enforcement by stealth through this schedule.

## PATENT LAW, HEALTH CARE AND ACCESS TO ESSENTIAL MEDICINES

In Australia, there was much debate as to what, if any, impact ACTA would have on health care. During the negotiations, the Department of Foreign Affairs and Trade denied that ACTA would deal, at all, with patent law. Surprisingly, the final text has only limited exclusions for patent law contained within footnotes. Members may choose to exclude patents from the entire civil enforcement section, and patents and protection of undisclosed information do not fall within the border measures section. Nonetheless, George Mina of the Department of Foreign Affairs and Trade insisted that ACTA would have a positive impact on health: "We had a seat at the negotiating table which enabled us to influence outcomes for the benefit of our exporters and for the health and safety of our consumers."[93] This position was disputed in the Australian debate.

Locally, Medicines Australia – which represents brand-name pharmaceutical drug manufacturers – has supported strong intellectual property protection for medicines.

Internationally, one of the main proponents of ACTA was the Pharmaceutical Research and Manufacturers of America (PhRMA).[94] The industry group, in a submission to the United States Trade Representative, argued that the definition of counterfeiting should embrace a wide range of medical products and pharmaceutical drugs. In addition to trademark reform, PhRMA called for a range of other sanctions for intellectual property infringements: "Even in countries with strong IP regimes, trademark laws are inherently incapable of protecting drug distribution channels against the full spectrum of activities that contribute to the proliferation of counterfeit medicines."[95] The group called for "a framework of strong, harmonised

92 Advisory Council on Intellectual Property, *Review of Trade Mark Enforcement*, Canberra: IP Australia, April 2004, http://www.acip.gov.au/library/reviewtmenforce.pdf

93 George Mina, 'Public Hearing', Hansard, Joint Standing Committee on Treaties, House of Representatives, 19 March 2012, 14.

94 Pharmaceutical Research and Manufacturers of America, 'Comments on the *Anti-Counterfeiting Trade Agreement*', the United States Trade Representative, 21 March 2008, https://sites.google.com/site/iipenforcement/civil-society-submissions

95 Ibid.

enforcement tools and remedies to combat the global proliferation of counterfeit medical products."[96]

There has been a long-standing debate over patent law and access to essential medicines in Australia, as well as internationally.[97]

Alphapharm – the Australian generic drugs manufacturer – has expressed concern that the agreement could adversely impact the dissemination of generic medicines.[98] Dr Martin Cross, the Managing Director of the company, gave evidence to the Joint Standing Committee on Treaties:

> By including patents, this creates major issues running forward (...) Because ACTA – unintentionally, we believe – has this extension into intellectual property, the possibility is that a totally legitimate generic medicine in Australia could now be considered a counterfeit under the agreement. This is extremely detrimental to our company's ability to bring the products to market, but, much more importantly to the Commonwealth, it has a huge impact on the cost of medicines for the Pharmaceutical Benefits Scheme.[99]

The concern remains that ACTA could have an impact on pharmaceutical drugs and access to medicines – either through an over-broad definition of piracy and counterfeiting, or through trademark enforcement or patent enforcement in respect of essential medicines.

The preamble of ACTA stresses that the treaty recognises "the principles set forth in the Doha Declaration on the TRIPS Agreement and Public Health, adopted on 14 November 2001, at the Fourth WTO Ministerial Conference." However, the actual text of ACTA provides no such recognition or acknowledgment of the principles in the Doha Declaration,[100] or the 2003 WTO General Council Decision.[101]

Notwithstanding the disclaimers, many fear that ACTA will have an adverse impact on access to essential medicines.

Brook Baker, for instance, has noted that "extending third-party enforcement and imposing provisional measures and permanent injunctions could interfere with the

96 Ibid.

97 Thomas Pogge, Matthew Rimmer and Kim Rubenstein (eds.) *Incentives for Global Public Health: Patent Law and Access to Medicines*. Cambridge: Cambridge University Press, 2010.

98 Alphapharm, 'Submission on the *Anti-Counterfeiting Trade Agreement* to the Joint Standing Committee on Treaties', 21 February 2012, http://www.aph.gov.au/Parliamentary_Business/Committees/House_of_Representatives_Committees?url=/jsct/21november2011/subs/sub5.pdf

99 Joint Standing Committee on Treaties, 'Public Hearing', Canberra: The Australian Parliament, 23 March 2012, 1.

100 *Declaration on the TRIPS Agreement and Public Health: Adopted on 14 November 2001*, WTO Doc WT/MIN(01)/DEC/2 (2001) ('the *Doha Declaration*').

101 *Implementation of Paragraph 6 of the Doha Declaration on the TRIPS Agreement and Public Health*, WTO Doc WT/L/540 (2003) (WTO General Council Decision of 30 August 2003).

goals of robust generic competition and access to medicine."[102] Similarly, Andrew Rens has expressed concerns that ACTA "threatens access to medicines through the indeterminacy of the terms 'counterfeit' and 'enforcement'," as well as through provisions on injunctions and border measures.[103] ACTA has also been criticised by a number of activists in the health sector, including Médecins Sans Frontières,[104] Oxfam[105] and Health Action International.[106]

There was also an uproar over customs interdicting generic medicines on the grounds of alleged intellectual property infringement following Dutch border officials' interception of a shipment of such medicines en route from India to Brazil.[107] While ACTA excludes patents and confidential information from the border measures section, it does not address other forms of intellectual property.

Sadly, Australia has been slow to implement international declarations and decisions on access to essential medicines such as the 2001 Doha Declaration on the TRIPS Agreement and Public Health and the 2003 WTO General Council Decision. The mechanism established by that decision has been rarely used thus far. In fact, there has been one instance of the scheme being used, when the Canadian generic manufacturer Apotex relied on the export mechanism to send drugs to Rwanda in 2008.[108] Up to now, too few countries have implemented an effective regime to allow for the export of essential medicines.

In 2007, the JSCOT recognised that providing better access to medicines to the world's poorest people is a worthy subject for an international treaty.[109] The committee supported "acceptance of the Protocol, followed by any necessary amendments to the Patents Act 1990 (Cth) to allow for compulsory licensing to enable export of cheaper versions of patented medicines needed to address public health problems

[102] Brook Baker, 'ACTA – Risks of Third-Party Enforcement for Access to Medicines' (2011) 26(3) *American University Journal of International Law* 579–599 at 581.

[103] Andrew Rens, 'Collateral Damage – The Impact of ACTA and the Enforcement Agenda on the World's Poorest Peoples' (2011) 26(3) *American University Journal of International Law* 784–809.

[104] Médecins Sans Frontières, 'A Blank Cheque for Abuse: The *Anti-Counterfeiting Trade Agreement* and its Impact on Access to Medicines', February 2012, http://www.msfaccess.org/sites/default/files/MSF_assets/Access/Docs/Access_Briefing_ACTABlankCheque_ENG_2012.pdf

[105] Oxfam, 'Statement Regarding ACTA and Public Health', October 2011, http://www.oxfamsol.be/fr/IMG/pdf/Oxfam_ACTA_analysis_FINAL.pdf

[106] Health Action International, 'ACTA and Access to Medicines: A Flawed Process, Flawed Rationale and Flawed Agreement', 27 February 2012, http://haieurope.org/wp-content/uploads/2012/02/27-Feb-2012-HAI-Europe-Policy-Brief-ACTA-and-Access-to-Medicines.pdf

[107] International Centre for Trade and Sustainable Development, 'Brazil, India Challenge Generic Drug Detentions', 12 May 2010, http://ictsd.org/i/news/bridgesweekly/75730/

[108] Matthew Rimmer, 'Race Against Time: The Export of Essential Medicines to Rwanda' (2008) 1 (2) *Public Health Ethics* 89–103.

[109] Joint Standing Committee on Treaties. *Protocol Amending the TRIPS Agreement*, Canberra: Australian Parliament August 2007, http://www.aph.gov.au/house/committee/jsct/9may2007/report/chapter9.pdf

to least-developed and developing countries."[110] However, the committee also noted that it shared my concerns that "the TRIPS Protocol requires intricate, time-consuming and burdensome procedures for the exportation of medicine, when what is needed is a simple, fast and automatic mechanism."[111]

Three years after the JSCOT report, IP Australia released its consultation paper entitled "Implementing the TRIPS Protocol" in April 2012.[112] After a long debate, in 2011, Trade Minister Craig Emerson and the then Innovation Minister Kim Carr had promised better access to medicines for countries in need.[113] Emerson observed: "Pandemics and other serious health issues remain a terrible problem in many of the world's poorest countries."[114] A draft legislative bill was released – the Intellectual Property Laws Amendment Bill 2012 (Cth) – to establish an export mechanism for compulsory licensing of essential medicines.[115] However, there have been doubts that this regime is too narrow and rigid in its construction to be effective with regard to generic drugs exports.

The parliamentary inquiry into ACTA reached a number of conclusions in the debate on patent law, trademark law and medicine. In Recommendation 7, the JSCOT addressed the question of patent law:

> In the event that the Australian Government ratifies the Anti-Counterfeiting Trade Agreement (ACTA), the Government prepares legislation to: Exclude patents from the application of the civil enforcement and border measures parts of ACTA; Ensure that products produced in Australia as a result of the invalidation of a patent or part of a patent in Australia are not subject to the counterfeiting prohibition in ACTA; and Ensure that the expression 'counterfeit' in ACTA is not applied to generic medicines entered or eligible for entry on the Australian Register of Therapeutic Goods.[116]

Anand Grover, the United Nations Special Rapporteur on the Right to Health, welcomed the rejection of ACTA, saying that the agreement "failed to address numerous concerns related to access to medicines, such as unnecessary inclusion of

[110] Ibid.

[111] Ibid.

[112] IP Australia, *Implementing the TRIPS Protocol*, Canberra: IP Australia, 2010.

[113] Senator Dr. Craig Emerson and Senator Kim Carr, 'Better Access to Medicines for Countries in Need', Australian Labor Party, 22 March 2011, http://www.alp.org.au/federal-government/news/better-access-to-medicines-for-countries-in-need/

[114] Ibid.

[115] *Intellectual Property Laws Amendment Bill* 2012 (Cth) http://www.ipaustralia.gov.au/46106/Exposure_Draft_of_Intellectual_Property_Laws_Amendment_Bill_2012.pdf

[116] Joint Standing Committee on Treaties, *Report 126 – Treaty Tabled on 21 November 2011: Anti-Counterfeiting Trade Agreement 2011*, Canberra: Australian Parliament, June 2012, http://www.aph.gov.au/Parliamentary_Business/Committees/House_of_Representatives_Committees?url=jsct/21november2011/report.htm

patents and civil trademark infringements and unjustified stricter civil enforcement provisions that could impede access to generic medicines."[117] Grover cautioned against "heightened enforcement standards, envisioned by agreements like ACTA, that would hinder the legitimate trade and transit of medicines and adversely affect the availability of, and access to, affordable generic medicines."[118] He expressed hope that "other signatories to ACTA and countries negotiating similar trade agreements would consider implications of such agreements on their people's right to the highest attainable standard of physical and mental health and allow for more public scrutiny of the agreements fundamental to their health."[119]

## TOBACCO CONTROL AND PLAIN PACKAGING

There has been concern that the tobacco industry has sought to use trade agreements such as ACTA and the Trans-Pacific Partnership to undermine tobacco control measures, including graphic health warnings and plain packaging of tobacco products, which have been contemplated by the World Health Organization (WHO) Framework Convention on Tobacco Control.[120] This issue has been particularly pertinent and significant in Australia since the Gillard government has been a world leader in tobacco control.

In 2011, the Australian government passed the groundbreaking Tobacco Plain Packaging Act (Cth) and accompanying regulations.[121] The legislation was designed to promote public health and implement the WHO Framework Convention on Tobacco Control. The regime was intended to address practices such as the use of tobacco packaging to recruit new consumers, engaging in misleading and deceptive advertising, and undermining and subverting health warnings.

The High Court of Australia has handed down a groundbreaking ruling on the plain packaging of tobacco products. Not only does the decision deal with questions of constitutional law; the court also considered the public purposes of intellectual property law. In the 2012 case of *JT International SA v. Commonwealth of Australia; British American Tobacco Australasia Limited v. The Commonwealth*, the tobacco industry challenged the constitutional validity of the Tobacco Plain Packaging Act

117 United Nations Office of the High Commissioner for Human Rights, 'Generic Drugs: UN Expert on Health Hails European Parliament's Rejection of *Anti-Counterfeiting Trade Agreement*', 9 July 2012, http://www.ohchr.org/en/NewsEvents/Pages/DisplayNews.aspx?NewsID=12332&LangID=E

118 Ibid.

119 Ibid.

120 *The World Health Organization Framework Convention on Tobacco Control* Opened for signature 21 May 2003, 2302 UNTS 166 (entered into force 27 February 2005).

121 For an overview, *see* Tania Voon, Andrew Mitchell and Jonathan Liberman with Glyn Ayres (eds.), *Public Health and Plain Packaging of Cigarettes: Legal Issues*, Cheltenham and Northampton, MA: Edward Elgar, 2012.

2011 (Cth) under the Australian Constitution.[122] The tobacco companies argued that various intellectual property rights – including trademarks, copyright, designs, patents and business reputation – had been acquired by the Commonwealth government without compensation. By a landslide majority of six to one, the High Court of Australia ruled that the federal government had not engaged in an acquisition of property on less than just terms. Hayne and Bell J pithily summed up the matter:

> The Tobacco Plain Packaging Act 2011 (Cth) neither permits nor requires the Commonwealth to use the packaging as advertising space. The Commonwealth makes no public announcement promoting or advertising anything. The packaging will convey messages to those who see it warning against using, or continuing to use, the product contained within the packaging. Statutory requirements for warning labels on goods will presumably always be intended to achieve some benefit: usually the avoidance of or reduction in harm. But the benefit or advantage that results from the tobacco companies complying with the Tobacco Plain Packaging Act 2011 (Cth) is not proprietary. The Commonwealth acquires no property as a result of their compliance with the Tobacco Plain Packaging Act 2011 (Cth).[123]

The regime is under challenge in international fora. For example, Ukraine and others have mounted a challenge to the plain packaging regime in the WTO, and Philip Morris has questioned it under an investment treaty between Australia and Hong Kong.[124]

It should be noted that the tobacco industry has been one of the main champions of ACTA.

British American Tobacco made an extensive submission to the United States Trade Representative on this issue:

> We applaud the efforts of the U.S. Government in negotiating the ACTA. We believe that ACTA will be a valuable tool to address the growing world market in counterfeit cigarettes. We would strongly advocate tobacco and tobacco products being prioritised in the course of the negotiations when specific areas of concern

[122] *JT International SA* v. *Commonwealth of Australia British American Tobacco Australasia Limited* v. *The Commonwealth* [2012] HCA 43. For a commentary, *see* Matthew Rimmer, 'Cigarettes Will Kill You: The High Court of Australia and Plain Packaging of Tobacco Products', (2013) 1 *WIPO Magazine* 20–23 http://www.wipo.int/wipo_magazine/en/2013/01/article_0005.html and Jonathan Liberman, 'Plainly Constitutional: The Upholding of Plain Tobacco Packaging by the High Court of Australia' (2013) *American Journal of Law and Medicine* http://papers.ssrn.com/sol3/papers.cfm?abstract_id=2215346

[123] *JT International SA* v. *Commonwealth of Australia British American Tobacco Australasia Limited* v. *The Commonwealth* [2012] HCA 43 at [188].

[124] *See* Matthew Rimmer, 'The High Court and the Marlboro Man: The Plain Packaging Decision', *The Conversation*, 18 October 2012, https://theconversation.edu.au/the-high-court-and-the-marlboro-man-the-plain-packaging-decision-10014

are being addressed (…). It is important that ACTA seek to create new IP protection and enforcement provisions that exceed already existing agreements.[125]

It is notable that British American Tobacco was calling for "TRIPS Double Plus" protection for its intellectual property – above and beyond any existing agreements. There has been much concern of late about tobacco companies using trade and investment agreements to frustrate the introduction and implementation of public health measures such as tobacco control.

In the Australian inquiry into ACTA, a number of submissions raised the issue of plain packaging and tobacco control, including the academics Matthew Rimmer, Anna George and Luigi Palombi, as well as Dr Martin Cross of Alphapharm.[126]

Another concern pertained to the fact that ACTA did not contain any exclusions or safeguards with respect to tobacco products – especially in light of Australia's landmark plain packaging regime and its ongoing battles with tobacco companies. In February 2013, New Zealand, too, announced that it would adopt the plain packaging for tobacco products.[127] The country has been involved in both the ACTA and the Trans-Pacific Partnership negotiations. A number of other countries that participated in the ACTA negotiations, including the United Kingdom and Canada, have also been contemplating stronger tobacco control measures. There is a need to ensure that ACTA does not have any adverse impact on the operation of the WHO Framework Convention on Tobacco Control. There are similar concerns in respect of the Trans-Pacific Partnership's text on tobacco control.[128]

## BORDER MEASURES

In the Australian debate, there was a strong discourse on ACTA's border measures. This tapped into a wider popular discourse in Australian politics, which was focused on national security and border protection.[129]

125 British American Tobacco, 'Comments on the *Anti-Counterfeiting Trade Agreement*', the United States Trade Representative, 2008, https://sites.google.com/site/iipenforcement/civil-society-submissions

126 The Joint Standing Committee on Treaties hearings on 19 March 2012, 23 March 2012, and 7 May 2012 at Canberra at the Australian Parliament.

127 Tariana Turana, 'Government Moves Forward with Plain Packaging of Tobacco Products', New Zealand Government, 19 February 2013, http://www.beehive.govt.nz/release/government-moves-forward-plain-packaging-tobacco-products and International Centre for Trade and Sustainable Development, 'New Zealand Confirms Plans for Introducing Cigarette Packaging Law' (2013) 17 (7) *Bridges Weekly Trade News Digest* 27 February 2013 http://ictsd.org/i/news/bridgesweekly/156105/

128 Peter Martin, 'Plain Packs: The New Kines of Attack. Big Tobacco Tries The WTO And TPPA' *The Age and The Sydney Morning Herald*, 20 August 2012, http://www.petermartin.com.au/2012/08/plain-packs-new-lines-of-attack-cancer.html; and Matthew Rimmer, 'Big Tobacco and The Trans-Pacific Partnership', (2012) 21 (6) *Tobacco Control* 526–7, http://tobaccocontrol.bmj.com/content/21/6/524.full?sid=3b0c6aa1-f2d4-4626-ad27-d7f562a7d158

129 See for instance, the popular Australian television series, Border Security, http://au.tv.yahoo.com/plus7/border-security/

Part 5, Division 7 of the Copyright Act 1968 (Cth) currently deals with seizure of imported copies of copyright material. Part 13 of the Trade Marks Act 1995 (Cth) deals with importation of goods infringing Australian trademarks.

ACTA would provide additional requirements. Its Section 3 on border measures places a great burden on customs and border authorities to police intellectual property infringements on behalf of intellectual property owners. This would involve a significant cost to the governments who become parties to ACTA. This cost had not been properly addressed in the National Interest Analysis. It was particularly pertinent as it has been reported that Australian Customs will suffer significant budget cuts.[130] Furthermore, customs lack significant, independent expertise in copyright law, trademark law and patent law. As such, there was a danger that customs and border authorities might be unduly influenced by intellectual property owners, both through the provision of information and the demand for remedies.

This section of ACTA failed to adequately take into account the interests of importers and exporters. There was also a concern that intellectual property owners could try to block the import and export of the legitimate goods in order to reduce or prevent competition in a particular sector.

Furthermore, ACTA Section 3 did not provide adequate protection for consumers, whether they were travellers or purchasers of goods by mail order or internet retailing. Consumers could be severely inconvenienced, both personally and financially, by the suspension, detention and destruction of their goods. This was a particularly significant problem given the sheer size and scale of online retailing and electronic marketplaces such as eBay.

In terms of international trade law, Section 3 could raise trade issues, particularly if customs and border authorities are overzealous in enforcing intellectual property rights and prohibit the entry of goods and chattels. This could arise, for instance, if customs and border authorities target goods from a particular country or region (for instance, China).

While the debate over ACTA was the cynosure of all eyes, the Australian Parliament rushed through the Intellectual Property Laws Amendment (Raising the Bar) Act 2012 (Cth), without substantive debate at the committee stage. Schedule 6 contained numerous amendments strengthening the position of intellectual property owners in respect of customs and border control measures. The Minister for Innovation, Industry, Science and Research, Senator Kim Carr, noted that the legislation enhanced the powers of the Australian Customs and Border Protection Service to intercept goods that infringed copyrights or registered trademarks at the

[130] Markus Mannheim, 'Top Customs Executives to Bear the Brunt of Cuts', *The Canberra Times*, 27 February 2012.

border.[131] The minister maintained that the legislation "protects people from imitations and fakes" and "provides better border protection systems and stronger sanctions against counterfeits."[132]

There has been much debate as to whether or not the Australian government engaged in a strategy of bait-and-switch with ACTA and the Intellectual Property Laws Amendment (Raising the Bar) Act 2012 (Cth). In any case, the end result was that the government passed heightened protection for intellectual property with regard to border and customs measures.

## INTERNATIONAL LAW

In Australia, there were worries over the fragmentation of international law in respect of intellectual property enforcement. The Hon. Melissa Parke was concerned that ACTA was "negotiated in an exclusive club approach in a secret and non-transparent manner outside of the usual fora established to address IP issues, namely the World Intellectual Property Organisation, WIPO, and the World Trade Organisation, WTO."[133] There was also debate about whether ACTA was conceived of as an intellectual property agreement, a trade agreement or a border security agreement.

The preamble to ACTA maintains that "this Agreement operates in a manner mutually supportive of international enforcement work and cooperation conducted within relevant international organizations." In fact, the treaty undermines the role of existing multilateral organisations, such as the World Intellectual Property Organization and the World Trade Organization, and duplicates and fragments international law on intellectual property enforcement.

ACTA Chapter IV deals with international cooperation on questions of intellectual property enforcement. Article 33 provides that "international cooperation is vital to realizing effective protection of intellectual property rights and that it should be encouraged regardless of the origin of the goods infringing intellectual property

[131] Senator Kim Carr, 'Second Reading Speech on the *Intellectual Property Laws Amendment (Raising the Bar) Bill*', Hansard, Senate, the Australian Parliament, 22 June 2011, 3425, http://parlinfo.aph.gov.au/parlInfo/search/display/display.w3p;query=Id%3A%22chamber%2Fhansards%2F3114f036-d57a-4423-a536-f8c05c168c6e%2F0024%22

[132] Senator Kim Carr, 'Debate on the *Intellectual Property Laws Amendment (Raising the Bar) Bill*', Hansard, Senate, the Australian Parliament, 27 February 2012, 888, http://parlinfo.aph.gov.au/parlInfo/search/display/display.w3p;db=CHAMBER;id=chamber%2Fhansards%2Faa88dae2-44ba-4705-833a-d8b10600a4d0%2F0230;query=Id%3A%22chamber%2Fhansards%2Faa88dae2-44ba-4705-833a-d8b10600a4d0%2F0224%22

[133] The Hon. Melissa Parke, 'Report 126: Treaty tabled on 21 November 2011 of the Joint Standing Committee of Treaties', the House of Representatives, Hansard, the Australian Parliament, 27 June 2012, 8174.

rights." Kimberlee Weatherall has analysed the discourse of "cooperation" in this treaty extensively.[134] The Australian Federation Against Copyright Theft argued that ACTA would facilitate international cooperation on cases such as the action against the New Zealand service Megaupload.[135] The industry group accused Megaupload of "digital theft," but this undermines its argument, given the controversy over the action against Megaupload in terms of due process and rule of law.[136]

Chapter V deals with institutional arrangements, most significantly the establishment of the ACTA Committee.[137] The remit of the committee is to review the implementation and operation of the agreement, consider any proposed amendments to the treaty, and consider any other matter that may affect its implementation and operation. This is a wide field of operations. Moreover, the ACTA Committee can establish ad hoc committees, working groups, seek the advice of groups or individuals, share information and take other actions in the exercise of its functions. The committee can determine, as well as amend, its rules and procedures.

The supporters of ACTA argued that the committee would be a democratic body, which would complement existing institutions such as WIPO and the WTO. Moreover, the treaty's advocates hoped that the committee would become an efficient international institution able to engage in quick decision making, without the problems of stalemate and deadlock that have afflicted many multilateral institutions.

A number of civil society groups criticised this institutional structure. James Love from Knowledge Ecology International has expressed concerns that the ACTA Committee would not operate in an open, transparent and inclusive manner.[138] He feared that it would be captured by industry groups and countries with a maximalist

[134] Kimberlee Weatherall, 'Politics, Compromise, Text, and the Failures of the *Anti-Counterfeiting Trade Agreement*' (2011) 33(2) *Sydney Law Review* 229–263. *See also* Weatherall, Chapter 23 in the current volume.

[135] The Australian Federation Against Copyright Theft, 'A Submission on the *Anti-Counterfeiting Trade Agreement* to the Joint Standing Committee on Treaties', 14 February 2012, http://www.aph.gov.au/Parliamentary_Business/Committees/House_of_Representatives_Committees?url=/jsct/21november2011/subs/sub15.pdf

[136] *United States of America* v *Dotcom* [2012] Nzhc 1353 (15 June 2012); *Dotcom* v *Attorney-General* [2012] Nzhc 1494 (28 June 2012); *United States of America* v *Dotcom* [2012] Nzhc 2076 (16 August 2012). Timothy Lee, 'New Zealand Prime Minister Apologizes For Illegal Dotcom Spying', *Ars Technica*, 28 September 2012, http://arstechnica.com/Tech-Policy/2012/09/New-Zealand-Prime-Minister-Apologizes-For-Illegal-Dotcom-Spying/. *See also* Charles Graeber, 'Inside the Mansion – and Mind – of Kim Dotcom, the Most Wanted Man on the Net', *Wired Magazine*, 18 October 2012, http://www.wired.com/threatlevel/2012/10/Ff-Kim-Dotcom/; and Karl Schaffarczyk, 'Can Kim Dotcom's Mega Beat The Law Where Megaupload Failed?', *The Conversation*, 29 January 2013, http://theconversation.edu.au/Can-Kim-Dotcoms-Mega-Beat-The-Law-Where-Megaupload-Failed-11826

[137] *See* Yu, Chapter 8 in this volume.

[138] James Love, 'KEI comment on US signing of ACTA', Knowledge Ecology International, 3 October 2011, http://keionline.org/node/1291

intellectual property agenda. He was also concerned that the new committee would have the authority to amend the agreement, engage in selective accreditation favouring intellectual property right holders and endorse best practices in relation to intellectual property enforcement.

Widney Brown from Amnesty International commented: "All global trade agreements must be negotiated transparently under the auspices of existing intergovernmental organizations such as the WIPO or the WTO."[139] He feared that the ACTA Committee would lack "accountability, transparency, participation, equality and sustainability."[140] Brown also expressed concern that "[t]he pact would set up an unelected ACTA Committee, which would have the power to set standards, negotiate accessions of new countries and promote best practices."[141] Moreover, the Amnesty representative commented: "It would also be the first port of call to interpret the meaning of the frequently vague text of the agreement – creating meaning after parliaments had given their approval."[142] Brown feared that civil society would excluded from its deliberations: "Most of these functions are already carried out by WIPO, where civil society has a voice and deliberations are generally transparent and predictable."[143]

According to the Electronic Frontier Foundation, "this institutional structure raises concerns for signatories' national sovereignty and ability to set appropriate domestic policy."[144]

In the Australian Parliament, the Joint Standing Committee on Treaties was concerned that ACTA would be a protean, mercurial treaty, subject to future revisions, without due oversight or scrutiny:

> It is possible for a circumstance to arise in which the development and entrenchment of guidelines that qualify provisions of ACTA could lead to a requirement for legislative change in Australia without amendments to the underlying treaty. Such changes would consequently occur without the benefit of public scrutiny required by a treaty making process.[145]

139 Amnesty International, 'EU Urged to Reject International Anti-Counterfeiting Pact',10 February 2012, http://www.amnesty.org/en/news/eu-urged-reject-international-anti-counterfeiting-pact-2012-02-10

140 Ibid.

141 Ibid.

142 Ibid.

143 Ibid.

144 Electronic Frontier Foundation, 'In the Matter of the Anti-Counterfeiting Trade Agreement', 15 February 2011, https://www.eff.org/sites/default/files/filenode//EFF%20ACTA%20submission%20110215.pdf

145 Joint Standing Committee on Treaties, *Report 126 – Treaty Tabled on 21 November 2011: Anti-Counterfeiting Trade Agreement* 2011, Canberra: Australian Parliament, June 2012, 17, http://www.aph.gov.au/Parliamentary_Business/Committees/House_of_Representatives_Committees?url=jsct/21november2011/report.htm

There was also a concern that the ACTA Committee was an unnecessary addition to the already densely crowded field of international organisations dealing with intellectual property. In particular, there was a worry that the committee would seek to usurp the role of existing international organisations, particularly multilateral entities such as WIPO,[146] WTO[147] and the Internet Corporation for Assigned Names and Numbers (ICANN).[148]

## CONCLUSION: TRICK OR TREATY? THE AUSTRALIAN PARLIAMENT AND INTELLECTUAL PROPERTY TREATIES

In Australia, there was anxiety that ACTA ran roughshod over domestic law reform processes, trammelled the role of the Australian Parliament in lawmaking on intellectual property and undermined the status and authority of international institutions such as WIPO, the WTO and the United Nations. The Australian economist, Peter Martin, observed plaintively: "Why do we negotiate free trade agreements in secret?"[149]

There has been much concern that ACTA was secretly negotiated by a cabal of trade representatives and diplomats from a limited number of nation states including the United States, Japan, the members of the European Union, Switzerland, Singapore, South Korea, Australia, New Zealand, Canada and Mexico. Although there was input from intellectual property industries, there was little in the way of democratic deliberations with civil society groups or affected industries and communities. Sean Flynn summarised these concerns about the lack of due process, transparency and accountability in the negotiations: "The negotiation process for ACTA has been a case study in establishing the conditions for effective industry

146 *World Intellectual Property Organization Development Agenda: 45 Recommendations*, http://www.wipo.int/ip-development/en/agenda/recommendations.html#c ('*WIPO Development Agenda* 2007'); and Andrew Rens, 'Collateral Damage – The Impact of ACTA and the Enforcement Agenda on the World's Poorest Peoples' (2011) 26(3) *American University Journal of International Law* 784–809.

147 Pascal Lamy, 'Letter to Members of the European Parliament', 4 May 2010, http://keionline.org/sites/default/files/WTO-Lamy_Answer-to-MEP-letter.pdf and Pascal Lamy, 'The Rise of Regional Trade Agreements could lead to "Policy Fragmentation"', The World Trade Organization, 20 September 2012, http://www.wto.org/english/news_e/sppl_e/sppl246_e.htm

148 The Internet Corporation for Assigned Names and Numbers, http://www.icann.org/ For a discussion of its role, *see* David Lindsay, *International Domain Name Law: ICANN and the UDRP*, Oxford and Portland: Hart Publishing, 2007; and Jacqueline Lipton, *Internet Domain Names, Trademarks and Free Speech*, Cheltenham and Northampton, MA: Edward Elgar, December 2010.

149 Peter Martin, 'Why Do We Negotiate Free Trade Agreements in Secret?', *The Sydney Morning Herald*, 22 May 2012, http://www.petermartin.com.au/2012/05/why-do-we-negotiate-free-trade.html *See also* Peter Martin, 'What's Our Trade Minister Up To? What's He Signing In Our Name?', *The Sydney Morning Herald*, 7 August 2012, http://www.petermartin.com.au/2012/08/whats-our-trade-minister-up-to-whats-he.html

capture of a lawmaking process."[150] Professor Peter Yu has called this a "country-club" approach to setting intellectual property standards.[151] He has observed that the treaty "militates against domestic legislative reforms and the development of future intellectual property laws and policies."[152]

In Australia, the Commonwealth power to make and implement treaties was reviewed in a 1995 report called *Trick or Treaty?*[153] The report emphasised the need for greater parliamentary involvement:

> International obligations are incurred at the point of entering into a treaty. However, the function of implementing the treaty is often reserved to the Commonwealth Parliament. Accordingly, it would be preferable to involve Parliament prior to ratification, so that it can make a free choice without the possibility of a potential breach of treaty obligations.[154]

The report recommended the establishment of the Joint Standing of Committees and treaty impact statements.

There was also considerable disquiet about the performance of the Department of Foreign Affairs and Trade (DFAT) in the ACTA negotiations. The department conducted desultory consultations with stakeholders on the treaty, but these were little more than a charade, since the text of the agreement and analysis was not made available during the negotiations. The DFAT issued a cursory statement extolling ACTA's virtues in its National Interest Analysis[155] but failed to provide a regulatory impact statement on the treaty. In addition, the DFAT did not provide any accompanying legislation, despite the fact that the obligations were over and above those found in existing international treaties that Australia is party to. Regrettably, there has been no independent analysis of the treaty's impact on economics, human rights or health care in Australia.

Similar concerns were expressed in other jurisdictions. Kader Arif, Rapporteur for ACTA in the European Parliament, said of the process: "I want to denounce in the strongest possible manner the entire process that led to the signature of this

150 Sean Flynn, 'ACTA's Constitutional Problem: This Treaty Is Not a Treaty', (2011) 26(3) *American University Journal of International Law* 903. *See also*, Flynn, Chapter 9, present book.

151 Peter Yu, 'ACTA and Its Complex Politics' (2011), 3 (1) *WIPO Journal* 1–16, http://www.wipo.int/about-wipo/en/wipo_journal/pdf/wipo_journal_3_1.pdf

152 Peter Yu, 'Six Secret (and Now Open) Fears of ACTA' (2011) 64 *SMU Law Review*, 101–249, http://ssrn.com/abstract=1624813 *See also* Yu, Chapter 10 in this volume.

153 Senate Legal and Constitutional References Committee, *Trick or Treaty? The Commonwealth Power to Make and Implement Treaties*, November 1995, http://www.austlii.edu.au/au/other/dfat/reports/tort-con.html

154 Ibid.

155 National Interest Analysis of the *Anti-Counterfeiting Trade Agreement* [2011] ATNIA 31, http://www.aph.gov.au/Parliamentary_Business/Committees/House_of_Representatives_Committees?url=jsct/21november2011/treaties/anti_counterfeiting_nia.pdf

agreement: no inclusion of civil society organisations, a lack of transparency from the start of the negotiations, repeated postponing of the signature of the text without an explanation being ever given, exclusion of the EU Parliament's demands that were expressed on several occasions in our assembly."[156] In the United States, Oregon Democratic Senator Ron Wyden put forward amendments calling for the US Congress to have greater oversight over international negotiations relating to intellectual property and trade.[157] Californian Republican Congressman Darrell Issa established a wiki to enable citizens to comment on the ACTA text.[158] Wyden and Issa have argued that there is a need for a digital bill of rights to protect consumers from overly expansive intellectual property laws and treaties.[159]

Like other legislative assemblies around the world, the Australian Parliament was concerned that the treaty would impinge on national sovereignty, and constrain its role to engage in policymaking on matters of intellectual property. The Joint Standing Committee on Treaties raised a number of concerns about the ACTA process in the Australian context. Observing that there was a lack of proper analysis of the treaty, the JSCOT recommended that "in future, National Interest Analyses of treaties clearly intended to have an economic impact include an assessment of the economic benefits of the treaty, or, if no assessment of the economic benefit of a treaty has been undertaken, a statement to that effect, along with an explanation as to why it was not necessary."[160]

The JSCOT also made a number of other recommendations with respect to the national interest analyses,[161] including that "the Australian Government commissions an independent and transparent assessment of the economic and social benefits and costs of ACTA,"[162] and that "in circumstances where a treaty includes the

[156] Ibid.

[157] *Amendment to Prohibit the President from Accepting or Providing for the Entry into Force of certain Legally Binding Trade Agreements without the formal and express approval of Congress*, HR 3606 http://infojustice.org/wp-content/uploads/2012/03/Wyden-ACTA-Amendment.pdf

[158] Representative Darrell Issa, 'Keep the Web Open', http://keepthewebopen.com/acta. *See also* Lance Ulanoff, 'ACTA is more dangerous than SOPA', Mashable Social Media, 26 January 2012, http://mashable.com/2012/01/26/acta-more-dangerous-than-sopa/

[159] Tamlin Bason, 'Wyden, Issa Say Digital Bill of Rights Needed to Prevent New Versions of SOPA', Bloomberg BNA, 12 June 2012, http://www.bna.com/wyden-issa-say-n12884909994/

[160] Joint Standing Committee on Treaties, *Report 126 – Treaty Tabled on 21 November 2011: Anti-Counterfeiting Trade Agreement 2011*, Canberra: Australian Parliament, June 2012, 12, http://www.aph.gov.au/Parliamentary_Business/Committees/House_of_Representatives_Committees?url=jsct/21november2011/report.htm

[161] Joint Standing Committee on Treaties, *Report 126 – Treaty Tabled on 21 November 2011: Anti-Counterfeiting Trade Agreement 2011*, Canberra: Australian Parliament, June 2012, http://www.aph.gov.au/Parliamentary_Business/Committees/House_of_Representatives_Committees?url=jsct/21november2011/report.htm

[162] Ibid.

introduction of new criminal penalties, the treaty's National Interest Analysis justify the proposed new penalties."[163]

Committee member Senator Simon Birmingham said of the report: "It is also positive in that it recommends a pathway forward and provides recommendations not just for the ACTA agreement but also for Australia's treaty, made in the process, that hopefully will encourage greater scrutiny and consideration of future agreements."[164]

The ACTA case study highlights the need for reform of international treaty-making by the Australian government. In their classic work, *No Country Is an Island*, leading international and public lawyers Hilary Charlesworth, Madelaine Chiam, Devika Hovell and George Williams lamented:

> The power to commit Australia to new international obligations lies with the executive alone. Especially in regard to bilateral agreements, governments continue to make key decisions outside the public eye and without parliamentary involvement. Whether or not this is appropriate, it is fair to say that, even after the 1996 reforms, the role of parliament in the treaty process is a minor one.[165]

ACTA's secretive origins highlight the need for greater transparency and information sharing about treaty negotiations; the necessity of democratic participation in policy formulation and development; and the demand for evidence-based policy-making informed by independent, critical research on the economic, social and political costs of treaties.

The role of the Department of Foreign Affairs and Trade in international intellectual property negotiations needs to be re-evaluated, both in light of its past performance and its current role in the discussions over the Trans-Pacific Partnership and other bilateral and regional free trade agreements. There should be a new lead agency to coordinate intellectual property negotiations in order to properly integrate the inputs from various government departments and stakeholders. As there is a need for evidence-based policymaking, so there should be a role for the Productivity Commission and the financial departments. Moreover, as envisaged by the Trick or Treaty reforms in the 1990s, there should be a greater critical role for the Australian Parliament and the Joint Standing Committee on Treaties in assessing and evaluating international treaties, particularly those relating to intellectual property.

[163] Ibid.

[164] Senator Simon Birmingham, 'Report 126: Treaty tabled on 21 November 2011 of the Joint Standing Committee of Treaties', the House of Representatives, Hansard, the Australian Parliament, 27 June 2012, 4716.

[165] Hilary Charlesworth, Madelaine Chiam, Devika Hovell and George Williams, *No Country Is an Island: Australia and International Law*, Sydney: UNSW Press, 2006, 153.

There have been concerns over the transparency of the current negotiations over the Trans-Pacific Partnership (TPP) – a blockbuster plurilateral free trade agreement spanning the Pacific Rim.[166] Senator Scott Ludlam of the Australian Greens was concerned that a similar approach would be taken by the Department of Foreign Affairs and Trade with regard to the TPP's intellectual property chapter: "We have not in the committee gone very much into detail and did not directly address the Trans-Pacific Partnership Agreement, which many are aware is coming down the pipeline directly behind ACTA, but I think this is the first domino being pushed over into the Trans-Pacific Partnership Agreement, and I think it heralds some very significant flaws there as well."[167]

The United States has aggressively pushed for high standards for intellectual property in the Transpacific Partnership talks. A draft proposal on the intellectual property chapter from the US Trade Representative was leaked in 2011.[168] The chapter sought to cover copyright law, trademark law, patent law, customs and border measures, and intellectual property enforcement. Sean Flynn and his colleagues provided a comprehensive analysis of the text, observing that "the US proposals, if adopted, would create the highest intellectual property protection and enforcement standards in any free trade agreement to date."[169] According to *Inside U.S. Trade*, Australia, New Zealand and Singapore have proposed replacing some elements of the US proposal on intellectual property enforcement with language drawn from ACTA.[170] This is disturbing, given that the Joint Standing Committee on Treaties recommended postponing ACTA's ratification. A further leak revealed that the United States and Australia had been seeking to confine copyright exceptions in the Trans-Pacific Partnership negotiations.[171] There has been much concern about the

166 The United States Trade Representative, *The Trans-Pacific Partnership*, http://www.ustr.gov/tpp and The Department of Foreign Affairs and Trade, *The Trans-Pacific Partnership Agreement Negotiations*, http://www.dfat.gov.au/fta/tpp/index.html

167 Senator Scott Ludlam, 'Report 126: Treaty tabled on 21 November 2011 of the Joint Standing Committee of Treaties', Senate, Hansard, the Australian Parliament, 27 June 2012, 4718.

168 Matthew Rimmer, 'A Mercurial Treaty: The Trans-Pacific Partnership and the United States', *The Conversation*, 15 June 2012, https://theconversation.edu.au/a-mercurial-treaty-the-trans-pacific-partnership-and-the-united-states-7471

169 Sean Flynn, Margot Kaminski, Brook Baker, and Jimmy Koo, 'Public Interest Analysis of the US TPP Proposal for an IP Chapter' (2011) *PIJIP Research Paper Series*. Paper 21. http://digitalcommons.wcl.american.edu/research/21

170 'Countries Offer ACTA Language to Replace U.S. Ipr Proposal', *Inside US Trade*, 14 May 2012, Http://Insidetrade.Com/201205142398797/Wto-Daily-News/Daily-News/Countries-Offer-Acta-Language-To-Replace-Us-Ipr-Proposal/Menu-Id-948.Html, And http://lists.keionline.org/Pipermail/A2k_Lists.Keionline.Org/2012-May/001218.html

171 Peter Martin, 'What's Our Trade Minister Up To? What's He Signing in Our Name?', *The Sydney Morning Herald*, 7 August 2012, http://www.petermartin.com.au/2012/08/whats-our-trade-minister-up-to-whats-he.html

Trans-Pacific Partnership investment chapter, especially since a draft text was leaked in 2012.[172] Concerns have also been expressed over the possibility that the investment chapter could be deployed in intellectual property disputes, such as those initiated at the WTO on plain packaging of tobacco products.[173] WikiLeaks have since published draft text of the Intellectual Chapter and the Environment Chapter of the Trans-Pacific Partnership in November 2013 and January 2014.

The Obama administration has reiterated its enthusiasm for regional trade agreements. In his 2013 State of the Union address, President Obama stressed his support for not only the Trans-Pacific Partnership but also a new pact between the United States and the EU called the Trans-Atlantic Free Trade Agreement.[174]

Instead of pursuing regional free trade agreements, the Australian Parliament and the Australian government would do better to endorse the Washington Declaration on Intellectual Property and the Public Interest 2011.[175] To that end, Australia should ensure that intellectual property reforms respect human rights, value openness and the public domain, strengthen intellectual property limitations and exceptions, support cultural creativity, check enforcement excesses, and implement the Doha Declaration on the TRIPS Agreement and Public Health, the 2001 WTO General Council Decision and the 2007 WIPO Development Agenda. It is particularly important that future domestic and international intellectual property reform is informed by evidence-based policy-making.

172 Zach Carter, 'Obama Trade Document Leaked, Revealing New Corporate Powers and Broken Campaign Promises', *The Huffington Post*, 13 June 2012, http://www.huffingtonpost.com/2012/06/13/obama-trade-document-leak_n_1592593.html; and Maira Sutton, 'Secretive Copyright Negotiations Continue at the 16th Round of TPP Talks', Electronic Frontier Foundation, 4 March 2013, https://www.eff.org/deeplinks/2013/03/secretive-copyright-negotiations-continue-16th-round-tpp-talks

173 Matthew Rimmer, 'A Dangerous Investment: Australia, New Zealand, and the Trans-Pacific Partnership', *The Conversation*, 2 July 2012, http://theconversation.edu.au/a-dangerous-investment-australia-new-zealand-and-the-trans-pacific-partnership-7440

174 Matthew Rimmer, 'The Two Treaties: Obama, Trade, and the State of the Union', *The Conversation*, 14 February 2013, https://theconversation.edu.au/the-two-treaties-obama-trade-and-the-state-of-the-union-12197

175 *Washington Declaration on Intellectual Property and the Public Interest* 2011, http://infojustice.org/washington-declaration-html

# 11

# A Brazilian Perspective

## Res Inter Alios Acta

*Denis Borges Barbosa*

### INTRODUCTION

According to the Latin maxim *"res inter alios acta … aliis nec nocet nec prodest,"* whatever is agreed among certain parties neither benefits nor harms non-parties to the treaty. Nothing could be less apropos to qualify the Anti-Counterfeiting Trade Agreement (ACTA), initially discussed among just a few parties. When the final text emerged in late 2012, it became obvious that the nations excluded from the negotiating process might well end up being harmed by the agreement, or at least not benefiting from it in any significant way.[1]

This chapter is a revised and updated version of Borges Barbosa, Denis, Untoward Restrictions to Trade and Abuses of Intellectual Property Rights: A Brazilian Perspective to the ACTA Exercise (June 22, 2010). Available at SSRN: http://ssrn.com/abstract=1628744 or http://dx.doi.org/10.2139/ssrn.1628744

[1] "From the outset, however, the negotiations were embroiled in controversy, for at least four reasons. First, while the negotiations were initially carried out behind closed doors, industry representatives were apparently being supplied with information that was not being disseminated to the public. Second, the 'plurilateral' nature of the negotiations aroused suspicions that the ACTA negotiations were but the latest example of 'forum-shifting' – a well-documented tactic that is apparently being deployed by owners of intellectual property (IP) in an effort to ratchet up international standards for the protection of private intellectual property rights (IPRs) […]. A particularly jolting development in the effort by critics to secure more specifics concerning the ACTA negotiations occurred in March 2009, when, notwithstanding President Obama's campaign promises of greater transparency in U.S. government policymaking, the Office of the U.S. Trade Representative (USTR) denied a Freedom of Information Act (FOIA) request for a copy of the ACTA discussion draft and related materials on the ground that they were "classified in the interest of national security." While the invocation of national security may have been simply a ruse to camouflage and avoid exacerbating growing divisions among the negotiating parties, it proved useful to take this national security claim at face value, as it offered a starting point for this chapter's predecessor – which sought "to provide two alternative tales of the treaty with a view to identifying and clarifying the various controversies currently surrounding the negotiations." McManis, Charles R. and Pelletier, John S., "Two Tales of a Treaty Revisited: The Proposed Anti-Counterfeiting Trade Agreement (ACTA) (May 1, 2012)." Washington University in St. Louis Legal Studies Research Paper No. 12–04–10. Available at SSRN: http://ssrn.com/abstract=2049673 or http://dx.doi.org/10.2139/ssrn.2049673. *See also* Levine, David S., Bring in

In October 2007, the United States, Japan, Switzerland and the European Union announced that they would launch negotiations for an Anti-Counterfeiting Trade Agreement (ACTA) with the aim of "providing a response to the increase in global trade of counterfeit goods and pirated copyright protected works."[2] A very peculiar characteristic of the initial phases of the proceedings was the secrecy surrounding the negotiating text. This was probably the aspect that generated the most dissatisfaction among civil society, particularly in the United States, Australia, Canada and EU countries. The fact that influential business associations such as the International Trademark Association, the Pharmaceutical Research and Manufacturers of America and International Intellectual Property Alliance had access to the text under negotiation, while other NGOs and third-party countries were held away, contributed to a sense of impending impropriety.[3]

ACTA has a broad scope[4]: it aims to supplement and develop the TRIPS level of enforcement.[5] Its Chapter II covers (a) general obligations; (b) civil enforcement; (c) border measures; (d) criminal enforcement; and (e) enforcement of intellectual property rights in the digital environment.

the Nerds: Secrecy, National Security and the Creation of International Intellectual Property Law (April 6, 2012). *Cardozo Arts & Entertainment Law Journal*, Vol. 30, No. 2, p. 105. Available at SSRN: http://ssrn.com/abstract=2038020.

2 "As of May 2012, the European Union and 22 of its 27 member states have joined Australia, Canada, Japan, Morocco, New Zealand, Singapore, South Korea and the United States as signatories of ACTA. Yet, the outlook for ratification by the May 1, 2013 deadline appears dismal. Mexico dropped out of early negotiations and is unlikely to sign, and in February 2012, the EU suspended ratification following widespread protests across Europe and riots in Poland. Effectively, ACTA has been declared dead on arrival." Stacy Wu, "United States: ACTA: The Public Revolt", 23 May 2012, found at http://www.mondaq.com/unitedstates/x/178644/Copyright/ACTA+The+Public+Revolt, visited 26/11/2012.

3 Until May 2008, these meetings for the negotiation of the agreement were made in absolute secrecy, until in May 22, 2008, a discussion paper with proposals on the settlement was disclosed in the site http://wikileaks.org/LEAK/ACTA-PROPOSAL-2007.PDF. The Brazilian Foreign Service has requested access to such text from the US Government, what was officially denied. The NGO Knowledge Ecology International also requested the USTR for such an access, on the basis of the US Freedom of Information Act. The application was refused on the grounds that the draft under negotiation was "Properly Classified in the interest of national security." In the EU, a similar request was presented by the Foundation for a Free Information Structure before the EU Council, which request was also rejected on the grounds that "disclosure of information could prevent the proper conduct of the negotiations, would weaken the position of the European Union and might affect negotiations and the relations with the third parties concerned." Similar requests were denied by the governments of Australia, Canada and New Zealand.

4 *See*, generally, The U.S. Trade Representative, "The Anti-Counterfeiting Trade Agreement–Summary Of Key Elements Under Discussion (2009)", available at http://www.ustr.gov/webfm_send/1479.

5 "Although ACTA is clearly an indictment of the TRIPS Agreement's failure to meet the enforcement needs and expectations of developed countries and their intellectual property industries, the agreement is also quite ambitious in scope. In addition to addressing the TRIPS Agreement's shortcomings in the area of crossborder enforcement, ACTA seeks to incorporate new measures to target digital and transnational challenges. While article 23.3 facilitates the introduction of anti-camcording laws,

While the ACTA text finally concluded in late 2010[6] did not include all the issues initially envisaged, it still sparked such a negative reactions from the general public and NGOs[7] that the European Parliament refused to endorse it.[8] The European Court of Justice was asked to consider the issue, but the European Commission eventually dropped the request.[9]

Brazil's foreign policy with regard to international IP obligations considers the terms negotiated during the TRIPS exercise as a *ceiling*. As stressed by Brazil during the FTAA initiative,[10] anything discussed after TRIPS – even under the argument that its enforcement standards were defective – must not go beyond the multilateral bargain achieved in 1994.

ACTA was a concern for the Brazilian government from the start. Brazil thought that the eventual conclusion of a multilateral instrument on "enforcement" might affect the balance of the intellectual property system and cause a negative impact on international trade.[11] The role of Brazil and like-minded emerging countries (none

article 23.4 includes new provisions that may create new criminal penalties for 'aiding and abetting' intellectual property infringements – penalties that do not yet exist in the United States." Yu, Peter K., "Enforcement, Enforcement, What Enforcement?" (October 23, 2011). *IDEA: The Journal of Law and Technology*, Vol. 52, 2012; Drake University Law School Research Paper No. 12–22. Available at SSRN: http://ssrn.com/abstract=1948326

6 Anti-Counterfeiting Trade Agreement, Dec. 3, 2010, opened for signature Mar. 1, 2011, available at http://www.ustr.gov/webfm_send/2417.

7 *See* European Academics, (2011), "Opinion of European Academics on Anti-Counterfeiting Trade Agreement", *Journal of Intellectual Property, Information Technology and E-Commerce Law* (JIPITEC) 2011, Vol. 2, 65 or http://www.iri.unihannover.de/acta-1668.html, visited Nov. 26, 2012.

8 On July 4, 2012. *See*, generally, Matthews, Duncan, "The Rise and Fall of the Anti-Counterfeiting Trade Agreement (ACTA): Lessons for the European Union" (October 15, 2012). Queen Mary School of Law Legal Studies Research Paper No. 127/2012. Available at SSRN: http://ssrn.com/abstract=2161764 or http://dx.doi.org/10.2139/ssrn.2161764.

9 The Court of Justice of the EU (CJEU) has to answer to the European Commission's request, on 22 February 2012, to clarify whether ACTA is incompatible, in any way, with the EU's fundamental rights and freedoms, including freedom of expression and information and data protection, and the right to property in the case of intellectual property.

10 "Brazil considers that IPRs constitute a 'systemic subject,' that will have to be discussed in the multilateral context, in the scope of the negotiations of the OMC [WTO], not in the context of the hemispherical negotiations. The MERCOSUL, however, would be available use, in the scope of the negotiations of the ALCA [FTAA], to accept the creation of mechanism of consultations in questions related to IPS, but it does not consider desirable the creation of mechanism of 'enforcement,' as considered by the North American party. Brazil considers that all the countries are liable the eventual imperfections in its IPRs system of protection. It is open to develop the cooperation in the area, but it does not consider desirable the creation of mechanism of 'enforcement' in the matter, on a hemispheric scope, as it considers that such mechanism could result in abuses and crossed retaliations in the case of eventual misunderstandings in the area IPRs." Brazilian Foreign Office letter to this author, of Feb. 6, 2006. Quoted in Borges Barbosa, Denis, "TRIPs art. 7 and 8, FTAs and Trademarks" (March 9, 2006). Available at SSRN: http://ssrn.com/abstract=889107.

11 Beyond the secrecy issue, the dubious nature of the negotiating strategy was noted by Yu, Peter K., "ACTA and Its Complex Politics" (November 3, 2011). *WIPO Journal*, Vol. 3, p. 1, 2011. Available at

of which negotiated or signed ACTA) may be significantly affected by an unbalanced enforcement treaty.[12]

## FORUM SHOPPING

Brazil has argued that intellectual property issues should be treated in specialised multilateral fora – WIPO and the WTO – where discussions are open to more than 140 countries, and deliberations are transparent and inclusive, with broad participation that includes representatives of both industrial interests and broader civil society values.

ACTA is part of the "forum-shopping" strategy of developed countries, which seek to promote their offensive interests in intellectual property outside the scope of specialised organisations such as WIPO and WTO through bilateral, plurilateral or other fora (WCO, UPU).[13] Forum shopping threatens the legal relevance of WIPO's Development Agenda,[14] the TRIPS Agreement and Doha Declaration on TRIPS and Public Health. This approach does not favour a balance between rights and obligations because in non-traditional fora, developed countries and the interests of their industries tend to wield disproportionate influence.

The ACTA negotiating parties were either (i) developed countries, or other high per capita income countries (Singapore, United Arab Emirates and Republic of Korea); (ii) OECD members (Mexico); or (iii) countries that had signed a free trade agreement with the United States (Jordan and Morocco).

The secrecy surrounding the negotiations was a major obstacle to the participation of non-governmental organisations, pro-consumer groups and other stakeholders beyond intellectual property right holders. All pro-ACTA non-governmental entities were associations linked to right holders.[15]

SSRN: http://ssrn.com/abstract=1953899. It is to be noted that similar secrecy surrounds the Trans-Pacific Partnership negotiations, the scope of which is limited to the Pacific countries. Chile and Peru are parties to the TPP, although they were excluded from the ACTA negotiations. Mexico signed ACTA in July 2012.

12 Barbosa, Denis Borges, "BRIIC: Laying a New Patent System," *International Review of Intellectual Property and Competition Law*, Vol. 43. No. 4, 2012.

13 A trend that this author had already noted in 2005 (Barbosa, Denis Borges, "Counting ten for TRIPS: Author rights and access to information – a cockroach's view of encroachment." In: Kors, J. and Remiche, B., *ADPIC, Première décennie: droits d´auteur et accès à l´information. Perspective latino-americaine. L´Accord ADPIC: dix ans après.* Belgica: LARCIER, 2007): "Professor Drahos has noticed that the USA used a 'forum-shifting' tactic to probe for a more advantageous instance in copyright issues, raising its TRIPs-plus interests in different international fora (e.g. WIPO, WTO, and UNESCO). The idea is to enlist the help of some 'progressive' developing countries to act as allies."

14 By the way, ACTA negotiations were launched two months after the Development Agenda, proposed by Argentina and Brazil, was adopted in WIPO.

15 According to the USTR site, among the organisations that had offered support to the agreement were the Business Software Alliance, the International Trademark Association, the Entertainment Industry

## REPRESSION

ACTA proposes a single remedy for counterfeiting and piracy – enforcement. Brazil recognises the importance of deterrence. The National Council to Combat Counterfeiting and Piracy – comprising government representatives, industry associations and civil society organisations – has been coordinating successful actions to seize counterfeit and pirated goods at the borders and within the national territory, enforced by the Federal Police, the Federal Highway Police and the Internal Revenue.

Brazil advocates, however, that a strategy to promote compliance with rights (i.e. enforcement) should always be integrated with socio-economic and educational measures, informed by a sophisticated and well-informed diagnosis about the global problem of piracy and of counterfeiting.

Plurilateral strategies based *exclusively* on repression threaten (i) the balance between rights and obligations, (ii) international trade in legitimate products, including generic drugs, and (iii) the rights of citizens, such as the presumption of innocence, the adversarial system and due process of law.

## SEIZURE OF GOODS IN TRANSIT

In May 2010, Brazil and India requested WTO dispute settlement consultations with the EU and the Netherlands on the seizure of generic drugs in transit, but the case is currently suspended.[16]

The final version of ACTA includes provisions allowing the seizure of goods in transit that allegedly infringe trademarks (no longer, as in the prior versions, covering broader intellectual property). Even this more restricted application affects unfavourably one of the cornerstones of the IP system, namely the principle of territoriality.

Guild Union, the Motion Picture Association of America, the Recording Industry Association of America and U.S. Chamber of Commerce.

16 "Several recent detentions of generic pharmaceutical products transiting through the European Union (EU) for suspected infringements of intellectual property rights raised serious concerns for public health advocates and threatened to expose systemic problems existing in the World Trade Organization's (WTO) Agreement on Trade-Related Aspects of Intellectual Property Rights (TRIPS). The detentions not only garnered international attention, but India and Brazil formally began WTO dispute settlement proceedings against the EU. The parties recently reached a mutually agreed solution to the matter and the proceedings have been halted, leaving unanswered the complex legal and technical questions raised by the detentions of pharmaceuticals in transit." Mercurio, Bryan Christopher, "'Seizing' Pharmaceuticals in Transit: Analysing the WTO Dispute that Wasn't" (2012). *International and Comparative Law Quarterly*, Vol 61, No. 2, 389–426. Available at SSRN: http://ssrn.com/abstract=2152457.

Intellectual property rights are essentially territorial – that is, they are made applicable in a particular jurisdiction. By seizing goods in transit, customs authorities assert jurisdiction on the flow of intellectual property goods bound exclusively for third countries, thus incurring an extraterritorial application of national legislation.

## THREAT TO THE RIGHT TO PRIVACY IN THE DIGITAL ENVIRONMENT

Brazil is especially concerned about enforcement rules that could lead to violations of privacy and restriction of individual freedom on the Internet. ACTA Section 4, which deals with the regulation of cyberspace, raises controversial topics such as technological protection measures, rights management information, obligations of providers to reveal the identity of their subscribers and procedures to disable access to the Internet. The final version of ACTA was careful enough to pay extensive lip service to the concerns of privacy.

## THE CONSTITUTIONALITY OF ACTA: A BRAZILIAN PERSPECTIVE

In the event that the Brazilian government decides to accede to ACTA or a similar international instrument, it is likely that significant constitutional issues would prevent its enactment under the country's legal system.[17]

First of all, there is a possible conflict with the privacy standards enshrined in the constitution as to the users of Internet.[18] These standards are being specified at the statutory level by a bill currently under discussion in the Brazilian congress.[19]

The industrial property provisions of the constitution (comparable to the IP clause in the US Constitution),[20] establish that the purpose of patents and trademarks is to

[17] *See* Patrícia Porto, "O interesse público brasileiro na adesão ao Anti-Counterfeiting Agreement (ACTA), Revista Eletrônica do IBPI", found at http://www.ibpibrasil.org/media/bceac241c78c151affff-802bac144226.pdf, visited Nov. 26, 2012. As to similar arguments raised in the European environment, Douwe Korff and Ian Brown, Opinion on the compatibility of the Anti-Counterfeiting Trade Agreement (ACTA) with the European Convention on Human Rights & the EU Charter of Fundamental Rights, found at http://rfc.act-on-acta.eu/fundamental-rights, visited on Nov. 23, 2012.

[18] Porto. Cit. "Se o governo brasileiro aderir a esse acordo violará vários direitos fundamentais previstos na Constituição nacional, como o direito à privacidade e ao sigilo das informações privadas, previstos nos incisos X, XII, do artigo 5, da CFRB/88. Ao permitir que se viole a privacidade dos usuários de computadores e Internet, por exemplo."

[19] Bill 2126/2011, "Marco Civil da Internet", found at http://www.camara.gov.br/proposicoesWeb/prop_mostrarintegra;jsessionid=48E53BDC65BC9914DC424FF0B78CC3A3.node1?codteor=912989&filename=PL+2126/2011, visited Nov. 26, 2012. Some comments classify such bill as an Anti-Acta proposal, *see* http://www.techdirt.com/articles/20121112/07295821015/will-brazils-anti-acta-marco-civil-be-subverted-copyright-lobbyists-last-moment.shtml, visited Nov. 22, 2012.

[20] "[t]o promote the Progress of Science and the Useful Arts." U.S. Const. Art. 1, 8. *See* Edward C. Walterscheid, To Promote the Progress of Science and the Useful Arts: The Background and Origin of the Intellectual Property Clause of the United States Constitution, 2 J. Intell. Prop. L. 1, 37–38 (1994).

fulfil the social interest and to promote the technical and economic development of Brazil.[21] Any imbalance in IP rights created by ACTA that conflicts with this constitutional target would prevent acceptance of the agreement.

Importantly, the constitutional requirement does not cover only the empowerment of the patent or trademark holder, but also imposes the reasonability of such protection in face of other constitutional interests. This does not seem entirely incompatible with the US constitutional interpretation of its own basic law.[22] This imbalance would also arguably conflict with some multilateral commitments in the TRIPS Agreement.[23]

Another important aspect is the eventual disproportion of sanctions, criminal or otherwise, which would be required by ACTA or its sequels.[24] Although some of the criminal sanctions included in Brazilian statutes also seem imbalanced,[25] any further aggravation would probably lead to close scrutiny by constitutional jurisdiction.

The wording of ACTA also raises other important issues that would probably defy constitutional inquiry,[26] especially with regard to the *maximum standards* provided

For a comparison of the Brazilian and US IP clauses, *see* Barbosa, Denis Borges, Ana Beatriz Nunes; Karin Grau-Kuntz. *A Propriedade Intelectual na Construção dos Tribunais Constitucionais*. Rio de Janeiro: Lumen Juris, 2009.

21 The Brazilian text is: "Art. 50 (...) XXIX – a lei assegurará aos autores de inventos industriais privilégio temporário para sua utilização, bem como proteção às criações industriais, à propriedade das marcas, aos nomes de empresas e a outros signos distintivos, tendo em vista o interesse social e o desenvolvimento tecnológico e econômico do País;" ["The statute shall ensure to the authors of industrial inventions a temporary privilege for its utilisation, as well as the protection of industrial creations, of the propriety of trademarks, of the trade names and of other distinctive signs, considering the social interest and the technological and economic development of the country"]

22 "Since Pennock v. Dialogue, 2 Pet. 1, was decided in 1829, this Court has consistently held that the primary purpose of our patent laws is not the creation of private fortunes for the owners of patents, but is 'to promote the progress of science and the useful arts' (Constitution, Art. I, § 8) – an object and purpose authoritatively expressed by Mr. Justice Story in that decision, saying: 'While one great object [of our patent laws] was, by holding out a reasonable reward to inventors and giving them an exclusive right to their inventions for a limited period, to stimulate the efforts of genius the main object was 'to promote the progress of science and useful arts." Motion Picture Patents Co. v. Universal Film Co., 243 U.S. 502 (1917).

23 Barbosa, Denis Borges, Chon, Margaret and von Hase Andrès Moncayo. "Slouching Towards Development in International Intellectual Property." *Michigan State Law Review*, Vol. 2007, No. 1, 2008, v. 2007, pp. 71–143.

24 Porto, cit.: "O ACTA fere os princípios da proporcionalidade e da razoabilidade, pois as sanções previstas no acordo são muito mais severas que as infrações. A sociedade como um todo seria criminalizada. O ACTA não distingue o uso justo e constitucional da contrafação e da pirataria e criminaliza toda e qualquer utilização de bens protegidos por direitos de exclusivas."

25 A number of state courts have been discussing the proportionality of such sanctions, especially the Supreme Court of the State of Minas Gerais.

26 Porto, cit.: "Se o governo brasileiro aderisse ao ACTA, violaria, ainda o artigo 5, inciso XXXII da CFRB/88, pois trataria os consumidores como criminosos e não observaria seus direitos. Violaria o artigo 5, LIV da CFRB/88, pois permitiria o confisco imediato e a destruição de produtos e bens de terceiros sem o devido processo legal."

by TRIPS on due process protection.[27] Moreover, considering the present mood of Brazilian civil society, the public reaction to the introduction of ACTA or any of its sequels would raise considerable difficulties in the congressional discussion and approval of such international instrument.

## CONCLUSION

Bringing IPR interests into the trade environment, as happened during the Uruguay Round, has certainly enhanced opportunities for right holders and other interested parties. By establishing a multilateral context where nineteenth-century intellectual property conventions were repositioned and some new obligations were added, IPR interests were advanced and an effective dispute resolution system was established.

This new situation has also brought two new requirements into the intellectual property arena. First, obtaining and enforcing patents, trademarks, copyrights and other similar property is no longer treated as an exception, albeit relevant, to trade considerations, as they were under the under Article XX of GATT 1947. Second, the need to balance eventual conflicting interests concerning IPRs was built up as a *trade* concern. Expediency and effectiveness in the enforcement of IPRs, while positive values in themselves, have now found a new limitation: any response to the increase in global trade of counterfeit goods and pirated copyright protected works (or an increase in the infringement of any other IP interest) may not be acceptable under the WTO if such response results in unreasonable harm to trade itself.

The TRIPS Agreement's balanced approach to this complex set of interests has established a strong set of procedural standards. Post-1994 IPR-related procedures may

[27] *See* Barbosa, Denis Borges, "Minimum Standards vs. Harmonization in the TRIPS context: the nature of obligations under TRIPS and modes of implementation at the national level in monist and dualist systems" in Carlos M. Correa (ed.), *Research Handbook on the Interpretation and Enforcement of Intellectual Property under WTO Rules*. London: Edward Elgar, 2010, v., p. 01–288. *See also* Josef Drexl, "The Evolution of TRIPS: Towards Flexible Multilateralism", in Kors, J and Remiche, B., *ADPIC, première décennie: droits d'auteur et accès à l'information. Perspective latino-americaine. L'Accord ADPIC: dix ans après*. Bruxelles: LARCIER, 2007, pp. 13–45: "Nevertheless, existing TRIPS standards may conflict with TRIPS-plus standards in bilateral agreements in cases in which the former do not only define minimum, but also maximum standards. Although it seems, according to Art. 1.1 TRIPS, that such maximum standards are inherently foreign to the concept of the TRIPS, the Agreement nevertheless prohibits "more intensive protection" in its provisions on enforcement of Part III to the extent that it fixes general procedural provisions to the benefit of any party to IP litigation. In some instances, the Agreement even explicitly provides for procedural rights of the defendant, like with regard to the level of legal certainty as a requirement for provisional measures (Art. 50.3 TRIPS) and the rights of the alleged infringer to be informed and to be heard within a reasonable time after provisional measures have been adopted inaudita altera parte (Art. 50.4 TRIPS). Most strikingly, Art. 48 TRIPS provides for a right to indemnification of the defendant in case of an abuse of enforcement procedures."

not ignore these standards, which – considering the interests of right holders – are to be taken as a *maximum* level of protection.

ACTA signatories, while purporting to make the enforcement of IPR interests more efficient, are subject to such standards. Any excess or abuse of the remedies provided under the proposed agreement shall be evaluated under the procedural guaranties set by WTO law, and the creation of separate institutional arrangements, or the exclusion of some parties to the benefit of the new rules, will not defeat the application of balanced and trade-filtered rules provided by the General Agreement and TRIPS.

An interesting aspect of international law helps to ensure that no ACTA provision may be applied in disregard of TRIPS *maximum standards*. Article 30 of the Vienna Convention on the Law of Treaties on the application of successive treaties relating to the same subject matter:

1. Subject to Article 103 of the Charter of the United Nations, the rights and obligations of States Parties to successive treaties relating to the same subject matter shall be determined in accordance with the following paragraphs.
2. When a treaty specifies that it is subject to, or that it is not to be considered as incompatible with, an earlier or later treaty, the provisions of that other treaty prevail. [...]

This provision also covers the relation of succeeding treaties on the same subject[28]:

4. When the parties to the later treaty do not include all the parties to the earlier one:
   (a) As between States Parties to both treaties the same rule applies as in paragraph 3;
   (b) As between a State party to both treaties and a State party to only one of the treaties, the treaty to which both States are parties governs their mutual rights and obligations.

Brazil's position, as a cautious observer from a comfortable distance, is that under the principle *pacta tertis nec nocent nec prossunt* – that is, "a treaty binds the parties and only the parties; it does not create obligations for a third state" – ACTA could not be *legally* applied to other non-signatory WTO members without full compliance with the TRIPS ceiling procedural guaranties. As a last resort, remedies under the Dispute Settlement Understanding would be available.

However, ACTA-like initiatives are proliferating. Even if negotiated in regional or otherwise limited contexts, the *economic* effects of such pacts are almost certain to affect a player like Brazil, whose cautious stance may become ever less comfortable.

[28] Nguyen Quoc Dinh, *Droit International Public*, 5th. ed., LGDJ, 1995, p. 267.

# 12

# Lessons to Be Drawn from the ACTA Process

## *An African Perspective*

*Andrew Rens*

### INTRODUCTION

What to make of ACTA? The European Parliament's unprecedented and overwhelming rejection of a treaty years in the making presents an unresolved anomaly in the narrative of intellectual property enforcement usually presented to African policymakers.

In the period leading up to the European Parliament vote in July 2012, five separate petitions were presented to its committees, while hundreds of thousands took part in street protests and nine countries halted ratification or declared that they would not ratify ACTA.[1] How could trade negotiators responsible to elected representatives, who are in turn accountable to citizens, come to be in such radical opposition to their citizens? What lessons might be drawn from the rapid advance and unforeseen failure of ACTA? How can these questions be answered from an African perspective?

Making sense of the history of ACTA is complicated by its proponents' choice of an opaque negotiating process that was neither open to observers nor openly reported. The text was initially kept secret, and only after repeated leaks and public criticism was a draft text made publicly available.

With the exception of Morocco, no African country was invited to participate in the drafting of ACTA. Some observers have suggested that the negotiators of the participating countries had planned to present developing countries with a finalised agreement on a "take it or leave it" basis.[2] African countries apparently were not the primary targets of the endeavour. So, what is ACTA's relevance to the continent?

[1] Eibauer, J. (2012) "Blessing or curse? The effects of transparency on the European Commission's success at the international ACTA negotiations", *PIPE – Papers on International Political Economy*, No. 14/2012.

[2] Geist, M. (2009) "The ACTA Threat to the Future of WIPO", *Intellectual Property Watch*, 14 April 2009, http://www.ip-watch.org/

Understanding ACTA from an African perspective is important for a number of reasons. The treaty would have caused both immediate and long-term negative effects on the poorest people in the world – many of them living in Africa – whether or not African countries acceded to it.[3] Some commentators suggest that ACTA was a response to developed countries' dissatisfaction over the failure to obtain their demands at WIPO,[4] or in the WTO-TRIPS Council,[5] or with TRIPS itself.[6]

ACTA was an undiluted manifestation of a multi-forum push for upward ratcheting of enforcement measures.[7] This ratcheting has imposed and will impose hardship on the world's poor, including those living in Africa. This chapter discusses some of the enforcement attempts that are particularly pertinent to the continent because they serve as practical examples of the treaty's likely effects. Particular attention is paid to the relationship between the enforcement attempts and the narrative proffered to justify them.

## THE ENFORCEMENT AGENDA

An emerging consensus explains ACTA as one in a series of strategic forum shifts, intended (amongst other things) to circumvent growing resistance and recruit new constituencies. These shifts did not result from simple domestic coalition building, but from densely internationally networked actors.[8] ACTA emerged as the product of a multi-nodal network in which many private and public actors sought to realise a process known as the Enforcement Agenda. Manifestations of this agenda conflate different types of intellectual property, collapse distinctions between private and commercial infringement and equate selling a poisonous fake medicine to downloading a digital recording of a song.[9]

[3] Rens, A. (2011) "Collateral Damage: The Impact of ACTA and the Enforcement Agenda on the World's Poorest People", *American University International Law Review* Vol. 26, No. 3, 783–809.

[4] Ibid. n. 2.

[5] Blakeney, M. (2012) "Intellectual Property Enforcement: A Commentary on the Anti-Counterfeiting Trade Agreement (ACTA)".

[6] McManis, C. R. and Pelletier, S. J. (2012) "Two Tales of a Treaty Revisited: The Proposed Anti-Counterfeiting Trade Agreement (ACTA)", *Washington University in St. Louis Legal Studies Research Paper Series* 12-04-10 (April) (available at http://ssrn.com).

[7] Sell, S. (2009) "From Forum-Shifters to Shape-Shifters: Rulemaking and Enforcement in Intellectual Property", *Annual ISA Conference, New York City*; Ibid. n. 3.

[8] Muñoz Tellez, V. (2009) "The Changing Global Governance of Intellectual Property Enforcement: A New Challenge for Developing Countries", in *Intellectual Property Enforcement International Perspectives*, Xuan Li and Carlos M. Correa, eds., 3, 10; Sell, S. (2010) "The Global IP Upward Ratchet, Anti-Counterfeiting and Piracy Enforcement Efforts: The State of Play". *PIJIP Research Paper* no. 15. American University Washington College of Law.

[9] Ibid.; Sell, S. (2011) "TRIPS Was Never Enough: Vertical Forum Shifting, FTAs, ACTA, and TPP", *Journal of Intellectual Property Law*, Vol. 3, 447, 464.

As a product of the Enforcement Agenda, ACTA contained a raft of measures designed to

- reduce, if not eliminate, procedural safeguards from infringement disputes;
- recruit police and customs as new constituencies to support current and expanded intellectual property regimes;
- shift the costs of enforcement from corporations to the public;
- impose liability on third parties.

Whether or not African countries became signatories to it, ACTA threatened them with decreased access to knowledge owing to measures in force in developed countries, disrupted global trade routes, decreased access to exports markets, anti-competitive blocking of exports and interception of medicines in transit.[10]

Although ACTA was probably intended to be expanded to other countries that were not given an opportunity to participate in its negotiation,[11] it is unlikely that African countries were the primary targets. Instead, the suffering imposed on Africans by some ACTA measures would be regarded as "collateral damage" by the negotiators.[12] Now that the agreement has been firmly rejected in Europe, it is unlikely that African and other developing countries will be faced with demands to agree to it; the treaty will no longer be the primary vehicle through which the Enforcement Agenda is driven. However, the abandonment of multilateralism that characterised ACTA continues. The Enforcement Agenda is already being pursued in other fora, such as the Transpacific Partnership (TPP) and the EU's bilateral free trade agreements with Canada (Comprehensive Economic and Trade Agreement, CETA) and India. Leaked drafts of earlier ACTA texts offer a useful indication of what at least some of its negotiators wanted.

The negative consequences of ACTA for developing countries did not stem only from the threat of being asked to agree to an agreement that they had no part in creating. Certain aspects of the treaty – such as the mandatory seizure of medicines in transit through ACTA signatory countries on the grounds of trademark infringement and the related construction of a "counterfeit medicine" discourse – continue to threaten to inflict considerable hardship on the world's poorest people, regardless of whether the countries in which those people live will be compelled to agree to ACTA or other multilateral trade agreements. Africans are likely to face similar enforcement moves in future.

[10] Ibid., n. 3.
[11] Ibid., n. 2.
[12] Ibid., n. 3.

## THE ENFORCEMENT AGENDA, ACTA AND ACCESS TO MEDICINES

In-transit seizures of medicines and the confusion of fake medicines with generics are both features of the Enforcement Agenda.[13] How these conjoined issues have affected Africans and people in other developing countries shows how ACTA-type provisions would likely be put into national law and practice.

The construction of a broad definition of "counterfeit medicines" sidesteps the important differences between fake medicines – which may be ineffective or harmful – on the one hand and safe, effective generic medicines that allegedly infringe the rights of intellectual property holders on the other.

The World Health Organisation International Medical Products Anti-Counterfeiting Task Force, which includes multinational corporations as well as government representatives, has declared that "counterfeit medicines may include products with the correct ingredients but fake packaging, with the wrong ingredients, without active ingredients or with insufficient active ingredients."[14] According to this description, a generic medicine could be claimed to be counterfeit. It blurs the distinctions between medicines without active ingredients, medicines with dangerous ingredients and medicines distributed without the authorisation of the trademark holder.

This description was adapted as part of the definition of counterfeit goods in the Kenyan Anti-Counterfeit Act 2008,[15] which threatened the supply of generic antiretroviral drugs to Africans whose lives depend on them in Kenya.[16] In *Ochieng v Attorney General*, the Attorney General of Kenya attempted to defend the provisions of the Kenyan Anti-Counterfeit Act 2008 as consistent with international best practice, including the WHO-IMPACT definition of counterfeit medicines. Since these provisions affect access to affordable and essential drugs and medications, and generic drugs in particular, the High Court held them to be a breach of the right to life, human dignity and health guaranteed by the Kenyan constitution.[17]

[13] Ibid., n. 10.

[14] World Health Organisation International Medical Products Anti-Counterfeiting Task Force (WHO IMPACT) 2006, Counterfeit Medicines Fact Sheet (14 November).

[15] von Braun, J. and Munyi, P. (2010) "New Enforcement Mechanisms Challenge the Legality of Generics in the Name of Public Health: The Emergence of Anti-Counterfeiting Legislation in Africa", *African Journal of International & Comparative Law* Vol. 18, 238–245.

[16] von Braun, J. and Munyi, P. (2010) "New Enforcement Mechanisms Challenge the Legality of Generics in the Name of Public Health: The Emergence of Anti-Counterfeiting Legislation in Africa", *African Journal of International & Comparative Law* Vol. 18, 238–245; Musungu, S. F. (2012) "Sections of the Kenya Anti Counterfeiting Act Struck Down as a Threat to Fundamental Human Rights", Iqsensato 23 April 2012 available at http://www.iqsensato.org/; *see also* Chapter 15 in this volume.

[17] Ibid., n. 20.

The conflation of consumer protection and intellectual property issues under the banner of counterfeit medicines played a role in EU member countries' seizure of generic medicines en route between developing countries. The seizures were carried out by the Netherlands and Germany based on alleged suspicions of patent and trademark infringement.[18] In the Netherlands, customs officials justified the seizures by reference to a legal fiction in Dutch law that treated the goods as manufactured in the Netherlands even though they were not. In 2009, an airborne shipment of drugs in transit to a least developed country through Germany was seized by German customs officials, who apparently found the international non-proprietary name Amoxicillan confusingly similar to the GlaxoSmithKlein trademark Amoxil.[19] When the seizures were challenged in the TRIPS Council, European officials claimed to be checking for counterfeits that constituted a danger to public health in developing countries.

Earlier drafts of the ACTA text required that border measures, including seizures of in-transit goods, should be mandated for alleged trademark, copyright and patent infringements, all of which were lumped under the undefined category of "suspect goods." The text was later modified so that patents were excluded from border measures. However, ACTA still mandates the seizure of goods in transit (including medicines bound for developing countries) that are considered "suspect goods" because they are alleged to infringe copyright or trademark in the country of transit.[20]

ACTA also requires a number of enforcement measures other than those at the border. These include the issuing of injunctions against third parties, referred to as "intermediaries," without the parties in question being heard, to prevent allegedly infringing goods from entering the channels of commerce. They also include the seizure and swift destruction of allegedly infringing goods without compensation.

While parties can elect to exclude patents from these provisions, they must apply them to alleged counterfeit trademark goods. The seizure of in-transit medicines in the Netherlands discussed earlier was based on the "manufacturing fiction." Although not required by ACTA, a similar fiction could be applied to in-transit goods, treating them as if manufactured in the country of transit.[21] ACTA's non-border enforcement measures would then operate against them. This could result in the seizure and destruction of generic medicines en route to developing countries.

[18] Ncube, C. (2009) "Enforcing Patent Rights against Goods in Transit: A New Threat to Trans-Border Trade in Generic Medicines", *South African Mercantile Law Journal* Vol. 21, 768; Rens, A. (2011) "Collateral Damage: The Impact of ACTA and the Enforcement Agenda on the World's Poorest People", *American University International Law Review* Vol. 26, No. 3, 783–809.

[19] ICTSD (2009) European Generic Drug Seizures Take Centre Stage at TRIPS Council Meeting, 13 BRIDGES WKLY. TRADE NEWS DIG. No. 21 June 10 http://ictsd.org

[20] Ibid., n. 24; Baker, B. K. (2011) "ACTA-Risks of Third-Party Enforcement for Access to Medicines", *American University International Law Review* Vol. 26, No. 3, 579–599.

[21] Ibid.

What could justify the threat to access to medicines in developing countries presented by ACTA and ACTA-type provisions? These are associated with a consistent narrative about the necessity of enforcement.

## THE ENFORCEMENT NARRATIVE AND ITS DIFFERENT MANIFESTATIONS

A notable feature of the opaque ACTA process was the nature of official pronouncements intended to justify the agreement. Press releases, FAQs and rejoinders to criticism of the treaty were remarkably consistent in presenting a uniform, if abbreviated, account for ACTA and the Enforcement Agenda. A typical example is the joint statement issued by the negotiators at the 2011 signing ceremony in Tokyo:

> The ACTA represents a significant achievement in the fight against the infringement of intellectual property rights, in particular the proliferation of counterfeiting and piracy on a global scale. (…) the ACTA will formalize the legal foundation for a first-of-its-kind alliance of trading partners, representing more than half of world trade. (…) The proliferation of counterfeit and pirated goods poses considerable challenges for legitimate trade and the sustainable development of the world economy. Trade in these goods causes significant financial losses for right holders and legitimate businesses. It also hinders sustainable economic development in both developed and developing countries and, in some cases, represents a health or safety risk to consumers. Expertise, innovation, quality, and creativity are the main factors for success in knowledge-based economies. Adequate protection and enforcement of intellectual property rights is a key condition for nurturing those factors. (…) The aim of the ACTA initiative was (…) an agreement that enhances international co-operation and contains effective international standards for enforcing intellectual property rights.[22]

This typical account, referred to as the "enforcement narrative" in this chapter, assumes rather than demonstrates its claims and the connections between them. The official champions of ACTA have neglected to present a full justification for the agreement, and so it would be idle for others to do so. The narrative advanced for ACTA, and for enforcement more generally, can be understood through an examination of how it draws on a variety of other narratives and frames. As will be seen, these are drawn from very different contexts, in which they perform different functions with regard to their role in the narrative of enforcement. References to global trade and successful economies attempt to link the enforcement narrative to a larger political story about intellectual property in which states are the primary

[22] Joint Press Statement of the Anti-Counterfeiting Trade Agreement Negotiating Parties (2011), Tokyo, http://www.ustr.gov/about-us/press-office/press-releases/2011/october/joint-press-statement-anti-counterfeiting-trade-ag

actors; each state is a rational actor intent on maximising its unitary interests. In this narrative, intellectual property is first and foremost an instrument by which developed countries entrench their comparative advantage in producing what are termed knowledge goods while bargaining with each other to advance their mutual interests. Developing countries are regarded primarily as consumers of the knowledge goods produced by developed countries, while simultaneously seeking to assert control over those types of knowledge goods that they are able to produce themselves, such as goods based on traditional knowledge.

Under this narrative, emerging economies will imitate the intellectual property laws of developed countries as their economies mature. The intellectual property narrative, often advanced by international organisations, explains the wealth of developed countries as owing, at least in part, to intellectual property law and policy, the former being presented as a policy "power tool" to encourage innovation.[23] In this story, developing countries lack expertise in intellectual property and therefore should adopt the policies recommended by developed country trade representatives and international experts. If developing countries do so, then – according to this narrative – innovation will result.[24]

The history of ACTA, culminating in its rejection by the European Parliament, does not fit easily into this narrative. The treaty did not fail because of developing country opposition, or because the negotiators were unable to reach agreement, but because of public opposition to the process and substance of the proposed treaty in developed countries. The extent of expert criticism and public opposition to ACTA destabilises this narrative because it cannot account either for radically divergent interests within a country or for the opposition between fundamental human rights and the measures sought in ACTA. While corporations that rely most on innovation and the most technologically sophisticated members of the population in both the United States and Europe united in opposition to ACTA, their trade representatives failed to pay much heed. The push for strategic enforcement measures is at odds with the interests of those who should, in the neorealist paradigm, be most invested in it.

The enforcement narrative presents ACTA as the outcome of a largely technical process in which experts from developed countries created a standard to which developing countries should adhere. However, when a group of international scholars warned of serious problems with ACTA,[25] the negotiators did not engage the

[23] Idris, K. (2002) *Intellectual Property: A Power Tool for Economic Growth*, Geneva: World Intellectual Property Organization (WIPO).

[24] Ibid.

[25] PIJIP (2010) "Urgent ACTA Communique International Experts Find that Pending Anti-Counterfeiting Trade Agreement Threatens Public Interests", Program one Information Justice and

experts. Although some changes were made between drafts – possibly in response to criticism by experts and global civil society – the opaque nature of the process makes it unclear whether this was due to reason or political expedience. Many of the problems raised by experts, but not addressed in the ACTA text, were regarded as fatal by the technical committees of the European Parliament, every one of which recommended the treaty's rejection. The expertise utilised in the formulation of ACTA's text was subject to epistemic myopia and suffered from sodalistic immunisation. The enforcement narrative thus appears unable to make a convincing case for either the political demand for certain enforcement measures or the defeat of ACTA.

According to the enforcement narrative, intellectual property infringement – characterised as growing "piracy" and "counterfeiting" – poses a threat serious enough to justify the "enforcement agenda." But if countries had acted rationally, they would have sought information as to the nature of the risk and possible remedies, engaging in a cost-benefit analysis and choosing to act only if likely benefits outweighed costs. This was not the behaviour of the trade representatives who negotiated ACTA.

There is no rigorous empirical evidence of the infringement problems that the agreement was apparently intended to address. Although willing to incur the expense of negotiating a treaty over several years, trade representatives were unwilling to pay for meticulous research. Quantitative claims by industry representatives have been shown to be largely spurious.[26] There has been no systematic attempt to gauge whether the measures in ACTA would make any difference to the empirically ungrounded threat it supposed to counter. How would it even be possible to gauge whether ACTA-type measures would be effective when the extent of the perceived threat has never been verified?

While the efficacy of the proposed measures is unprovable, what we do know is that they would impose significant costs, not least on access to medicines for the world's poorest people. Why were the governments of the wealthiest countries in the world willing to expend considerable resources, including national and international capital, on ACTA but chose not to commission independent empirical research into the threat? The insistence on proceeding with ACTA (despite its known costs) to counter an unclear threat, just to be seen as doing something even if it should prove unhelpful, amounts to "enforcement theatre."[27] Although engaging in enforcement theatre might be rational for corporate lobbyists and trade representatives, it is not rational for countries as envisaged in the "neorealist paradigm."

Intellectual Property, American University Washington College of Law, Washington, DC, http://www.wcl.american.edu/pijip

26 Ibid., n. 24.

27 Rens, A. (2012) "Enforcement Theater, the Enforcement Agenda and the Institutionalization of Enforcement Theater in the Anti-Counterfeiting Trade Agreement", *Suffolk Transnational Law Review* Vol. 35, 519.

An additional element of the enforcement narrative – largely, although not entirely, absent from official communications – is the action movie framing of enforcement in which intellectual property infringers are criminal masterminds and enforcement agencies and ACTA are heroic defenders of public order. Although this trope is common in journalistic accounts, it can also be found in some of the rare defences of ACTA made in academic contexts.

"Surreptitious negotiations, covert drafts, leaked documents and swift announcements at the eleventh-hour – such is the stranger-than-fiction story of the 'Piracy Treaty' signed by several world powers in the past week. (…) ACTA contains several provisions for the speedy, procedure-free enforcement of IP rights." This is how professor Owen Dean begins his panegyric of ACTA,[28] while a law review article defending the necessity of ACTA applauds the FBI's arrest of "criminal mastermind" Kim Dotcom – operator of a file-sharing website accused of facilitating copyright infringement by repeating a journalistic account of circling helicopters, shotguns and seizures of luxury goods. The raid was ostensibly carried out under the authorisation of current law, its link to ACTA is never made clear.[29]

The action movie account of ACTA seeks to make a virtue of the secrecy of surrounding the treaty's negotiating process, praising the abandonment of due process, describing infringement with legally inaccurate emotive language such as "theft" and referring to widely publicised enforcement operations as a justification for ACTA.[30] The action movie trope seeks to link intellectual property enforcement to fictional accounts of espionage and policing rather than their more quotidian realities.

In the action movie trope, the necessity and efficacy of enforcement measures are assumed rather than demonstrated. The narrative's focus on the glamour of enforcement negotiations and operations distracts from the political choices being made rather than explain the reasons for those choices. Collateral damage is either ignored or justified. The action movie trope cannot explain opposition by commercial corporations or experts. Under this scenario, only criminals or dupes of criminals would oppose ACTA, and therefore anyone who opposed ACTA must either be a criminal or a dupe. While this narrative tends to silence initial opposition to upward-ratcheting enforcement measures, once opposition becomes sufficiently sophisticated and prominent, the action movie trope is shown to be a distraction from the political choices being made.

28 Dean, O. (2012) "ACTA – a sting in the tail for IP rights enforcement", Anton Moster Chair of Intellectual Property Blog, University of Stellenbosch, March 2012, http://blogs.sun.ac.za/iplaw

29 Rice, N. W. (2012) "Head-in-the-Clouds: The Public's Failure to Recognize How the Anti-Counterfeiting Trade Agreement Protects the Global Intellectual Property Marketplace in the Digital Age", *Suffolk Transnational Law Review* Vol. 35, 631.

30 Ibid., n. 36.

Since the enforcement narrative is unsatisfactory, what is the alternative? An alternative account of ACTA – is that it is the product of densely networked global political actors responding not to the threat of growing infringement but rather that it was – until its defeat in May 2012 – the most salient manifestation of an agenda manufactured for political reasons. Since the enforcement agenda and therefore ACTA is the product not of domestic political alliances, but of a global network of trade officials and agents seeking to act on behalf of multinational tobacco, pharmaceutical, consumer goods and entertainment corporations, it necessarily had to conflate online infringement with fake consumer goods and medicines. Because ACTA was formulated as a non-negotiable secret treaty-making process outside of a multilateral process, it took no account of the impact on the world's poorest people, many of whom live in Africa.

ACTA proponents sought to justify the pact as a necessary response to an existential threat to a large number of industries, and thus could not moderate their demands or take into account the treaty's negative consequences for privacy, freedom of expression and online innovation in developed countries. The multi-nodal international network is formed by mutual allegiance to a narrative of growing intellectual property infringement. It upholds the necessity and likely efficacy of the enforcement measures sought in ACTA and other manifestations of the enforcement agenda. The perceived threat, necessity and presumed efficacy of the desired enforcement measures thus cannot be questioned within the network.

Seizures of generic medicines in transit may recur. The effort to recruit developing world constituencies through linking increased institutional resources, such as customs and the police, to an interest in enforcing trademarks, even against generic medicines may well continue. With the enforcement agenda continuing in other fora, why did ACTA fail?

## BEYOND ACTA

The defeat of ACTA in Europe followed the defeat of the proposed SOPA (Stop Online Piracy Act) and PIPA (Protect IP Act) Bills in the US Congress in January 2012. These defeats – largely attributable to public opposition – indicate that some intellectual property issues have entered mainstream politics in the United States and Europe. There seems to be growing public dissatisfaction with the international alliance of brand-name pharmaceutical corporations, fashion goods brand owners, tobacco multinationals, as well as music recording and cinematographic production companies, which had obtained repeated expansion of intellectual property laws domestically in the United States, Europe and elsewhere.

The public discourse around intellectual property law is beginning to mature and increasingly sophisticated analyses now appear in the mainstream press. But will growing public dissatisfaction inhibit trade representatives from advancing the enforcement agenda in their dealings with developing countries?

Since the TPP, CETA and TAFTA negotiations are secret, it is difficult to gauge what difference public opposition to SOPA and ACTA may have made. It seems likely that proponents of the enforcement agenda will continue to seek fora in which to pursue it. The history of ACTA, however, undermines the credibility of the enforcement narrative deployed to justify it, directing attention instead to the networks of global politics that underlie the efforts to ratchet up intellectual property protection.

**PART III**

# Impact on Related Processes

# 13

# Three Steps Taken toward a Reinterpreted Three-Step Test

## *The Impact of ACTA and SOPA on TPP*

*Jonathan Band*

### INTRODUCTION

The public opposition to the Anti-Counterfeiting Trade Agreement (ACTA) and the Stop Online Piracy Act (SOPA) has already had a positive impact on the proposed Transpacific Partnership (TPP) Agreement. The text concerning copyright limitations and exceptions, leaked in August 2012, reflects two basic approaches – one proposed by the United States, the other proposed by New Zealand, Chile, Malaysia, Vietnam and Brunei. In general, both approaches represent improvement over the copyright exception language in existing US free trade agreements (FTAs). Accordingly, there is reason to hope that the final TPP Agreement will include strong language on copyright exceptions that will lead to balanced copyright regimes in the TPP region.

Because of the lack of transparency of the TPP negotiations, it is difficult to reconstruct a precise timeline of when specific language was proposed, who proposed it, and why. However, a combination of leaked drafts and public statements provides evidence of the positive impact that the collapse of SOPA in the United States and of ACTA in the EU may have had on the TPP provision addressing copyright exceptions and limitations.

### STEP 1. THE US IP CHAPTER PROPOSAL

In February 2011, the US proposal for the IP chapter of the TPP was leaked. At Article 4.8, it contained the following bracketed language: "Placeholders for provision on (1) exceptions and limitations, (2) Internet retransmission, and (3) any other appropriate copyright/related rights provision."[1]

1 Trans-Pacific Partnership Intellectual Property Rights Chapter. Feb. 10, 2011. Available at http://keionline.org/sites/default/files/tpp-10feb2011-us-text-ipr-chapter.pdf.

## STEP 2. THE COMPETING COPYRIGHT LIMITATIONS AND EXCEPTIONS PROPOSALS

At some point between February 2011 and July 2012, two competing proposals on copyright limitations and exceptions were introduced to replace the bracketed language in the leaked February 2011 draft. First, a proposal supported by the United States and Australia reads as follows:

> With respect to this Article [Article 4 on copyright and Article 5 and 6 (which deal with copyright and related rights section and the related rights section)], each Party shall confine limitations or exceptions to exclusive rights to certain special cases that do not conflict with a normal exploitation of the work, performance, or phonogram, and do not unreasonably prejudice the legitimate interests of the right holder.[2]

It is unclear whether the United States and Australia jointly submitted this language, or one delegation introduced it and the other subsequently signalled support. For convenience, this chapter will attribute this language to the United States.

Second, a proposal supported by New Zealand, Chile, Malaysia, Brunei and Vietnam provides:

> 1. Each party may provide for limitations and exceptions to copyrights, related rights, and legal protections for technological protections measures and rights management information included in this Chapter, in accordance with its domestic laws and relevant international treaties that each are party to.
> 2. Paragraph 1 permits a party to carry forward and appropriately extend into the digital environment limitations and exceptions in its domestic laws. Similarly, these provisions permit a Party to devise new exceptions and limitations for the digital environment.[3]

Once again, it is unclear whether this group of five countries jointly submitted this language, or one delegation introduced it and the others joined later.

The US proposal is the familiar three-step test, incorporated in various forms in the Berne Convention, the TRIPS Agreement and the various US FTAs. The formulation in the US proposal is the same as in the FTAs, without the clarifying (and limiting) language found in some of the FTAs – including the Australia-US FTA (AUSFTA).[4]

[2] Knowledge Ecology International. "Leak of TPP text on copyright Limitations and Exception". Aug. 3, 2012. Available at http://keionline.org/node/1516 (August 2012 text).

[3] It is unclear whether both paragraphs were introduced at the same time.

[4] These limitations are discussed later in the chapter. ACTA does not include any reference to the three-step test or copyright exceptions because it addresses IP enforcement rather than substantive IP rights.

The second paragraph of the "Group of Five" proposal derives from footnote 9 of the WIPO Copyright Treaty. Similar language appears in footnote 17 of the IP chapter of the Chile-US FTA. The first paragraph appears to be a new alternative to the three-step test, presumably reflecting the concerns raised by scholars and civil society that the three-step test is unduly restrictive.[5]

The United States and Australia opposed the Group of Five proposal. Likewise, the Group of Five opposed the US proposal. Singapore and Peru indicated that they could support either the US proposal or paragraph 1 of the Group of Five proposal.

## STEP 3. THE JULY 2012 US PROPOSAL

On 3 July 2012, during the round of TPP negotiations in San Diego, California, the United States issued a statement concerning copyright exceptions and limitations. The United States declared:

> The balance of rights and exceptions and limitations achieved in U.S. law provides diverse benefits for large and small businesses, consumers, authors, artists, and workers in the information, entertainment, and technology sectors.
>
> A robust copyright framework ensures that authors and creators are respected, investments (both intellectual and financial) are promoted, that limitations and exceptions provide an appropriate balance, and that enforcement measures are effective.
>
> An important part of the copyright ecosystem is the limitations or exceptions placed on the exercise of exclusive rights in certain circumstances. In the United States, for example, consumers and businesses rely on a range of exceptions and limitations, such as fair use, in their businesses and daily lives. Further, under the U.S. Digital Millennium Copyright Act (DMCA), the United States provides safe harbors limiting copyright liability, which help to ensure that legitimate providers of cloud computing, user-generated content sites, and a host of other Internet-related services who act responsibly can thrive online.[6]

While US government officials have previously made comments supportive of exceptions in international fora, this language seems unprecedented in its sweeping and detailed nature.

After this introduction stressing the importance of copyright exceptions, the United States announced:

5 *See*, e.g., Max Planck Institute for Intellectual Property and Competition. "Declaration on the 'Three-Step Test'". Available at http://www.ip.mpg.de/files/pdf2/declaration_three_step_test_final_english1.pdf.

6 Office of the U.S. Trade Representative. "USTR Introduces New Copyright Exceptions and Limitations at San Diego TPP Talks". July 3, 2012, http://www.ustr.gov/about-us/press-office/blog/2012/july/ustr-introduces-new-copyright-exceptions-limitations-provision.

> For the first time in any U.S. trade agreement, the United States is proposing a new provision, consistent with the internationally-recognized '3-step test,' that will obligate Parties to seek to achieve an appropriate balance in their copyright systems in providing copyright exceptions and limitations for purposes such as criticism, comment, news reporting, teaching, scholarship, and research.[7]

The United States followed this description of its new proposal by asserting that

> [t]hese principles are critical aspects of the U.S. copyright system, and appear in both our law and jurisprudence. The balance sought by the U.S. TPP proposal recognizes and promotes respect for the important interests of individuals, businesses, and institutions who rely on appropriate exceptions and limitations in the TPP region.[8]

On 3 August 2012, the precise language of the new US proposal was leaked. Consistent with the 3 July announcement, the proposal contained a new paragraph 2 which would come after the three-step test language previously supported by the United States and Australia:

> 2. Subject to and consistent with paragraph (1), each Party shall seek to achieve an appropriate balance in providing limitations or exceptions, including those for the digital environment, giving due consideration to legitimate purposes such as, but not limited to, criticism, comment, news reporting, teaching, scholarship and research.[9]

The proposal also contained the following footnote:

> For purposes of greater clarity, a use that has commercial aspects may in appropriate circumstances be considered to have a legitimate purpose under paragraph 2.[10]

The text of the 3 July US statement, combined with this new paragraph 2, clearly represents a more favourable attitude on the part of the United States toward exceptions and limitations than the bare three-step test language it had previously proposed. How much more favourable is discussed later in the chapter. First we pause to consider what may have precipitated the introduction of this new language.

The fact that the United States made this proposal in July 2012, just six months after the defeat of SOPA and PIPA in the US Congress and five months after protests against ACTA swept across the EU, suggests that the United States was influenced by those events.[11] Perhaps it concluded that unless TPP contained positive language concerning exceptions and limitations, the civil society and technology associations

7 Ibid.

8 Ibid.

9 August 2012 text.

10 Ibid.

11 The European Parliament rejected ACTA on 4 July 2012, the day after the United States announced its new proposal. However, in the weeks leading up to vote in the European Parliament, ACTA's

that supported such exceptions – and had opposed SOPA – would mobilise powerful political resistance against the United States joining TPP. Likewise, civil society in the other TPP countries might succeed in rallying strong domestic opposition to the agreement. To be sure, correlation does not prove causation. Nonetheless, the timing of this major change in position certainly implies that it was, at least in part, a reaction to the SOPA and ACTA defeats.

## A TALE OF TWO PARAGRAPHS

The US announcement on 3 July 2012 concerning copyright exceptions and limitations met with immediate criticism from a group of public interest groups, including the Electronic Frontier Foundation (EFF), Public Knowledge, Public Citizen, Innovarte, Derechos Digitales and Knowledge Ecology International.[12] In contrast, other groups that also support balanced copyright policy, such as the Computer & Communications Industry Association (CCIA) and the Library Copyright Alliance (LCA), reacted positively to the US announcement.[13]

The apparent inconsistency can be explained by the fact that EFF and other opponents were criticising the original first paragraph of the US proposal, which repeats the three-step test, while CCIA and LCA were applauding the new second paragraph. Thus, the Joint Statement of Civil Society Groups expressed concern that inclusion of the three-step, depending on its scope and interpretation, could "restrict fair use and other copyright exceptions and limitations crucial for the progress and access of culture, science, education, and innovation."[14] The Joint Statement noted that the WTO had interpreted the three-step test narrowly in a case concerning section 110.5 of the US Copyright Act.[15] Moreover, the Joint Statement opposed the possible extension of the three-step test to existing exceptions and limitations that

prospects appeared progressively dimmer. For example, on 7 May 2012, Neelie Kroes, the European Commissioner for Digital Agenda, questioned whether the EU would ultimately ratify ACTA. *See* Aaron Souppouris. "ACTA Unlikely to Happen, Says European Commissioner". *The Verge*, 7 May 2012. Available at http://www.theverge.com/2012/5/7/3004275/european-commissioner-digital-agenda-acta-unlikely-to-happen. For a more detailed discussion of the protests against SOPA and ACTA, *see* Jonathan Band. "The SOPA/TPP Nexus". PIJIP Research Paper no. 2012-06, http://digitalcommons.wcl.american.edu/research/28/. As discussed in that paper, the US government actually voiced serious concerns with SOPA days before the online protest on 18 January 2012.

12 Joint Statement of Civil Society Groups on U.S. TPP Copyright Proposal. July 3, 2012. Available at https://www.eff.org/deeplinks/2012/07/joint-statement-civil-society-groups-us-tpp-copyright-proposal.

13 Computer and Communications Industry Association. "Internet-friendly Language Proposed in Trade Agreement". July 3, 2012. Available at http://www.ccianet.org/index.asp?sid=5&artid=308&evtflg=False; Adler, Prudence. "Library Copyright Alliance Letter to U.S. Trade Representative Ron Kirk". Aug. 15, 2012. Available at http://www.librarycopyrightalliance.org/bm~doc/lt_kirktpp14aug12.pdf.

14 Joint Statement of Civil Society Groups.

15 *See* World Trade Organization. "Trade Related Intellectual Property Agreement". Available athttp://www.wto.org/english/tratop_e/dispu_e/1234da.pdf.

now fall outside it. "In particular, we note that the Berne Convention and the Rome Convention both have several articles that specifically provide for copyright limitations and exceptions without a 3-step test."[16]

In contrast, CCIA focused on the language of the second paragraph. After explaining that industries dependent on fair use and other copyright limitations represent one-sixth of the US GDP, CCIA stated that "this is the first time the US government has committed to export the 'balancing' exceptions and provisions of US law, not just the IP protections of US law. Exceptions like fair use are essential components of IP law and we commend this initiative."[17] CCIA added that "this is a positive development for all nine countries negotiating the TPP. Part of the success of the US tech industry is owed to the balance infused into our copyright laws. For the US to negotiate in good faith with its trading partners, it makes sense to export our complete formula for a successful Internet sector – both our IP enforcement measures and our copyright limitations and exceptions."[18]

LCA likewise praised the new second paragraph. The group observed that the list of legitimate purposes contained in paragraph 2 derives from 17 U.S.C. § 107, which codifies the fair use privilege. LCA welcomed the inclusion of this language for three reasons. First, "this language would insure that nothing in TPP would in any direct or indirect way undermine the fair use right. … Fair use is critical to the operation of libraries and the activities of their users, and no international agreement should ever abridge it in any manner."[19]

Second, LCA asserted that "this language would enhance the ability of libraries overseas to serve their users."[20] According to LCA,

> The copyright laws of several of the other TPP countries do not contain the robust framework of exceptions for libraries and educational institutions found in the U.S. Copyright Act. Paragraph 2 obligates Parties to seek to achieve a balance in their copyright laws by adopting limitations and exceptions for legitimate purposes such as criticism, teaching, scholarship, and research – the very purposes for which libraries exist. Thus, paragraph 2 would lead to libraries throughout the TPP region benefiting from the same exceptions as U.S. libraries.[21]

Finally, LCA observed that "this language demonstrates U.S. leadership in the promotion of exceptions and limitations in perhaps the most visible and forceful manner of any U.S. Administration."[22]

16 Joint Statement of Civil Society Groups.
17 CCIA Press Release.
18 Ibid.
19 LCA Letter.
20 Ibid.
21 Ibid.
22 Ibid.

The juxtaposition of paragraphs 1 and 2 raises two questions.

### *(i) Is Paragraph 1 as Problematic as the Joint Statement Suggests?*

On its face, the formulation of the three-step test in paragraph 1 appears less favourable to exceptions than formulations in other agreements.

- In the Berne Convention, the three-step test applies only to exceptions to the reproduction right, and does not apply to the "small exceptions" for quotations and other purposes in Articles 10 and 10bis.
- TRIPS Article 13 extended the three-step test to exceptions for all rights, but Article 6 excluded exhaustion from its scope.
- The World Intellectual Property Organization (WIPO) Copyright Treaty (WCT) and Performances and Phonograms Treaty (WPPT) likewise extended the three-step test to exceptions to all rights,[23] but excluded exhaustion from its scope.[24] Additionally, a footnote to Article 10 of the WCT stated:

> [I]t is understood that the provisions of Article 10 permit Contracting Parties to carry forward and appropriately extend into the digital environment limitations and exceptions in their national laws which have been considered acceptable under the Berne Convention. Similarly, these provisions should be understood to permit Contracting Parties to devise new exceptions and limitations that are appropriate in the digital network environment. It is also understood that Article 10.2 neither reduces nor extends the scope of applicability of the limitations and exceptions permitted by the Berne Convention.

This agreed statement also applied to WPPT Article 16. Various FTAs contained language similar to the WCT's limitations on the three-step test. The Chile-US FTA provided that the three-step test language "neither reduces nor extends the scope of applicability of the limitations and exceptions permitted by the Berne Convention, the WIPO Copyright Treaty (1996), and the WIPO Performances and Phonograms Treaty (1996)."[25] The Chile-US FTA also stated:

> These provisions permit a Party to carry forward and appropriately extend into the digital environment limitations and exceptions in its domestic laws which have been considered acceptable under the Berne Convention. Similarly, these provisions permit a Party to devise new exceptions and limitations that are appropriate in the digital network environment.[26]

23 WCT Article 10; WPPT Article 16.
24 WCT Article 6(2); WPPT Articles 8 and 12.
25 IP Chapter, Chile-US Free Trade Agreement n. 17.
26 Ibid.

- AUSFTA provided that nothing in the three-step test provision "shall be construed as reducing or extending the scope of applicability of the limitations and exceptions permitted under the agreements referred to in Articles … and the TRIPS Agreement."[27]
- The three-step test in the Korea-US Free Trade Agreement has an even narrower scope. It applies only to the reproduction right. Moreover, it clarified that "each Party may adopt or maintain limitations or exceptions to the [reproduction right] for fair use," as long as the limitation complies with the three-step test.

At the same time, the FTAs with Singapore,[28] Central America and the Dominican Republic,[29] Bahrain[30] and Morocco,[31] contain the same "bare" formulation of the three-step test as does paragraph 1 of the US TPP proposal. Thus, paragraph 1 is no worse than the status quo of many of the FTAs.

Moreover, paragraph 1 does not exist in isolation; it is accompanied by paragraph 2. The relationship of paragraphs 1 and 2 is discussed later in the chapter.

Furthermore, on 8 September 2012, three professors from the Washington College of Law at the American University in a letter to Ambassador Kirk laid out their understanding of the US government's interpretation of paragraph 1 pursuant to meetings they had with US officials. The letter states:

- "The United States considers (…) that the so-called Berne 'small exceptions' for quotations and other purposes are in compliance with the three-step test in its TPP proposal, were it to be applied to them."[32]
- "The U.S. specifically affirms and supports the Agreed Statement to WCT article 10,"[33] quoted above.
- "The United States proposed three-step test would apply only to limitations and exceptions to exclusive rights granted to copyright owners rather than to provisions that delineate the scope of such rights. For example, the absence of an exclusive right of private performance if a copyrighted work in U.S. law would not be a limitation or exception subject to the three-step test."[34]

[27] AUSFTA Article 17.4.10(c).

[28] Singapore-US FTA Article 16.4.10.

[29] Central America-Dominican Republic FTA Article 15.5.10(a).

[30] Bahrain-US FTA Article 14.5.10(a).

[31] Morocco-US FTA Article 15.6.11(a).

[32] Letter from Profs. Peter Jaszi, Michael Carroll, and Sean Flynn to U.S. Trade Representative Ronald Kirk, September 8, 2012, available at http://infojustice.org/wp-content/uploads/2012/09/PIJIP-letter-to-Kirk-September-8-2012.pdf.

[33] Ibid. at 2.

[34] Ibid. at 2–3.

- "The United States takes the position that nothing in existing U.S. copyright law, as interpreted by the federal courts of appeal, would be inconsistent with its proposed three step test."[35] The letter specifically references the transformative use standard recognized in *Bill Graham Archives v. Doring Kindersley Publishing, Inc.*, 448 F.3d 605 (2d Cir. 2006) and the definition of copy in *Cartoon Network, LP v. CSC Holdings, Inc.*, 536 F.3d 121 (2d Cir. 2008).

While these statements are reassuring, they obviously have no force of law. According to the American University professors, "the United States is not categorically opposed to the adoption of Agreed Statements as part of the TPP, although it has not done so for other free trade agreements, and it does not have a position on this matter at present."[36] Additionally, as noted earlier in the chapter, the Chile, Australia and Korea FTAs all contain language that clarifies or limits the applicability of the three-step test. Accordingly, any concerns that the US proposal for the three-step test in TPP is more restrictive than the three-step test in the FTAs or other international agreements, or than existing US law, could easily be addressed by including clarifying language such as that found in the WCT and the Chile FTA.

### *(ii) Is Paragraph 2 as Helpful as CCIA and LCA Suggest?*

On its face, paragraph 2 appears hospitable to exceptions. "Each Party shall seek to achieve an appropriate balance in providing limitations or exceptions (…) giving due consideration to legitimate purposes" such as criticism, comment, news reporting, teaching, scholarship and education. These six purposes are the same as those listed in the fair use provision in the US Copyright Act, 17 U.S.C. § 107. The US 3 July announcement makes clear that this is no accident; the United States indicates that it seeks to have the exceptions in US law, including fair use, reflected in TPP. Importantly, the exceptions can apply in "the digital environment" and to "a use that has commercial aspects."

The 3 July announcement is correct in that the United States has never previously proposed language in an international agreement that would "obligate Parties to seek to achieve an appropriate balance in their copyright systems (…)."[37] Nonetheless,

35 Ibid. at 3.

36 Ibid. at 2.

37 Other international agreements do, however, reference the balance of interests in intellectual property law. Article 7 of the TRIPS agreement, entitled "Objectives," provides that "the protection and enforcement of intellectual property rights should contribute to the promotion of technological innovation and to the transfer and dissemination of technology, to the mutual advantage of producers and users of technological knowledge and in manner conducive to social and economic welfare, and to a balance of rights and obligations." The preamble to the WCT states: "Recognizing the need to maintain a balance between the rights of authors and the larger public interest, particularly education, research and access to information, as reflected in the Berne Convention." The Preamble to

some have suggested that the language of paragraph 2 actually may not be as effective as it seems at first blush. First, the obligations of paragraph 2 are preceded with the phrase "subject to and consistent with" the three-step test in paragraph 1. The words "subject to" seem to restrict paragraph 2 to what is otherwise permitted by the three-step test. On the other hand, the words "consistent with" suggest that paragraph 2 is interpreting the three-step test. That is, "consistent with" implies that exceptions that achieve an appropriate balance for a legitimate purpose are by definition consistent with the three-step test. Any ambiguity in the relationship between paragraphs 1 and 2 should be clarified by removing the words "subject to."

Second, the phrase "each Party shall seek to achieve an appropriate balance in providing limitations and exceptions" is susceptible to different interpretations, depending on the meaning of the word "in." If "in" means "when," then a party must seek to achieve a balance when it is adopting exceptions, but the party has no obligation to adopt any exceptions. Conversely, if "in" means "by," then a party has an affirmative obligation to attempt to achieve a balance by adopting exceptions. This ambiguity should be eliminated by replacing "in" with "by."

Even if the text of paragraph 2 is included in the final TPP agreement without amendment, an expansive interpretation would align not only with the objectives set forth in the 3 July announcement but also with the statements made by US officials to the American University professors:

> The goal of the United States in proposing an obligation in the TPP concerning limitations and exceptions is not to further limit policy discretion to devise and implement limitations and exceptions at the national level that comply with the existing multilateral treaties on copyright, but rather to expand this discretion through a new provision that would oblige TPP Members to 'seek to achieve a balance' through adoption of limitations and exceptions.[38]

Evidently, the United States intends for paragraph 2 to create an obligation to seek to achieve a balance through exceptions, thereby expanding the policy discretion to devise exceptions for legitimate purposes. Moreover, the United States believes that this policy discretion is consistent with the three-step test.

In this light, paragraph 2, even in its current form, represents a major step forward in fostering the adoption in the TPP region of exceptions comparable to those in the United States. It also places a helpful gloss on the application of the three-step test in countries outside the TPP region because it makes clear that a major trading

ACTA states "Desiring to address the problem of infringement of intellectual property rights, including infringement taking place in the digital environment, in particular with respect to copyright or related rights, in a manner that balances the rights and interests of the relevant right holders, service providers and users."

38 American University Professors Letter at 2.

bloc has interpreted the tree-step test to allow a robust framework of exceptions and limitations.

## CONCLUSION

Paragraph 2 of the US TPP proposal regarding copyright exceptions and limitations, which is based on language appearing in the fair use provision, 17 U.S.C. § 107, constitutes an important shift in the US negotiating position in IP international negotiations in general and the TPP negotiations in particular. Given the timing of the introduction of this proposal on 3 July 2012, it is safe to assume that the shift in position was caused to some degree by the defeat of SOPA and PIPA in the US Congress and opposition to ACTA in the EU earlier in 2012. This increased balance in the copyright section, however, does not necessarily suggest any moderation by the United States on other controversial issues in TPP, such as pharmaceutical patents.

# 14

# ACTA and the Future of Access to Knowledge in the Digital Environment

## *US Enforcement Trends as a Global Predictor*

*Annemarie Bridy*

### INTRODUCTION

This chapter considers ACTA's impact on access to knowledge by focusing on two provisions that have the potential to undermine the public's right to transmit and receive lawful information over the Internet. The first of these is the "cooperative efforts" provision in the section on enforcement in the digital environment. The second is the seizure provision in the section on civil enforcement. Neither provision appears on its face to threaten the public's exercise of expressive rights on the Internet; however, recent enforcement trends in the United States foreshadow how each could be implemented to limit communicative freedom online, with little or no due process of law.

The cooperative efforts provision encourages the privatisation of online copyright enforcement pursuant to business agreements designed for the benefit of ISPs and copyright owners. Such agreements become binding on Internet users through terms of service drafted unilaterally by ISPs and presented to users on a "take it or leave it" basis. The contractual enforcement arrangements that result from cooperative efforts may displace flexibilities and consumer protections guaranteed under public law. When they do, Internet users will generally be left without judicial recourse because users formally consent to terms of service when they open their accounts.

The civil seizure provision, which falls under ACTA's general obligation to provide "expeditious remedies" for IPR owners, may be implemented to undermine due process of law by allowing the government to seize and retain suspect domain names on thin and untested evidence of criminal infringement. Moreover, if the US law of civil seizure becomes a model for ACTA parties, law enforcement authorities will be empowered to seize domain names belonging to non-citizens, as long as the domain names are registered within a party's territorial limits. Where a seized domain provides access to non-infringing as well as infringing material, the non-infringing content will become unavailable to users. If the seizure results in a permanent forfeiture, which is the intended course of events, access to that lawful content will never be restored.

## VOLUNTARY COOPERATIVE EFFORTS

### *Graduated Response*

ACTA's cooperative efforts provision requires parties to promote inter-industry partnerships between right owners and Internet intermediaries to curb repeat infringement online. This provision refers implicitly to privately designed graduated response or "three strikes" copyright enforcement regimes, which usually culminate in termination or suspension of Internet access for the accused repeat peer-to-peer (P2P) infringers. Given the vital role that Internet access plays in contemporary social, cultural and political life, there is a strong case to be made that cutting off Internet access, even temporarily, is an inherently disproportionate sanction for the violation of copyright laws. Although graduated response regimes do not necessarily culminate in loss of Internet access, they do pose a very real threat to affected users' communicative freedoms. That threat increases with the duration of permitted access sanctions, which might range from a few days to a year or more.

A few ACTA parties (e.g., Korea, New Zealand, France, and Great Britain) have incorporated graduated response mandates into their domestic copyright regimes. The majority, however, have not. For corporate copyright owners, privately developed codes of conduct negotiated with Internet service providers (ISPs) represent an attractive under-the-radar alternative to government mandates, which have proven to be politically controversial in the handful of countries that have enacted them. In France, for example, public and parliamentary resistance to the Hadopi graduated response system threatened to derail the initiative. Opponents of the legislation delayed implementation and forced a game-changing amendment that initially required judicial oversight of all Internet disconnections. In 2013, with public opposition still going strong four years after implementation, the law was amended to eliminate disconnection as an available sanction. In New Zealand, a similar narrative unfolded over Section 92A, a 2008 amendment to the Copyright Act requiring account termination for repeat infringers. After public outcry, Section 92A was repealed before it went into effect and was subsequently revised to incorporate greater consumer protections. When government officials work behind the scenes to pressure ISPs to become copyright enforcers, as ACTA contemplates, public scrutiny of the resulting private collaborations is minimized or altogether avoided. New enforcement arrangements can be negotiated in secret and presented to the public as a fait accompli.

A case in point is the privately developed Copyright Alert System (CAS) in the United States.[1] CAS, which is a "six strikes" graduated response system, is the end product of a government-initiated, multi-year, confidential negotiation between major broadband providers and corporate copyright owners. It is exactly the kind of inter-industry partnership that ACTA's architects had in mind when they drafted the cooperative efforts provision. In a negotiating environment like the one that produced CAS, the public's interest is advanced only to the extent that it coincides with the interests of one or more of the participating corporations. After a deal is struck, consumers' ability to opt out can be severely limited by lack of competition among ISPs in local markets. This economic reality effectively gives cooperative efforts the force and reach of public law, but without the public benefit of democratic process.

Another reason why corporate copyright owners might prefer cooperative efforts to government mandates is that government-administered graduated response systems are subject to shifting political winds. When French president Nicolas Sarkozy, perhaps Europe's staunchest supporter of graduated response, lost the presidential election to his Socialist opponent François Hollande in 2012, Hadopi's very survival was put in doubt. During the campaign, Hollande vowed to shut down Hadopi.[2] He softened his position after winning the election, but the fact that Hadopi became a campaign issue at all reveals the political vulnerability of public graduated response regimes. Unlike government-run anti-piracy efforts, voluntary cooperative efforts are enshrined in contracts, which are both legally enforceable and immune to the vagaries of electoral politics.

The call for increased cooperative efforts between copyright owners and ISPs goes beyond ACTA. So, even if ACTA never enters into force, the campaign to make government pressure on ISPs an integral part of the global "war on piracy" will continue in other international fora. One such forum is the Organization for Economic Co-operation and Development (OECD), which counts among its members many of the ACTA parties. In 2011, with ACTA's fate uncertain, the OECD Council issued a Recommendation on Principles for Internet Policy Making. The Recommendation contains its own co-operative efforts provision and encourages

1 Bridy, A. (2012). "Graduated Response American Style: 'Six Strikes' Measured against Five Norms". *Fordham Intellectual Property, Media & Entertainment Law Journal* 23(1); LaFrance, M. (2012). "Graduated Response by Industry Compact". *Cardozo Arts & Entertainment Law Journal* 30(2):165–186.

2 Oberti, C. (2012). "Hadopi: La police du Web Fliquée par Aurélie Filippetti". France 24, obtained at France24.com.

governments to "foster voluntarily developed codes of conduct" that are backed, if necessary, by government enforcement.[3]

Another major international forum is the Transpacific Partnership (TPP) Agreement, for which negotiations started before ACTA's negotiations finished. Like ACTA, the TPP is being negotiated out of public view, and negotiating drafts are treated as a closely guarded secret. A leaked draft of the TPP's Intellectual Property Chapter contains both a "repeat infringer" provision, which conditions limited liability for claims of third-party copyright infringement on an ISP's adoption and implementation of a policy to terminate the accounts of repeat infringers, and a cooperative efforts provision, which requires parties to provide "legal incentives for service providers to cooperate with copyright owners in deterring the unauthorized storage and transmission of copyrighted materials."[4] ACTA's cooperative efforts provision is less prescriptive than TPP's in that it does not require parties to provide legal incentives.

When it comes to cooperative efforts to implement graduated response to control unlawful P2P file sharing, corporate right owners have shrewdly diversified their international policy portfolio. What that diversification means for proponents of digital access to knowledge is that there are and will continue to be many sources of pressure on governments to browbeat ISPs into adopting graduated response systems. Regardless of what happens with ACTA, A2K activists will need to be vigilant about the kinds of graduated response models that result from cooperative efforts. From the point of view of communicative freedom, not all graduated response protocols are created equal. Those that incorporate termination of Internet access as a sanction should be singled out for the most vigorous opposition.

### *Voluntary Content Filtering*

ACTA's cooperative efforts provision also encompasses enforcement agreements between major copyright owners and Web 2.0 content-hosting platforms like YouTube. YouTube's proprietary Content ID filtering system is a prominent example of a private copyright enforcement regime. The fully automated system compares user-uploaded content to a database of reference files provided to YouTube by copyright owners. Content ID lets copyright owners choose what to do when uploaded content completely or even only partially matches their reference files. They can opt to share revenue from ads running alongside the content, to receive statistics on

3 OECD Council Recommendation on Principles for Internet Policy Making (2011), obtained from oecd.org.

4 Trans-Pacific Partnership Agreement Intellectual Property Rights Chapter, leaked draft dated February 10, 2011, obtained from keionline.org.

user traffic to the content, or to block the content from being uploaded to the site altogether. The automated match serves as a proxy for a finding of infringement, and the prerogative to block belongs solely to copyright owners. YouTube users whose uploaded content matches reference files three times are suspended from the service, pursuant to YouTube's own repeat infringer policy.[5]

The problems with using automated filters to screen for infringing digital content are well documented. An incident involving Content ID and public domain footage of the Mars Curiosity rover illustrates the danger of over-blocking and the probability that a system engineered to screen hundreds of thousands of files a day will generate false positives that deny access to lawful content. The video footage in question was publicly released by the US National Aeronautics and Space Administration (NASA) to document and promote the Curiosity mission. As a "government work," NASA's footage is not subject to copyright under US law. Nevertheless, Curiosity footage that NASA posted to YouTube was taken down and replaced with a message indicating that the video had been blocked by Scripps Local News, which claimed copyright in it through the Content ID system.[6] The video was later restored when NASA complained to YouTube. In a similar incident, a political campaign advertisement showing President Barack Obama singing a line from an Al Green song was taken down because it matched a file provided by BMG.[7] These two false positives – one in which a copyright owner made a claim to public domain content, the other in which a copyright owner was permitted to pre-empt a colourable fair use of its work – highlight the limits of algorithmic blocking as an adequately speech-protective method of online copyright enforcement. Where systems like YouTube's allow blocking of uploads even if they only partially match the content of reference files, many fair uses are likely to be blocked.

YouTube's implementation of the Content ID system as a means of playing nicely with corporate copyright owners was neither required by US law nor debated in any public forum. US copyright law expressly does not require online service providers to monitor their networks for infringing content. In the cooperative efforts that produced the Content ID system, however, YouTube chose to go above and beyond its legal obligations for the benefit of corporate copyright owners. As with cooperative efforts to control infringement in the P2P environment, cooperative efforts between copyright owners and user-generated content (UGC) platforms must be monitored carefully to insure that the public has access to non-infringing content and that the

5 Information about YouTube's Content ID system and its "three strikes" protocol was obtained from youtube.com.

6 Lee, Timothy B. (2012). "As Curiosity Touches Down on Mars, Video Is Taken Down from YouTube". Ars Technica, obtained from arstechnica.com.

7 Lee, Timothy B. (2012). "Music Publisher Uses DMCA to Take Down Romney Ad of Obama Crooning". Ars Technica, obtained from arstechnica.com.

public's ability to take full advantage of copyright exceptions and flexibilities is not systematically compromised.

### *Civil Seizures of Internet Domain Names*

ACTA's civil seizure provision requires parties to empower their judicial authorities to order the seizure of "materials and implements" used to infringe copyright or related rights.[8] Civil seizures are designed to culminate in the forfeiture of the subject property to the government. ACTA's seizure provision could be interpreted to apply only to machinery used to manufacture infringing hard goods like DVDs. It could also be read and implemented more broadly, however, to reach Internet domain names. The US Department of Justice, working in cooperation with the National Intellectual Property Rights Coordination (IPR) Center, relies on similar provisions in US domestic law to seize the domain names of what are sometimes referred to as "rogue sites."[9] Such sites are typically defined as sites dedicated to intellectual property infringement, including the distribution and/or streaming of copyrighted content.

Based on the domestic experience in the United States, there is good reason to believe that corporate copyright owners will pressure ACTA parties to implement the agreement's civil seizure provision to reach Internet domain names registered within their territorial limits. Because domains that facilitate content sharing often provide users with access to lawful content in addition to infringing content, their seizure by law enforcement authorities pursuant to evidentiary standards as relaxed as those in US copyright law raises global A2K concerns. When seizure laws are drafted as they are in the United States to require no more than a showing of probable cause to believe the targeted property has been used to commit or facilitate criminal copyright infringement, the potential for mistake and abuse by law enforcement authorities is great. That potential is amplified when zealous enforcement of IPRs becomes an institutional priority for law enforcement, as it has in the United States, where specialized multi-agency teams focus their energies on IPR enforcement.

Some background on a US law enforcement initiative called "Operation In Our Sites" is helpful for understanding how ACTA parties could implement ACTA's

8 Civil seizure and forfeiture differ from criminal seizure and forfeiture in that civil forfeiture operates on "guilty" property; criminal forfeiture, by contrast, is imposed as part of a convicted criminal's punishment. Garretson, H. (2008). "Federal Criminal Forfeiture: A Royal Pain in the Assets". *Review of Law and Social Justice* 18(1):45–77.

9 The provisions were part of the Prioritizing Resources and Organization for Intellectual Property (PRO-IP) Act of 2008, which also created the Office of the Intellectual Property Enforcement Coordinator (IPEC) to coordinate IPR enforcement across a range of federal law enforcement agencies.

civil seizure provision to shut down entire Internet domains with almost no due process of law. Under US law, the owner of property targeted by the government gets notice of its seizure, but the property owner's only recourse is to contest the action ex post, with the subject property already in the hands of the government. When the US government seizes a domain name, the registrar is directed to "restrain and lock" it, pending transfer of its title to the United States upon completion of forfeiture proceedings.[10] The registrar is further ordered to point that domain's traffic to an IP address belonging to the US government, at which a banner is displayed to users indicating that the domain has been seized for criminal violation of copyright law.[11] Finally, the registrar is ordered to change the WHOIS information associated with the domain name to identify the US government as the contact, effectively erasing the identity of the domain name owner.[12] All of this occurs without any adversarial judicial hearing on the merits of the underlying criminal infringement charges. If the owner of the domain name, who may not even reside in the United States, does not retain counsel and appear in court to contest the seizure, the "offending" property is automatically forfeited to the government. Users of affected sites receive no notification of the seizure beyond the information displayed on the banner, and they have no legal standing to contest the seizure.

In 2011, US law enforcement authorities operating under the auspices of Operation In Our Sites seized 270 domain names, of which 22 were seized for allegedly distributing copyrighted digital content.[13] Ten of the 22 sites hosted no copyrighted content at all and simply linked to other sites at which allegedly infringing content was available.[14] Even though the government had questionable legal grounds for its theory that linking to infringing material gives rise to criminal liability, the seizure warrants were issued. Moreover, they were issued under seal, meaning that the public could not access them. The Spanish operator of two of the seized domains, Rojadirecta.com and Rojadirecta.org, retained US counsel and contested the impending forfeiture.[15] No fewer than eighteen months after the seizure, attorneys for the US government voluntarily dismissed the forfeiture complaint with little explanation, citing

[10] *United States v. HQ-Streams.com*, S.D.N.Y., No. 11 MAG 262, affidavit unsealed February 2, 2011.

[11] Ibid.

[12] Ibid.

[13] US 2011 Intellectual Property Enforcement Coordinator Annual Report on Intellectual Property Enforcement (2012), obtained from ipec.gov.

[14] US Immigration and Customs Enforcement (ICE) Press Release dated February 2, 2011, obtained from ice.gov.

[15] The operators also promptly registered the Rojadirecta name in other top-level domains, from which they continued to operate the sites during the pendency of the forfeiture action. The ease with which domain name seizures can be circumvented raises serious questions about their efficacy as a law enforcement tool. Due process is undermined, but there is no meaningful countervailing law enforcement benefit.

only "certain recent judicial authority involving issues germane" to the case.[16] Given the timing of the request for dismissal, the referenced authority is likely a federal appellate case decided only days before, which held that a social-bookmarking site that provided embedded video streamed to users from another site's server was not liable for infringement.[17] Following the government's surprise request to vacate the seizure warrant, no compensation was paid to the Spanish operator of the sites, and there were no repercussions for the government's apparent overreaching.

The Rojadirecta case exposes the threats to due process and access to knowledge that inhere in the US law of civil seizure and forfeiture as applied in the context of online copyright infringement. If ACTA parties pass laws that resemble the seizure provisions in US copyright law, operators and users of web sites registered in those countries may be deprived of important procedural safeguards that exist to protect the property of accused wrongdoers from improper or premature expropriation by the government.

## CONCLUSION

Access-to-knowledge advocates should view developments in domestic IPR enforcement in the United States since 2008, when ACTA negotiations opened, as a harbinger of things to come in countries that are parties to ACTA. Given the reputation of the United States as an IPR norm exporter, two ACTA provisions that warrant monitoring in their implementation are the cooperative efforts provision and the civil seizure provision. Both provisions are already part of the US enforcement agenda, and both substantially raise the risk of over-enforcement at the expense of Internet users and their communicative freedoms.

16 Frey, C. (2012), Letter dated August 29, 2012 to the Honorable Paul A. Crotty, US District Judge for the Southern District of New York Re: United States of America v. Rojadirecta.org, et al., obtained from wired.com.

17 Flava Works, Inc. v. Gunter, 689 F.3d 754 (7th Cir. 2012).

# 15

# ACTA, East African Enforcement Legislation and Generic Medicines

## *A Comparison*

*Christoph Spennemann*

### INTRODUCTION

It is not the purpose of this chapter to provide yet another analysis of the possible implications of the Anti-Counterfeiting Trade Agreement (ACTA) for trade in generic medicines. This has been done in detail by various scholars.[1] Instead, the present chapter seeks to shed some light on the legal frameworks regarding intellectual property rights (IPRs) enforcement in the East African Community (EAC) and some of its partner states, namely Kenya, Uganda and Tanzania, as compared to parallel provisions in ACTA. These countries are in the process of adopting, at the regional and/or the national level, specific anti-counterfeiting legislation that to some extent exceeds minimum standards established under the World Trade Organization's (WTO) Agreement on Trade-Related Aspects of Intellectual Property Rights (TRIPS Agreement) as well as comparable provisions under ACTA. At the same time, these countries have been proactively pursuing policies of implementing public health-related TRIPS flexibilities in their domestic intellectual property (IP) legislation, which are at least partly affected by "TRIPS-Plus" obligations in the area of IPR enforcement. The present chapter illustrates the need for policy coherence between the areas of IP, trade and public health.

[1] *See*, for example, Ruse-Khan, Chapter 5 of this volume; *see also* Ruse-Khan, Henning Grosse. "A Trade Agreement Creating Barriers to International Trade?: ACTA Border Measures and Goods in Transit", *American University International Law Review* 26 no. 3 (2011): 645–726.

## ANTI-COUNTERFEIT LEGISLATION IN THE EAC – LATEST DEVELOPMENTS

In 2010, the EAC Secretariat made available to partner states[2] an EAC Anti-Counterfeit Bill as drafted pursuant to a consultancy by two Nairobi-based law firms. The 2010 version received comments from partner states governments and underwent a number of minor modifications. Consultations between the EAC secretariat and partner states are currently pursued on the basis of the 2011 version of the bill.[3] It is important to note that this piece of law, once adopted, is envisaged to take "precedence over all the laws of the Partner States with respect to any matter to which its provisions relate."[4]

In Kenya, the High Court in a 20 April 2012 judgment declared parts of the 2008 national Anti-Counterfeit Act unconstitutional for potential violations of the rights to life, human dignity and health and requested the Kenyan legislator to amend the Act.[5] The Kenyan law has provided a template for anti-counterfeit draft legislation in other EAC partner states and the EAC secretariat.

In Uganda, the 2009 version of the Counterfeit Goods Bill is under consideration among government agencies. Local civil society and the Ministry of Tourism, Trade and Industry played an important role in amending a previous version from 2008 to better reflect concerns related to public health and generic competition.

Tanzania has for the time being no specific domestic (draft) anti-counterfeit legislation. Patent legislation in Tanzania is divided between Tanzania-Mainland and the island of Zanzibar. In an effort to implement TRIPS Agreement public health-related flexibilities, Tanzania-Zanzibar adopted the 2008 Patents Act, which in cases of patent infringement and counterfeit trademarked goods provides for remedies comparable to TRIPS Agreement minimum standards. Tanzania-Mainland still relies on the pre-TRIPS Patents Act of 1995.

## THE DEFINITION OF COUNTERFEITING

While the final version of ACTA does not expand the notion of counterfeiting beyond counterfeit trademark goods (Section 2.d), relevant East African (draft) legislation has introduced a much broader definition.

2 Partner states of the EAC are Burundi, Kenya, Rwanda, Uganda and the United Republic of Tanzania.

3 Version 080411 of 2011, on file with the author.

4 Section 1.4 of the EAC Anti-Counterfeit Bill.

5 Judgment of the High Court of Kenya in *Patricia Asero Ochieng, Maurine Atieno and Joseph Munyi v The Republic*, 20 April 2012 [hereinafter Kenyan High Court decision].

The Kenyan Anti-Counterfeit Act in Section 2 states:

> '[C]ounterfeiting' means taking the following actions without the authority of the owner of intellectual property right subsisting in Kenya or elsewhere in respect of protected goods
> (a) the manufacture, production, packaging, re-packaging, labelling or making, whether in Kenya or elsewhere, of any goods whereby those protected goods are imitated in such manner and to such a degree that those other goods are identical or substantially similar copies of the protected goods;
> (b) the manufacture, production or making, whether in Kenya or elsewhere, the subject matter of that intellectual property, or a colourable imitation thereof so that the other goods are calculated to be confused with or to be taken as being the protected goods of the said owner or any goods manufactured, produced or made under his licence;
>
> [...]
>
> (d) in relation to medicine, the deliberate and fraudulent mislabelling of medicine with respect to identity or source, whether or not such products have correct ingredients, wrong ingredients, have sufficient active ingredients or have fake packaging; Provided that nothing in this paragraph shall derogate from the existing provisions under the Industrial Property Act.

Paragraph (d) on medicines was not part of the original draft provision. It was added to respond to concerns voiced about the impact the definition especially in paragraph (a) may have on the legitimate generic production of medicines. The chapeau to the provision establishes that the authorisation from the IPR holder shall be the key criterion for determining counterfeiting. Section 2 also provides that the notion of "intellectual property rights" includes "any right protected under the Industrial Property Act, 2001" (i.e. especially patents).

It is obvious that, without the subsequently added paragraph (d), the broad definition of counterfeiting would have encompassed activities by generic producers that do not necessarily meet the patent right holder's approval, such as the use of the regulatory review exception for early generic market entry, reliance on the research exception for seeking incremental improvements and especially the marketing of generic copies during the patent term in cases where the generic producer has reason to believe that the right holder's patent is weak and may be challenged in infringement litigation. Consequently, generic producers engaged in these legitimate activities would have been exposed to criminal sanctions, which are triggered by activities that meet the definition of counterfeiting.[6]

[6] See section on applicable remedies later in the chapter for details.

Compared to this very broad approach (which has also been used in Uganda and to some extent at the EAC level), even ACTA's earlier versions never attempted to link the term "counterfeiting" to the authorisation of competitors' activities by the IP right holder. This raises the question of the origins of the approach taken in East Africa.

According to the Ugandan commissioner for customs, it was mainly a seminar organised by the World Customs Organization (WCO) in Kampala in 2006 that influenced the drafting of the Kenyan law.[7] The meeting was reportedly funded by a number of multinational companies, including some major pharmaceutical players.[8] In 2008, a number of multinational pharmaceutical firms through their Kenyan affiliates established an anti-counterfeit committee within the Kenya Association of Manufacturers (KAM) and submitted a position paper on IP enforcement to the Kenyan Parliament's committee in charge of anti-counterfeiting legislation. This was followed by considerable lobbying efforts by KAM within this committee.[9] KAM succeeded to convince the initially reluctant Kenyan government to speed up the parliamentary approval process of the Anti-Counterfeit Act by referring to the losses to be expected in the pharmaceutical industry as a result of counterfeit trade.[10] The parliamentary committee in charge of the draft legislation received technical advice from KAM and its member companies.[11] Meanwhile, in Uganda, funds received in 2009 from the European Union in the context of implementing the Economic Partnership Agreement between the EU and East African nations were employed to hire a consultant for the elaboration of the country's Counterfeit Goods Bill.[12]

Turning back to paragraph (d) of the Kenyan definition of counterfeiting, quoted earlier, this was drafted along the lines of the World Health Organization's (WHO) definition of spurious/falsely labelled/falsified/counterfeit (SFFC) medicines.[13]

7 Wambi Michael, "East Africa: Global Players Behind Anti-Counterfeit Law Campaign", Inter Press Service (IPS) News Agency, 21 May 2010 (http://www.ipsnews.net/2010/05/east-africa-global-players-behind-anti-counterfeit-law-campaign/) (last visited 28 February 2013), quoting Peter Malinga, Ugandan commissioner for customs and WCO chairperson for East and Southern Africa.

8 Ibid.

9 Suleiman Mbatiah, "Kenya: Pharmaceutical Companies Pushing Anti-Counterfeit Law", IPS, 14 June 2010, (http://www.ipsnews.net/2010/06/kenya-pharmaceutical-companies-pushing-anti-counterfeit-law/) (last visited 28 February 2013), quoting Joseph Wairiuko, KAM executive officer for policy research and advocacy.

10 Ibid., quoting J. Wairiuko.

11 Ibid., quoting GlaxoSmithKline's managing director for Kenya, John Musunga.

12 Wambi Michael, "HEALTH UGANDA: EU Supports Law Threatening Access to Medicines" (http://www.ipsnews.net/2010/03/health-uganda-eu-supports-law-threatening-access-to-medicines/) (last visited 28 February 2013), quoting Alex Nakajo, trade operations officer at the EU delegation to Uganda, as stating that the bill "targets only people who infringe on protected intellectual property rights," while "counterfeits should not … be confused with generic drugs."

13 *See* http://www.who.int/mediacentre/factsheets/fs275/en/ (last visited 15 November 2012).

While this paragraph, read in isolation, makes clear that the qualification of a drug as counterfeit hinges on deliberate and fraudulent mislabelling and is not necessarily related to an authorisation by an IP holder, its relationship with the chapeau of the provision is not obvious. In particular, it is unclear to what extent the IP holder authorisation requirement continues to apply to medicines-related activities. This ambiguity may have been the result of hasty drafting. In any case, it was criticised by the Kenyan High Court's 20 April 2012 decision as not providing a sufficient safeguard for the right to life, dignity and health against IP enforcement actions targeting generic medicines.[14] The Court drew the conclusion that Section 2 of the domestic Anti-Counterfeit Act threatens to violate the petitioners' right to life, human dignity and health as provided under Kenya's constitution.[15]

The EAC Anti-Counterfeit Bill in its (still bracketed) Section 3.1 basically copies the definition of counterfeiting used in the Kenyan law as previously discussed, with one exception: there is no specific proviso on the application of this definition in the context of medicines. While this could be understood as including in the definition of counterfeiting generic producers' activities as they relate to patented products, the EAC bill applies a much narrower definition of intellectual property rights than the Kenyan Anti-Counterfeit Act. Section 3 of the EAC bill specifies that the meaning of intellectual property right is limited to trademarks, copyright and related rights. Thus, the seemingly broad definition of counterfeiting does not include activities related to the copying of patent-protected substances. However, the inclusion of trademarks raises the question of whether legitimate or non-intentionally infringing generic branding could potentially be considered counterfeiting, generating inter alia criminal liability. In this respect, Section 3.1 of the EAC bill states:

> 'Counterfeiting' means:
>
> (a) the manufacturing, producing or making, packaging, repackaging and labelling whether in the Community or elsewhere, of any goods whereby those protected goods are imitated in such manner and to such a degree that those other goods are substantially identical copies of the protected goods without the authority of the Owner of any Intellectual Property Right subsisting in the relevant Partner State in respect of Protected Goods;
> (b) the manufacturing, producing or making or applying to goods, whether in the Community or elsewhere, the subject matter of that Intellectual Property Right, or a colourable imitation thereof so that the other goods are calculated to be confused with or to be taken as being the Protected Goods of the said Owner or any goods manufactured, produced or made under his licence without the authority of the

[14] Kenyan High Court decision, p. 44/para. 84.
[15] Ibid., para. 87.

> Owner of any Intellectual Property Right subsisting in the relevant Partner State in respect of the Protected Goods.

In principle, the reference in paragraph (b) to "applying to goods (...) the subject matter of that Intellectual Property Right" in conjunction with consumer confusion as to the true origin of the goods indicates the applicability of this definition to branding activities. However, the reference to the "calculation" on the part of the alleged infringer to confuse consumers makes clear that innocent trademark infringement does not fall under this definition of counterfeiting, which requires some intent. Innocent trademark infringement could especially happen due to the tendency of generic manufacturers in many countries to name products according to their active pharmaceutical ingredients (i.e. the international non-proprietary name, INN).[16]

The definition of counterfeiting in Uganda's 2009 Counterfeit Goods Bill is essentially a copy of the Kenyan definition, stating:

> 'Counterfeiting' means without the authority of the owner of any intellectual property right subsisting in Uganda in respect of protected goods –
> (a) The manufacturing, producing, packaging, repackaging, labelling or making, whether in Uganda or outside Uganda, of any goods by which those protected goods are imitated in such manner and to such a degree that those other goods are identical to or substantially similar to protected goods;
>
> [...]
>
> (c) In the case of medicines, *includes* the deliberate and fraudulent mislabelling of medicines with respect to identity or source, whether or not such products have correct ingredients, wrong ingredients, have sufficient active ingredients or have fake packaging. (emphasis added)

As in the case of the Kenyan definition, the relationship between the chapeau and the specific paragraph on medicines is unclear. In the case of Uganda, the situation is made even more difficult by the use of the term "includes" (as emphasised in the preceding quote), which is not used in the Kenyan provision. This could be misunderstood as implying that paragraph (a) regarding manufacturing activities still

16 In many cases, pharmaceutical producers brand their products on the basis of the international non-proprietary name (INN) of the active pharmaceutical ingredients (APIs). *See* SEATINI, "A briefing paper on the utilization of TRIPS flexibilities in the EAC Region", briefing paper produced by Health Action International Africa, 2012, available at http://www.seatiniuganda.org/a-briefing-paper-on-the-utilization-of-trips-flexibilities-in-the-eac-region/ (last visited 14 November 2012) [hereinafter SEATINI]. This could result in similarity of pharmaceutical trademarks among various producers, resulting in a likelihood of consumer confusion. Such non-intentional trademark infringements (see Article 16.1, TRIPS Agreement) have to be distinguished from the intentional use of someone else's trademark to benefit from the goodwill associated to the latter (i.e. what the TRIPS Agreement refers to as "counterfeit goods" in Article 51, footnote 14(a)).

applies in addition to paragraph (c), thus qualifying generic producers' activities as counterfeiting.[17] The criticism advanced by the Kenyan High Court (see discussion earlier in the chapter) applies to an even greater extent to this Ugandan provision. As in Kenya, and unlike under the EAC bill, the definition of intellectual property rights in the Ugandan bill also includes patents, thus potentially targeting generic pharmaceutical production activities.

Finally, a striking feature in all three legal texts (i.e. EAC, Kenya and Uganda) is the extraterritorial application of IPRs existing in these jurisdictions to activities occurring in third countries. According to the original drafting of the definition of counterfeiting in Kenya and Uganda, an IPR holder in these countries could have qualified manufacturing activities in a third country, such as India, for example, where its product enjoys no IPR protection, as counterfeiting.[18] Domestic subsidiaries of these foreign manufacturers operating in Uganda would potentially have been exposed to sanctions related to counterfeiting, such as criminal remedies (fines and imprisonment). Considering the important presence of particularly Indian generic investors in the EAC partner states,[19] this could have a serious impact on decisions related to foreign investment in Uganda.

## APPLICABLE REMEDIES IN CASE OF PATENT AND TRADEMARK INFRINGEMENT

### *ACTA*

Under ACTA, the scope of application of civil and criminal enforcement as well as border measures varies according to the category of the IPR at issue. Civil enforcement in general applies to all categories of IPRs as provided under Sections 1 through 7 of part II of the TRIPS Agreement, while ACTA parties may opt to exclude patents and the protection of undisclosed information from the scope of civil enforcement measures.[20] A reason for such exclusion could relate to concerns that some ACTA

[17] *See* UNCTAD-ICTSD, "Development Dimensions of Intellectual Property in Uganda: Transfer of Technology, Access to Medicines and Textbooks", available at http://unctad.org/en/docs/diaepcb200913_en.pdf (last visited 7 November 2012), p. 53 [hereinafter UNCTAD, DDIP Uganda].

[18] This shows the importance of the (subsequent) introduction of the specific proviso on medicines, as quoted earlier. Note that the broad approach to "counterfeiting", as originally envisaged for Kenya and Uganda, would be more difficult to support in the context of the EAC Anti-Counterfeit Bill, which does not apply to patents or ordinary trademark infringement.

[19] For example, the Indian pharmaceutical firm Cipla in a joint venture with Uganda's Quality Chemicals formulates anti-retroviral drugs at a site near Kampala (see UNCTAD, DDIP Uganda, pp. 6–7). The active pharmaceutical ingredients (APIs), which could potentially be patented in Uganda, are imported by Cipla from India.

[20] *See* Kamperman, Chapter 4, present volume.

provisions on civil enforcement like damages (Article 9.1), provisional measures (Article 12) and abuse deterrence (Articles 12.5, 18) could be used to the detriment of generic manufacturers.[21] In should be noted in this context that civil remedies under ACTA only differ slightly from the minimum standards under Articles 45 and 50 of the TRIPS Agreement.[22]

Under ACTA, patents and undisclosed information do not fall within the scope of border measures.[23] This responds to concerns voiced during ACTA negotiations that patent holders could invoke border measures to stop shipments of generic medicines in transit in the jurisdiction where the patent is registered, irrespective of the fact that the drugs may be off-patent in the country of origin as well as the country of destination.[24] A point of concern for generic producers, however, is the mandatory extension of border measures under ACTA Article 13 to all categories of IPRs (except patents and undisclosed information), including cases of non-intentional ("ordinary") trademark infringement, coupled with the optional extension of border measures to goods in transit.[25] Unlike under Article 51 of the TRIPS Agreement, generic pharmaceuticals displaying confusingly similar signs may thus be suspended at the border when transiting a country, provided that country has opted to apply border measures to transit cases. While it is clear that the right holder must have remedies available to prevent the use of confusingly similar trademarks, the question arises whether goods bearing such trademarks can effectively curb the trademark holder's rights and economic interests when only in transit. It has been observed in the literature that only "few countries are likely to apply such a broad notion of protection for an IP right to transit cases that lack any real link to their territory."[26] The main concern relates to the loss of time generated by detentions of shipments

[21] *See*, for instance, Health Action International (HAI) Europe, "ACTA and Access to Medicines: A Flawed Process, Flawed Rationale and Flawed Agreement", 27 February 2012 [hereinafter HAI, 2012], available at http://haieurope.org/wp-content/uploads/2012/02/27-Feb-2012-HAI-Europe-Policy-Brief-ACTA-and-Access-to-Medicines.pdf (last visited 15 November 2012).

[22] But see HAI, 2012, for a more critical assessment of ACTA provisions on civil enforcement.

[23] See footnote 6 to Article 13, ACTA.

[24] *See* Chapter 7, present volume and also Ruse-Khan, 2011 (supra ft 1), p. 662, citing authorities and providing further analysis. This concern is based on concrete experiences, namely the practice by some European customs authorities in 2008 and 2009 to stop and return several shipments of generic drugs that were transiting the EU, en route from India to ports in mainly Latin American and African countries. These drugs were off-patent in both the country of origin of the shipment and the country of destination, but were patented in the relevant member states of the EU. *See*, for instance, Frederick M. Abbott, "Worst Fears Realised: The Dutch Confiscation of Medicines Bound from India to Brazil", *Bridges Monthly*, No. 1, February–March 2009. It would go beyond the scope and objective of this chapter to revisit the arguments advanced by the EU regarding its system of border measures.

[25] Article 16.2, ACTA makes the adoption of border measures optional in the case of transits, as opposed to the cases of imports and exports, where border measures are mandatory under Article 16.1, ACTA.

[26] Ruse-Khan, 2011 (supra ft 1), p. 689.

of generic drugs until customs authorities have determined their (non-)infringing character.[27] It appears essential for competent authorities to make the initiation of border measure procedures dependent on the submission by the right holder of convincing evidence for prima facie trademark infringement in cases of transit, such as the showing of a concrete and credible likelihood of trade diversion into the national territory of the country of transit. The mere possibility of trade diversion should in any case be regarded as insufficient in this context.[28]

Finally, criminal sanctions under ACTA do not in principle apply to cases of patent and ordinary trademark infringement.[29]

Summing up, under ACTA, the main public health–related concern arises from the potential application of border measures to generic medicines in transit that bear trademarks of confusing similarity with originator brands, possibly causing delays of shipments and legal uncertainty for generic suppliers.

### *Kenya, Uganda and Tanzania*

As the Ugandan Counterfeit Goods Bill is largely a blueprint of the Kenyan Anti-Counterfeit Act, the following observations apply to both pieces of legislation. Under both, the application of remedies such as criminal sanctions and border measures entirely depends on the qualification of an activity as counterfeiting. Based on the specific proviso on medicines in the definition of counterfeiting in the Kenyan and Ugandan laws, it should be argued that none of the available remedies apply to generic drugs, as these do not imply any "deliberate and fraudulent mislabelling." On the other hand, the unclear interpretation of this definition as observed by the Kenyan High Court (and the even greater uncertainty in the Ugandan bill, due to poor drafting; see discussion in the previous section) could encourage some holders of pharmaceutical patents to claim unauthorised production and labelling activities as falling under the term of "counterfeiting." Such uncertainty could potentially generate a chilling effect on generic production activities.

Criminal sanctions under both pieces of legislation range from certain fines to imprisonment up to five years or, in the case of Kenya, up to fifteen years in case of a secondary or subsequent conviction.[30] Sanctioned activities encompass

[27] Ibid. Article 19, ACTA provides that competent authorities shall make such a determination "within a reasonable period after the initiation of the procedures" on border measures.

[28] This is the position adopted by the International Association for the Protection of Intellectual Property (AIPPI) in its Resolution on "Question Q230 – Infringement of trademarks by goods in transit", Congress Seoul 2012, 23 October 2012.

[29] Article 23, ACTA provides Parties with the discretion to extend the application of criminal measures beyond the specific cases of trademark counterfeit goods and copyright piracy.

[30] See Section 35.1 of the Kenyan Anti-Counterfeit Act, Section 17.3 of the Ugandan Counterfeit Goods Bill.

any domestic activities undertaken "in the course of trade," as well as imported, exported, transited or transhipped products.[31] The reference to the "course of trade" in this regard is quite striking, as it illustrates the true intention behind these laws. As observed by the Kenyan High Court,

> Clearly, as the above provisions [i.e. Sections 32–34 of the Kenyan Anti-Counterfeit Act] show, the tenor and object of the Act is to protect the intellectual property rights of individuals. [...] Had the primary intention been to safeguard consumers from counterfeit medicine, then the Act should have laid greater emphasis on standards and quality.[32]

While transits and transhipments may thus give rise to criminal sanctions, neither the Kenyan law nor the Ugandan bill provides for border measures in these cases. Seizures and detentions of counterfeit products are only provided in the case of importation.[33]

Finally, it is important to note that the Kenyan Patents Act complements the Anti-Counterfeit Act in terms of criminal sanctions for patent infringements. Section 109 of the Patents Act provides, inter alia, for imprisonment between three and five years for any act of intentional patent infringement. Thus, even if it may be argued that the Anti-Counterfeit Act has to be interpreted as not applying criminal sanctions to patent infringements, the Patents Act may be used to fill this "gap." This is likely to deter generic producers from launching a generic copy of a patented drug at any time during the term of the patent, in case the patent appears to be of low quality.[34] Civil liability alone would not have such a deterring effect. Generic producers still have the possibility to challenge the patent grant directly before the courts, but the Kenyan Industrial Property Act only allows such action within a period of nine months from the date of publication of the patent grant.[35]

Tanzania-Zanzibar in 2008 adopted the new Patents Act, which provides only civil remedies in all cases of patent infringement.[36] The Act provides for border measures only in case of "counterfeit trademark goods" within the meaning of Article 51 of the TRIPS Agreement. By contrast, Tanzania-Mainland relies on the 1995 Patents

[31] See Section 32 of the Kenyan Anti-Counterfeit Act, Section 17.1 of the Ugandan Counterfeit Goods Bill.

[32] Kenyan High Court decision, para. 82.

[33] Section 34.1 of the Kenyan Anti-Counterfeit Act, Section 20.1 of the Ugandan Counterfeit Goods Bill.

[34] This may constitute an important means for generic producers to challenge pharmaceutical patents. Upon the launch of the generic product, the patent holder may be expected to claim patent infringement, which may then be countered by the generic producer based on the defense of patent invalidity.

[35] See Section 103.2 of the Kenyan Industrial Property Act.

[36] See Sections 73, 82, 84, 85 of the 2008 Zanzibar Patents Act.

Act, which does not provide for specific border measures. It mandates, inter alia, a maximum term of imprisonment of five years in cases of intentional patent infringement.[37] Unlike the corresponding legislation in Kenya, however, the 1995 Patents Act imposes no time limitation for third-party requests to invalidate a patent before the courts.

In Uganda, general patent law provides no criminal sanctions in the case of intentional patent infringement.[38] Generic producers may therefore consider, at any time during the patent term, challenging a pharmaceutical patent by means of invoking its invalidity in the course of patent infringement litigation.

### *The EAC*

Because the EAC Anti-Counterfeit Bill is limited to unauthorised activities in the areas of trademark and copyright, remedies under this bill do not address patent-infringing activities by generic producers. All other remedies, in particular criminal sanctions (Section 15) and seizures, as well as detentions of products (Section 19.1(a)), only apply to intentional trademark infringement, as opposed to the innocent design of confusingly similar trademarks, which could occur in the course of generic branding based on the INN of pharmaceutical products. As compared to the domestic approaches in Kenya and Uganda, generic producers gain considerably in legal certainty under the EAC bill as a result of the exclusion of patents and pharmaceutical test data from the scope of the legislation.

### *Summary of Key Observations*

Summing up the preceding analysis from the perspective of legitimate generic production and trade, ACTA appears to be more problematic in the area of trademarks, whereas East African legislation raises more concerns with respect to patents.

The final version of ACTA does not apply border measures to generic activities related to patents or pharmaceutical test data. But goods in transit may be caught in border measure procedures upon allegation of ordinary trademark infringement, depending on national law.

Under the reviewed East African national legislation, the situation is quite the opposite: because of vague definitions of counterfeiting in the Kenyan and Ugandan laws, and owing to criminal sanctions for intentional patent infringements under Kenyan and Tanzanian patent law, generic producers' typical activities as they relate

[37] See Section 70 of the 1995 Patents Act.

[38] Both the 1993 Patents Act and the 2009 Industrial Property Bill only foresee civil remedies to address patent infringements.

to the copying of pharmaceutical substance are potentially at risk, depending on the judicial interpretation of the relevant national provisions. Border measures, by contrast, do not appear to pose a particular problem to legitimate generic trade in transit in any of these countries, as they only apply to imports, or, in the case of Tanzania-Zanzibar, only address counterfeit goods within the meaning of the TRIPS Agreement minimum standards. But again, much depends on judicial interpretation of key terms such as "counterfeiting" in Kenyan and Ugandan domestic laws.

Finally, the EAC Anti-Counterfeit Bill appears to have been modified to an extent that arguably takes care of patent and trademark issues. Through its limitation to certain forms of trademark and copyright infringement, remedies such as criminal sanctions and border measures do not apply to typical generic activities such as drugs production and branding. This being said, its interpretation as regards the types of covered trademark infringements is not obvious and demands some awareness on the part of the judiciary of possible implications of different interpretations for generics trade. This is of particular relevance in light of the fact that EAC regional legislation has a supranational character and will thus supersede any relevant domestic laws, including in the area of IP enforcement.[39]

## CONCLUSIONS

The analysis in this chapter has sought to provide a comparison of the impact on generic producers generated by certain enforcement provisions in ACTA and East African regional and national legislative initiatives. In general, it may be stated that all of the analysed legal frameworks have addressed a number of concerns related to potential abuses of enforcement provisions to stifle legitimate generic production and trading activities. However, it is clear that a number of concerns remain. All of the reviewed initiatives were originally much more problematic from a generic producers' point of view, and it is thanks to increasing involvement of civil society organisations that the most burning issues were addressed.[40] This, however, does not mean that any of the analysed legal frameworks provide a template to be followed by countries that seek to address the problem of SFFC medicines. As highlighted by the Kenyan High Court, such legislation should be much more concerned with drugs quality standards than with intellectual property infringements. The result of controversial debates around the East African anti-counterfeit laws is a piecemeal

39 See Article 8.4. of the EAC Treaty: "Community organs, institutions and laws shall take precedence over similar national ones on matters pertaining to the implementation of this Treaty."

40 For instance, as far as anti-counterfeit legislation in Uganda and the EAC is concerned, Ugandan health activists such as the Coalition for Health Promotion and Social Development (HEPS Uganda) have been instrumental in raising awareness of government entities regarding potential implications for generic production and access to medicines.

collection of rather poorly drafted and vague provisions, unclear in scope and interpretation. The last-minute insertion of public health safeguards is obvious to intellectual property and public health specialists, who would be in a position to correctly apply such safeguards in order to ensure the legitimate interests of generic producers. But the crux of the matter is that domestic judges, who in many cases are less aware of the implications of certain interpretations for generic competition, may find it considerably challenging to apply these unclear provisions.

For example, a possible extension of criminal enforcement measures to generic producers (which could happen through uninformed judicial interpretation of the definition of counterfeiting) would generate a chilling effect on generic activities. Such a result would be in stark contrast with other policy developments in the EAC, where remarkable efforts have been made to prepare a policy environment that is conducive to local generic production and trade within the EAC, mainly by agreeing on regional harmonisation of drug regulation,[41] phasing out tariffs on pharmaceutical products among partner states and designing public procurement regimes that take account of industrial policy objectives.[42]

The abovementioned initiatives for the promotion of local generic production on the one hand and the preparation of the regional and national laws or drafts on counterfeiting on the other happened in parallel, mainly during the years 2008/9 – 2011. In October 2011, EAC health ministers, with the assistance of German International Cooperation (GIZ), tabled a counterproposal to the EAC bill, suggesting a number of fundamental amendments to avoid any potentially negative impact of the bill on public health–oriented initiatives in the areas of IP flexibilities and generic drugs trade.

All of the analysed anti-counterfeit legislation, if interpreted and applied in unawareness of potential implications for generic producers, could undermine public health–oriented initiatives, especially because the EAC Anti-Counterfeit Bill, once adopted, will be binding in all partner states,[43] whereas recently adopted EAC treaties on public health-related TRIPS flexibilities are non-binding instruments.[44]

41 *See* "EAC Pushes Towards Drug Registration Harmonisation and Integration", *AfriPharma Focus* Volume 1, Issue 1, February 2012, available for subscription at http://www.pharmaafrica.com/eac-pushes-towards-drug-registration-harmonisation-and-integration/ (last visited 14 November 2012).

42 For the case of Uganda, *see* UNCTAD, DDIP Uganda, p. 34.

43 *See* Section 39 of the EAC Bill: "This Act binds all the Partner States."

44 Personal e-mail communication to the author from the EAC-GIZ Programme on Regional Integration, Arusha, Tanzania, 2 February 2012 (on file with the author). In 2011, EAC Health Ministers adopted two important but non-binding instruments regarding the interface of IP and public health: (1) the "EAC Regional Intellectual Property Policy on the Utilisation of Public Health Related WTO-TRIPS Flexibilities and the Approximation of National Intellectual Property Legislation" and (2) the "EAC Regional Protocol on Public Health Related WTO-TRIPS Flexibilities."

Considering the current situation in the EAC, it is difficult to come up with a more obvious example for the urgent need for policy coherence in the areas of IP standards, IP enforcement and public health. While the EAC is a good example of policy coherence in the areas of TRIPS flexibilities, local pharmaceutical production, industrial development and harmonised regulatory and trade rules, there was apparently a lack of awareness of the implications of vaguely drafted anti-counterfeit standards. In this context, the involvement of local public health groups and other stakeholders plays a key role. Their awareness of public health implications of IP standards and their enforcement appears crucial to inform the national and regional process of adopting legal frameworks. At the same time, government officials and policy makers should be sensitised to understand the consequences of their decisions. Last but not least, a knowledgeable judiciary is indispensable in overcoming the shortcomings of the legislators by applying, to the extent possible, an interpretation to the domestic law that strikes a fair balance between opposing interests.

Drawing a comparison between ACTA and EAC anti-counterfeit legislation, it is clear that in both cases, the objective of these initiatives was the strengthening of IP enforcement mechanisms beyond TRIPS Agreement minimum standards. A legitimate policy objective (i.e. reducing trade in counterfeit products) was employed to promote the commercial interests of IPR holders vis-à-vis their competitors, arguably at a higher degree in the EAC than under ACTA. Under both initiatives, there were attempts to pass legislation without broad stakeholder consultation: in the case of ACTA through a non-transparent negotiation process, and in the case of the Kenyan law through lobbying pressure on decision makers to pass legislation within a very limited amount of time that excluded lengthy stakeholder consultations.

On the other hand, the processes leading to ACTA and the EAC legislation differed considerably in their approaches. In the case of ACTA, negotiating parties never conceived the agreement as having a particular health-related objective.[45] By contrast, East African anti-counterfeiting legislation was promoted under a public health objective,[46] thus potentially avoiding critical comments in the early phases of drafting.[47] In

45 See the ACTA Preamble, which refers to objectives such as economic growth, legitimate trade and sustainable development.

46 See the position of the Kenyan Attorney General, supported by the Chairman of the Board of the Kenyan Anti-Counterfeit Agency, during the proceedings leading to the High Court's decision of 20 April 2012: "According to the respondents, the duties of the state under Article 43 [of the Kenyan Constitution] are to ensure that its people attain the highest standard of healthcare. It is also the duty of the state to ensure that they enjoy the right to life. This is why the state enacted the Anti-Counterfeit Act as allowing counterfeit drugs will lead to death, and the Act was intended to protect citizens. […] The intention of the Act was to protect the lives of Kenyans from those few individuals who would deal with counterfeit goods, including drugs, for profit." (paras. 39, 43 of the Kenyan High Court decision).

47 A similar objective was pursued by ACTA negotiating parties by keeping negotiations confidential as long as possible.

addition, strong lobbying efforts by multinational firms created the impression with local policy makers that expansive anti-counterfeiting legislation would be beneficial to the local economy. This may be the reason for a striking degree of policy incoherence within the EAC and its partner states. The very same African governments that are involved in the design of the analysed anti-counterfeiting legislation have been at the forefront of implementing public health–related TRIPS flexibilities in their domestic laws. These flexibilities – including certain exclusions from patentability, a strict application of patentability requirements and solid research and regulatory review exceptions – seek to ensure a balance between exclusive rights and generic competition by granting generic competitors a certain amount of freedom to operate, in consideration of national development objectives such as access to affordable, quality medicines and the promotion of local pharmaceutical production. Such balance may be at risk when IPRs are enforced in disregard of legitimate rights and interests of alleged infringers.

# 16

# The EU and Its IP Policies

## *ACTA and Third Countries*

*Anselm Kamperman Sanders*

### INTRODUCTION

Europe's trade relations with Asia are increasingly advanced through so-called Broad-based Trade and Investment Agreements (BTIAs). After the conclusion of its free trade agreement (FTA) with South Korea, the EU is actively negotiating with India, and talks with Singapore are well under way. Further talks with Japan and a number of other Asian partners are expected.

In terms of innovation policy and technology transfer, intellectual property rights and their protection feature strongly in the BTIA template that the EU has been fine-tuning since it concluded FTAs with the Caribbean Community (CARICOM), as well as Colombia and Peru and, more recently, South Korea. The EU was also to become a party to the Anti-Counterfeiting Trade Agreement (ACTA), but since the European Parliament's rejection of the treaty on 4 July 2012, it is clear that less ambitious bilateral arrangements are the way forward.

The ongoing negotiations on the EU-India FTA show that, despite ACTA being off the table, intellectual property remains a contentious issue. In addition, new bilateral deals are currently being brokered or have been announced. EU-Singapore and EU-Malaysia talks have been under way since 2010, EU-Vietnam talks since June 2012 and EU-Japan FTA trade negotiations were announced on 29 November 2012. Many other Asian nations are currently involved in negotiations on the Transpacific Partnership Agreement (TPP) with the United States, which demands US-style protection of intellectual property rights from its trading partners.

The essential question is the extent to which the specificities of EU-Asia relations will be influenced by ACTA and current and future BTIAs. The announcement in early 2013 that the EU and the United States will attempt to establish a transatlantic FTA as early as 2015 was accompanied by a statement that there was "no low-hanging fruit" on which agreement could easily be reached. With import tariffs for goods currently averaging just 4 per cent, it is clear that the EU-US negotiations will focus on much more contentious issues such as services, standards, agricultural subsidies, public procurement and intellectual property.

## THE EU NEGOTIATION STRATEGY

The European Commission has traditionally been in charge of negotiations on trade agreements. Prior to the Treaty of Lisbon, resulting in the Treaty for the Functioning of the European Union (TFEU), it had exclusive competence only over goods, agriculture and most services. While this did not formally extend to services that did not affect cross-border trade or intellectual property rights (IPRs),[1] in practice the member states effectively gave the Commission an all-encompassing mandate.

At present, TFEU Article 3.1(e) provides the EU with the exclusive competence to deal with common commercial policy. This includes tariff and trade agreements that comprise, according to Article 207.1 TFEU, commercial aspects of intellectual property.

In this context we also have to consider the ERTA doctrine contained in TFEU Article 216(1), which is the codification of the decision of the European Court of Justice (ECJ) in *Commission v Council* (ERTA).[2] The Court laid down an obligation of loyal cooperation by the member states with regard to dealing with third parties, first of all where rules have been adopted by the Community collectively, but also in relation to the broader ambitions of bringing about the Common Market. In this judgment, the ECJ held:

> Each time the Community (…) adopts provisions laying down common rules (…), the Member States no longer have the right, acting individually or even collectively, to undertake obligations with third countries which affect those rules. (…) When such common rules come into being, the Community alone is in a position to assume and carry out contractual obligations towards third countries affecting the whole sphere of application of the Community legal system. (…) To the extent to which Community rules are promulgated for the attainment of the objectives of the Treaty, the Member States cannot, outside the framework of the Community institutions, assume obligations which might affect those rules or alter their scope.

All this means that it is arguable that agreements that deal only with intellectual property are not covered by TFEU Article 207.1, or that reliance on the "ERTA doctrine" would bring the negotiation of such an agreement within the exclusive competence of the EU. TFEU Article 207.6 states:

[1] Woolcock, S. (2010) 'The Treaty of Lisbon and the European Union as an actor in international trade', ECIPE Working paper, 1/2010. ECIPE, Brussels, Belgium.

[2] Case 22–70, *Commission v Council* (ERTA), 1971 E.C.R. 263.

> The exercise of the competences conferred by this Article [to conclude international agreements] in the field of the common commercial policy shall not affect the delimitation of competences between the Union and the Member States, and shall not lead to harmonization of legislative or regulatory provisions of the Member States in so far as the Treaties exclude such harmonization.

This makes it clear that the EU and its member states have shared competence over IP-only or mixed agreements. This was the case in the negotiation of ACTA, which is an IP-only agreement that includes both harmonised IP law and provisions that are neither harmonised nor unitary in the EU – specifically those dealing with criminal sanctions. It is for this reason that ACTA has been labelled a trade agreement rather than an intellectual property treaty.

Economic research[3] shows that neither strong IPRs nor FTAs automatically yield an increase in technology transfer and foreign direct investment (FDI). Figures show that countries with weak IPR protection or enforcement, such as Brazil and China, have been more successful in attracting FDI than many other developing countries that have made strong IPRs central to their development strategies.[4] Brazil, India and China are large, high-growth market economies with an increasingly adequate regulatory system involving taxes, investment regulations, production incentives, trade policies and even a hint of competition rules. In other words, the strength of IPR protection is clearly not the only factor in investment decision making.

Although econometric evidence of positive effects of strong IPR protection on FDI and technology transfer is not conclusive,[5] strengthening IPRs and providing effective enforcement is seen as a strong signal indicating that a country is willing to provide a more business-friendly environment capable of absorbing and safeguarding foreign investment and technology transfer interests. Empirical economic studies show that the relationship between IPRs and FDI in developing countries varies highly in respect of industry type, the stage of economic development factors (for example, transparency, openness, stable financial institutions, sound economic governance, competition law, low corruption) and the natural and labour resources of the country in question.

3 Correa, C. (2004), 'Bilateral investment agreements: Agents of new global standards for the protection of intellectual property rights?' GRAIN, available at www.grain.org, at 3.

4 Maskus, K. (1998) 'The Role of Intellectual Property Rights in Encouraging Foreign Direct Investment and Technology Transfer', *Duke Journal of Comparative and International Law*, 9(1), 109–161.

5 Maskus, K. (2005) 'The Role of Intellectual Property Rights in Encouraging Foreign Direct Investment and Technology Transfer', in Fink, C. and Maskus, K. (eds.) *Intellectual Property and Development – Lessons from Recent Economic Research* (New York: World Bank/Oxford University Press), 54.

### *EU-India: Access to Affordable Medicines*

BTIA talks between the EU and India, started in 2007, came to a standstill over IPRs, particularly with regard to the contentious issue of protection for pharmaceutical products and the exclusivity over clinical trial test data desired by the EU. The negotiations were officially expected to conclude in 2012, but that timeline proved too optimistic.[6] The key priority of India's strong domestic pharmaceutical industry and civil society is access to affordable medicines, as guaranteed by the Agreement on Trade-Related Aspects of Intellectual Property Rights (TRIPS) and the 2001 Doha Declaration on the TRIPS Agreement and Public Health. India is also asking the EU to screen the validity of European patents against prior use in traditional Indian medicine and knowledge related to Indian genetic resources.

### *China: Treatment of Audio-Visual/Cultural Products*

For a country like China, the need to acquire growth-enhancing intellectual property through technology transfer should be an incentive for strengthening IP protection.[7] However, the country's industry is still at a transformative stage, and the road towards value-added innovative production is long. Meanwhile, China remains the world's main supplier of counterfeit and pirated goods.[8] The fact that China is the "factory of the world" means that it can – despite being a member of the World Trade Organisation and thus bound by TRIPS[9] – afford to hold out on signing any FTA that would interfere with its ability to pursue its own industrial strategy, and set its own pace in strengthening IPR enforcement. This is especially noticeable in sectors engaged in the production and dissemination of audio-visual media and cultural products.

China's desire to monitor and censor media and cultural products or expressions, as well as to limit and control the legitimate market for them, explains in part the country's high piracy rates. Only a few Chinese companies have been granted rights to import foreign films, and these importers are responsible for seeking compliance with the censor. When the United States complained about this practice at the WTO, China argued that its regulatory regime for films for theatrical release was akin to regulating services: "Films for theatrical release are not goods because they

6 *See* http://ec.europa.eu/trade/creating-opportunities/bilateral-relations/countries/india/

7 Schiappacasse, M. (2004) 'Intellectual Property Rights in China: Technology Transfers and Economic Development', *Buffalo Intellectual Property Law Journal* 2, 164.

8 Chow, D. (2006) 'Why China Does Not Take Commercial Piracy Seriously', *Ohio Northern University Law Review* 32, 2003.

9 Yu, P. (2006) 'From Pirates to Partners (Episode II): Protecting Intellectual Property in Post-WTO China', *American University Law Review* 55, 901.

are exploited through a series of services; because the commercial value of films for theatrical release lies in the revenue generated by these services; and because the delivery materials containing the content of films are mere accessories of such services and have no commercial value of their own."[10]

The Appellate Body rejected this reading and concluded that, although services are involved, ultimately and inevitably there will be an act of importation of a physical carrier. The result is that China will have to allow imports on a non-discriminatory basis, although censors retain the authority to either approve or disapprove films for circulation.[11]

Another cause for concern is that overlap and division in competences between competing government agencies responsible for regulating these sectors does not result in effective IP enforcement.[12] And, finally, due to regional and local interests, national policy percolates very slowly from Beijing down to the regions.[13] Local protectionism and interdependence between counterfeiting/piracy and the legitimate economy is a norm rather than an exception.

## ENCIRCLEMENT OF CHINA

Innovative IPR-driven Asian economies (Japan, South Korea and Singapore), Australia, New Zealand, the United States and the EU are all seemingly engaged in a policy of "encirclement" of China, that is, ensuring that China's major and regional trading partners are committed to providing more effective IP enforcement, especially with regard to border controls and customs controls aimed at preventing trade in and importation of pirated and counterfeit goods. It is in this context that initiatives such as ACTA and TPP are relevant. Japan took the initiative for ACTA in 2005.[14] The United States quickly came on board in 2006, after which formal negotiations were launched in October 2007.

10 WT/DS363 China (Measures Affecting Trading Rights and Distribution Services for Certain Publications and Audiovisual Entertainment Products), adopted by the DSB on 19 January 2010, para. 173.

11 Conconi, P. and Pauwelyn, J. (2011) 'Trading Cultures: Appellate Body Report on China – Audiovisuals', *World Trade Review* 10(1), 95.

12 Creemers, R. (2012) *Explaining Audiovisual Media Piracy in China* (Maastricht University PhD 02-02-2012).

13 Mertha, A. (2005) *The Politics of Piracy: Intellectual Property in Contemporary China* (Ithaca, NY: Cornell University Press); Massey, J. (2006) 'The Emperor Is Far Away: China's Enforcement of Intellectual Property Rights Protection, 1986–2006', *Chicago Journal of International Law* 7, 231; Jingzhou, T. (2007) 'Problems and New Developments in the Enforcement of Intellectual Property Rights in China', in Torremans, P., Shan, H. and Erauw, J. (eds.) *Intellectual Property and TRIPS Compliance in China: Chinese and European Perspectives* (London: Edward Elgar), 107.

14 Gerhardsen, T. (2005) 'Japan Proposes New IP Enforcement Treaty', Intellectual Property Watch, 15 November, www.ip-watch.org/weblog/index.php?p=135.

The EU joined the talks only in 2008, as the mandate to negotiate had to be obtained from the member states. The Commission obtained a mandate from the Council to negotiate on issues covered by the EU *Acquis Communautaire*. In relation to other matters, such as criminal enforcement, negotiations were undertaken by the Presidency of the Council on behalf of the member states.

ACTA is in many ways a forum-shifting exercise born out of the frustration over the lack of progress on the fight against piracy and counterfeiting at the WTO.[15] Countries such as Brazil, India and China have systematically blocked the topic of intellectual property enforcement from the agenda of the WTO Council for TRIPS.[16] Equally, at the World Intellectual Property Organization (WIPO), issues of enforcement are discussed merely at the level of an advisory committee.[17]

ACTA can also be seen as a consolidation of provisions related to the enforcement of IPRs contained in the parties' bilateral and regional FTAs; in fact, all ACTA states are connected through FTAs in one way or another.[18] The United States is continuing its own strategy of extending the influence of the Asia-Pacific region by building on ACTA through the expansion of the original 2005 Trans-Pacific Strategic Economic Partnership Agreement (TPSEP or P4) between Brunei, Chile, New Zealand and Singapore with the addition of new members such as Australia, Japan, Malaysia, Peru and Vietnam.

## ACTA AND ITS HISTORY

The ACTA negotiations were concluded, after eleven rounds, in October 2010 in Tokyo. The final text was published on 3 December 2010.[19] On 1 October 2011, Australia, Canada, Japan, Morocco, New Zealand, South Korea, Singapore and the United States signed the agreement during a ceremony in Tokyo. The EU member states, as well as Switzerland and Mexico, were represented at the ceremony but did not sign.

On 27 January 2012, twenty-two EU member states (the United Kingdom, Austria, Belgium, Bulgaria, Czech Republic, Denmark, Finland, France, Greece, Hungary, Ireland, Italy, Latvia, Lithuania, Luxemburg, Malta, Poland, Portugal, Romania, Slovenia, Spain and Sweden) signed ACTA. The five remaining member

15 Kaminski, M. (2009) 'Recent Development: The Origins and Potential Impact of the Anti-Counterfeiting Trade Agreement (ACTA)', *Yale Journal of International Law* 34, 247.

16 *See* 'Minutes of Meeting Held in the Centre William Rappard on 8–9 June 2010', Council on Trade-related Aspects of Intellectual Property, IP/C/M/63, 4 October 2010.

17 WIPO 'Mandate of WIPO Advisory Committee on Enforcement', WO/GA/28/7, www.wipo.int/meetings/en/doc_details.jsp?doc_id=14890

18 *See* www.bilaterals.org

19 *See* http://ec.europa.eu/trade/creating-opportunities/trade-topics/intellectual-property/anti-counterfeiting/ for the official text

states – Cyprus, Germany, Estonia, the Netherlands and Slovakia – did not. Aside from ratification at member state level, ACTA also had to pass the European Parliament in order to satisfy all requirements in relation to this mixed agreement. In the run-up to ratification, ACTA was hotly debated. The Committee on International Trade of the European Parliament (INTA) commissioned a study[20] on ACTA's compatibility with the EU's international obligations, most notably the WTO TRIPS, and the EU *Acquis*.

During the negotiations, many critical questions had been raised over to the lack of transparency and the nature and content of the treaty. European academics were unreservedly critical about ACTA,[21] which prompted the European Commission to respond directly to this criticism,[22] even to an unprecedented extent in a statement entitled *10 Myths About* ACTA.[23] This document was quickly dismissed by the Foundation for a Free Information Infrastructure as "pure propaganda."[24]

Equally remarkable was the fact that ahead of a public hearing organised by the European Parliament on 1 March 2012, Euro MP Kader Arif – the ACTA rapporteur to the Parliament – resigned on 27 January 2012. Arif stated at that time: "I condemn the whole process which led to the signature of this agreement: no consultation of the civil society, lack of transparency since the beginning of negotiations, repeated delays of the signature of the text without any explanation given, rejection of Parliament's recommendations as given in several resolutions of our assembly."[25]

In a final salvage attempt, the European Commission announced on 22 February 2012 that it intended to refer ACTA to the European Court of Justice (ECJ) in order to "assess whether ACTA is incompatible – in any way – with the EU's fundamental rights and freedoms." Ultimately, following a workshop at the European Parliament (webcast over the Internet on 1 March 2012),[26] ACTA was rejected on 4 July 2012 by

20 INTA study for the European Parliament DG EXPO Policy Department (2011) *The Anti-Counterfeiting Trade Agreement (ACTA): An Assessment* (Brussels: European Parliament). *See* www.europarl.europa.eu/studies. I have contributed to this study.

21 'Opinion of European Academics on the Anti-Counterfeiting Trade Agreement', February 2011, www.iri.uni-hannover.de/tl_files/pdf/ACTA_opinion_110211_DH2.pdf (last accessed 9 September 2011).

22 *See* Commission Services Working Paper, 'Comments on the "Opinion of European Academics on Anti-Counterfeiting Trade Agreement"', 27 April 2011, http://trade.ec.europa.eu/doclib/docs/2011/april/tradoc_147853.pdf

23 *See* '10 MYTHS ABOUT ACTA', http://trade.ec.europa.eu/doclib/docs/2012/january/tradoc_148964.pdf [PR:(last accessed 29 May 2014)]

24 FFII ACTA Blog, (2012) EU Commission Propaganda on ACTA. 26 January, http://acta.ffii.org/?p=1082

25 *See* 'European Parliament rapporteur quits in Acta protest', http://www.bbc.co.uk/news/technology-16757142

26 *See* http://www.europarl.europa.eu/ep-live/en/committees/video?event=20120301-0900-COMMITTEE-INTA for the full videostream of the hearing.

478 votes to 39, with 165 abstentions. The Commission's reference of ACTA to the ECJ was subsequently withdrawn.

## A CONTROVERSIAL AGREEMENT

Until April 2010, ACTA negotiations were conducted in secret, as the treaty was characterised as a trade agreement. Statements made to justify the secrecy even went so far as to state that ACTA was an issue of national security.[27]

The lack of transparency and the various draft documents that came out through WikiLeaks since 2008[28] did not result in a positive public perception of the treaty. Upon the release of the official text, some of the worst fears of anti-ACTA activists proved to be unjustified – including controversial issues such as the "three strikes" rule for illegal downloading and customs controls of the contents of MP3 players, laptops and the like. Nevertheless, there was still pressure to stop the negotiations as late as 2010,[29] with many Euro MPs asking critical questions: (1) when would the Commission make all negotiating documents public; (2) whether the chairperson and coordinators of the INTA Committee had access to the negotiating documents; (3) why a secretive forum was chosen rather than a more transparent multilateral venue such as WIPO; and (4) why an apparent mismatch between access to ACTA documents by industry lobby groups and lack of access by parliamentarians and public interest organisations.[30] In Mexico, similar issues[31] were raised in the Senate, resulting in a widely carried rejection of ACTA on 7 September 2011.[32]

ACTA proponents presented the treaty as a mere restatement of best practices in IP protection and enforcement in the participating countries. A 2008 OECD study on the effects of counterfeiting on the economy was widely used to justify joint action. The United States in particular felt that ACTA was a mere repetition of existing US practice, thus allowing the administration to ratify ACTA by means of an

[27] McCullagh, D. (2009) 'Copyright Treaty Is Classified for National Security', *CNET NEWS*, http://news.cnet.com/8301-13578_3-10195547-38.htm

[28] *See* the leaked documents at http://keionline.org/acta

[29] *See* 'Lawmakers call for halt to ACTA deal', 5 October 2010, www.euractiv.com/en/infosociety/lawmakers-call-halt-acta-deal-news-498442

[30] Ad 1): Written Question E-2079/10 by Morten Messerschmidt (EFD) to the Commission; Ad 2) Written Question E-0147/10 by Alexander Alvaro (ALDE) to the Commission; Ad 3) Written Question E-0147/10 by Alexander Alvaro (ALDE) to the Commission; Ad 4) Written Question E-1391/10 by Andreas Mölzer (NI) to the Commission.

[31] Resolution of the Mexican Senate, 5 October 2010, www.senado.gob.mx/index.php?ver=sp&mn=2&sm=2&id=5264&lg=61

[32] Resolution of the Mexican Senate, 6 September 2011, www.senado.gob.mx/sgsp/gaceta/61/3/2011-09-06-1/assets/documentos/GrupoPlural_ACTA.pdf

Executive Order,[33] without the involvement of Congress. A study by the US Trade Representative, however, indicates that neither the general public nor the Congress supported this view.[34]

A Congressional Research Service report on the legality of ACTA prepared for the Senate at the request of Senator Ron Wyden has been suppressed. The advocacy group Knowledge Ecology International (KEI) called for the study to be made public under the Freedom of Information Act, but the request was rejected in March 2011.[35] ACTA is said to remain controversial in the United States for this reason, particularly as negotiations with Brunei, Chile, New Zealand, Singapore, Australia, Malaysia, Peru and Vietnam on the TPP are set to include ACTA-like, if not stronger,[36] norms in relation to enforcement of IPRs.

The Obama administration characterises ACTA as a "sole executive agreement," which means that implementing legislation or changes to the national regime are not foreseen. Since Congress will not be involved,[37] however, there is a risk that the United States will not be able to fulfil its international obligations if ACTA turns out to have an effect on US domestic law after all. In such a case, the constitutionality of ACTA would immediately be called into doubt.

## THIRD COUNTRIES

Third countries have also been vocal in their rejection of ACTA and its genesis. Paradoxically, the treaty prompted the tabling of the issue of enforcement on the agenda in the TRIPS Council for the first time.

The Indian delegation remarked in October 2009 that "the ACTA Agreement was being negotiated in secrecy and with the exclusion of a vast majority of countries, including developing countries and LDCs."[38] In June 2010, China, India and

33 Goldsmith, J. and Lessig, L. (2010) 'Anti-counterfeiting Agreement Raises Constitutional Concerns', *Washington Post*, 26 March.

34 Comment to ACTA could be submitted until 15 February 2011 at www.regulations.gov, docket number USTR-2010-0014

35 Masnick, M. (2011) 'USTR Refuses to Release Congressional Research Service Study on Legality of ACTA', *TechDirt*, 28 March, www.techdirt.com/articles/20110325/04480513628/ustr-refuses-to-release-congressional-research-service-study-legality-acta.shtml

36 Geist, M. (2011) 'U.S. Intellectual Property Demands for TPP Leak: Everything It Wanted in ACTA But Didn't Get', Michael Geist Blog, 11 March, www.michaelgeist.ca/content/view/5686/125/; Anderson, N. (2011) 'Son of ACTA: meet the *next* secret copyright treaty', *Ars Technica*, 11 March, http://arstechnica.com/tech-policy/news/2011/03/son-of-acta-meet-the-next-secret-copyright-treaty.ars?utm_source=twitterfeed&utm_medium=twitter&utm_campaign=rss

37 Flynn, S. (2011) *'ACTA's Constitutional Problem: The Treaty That Is Not a Treaty (Or An Executive Agreement),'* PIJIP Research Paper no. 19, American University Washington College of Law, Washington, DC; *see* Flynn, Chapter 9, present volume.

38 'Minutes of Meeting Held in the Centre William Rappard on 27–28 October and 6 November 2009', Council on Trade-Related Aspects of Intellectual Property, IP/C/M/61, 12 February 2010, para. 264.

Brazil commented on draft versions of ACTA,[39] stating that ACTA was inconsistent with the letter and spirit of the TRIPS Agreement. In October 2010,[40] again in the TRIPS Council, India complained about the fact that ACTA bypassed the multilateral process and completely ignored the interests of other WTO members.[41] India also voiced its concern over the nature and scope of ACTA with regard to transit procedures, injunctions and the way in which treaty reinterprets the term "commercial scale." This criterion is of paramount importance to set mere intellectual property infringements apart from large-scale economically harmful activities such as piracy and counterfeiting.

In the WTO case *China – Measures Affecting the Protection and Enforcement of Intellectual Property Rights*,[42] one of the issues revolved around the question of how many infringing copies would have to be found in order to hold that the infringer had acted on a commercial scale, as defined in Article 61 of the TRIPS Agreement. This elevates the trader of such items from a mere infringer to a counterfeiter or pirate, in which case criminal sanctions could be imposed, rather than just civil claims for injunctive relief or damages.

The panel held that the United States, the complainant in this case, did not convincingly prove that the contested thresholds impacted the commercial marketplace.[43] It then clarified that the threshold for criminal enforcement covering activities on a commercial scale was set at "counterfeiting or piracy carried on at the magnitude or extent of typical or usual commercial activity with respect to a given product in a given market." ACTA replaces this test and rather focuses on the question of whether the infringer is engaged in wilful activity that has somehow resulted in an economic or commercial advantage, thus lowering the threshold set by TRIPS.

## CONCLUSION: ACTA CASTING ITS SHADOW?

Given that the trade of third parties with ACTA states is going to be influenced by the treaty, the agreement has the potential to affect the multilateral trading system and casts a negative shadow on the progress of multilateral negotiations[44] in the

[39] 'Minutes of Meeting Held in the Centre William Rappard on 8–9 June 2010', Council on Trade-related Aspects of Intellectual Property, IP/C/M/63, 4 October 2010, para. 252.

[40] 'Minutes of Meeting Held in the Centre William Rappard on 26–27 October 2010', Council on Trade-related Aspects of Intellectual Property, IP/C/M/64, 17 February 2011.

[41] 'Minutes of Meeting Held in the Centre William Rappard on 26–27 October 2010', Council on Trade-related Aspects of Intellectual Property, IP/C/M/64, 17 February 2011, para. 444.

[42] 'China – Measures Affecting the Protection and Enforcement of Intellectual Property Rights', WT/DS362, adopted by the Dispute Settlement Body on 20 March 2009.

[43] Appellate Body Report on 'China – Measures Affecting the Protection and Enforcement of Intellectual Property Rights', p. 131.

[44] 'Minutes of Meeting Held in the Centre William Rappard on 26–27 October 2010', Council on Trade-related Aspects of Intellectual Property, IP/C/M/64, 17 February 2011, para. 451.

area of intellectual property law.[45] The latter point is relevant in the context of the unstated ambition of ACTA states to influence not only future multilateral negotiations but to use the treaty as a template for regional and bilateral agreements as well. Indeed, the ACTA negotiations have been described as "a new kind of international IP lawmaking,"[46] as the agreement places its members in plurilateral framework with strong enforcement obligations but without matching limitations and exceptions.[47] This puts ACTA members in a strong negotiating position with third parties where the rights of IP owners are concerned. Because ACTA does not foresee the establishment of a secretariat or permanent institutional mechanism, the implementation, future development or accession of new members remain subject to bilateral consultations, which will remain confidential and secret.

Intellectual property protection, most notably in the field of pharmaceuticals, is the most contentious issue in the EU's BTIA negotiations with Canada and India. As the EU continues to negotiate trade liberalisation with ACTA members in Asia, it is clear that once IPRs come up, ACTA-like obligations may have to be revisited. Even more interesting will be the upcoming negotiations on the EU-US Transatlantic Agreement, where both parties aim to blast their way out of the economic crisis. With intellectual property relegated to just one of the many topics in a wider negotiating package, parliaments may be far less critical if the overall deal promises economic growth and more jobs.

45 'Minutes of Meeting Held in the Centre William Rappard on 26–27 October 2010', Council on Trade-related Aspects of Intellectual Property, IP/C/M/64, 17 February 2011, para. 453.

46 Weatherall, K. (2010) '*ACTA as a New Kind of International IP Law-Making*', 9 January, PIJIP Research Paper no. 12, American University Washington College of Law, Washington, DC.

47 *See also* Weatherall, Chapter 23 in the present volume.

## PART IV

# Views from Stakeholders: Lessons

# 17

# Lessons Learned from the ACTA Process

## *An Industry Perspective*

*Candice Li*

### INTRODUCTION

After decades of exponential growth in trademark counterfeiting and copyright piracy, ten countries and the twenty-seven member states of the European Union announced in June 2008 the launch of negotiations for the Anti-Counterfeiting Trade Agreement (ACTA).[1] Following traditional trade negotiation protocols, the negotiators of ACTA released an agreement on May 2011[2] aimed at tackling counterfeiting and piracy at a global level.

Fourteen months later, the European Parliament voted not to approve ACTA,[3] effectively blocking any further progress of the agreement in the EU. Although subsequently there was positive news for ACTA with Mexico signing it in July 2012 and Japan ratifying the agreement in September 2012, industry supporters knew that ACTA's progress faced an uphill challenge in getting additional signatories and actual implementation. What clearly emerged after a four-year effort to support the trade agreement was that the perceived impact of ACTA on the Internet had become one of the most controversial issues facing policy makers, enforcement officials and industry battling to protect businesses and consumers exposed to fraud and theft online. Without a doubt, efforts will need to be redoubled to increase public awareness of the value of intellectual property (IP) and the harms of IP infringement, particularly on the Internet.

Industry organisations such as the International Trademark Association (INTA) view ACTA as an important initiative in the fight against counterfeiting and piracy.

[1] For available information, *see* http://www.ustr.gov/about-us/press-office/press-releases/archives/2008/august/statement-ustr-spokesman-scott-elmore-a

[2] Intellectual Property Watch, 27 May 2011, http://www.ip-watch.org/2011/05/27/new-final-acta-text-published-open-for-signature/

[3] http://www.europarl.europa.eu/news/en/pressroom/content/20120703IPR48247/html/European-Parliament-rejects-ACTA

As the largest trademark association in the world with more than 6400 members in 190 countries. INTA believes that ACTA will provide a much-needed framework for stronger enforcement and for additional cooperation and sharing of resources at an international level. ACTA also addresses, in Article 27, today's most pressing challenge with anti-counterfeiting and anti-piracy: the flood of counterfeit and pirated material available over the Internet.

To be sure, the Internet presents far-reaching benefits to global commerce and promotes the sharing of information and public discourse. However, the very elements of the Internet that make it a catalyst for productive exchanges – global reach, instantaneous connection and anonymity – also enable criminals to engage in all manner of illegal and unscrupulous activities. These include fraud, cybersquatting, child pornography and counterfeiting, which, while committed in a virtual space, have real life consequences. To understand industry's concern about counterfeiting on the Internet, one must first understand the problem in the brick-and-mortar world, the scope and scale of which are greatly expanded in the virtual world.

## COUNTERFEITING: AN ISSUE FOR ALL

Intellectual property is an important driver of economic growth. Strong IP protection provides a financial incentive for risk taking and investment. Studies have found a positive correlation between the strengthening of a country's IP system and subsequent economic growth. A US Commerce Department's 2012 report, "IP and the US Economy: Industries in Focus,"[4] shows that IP-intensive industries were directly responsible for 27.1 million jobs in the United States, 22.6 million of which were related to trademark-intensive industries. These IP-intensive industries also indirectly supported an additional 12.9 million supply-chain jobs throughout the economy. This means that every two jobs in IP-intensive industries support an additional job elsewhere in the economy. In total, 40 million jobs, or 27.7 per cent of all jobs, were directly or indirectly attributable to the most IP-intensive industries, which also accounted for about US$5.06 trillion in value added, or 34.8 per cent of US gross domestic product (GDP) in 2010.[5] Similar benefits of intellectual property are realised in other countries and are recognised as essential building blocks to economic growth.

Because of the tremendous value derived from intellectual property and trademarks in particular, counterfeiting is by far the most serious form of trademark

4 *Intellectual Property and the US Economy: Industries in Focus*, report prepared by the Economics and Statistics Administration and the US Patent and Trademark Office, March 2012, pp. vi–vii, http://www.uspto.gov/news/publications/IP_Report_March_2012.pdf

5 Ibid. at vii.

infringement. Counterfeiting is the illegal production and sale of goods, including packaging, bearing without authorisation a trademark which is identical to a validly registered trademark, or which cannot be distinguished from the genuine trademark. Counterfeits can be found in all categories of products – luxury and basic consumer goods, medicines, electronics, and automotive and aeronautical parts and equipment. The quality of counterfeit products is often substandard and poses the greatest threat to public health and safety and even to national security. So, contrary to public perception, counterfeiting is not a victimless crime. In addition to the harm to legitimate businesses, consumers and governments at all levels are duped and adversely impacted by counterfeiters.

According to a 2011 report by Frontier Economics entitled "Estimating the Global Economic and Social Impacts of Counterfeiting and Piracy," the impact of counterfeiting and piracy is estimated at US$650 billion annually. This includes costs to both the trademark owners in lost profits as well as costs to national economies. The Frontier Economics report also states that G20 governments lose US$125 billion annually in tax revenue – revenue that is badly needed for government programmes. In 2004, the office of the New York City Comptroller reported that New York City's counterfeiting trade (equal to about 12 per cent of the total counterfeit trade in the United States) accounted for more than US$1.6 billion in lost sales and tax revenues.[6]

Seizures of counterfeit products posing health and safety risks are on the rise globally as evidenced through numerous official reports of actual seizures of counterfeits. According to the US Customs and Border Protection Fiscal Year 2011 Intellectual Property Rights Report,[7] the top five categories of IPR-infringing products seized were pharmaceuticals, health/personal care, eyewear/parts, critical technology components and electronic articles. The value of these domestic seizures increased by 41 per cent compared to 2010,[8] with pharmaceuticals accounting for 28 per cent of the total.[9] The value of consumer safety and critical technology IPR seizures increased 44 per cent to more than US$60 million, owing to the increase in pharmaceutical and perfume seizures.[10]

In its Operation Pangea IV initiative, which involved eighty-one countries, INTERPOL,[11] the world's largest international police organisation, was successful

6 William Thompson, *Bootleg Billions: The Impact of Counterfeit Goods Trade on New York City*, report by the City of New York's Office of the Comptroller, November 2004, http://www.comptroller.nyc.gov/bureaus/bud/04reports/Bootleg-Billions.pdf

7 *Intellectual Property Rights – Fiscal Year 2011 Seizure Statistics*, report prepared by the U.S. Customs and Border Protection Office of International Trade; Table 5: FY 2010 – FY 2011 Consumer Safety and Critical Technology, http://www.ice.gov/doclib/iprcenter/pdf/ipr-fy-2011-seizure-report.pdf

8 Ibid. at Executive Summary.

9 Ibid. at Table 5.

10 Ibid. at Executive Summary.

11 http://www.interpol.int/News-and-media/News-media-releases/2011/PR081

in seizing 2.4 million counterfeit pills valued at US$6.3 million in just one week. The World Health Organization estimates that counterfeit drugs account for 10 per cent of all pharmaceuticals,[12] with this figure rising as high as 60 per cent in developing countries in Africa and East Asia. According to organisations such as the United Nations Office on Drugs and Crime, this has serious implications because counterfeit medicines have a direct impact on increased medical costs attributable to prolonged treatment periods and medical complications in the spread of treatment-intensive diseases.

Counterfeit food items pose similar health concerns as counterfeit medicines do to the public. According to the US Pharmacopeial Convention,[13] the top counterfeited food items worldwide include: olive oil (16 per cent of the olive oil market), milk (14 per cent of the dairy market), fish (9 per cent of the fish market), honey (7 per cent of the honey market) and saffron (5 per cent of the saffron market). In 2011, INTERPOL launched a week-long initiative in Europe, Operation Opson,[14] focused on counterfeit foods, which resulted in the recovery of more than 13,000 bottles of substandard olive oil, 30 tons of fake tomato sauce, approximately 77,000 kilogrammes of counterfeit cheese, more than 12,000 bottles of substandard wine (worth more than US$350,000), five tonnes of substandard fish and seafood and nearly 30,000 counterfeit candy bars.

Another major safety risk is counterfeit electronics. These counterfeits affect personal safety when consumers purchase electronics that were made with inferior materials that are unsafe for use. The Loss Prevention Concepts Organization reports that airliners and helicopters have crashed because of counterfeit components. Counterfeit auto parts, notably brake pads, have also caused deaths.[15] According to the 2012 report "Intellectual Property and the US Economy: Industries in Focus," counterfeiting is estimated to cost the global automotive parts industry US$12 billion a year in lost sales, with US$3 billion in phony auto parts sales in the United States. In October 2012, US enforcement agencies reported[16] the indictment of a man who sold counterfeit automobile airbags to unsuspecting consumers. At least 7,000 airbags were sold online earning him revenue of at least US$1.4 million.

[12] Fakes! *Business Week*, 6 February 2005, http://www.businessweek.com/stories/2005-02-06/fakes

[13] Jeffrey C. Moore, John Spink and Markus Lipp. 'Development and Application of a Database of Food Ingredient Fraud and Economically Motivated Adulteration from 1980 to 2010', *Journal of Food Science* 77, no. 4. 2012. Available at http://onlinelibrary.wiley.com/doi/10.1111/j.1750-3841.2012.02657.x/full

[14] http://www.interpol.int/Crime-areas/Trafficking-in-illicit-goods-and-counterfeiting/Operations/Operations/Operation-Opson

[15] http://www.washingtontimes.com/news/2007/may/15/20070515-083952-9160r/?page=all

[16] http://www.ice.gov/news/releases/1210/121010washingtondc.htm

Follow-up testing of the airbags showed that they did not properly inflate, or in the most extreme case exploded in flames.

Counterfeiting is a threat not just to the individual consumer but also to national and public safety in general. The 2012 Senate Armed Services Committee's report showed that a year-long investigation of the US military found 1,800 cases of counterfeit parts in military equipment.[17] It would be reasonable to conclude that other countries face similar risks.

These numbers are significant, and counterfeiting, which is among the largest threats to IP innovation, remains rampant. There are many reasons why this is so.

- Counterfeit manufacturing, labelling, packaging and distribution practices are increasing in sophistication, making counterfeits more difficult to distinguish from genuine goods. This is especially alarming when trying to differentiate between fake and genuine drugs, auto parts or food. While the quality of the counterfeits appears to have improved, the components of the fakes often remain substandard and overall do not follow safety standards.
- The Internet allows counterfeiters to attract all types of consumers through professional-looking websites or descriptions that can easily dupe consumers. Some counterfeiters will show pictures of genuine products but ship fakes. Others may price fake goods at a price similar to the genuine product in order to appear as if they are giving a reasonable discount on a genuine item. Rogue websites selling counterfeit physical goods attract more than 87 million visits[18] per year, amounting to US$135 billion in global sales,[19] according to MarkMonitor in 2011.
- Through the Internet, counterfeiters are able to sell anonymously and move from one site to another, allowing them to escape detection easily.
- Inconsistent laws and regulations among countries also continue to be a major challenge in the battle against counterfeiters, who are not bound by the same jurisdictional limitations as enforcement authorities are.
- Awareness remains low as to the extent to which counterfeiting harms the public, reduces government revenue and promotes criminal activity. The sluggish global economy exacerbates the demand for counterfeits as consumers look for cheaper products, while government and industry experience a lack of resources to comprehensively address this problem.

17 Inquiry into the Counterfeit Electronic Parts in the Department of Defense Supply Chain, report of the Committee on Armed Services, US Senate, May 2012, page I, http://www.armed-services.senate.gov/Publications/Counterfeit%20Electronic%20Parts.pdf

18 MarkMonitor, *Traffic Report: Online Piracy and Counterfeiting*, January 2011, p. 7, https://www.markmonitor.com/download/report/MarkMonitor_-_Traffic_Report_110111.pdf

19 MarkMonitor, *Seven Best Practices for Fighting Counterfeit Sales Online*, September 2010, p. 3, https://www.markmonitor.com/download/wp/wp-Fighting_Counterfeit_Sales.pdf

ACTA: AN INDUSTRY PERSPECTIVE

Faced with mounting problems in curbing counterfeiting, industry groups view ACTA as an opportunity to address the issue more effectively beyond current international agreements such as the World Trade Organization's Agreement on Trade-Related Aspects of Intellectual Property Rights (TRIPS), which went into effect in stages starting in 1995. Equally important, ACTA would provide an additional framework for countries to coordinate enforcement efforts and consumer education, which are necessary to address the issue effectively at the international level.

Industry associations such as INTA quickly found support among its membership and from other organisations around the world that recognised the value of a trade agreement like ACTA. Together with the International Chamber of Commerce's Business Action to Stop Counterfeiting and Piracy, INTA coordinated with more than twenty IP-related organisations from Switzerland, Japan, Morocco, Mexico, United States, Italy and France, among others, to express support for the agreement.[20] Collaboration with other associations started as early as 2008, and by 2012 more than 150 associations in Europe alone joined efforts to express support for ACTA. The associations included those advocating for the protection of IP, industry federations, labour unions, manufacturers and chambers of commerce, thereby demonstrating that concerns about counterfeiting and piracy were shared by a range of stakeholders.

Given the support for international action, some thirty-seven countries, which include the twenty-seven member states of the EU, joined in the negotiations. These countries together represent more than 50 per cent of world trade.[21] The negotiations, which lasted from 2008 to 2010, were kept confidential at first, following traditional trade negotiating protocols in order to provide the participants the flexibility to consider proposals that may or may not be contained in the final agreement. As the framework of the ACTA text began to take form, negotiators began to release parts of the agreement for public review. Additionally, some of the negotiating parties such as the EU, United States, Australia and New Zealand conducted public consultations and held meetings with stakeholders to provide updates.

Despite this process, concerns about transparency, the impact on the Internet and other issues began to mount. Increasing public resistance to ACTA was largely spurred by unsubstantiated fears that the agreement was an international version of draft legislation that was being considered in the United States in 2012 to address specifically counterfeiting and piracy on the Internet. The Protect Intellectual Property

[20] http://www.inta.org/Advocacy/Documents/ACTAJune2008BRGMemo.pdf
[21] http://www.theglobalipcenter.com/us-chamber-applauds-signing-anti-counterfeiting-trade-agreement/

Act (PIPA) and the Stop Online Piracy Act (SOPA) were withdrawn from consideration in the US Congress following public protests and illegal tactics such as cyber attacks. Even though ACTA did not contain the same provisions as the US legislation, it became enmeshed in the SOPA/PIPA controversy and was perceived by its detractors as potentially restricting Internet freedom, free speech and, ultimately, democracy.[22] The objectives of the plurilateral trade agreement and its differences from the US legislation were lost in calculated misinformation and hyperbole. The same tactics quickly took root in Europe, which accounts for the negative vote by the European Parliament.

Some of the harshest criticisms of ACTA have been based on distorted interpretations of the agreement's text. One major misconception about the treaty is that it would force Internet service providers (ISPs) to monitor users' activities, thereby implying that ISPs would censor their users in their quest to stop counterfeit sales and piracy over the Internet. In reality, ACTA does not require ISPs to oversee sites, but rather requires them to "promote cooperative efforts within the business community to effectively address trademark and copyright" infringement while preserving legitimate competition, freedom of speech and privacy. ACTA does not require ISPs to check for counterfeits or copyrighted material on their servers, and its minimum requirement of cooperative efforts with the business community against infringements can be satisfied in many non-restrictive ways.

An additional argument put forward by detractors is that ACTA would impede the flow of generic medicines and block a developing country's access to drugs. However, this is clarified in the agreement's border measures section, which allows countries to not apply customs measures under ACTA to patents and protection of undisclosed information. These exclusions are also available under the civil enforcement section of the treaty.

Like all international agreements, ACTA's text is broad and should be interpreted according to the fundamental rule of treaty interpretation as set out in Article 31.1 of the Vienna Convention on the Law of Treaties: "in good faith in accordance with the ordinary meaning given to the terms of the treaty in their context and in the light of its object and purpose." It is the hope of trade and industry associations that the potential for ACTA to provide participating governments with a framework to protect consumers and national economies more effectively from counterfeiting and piracy will be fully realised.

[22] Trevor Timm, https://www.eff.org/deeplinks/2012/01/how-pipa-and-sopa-violate-white-house-principles-supporting-free-speech; Jenna Wortham, http://www.nytimes.com/2012/01/18/technology/web-wide-protest-over-two-antipiracy-bills.html

## LESSONS LEARNED

The scope and intensity of the public's adverse reaction to ACTA, as well as the means through which public opinion was formed through misinformation and fear tactics spread over the Internet, social networks and media platforms, were unprecedented learning experiences for those who support the value that IP brings to society.

The public clamour highlighted a deficient, even distorted understanding of the role of IP in general, as media coverage and groups such as Anonymous propagated the view that IP is merely a tool for large businesses to take advantage of smaller ones and of consumers. In fact, IP is critical for all businesses, particularly the small and medium-sized enterprises that need to protect their products, services and innovations. They too are prey to counterfeiters and pirates. Consequently, the ACTA process also demonstrated to industry the need for increased efforts to raise more effectively awareness about the value of intellectual property to all stakeholders and to the public.

Going forward, IP protection and its proper enforcement should continue to be a priority for industry stakeholders and governments around the world. However, there is an urgent need to engage with a broader set of stakeholders. We must establish among the public informed awareness of the value of intellectual property not just to businesses but also to the economy, investment, innovation, creativity and jobs. We must also demonstrate the dangers of rampant IP theft including that occurring online, and the criminal activity connected with it and its social, economic and health consequences. The time is now. The need is more critical than ever before.

# 18

# Lessons Learned from the ACTA Process

## *The View of Creators*

*Adriana Moscoso del Prado*

### INTRODUCTION

ACTA has been a failure, not only from the perspective of international policy but also from the perspective of intellectual property rights protection. Although the European Court of Justice has not ruled on whether the agreement goes beyond the *acquis communautaire* and, therefore, infringes on EU legislation, the amount of criticism it has sparked seems to make it impossible to save a treaty that faces so many obstacles.

Some of the obstacles were created by ACTA's very promoters, who failed to respond adequately to parliamentarians' and NGOs' criticisms regarding the lack of transparency of the negotiating process. Other obstacles, however, were created by opinion makers who succeeded in misinforming and manipulating civil society organisations, and public opinion more generally, making them believe that ACTA was a threat to fundamental rights and civil liberties, something that is certainly not true. The campaign against ACTA should be seen in the context of a global effort by interested parties to depict IPRs as contrary to rights of freedom of expression and to privacy.

As matters stand, the treaty has been signed by the United States, Australia, Canada, South Korea, Japan, New Zealand, Morocco, Singapore and Mexico, plus the European Union and twenty-two of its twenty-seven members; however, so far it has been ratified only by Japan, and rejected by the European Parliament.

At this point, we must ask ourselves what we have gained and lost from this experience. This chapter focuses in particular on what we have lost from the point of view of talent and creativity. The main goal of ACTA is to fight the counterfeiting of goods and copyright piracy. These are, of course, areas of major concern for all countries, whether developed or developing, because they entail the loss of professional opportunities, employment, cultural diversity and prosperity.

Why, then, is it so hard to move on in the harmonisation of international legislation for the protection of IPRs?

## COPYRIGHT INFRINGEMENT: WHO IS CONCERNED?

Most of the emotional criticisms toward ACTA have tried to show that it is an instrument tailored to the interests of big content-providing companies, helping them to reinforce their bargaining power and limit consumers' rights and choices. In fact, however, copyright law is even more crucial to individuals and small- and medium-size firms. Copyright infringement not only deprives business from gaining more or fewer benefits; it also reduces employment (direct and indirect jobs) from the creative industries and frustrates artistic and scientific careers, wasting away the creative potential of individuals and, as a consequence, the culture, plurality and democratic quality of our societies. In the current economic crisis, this reality has become even harsher. I need not look very far to illustrate this situation as, unfortunately, there is an excellent example in my home country, Spain.

According to a recent GfK study published for the Spanish Right Holders Coalition,[1] half of Spanish Internet users regularly access illegal content. In 2012, musical content was illicitly accessed more than 2,1 billion times, while the corresponding figures for films and videogames were 536.2 million and 168 million, respectively. Translated into jobs and taxes, these numbers show that Spanish tax authorities failed to receive €249.6 million and 24,766 jobs were lost. The progressive disappearance of the music industry in Spain is evidenced by fact that there are no new Spanish artists in international sales lists since 2008 and the music market has been reduced to a third of what it was in 2001. In the words of Rob Wells, president of Universal Music Publishing, "Spain, which should be the powerhouse of repertoire for Latin America and the US Latin market, is effectively a dead market."[2]

The 2013 International Intellectual Property Alliance (IIPA)[3] annual report recommends that Spain be placed back on the Special 301 Watch List in view of the "extreme slowness in responding to right-holders complaints" of the new IP Commission that has the mandate to fight online piracy. Of course, one may say that these data are given by an interested party – the right holders. This is why initiatives such as the European Observatory on Infringements on Intellectual Property[4] are more than welcome.

[1] Accessible at http://lacoalicion.es/wp-content/uploads/Observatorio_Pirateria-2012_Final.pdf

[2] IFPI Digital Music Report 2011 (http://www.ifpi.org/content/library/dmr2011.pdf) and IFPI Digital Musical Report 2012 (http://www.ifpi.org/content/library/DMR2012.pdf)

[3] http://www.iipa.com/rbc/2013/2013SPEC301SPAIN.PDF

[4] http://oami.europa.eu/ows/rw/pages/OBS/index.en.do

Spain represents one of the worst-case scenarios for copyright infringement today. It is a glaring example of the damage that the destruction of an economic sector can create in terms of jobs, taxes and welfare. Several reports also show revealing data on the rest of the EU and many other countries. For instance, the OECD project on counterfeiting and piracy concluded in 2007 that international trade in counterfeit and pirated goods (digital contents were not included in the analysis) "could have accounted up to US$200 billion in 2005"[5] and that "counterfeit and pirated goods in international trade grew steadily over the period 2000–2007 and could amount up to US$250 billion in 2007."[6] The study concluded that "the share of counterfeit and pirated goods in world trade is also estimated to have increased from 1.85 per cent in 2000 to 1.95 per cent in 2007."[7]

The 2013 annual report[8] of the International Federation of the Phonographic Industries (IPFI) shows more positive results for a second year consecutively.[9] However, it also "highlights major hurdles that need to be addressed to unlock the huge potential for further growth. Illustrating the continued serious impact of Internet piracy, IFPI estimates, based on data from both Nielsen and ComScore, that as many as a third of all internet users (32 per cent) still regularly access unlicensed sites."[10]

Finally, another report conducted by TERA Consulting – commissioned by the International Chamber of Commerce/BASCAP[11] in 2010 – focuses on the relevance, in Europe's digital economy, of saving jobs in the creative industries. The report estimates that creative industries "represent a major European economic force, corresponding to 6.9 per cent of European GDP, and 6.5 per cent of the European workforce. This translates into €860 billion in revenues and 14 million jobs." As a conclusion, the report provides two scenarios for Europe in 2015, if no measures to fight piracy are taken:

> Further growth in broadband penetration and the ongoing digitalisation of creative industry products will accelerate and, without sustained and effective action, this trend will greatly facilitate the continued expansion of digital piracy in Europe.

5 OECD Project on Counterfeiting and Piracy. http://www.oecd.org/industry/ind/oecdprojectoncounterfeitingandpiracy.htm

6 Ibid.

7 Ibid.

8 IFPI Digital Music Report 2013. http://www.ifpi.org/content/section_resources/dmr2013.html

9 Global recorded music industry revenues increased by an estimated 0.3 per cent in 2012, the first year of industry growth since 1999, to US$16.5 billion, and digital revenues increased by an estimated 9 per cent to US$5.6 billion in 2012, now accounting for around 34 per cent of global industry revenues.

10 Ibid.

11 "Building a Digital Economy: The Importance of Saving Jobs in the EU's Creative Industries". TERA Consultants, http://www.iccwbo.org/Advocacy-Codes-and-Rules/BASCAP/BASCAP-Research/Economic-impact/Building-a-Digital-Economy-TERA-study/

> This study provides two scenarios of estimated piracy-driven losses escalating from 2008 to 2015 based on Cisco System's Internet traffic forecasts and assuming that no measures are taken to address piracy. In Scenario 1, digital piracy growth follows 'file-sharing' traffic trends and assumes that piracy behaviour continues to be centred on P2P. For the same creative industries, retail losses will reach approximately €32 billion by 2015, while cumulative job losses will reach 610,000 in the EU. In Scenario 2, digital piracy growth follows 'global consumer IP' traffic trends in Europe. This scenario assumes that digital piracy techniques will be further diversified and leads to retails losses equalling €56 billion in 2015 and to 1.2 million cumulative job losses by 2015.[12]

These are the main reasons why ACTA was supported by a group of more than forty European associations representing thousands of companies of all sizes, as well as right holders and millions of workers in dozens of sectors crucial to the European economy. All of them addressed a letter to the members of the European Parliament and national governments[13] asking them to support ACTA, as an agreement that would establish common procedures for dealing with IPR infringements across countries accounting for 50 per cent of world trade.

Another recurrent argument against ACTA was the assault it supposedly inflicted on the freedom of expression and privacy rights. Before looking at the text of ACTA in this respect, it is important to draw attention to something that many people in this debate seem to forget: authors' rights are also fundamental rights. Article 27.1 of the Universal Declaration of Human Rights states that "everyone has the right freely to participate in the cultural life of the community, to enjoy the arts and to share in scientific advancement and its benefits." Further, Article 27.2 confirms that "everyone has the right to the protection of the moral and material interests resulting from any scientific, literary or artistic production of which he is the author." Article 15.1(c) of the International Covenant on Economic, Social and Cultural Right contains similar wording, while the Charter of Fundamental Rights of the European Union recognises in Article 17 the protection of intellectual property.[14] Several constitutions

[12] Ibid.

[13] Letter dated February 10, 2012 signed by ACG; Alliance Against IP Theft; ANDEMA; AIM; APM; AFP; AGPP; BAMP; BASCAP; BBB; BEA; BIEM; BPI; BREIN; BVA; BVMI; CIPR; EACA; ECTA; EPC; EURATEX; EUROCINEMA; FAMA; FEP-FEE; FESI; FIAPF; FIAD; FIMI; GESAC; IFPI; INDICAM; INTA; IRMA; ISFE; IVF-, MAHASZ; MARKEVERBAND; NVPI; SAGC; TIE; TABD; TUOTOS; UNIFAB; VKE

[14] Article 17. Right to property:

1. "Everyone has the right to own, use, dispose of and bequeath his or her lawfully acquired possessions. No one may be deprived of his or her possessions, except in the public interest and in the cases and under the conditions provided by law, subject to fair compensation being paid in good time for their loss. The use of property may be regulated by law in so far as it is necessary for the general interest."
2. "Intellectual property shall be protected."

also recognise the human rights dimension of intellectual property rights, including those of Spain (Art. 20.1(b))[15] and the United States (Art. 1.8).[16]

However, we also know that fundamental rights are not absolute. Limits to fundamental rights are usually found where these rights conflict with other rights. Moreover, the laws of countries that have recognised human rights in their legal systems have established a set of procedures aimed at ensuring that the application of such limits is done through a legal process that guarantees no extra limitations or abuses in their application by public authorities. In my opinion, the search for such balance is the principle that prevailed with the promoters of ACTA, as illustrated in the following provisions dealing with enforcement issues in the digital environment (emphasis added):

> Art. 27.2 Further to paragraph 1, each Party's enforcement procedures shall apply to infringement of copyright or related rights over digital networks, which may include the unlawful use of means of widespread distribution *for infringing purposes*. These procedures shall be implemented in a manner that avoids the creation of barriers to legitimate activity, including electronic commerce, and, consistent with that Party's law, *preserves fundamental principles such as freedom of expression, fair process and privacy*.
>
> 27.3 Each party shall endeavour to promote cooperative efforts within the business community to effectively address trademark and copyright or related rights infringement while preserving legitimate competition and, consistent with that Party's law, *preserving fundamental principles such as freedom of expression, fair process, and privacy*.
>
> 27.4 A party may provide, in accordance with its laws and regulations, its competent authorities, with the authority to order an online service provider to disclose expeditiously to a right holder information sufficient to identify a subscriber whose account was allegedly used for infringement, where that right holder *has filed* a legally sufficient *claim* of trademark or copyright or related rights infringement, and where such information is being sought for the *purpose of protecting or enforcing those rights*. These procedures shall be implemented in a manner that avoids the creation of barriers to legitimate activity, including electronic commerce and, consistent with that Party's law, *preserve fundamental principles such as freedom of expression, fair process and privacy*.
>
> 27.8 In providing adequate legal protection and effective legal remedies pursuant to the provisions of paragraphs 5 and 7, a Party may *adopt or maintain appropriate*

15 "Se reconocen y protegen los derechos: a) A expresar y difundir libremente los pensamientos, ideas y opiniones mediante la palabra, el escrito o cualquier otro medio de reproducción. b): A la producción y creación literaria, artística, científica y técnica (…)."

16 "Congress shall have the power to promote the progress of science and useful arts by securing for limited times to authors and inventors the exclusive right to their respective writings and discoveries."

> *limitations or exceptions* to measures implementing the provisions of paragraphs 5, 6, and 7. The obligations set forth in paragraphs 5, 6 and 7 are *without prejudice to the rights, limitations, exceptions, or defences to copyright* or related rights infringement under a Party's law.

In the letter mentioned earlier, authors' and composers' associations reminded the European Parliament and EU governments of creators' steadfast support for fundamental rights and liberties. Artistic works are among the best instruments to condemn injustice, and authors have always been, and remain today, at the vanguard of the fight against censorship and violation of human rights. At the same time, free creation is not possible without freedom of expression. This does not, however, mean that artistic works can be used and exploited without authorisation or remuneration.

The defence of copyright, and IPRs more generally, is not only an issue for developed countries, as we often heard during the ACTA process. As Professor Charles R. McManis states, "there are ample reasons for developing countries [...] to be concerned with international trade in counterfeit and pirate goods, as a mounting body of empirical evidence has linked trade in counterfeit and pirate goods with threats to public health and the involvement of organised crime and terrorist organizations."[17]

International Criminal Police Organization's (INTERPOL) information and reports recalled in professor McManis's article are disturbing. They show the damage that counterfeiting inflicts on legal commerce and the close link to organised crime and international terrorism, plus the major risk that, according to INTERPOL, counterfeit medical products pose to public health, particularly in Africa, Asia and Latin America. A different report to which McManis refers – the RAND Corporation's study on *Film Piracy, Organized Crime and Terrorism*[18] – offers "a cogent illustration of how international trade in pirated goods, like that in counterfeit medicines, can adversely impact developing countries." It is also easy to understand why organised crime enters into piracy and counterfeiting: the "profit margin[s] (though not yet the total profits) are much higher than those of illegal drugs, while the criminal penalties are relatively light in comparison to those for drug trafficking."[19]

Developing countries and emerging economies should be deeply involved in the fight against counterfeiting and piracy. A recent UNESCO report evidences the contribution of culture to development and its influence on economy and poverty

[17] Charles R. McManis and John S. Pelletier, "Two Tales of a Treaty Revisited: The Proposed Anti-Counterfeiting Trade Agreement (ACTA). Legal Studies Research Paper Series. Paper no. 12-04-10. Washington University in St. Louis. School of Law. April 2012. Available at http://ssrn.com

[18] Available at http://www.rand.org/content/dam/rand/pubs/monographs/2009/RAND_MG742.pdf

[19] Ibid. at 12.

alleviation.[20] The report underlines that "throughout the past decade, statistics, indicators and data[21] on the cultural sector, as well as operational activities have underscored that culture can be a powerful driver for development, with community –wide social, economic and environment impacts."[22] Investment in culture and creativity has proven to be an excellent tool to revitalise the economy of cities, has generated new jobs, new market opportunities, and higher levels of income that "have improved living conditions and fostered community based economic growth, and contributed to empowering individuals." Moreover, culture-led development also brings an important range of non-monetised benefits, such as "greater social inclusiveness and rootedness, resilience, innovation, creativity and entrepreneurship for individuals and communities, and the use of local resources, skills and knowledge."[23]

Thus, developing countries have in culture a precious tool for sustainable development and economic growth. IP protection is a fundamental part of this.

## THE PROBLEMS WITH ACTA

The main criticisms of ACTA's drawn-out drafting process could be summarised as follows:

- Lack of transparency concerning the negotiations.
- Lack of clarity on several provisions, related to the lack of commitment of the negotiating parties to truly harmonise standards for IP enforcement. This has resulted in a text that allows multiple approaches and interpretations.
- Negotiations conducted outside the multilateral processes of WIPO or WTO.
- Negotiations conducted only among like-minded countries (resulting in what some have called a "country club" agreement).
- Possible conflict of competence between the EU and its member states.
- Regulation that goes beyond the *Acquis Communautaire* in fields such as criminal measures.
- Threats to the fundamental rights of freedom of expression and privacy.

The European Commission reacted to concerns over the perceived lack of transparency on several occasions, reminding critics that the text of the treaty had been

[20] Culture: a driver and an enabler of sustainable development. Thematic Think Piece. UNESCO. UN System Task Team on the post-2015 UN Development Agenda. May 2012. http://www.un.org/en/development/desa/policy/untaskteam_undf/thinkpieces/2_culture.pdf

[21] *See also* "The impact of culture on creativity". A report made by KEA Consultancy for the European Commission. http://ec.europa.eu/culture/documents/study_impact_cult_creativity_06_09.pdf

[22] UNESCO, op. cit.

[23] Ibid.

publicly available since November 2010 and that the Commission had organised four stakeholder conferences on ACTA.[24] In March 2013, the European General Court (Second Chamber), gave some support to the Commission's arguments in response to a complaint filed by MP Sophie in 't Veld (Liberal Party Group).[25] The Court considered that the Commission acted correctly in withholding some documents reflecting the position of EU members on criminal law enforcement provisions contained in ACTA, as well as when it did not facilitate daily emails between negotiators, on the basis of Article 4 of EU Regulation 1049/2001. The Commission had argued that "[t]he unilateral disclosure of those documents by the European Union, in the context of international negotiations based on mutual trust between negotiating parties, would have undermined the protection of the public interest as regards international relations."

The issue surrounding a lack of clarity in several provisions, as well as lack of commitment of the negotiating parties to truly harmonise law in this field, is difficult to resolve, because any possible solution is hampered by the necessity of bringing together different positions and legal backgrounds inherent within the ACTA negotiating process. The ACTA text should probably be the point of departure for further negotiations, not the endpoint. More time and more multilateral participation would have probably helped in this regard.

With regard to criticism concerning the small like-minded group of countries that negotiated ACTA, it has to be pointed out that many international agreements have started among a reduced group of countries and ended up as multilateral instruments. The initial involvement of only some countries in the negotiations was probably the most realistic option at the time, and could have helped parties to "develop a preliminary common position."[26] At some point, however, it would have been necessary to secure the adherence of more developing countries and emerging economies. Furthermore, multilateral organisations, such as WIPO or WTO, should be the appropriate fora to enact new international legislation.

However, developments after ACTA suggest that many countries will choose bilateral and plurilateral approaches to advancing their trade-related interests. In March 2013, the United States Trade Representative notified the US Congress of the intention to negotiate a Transatlantic Trade and Investment Partnership with the EU, with intellectual property rights among the specific negotiation objectives.[27]

[24] "What ACTA is about". European Commission:http://trade.ec.europa.eu/doclib/docs/2012/january/tradoc_149003.pdf

[25] http://curia.europa.eu/juris/document/document.jsf?text=&docid=135225&pageIndex=0&doclang=EN&mode=lst&dir=&occ=first&part=1&cid=173202

[26] Peter K. Yu, "ACTA and Its Complex Politics". Drake University. Legal Studies Research Paper Series. Research Paper no. 12–16. Available at http://ssrn.com

[27] See the press release of the Office of the US Trade Representative: http://www.ustr.gov/about-us/press-office/press-releases/2013/march/administration-notifies-congress-ttip

Also in March 2013, we witnessed an agreement reached by the BRICS[28] to conclude a trade and investment cooperation framework that includes IPRs and cooperation in this field.[29]

Finally, with respect to observations touching upon EU competences and the threats to human rights, a decision by the European Court of Justice would certainly have been very helpful in view of the widely diverging positions taken by the European Commission and Parliament. Unfortunately, the Commission withdrew the referral of ACTA to the ECJ in December 2012. Nevertheless, the ACTA experience is likely to have an influence on future EU initiatives regarding copyright protection, particularly as all parties are now much more conscious of the EU *Acquis*.

## CONCLUSIONS

The ACTA process has been both a lost opportunity and a lesson for the future. Indeed, it has been a lesson for our representatives. Citizens of the information society are now much more demanding and involved in legislative initiatives promoted by their representatives. Moreover, one of the prominent characteristics of the information society is the rapid and abundant flow of heterogeneous opinions, many of them inaccurate and far from objective but still very influential. Some of the undertakings adopted in international treaties for the enforcement of IPRs touch upon complex issues. They are thus difficult to explain and give rise to intense debates. Our representatives have the duty to explain these compromises and must be courageous when silencing rumours. Always with the aim of reaching consensus, they must defend what they think is most appropriate for their nations, regardless of potential unpopularity. The failure of ACTA is also attributable to a lack of leadership from our politicians. In this respect we have gained something: the opening of the eyes of our governments, although the question is still unanswered concerning whether they have learned something that will make them act differently next time.

With regard to copyright infringement, we have lost again. On the side of the right holders, it is time to stop feeling guilty for defending authors' rights. It is also time to fight more courageously against misleading information and strategies that, under the broad claim of defending consumer's rights, serve the interests of some multinational corporations with dominant positions and huge profits on the Internet market.

[28] Brazil, Russia, India, China and South Africa.

[29] http://www.brics5.co.za/search/trade+framework

Copyright protection is a matter of concern for all: creators, companies, users, consumers, governments and citizens. Authors and creative industries are not against the development of the Internet. They just wish that their efforts, work and investments be recognised and protected under the same legal principles they are in the analogue world.

# 19

# ACTA, a View from the Eye of the Storm

*Marietje Schaake*

## INTRODUCTION

On 4 July 2012, the European Parliament voted against the Anti-Counterfeiting Trade Agreement (ACTA). The vote was groundbreaking both in terms of substance, and because it was the first time the European Parliament used its consent procedure (Articles 207 and 218 TFEU) on an international trade agreement. The Parliament's rejection of ACTA has led to critical reflections, mostly by those who would have liked to see the treaty pass.

As a member of the European Parliament closely involved with ACTA in the International Trade Committee, and as a defender of digital freedoms, I argue that those who sought the dismissal must also reflect. While "anti-ACTA" networks happily recalled and celebrated the victory, there are lessons to be learned from the whirlwind that swept through European capitals and EU institutions.

Beyond the surface and the headlines, I want to explore the broader social and political context in which the Parliament's consideration and, ultimately, its vote on ACTA took place. This should shed light on the challenges we can expect in the future when seeking to preserve digital freedoms while pursuing an ambitious trade agenda.

## A BRIEF HISTORY

Official negotiations on ACTA began in Geneva in 2008 and took place behind closed doors, based on confidential or secret draft texts as is common practice for all trade agreements given their potential market impact. The information that was publicly available came through leaked negotiating texts published on WikiLeaks[1] and other online platforms.

[1] http://wikileaks.org/wiki/Proposed_US_ACTA_multi-lateral_intellectual_property_trade_agreement_%282007%29

Concern about the non-transparent process and ACTA's potential restrictive and repressive consequences initially came from a select group. Lawyers, academics and consumer rights organisations considered ACTA an undesirable agreement, because leaked drafts, discussion papers or negotiating positions hinted at the introduction of new and controversial concepts in global intellectual property rights (IPRs) enforcement. These included promoting cooperation between right holders and Internet service providers (ISPs) in assessing customers' net surfing patterns in search of "illegal downloads" or piracy. This kind of self-regulation would lack democratic oversight and jeopardise the separation of powers by practically privatising law enforcement online.

When confronted with initial questions and concerns by members of the European Parliament, the European Commission (as lead negotiator on behalf of the EU) replied by publishing a letter stating that there was no cause for alarm.[2] However, those concerned about the lack of transparency in the negotiations, including several NGOs[3] and academics,[4] remained unconvinced by the Commission's arguments.

In mid-2010, I hosted a hearing[5] on ACTA in the European Parliament together with a colleague. It became increasingly clear that the treaty's initial scope of fighting trade in counterfeit (tangible) goods had been widened to include indications of country of origin, as well as ending piracy of (non-tangible) content. We refer to such piling of issues in agreements or parliamentary resolutions as a "Christmas tree."

## TESTING THE WATERS

Around the same period, one of the first procedures in the current Parliament's legislature on intellectual property rights enforcement took off. It proved an important precursor to what lay ahead with regard to ACTA. The main thrust of a report on Enforcement of Intellectual Property Rights in the Internal Market[6] by Marielle Gallo (Christian Democrats/EPP) was to strengthen the enforcement of IPRs online.

In often heated debates on the report, I sought to convince fellow MEPs and stakeholders of the need to reform the fragmented European system and to increase flexibility. Certain business models must not be favoured over competition and

[2] http://trade.ec.europa.eu/doclib/docs/2008/october/tradoc_140836.11.08.pdf

[3] http://www.publicknowledge.org/pdf/acta-letter-20091105.pdf

[4] http://www.wcl.american.edu/pijip/go/blog-post/academic-sign-on-letter-to-obama-on-acta; http://www.iri.uni-hannover.de/tl_files/pdf/ACTA_opinion_200111_2.pdf

[5] http://www.marietjeschaake.eu/2010/04/event-alde-conference-acta-anti-counterfeiting-trade-agreement/

[6] http://www.europarl.europa.eu/oeil/popups/ficheprocedure.do?id=581763

innovation or over the public interest more broadly. Outdated laws currently favour incumbents. Existing copyright models have lost legitimacy and relevance among Europeans; they hamper economic development and access to culture and knowledge in the digital era. Reform and harmonisation are needed to ensure opportunities for consumers, SMEs and business development alike, while respecting people's fundamental rights.

The non-binding report was adopted with 328 votes in favour, 245 against and 81 abstentions.[7] While the lack of a large majority indicated a shift of balance in the Parliament's thinking on copyrights, the report still seemed to clear the way for parliamentary approval of ACTA. Many points made in the Gallo report could be compared to provisions in ACTA.

The first real yardstick for the ACTA negotiations after the Gallo report was an interim resolution[8] initiated by the European People's Party (EPP) preparing for the eventual consent vote. The EPP draft resolution supported the European Commission's direction in the ACTA negotiations. Other political groups and individual MEPs who did not agree with this reading decided to write an alternative resolution, which was very critical of the process and the content of the negotiations. It stressed the lack of balance between corporate interests and consumer freedoms in leaked negotiating texts available at the time.

When I made a draft version available online asking for public input,[9] I received many constructive comments. After carefully reviewing the suggestions and recommendations, the draft resolution was amended accordingly, and then put up for a vote. The "crowd-sourced" resolution was voted down by a close margin of only 16 votes (in favour: 306, against: 322, abstentions: 26)[10] and the more conservative resolution was adopted. Although the loss was a disappointment, it revealed that a decisive tilt in the balance between "enforcers" and "reformers" was within reach. And there was still time before the final vote on ACTA.

In defending the need to reform IPRs, push for updates of enforcement regimes and retain relevance in the digital era, the importance of improving my colleagues' knowledge became clear, as the impact technological developments actually have on people's lives was not plain to everyone. Also, there was a significant lack of knowledge about IPRs in our legal systems. Terms such as "copyright theft" and "piracy" were accepted widely. Yet, theft implies a criminal act, while IPR enforcement in all

7 http://www.votewatch.eu/en/enforcement-of-intellectual-property-rights-in-the-internal-market-motion-for-a-resolution-vote-reso.html

8 http://www.europarl.europa.eu/sides/getDoc.do?type=MOTION&reference=B7-2010-0618&language=EN

9 http://www.marietjeschaake.eu/2011/11/draft-resolution-about-acta-crowdsourced/

10 http://www.votewatch.eu/en/anti-counterfeiting-trade-agreement-acta-version-drafted-by-the-centre-left-alde-s-d-greens-efa-gue–45.html

EU member states is a civil law matter. Education was needed, and several seminars and other activities were organised to that end.

## MOMENTUM

Meanwhile, the revolutionary impact of technological developments on our societies, citizens' lives and economic development became clearer with every day that passed. This gradually led to a critical momentum before the votes on ACTA in the relevant committees and later in the full plenary of the European Parliament in Strasbourg in July 2012.

In late 2011, the focus had been on the United States, where two controversial bills were introduced in Congress. The Stop Online Piracy Act (SOPA) and the Protect Intellectual Property Act (PIPA) caused waves of concern among Internet users who feared the privatisation of law enforcement and even censorship of the Internet. One of the most visible acts of protest was the blackout of Wikipedia for a day. The division between the entertainment industry interests and the growing voice of Internet companies surfaced. This fight was commonly referred to as Hollywood versus Silicon Valley. The music and film industries pushed for stronger enforcement of IPRs online, while Internet companies focused on the opportunities for accessing online content. The latter could be hampered by protecting certain vested (business) interests through new and expanded legal measures. These businesses practically pushed lawmakers to sacrifice democratic control for the sake of corporate vigilantism.

The successful global online protests and campaigns against these controversial bills in the United States created increased self-awareness in civil society and empowerment of the individual through the Internet. On the tail of SOPA and PIPA, public awareness of ACTA grew. Many people involved in the protests against the two bills also opposed ACTA. National borders did not matter in the lobbying efforts, as the impact of the agreement would reach far beyond these nations' borders. I wrote a letter to members of Congress, co-signed by a number of other MEPs, as well as European businesses and NGOs expressing concern over the potential extraterritorial impact of SOPA and PIPA. A vast and borderless network of people rallied behind this issue and prevented the laws from passing. We witnessed the increasingly connected and organised manifestation of an "Internet public."

To help people gain insight into the political process and upcoming timelines for the consideration of ACTA by several committees in the European Parliament, I posted the timeline and decisive moments in the process on Reddit.com.[11] I also

[11] http://www.reddit.com/r/politics/comments/ow1v5/acta_note_from_marietje_schaake_member_of_the/

believed that the more people would know about ACTA, the more likely they would be to vote against it. Getting information out was important.[12] It also proved essential to connect stakeholders with varying concerns about ACTA. While the protests by digital freedom activists were more visible, development aid organisations, consumer rights groups, academics, SMEs and ISPs were equally important in conveying the diversity of impact and opposition.

## MOBILISATION AND MYTHS

The swelling voices against ACTA raised a number of concerns. The lack of transparency – a common feature in negotiations of trade agreements more broadly – was seen as a major obstacle to public involvement and scrutiny. I came to consider ACTA as an enforcement agreement rather than as an international trade agreement. The European Commission did not share this view, although Trade Commissioner De Gucht later spoke of an enforcement agreement several times. A trade agreement could be kept secret, whereas an enforcement agreement would be up for public and parliamentary scrutiny. Although EU negotiators were not in favour of this lack of transparency, other countries insisted that relevant documents stay officially secret.

While ACTA raised a number of relevant questions, the treaty's effect on ending the production of counterfeit and dangerous products would be minimal, given that the main producers (i.e. China and India) were not signatories of ACTA. Furthermore, the way in which counterfeit would have to be differentiated from authentic goods caused concern among development organisations. They feared that the lengthy assessment process would lead to generic (legal) medicines being held up by customs, thus preventing the drugs from reaching areas struck by epidemics in time. The inclusion of piracy in ACTA caused concern among Internet users about their rights. Consumer rights organisations and ISPs agreed that piracy should not be enforced either on the individual consumer level or by letting private companies assess the surfing behaviour of customers. The lack of guarantees to that end in the text failed to meet these concerns.

The Commission insisted that the EU body of regulations and directives (the so-called *acquis*) would not change if ACTA was enacted, but they failed to convince the public. For those who believed that EU laws should be revised or reformed, the argument that nothing would change after ACTA was actually a cause for concern rather than a confidence boost.

To clarify confusion and conflicting information about ACTA, the European Parliament requested several studies, legal opinions and organised official hearings.

12 https://torrentfreak.com/we-need-copyright-reform-not-acta-120204/

The hope was that impartial information about ACTA would give guidance. To some extent it did, but as time went on, fact-based discussions were replaced by allegations of partiality. As the trenches got deeper, more and more politicians jumped sides. This included ministers and ambassadors who believed their decision to support ACTA was misinformed. Politicising the debate ensured that politicians would be held accountable for their vote. Many got informed about the technical details, but some in favour of ACTA admitted they were unwilling to take the political heat. Others believed the anti-ACTA lobby was heavily inflated and misguided. As most of the opposition was voiced online, and came from all corners of the globe, it was difficult to get a sense of who was representing whom.

## LAST PUSH

The real tipping point came when demonstrations went from the web to the streets. While 2.5 million online signatures against ACTA was already impressive, European capitals filled with young people defending digital freedom put a face on the names. The largest protests were seen in Eastern Europe, especially in Poland. The reasons behind these broad protests were probably the relatively high prices Eastern Europeans pay for legal access to culture online (lower wages but same price for media as in Western Europe), as well as the recent memory of the secret police monitoring people and their communications in the Soviet era.

The protests prompted national government officials to speak out against ACTA, setting off a domino effect throughout the EU. Within a few weeks, governments of several EU member states either spoke out against ACTA or decided to wait for the European Parliament's final verdict. Beyond the pan-European movement, people from all over the world lobbied the European Parliament. In the United States, ACTA was considered merely an executive decision, which did not require approval by Congress. This may explain why many Americans reached out across the Atlantic to share their concerns with members of European Parliament.

While ACTA figured prominently on the political agenda, there was still much misinformation floating around. Some of this misinformation was probably spread intentionally or was not fact-checked or corrected properly. The pro-ACTA lobby in turn used the confusion among citizens and policy makers to denounce the critical analysis and blame activists for spreading misinformation. The enormous amount of mass emails sent to MEPs led some of them to speak of a cyberattack. Others called the public attention and action a "soft form of terrorism." While these statements were extreme, they revealed the negative impression made by the anti-ACTA lobby.

Before the International Trade Committee would give its leading recommendation for the final plenary vote on ACTA, several parliamentary committees gave their "opinion" on the agreement. These ranged from legal points of view to a development cooperation angle, acting as a series of test cases for the final vote. After tense debates in packed committee rooms, all committees adopted opinions or amendments which heavily criticised the final text of ACTA and called for the Parliament to withhold its consent.[13]

The final vote on ACTA took place on 4 July 2012 with 478 MEPs voting against and only 39 in favour, and 146 MEPs abstaining.[14] This was a veritable landslide compared to the results on the Gallo report and the ACTA resolution a year and a half earlier. The European Commission did not hide its disappointment and announced it would persist in its efforts to seek a legal opinion from the EU's highest court. However, the Commission decided on 19 December 2012 that it would no longer pursue this quest.

Underpinning the new decision-making powers was the Lisbon treaty, which granted the European Parliament (albeit passive) co-legislative powers in concluding international (trade) agreements. When the ACTA negotiations started in 2008, the European Commission and the Council were not legally obliged to consider the European Parliament. After the Lisbon treaty entered into force on 1 December 2009, we had a binding voice. By voting ACTA down, the Parliament representing European citizens took on a new role in checking and balancing the other two EU institutions.

## LOOKING AHEAD

After ACTA was rejected by the European Parliament, I have been asked to speak about the path leading to this decision to groups of lobbyists, students and digital freedom activists alike. The process around ACTA became a cocktail of organised and spontaneous protests that swelled from a breeze to a sweeping storm. From the eye of that storm I could see the successful result, which I actively pursued.

At the same time, going forward and facing upcoming challenges around IPR reform and enforcement, as well as new trade negotiations, all sides need to cool down. We need to work on a rational, fact-based debate to make policies that benefit European business, creative industries as well as Internet users and consumers. As technological developments more often show up on political agendas, and have a growing role in policy decisions, a mature and professionally operating network of stakeholders will be an essential voice.

13 http://www.europarl.europa.eu/news/nl/pressroom/content/20120529IPR45936/html/ACTA-now-rejected-by-four-EP-committees; http://www.europarl.europa.eu/news/en/pressroom/content/20120614IPR46889/html/Parliament-should-say-NO-to-ACTA-says-International-Trade-Committee

14 http://www.votewatch.eu/en/anti-counterfeiting-trade-agreement-between-the-eu-and-its-member-states-australia-canada-japan-the--2.html

While the EU is better off without ACTA, politicians bear responsibility for finding alternatives that better address the harmful impact of counterfeit products. Sectoral IPR agreements could be a more targeted approach. We must also make sure the EU does not fall into global trade isolation, and break the suffocating status quo around IPR enforcement in Europe that neither serves our citizens' rights and freedoms nor fosters creative industries.

It may be all quiet now on the ACTA front, but new storms are sure to emerge. The Parliament has drawn a clear red line and forced the European Commission to refrain from negotiating ACTA-like provisions in other international agreements such as the Comprehensive Economic and Trade Agreement with Canada and the recently concluded FTA with Singapore. However, the upcoming Transatlantic Trade and Investment Partnership (TTIP) negotiations between the EU and the United States are likely to see tough bargaining over the IPR chapters.[15] Those seeking relevant policies that do justice to the revolutionary impact of the digital era need to brace themselves. Working towards viable alternatives is more challenging than saying "no" to a proposal.

More broadly speaking, recent developments at the 2012 meeting of the International Telecommunications Union (WCIT) in Dubai – where a majority of countries expressed favourable views of an increased role for government control over the global governance of the Internet – mark the true start of an era of Internet politics of which the IPRs debate is just one aspect.

The emancipation of citizens as well as the emergence of an "Internet public," allow for transparency and participation in policy and lawmaking. A failure by politicians and institutions to constructively meet the possibilities of the networked society with more openness will lead to destructive confrontations. More progress can be made when support from new stakeholders is weighed against strong vested interests. The ACTA negotiating and ratification process has shown the need for a fundamentally different approach to negotiating international agreements. The EU should embrace new forms of multi-stakeholder cooperation, especially when working on agreements and laws that impact people's fundamental rights.

[15] http://www.marietjeschaake.eu/2013/06/faq-transatlantic-trade-and-investment-partnership-ttip/

## 20

# ACTA, the EU, and Economic, Social, and Cultural Rights in the Digital Environment

*Ante Wessels*

### INTRODUCTION

During the debates sparked by ACTA, civil rights, such as privacy and freedom of expression in the digital environment, attracted a great deal of attention while hardly any scrutiny was expended on economic, social and cultural rights such as access to knowledge and culture, remix artists, patent trolls and sequential innovation.

This chapter applies an economic, social and cultural human rights analysis to the four issues largely ignored by the debate. It discusses three human rights that are relevant to the digital environment: the right to access to knowledge, the right to access to culture, and authors' rights – all of which are enshrined in the Universal Declaration of Human Rights and the UN International Covenant on Economic, Social, and Cultural Rights (ICESCR).

### BACKGROUND

After massive street protests against ACTA, the European Commission requested that the European Court of Justice (ECJ) rule on the agreement's compatibility with the Charter of Fundamental Rights of the European Union in April 2012. However, in December 2012, the Commission withdrew the court referral, explaining that the decision was made on the grounds that there was "not any realistic chance that the Council and the European Parliament will agree to the proposed treaty."[1]

Indeed, the Parliament had not waited for the ECJ's opinion and it resoundingly rejected ACTA on 4 July 2012 by a majority vote of 478 to 39 with 165 abstentions. Prior to this vote, various opinions had found the agreement incompatible with fundamental rights instruments. Such concerns were voiced, inter alia, by European

[1] European Commission, (2012) statement on withdrawal of ACTA referral, http://www.youtube.com/watch?v=VCBTFh3IhQY

Academics (2011), Korff and Brown,[2] the European Data Protection Supervisor,[3] ARTICLE 19[4] and the European Parliament's committee on Civil Liberties, Justice and Home Affairs.[5]

In defence of ACTA, the European Commission,[6] the European Parliament's legal service,[7] Gallo[8] and Vrins[9] argued that the agreement contained horizontal safeguards. They also pointed out that the obligations imposed by an international agreement could not have the effect of prejudicing the constitutional principles of the EU, which include the principle that all EU acts must respect fundamental rights.

The ACTA proponents' argument that all EU acts must respect fundamental rights raises the question whether this extends to economic, social and cultural rights. The Foundation for a Free Information Infrastructure (FFII) submitted an *amicus curiae* brief which focused on these rights to the ECJ.[10]

[2] Korff, D. and Brown, I., (2011) Opinion on the compatibility of the Anti-Counterfeiting Trade Agreement (ACTA) with the European Convention on Human Rights & the EU Charter of Fundamental Rights, obtained from rfc.act-on-acta.eu

[3] EDPS, (2010), Opinion of the European Data Protection Supervisor on the current negotiations by the European Union of an Anti-Counterfeiting Trade Agreement, (2010/C 147/01), obtained from Edps.europa.eu; EDPS, (2012), Opinion of the European Data Protection Supervisor on the proposal for a Council Decision on the Conclusion of the Anti-Counterfeiting Trade Agreement between the European Union and its Member States, Australia, Canada, Japan, the Republic of Korea, the United Mexican States, the Kingdom of Morocco, New Zealand, the Republic of Singapore, the Swiss Confederation and the United States of America, obtained from Edps.europa.eu

[4] ARTICLE 19, (2011) European Parliament: Reject Anti-Counterfeiting Trade Agreement (ACTA), obtained from Article19.org

[5] LIBE, 2012, European Parliament Committee on Civil Liberties, Justice and Home Affairs, (2012) Opinion of the Committee on Civil Liberties, Justice and Home Affairs for the Committee on International Trade on the compatibility of the Anti-Counterfeiting Trade Agreement between the European Union and its Member States, Australia, Canada, Japan, the Republic of Korea, the United Mexican States, the Kingdom of Morocco, New Zealand, the Republic of Singapore, the Swiss Confederation and the United States of America with the rights enshrined in the Charter of Fundamental Rights of the European Union (12195/2011 – C7-0027/2012 – 2011/0167(NLE)), obtained from Europarl.europa.eu

[6] European Commission, (2011) Commission Services Working Paper, "Comments on the 'Opinion of European Academics on Anti-Counterfeiting Trade Agreement'", *Journal of Intellectual Property, Information Technology and E-Commerce Law* (JIPITEC) 2011, Vol. 2, 171, obtained from Trade.ec.europa.eu

[7] European Parliament legal service, (2011) Legal Opinion, Re: Anti-Counterfeiting Trade Agreement (ACTA) – Conformity with European Union law, obtained from lists.act-on-acta.eu

[8] Gallo, M. (2012) Draft Opinion on the draft Council decision on the conclusion of the Anti-Counterfeiting Trade Agreement between the European Union and its Member States, Australia, Canada, the Republic of Korea, the United States of America, Japan, the Kingdom of Morocco, the United Mexican States, New Zealand, the Republic of Singapore and the Swiss Confederation – Committee on Legal Affairs PE 487.684v01-00 10 April 2012, obtained from Europarl.europa.eu

[9] Vrins, O. (2012) The Impact of ACTA on the EU Acquis and Civil Liberties, European Parliament Policy Department DG External Policies, obtained from Europarl.europa.eu

[10] FFII, (2012) amicus curiae brief on ACTA, obtained from Acta.ffii.org

## THE INTERNATIONAL COVENANT ON ECONOMIC, SOCIAL AND CULTURAL RIGHTS

All EU member states have ratified the International Covenant on Economic, Social and Cultural Rights (the EU itself is not a party to the ICESCR). The EU's obligation to respect, protect and fulfil the human rights enshrined in the ICESCR results from the constitutional traditions common to the member states (Article 6.3, Treaty on European Union).

Three ICESCR rights are relevant to the digital environment: the right to access to knowledge, the right to access to culture and authors' rights. Access to knowledge and culture are protected at the level of human rights. ICESCR Article 15.1(a) and (b) recognises the right of everyone to take part in cultural life, and to enjoy the benefits of scientific progress and its applications.

### *Rights to Access to Knowledge and Culture*

The UN Committee on Economic, Social and Cultural Rights clarifies the right of everyone to take part in cultural life in its authoritative interpretation, General Comment No. 21. It states that the right to take part in cultural life includes the rights to access to cultural goods, to benefit from the cultural heritage, to be involved in creating the spiritual, material, intellectual and emotional expressions of the community, to seek and develop cultural knowledge and expressions, and to share them with others.[11]

### *Authors' Rights*

The covenant balances access to knowledge and culture rights with authors' rights. Under ICESCR 15.1(c), authors have the right to benefit from the protection of their moral and material interests resulting from any scientific, literary or artistic production.

These different human rights may lead to conflicts, for instance between the right to access to knowledge and authors' rights. To solve such conflicts, a balance has to be found. Peter Yu[12] has argued that individuals have a right to access to knowledge

[11] ECOSOC (2009) Committee on Economic, Social and Cultural Rights, General comment No. 21, Right of everyone to take part in cultural life (art. 15, para. 1 (a), of the International Covenant on Economic, Social and Cultural Rights), E/C.12/GC/21, obtained from Ohchr.org; http://www2.ohchr.org/english/bodies/cescr/comments.htm

[12] Yu, P. K. (2011) "Intellectual Property and Human Rights in the Nonmultilateral Era", *Florida Law Review*, Vol. 64, pp. 1045–1100, Drake University Law School Research Paper No. 11 – 04, obtained from Ssrn.com

while the author has a right to just remuneration. According to Yu, "Under this approach, authors and inventors hold a right to remuneration (rather than exclusive control), while individuals obtain a human rights-based compulsory license (as compared to a free license)."[13]

Other conflicts between human rights and intellectual property rights may also arise, for instance between patents and the right to access to knowledge. In this regard, it is important to note that there are fundamental differences between ICESCR authors' rights and intellectual property rights.

The Committee on Economic, Social and Cultural Rights emphasises that intellectual property rights are not be equated with ICESCR authors' rights:

> Human rights are fundamental as they are inherent to the human person as such, whereas intellectual property rights are first and foremost means by which States seek to provide incentives for inventiveness and creativity, encourage the dissemination of creative and innovative productions, as well as the development of cultural identities, and preserve the integrity of scientific, literary and artistic productions for the benefit of society as a whole. [...] Whereas the human right to benefit from the protection of the moral and material interests resulting from one's scientific, literary and artistic productions safeguards the personal link between authors and their creations and between peoples, communities, or other groups and their collective cultural heritage, as well as their basic material interests which are necessary to enable authors to enjoy an adequate standard of living, intellectual property regimes primarily protect business and corporate interests and investments. Moreover, the scope of protection of the moral and material interests of the author provided for by Article 15, paragraph 1 (c), does not necessarily coincide with what is referred to as intellectual property rights under national legislation or international agreements (Authoritative interpretation General Comment No. 17).[14]

Furthermore, only natural persons can be authors under ICESCR. General Comment No. 17 clarifies that under ICESCR Article 15, paragraph 1(c), legal entities are not protected at the level of human rights. This gives individuals a strong position.

States may limit ICESCR rights, but only under three cumulative conditions as defined in ICESCR Article 4:

> The States Parties to the present Covenant recognize that, in the enjoyment of those rights provided by the State in conformity with the present Covenant, the State may subject such rights only to such limitations as are determined *by law* only

[13] Ibid.

[14] ECOSOC, (2006) Comm. on Econ., Soc. & Cultural Rights (CESCR), General Comment No. 17: The Right of Everyone to Benefit from the Protection of the Moral and Material Interests Resulting from Any Scientific, Literary or Artistic Production of Which He Is the Author (Article 15, Paragraph 1(c), of the Covenant), 4, U.N. Doc. E/C.12/GC/17 (Jan. 12, 2006), obtained from Ohchr.org

> in so far as this may be *compatible with the nature of these rights* and solely for the purpose of *promoting the general welfare in a democratic society* (emphasis added).

This provides us with a tool to consider the following four issues in the digital environment.

### *Access to Knowledge and Culture Deficiencies in Emerging Economies*

In emerging economies, there are serious deficiencies with regard to access to knowledge and culture. Karaganis et al.[15] show that relative to local incomes in Brazil, Russia or South Africa, the price of a CD, DVD or copy of Microsoft Office is five to ten times higher than in the United States or Europe. As there is no distribution of legal CDs and DVDs outside the capitals, up to 90 per cent of the people in emerging economies can only turn to illegal copies.

Such problems also exist in eastern European emerging economies. Euractive.com[16] reports: "Ivan Dikov writes in an op-ed with the Bulgarian news website Novinite that Bulgaria is a country much poorer than the remaining ACTA signatories and could not in fact assume the same responsibilities. Torrent sites such as Zamunda and Arena are the most popular websites in Bulgaria. The reason for that is not just the enormous amount of music, films, software, and books that they make available to anybody for free. The sites are not accessible from outside the country. These torrent sites are technically in violation of all sorts of copyright laws but what they offer has no alternative for the people in Bulgaria for the time being given the country's social and economic development, Dikov argues."

In emerging economies, digital technology helps to solve deficiencies in access to knowledge and culture, but intellectual property laws hinder this access. In these countries, intellectual property laws nullify or impair the rights to access to knowledge and culture for many. This is neither compatible with the second condition of ICESCR Article 4, "compatible with the nature of these rights," nor with the third, "promote the general welfare in a democratic society."

### *Remix Artists*

It is often impossible to obtain (affordable) licenses for remixing music and movies. This interferes with various human rights. As ICESCR does not exclude any author ("everyone"), artists remixing music or movies are protected at the level of human rights. The absence of affordable licenses also interferes with the artist's as well as the public's rights to access to culture.

[15] Karaganis, J. (ed.), (2011) Media Piracy in Emerging Economies, SSRC books, obtained from piracy.americanassembly.org

[16] Euractive (2012) ACTA activates European civil society, obtained from Euractiv.com

Under current copyright law, remix artists face injunctions and damages. This nullifies or impairs the rights of remix artists and the public. An ICESCR-compatible solution could be that individual original authors have a right to remuneration and the individual remix artists obtain a human rights-based compulsory license.

### *Software Patent Trolls*

A software developer may never look at patents and still infringe them. Patents create a legal minefield in the software sector, where there are many trivial and overbroad patents. This situation is abused by non-practicing entities or patent trolls. They acquire patents at low cost, for instance by buying bankrupted companies. Their patents tend to have broad claims on trivial methods so that infringement is unavoidable. All software developers ignore software patents to some extent, simply because every single useful program they write may infringe several patents.

Patent trolls, as legal entities acquiring patents, are not protected under ICESCR Article 15.1(c), while individual software developers are. But injunctions and damages nullify or impair the rights of these developers, even when no copying takes place at all. This phenomenon contradicts the second condition mentioned in the ICESCR's Article 4 ("compatible with the nature of these rights"). A human rights–based independent rediscovery defence for individual developers could be a solution. If no copying takes place, there is no ground for remuneration.

Arguably, injunctions and damages are also incompatible with the third condition of ICESCR Article 4 ("promoting the general welfare in a democratic society"). Ewing and Feldman[17] note that the patent world is quietly undergoing a change of seismic proportions. They describe entities that have amassed vast treasuries of patents on an unprecedented scale: "Most important, the basic business model of mass aggregation is troubling. The successful aggregator is likely to be the one that frightens the greatest number of companies in the most terrifying way. This may not be an activity that society wants to encourage." Injunctions and damages that encourage mass aggregation do not promote the general welfare in a democratic society.

### *Harm to Follow-Up Innovation in the Software Sector*

Patents, whether trivial or brilliant, are exclusive rights; the right holder can block sequential innovation. Hargreaves[18] notes that for sequential inventions,

[17] Ewing, T. and Feldman, R. (2012) The Giants Among Us, Stan. Tech. L. Rev. 1, obtained from Stlr.stanford.edu

[18] Hargreaves, I., (2011) Digital Opportunity, A review of Intellectual Property and Growth, obtained from Ipo.gov.uk

> higher welfare and more innovation may be more likely to result from the absence of patenting opportunities. Over time, as digital technology becomes pervasive across the economy, this represents a serious concern. [...] Given the pace of change in the digital world and the strongly sequential nature of innovation in computer programs, the problems arising from thickets in this environment are particularly severe and it is essential that changes do not worsen the situation.

Software developers involved in sequential invention are authors under ICESCR article 15.1(c). In search of an ICESCR-compatible solution it is proposed that the individual first inventor(s) have a right to remuneration and the individual sequential inventor(s) obtain a human rights-based compulsory license.

## EUROPEAN HUMAN RIGHTS INSTRUMENTS

Europe's two regional human rights instruments – the Council of Europe's European Convention on Human Rights (ECHR) and the EU Charter of Fundamental Rights – do not formulate general rights to access to knowledge and culture, nor do they recognise an author's right.

As we saw from the earlier discussion, a number of countries – including, for instance, Bulgaria – face serious deficiencies in accessing knowledge and culture. This market is underserved. As EU law does not have an underserved market exception, the strong EU enforcement measures, including injunctions and damages, also apply in Bulgaria. The European human rights instruments do not provide a safeguard against this.

Both European human rights instruments protect the right to enjoy property after it is lawfully acquired. The protection includes intellectual property. The author of a novel, for example, is protected by copyright, European human rights instruments and ICESCR. A software patent troll is protected by patent law and the European human rights instruments, but (as a legal entity acquiring patents) not by ICESCR. A software developer who writes his software from scratch and who has to defend himself against a patent troll is not protected by patent law or the European human rights instruments. He may argue that he has an ICESCR-based independent rediscovery defence. The outcome is uncertain.

Both European human rights instruments recognise the right to freedom of expression. Article 17 EU Charter of Fundamental Rights says: "Everyone has the right to freedom of expression. This right shall include freedom to hold opinions and to receive and impart information and ideas without interference by public authority and regardless of frontiers."

A broad interpretation of the right to freedom of expression, including the right to receive and impart information, could possibly act as a substitute of ICESCR authors' right, and access to knowledge and culture rights. However, Europe's human rights courts take the opposite approach: they limit the right to freedom of expression.

An example is the recent case of Ashby Donald and Others versus France. In this case, Ashby Donald and Marcio Moraes posted photos of Paris fashion shows (taken by Olivier Claisse in 2003) on their Internet site without permission of the fashion houses concerned. French copyright law forbids the unauthorised publication of pictures taken at fashion shows, even when the pictures are published by the individual who took them. A French court ordered the photographers to pay fines between €3,000 and €8,000 (US$4,000–10,500) and damages amounting to €255,000 (US$335,000).

The photographers appealed to the European Court of Human Rights, complaining that the French court breached their right to freedom of expression and information under the European Convention on Human Rights. The court acknowledged that the conviction for breach of copyright and the award of damages was an interference with their right to freedom of expression. But it also saw the fashion photos as "commercial speech," not of general interest for society. It thus saw no reason to step in and gave a wide margin of appreciation to the domestic authorities. The photographers lost the case.[19]

This demonstrates that the European Court of Human Rights limits the right to freedom of expression and information in cases of commercial speech. There is no such limitation under ICESCR; on the contrary, authors have the right to benefit from their work. An ICESCR interpretation of this case could lead to a different result.

French copyright law clearly protects fashion houses against photographers. The latter cannot freely express their vision on fashion shows. The law thus interferes with the rights of the photographers as authors, with the rights of the public to access cultural resources, and with the rights concerning the ability to be involved in the creation and sharing of spiritual, material, intellectual and emotional outputs of a community, which seek and develop cultural knowledge and expressions. Injunctions, damages and fines nullify or impair these rights. Under ICESCR, a human rights–based compulsory license combined with just remuneration could provide a solution.

## RESOLVING THE CONFLICT

Economic, social and cultural human rights may help to bridge the deep divide over intellectual property rights that persists in our societies. This next two sections will

[19] Voorhoof, D. and Høedt-Rasmussen, I. (2013) ECHR: Copyright vs. freedom of expression, obtained from Kluwercopyrightblog.com

seek to (1) resolve the conflict between European human rights instruments and ICESCR, and (2) assess whether ACTA is compatible with ICESCR.

ICESCR rights are freedoms: Article 15 starts with "The States Parties to the present Covenant recognize the right of everyone [...]." We saw above that human rights are fundamental as they are inherent to the human person as such,[20] and that interference with ICESCR rights is only allowed if compatible with the covenant's Article 4.

European human rights instruments take a different approach. They protect the right to enjoy property (including intellectual property), after it is lawfully acquired; but the protection is limited. Article 17 of the EU Charter of Fundamental Rights reads:

> Right to property
>
> 1. Everyone has the right to own, use, dispose of and bequeath his or her lawfully acquired possessions. No one may be deprived of his or her possessions, except in the public interest and in the cases and under the conditions provided for by law, subject to fair compensation being paid in good time for their loss. The use of property may be regulated by law in so far as is necessary for the general interest.
> 2. Intellectual property shall be protected.

Intellectual property rights are not rights inherent to the human person as such. They are granted by law – that is, they are rule-based privileges. While copyright arises automatically, it does so on the basis of laws that should be ICESCR-compatible. Interference with those rights is only allowed if the interference is compatible with ICESCR Article 4.

In case of a conflict between ICESCR rights and intellectual property rights, the first step is to identify and balance the ICESCR rights. The next step is to assess whether interference of intellectual property rights with ICESCR rights is compatible with the covenant's Article 4. As we saw in the earlier discussion, injunctions, damages and criminal measures, in so far as they nullify or impair the enjoyment of ICESCR rights, are not compatible with the nature of these rights; they fail the Article 4 test.

## ACTA AND ICESCR

States party to ICESCR and the EU are obliged to respect, protect and fulfil the human rights enshrined in the covenant. They must desist from acts and omissions that create a real risk of nullifying or impairing the enjoyment of ICESCR rights.

[20] Ibid. n.13

ACTA contains mandatory injunctions, damages and criminal measures which may nullify or impair the enjoyment of ICESCR rights. ACTA also contains non-mandatory provisions. While ACTA parties may exclude patents and protection of undisclosed information from the scope of the civil section (ACTA footnote 2), inclusion of patents remains the default position. ACTA also invites countries to strengthen the rights of patent owners, including software patent trolls. Implementation of such measures may further nullify or impair the enjoyment of ICESCR rights.

ACTA contains horizontal safeguards, but not with regard to ICESCR, which is not even referenced in the agreement (nor are the rights to knowledge and culture or authors' rights). Article 27, which is a part of ACTA's digital environment section, refers three times to "fundamental principles such as freedom of expression, fair process, and privacy." These principles do not suggest that these safeguards could extend to economic, social and cultural rights obligations.

In conclusion, ACTA contains measures which may nullify or impair the enjoyment of ICESCR rights, while neither ACTA nor European human rights instruments provide safeguards against this.

Citizens may try to protect their economic, social and cultural human rights by invoking ICESCR. With the exception of Singapore, the EU and the United States, all ACTA parties have either ratified or acceded to ICESCR (the United States has signed but has not ratified the covenant).

On a related note, one should consider the process through which ACTA was created. The secretive negotiations were not compatible with the right of everyone "to take part freely in an active and informed way, and without discrimination, in any important decision-making process that may have an impact on his or her way of life and on his or her rights under Article 15, paragraph 1 (a)."[21]

Furthermore, states party to ICESCR and the EU involved in the ACTA negotiations also violated their international obligations, as formulated in ICESCR Article 2:

> Each State Party to the present Covenant undertakes to take steps, individually and *through international assistance and co-operation*, especially economic and technical, to the maximum of its available resources, with a view to achieving progressively the *full realization* of the rights recognized in the present Covenant by all appropriate means, including particularly the adoption of legislative measures. (emphasis added)

[21] ECOSOC (2009) Committee on Economic, Social and Cultural Rights, General comment No. 21, Right of everyone to take part in cultural life (art. 15, para. 1 (a), of the International Covenant on Economic, Social and Cultural Rights), E/C.12/GC/21, obtained from Ohchr.org; http://www2.ohchr.org/english/bodies/cescr/comments.htm

As a final remark, the essential question is whether the European Court of Justice or the European Court of Human Rights will have the final judgement on laws. Individual member states of the EU have signed many international agreements containing investor-state dispute resolution mechanisms, and the EU may do this as well. According to Kelsey and Wallach,[22] international arbitrators are not ordinarily well versed in human rights. An international arbitration tribunal interpreting the implementation of ACTA or similar agreements could severely harm human rights.

22 Kelsey, J., and Wallach, L., (2012) "Investor-State" Disputes in Trade Pacts Threaten Fundamental Principles of National Judicial Systems, obtained from Tpplegal.files.wordpress.com

PART V

# What Lies Ahead ACTA

# 21

# Assessing the Implications of ACTA for the European Union

## *Legitimate Aim but Wrong Means*

*Christophe Geiger*

### INTRODUCTION

The Anti-Counterfeiting Trade Agreement (ACTA) is a plurilateral agreement aimed, according to its Preamble, at providing effective and appropriate means for the enforcement of intellectual property rights. The issue is obviously important, since the attractiveness of intellectual property rights risks being seriously undermined if they cannot be enforced in an appropriate manner. For this reason, the creation of an effective system to secure a proper enforcement of intellectual property rights and to combat counterfeiting has been a constant preoccupation of the European Union (EU) over the last few years. Serious efforts have been made and numerous initiatives undertaken by the EU and its member states to improve the European legal framework in this regard. Following an evaluation report published on 22 December 2010,[1] the European Commission has announced its intention to

This article draws on an assessment paper on the Anti-Counterfeiting Trade Agreement prepared for the Committee on International Trade (INTA), Directorate-General for External Policies of the European Parliament, March 2012. Its conclusions have been presented at the European Parliament in Brussels on 1 March 2012 during a workshop on ACTA organized by INTA. An earlier version was published with the title "Weakening Multilateralism in Intellectual Property Lawmaking: A European Perspective on ACTA", WIPO J. 2012, Vol. 3, Issue 2, 166. The author is thankful to Oleksandr Bulayenko and Elena Dan, research assistants at the CEIPI, for their research and editorial assistance.

1 Report from the Commission to the European Parliament, the Council, the European Economic and Social Committee and the Committee of the Regions on the application of Directive 2004/48/EC of the European Parliament and the Council of 29 April 2004 on the enforcement of intellectual property rights COM(2010) 779 final. For a comment, *see* Ch. Geiger, J. Raynard and C. Rodà, What Developments for the European Framework on Enforcement of Intellectual Property Rights? A Comment on the Evaluation Report of the European Commission dated 22 December 2010, EIPR 2011, p. 543.

revise the reference text on the topic,[2] the Directive of 29 April 2004,[3] which has now been implemented in all the member states.[4] Work has also started on an amendment of the regulation of 22 July 2003[5] concerning customs action against goods suspected of infringing certain intellectual property rights.[6] In 2009, the Commission also set up a European Observatory on Counterfeiting and Piracy,[7] one of whose principal objectives is to collect and transmit data on the economic and social consequences of counterfeiting, and whose powers were recently considerably increased.[8] It is only in the sensitive field of criminal penalties for counterfeiting that harmonisation has not yet succeeded, mostly because of the considerable opposition that a proposed directive on this matter encountered within the European Parliament.[9] This resistance ultimately led to the text being withdrawn by the European Commission on 18 September 2010.[10]

This withdrawal took place shortly before the publication of the consolidated version of the plurilaterally agreed draft ACTA text. The agreement, negotiated over a period of three years outside multilateral bodies by the European Commission (for the EU and its member states) and ten other countries,[11] has led to and is continuing

[2] *See* the Communication of the Commission, A Single Market for Intellectual Property Rights – Boosting creativity and innovation to provide economic growth, high quality jobs and first class products and services in Europe, Brussels, 24 May 2011, COM(2011) 287 final, p. 20 et *seq*.

[3] Directive 2004/48/EC of the European Parliament and of the Council of 29 April 2004 on the enforcement of intellectual property rights, OJEU L 157 of 30 April 2004 corrected in OJEU L 195 of 2 June 2004, p. 16.

[4] For a comparative analysis, *see* C. Rodà, *Les conséquences civiles de la contrefaçon des droits de propriété industrielle: droits français, belge, luxembourgeois, allemand, anglais*, Paris, Litec, CEIPI Series, 2011.

[5] Council Regulation (EC) No 1383/2003 of 22 July 2003 concerning customs action against goods suspected of infringing certain intellectual property rights and the measures to be taken against goods found to have infringed such rights, OJEU L 196 of 2 August 2003, p. 7.

[6] Proposal for a Regulation of the European Parliament and of the Council concerning customs enforcement of intellectual property rights of 24 May 2011, COM(2011) 285 final, 2011/0137 (COD), C7-0139/11.

[7] Communication from the Commission on enhancing the enforcement of intellectual property rights in the internal market, Brussels, 11 September 2009, COM(2009) 467 final, p. 5 et *seq*.

[8] Regulation (EU) No 386/2012 of the European Parliament and of the Council of 19 April 2012 on entrusting the Office for Harmonization in the Internal Market (Trade Marks and Designs) with tasks related to the enforcement of intellectual property rights, including the assembling of public and private-sector representatives as a European Observatory on Infringements of Intellectual Property Rights, OJEU L 129 of 16 May 2012, p. 1.

[9] Amended proposal for a Directive of the European Parliament and of the Council on criminal measures aimed at ensuring the enforcement of intellectual property rights of 26 April 2006, COM(2006) 168 final, 2005/0127 (COD).

[10] OJEU C 252 of 18 September 2010, p. 9.

[11] These countries are Australia, Canada, the Republic of Korea, the United States of America, Japan, the Kingdom of Morocco, the United Mexican States, New Zealand, the Republic of Singapore and the Swiss Confederation.

to lead to the spilling of much ink.[12] The secrecy of the negotiation process has contributed considerably to the development of mistrust among the general public and has given rise to widespread speculation on the content and the objectives of the agreement.[13] Many concerns have been expressed, for example, regarding an excessive tightening of penalties in the field of intellectual property, specifically in the context of the use of works on the Internet by means of peer-to-peer networks, or regarding excessive restrictions of certain fundamental rights. It is for this reason that the European Parliament, echoing many of the worries expressed, adopted in March

[12] For a comment on this text, *see* for example H. Grosse Ruse-Khan, R. D'Erme, Ch. Geiger, C. Heinze, T. Jaeger, R. Matulionyte and A. Metzger, The Impact of the Anti-Counterfeiting Trade Agreement on the Legal Framework for IP Enforcement in the European Union, in: Ch. Geiger (ed.), *Constructing European Intellectual Property: Achievements and New Perspectives*, EIPIN Series Vol. 1, Cheltenham, UK / Northampton, MA: Edward Elgar, 2013, p. 394; P. Arhel, L'accord commercial anticontrefaçon: version finale, Propr. industr. March 2011, p. 13; J.-C. Galloux, RTDcom. January/March 2011, p. 81; see also the study of the Institute for Globalisation and International Regulation (IGIR) of the University of Maastricht for the European Parliament, The Anti-Counterfeiting Trade Agreement (ACTA): An Assessment, June 2011 (Kamperman Sanders et al.), and the special edition of the American University International Law Review, entitled: Intellectual Property Law Enforcement and the Anti-Counterfeiting Trade Agreement, *Am.U.Int'l L.Rev* 2011, Vol. 26, No. 3; K. Weatherall, Politics, Compromise, Text and the Failures of the Anti-Counterfeiting Trade Agreement, *Sidney Law Review* 2011, Vol. 33, p. 229; M. Stieper, Das Anti-Counterfeiting Trade Agreement (ACTA), GRUR Int. 2011, p. 124; Ch. Geiger, Of ACTA, 'Pirates' and Organized Criminality: How 'Criminal' Should the Enforcement of Intellectual Property Be?, IIC 2010, p. 629 and from the same author: Quelle mise en œuvre des droits de propriété intellectuelle au niveau international ? Retour sur l'Accord commercial anti-contrefaçon (ACTA), *Propr. intell.* 2012, No. 43, p. 201; L. P. Devigne, P. Velasco-Martins and A. Iliopoulou, Where Is ACTA Taking Us? Policies and Politics, in: I. A. Stamatoudi (ed.), *Copyright Enforcement and the Internet*, Alphen aan den Rijn, Kluwer Law International, 2010, p. 29; E. Ayoob, Recent Development: The Anti-Counterfeiting Trade Agreement, *Cardozo Arts & Ent. L.J.*, Vol. 28, 2010, p. 175; B. Mercurio, Beyond the Text: The Significance of the Anti-Counterfeiting Trade Agreement, *Journal of International Economic Law* 2012, Vol. 15, No. 2, p. 361; D. Matthews, The Rise and Fall of the Anti-Counterfeiting Trade Agreement (ACTA): Lessons for the European Union, Queen Mary University of London, School of Law, Legal Studies Research Paper No. 127/2012; M. Blakeney, *Intellectual Property Enforcement A Commentary on the Anti-Counterfeiting Trade Agreement (ACTA)*, Cheltenham UK / Northampton, MA, Edward Elgar, 2012.

[13] On the impact of the lack of transparency in the negotiations on the perception of the agreement in public opinion, *see* for a European perspective for example A. Metzger, A Primer on ACTA, What Europeans Should Fear about the Anti-Counterfeiting Trade Agreement, *JIPITEC* 2010, p. 109. For an international perspective, *see* P. K. Yu, Six Secret (and Now Open) Fears of ACTA, *SMU Law Review* 2011, Vol. 64, No. 3, p. 975; C. R. McManis, The Proposed Anti-Counterfeiting Trade Agreement (ACTA): Two Tales of a Treaty, *Houston Law Review* 2009, Vol. 46, No. 4, p. 1235; M. Kaminski, The Origins and Potential Impact of the Anti-Counterfeiting Trade Agreement (ACTA), *Yale J. Int'l L.* 2009, No. 24, p. 247; M. Geist, ACTA's State of Play: Looking Beyond Transparency, *Am.U.Int'l L.Rev* 2011, Vol. 26, No. 3, p. 543; T. Hoeren, ACTA ad acta? Überlegegungen zum urheberrechtlichen "Shitstorm", MMR 2012, p. 137; D. S. Levine, Transparency Soup: ACTA Negotiating Process and 'Black Box' Lawmaking, *Am.U.Int'l L.Rev.* 2011, Vol. 26, No. 3, p. 813, according to whom "the lack of transparency placed leaked documents and hearsay at the center of public policy discussions, caused debates over both real and imagined issues, and brought about a general erosion of public knowledge and confidence in the ACTA process."

2010 a resolution demanding full information about the progress of the negotiations on the proposed agreement.[14] As a result of this resolution, the Commission finally published the first version of the proposed agreement on 21 April 2010,[15] followed by a consolidated version on 2 October 2010[16] and a final version on 3 December 2010, subsequent to the legal verification meeting in Sydney.[17] For a long time only available in English,[18] this last version of the agreement was then published in a number of different languages on 23 August 2011.[19] ACTA was signed on 1 October 2011 in Tokyo by the representatives of eight of the negotiating countries (Australia, Canada, Japan, the Republic of Korea, the Kingdom of Morocco, New Zealand, the Republic of Singapore and the United States)[20] and on 26 January 2012 by the EU and twenty-two of its member states.[21] The agreement was submitted to the European Parliament for examination and needed to be adopted by the entirety of the member states according to the requirements of their national constitutions, as it constitutes a mixed agreement for which the EU's competence is shared with that of the member states.[22] After heated discussions at the EU and national levels, the European Parliament rejected ACTA on 4 July 2012 with an overwhelming majority.[23] The future of the agreement in the EU and in other negotiating countries is therefore uncertain.[24]

[14] *See* European Parliament resolution of 10 March 2010 on the transparency and state of play of the ACTA negotiations, P7_TA (2010)0058).

[15] ACTA, consolidated text prepared for public release, April 2010, available at: http://trade.ec.europa.eu/doclib/docs/2010/april/tradoc_146029.pdf (last accessed 25 January 2013).

[16] Anti-Counterfeiting Trade Agreement, Consolidated text, reflects changes made during September 2010 Tokyo Round, Informal Predecisional/Deliberative Draft 2 October 2010.

[17] Which, however, only had very little impact on the final text.

[18] Which might explain why most of the comments have been written in English so far.

[19] Council of the European Union, 23 August 2011, 12196/11, Interinstitutional File: 2011/0166 (NLE).

[20] The United Mexican States signed ACTA on 11 July 2012.

[21] These countries are Austria, Belgium, Bulgaria, the Czech Republic, Denmark, Finland, France, Greece, Hungary, Ireland, Italy, Latvia, Lithuania, Luxembourg, Malta, Poland, Portugal, Romania, Slovenia, Spain, Sweden and the United Kingdom.

[22] This results from the fact that a significant part of the Agreement is devoted to criminal enforcement (see below), for which the European Union enjoys very limited competence (Article 83.2 TFEU). For this reason, the competence of the EU to adopt ACTA has been the subject of serious doubts (see on this issue in particular A. Ramalho, The European Union and ACTA – Or Making Omelettes without Eggs (Again), IIC 2011, p. 97; Ch. Geiger, The Anti-Counterfeiting Trade Agreement and Criminal Enforcement of Intellectual Property: What Consequences for the European Union?, in: J. Rosen (ed.), *Intellectual Property at the Crossroads of Trade*, Cheltenham UK / Northampton, MA, Edward Elgar, 2012, 167.

[23] *See* European Parliament legislative resolution of July 4, 2012 on the draft Council decision on the conclusion of the Anti-Counterfeiting Trade Agreement between the European Union and its Member States, Australia, Canada, Japan, the Republic of Korea, the United Mexican States, the Kingdom of Morocco, New Zealand, the Republic of Singapore, the Swiss Confederation and the United States of America (12195/2011 – C7-0027/2012 – 2011/0167(NLE)), P7_TA-PROV(2012)0287).

[24] On 26 June 2012 the Dutch Government decided not to sign ACTA, while the Swiss Confederation postponed its signature. Bulgaria, which has signed ACTA, is the first EU country that has stopped

## THE EU CONTEXT OF ACTA

The general context of ACTA is the proliferation of counterfeiting in third countries, notably in developing countries,[25] combined with a certain degree of weakness in international intellectual property law regarding enforcement mechanisms.[26] Developed countries therefore pushed for the adoption of stricter multilateral rules in the context of international organisations such as the World Intellectual Property Organization (WIPO) and the World Trade Organization (WTO), but encountered

ratification process of the Agreement after the European Parliament rejected it. Moreover, the discussion in European Parliament had a strong impact within other negotiating countries, such as Australia for example (see chapter by Rimmer, present volume), where the Australian Parliament's Joint Standing Committee on Treaties, issued its report on ACTA on 27 June 2012 stating: "It is prudent, therefore, that ACTA not be ratified by Australia until this Committee has received and considered the assessment of the economic and social benefits and costs of the Agreement (…). In considering its recommendation to ratify ACTA, a future Joint Standing Committee on Treaties should have regard to events related to ACTA in other relevant jurisdictions, including the EU and the US." Report 126, Treaty tabled on 21 November 2011, Anti-Counterfeiting Trade Agreement (Tokyo on 1 October 2011), the Parliament of the Commonwealth of Australia, Canberra, June 2012, para. 8.16. Anyhow, it should also be noted that the signatory party Japan ratified the Agreement on 6 September 2012, meaning ACTA could be revived, since with six ratifications the Agreement will take effect within those parties.

25 See in particular the impressive figures quoted in the OECD study, The Economic Impact of Counterfeiting and Piracy, Paris, OECD Publishing, 2008, updated in 2009: OECD, Magnitude of counterfeiting and piracy of tangible products: an update, November 2009, p. 1.

26 The "weakness" of the international provisions for enforcing intellectual property rights would be illustrated by the WTO Panel decision in a case brought by the United States against China (China – Measures affecting the protection and enforcement of intellectual property rights, Report of the Panel, January 26, 2009, WT/DS362/R). The United States accused China of not providing for criminal penalties in its national legislation for the infringement of copyright on a commercial scale, thus failing to comply with Article 61 of the TRIPS Agreement. The WTO Panel adopted a cautious interpretation of the concept of "commercial scale," explaining that this referred "to counterfeiting or piracy carried on at the magnitude or extent of typical or usual commercial activity with respect to a given product in a given market", para. 7.577. While the flexible interpretation of the provisions of the TRIPS Agreement by the Panel was welcomed by many commentators, permitting the adjustment of the obligations under the agreement in terms of penalties to the specific circumstances and needs of the country in question, many developed countries saw it as confirmation of the inadequacies of the existing international provisions. For a comment on the case *see* for example R. Creemers, The Effects of World Trade Organization Case DS362 on Audiovisual Media in China, EIPR 2009, p. 568; H. Xue, Enforcement For Development: Why Not an Agenda For the Developing World?, in: X. Li and C. M. Correa (eds.), *Intellectual Property Enforcement, International Perspectives*, Edward Elgar, Cheltenham, UK / Northampton, MA, Edward Elgar, 2009, p. 133, and, by the same author *see* An Anatomical Study of the United States versus China at the World Trade Organization on Intellectual Property Enforcement, EIPR 2009, p. 292; D. Gervais, China – Measures Affecting the Protection and Enforcement of Intellectual Property Rights, *Am. J. Int'l L.* 2009, p. 549; H. Grosse Ruse-Khan, Criminal Enforcement and International IP Law, and P. K. Yu, Shaping Chinese Criminal Enforcement Norms through the TRIPS Agreement, in: Ch. Geiger (ed.), *Criminal Enforcement of Intellectual Property: A Handbook of Contemporary Research*, Cheltenham, UK / Northampton, MA, Edward Elgar, 2012; P. K. Yu, The U.S. China Dispute over TRIPS Enforcement, Drake University

some difficulties in imposing such changes on the international framework rapidly and without making concessions.

The EU, aware of the difficulty of enforcing intellectual property rights effectively in certain regions of the world, adopted in 2005 a strategy aimed at ensuring the enforcement of intellectual property rights in third countries.[27] Annex I of the text clearly identifies the nature of the problem:

> The TRIPS Agreement establishes for the first time a single, comprehensive, multilateral set of rules covering all kinds of IPR. It contains also a detailed chapter setting minimum standards of IPR enforcement to be adopted by all members of the WTO. However, despite the fact that, by now, most of the WTO members have adopted legislation implementing such minimum standards, the levels of piracy and counterfeiting continue to increase every year. These activities have, in recent years, assumed industrial proportions, because they offer considerable profit prospects with often a limited risk for the perpetrators. It has thus become clearly insufficient to limit the efforts of the EC to merely monitoring the creation of general legislative frameworks in WTO member countries. It is essential that the EC increasingly focuses on vigorous and effective implementation of the enforcement legislation.[28]

The EU thus implicitly recognised that its efforts to improve the enforcement of intellectual property rights outside the territory of the Union would be in vain, and that it was therefore desirable for stricter rules to be adopted in the countries where large-scale infringements were occurring.

As a result, the EU, along with a number of other countries with the same concerns, pushed for rapid action to tighten civil and criminal penalty provisions in international negotiations, but with little success because of the opposition from developing countries that did not necessarily share the EU's interests and concerns.[29]

Law School, Occasional Papers in Intellectual Property Law No. 5, 2010, and, by the same author *see* The TRIPS Enforcement Dispute, *Nebraska Law Review* 2011, Vol. 89, No. 4, p. 1046; A. Adam, What is 'Commercial Scale'? A Critical Analysis of the WTO Decision in WT/DS362/R, EIPR 2011, p. 342; Ch. Geiger, Comment of the decision of the WTO Panel of 26 January 2009, with M. Viviant, *Propr. intell.* 2010, No. 35, p. 747.

27 Strategy aimed at ensuring the enforcement of intellectual property rights in third countries, OJEU C 129 of 26 May 2005, p. 3.

28 OJEU, C 129 of 26 May 2005, p. 12.

29 Interestingly, some scholars have demonstrated that most of today's developed countries went through a period of intellectual property piracy or at least uncompensated uses of the intellectual property of other more developed nations in order to foster their own innovation capacities (see for example on this issue the interesting article by L. J. Gibbons, Do as I Say (Not as I Did): Putative Intellectual Property Lessons for Emerging Economies from the Not So Long Past of the Developed Nations, *SMU Law Review* 2011, Vol. 64, No. 3, p. 923.

Therefore, given the difficulty in achieving satisfactory rules within the classical multilateral framework,[30] a number of like-minded countries engaged in what has been termed "forum shifting"[31] opted to negotiate amongst themselves (and in secret) a stricter agreement, ACTA.[32] The Preamble of the agreement is clear on this issue: it states that the new text aims at providing effective and appropriate means for enforcing intellectual property rights *complementary* to the Agreement on Trade-

[30] This questioning of the multilateral system concerning the enforcement of intellectual property rights was clearly expressed by the European Commission in 2009 as follows: "It is necessary to stress that attempts by the European Union and other supporters of an effective IPR system to constructively address enforcement problems in multilateral fora (World Trade Organisation, World Intellectual Property Organisation, World Customs Organisation) have been opposed by countries like Brazil and India, often supported by China, Argentina and others. This has prevented some of these institutions from addressing pressing IPR enforcement issues that could suitably be resolved multilaterally", *see* Commission Staff Working Document, IPR Enforcement Report 2009, Brussels, SEC(2009) 1360, p. 4, available at: http://trade.ec.europa.eu/doclib/docs/2009/october/tradoc_145204.pdf (last accessed 25 January 2013).

[31] P. K. Yu, Six Secret (and Now Open) Fears of ACTA, *supra* note 13, p. 1075; K. Weatherall, Politics, Compromise, Text and the Failures of the Anti-Counterfeiting Trade Agreement, *supra* note 12; M. Kaminski, The Origins and Potential Impact of the Anti-Counterfeiting Trade Agreement (ACTA), *supra* note 13. Very critically on this tendency in recent international intellectual property law making, *see* S. K. Sell, Everything Old Is New Again: The Development Agenda Then and Now, *WIPO J.* 2011, Vol. 3, p. 20, stating that "in the years since TRIPs, governments that are homes to intellectual property-based multinational corporations have continued to ratchet up standards of intellectual property protection outside of multilateral channels. US Free Trade Agreements, bilateral investment treaties, European Economic Partnership Agreements, and plurilateral efforts like the Anti-Counterfeiting Trade Agreement and the Trans-Pacific Partnership negotiations have all included stricter standards for protection and enforcement of intellectual property rights." The same author defines ACTA-like initiatives as a "vertical forum shifting": "At the same time, the international intellectual property policymaking arena has grown ever more congested and complex. This multi-level policy arena has expanded horizontally, across more multilateral institutions, and it has expanded vertically, from the multilateral level to the most granular – even down to individuals. While it may be too soon to tell if and when the complicated, competing, and inconsistent norm-setting and rule-making processes may find an equilibrium, it seems that the horizontal forum-shifting has provided some opportunities for crusaders for expanded access to intellectual property. The vertical forum shifting, from the multilateral down to the individual, with multiple levels in-between, thus far has redounded to the benefit of stronger parties who seek to ration access to intellectual property." *See* S. K. Sell, TRIPS was Never Enough: Vertical Forum Shifting, FTAs, ACTA, and TPP, *J. Intell. Prop. L.*, 2011, Vol. 18, No. 2, p. 449. The strategy of "regime shifting" has also been used by developing countries, *see* L. Helfer, Regime Shifting: The TRIPs Agreement and New Dynamics of International Intellectual Property Lawmaking, *Yale J. Int'l. L* 2004, Vol. 29, p. 1.

[32] In a text entitled "10 Myths about ACTA (Anti-Counterfeiting Trade Agreement)" published on the DG Trade site, the European Commission explicitly concedes that it "would have preferred to address IPR enforcement problems in the WTO or in WIPO, and made many proposals to that effect. The point is that certain other Members of these organisations opposed any enforcement debate there. ACTA sets international IPR standards, and more countries are welcome to join this multilateral treaty", available at: http://trade.ec.europa.eu/doclib/docs/2012/february/tradoc_149112.pdf (last accessed 25 January 2013).

Related Aspects of Intellectual Property (TRIPS).[33] However, the majority of the states that negotiated the agreement have in their national legislation legal provisions on IP enforcement that are often sufficiently developed and at times stronger than those provided for by ACTA.

One of the arguments frequently advanced by the European Commission and the governments of the signatory parties to reassure the opponents of the agreement is that the latter in no way modifies the legal provisions applicable in the field. Therefore, the Commission has on several occasions emphasised that ACTA is fully compatible with the *Acquis Communautaire*,[34] and the European Parliament also adopted a resolution in this sense on 24 November 2010.[35] Hence, it can be wondered why so much effort has been expended negotiating a text that, according to its main protagonists, will not change anything in the existing law.

The answer is that the agreement seems to be mainly addressed at *non-signatory* emerging countries,[36] who will later be invited to "join the club"[37] by ratifying the text or by signing bilateral agreements.[38] The Preamble confirms that ACTA's aim is "global" and that it concerns the "world economy and not merely the economies of the signatory countries."[39] Moreover, the establishment of a special body

[33] The TRIPS Agreement is reproduced as Annex 1.C of the Marrakesh Agreement Establishing the World Trade Organization, signed in Marrakesh on 15 April 1994.

[34] See in particular the Communication of the Commission, *supra* note 2, p. 24.

[35] European Parliament resolution of 24 November 2010 on the Anti-Counterfeiting Trade Agreement (ACTA), P7_TA(2010)0432.

[36] As an example, countries like China, Brazil, Russia and India were not invited to take part in the negotiations although they are regularly identified by certain signatory states as being the principal origin of counterfeit products (see in particular the "IPR Enforcement Report 2009" by the European Commission, *supra* note 30). According to Professor Galloux, the fact that the emerging countries were not involved or were not invited "constitutes beyond doubt one of the weaknesses of this project" (*supra* note 12, p. 81). *See also* in this sense A. Rens, Collateral Damage: The Impact of ACTA and the Enforcement Agenda on the World's Poorest People, PIJIP Research Paper No. 5, American University Washington College of Law, Washington, DC, 2010.

[37] To quote an expression used by Professor Gervais, *supra* note 26, p. 555: "The approach is neither regional nor truly multilateral; it is a 'club approach' in which like-minded jurisdictions define enforcement 'membership' rules and then invite other countries to join, presumably via other trade agreements." *See also* P. K. Yu, ACTA and Its Complex Politics, *WIPO J.* 2011, Vol. 3, No. 1, p. 3; IGIR, The Anti-Counterfeiting Trade Agreement (ACTA): An Assessment, *supra* note 12, p. 11.

[38] *See also* Kamperman Sanders et al., The Anti-Counterfeiting Trade Agreement (ACTA): An Assessment, *supra* note 12, p. 9. The European Commission explicitly denies this in a text entitled "10 Myths about ACTA (Anti-Counterfeiting Trade Agreement)" (*supra* note 32): "There is no intention to do so, and this has not been proposed in bilateral trade negotiations conducted by the EU." Moreover, for an interesting perspective on bilateral agreements between developing and developed countries, *see* B. H. Malkawi, A Long 'TRIP' Home: How the Berne Convention, TRIPS Agreement, and Other Instruments Complement the International Copyright System, EIPR 2013, Vol. 35, No. 2.

[39] According to the Preamble, "the proliferation of counterfeit and pirated goods, as well as of services that distribute infringing material, undermines legitimate trade and sustainable development of the world economy, causes significant financial losses for right holders and for legitimate businesses, and, in some cases, provides a source of revenue for organized crime and otherwise poses risks to the

to implement the agreement, the "ACTA Committee,"[40] whose functions are to examine "matters concerning the development of the Agreement," to decide upon "the terms of accession to this Agreement of any member of the WTO" and to invite "those signatories not parties to this Agreement to participate in the Committee's deliberations on those rules and procedures,"[41] likewise reinforces the view that the prime addressees are third countries. However, it is not certain, contrary to what has often been claimed by the European Commission, that agreement would not have an impact on the legislations of the EU and its member states.

## THE POSSIBLE IMPACT OF ACTA ON THE EU LEGISLATION

The objective here is not to present an in-depth analysis of the proposed provisions, since this would go far beyond the framework of this chapter, but rather to make some observations and a general assessment of the differences between the text and current EU legislation.

ACTA consists of five chapters, the most important within the context of the present article being the first two. The first chapter contains the initial provisions, general definitions (concerning in particular the relationship with other agreements), the nature and the scope of the obligations and the general principles relating to the agreement. The second chapter lays down the legal framework for improving the enforcement of intellectual property rights. It also constitutes the core of the proposed regulation and contains in particular the provisions concerning civil enforcement, border measures, criminal enforcement and an additional section on the specific measures aimed at enforcing intellectual property rights in the digital environment (the "digital chapter" of the agreement).

The complexity and technical nature of the agreement, combined with the lack of transparency concerning the negotiation process, has given rise to numerous misunderstandings about its contents. First of all, it should be noted that in the final version of the treaty, numerous controversial provisions envisaged during the negotiations, specifically regarding the implementation of "graduated response" systems for combating file sharing on the Internet, have been dropped or had their scope considerably narrowed.[42] In this regard, it is probable that the publication of the draft agreement by the Commission under the pressure of the European Parliament

public"; for this reason, the parties to the Agreement desire "to combat such proliferation through enhanced international cooperation and *more effective international enforcement*" (emphasis added).

40 ACTA Article 36.

41 ACTA Article 36.2(b), Article 36.2(d) and Article 36.5. For a comment *see* P. K. Yu, The ACTA Committee, Drake University Legal Studies Research Paper Series, Research Paper 2012 No. 12–34, and chapter 8 in this same publication.

42 *See* also Kamperman Sanders et al., The Anti-Counterfeiting Trade Agreement (ACTA): An Assessment, *supra* note 12, p. 60; T. Hoeren, *supra* note 13, p. 137.

contributed to the abandonment of some of these provisions, although it is known that they were envisaged by the negotiators. As a result, the "digital chapter" is less problematic, even if doubts persist as to the scope of certain provisions and how to safeguard uses covered by exceptions and limitations.[43] Anyhow, the criticism of ACTA is not unique in this regard. The same sort of difficulties had already arisen in the EU following the adoption of the Directive of 22 May 2001 on the harmonisation of certain aspects of copyright and related rights in the information society,[44] which has been criticised exactly for the same reason.[45]

Second, it should be noted that major efforts have been made to include, specifically in the treaty's general provisions, a number of rules aimed at guaranteeing balanced procedures.[46] As an example, the agreement refers to the principles and objectives of the TRIPS Agreement (Articles 7 and 8) and lays down that they apply *mutatis mutandis* (Article 2.3). These articles can generally be regarded as having a "balancing" function, given that they can be used as an interpretive guideline that allows the different interests involved to be taken into account when defining the scope of the agreement.[47] It should be noted, however, that these TRIPS provisions have rarely been used by the WTO in its various panel reports.[48] ACTA Article 6.2 also lays down that "procedures adopted, maintained or applied to implement

[43] On the topic *see* in detail R. Matulionyte, ACTA's Digital Chapter: Remaining Concerns and What Can Be Done, *QMJIP* 2011, Vol. 1, No. 3, p. 248, and the Opinion of European Academics on Anti-Counterfeiting Trade Agreement, 2011 *Journal of Intellectual Property, Information Technology and E-Commerce Law* (JIPITEC) 2011, Vol. 2, p. 65, para. 15 et *seq*. For an analysis of the ACTA provisions concerning internet service providers (Article 27.4) and the disclosure of data relating to their subscribers with regard to their compatibility with the *acquis communautaire*, *see* I.A. Stamatoudi, ACTA, Internet Service Provider and the Acquis Communautaire, in: J. Rosen (ed.), IP Rights at the Crossroads of Trade, *supra* note 22. *See also* Matulionnyte, Chapter 7, present volume.

[44] Directive 2001/29/EC of the European Parliament and of the Council of 22 May 2001 on the harmonisation of certain aspects of copyright and related rights in the information society, OJEU, L 167/10 of 22 June 2001.

[45] *See* for example Ch. Geiger, The Future of Copyright in Europe: Striking a Fair Balance between Protection and Access to Information, Report for the Committee on Culture, Science and Education – Parliamentary Assembly, Council of Europe, Strasbourg, July 2009 (extended version published in: *Intellectual Property Quarterly* (IPQ) 2010, p. 1).

[46] For an extensive comment, *see* in this same publication, X. Seuba, ACTA Initial Provisions and General Obligations, stating that some of the provisions of Chapter I "are expected to play an important balancing function."

[47] *See* Ch. Geiger, Exploring the Flexibilities of the TRIPs Agreement Provisions on Limitations and Exceptions, in: A. Kur and V. Mizaras (eds.), *The Structure of Intellectual Property Law – Can One Size Fit All?*, Cheltenham, UK / Northampton, MA, Edward Elgar, 2011, p. 287; P.K. Yu, The Objectives and Principles of the TRIPs Agreement, *Houston Law Review* 2009, p. 979.

[48] *See* H. Grosse Ruse-Khan, Criminal enforcement and international IP law, in: Ch. Geiger (ed.), *Criminal Enforcement of Intellectual Property: A Handbook of Contemporary Research*, *supra* note 26. *See also* from the same author: The (Non) Use of Treaty Object and Purpose in Intellectual Property Disputes in the WTO, Max Planck Institute for Intellectual Property & Competition Law Research Paper No. 11–15, 19 October 2011.

the provisions of this Chapter shall be fair and equitable, and shall provide for the rights of all participants subject to such procedures to be appropriately protected. These procedures shall not be unnecessarily complicated or costly or entail unreasonable time limits or unwarranted delays." Paragraph 3 further provides that "in implementing the provisions of this Chapter, each Party shall take into account the need for proportionality between the seriousness of the infringement, the interests of the parties, and the applicable measures, remedies and penalties." By emphasising that the procedures must be "fair" and "equitable," and by referring to the principle of proportionality, the agreement introduces several notions which could have a positive influence on its interpretation, specifically by guaranteeing a balanced understanding. Finally, Article 27.2 further lays down that the procedures for the enforcement of copyright in digital networks must preserve "fundamental principles such as freedom of expression, fair process, and privacy."

These provisions are all the more important because the secret nature of the negotiations makes it more difficult to understand the text, since the negotiating record is neither known nor accessible, unlike the multilateral agreements adopted within the WTO or WIPO, where the debates are documented.[49]

Nevertheless, as noted earlier in the chapter, the vague and uncertain nature of some provisions and the lack of clear limits may be the source of difficulties.[50] The discretion left to member states in the implementation of the agreement may also allow "maximalist" readings of the provisions. Moreover, the treaty still contains a number of controversial provisions that have for the most part been worded in a non-binding manner. Of course, this does not lead to a direct obligation to implement them, but can nevertheless reflect an intention to induce the parties to introduce those provisions into their national law.[51] For example, Article 23.3 states that "a Party may provide criminal procedures and penalties in appropriate cases for the unauthorised copying of cinematographic works from a performance in a motion picture exhibition facility generally open to the public." Leaving aside the fact that Article 23.1 specifies that criminal penalties are in principle reserved to wilful counterfeiting "on a commercial scale" (and that this condition is not repeated in the context of paragraph 3), under existing legislation it is not the copy itself that

[49] *See* Kamperman Sanders et al., The Anti-Counterfeiting Trade Agreement (ACTA): An Assessment, *supra* note 12, p. 17. *See also* Article 6 of the European Parliament resolution of 10 March 2010 on the transparency and state of play of the ACTA negotiations, (*supra* note 14), in which the Parliament "deplores the calculated choice of the parties not to negotiate through well-established international bodies, such as WIPO and WTO, which have established frameworks for public information and consultation."

[50] See in this sense T. Hoeren, *supra* note 13, p. 138, stating that the interpretation of the agreement remains very unclear.

[51] *See also* the Opinion of European Academics on the Anti-Counterfeiting Trade Agreement (ACTA), *supra* note 43.

constitutes the problematic use,[52] but rather its dissemination such as by means of file-sharing sites on the Internet. Even if the text refers to the "unauthorised" copy, this is still ambiguous because it is not apparent who is entitled to give the authorisation: Is it the right holder (in which case, this would imply that the exceptions and limitations are to be left to the decision of the right holder) or is it the legislature, and if so, which (as the private copy exceptions are not harmonised and the national laws vary considerably on this point)? This is a good illustration of the difficulties related to an unclear interpretation of the text.

More generally, the agreement contains a certain number of differences to provisions of European and international intellectual property law, specifically regarding civil enforcement, border measures, criminal enforcement and the provisions concerning the enforcement of the IP rights in the digital environment. These differences were pointed out by a group of European academics in an opinion, the aim of which was to bring to the attention of the EU institutions, and the European Parliament in particular, that the ratification of the agreement could lead to possible modifications of European law.[53] The objective of the opinion was to provide the legal analysis required for an informed decision by the EU institutions (ACTA having been described a little too quickly by the European Commission and the European Parliament as being "entirely compatible with the *acquis communautaire*"). The opinion led to an official reply on the part of the European Commission,[54] a fact that deserves to be mentioned because this is very rare for a text written by academics. Some of the explanations given in the reply are convincing and help to specify the scope of certain ambiguous provisions. The problem is that the interpretations proposed by the European Commission are not binding on the EU institutions. Therefore, if the text were to be adopted, it would be highly desirable to publish some clear interpretative guidelines as an annex to complement the treaty text. The precise understanding of the various ambiguous provisions should then first be the subject of an open and transparent debate, thus helping to clarify the scope of the legal commitment that the adoption of ACTA would imply.

[52] Indeed reproduction can be permitted by means of an exception, in particular the private copy exception, and thus constitute a perfectly legitimate act. See the Opinion of European Academics on the Anti-Counterfeiting Trade Agreement (ACTA), *supra* note 43, para. 9, according to which "ACTA prompts Contracting Parties to criminalize such an action (unauthorised copying of cinematographic works) without the commercial scale assessment and without any assessment of the intention of the defendant. Again, this disregards the exception in relation to fair use and copying for private and not-for-profit purposes repeatedly stressed by the EP."

[53] Opinion of European Academics on the Anti-Counterfeiting Trade Agreement, *supra* note 43. A French translation of the Opinion was published in Issue 6 of the Journal Auteurs et Médias 2011, p. 583. The text was sent to the European Parliament and the European Commission in February 2011.

[54] Comments on the Opinion of European Academics on Anti-Counterfeiting Trade Agreement, 27 April 2011, Commission Services Working Paper, reproduced in: *Journal of Intellectual Property, Information Technology and E-Commerce Law* (JIPITEC) 2011, Vol. 2, p. 171.

The Commission's response to the opinion, however, was less convincing when it came to the ACTA criminal provisions in the agreement,[55] probably the most problematic aspect. Article 23.1 provides that "each Party shall provide for criminal procedures and penalties to be applied at least in cases of wilful trademark counterfeiting or copyright or related rights piracy on a commercial scale." The term "commercial scale" is defined broadly as comprising at least acts carried out "as commercial activities for direct or indirect economic or commercial advantage," which expands the notion considerably and is less flexible than market/product-based interpretation of the TRIPS Agreement by the WTO Panel.[56] The parties agree to introduce criminal penalties into their legislation; however, within the EU legislative framework, there are currently no provisions concerning criminal penalties for the infringement of intellectual property rights.

This is problematic because the harmonisation of criminal law at European and international levels has always been a highly sensitive issue and would have needed some further discussions, since criminal law is closely linked to moral and cultural conceptions at national level.[57] Criminal enforcement of intellectual property has some economic but also ethical, historical and even psychological implications[58] that were not addressed by the ACTA treaty.

## CONCLUSION

ACTA aims to complete the international legal system concerning the enforcement of intellectual property rights that resulted from the TRIPS Agreement. Sometimes weaker than the obligations laid down in EU law and national law of the negotiating parties in the field of civil and criminal enforcement, ACTA appears primarily addressed to non-signatory third countries which will be later invited to "join the club," either by ratifying the agreement a posteriori or by concluding bilateral agreements.

Some dark areas remain concerning the exact impact of the provisions of the treaty on EU law. After announcing the referral of ACTA to the Court of Justice

[55] On this question, *see* Chapter 6 in this volume.

[56] *See* in this sense H. Grosse Ruse-Khan, Criminal enforcement and international IP law, in: Ch. Geiger (ed.), *Criminal Enforcement of Intellectual Property, supra* note 26, p. 171 *sq*. The WTO Panel (*supra* note 26) referred to "counterfeiting or piracy carried on at the magnitude or extent of typical or usual commercial activity with respect to a given product in a given market", para. 7.577.

[57] *See* Ch. Geiger, The Anti-Counterfeiting Trade Agreement and Criminal Enforcement of Intellectual Property: What Consequences for the European Union?, in: J. Rosen (ed.), *IP Rights at the Crossroads of Trade, supra* note 22, p. 169.

[58] For a historical, economic and psychological perspective on criminal enforcement, *see* the chapters by D. Lefranc, A. Wechsler and A. Peukert, in: Ch. Geiger (ed.), Criminal Enforcement of Intellectual Property, *supra* note 26.

of the EU[59] in order to verify its compatibility with primary EU legislation,[60] and specifically with fundamental rights[61] (which, with the entry into force of the Treaty of Lisbon, acquired "the same legal value as the Treaties"),[62] the European Commission has finally withdrawn its request on 19 December 2012. Anyhow, a clarification of the exact implications for the *acquis communautaire* and the law of the member states would also have been helpful. Certainly, as the European Commission rightly asserts, ACTA as an international agreement is not required to comply with EU secondary legislation. Nevertheless, it is possible that it will have consequences on the latter by requiring (and/or strongly suggesting) changes or new legislative initiatives. Indeed, as we have emphasised, the scope of many provisions is vague, and there are currently uncertainties about the interpretation that will be given to the text. It would therefore be desirable, if the agreement should ever be adopted in its current or in a modified version (what seems very unlikely for the moment), to complement it by means of binding interpretive guidelines that would give more clarity and be the subject of a transparent debate. Moreover, the adoption of ACTA by the EU would mean that the latter would integrate its legal system, with

59 *See* Statement by Commissioner Karel De Gucht on ACTA (Anti-Counterfeiting Trade Agreement), 22 February 2012, MEMO/12/128, available at: http://europa.eu/rapid/pressReleasesAction.do?reference=MEMO/12/128 (last accessed 18 January 2013). The referral took place on 10 May 2012 (European Commission officially referred ACTA to the European Court of Justice Statement by John Clancy, EU Trade Spokesman, Notice, Brussels, 11 May 2012).

60 The Court might have been able to provide useful guidance on this issue since fundamental rights are now increasingly applied by the Court of Justice to interpret EU legislation in the field of intellectual property. As an example, the Court recently ruled on the balance of rights laid out in the European Union Charter of Fundamental Rights in relation with intellectual property enforcement measures, where it stated that national courts cannot order internet service providers or social networks to introduce monitoring or general filtering systems to identify potential infringers and prevent illegal file-sharing, *see Belgische Vereniging van Auteurs, Componisten en Uitgevers CVBA (Sabam) v Netlog NV* (C 360/10), unreported 16 February 2012.

61 Expressing doubts in this respect, *see* the Opinion of the European Economic and Social Committee on the Communication from the Commission to the European Parliament, the Council, the European Economic and Social Committee and the Committee of the Regions – A Single Market for Intellectual Property Rights – Boosting creativity and innovation to provide economic growth, high quality jobs and first class products and services in Europe, Brussels, 18 January 2012, COM(2011) 287 final, CESE 143/2012 – INT/591. According to the Committee, ACTA's exclusive focus "on increasing protection for right holders by means of customs, police and administrative cooperation measures continues to favour a certain view of rights ownership. Other doubtless more fundamental human rights, such as the right to information, health, sufficient food, the right of farmers to select seeds and the right to culture, are not taken sufficiently into consideration, and this will impact on future European legislation geared towards the harmonisation of Member States' legislation", (para. 3.13; D. Korff and I. Brown, Opinion on the Compatibility of ACTA with the ECHR and EU Charter of Fundamental Rights, Study prepared at the request of the Greens/European Free Alliance in the European Parliament, October 2011, available at: http://rfc.act-on-acta.eu/fundamental-rights (last accessed 25 January 2013).

62 Article 6.1.1 TEU.

the consequence that any future directive or regulation would have to comply with it and be interpreted in its light. As a minimum, it is thus the interpretation of the *acquis communautaire* that will be affected.[63] From this point of view, one might ask whether it is advisable for the EU to adopt an additional instrument that could lead to complications, given that ACTA is not identical with EU law in terms of its provisions and scope.

Ultimately, it is perhaps not so much the content of the agreement that is the most problematic, but rather the method of its adoption.[64] A secret negotiation of the future of intellectual property law between a few like-minded countries, outside the competent international organisations, is clearly a bad method and by no means a guarantee of success.[65] On the contrary, it tends to undermine the credibility of multilateralism in the field of intellectual property law and in the long term risks to weaken considerably the WTO and WIPO that are responsible for such legislation at international level.[66] At a time when intellectual property is more

63 *See* in this sense Legal Opinion of the Legal Service of the European Parliament, SJ-0501/11, IDP/DG/NG/mm, D(2011)47454, Brussels, 5 October 2011 requested by the International Trade Committee (INTA), para. 18: "This implies that when the EU concludes agreements, it is bound by them in the sense that legislation which the Union will subsequently adopt has to be compatible with their provisions. Moreover, if an international agreement implies a modification of existing legislative acts, the latter must be modified accordingly."

64 *See* B. Mercurio, Beyond the Text: The Significance of the Anti-Counterfeiting Trade Agreement, *supra* note 12, p. 361, arguing that "the real significance of ACTA lies not in its textual obligations but more in the effect it will potentially have as a starting point in multilateral and bilateral trade negotiations, as an alternative forum for IP lawmaking and on the 'governance' of international IP more generally."

65 On this point, one might recall the failure of the Multilateral Agreement on Investment (MAI), which was negotiated in secret within the OECD between 1995 and 1997 with the intention of subsequently extending it to non-members, and which encountered huge opposition among the general public until it was finally abandoned in October 1998 (*see* on the question in particular D. Henderson, L'accord multilatéral sur l'investissement, Leçons d'un échec, Paris, GEM, 1999). While an international regulation of investments was certainly desirable, the method adopted blocked any progress on the topic for many years. It is possible for this scenario to be repeated with ACTA.

66 *See also* P.K. Yu, Six Secret (and Now Open) Fears of ACTA, *supra* note 13, p. 1078: "By developing intellectual property protection outside the traditional fora, like WIPO and the WTO, the negotiation of ACTA undermined the stability of the international trading system and the preference for the multilateral process. It also alienated the trading partners of ACTA negotiating parties, making it more difficult to undertake future multilateral discussions." *See also* by the same author, ACTA and Its Complex Politics, *supra* note 37, p. 1: "This approach is likely to have serious ramifications for both the structural integrity and continued vitality of the existing international intellectual property regime." The WIPO Director General has also expressed his reservations about such a procedure, arguing that the approach adopted by the ACTA signatories risked damaging the multilateral intellectual property system, *see* the discussion reported by C. Saez, ACTA a Sign of Weakness in Multilateral System, WIPO Head says, Intellectual Property Watch, 30 June 2010. According to Francis Gurry, "a number of countries feel (there is) an important area of public policy they are not able to address in the multilateral forum, and so have gone outside the multilateral framework to satisfy their desire for creating some form of 'international cooperation'. (...) That's the challenge for us. And whether it

than ever a major aspect of the global economy, this is undoubtedly an undesirable signal.[67] The struggle against counterfeiting and the adequate enforcement of intellectual property rights are perfectly legitimate objectives that can be defended effectively and probably successfully within the multilateral system.[68] Equally, convincing emerging countries that it is in their interest to have effective enforcement mechanisms does not seem to be an impossible task, particularly since several of these countries have gradually developed strategies for stronger protection of their intellectual property rights. Obviously, such a multilateral approach will very likely require compromises and to take into account the equally legitimate demands of many developing countries, such as in the field of limitations and exceptions to copyright, the protection of traditional knowledge or access to medicines. This will surely need efforts on both sides, but in the long term is likely to be much more effective than the iron fist which is currently being wielded by the rich countries and the equivalent defensive posture of developing countries as concerns the governance of intellectual property.[69] In the meantime, it is the legitimacy of the entire system that is at risk.[70]

concerns enforcement, ACTA, or any other area, that, on whole, is a bad development for a multilateral agency, that member states start to do things outside." In this sense, *see* S. Bannerman, WIPO and the ACTA Threat, *Int. J. Technology and Law* 2012, Vol. 1, No. 1, p. 3.

67 *See* L. Floridi, ACTA – The Ethical Analysis of A Failure, and Its Lessons, ECIPE Occasional Paper, No. 4/2012, p. 11: "One of the most serious collateral damages caused by ACTA's failure is that it has now made it more difficult to reach an international agreement on how best to protect IPR."

68 Strengthening the enforcement mechanisms of IP rights is probably not the only solution to diminish piracy in developing countries. According to a recent study, the efficiency of these measures would even be quite uncertain. *See* J. Karaganis (ed.), Media Piracy in Emerging Economies, Social Science Research Council, 2011, Executive Summary iii, the authors of the study concluding that "they have seen little evidence – and indeed few claims – that enforcement efforts to date have had any impact whatsoever on the overall supply of pirated goods. Our work suggests, rather, that piracy has grown dramatically by most measures in the past decade, driven by exogenous factors – high media prices, low local income, technological diffusion, and fast changing consumer and cultural practices." See also in this sense, but with regard to Internet piracy, I.A. Stamatoudi, ACTA, Internet Service Provider and the Acquis Communautaire, in: J. Rosen (ed.), IP Rights at the Crossroads of Trade, *supra* note 22, concluding that "internet piracy cannot be solved solely through the vehicle of law", but also by new business models and affordable prices.

69 For a consideration on the future of the international intellectual property system *see* A. Abdel- Latif, Change and Continuity in the International Intellectual Property System: A Turbulent Decade in Perspective, *WIPO J.* 2011, Vol. 3, No. 1, p. 36.

70 In this sense, at the European Union level it seems that the European Commission seeks to renew the consensus on the intellectual property rights enforcement and adopted on 1 July 2014 two new communications: 'Trade, growth and intellectual property – Strategy for the protection and enforcement of intellectual property rights in third countries', COM(2014) 389 final and 'Towards a renewed consensus on the enforcement of intellectual property rights: An EU Action Plan', COM(2014) 392/2.

# 22

# ACTA

## *Anatomy of a Failed Agreement*

*Bryan Mercurio*

### INTRODUCTION

The Anti-Counterfeiting Trade Agreement (ACTA or "the agreement") is a failed agreement, and represents a failure of international lawmaking. The validity of this statement is not dependent on whether the agreement ever enters into force. Promoted as a "twenty-first-century" agreement aimed at deepening international cooperation and promoting strong enforcement practices, the final text of ACTA accomplishes neither objective.

On the one hand, this failure is unfortunate, as counterfeiting and piracy have rapidly expanded over the past decade and in certain cases represent a serious threat to public health and safety.[1] On the other hand, the failure of ACTA is not necessarily an undesirable result. Beyond the rhetoric, the negotiating objectives of the agreement were ill-defined and the negotiating parties never fully committed to negotiating an agreement which harmonised enforcement standards or truly engaged in serious standard setting. Instead, all of the major negotiating parties simply sought to "harmonise" through the exportation of their own laws to the other parties. With domestic laws diverging in several respects between and among the negotiating parties, the agreement's original aims slowly faded into the background and the priority became simply to conclude *an* agreement as opposed to conclude a *meaningful* agreement. The result is a patchwork of vague legal standards allowing for multiple approaches and interpretations.

Thus, while many have concluded that public pressure and demonstrations directly led to the demise of ACTA,[2] this chapter contends that the treaty failed as

[1] *See* Chaudhry, P. and Zimmerman, A. (2009). *The Economics of Counterfeit Trade*. Springer, Heidelberg. Germany; International AntiCounterfeiting Coalition, obtained from http://www.iacc.org; World Intellectual Property Organization (2009). "Counterfeiting and Piracy Endangers Global Economic Recovery Say Global Congress Leaders". WIPO Press Release PR/2009/621.

[2] Lee, D. (11 February 2012). "Acta protests: Thousands take to streets across Europe". BBC News, obtained from http://www.bbc.co.uk

a piece of international lawmaking long before the public protests and European Parliament vote to reject ACTA. Of course, without the inclusion of the digital environment in ACTA, it would have in all likelihood come into force sometime in 2013 and simply been a failed agreement. The inclusion of the digital environment directly led to unwanted media attention, public pressure and demonstrations and may have effectively killed ACTA as an international agreement. In retrospect, the agreement would likely have escaped the attention of a sceptical public if it had excluded provisions relating to the Internet/digital environment and solely focused on the counterfeiting and piracy of tangible goods. The point to be made in this chapter, however, is that the resulting agreement would nevertheless have still represented a failure of international lawmaking.

The chapter uses examples to demonstrate that the negotiating parties failed to understand the significance of the differences in general approach taken and disparity of legal architecture in the domestic setting of each of the negotiating parties. These differences, coupled with the aforementioned goal of exporting one's own legal architecture and approach, led to direct conflict and ultimately compromise in the form of vague and permissive standards which in many cases represented little more than the status quo. The final section contains concluding analysis which touches upon the impact of ACTA on future trade negotiations.

## NEGOTIATION OF ACTA: COMMON GOAL, DIFFERING VISION

ACTA failed as an instrument in international lawmaking primarily as a result of the failure of the parties to realise (and adequately account for) the laws and regulations among and between the negotiating parties differed widely. Even though the negotiating parties all maintain high levels of IP protection and enforcement standards, the particulars of each regime significantly differ in a number of areas. Of course, such a result should not have been unexpected, as every international effort aimed at harmonising standards requires compromise and ultimately legislative and/or administrative modifications.

In regard to ACTA, this reality became problematic as a large number of negotiating parties intended on achieving the objective of harmonisation simply through the exportation of their own law and regulations. Thus, with negotiating parties such as Australia, Canada, European Union, Switzerland and the United States never intending for ACTA to require any domestic legislative modifications, the parties were bound to discover areas where the domestic law of one party was not in sync with other negotiating parties. Again, if harmonisation were to be achieved, the parties would have had to agree on a position and set a single international standard. This did not occur, however, and in several areas the final text of ACTA simply allows for multiple positions. This is despite the fact that these issues were heavily negotiated, which itself indicates both the intent for the parties to export their own laws and unwillingness to agree to a standard which requires a legal change. Taken together, and simply stated, the result is an agreement which simply maintains the status quo of all of the negotiating parties to the detriment of harmonisation and international standard setting.

This is not to say that ACTA does not contain provisions which advance the agenda beyond the TRIPS Agreement. To the contrary, ACTA contains several provisions which go beyond what is required in the TRIPS Agreement, including Article 8 (injunctions applying to imports and exports whereas Article 44.1 of TRIPS only applies to imports) and Article 9 (potential calculation of damages is more prescriptive than Article 24.1 of TRIPS). There simply would have been no point even to begin negotiations if the aim was to repeat existing international obligations. But even here, most if not all of the advancements beyond TRIPS already form part of the domestic law in most of the negotiating parties. So, while the provisions advance beyond what is required in TRIPS, they merely codify existing domestic law of the respective negotiating parties. Thus, the fact that ACTA contains some "TRIPS-plus" provisions does not detract from the broader point that ACTA maintains the status quo of the negotiating parties to the detriment of harmonisation and international standard setting.

Examples of this broader point include Article 9.3 relating to damages, which states:

> At least with respect to infringement of copyright or related rights protecting works, phonograms, and performances, and in cases of trademark counterfeiting, each Party shall also establish or maintain a system that provides for one or more of the following: (a) pre-established damages; or (b) presumptions for determining the amount of damages sufficient to compensate the right holder for the harm caused by the infringement; or (c) at least for copyright, additional damages.

This provision was apparently subject to heavy negotiation in a number of negotiating rounds, and the aim of at least some of the parties was harmonisation and standard setting. In the end, however, the parties failed to compromise, and the result is an article which fails as an instrument of harmonisation and international standard setting. Instead, Article 9.3 allows for a variety of different methods in line with existing practice of ACTA negotiating parties. Moreover, and perhaps for the better, the provision is limited to "at least" copyright and trademark, which allows each party to determine whether to establish or maintain any of the three options (pre-established damages, presumptive damages or additional damages) for other IPRs. More damning, the article does not even attempt to harmonise the rationale behind the three options. To illustrate, whereas both the United States and the EU utilise "pre-established damages," their respective reasons for doing so differ quite radically: in the United States, pre-established damages are used in part to punish infringers and as a deterrent, whereas the EU uses them only against unintentional infringers as a way of compensating IP owners. Similarly, the rationale for including "additional damages" in Australia (compensation awarded following the principles of aggravated and exemplary damages at common law) differs from that of England and Wales (restitution through the use of aggravated damages). Given such varying interpretations of the terms in the domestic setting of each of the parties, it will be difficult if not impossible to find a common meaning of the language used in the treaty text. While this will cause obvious interpretative difficulties, the main point for our purposes is the attempt by each party to allow for the continuation of its own laws and correspondingly the failure of the parties to harmonise or set an international standard.

Likewise, the parties heavily negotiated Section 3 of ACTA relating to border measures, which caused many in the public health community to worry that ACTA would threaten to destabilise the hard-fought gains of developing countries and public health campaigners in the area of access to essential medicines. Such fears centred on whether the terms "counterfeiting" and "piracy" would be extended to include the manufacture, sale and import/export of generic pharmaceuticals and thus potentially severely curtail trade in generic pharmaceuticals and add significant costs to the procurement of essential medicines.[3]

Such concerns were legitimate given the ACTA negotiations coincided with the seizure/detention of at least nineteen shipments of generic pharmaceuticals while transiting through the EU on their way from and to developing countries where a patent was not in place.[4] While the legality of the customs measures with World Trade Organization (WTO) and EU law continues to evoke considerable debate,[5] the relevant point for our purposes is that the negotiation of ACTA could have opened up a separate avenue to legitimise the seizures/detentions. This could have occurred in two ways.[6] First, the definitions of counterfeit and/or piracy could have been drafted or interpreted in an expansive manner so as to clearly allow for the seizure of generic

[3] *See* Grosse Ruse-Khan, H. (2011). "A Trade Agreement Creating Barriers to International Trade? ACTA Border Measures and Goods in Transit". *American University International Law Review* 26: 645–726; Chapter 5 of this volume; Inside US Trade (30 April 2010). "Consumer Groups Fear ACTA Could Encourage Generic Drug Seizures". *Inside US Trade*; Yu, P. (2010). "*Six* Secret (and Now *Open*) *Fears* of ACTA". *Southern Methodist University Law Review* 64: 975–1094.

[4] Mercurio, B. (2012). "Drugs Seized in Transit: The Case that Wasn't". *International and Comparative Law Quarterly* 61(2): 389–426.

[5] Ibid. n. 4; Court of Justice of the European Union, Joined Cases C-446/09 *Koninklijke Philips Electronics NV v Lucheng Meijing Industrial Company Ltd and others* and C-495/09 *Nokia Corporation v Her Majesty's Commissioners of Revenue and Customs*, obtained from http://www.eulaws.eu

[6] Atik, J. (2012). "ACTA and the Destabilization of TRIPS" in *Sustainable Technology Transfer: A Guide to Global Aid and Trade Development*. Lidgard, H. H., Atik, J., and Nguyen, T. T., eds.

pharmaceuticals transiting through the territory of ACTA members. Second, ACTA could have been drafted in such a manner so as to require the seizure of transiting goods which violate the IPRs in the country of transit.

The final text, however, represents far less of a threat to the trade in generic pharmaceuticals, for a number of reasons. First, while ACTA continues to include all of the TRIPS-covered areas of IPRs in its mandate (Article 5), it restricts the definitions of both counterfeit and piracy to trademark in the former and copyright in the latter. Thus, infringements of patents are not included in the terms "counterfeit" or "piracy." Second, the language of Article 16.2 provides that parties may, but are not required to, adopt or maintain procedures leading to the suspension of release with respect to in-transit goods. Finally, a footnote (FN 6) to Article 13 (which provides for the scope of border measures and calls for enforcement in a manner that does not discriminate unjustifiably between IPRs and in a manner which avoids the creation of barriers to legitimate trade) excludes patents and protection of undisclosed information from the scope of Section 3.

Thus, while ACTA does not require parties to enforce domestic IPRs with respect to goods in transit, it takes an equivocal position by maintaining the status quo. Through silence, ACTA thus allows parties to adopt such procedures if and when they see fit, and in so doing does not depart very far from the position taken in Part IV of the TRIPS Agreement. I would be remiss to omit, however, that Article 5 of ACTA does depart from TRIPS in that it defines counterfeiting and piracy "under the law of the country in which the procedures (…) are invoked," whereas Article 52 and footnote 14 of TRIPS sets out an uncertain standard of the "country of importation," which could be interpreted to be either the country of transit or the country of final destination. The latter would imply the rather odd scenario of customs officials and/or judges in one country being forced to interpret the laws of another country. While such a scenario is contemplated and enshrined in the domestic law of a few jurisdictions, such as Switzerland,[7] the legal issue remains unresolved at the WTO.

While public health campaigners would have preferred ACTA to prohibit the seizures/detentions of generic pharmaceuticals in transit, the final text is perhaps the best realistic outcome for such interested observers given the (then) ongoing dispute between the EU/Netherlands and India and Brazil at the WTO. What is more, the result could have been far more threatening, as it appears the issue of border measures was among the most contentious negotiating topics, and one that threatened to derail the entire agreement.[8] Moreover, the drafts of the negotiating

7 Seuba, X. (2010). "Free trade of pharmaceutical products: the limits of intellectual property enforcement at the border", Issue Paper no. 27, Geneva: ICTSD.

8 Inside US Trade (16 July 2010) "De Gucht Lashes Out at US over ACTA, Geographical Indications" 28(28) *Inside US Trade*.

text were expansive in scope and covered all forms of IPRs contained in the TRIPS Agreement (including patents), and even the July 2010 draft text provided for the possibility of mandatory injunctions for IPR infringements of in-transit goods.

In the end, the aims of harmonisation and an international standard gave way to a political compromise which allowed the EU to claim victory through the inclusion of at least a portion of its domestic regulations regarding the seizure/detention of in-transit goods suspected of patent infringement into ACTA and for extending Section 4 to cover all IPRs (less patents and undisclosed information), which potentially allows for enhanced recognition and protection of geographical indications through ACTA.[9] At the same time, the compromise allowed the United States, the EU, Australia and others to announce that nothing in these provisions will require amending domestic law.[10]

This pattern of an issue being heavily negotiated – and potentially containing provisions which would have caused significant shifts in the law of several negotiating parties – before being whittled down to little more than the status quo repeats to a certain extent in almost every section of ACTA, and certainly can be further illustrated in the sections on civil enforcement (Section 2) and the digital environment (Section 5). While space does not permit a full review of either section, given the extensive attention Section 5 received in the media (and on the streets), it is worth highlighting a few provisions which illustrate the significant backtrack in the negotiations and ultimate agreement which allows for countries to maintain their existing regime without amendment.

For example, it is clear from the draft texts that for some time the negotiations included the possibility of requiring a graduated response (also referred to as "three strikes law"), notice-and-takedown provisions and other measures relating to copyright violations over the Internet, which potentially encroach on civil liberties. Intense negotiations over these issues, however, produced a final text which is much more restrained. All of the provisions some saw as being nefarious in nature have not been retained in the final text. In addition, and in contrast to the early drafts, the final text contains a number of general "safeguards" (for instance, Preamble, Article 1, Article 2.3, Article 4, Article 6.2 and Article 6.3), while Section 5 contains several specific safeguards. Thus, while Article 27.1 extends the enforcement proceedings mandated in Sections 2 (Civil Enforcement) and 4 (Criminal Enforcement) to the digital environment, Article 27.2 calls for implementation "in a manner that avoids the creation of barriers to legitimate activity, including electronic commerce, and, consistent with that Party's law, preserves fundamental principles such as freedom of

[9] Ibid. n. 8.

[10] Weatherall, K. (2011). "Politics, Compromise, Text and the Failures of the Anti-Counterfeiting Trade Agreement". *Sydney Law Review* 33: 229–263.

expression, fair process, and privacy." Article 27.4 provides another example of the flexibility of ACTA in providing:

> A Party *may* provide, *in accordance with its laws and regulations*, its competent authorities with the authority to order an online service provider to disclose expeditiously to a right holder information sufficient to identify a subscriber whose account was allegedly used for infringement, where that right holder has filed a legally sufficient claim of trademark or copyright or related rights infringement, and where such information is being sought for the purpose of protecting or enforcing those rights. These procedures shall be *implemented in a manner that avoids the creation of barriers to legitimate activity, including electronic commerce, and, consistent with that Party's law, preserves fundamental principles such as freedom of expression, fair process, and privacy*. (emphasis added)

While the provision calls on parties to order online service providers to disclose information which could identify the identity of a subscriber alleged to have infringed IPRs, the provision is discretionary; that is, parties are not required to implement the provision. Moreover, where a party chooses to implement the provision, Article 27.4 explicitly states that such implementation is subject to existing laws and regulations of the party. Finally, the article repeats the language used in Article 27.2 as a general safeguard and nod to civil liberties. While such drafting may be preferable to harmonisation and setting a mandatory international standard in this emerging and important area, it perfectly illustrates the failure of the parties to meet their negotiating objectives and instead agreeing to text which requires few (or in this case, no) change of practice. This cycle repeats in a number of areas related to the digital environment, including the limiting effect of Article 27.8 on the substantive provisions relating to the circumvention of effective technological measures and electronic rights management information.

Again, the point of illustration through these examples is not that the agreement failed as it did not contain maximalist IP provisions, but that the agreement failed to meet its objectives of harmonisation and international standard setting because of its ambiguous and permissive text. This section further posited that the intention of several parties from the outset was harmonisation and standard setting through the export of their own domestic law. Where the laws of the parties differed, treaty language was drafted to allow for positions and interpretations suitable to all parties current law. For this reason, ACTA is a failure as an instrument in international lawmaking.

## CONCLUSION

For better or for worse, what started as an ambitious undertaking targeted at reducing the scourge of counterfeiting and piracy through increased cooperation and new international standards became little more than a codification of the status quo among the negotiating parties. ACTA does not significantly advance the IP agenda beyond the TRIPS Agreement, while at the same time it allows wide discretion in implementation and little harmonisation or standard setting. Moreover, the negotiations became a public relations disaster, the blowback of which will likely affect current and future international trade, investment and IP negotiations.

While the negotiating parties agreed to the rhetoric in promoting ACTA, they discovered that massive divergences lay beyond the rhetoric and, instead of agreeing to international standards, they negotiated an agreement which contains few mandatory provisions, allows for wide interpretive scope and (at least according to the parties) does not require any domestic legislative changes in a number of signatory countries. The wisdom of such a strategy should be questioned, as one wonders how these negotiating parties intended for ACTA to combat the real (and increasing) problem of counterfeiting and piracy through an agreement that requires no change of domestic law. If one accepts that the current international and domestic regimes are failing to adequately curtail counterfeiting and piracy, it does not follow that an agreement which does not require any domestic modifications will address the problem.

Tellingly, leaked draft texts of the intellectual property chapter of the Transpacific Partnership (TPP) contain many provisions which were raised, discussed and rejected in the context of the negotiations of ACTA. These drafts reveal that at least one negotiating party to ACTA – the United States – does not view the standards set in ACTA as sufficient to effectively manage and curtail counterfeiting and piracy. Similarly, other negotiations and recently completed trade agreements are not referencing, referring to or being constrained by the text of ACTA. Instead, it again appears that the early ACTA proposals of some of the more influential negotiating parties are simply being repeated in a different forum, despite the fact that these proposals were considered and rejected in ACTA. This leads to a more systemic point: the fact that ACTA is seemingly irrelevant to current FTA negotiations casts doubt on its long-term relevance, regardless of whether it enters into force.

As is well known, other problems plagued ACTA. It is clear that the negotiating parties failed to appreciate both the level and volume of dissent the inclusion of counterfeiting and piracy over the digital environment would cause, as well as the discontent stemming from what many viewed as excessive secrecy throughout the negotiations. Both directly led to the widespread dissemination of misleading and false information, which the parties never successfully combated.[11] Moreover, this failure directly resulted in some influential politicians and parliaments viewing

[11] Schusterman, M. (2011). "How ACTA will take down the Internet, healthcare, and farming". [Infographic], obtained from http://matadornetwork.com

ACTA unfavourably and voting as such, as opposed to engaging in any meaningful review of the text. These issues, as well as others, are comprehensively addressed elsewhere in this book.

Thus, a multitude of factors combined to form a "perfect storm" which derailed ACTA. Based on the final text of ACTA, perhaps such a result is neither unwarranted nor to the detriment of international intellectual property. But counterfeiting and piracy are not abating, and something must be done proactively in the near future to address the problem. ACTA therefore represents not only a failure in international lawmaking but also a missed opportunity.

# 23

# What Was Left Out of ACTA

*Kimberlee Weatherall*

## INTRODUCTION

ACTA is a fascinating and in places disturbing document. But it is worthy of attention not only for what is there on the page, but for what is *not* there. I hope to convince you that we all – governments, trade negotiators, right holders, civil society and user interests – have as much to learn from the absences in ACTA as from its black-and-white text.

## FROM AMBITION TO VAGUE ASPIRATIONAL STATEMENTS AND OPTIONAL EXTRAS

The ACTA negotiations started out with high, evangelical ambitions: to promote IP enforcement through global cooperation and to establish the "gold standard" for IP enforcement rules and procedures.[1] Early leaked texts showed how major players like the United States and the European Union aspired to export their own detailed, right holder–friendly systems.

The United States wanted its digital copyright regulations: comprehensive rules against "hacking" technological protections like encryption and copy controls, and safe harbours for Internet intermediaries conditioned on those intermediaries becoming Internet police, removing infringements and kicking the intransigent off the Internet entirely. The United States also wanted extensive rules criminalising even non-commercial copyright infringements – based on its own No Electronic Theft Act of 1999.

The EU wanted extensive measures for intercepting IP infringement at the border, including requirements to stop infringing goods "in transit," as well as at the

[1] On ACTA's ambitions, *see* Kimberlee Weatherall, 'Politics, Compromise, Text, and the Failures of the Anti-Counterfeiting Trade Agreement' (2011) 33 *Sydney Law Review* 229, 238 and following.

point of import or export, and the extension of these measures and other enforcement measures to patents, designs, and the EU's own favoured form of IP protection: geographical indications.

Many of these early ambitions ended up being significantly watered down in the final text. This was particularly evident in digital enforcement, where the United States gradually caved on its most ambitious proposals. The digital copyright rules were reduced to an uncertain and vague shadow of their earlier selves. The final text contains little more than aspirational statements about ensuring that enforcement procedures are available and encouraging companies to cooperate (Article 27). Proposals for Internet intermediaries to take on a role as Internet police disappeared entirely, replaced with a vague reference in Article 27.1 to "enforcement procedures [applying to] infringement of copyright or related rights over digital networks," and footnote 13 which gives Internet safe harbours as one possible example of such a procedure.[2]

The final rules on criminalising copyright also looked very different from early proposals – taking out any reference to "private financial gain" and acts "that have no direct or indirect motivation of financial gain" – and requiring only criminalisation of copyright infringement "carried out in the context of commercial activity for direct or indirect economic or commercial advantage."[3] File-sharing individuals are not criminals on this text, although businesses using pirated software are.

Nor was the EU successful in gaining acceptance for its more ambitious ideas. Patents and trade secrets were left out of the border measures entirely (footnote 6), and other IPRs can be excluded provided there is no "unjustifiable" discrimination (Article 13). Having systems for seizure of goods in transit is optional (Article 16). Patents and trade secrets are also an optional exclusion from the general civil enforcement provisions (footnote 2).

## OTHER NOTABLE ABSENCES: THE EXCLUSION OF USER RIGHTS AND PROTECTIONS

If the final version of ACTA left out some of the US' and EU's more zealous suggestions, it also left out a lot of things user interests might have wanted.

Perhaps most mystifying is the failure to replicate in ACTA procedural safeguards in enforcement already agreed to in TRIPS. For example, consider the rules on search and seizure of alleged infringing articles before the defendant can have a

2 For a detailed review of these changes – and the reasons behind them – *see* Kimberlee Weatherall, 'ACTA as a New Kind of International IP Lawmaking' (2011) 26(3) *American University International Law Review* 839, 858–866.

3 *See* ibid. 866–869.

court hearing. Such measures – for example, the *Anton Piller* or search order – may be justified by the need to ensure that important evidence is not destroyed. But they also contravene a basic principle that everyone has a right to be heard before being exposed to a court order, and so ought to be carefully circumscribed. Article 50.4 of TRIPS requires that where orders are made, affected parties must be given notice without delay and, at their request, a hearing must occur to determine whether the measures should be modified, revoked or confirmed. Article 12 of ACTA, bizarrely, contains no such safeguards. Article 1 of ACTA – which reaffirms TRIPS obligations – in my view means that parties to ACTA will still be obliged to provide these safeguards, even where procedures are applied to IPRs, such as patents, that are not covered by TRIPS Article 50.[4] This simply makes the absence of such safeguards more strange. Including the safeguards would have made the position clearer and prevented the belief forming among some commentators that TRIPS safeguards had been abrogated.[5] To the extent that ACTA is meant to set out the "gold standard" of enforcement, surely that includes gold standard safeguards. If not, why not?

Also mostly absent from ACTA are real procedural protections for defendants in IP cases. Admittedly, some fairly vague standards are there – in Article 6, procedures have to be "fair and equitable" and must "provide for the rights of all participants subject to such procedures to be appropriately protected." Governments must "*take into account* the need for proportionality between the seriousness of the infringement, the interests of third parties, and the applicable measures, remedies and penalties."[6] Note, however, that this is not an *obligation* to ensure proportionality: a government could, consistently with ACTA, argue that the need for deterrence outweighs the importance of proportionality, and set damages, fines or terms of imprisonment at draconian and utterly disproportionate levels. Nor is it an *obligation* to protect the interests of innocent third parties. Nor on the face of it does the obligation in Article 6.2 that *procedures* be fair and equitable require that *remedies* be proportionate (and so Article 6.3 cannot really be seen as an elaboration of Article 6.2). And while there is excruciating detail on how damages are to be calculated (Article 9), no similar

4 Anselm Kamperman Sanders, Dalindyebo Bafana Shabalala, Anke Moerland, Meir Pugatch, Paolo Vergano, *The Anti-Counterfeiting Trade Agreement (ACTA): An Assessment*, Report for the Directorate-General for External Policies of the Union, Directorate B, June 2011, 21; *see also* Weatherall, ' Politics, Compromise, Text, and the Failures of the Anti-Counterfeiting Trade Agreement' (2011) 33 *Sydney Law Review* 259–260.

5 *See* e.g. European Academics (Axel Metzger et al.), *Opinion of European Academics on ACTA*, Institute for Legal Informatics, http://www.iri.uni-hannover.de/acta-1668.html; *see also* Margot Kaminski, 'An Overview and the Evolution of the Anti-Counterfeiting Trade Agreement (ACTA)' (PIJIP Research Paper No 17, American University Washington College of Law, 1 January 2011), http://digitalcommons.wcl.american.edu/research/17.

6 The form of words comes from TRIPS Article 46. TRIPS does not create an obligation to ensure proportionality in implementing enforcement measures. The absence of such an obligation is more serious in ACTA, however, owing to the greater stringency of the enforcement provisions and their potential to impact on a broader range of legitimate activities.

effort has been expended to set out what fairness or equity for a defendant might mean when faced with seizure of assets or suspension of the right to trade – unlike in TRIPS, in which specific procedural protections are provided.[7]

The contrast between protections for individuals and for companies is also telling. For example, Article 4 deals with privacy and with (commercial) trade secrets. Individual privacy is only protected as far as a country's law already requires (if at all). Commercial trade secrets are specifically protected from disclosure that would prejudice legitimate commercial interests.

More broadly, ACTA fails to reflect broader civil society concerns with limits on IPRs in the interests of the public. For example, there is nothing in ACTA about exceptions to IPRs. You might think this is natural: that a treaty about enforcement ought to have little to do with exceptions and limitations. However, strengthening enforcement across the board *without* thinking about and expanding exceptions risks demonising behaviour which has been tolerated with benefits for social welfare. The US early proposals for criminalising copyright infringement for private financial gain could have criminalised great swathes of the population in a country with no exceptions to allow copying of songs onto mp3 players. Even the final text could create some nasty consequences for companies undertaking commercial research in countries with no copyright exceptions to allow such research.

ACTA also failed – strangely, for an agreement that purports to be an Anti-Counterfeiting *Trade* Agreement – to put any real limits on IP enforcement in the interests of free trade. For example, countries other than the United States might have been well advised to impose limits on that country's recent unilateralism in IP enforcement. With the United States now treating seizure of foreign websites and domain names as an ordinary tool of domestic enforcement, you might have thought other countries could have taken the opportunity to put some limits on that activity. Apparently not.

## WHAT DOES IT ALL MEAN?

So what do these absences and exclusions tell us?

First, they tell us something about the dynamics of international IP lawmaking as it is playing out today. I am sure that there was some expectation on the part of ACTA supporters and commentators that the final agreement would look considerably stronger than it did in the end. ACTA was, after all, negotiated between a group of hand-picked participants: countries with historically strong IP protections (such as the United States, the EU, Japan, Switzerland and Australia) and a "coalition of the willing" – most countries (like Singapore, South Korea and Morocco) who

7 See, for example, TRIPS Articles 50.3–50.8, 52–58.

have bilateral trade agreements with the United States or those (like New Zealand) who aspire to one, and who have therefore adopted, or are prepared to adopt, the detailed IP rules the United States requires as a condition of entry into such a trade relationship.

People seem to have assumed that IP obligations could only ever go up, and up again: that rules found in bilateral agreements would, eventually, be reflected by similar rules at a multilateral level.[8] ACTA shows that sometimes this does not happen. The detailed rules that the United States has been busily promulgating in its bilateral agreements could not be agreed to in ACTA – because they were inconsistent with EU law. The detailed rules the EU has been pushing on geographical indications and customs rules could not be agreed to – because they were inconsistent with US law.

So what do we have in international IP lawmaking? Not the inexorable rise of IP standards so much as the proliferation of multiple (inconsistent) standards: US standards in its FTAs, EU standards in its FTAs, and different ones again in ACTA. This is not so much a one-way ratchet as an every-which-way global IP ratchet.[9]

This has costs for everyone, including right holders and governments. The more inconsistent standards you have, the more risk there is of confusion and fragmentation. Governments and right holders would be well advised to consider whether the strategy of seeking the strongest possible rules in every agreement is producing more costs than benefits.

With bilateral agreements, multilateral agreements, and treaties like ACTA, governments will be subject to multiple overlapping requirements found in multiple overlapping agreements. This is not good for government efficiency. It may give domestic and international bureaucrats and lobbyists something (actually lots of things) to do, but it is unlikely to actually reduce counterfeiting. What would a government rather be doing – providing money to support innovation, or box ticking on their customs processes to check compliance with the multiple different obligations in different treaties and flying its public servants around the world for the latest anti-counterfeiting meeting?

In addition, for right holders who want higher standards, ACTA represents a significant public relations failure. By failing to achieve a higher standard in negotiations between high-protection countries, ACTA has the potential to undermine the push for higher standards, and to validate a claim by opponents that the bilateral provisions are unacceptable, excessive and a source of conflict with other potential

8 Peter Drahos with John Braithwaite, *Information Feudalism: Who Owns the Knowledge Economy?* (Earthscan, 2002); Bryan Mercurio, 'TRIPS-Plus Provisions in FTAs: Recent Trends', in Lorand Bartels and Federico Ortino (eds) *Regional Trade Agreements and the WTO Legal* System (2006).

9 For more detail, see Weatherall, 'ACTA as a New Kind of International IP Lawmaking' (2011) 26(3) *American University International Law Review*, 844–856.

trade partners. It cannot, after all, be argued that the ACTA negotiators are a lowest-common-denominator group. In reality, a watered-down ACTA allows opponents to say that there were things that the United States does that not even Europe, with its concerns for strong IPRs, considers appropriate or justifiable. A country wanting to negotiate trade agreements with both the United States and the EU now has concrete evidence that detailed agreement with one could be a barrier to agreement with the other – and a precedent to use in its push for lower standards.

For civil society, the watering down of ACTA over time shows the importance of local models, particularly in important negotiating countries. Changes were wrought in the ACTA text over the course of negotiations in those areas where the EU model differed from that in the United States. This suggests developing local models in *other* important countries – such as India, Brazil, China and others – as a strategy to counter the attempt to "multilateralise" any harmful ACTA or other IP provisions.

These absences and exclusions also reveal the importance – for *everyone*, including governments, trade negotiators, right holders, civil society and users – of giving serious thought to developing model treaty provisions on both exceptions and limitations to IPRs, and on procedural protections. The absence, in ACTA, of real and substantive provisions on exceptions and on the protection of defendants involved in enforcement procedures has surely been a factor in the public rejection of ACTA following its conclusion.

Part of the reason for this absence was no doubt due to pressure from right holders to get the strongest possible protection. But I suspect that a second reason for the absence of such provisions was, quite simply, that negotiators did not have good precedents. And so we need to develop some – whether through international negotiations on exceptions in WIPO; academic projects like Hugenholtz and Okediji's 2008 project, *Conceiving an International Instrument on Limitations and Exceptions to Copyright*,[10] or the Max Planck Institute for Intellectual Property, Competition and Tax Law's project *Intellectual Property Rights in Transition*; or other civil society efforts. If we can develop better precedents, I suspect that international trade negotiators could be open to having some way to respond to the growing public opposition to IP chapters following ACTA.

It is in the interests of governments and right holders to respond to this public concern. A perception that IP law is fair between stakeholders is critical to its future. IPRs need support from the public in order to be effective. To receive such support, IP law needs to address the needs of all stakeholders – it needs to be fair, and to be

[10] P. Bernt Hugenholtz, and Ruth Okediji, *Conceiving an International Instrument on Limitations and Exceptions to Copyright: Final Report*, 6 March 2008.

*seen* to be fair. Treaties that strengthen enforcement without addressing the needs of others look (and are) unfair and will bring IP law even further into disrepute.

Future IP negotiating efforts that obdurately refuse to concede the need for exceptions and for procedural rights in addition to enforcement risk a backlash from an organised, motivated set of people with well-developed ideas. They will also make it easier for third countries to reject their outcomes out of hand. Including genuine limitations will not guarantee that any IP treaty is welcomed with open arms – there will always be opponents – but it would help.

And so I would argue that ACTA, with its absences and exclusions and the public reaction to some of those absences, holds lessons for all of us – for governments, right holders, and civil society at large. It has been, unfortunately, an object lesson in how *not* to go about giving IP law the balanced, credible international future it deserves and could have.

# 24

# Slaying the ACTA Myths

*Michael Geist*

## INTRODUCTION

On 23 October 2007, the United States, the European Union, Canada, Japan and a handful of other countries announced plans to negotiate the Anti-Counterfeiting Trade Agreement (ACTA). The behind-the-scenes discussions had apparently been ongoing for several years, leading some countries to believe that a full agreement could be concluded within a year to coincide with the end of the second Bush administration. Few paid much attention as the agreement itself was shrouded in secrecy. ACTA details slowly began to emerge, however, including revelations that lobby groups had been granted preferential access, the location of various meetings, and troubling details about the agreement itself.

As the public pressure mounted, the talks dragged on, with participating countries increasingly defensive about the secrecy and the substance. ACTA was ultimately concluded in 2010 – years after the initial target – and some of the most troubling provisions were abandoned. Yet, the final agreement still raised serious concerns, for the way the treaty was concluded as well as its substance.

When ACTA was formally signed by most participants in October 2011 in Tokyo, Japan, few would have anticipated that less than a year later it would face massive public protests and abandonment by leading countries. With tens of thousands taking to the streets in Europe in the spring of 2012, ACTA became the poster child for secretive, one-sided IP agreements that do not reflect the views and hopes of the broader public. In July 2012, the European Parliament voted overwhelmingly against the agreement, effectively killing ACTA within the EU.

ACTA is not yet dead – it may still eke out the necessary six ratifications for it to take effect – but it is badly damaged and will seemingly never achieve the goals of its supporters as a model for other countries to adopt and to emerge as a new global standard for IP enforcement. While much credit goes to the activists who worked tirelessly to raise public awareness and convince the European Parliament to reject the treaty, the foundation of the opposition lay with the efforts of ACTA critics to forcefully challenge three pervasive myths perpetuated by the agreement's supporters. These myths – which revolved around the transparency of the negotiations, the substance of the treaty and the flexibility associated with permissive provisions – each needed to be fully addressed in order to convince thousands of concerned citizens that their mounting fears were warranted.

## TRANSPARENCY

ACTA's lack of transparency was a consistent source of concern throughout the negotiation process. In December 2007, before formal negotiations began, the US government asked other participating countries to agree to a confidentiality agreement. The agreement classified all correspondence between ACTA parties as "national security" information on the grounds that it was confidential "foreign government information."[1]

The first few rounds of negotiations were held in secret locations, with each participating country offering near-identical cryptic press releases that did little more than fuel public concern about the potential scope of the treaty and the prospect that it might be concluded without public input or review. This highly unusual level of secrecy, particularly for an agreement focused on intellectual property, led not only to an outcry from citizens and civil society groups[2] but also to a steady stream of parliamentary resolutions[3] and political demands for transparency[4] coming from around the globe.

Notwithstanding the mounting public outrage, ACTA participants responded with little more than vague discussions about transparency and inadequate promises

[1] Eddan Katz and Gwen Hinze, The Impact of the Anti-Counterfeiting Trade Agreement on the Knowledge Economy: the Accountability of the Office of the U.S. Trade Representative for the Creation of IP Enforcement Norms Through Executive Trade Agreements, Volume 35 (Fall 2009) *Yale Journal of Int'l Law*.

[2] *See*, e.g., CIPPIC, "Re: Anti-Counterfeiting Trade Agreement (ACTA)" (30 April 2008), http://www.cippic.ca/uploads/CIPPIC_LT_DFAIT-ACTA-30%20April%2008.pdf; Mart Kuhn, "ACTA means trouble, but don't take our word for it", *Public Knowledge* (June 10, 2010), http://www.publicknowledge.org/node/3155; La Quadrature du Net, "Three Core Reasons for Rejecting ACTA" (29 March 2010), http://www.laquadrature.net/en/three-core-reasons-for-rejecting-acta

[3] European parliament, Press release, "Access to documents: The European parliament demands more transparency" (11 March 2009), http://www.europarl.europa.eu/news/expert/infopress_page/019-51409-068-03-11-902-20090310IPR51408-09-03-2009-2009-false/default_es.htm

[4] E.g. Letter from Senator Bernard Sanders and Senator Sherrod Brown to Honorable Ron Kirk (23 November 2009), http://keionline.org/sites/default/files/sanders_brown_acta.pdf; MP Clare Curran, "ACTA, secrecy, Copyright and delays" (16 December 2009), http://blog.labour.org.nz/index.php/2009/12/16/acta-secrecy-copyright-and-delays/?utm_source=wordtwit&utm_medium=social&utm_campaign=wordtwit

to solicit greater public feedback. In November 2009, as a response to demands for more transparency, ACTA partners released a joint statement claiming that "it is accepted practice during trade negotiations among sovereign states to not share negotiating texts with the public at large, particularly at earlier stages of the negotiation."[5]

Yet, a closer examination of similar international IP negotiations reveals that ACTA's opaque approach was not "an accepted practice," but rather was out-of-step with many other global norm-setting exercises. The World Trade Organization (WTO), World Intellectual Property Organization (WIPO), World Health Organization (WHO) and an assortment of other organisations are all far more open than ACTA is. For example, the WIPO Internet treaties, which offer the closest substantive parallel to the ACTA Internet provisions, were by comparison very transparent, with full texts made readily available to the public well in advance of the final agreement.[6]

Internal US government documents confirm that European government officials privately acknowledged the transparency problem. For example, a November 2008 US cable released by Wikileaks noted that the Italian head of the intellectual property office within the Ministry of Foreign Affairs expressed concern over the lack of transparency and effective consultation:

> The level of confidentiality in these ACTA negotiations has been set at a higher level than is customary for non-security agreements. According to Mazza, it is impossible for member states to conduct necessary consultations with IPR stakeholders and legislatures under this level of confidentiality. He said that before the next round of ACTA discussions, this point will have to be renegotiated.[7]

A year later, a Swedish official who represented the EU Presidency at the ACTA negotiations told US officials:

> The secrecy issue has been very damaging to the negotiating climate in Sweden. All political parties have vocal minorities challenging the steps the government has taken to step up its IPR enforcement. For those groups, the refusal to make ACTA documents public has been an excellent political tool around which to build

5 ACTA negotiating parties, Press release, "The Anti-Counterfeiting Trade Agreement – Summary of Key Elements Under Discussion" (6 November 2009), http://www.ustr.gov/webfm_send/1479

6 Knowledge Ecology International, "ACTA is secret. How transparent are other global norm setting exercises?" (21 July 2009), http://www.keionline.org/misc-docs/4/attachment1_transparency_ustr.pdf; the EU references the openness of the WIPO process in their ACTA resolution on transparency: European Parliament, *Resolution on the transparency and state of play of the Anti-Counterfeiting Trade Agreement* ACTA, http://www.europarl.europa.eu/oeil/FindByProcnum.do?lang=en&procnum=RSP/2010/2572

7 The Guardian, "US embassy cables: Italy, the EU and the Anti-Counterfeit Trading Agreement" (22 December 2010), http://www.guardian.co.uk/world/us-embassy-cables-documents/176810

> speculation about the political intent behind the negotiations. If the instrument for example had been negotiated within the World Intellectual Property Organization (WIPO) critics say, WIPO's Secretariat would have made public initial draft proposals. In Johansson's opinion, the secrecy around the negotiations has led to that the legitimacy of the whole process being questioned.[8]

The same cable expressed additional concern that the US was providing access to various industry lobby groups, while other countries were unable to consult with their stakeholders. The cable notes:

> European Commission is concerned that the USG [US government] has close consultation with US industry, while the EU does not have the same possibility to share the content under discussion in the negotiations.[9]

These concerns are unsurprising given that the ACTA negotiations were demonstrably more secretive than comparable past processes. They represented a major shift toward greater secrecy in the negotiation of international treaties on intellectual property, in what appeared to be an attempt to avoid public participation and scrutiny.

A draft version of the ACTA text was only released after years of negotiation in April 2010. Two documents, leaked in early 2010, were instrumental in the release. The first leak involved internal Dutch government documents describing the positions of many ACTA participants on treaty transparency.[10] Up to that point, a standard evasive response from many governments to transparency criticisms had been to claim that they favoured releasing the ACTA text to the public, but that other unnamed countries did not. Therefore, because there was no consensus, the text could not be released. The Dutch leak succeeded in blowing the issue wide open by identifying which countries posed barriers to transparency.

The second major leak came in March 2010, in the form of a copy of a draft agreement dating from January 2010. Even after this leak, countries maintained their official pretence of treaty secrecy, despite the full, albeit unconfirmed, draft text – including negotiating positions – being available to anyone with Internet access. Because the text had not been officially released, government officials refused to comment on substantive provisions revealed by the leaked document.

The combined effect of the two leaks was a reversal on the transparency issue several months before the conclusion of the negotiations at the April 2010 round of

[8] The Guardian, "US embassy cables: Sweden's concerns about Anti-Counterfeit Trading Agreement negotiations" (22 December 2010), http://www.guardian.co.uk/world/us-embassy-cables-documents/236363

[9] Ibid.

[10] Brenno de Winter, "Dutch internal ACTA documents" (25 February 2010), http://www.bigwobber.nl/2010/02/25/dutch-internal-acta-documents/

discussions in New Zealand. Several days after those talks concluded, a draft version of the ACTA text was publicly released. Even though this official release had been purged of references to parties' negotiating positions that were present in the leaked March version, the release quieted much criticism about the lack of transparency.

The commitment to transparency was short-lived, however. Parties were unable to agree to release an updated text at the July 2010 Lucerne round, a pattern that repeated itself a month later at the August 2010 Washington round. European and Swiss officials publicly indicated that they supported releasing an updated text.[11] Given the long-standing support for public release from countries such as Canada, Australia and New Zealand, it appeared likely that the United States reverted back to its original position favouring secrecy.

In fact, US opposition to public release extended to secrecy in the Freedom of Information process. Efforts to obtain information about the agreement through the Freedom of Information Act process proved largely unsuccessful. For example, a lawsuit brought by the Electronic Frontier Foundation and Public Knowledge in 2008 resulted in the release of 159 pages of information, but 1,362 pages were withheld under a national security classification.[12]

Opposition to transparency extended to other ACTA participants. In Europe, the European Digital Rights (EDRi) counted numerous instances where access requests were refused. In light of the lack of transparency, in July 2010, the Green group in the European Parliament issued a call for the European Commission to suspend all negotiation on ACTA until a proper agreement was in place for full transparency.[13]

In South Korea, IPLeft, a Korean digital rights activist group founded in 1999, demanded that the country's government disclose relevant information about its stance on the negotiation of ACTA in August 2008. The disclosure was denied, and the reason for the denial was that "disclosure would result in a harmful effect on a diplomatic relationship with foreign countries and severe damage to considerable national interests."[14]

No further texts were released until the ACTA negotiations concluded in October 2010. The lack of transparency throughout the ACTA process eroded public confidence in the entire agreement, with reverberations that are still being felt today. While ACTA supporters have pointed to secret releases to European Parliament

[11] Monika Ermert, "ACTA Negotiators Vow To Mesh With National-Level Rights; Withhold New Text", *Intellectual Property Watch* (2 July 2010), http://www.ip-watch.org/weblog/2010/07/02/acta-negotiators-vow-to-mesh-with-national-level-rights-withhold-new-text/

[12] Defendant's Motion for Summary Judgment, Elec. Frontier Found. v. Office of the U.S. Trade Representative, No. 081599 (D.C. Cir. 17 Sept. 2008).

[13] Andrew Macpherson, "EU crossed wires over ACTA", 11 July 2010, http://www.iptegrity.com/index.php/acta/545-eu-gets-wires-crossed-over-acta-transparency

[14] Danny O'Brien, Blogging ACTA Across the Globe: Lessons from Korea (29 January 2010), Electronic Frontier Foundation, https://www.eff.org/deeplinks/2010/01/acta-and-korea

committees, the exclusion of the public from the consultation process has bred enormous distrust in the entire agreement.

## SUBSTANTIVE CONCERNS

In a speech to the European Parliament in September 2010, Commissioner of Trade Karel De Gucht assured members of the European Parliament that "ACTA is only about enforcement of existing intellectual property rights. It will not include provisions modifying substantive intellectual property law."[15] Yet, despite the assurances and ongoing efforts to discount public concern over the substance of the agreement, critics were able to demonstrate that ACTA represents a shift in intellectual property law that extends beyond mere enforcement.

ACTA raises several concerns with respect to the expansion of international intellectual property laws. The emphasis on secondary liability, which potentially holds third parties liable for the infringing actions of others, represents a significant shift in international intellectual property law. While many countries have codified secondary liability principles within their domestic laws, there are relatively few provisions aimed at secondary liability at the international level. Within ACTA, Article 8 on Injunctions applies to both infringers and third parties as does Article 12 on Provisional Measures, which can be applied to third parties. Both Article 8 and Article 12 apply in a civil enforcement context. There are concerns these provisions could be used to target active ingredient suppliers of generic medicines.[16]

ACTA also extends secondary liability to its criminal provisions. Articles 23.4 and 24 on Criminal Offences requires parties to add "aiding and abetting" to their laws. Aiding and abetting is designed specifically to target third parties rather than primary infringers.

The Internet provisions within ACTA also target third parties. Article 27.2 provides that "each Party's enforcement procedures shall apply to infringement of copyright or related rights over digital networks, which may include the unlawful use of means of widespread distribution for infringing purposes."[17] In other words, the potential liability extends beyond those infringing to those who are seen to facilitate infringing activity. In fact, the provision could be applied to peer-to-peer networks, blogging platforms and other technologies that facilitate the dissemination of content.

[15] Karel de Gucht, "Speaking Points: State of play of negotiations on the Anti-Counterfeiting Trade Agreement (ACTA)", 8 September 2010, http://trade.ec.europa.eu/doclib/docs/2010/september/tradoc_146465.pdf

[16] Sean Flynn and Bijan Madhani, "ACTA and Access to Medicines", http://rfc.act-on-acta.eu/access-to-medicines

[17] Anti-Counterfeiting Trade Agreement, Article 27.2.

In addition to secondary liability concerns, ACTA significantly broadens the reach of criminal provisions in copyright and trademark cases. For example, Article 23.1 provides:

> Each Party shall provide for criminal procedures and penalties to be applied at least in cases of wilful trademark counterfeiting or copyright or related rights piracy on a commercial scale. For the purposes of this Section, acts carried out on a commercial scale include at least those carried out as commercial activities for direct or indirect economic or commercial advantage.[18]

This provision creates considerable uncertainty because "commercial scale" is undefined (other than the reference to commercial activities for direct or indirect economic or commercial advantage). Given the requirement on parties to include the provision within their domestic criminal laws, Article 23.1 is far too vague and open to interpretation. The provision does not feature any safeguards and should have been limited to clearly commercial activities.

ACTA also expands intellectual property law with respect to border measures provisions. Article 13, which provides for "effective border enforcement of intellectual property rights," applies to many forms of intellectual property rights extending the law found in many countries that limit such rules to counterfeit goods only. This is particularly problematic given the wide powers granted to officials in Article 19, which enables "competent authorities" to reach determination on whether suspect goods infringe an intellectual property right. Article 19 does not require any court oversight or provide for an appeal process.

These substantive concerns are exacerbated by the absence of balancing provisions and procedural safeguards. Unlike comparable international intellectual property agreements that have identified the need for balance and proportionality, with the exception of several general provisions at the start of the agreement, ACTA is almost single-minded in its focus on increasing enforcement powers. The treaty's Article 9 removes safeguards from the damages provision; Article 11 on the provision on information removes the proportionality provision found in the TRIPS equivalent; and ACTA Article 18 does not include rules for compensation in cases of wrongful detentions.

The missing balancing provisions and procedural safeguards do not end there. ACTA Article 12.2 provides for "provisional measures *inaudita altera parte* where appropriate." The provision does not include specific safeguards or procedural guarantees.

ACTA Article 26 on Ex Officio Criminal Enforcement strengthens criminal enforcement powers but does not build in procedural safeguards to ensure due

[18] Anti-Counterfeiting Trade Agreement, Article 23.1.

process. The Foundation for a Free Information Infrastructure (FFII) notes that in 2007, the European Parliament adopted the following amendment during its review of IPRED2[19]:

> Member States shall ensure that, through criminal, civil and procedural measures, the misuse of threats of criminal sanctions is prohibited and made subject to penalties. Member States shall prohibit procedural misuse, especially where criminal measures are employed for the enforcement of the requirements of civil law.

No similar provision is contained in ACTA.

## THE FLEXIBILITY OF PERMISSIVE PROVISIONS

In an attempt to resolve ongoing conflicts over several substantive areas, the ACTA negotiators agreed to make many provisions permissive rather than mandatory. Supporters frequently pointed to the non-mandatory nature of several contentious provisions as evidence that there was little reason for concern with the substantive elements of ACTA.

The permissive approach may be a useful mechanism to achieve consensus, but critics noted that it provides cold comfort to those concerned with the long-term implications of the agreement. The experience with other treaties, such as the WIPO Internet treaties, indicates that flexible, permissive language is gradually transformed into mandatory, best practice language.

Many of ACTA's most contentious areas feature permissive language stipulating that parties "may" include certain provisions but are not required to do so. Notable examples include:

- Article 9.3 on Damages, which grants parties three options for implementing damages provisions similar to those found in the United States as statutory damages
- Article 10.3 on Other Remedies, which states that parties "may provide for the remedies described in this Article to be carried out at the infringer's expense"
- Article 14.2 on Small Consignments and Personal Luggage, which states that parties "may exclude from the application of this Section small quantities of goods of a non-commercial nature contained in travellers' personal luggage"
- Article 16.2 on Border Measures, which states that parties "may adopt or maintain procedures with respect to suspect in-transit goods or in other situations where the goods are under customs control"

[19] FFII, Copyright Criminal measures in ACTA, (8 October 2010), http://acta.ffii.org/wordpress/?p=34

- Article 22 on Disclosure of Information, which states that parties "may authorize [their] competent authorities to provide a right holder with information about specific shipments of goods, including the description and quantity of the goods, to assist in the detection of infringing goods"
- Article 23.3 on Criminal Offences, which states that parties "may provide criminal procedures and penalties in appropriate cases for the unauthorized copying of cinematographic works from a performance in a motion picture exhibition facility generally open to the public"
- Article 27.4 on Enforcement in the Digital Environment, which states that parties "may provide, in accordance with its laws and regulations, its competent authorities with the authority to order an online service provider to disclose expeditiously to a right holder information sufficient to identify a subscriber whose account was allegedly used for infringement"

The net effect of these provisions is to open the door to statutory damages, detention of in-transit goods, disclosure of information to rights holders, creation of criminal provisions for unauthorised camcording and a requirement that Internet service providers disclose information about their subscribers.

While it is true that ACTA parties will not be required to implement these provisions in order to be compliant with the agreement, there will be considerable pressure to reinterpret these provisions as mandatory rather than permissive. The International Intellectual Property Alliance (IIPA), whose members include Association of American Publishers, Business Software Alliance, Entertainment Software Association, Independent Film & Television Alliance, Motion Picture Association of America, National Music Publishers' Association and Recording Industry Association of America, filed a submission in 2012 with the US government recommending that several ACTA parties be placed on the US Special 301 list for providing inadequate intellectual property protections due in part to the failure to include these provisions within their domestic legislation.[20]

For example, IIPA cited Greece for failing to provide for mandatory disclosure of personal information by Internet providers, noting "there has been no progress in the past year to amend Article 4 of the Data Protection Law (Law 2225/1994) to require ISPs to disclose the identity of users suspected of copyright infringement."[21] IIPA also took issue with Switzerland's failure to include anti-camcording provisions within its domestic law.[22]

[20] International Intellectual Property Alliance, 2012 Special 301 Report, Online at http://www.iipa.com/2012_SPEC301_TOC.htm

[21] Ibid., http://www.iipa.com/rbc/2012/2012SPEC301GREECE.PDF.

[22] Ibid., http://www.iipa.com/rbc/2012/2012SPEC301SWITZERLAND.PDF

Mexico was cited for the decline of in-transit seizures, with IIPA noting that the Attorney General "halted its seizure of in-transit containers, claiming a lack of authority. It is expected that this may be corrected in 2012 with a new 'protocol' between PGR and Customs officials."[23] Canada was also targeted for its border measures provisions, with IIPA arguing that it should "make legislative, regulatory or administrative changes necessary to empower customs officials to make ex officio seizures of counterfeit and pirate product at the border without a court order."[24]

IIPA recommended new search powers in Romania, arguing that "the law should be amended to provide that the mere verification of the existence of software installed on computers should not require such a search warrant."[25] Spain[26] and Latvia[27] were also cited for needing stronger criminal provisions, including the availability of larger damages awards.

In other words, while ACTA states that implementation of these provisions is optional, leading copyright lobby groups are already urging the US government to include ACTA countries on its piracy watch list for failing to include the rules within their domestic legal frameworks.

There is ample precedent for this approach with other international intellectual property agreements. The WIPO Internet treaties, which are the source of technological protection measures found in some domestic laws and in ACTA Article 27, provide a good illustration of the gradual transition away from flexibility.[28] The treaties were concluded at a Diplomatic Conference in December 1996, which featured debate in both the Main Committee and within the Plenary on the anti-circumvention provisions.

The starting point for the Diplomatic Conference was the US-backed "Basic Proposal" that provided:

> (1) Contracting Parties shall make unlawful the importation, manufacture or distribution of protection-defeating devices, or the offer or performance of any service having the same effect, by any person knowing or having reasonable grounds to know that the device or service will be used for, or in the course of, the exercise of rights provided under this Treaty that is not authorized by the rightholder or the law.
>
> (2) Contracting Parties shall provide for appropriate and effective remedies against the unlawful acts referred to in paragraph (1).

[23] Ibid., http://www.iipa.com/rbc/2012/2012SPEC301MEXICO.PDF

[24] Ibid., http://www.iipa.com/rbc/2012/2012SPEC301CANADA.PDF

[25] Ibid., http://www.iipa.com/rbc/2012/2012SPEC301ROMANIA.PDF

[26] Ibid., http://www.iipa.com/rbc/2012/2012SPEC301SPAIN.PDF

[27] Ibid., http://www.iipa.com/rbc/2012/2012SPEC301LATVIA.PDF

[28] "The Case for Flexibility in Implementing the WIPO Internet Treaties: An Examination of the Anti-Circumvention Requirements", in *From "Radical Extremism" to "Balanced Copyright": Canadian Copyright and the Digital Agenda*, (M. Geist, ed.) (Toronto, Irwin Law) 204–46 (2010).

The record indicates that there were *no* unqualified endorsements of the Basic Proposal's provisions on Technological Measures in the Summary Minutes of the Plenary. Given the opposition at the Diplomatic Conference and in the months leading up to it at the Committee of Experts, it should come as no surprise that the Basic Proposal – the only document that required prohibitions against trafficking in circumvention devices – did not achieve consensus.

The compromise position was to adopt the far more ambiguous "to provide adequate legal protection and effective legal remedies" standard. Not only does this language not explicitly require a ban on the distribution or manufacture of circumvention devices; it does not specifically target either access or copy controls. In fact, the record makes it readily apparent that the intent of the negotiating parties was to provide flexibility to avoid such an outcome. Countries were free to implement stricter anti-circumvention provisions consistent with the Basic Proposal (as the United States ultimately did), but consensus was reached on the basis of leaving the specific implementation to individual countries with far more flexible mandatory requirements.

In the years since the conclusion of the WIPO Internet treaties, the United States has worked tirelessly to shift the flexible language found in the treaties toward the more restrictive approach that was rejected during the negotiations. As discussed earlier in the chapter, ACTA contains anti-circumvention provisions that extend beyond the requirements within the WIPO Internet treaties.

The experience with the WIPO Internet treaties is likely to be replicated with ACTA, because permissive language provides a false sense of security to those concerned with the potential of the agreement to foster dramatic changes to domestic laws. Given the current efforts of groups such as IIPA, it is readily apparent that the shift from permissive to mandatory is already under way. In fact, ACTA Article 36.3(c) envisions the establishment of implementation "best practices" by the ACTA Committee that seems likely to be used to strongly encourage the adoption of permissive provisions into national law.

## CONCLUSION

The anti-ACTA movement is part of a broader backlash against secretive intellectual property agreements that are either incorporated into broad trade agreements or raise critical questions about prioritising IP enforcement over fundamental rights. The opposition to ACTA and ACTA-style treaties (which include the Transpacific Partnership and earlier iterations of bilateral agreements such as the Canada-EU Trade Agreement) is part of a growing international trend, as elected officials and independent policy officials around the world voice their objection to these treaties.

Notwithstanding efforts to dismiss ACTA critics as misinformed, the success of the anti-ACTA process owes much to their detailed analysis and research on the treaty's likely effects. Indeed, given ACTA's corrosive effect on transparency in international negotiations, the damage to international intellectual property institutions, the exclusion of the majority of the developing world from the ambit of the agreement, the potentially dangerous substantive provisions and the uncertain benefits in countering counterfeiting, there were ample reasons for the public and politicians to reject the agreement.

# 25

# Developing Countries and the Contestation of ACTA at the TRIPS Council

*Ahmed Abdel-Latif*

## INTRODUCTION

Developing countries set an important precedent in their contestation of ACTA, which has gone relatively unnoticed. For the first time, they have formally questioned at the WTO an entire plurilateral agreement containing TRIPS-plus obligations negotiated and concluded outside the organization. While many developing countries have had concerns about TRIPS-plus standards in regional and bilateral trade agreements for several years, never have such concerns been so forcefully articulated from the point of view of their "systemic" implications for the TRIPS Agreement and the WTO. The use of the TRIPS Council as a platform for such contestation is also rather remarkable and unprecedented.

In this context, this chapter examines the positions of developing countries, particularly emerging economies, towards ACTA at the WTO TRIPS Council and how they evolved in a short time period towards open defiance. While there has been extensive analysis of concerns amongst developing countries regarding specific provisions in ACTA, there has been relatively less attention to their concerns about the Agreement's systemic implications, as well as the broader dynamics of their significance for the international intellectual property (IP) system.

While developing countries were ultimately not behind the coup de grâce that led to ACTA's de facto political demise, their hostility towards it certainly contributed to that outcome, amidst a growing opposition movement arising from different quarters. At the same time, the responses of developing countries to ACTA illustrate some of the limitations and weaknesses they face in addressing such initiatives at the international level.

## ACTA: AN AGREEMENT TARGETING DEVELOPING COUNTRIES YET NEGOTIATED WITHOUT THEM

Since the formal launch of negotiations in 2007, key countries promoting ACTA considered that enticing the support of developing countries, in particular emerging economies with high level of piracy and counterfeiting, would be a measure of the agreement's success and value. A 2007 discussion paper by the Australian Department of Foreign Affairs and Trade underlined that the "extent to which ACTA would attract support from countries where counterfeiting and piracy is more problematic would be critical in determining its real value."[1] The United States, on its part, said it expected other trading partners to "join in the emerging consensus for stronger IPR enforcement," including developing countries, which also have "a major stake in fighting counterfeiting and piracy." In May 2010, the European Commission (EC) mentioned that "large emerging economies, where IPR enforcement could be improved, will sign up to the agreement." It expressed its confidence that "in light of the growing international consensus on IPR enforcement (...) more countries will join ACTA."[2] After ACTA's conclusion, in 2012, the EC continued to voice its hope that "major countries facing the same counterfeiting and piracy problems will eventually accede to it."[3]

So rather than just being an agreement among like-minded countries seeking to "align" their enforcement practices, ACTA had developing countries in mind from its inception to its conclusion. Yet, at no moment were developing countries, in particular emerging economies, invited to formally join the negotiation process, though "there is no doubt that these emerging countries are important to the successful operation of the international enforcement regime."[4] This was confirmed by a study assessing ACTA commissioned by the European Parliament, which indicated that "the major emerging economies, China, Brazil and India appear not to have been formally invited to participate."[5] Only a handful of developing countries (Jordan, Morocco, Singapore and the United Arab Emirates) with already high levels of intellectual property protection and enforcement participated in some or all rounds of ACTA negotiations. Ultimately, only Morocco and Singapore became ACTA signatories and both countries already have FTAs in place with the United States.[6]

The fallacy of negotiating an agreement targeting developing countries but without involving them revealed itself to be a serious flaw in the ACTA narrative, as promoted by its backers. Indeed, it would make little sense, in terms of combating

1 Department of Foreign Affairs and Trade, Australia, *Discussion Paper: An International Proposal for a Plurilateral Anti-Counterfeiting Trade Agreement (ACTA)*, 13 November 2007.

2 European Commission, *Follow-up to the European Parliament Resolution on the transparency and state of play of the ACTA negotiations*, adopted by the European Commission on 12 May 2010.

3 European Commission, *What ACTA is about*, 2012.

4 P. Yu, ACTA and its Complex Politics, *WIPO Journal*, Vol. 3, pp. 1–16, 2011, p. 7.

5 A. Kamperman et al., *The Anti-Counterfeiting Trade Agreement (ACTA): An Assessment*, European Parliament Directorate-General for External Policies, 2011, p. 17.

6 Mexico, being an OECD member, is not considered a developing country here. The Mexican government signed ACTA on 12 July 2012, but the Mexican Senate rejected this signature on 25 July 2012.

piracy and counterfeiting, to have ACTA confined to mainly industrialised countries, which already have strong intellectual property rights (IPRs) enforcement standards. At the same time, if ACTA was an agreement targeting developing countries but negotiated without them, it simply meant that it was intended to be a *fait accompli*, a "country club" agreement that new members would join based on membership rules already established and difficult to change.[7] This has been subsequently confirmed: a high-ranking Japanese official was reported to state explicitly "that the purpose of ACTA is to address the IPR problems of third-nations such as China, Russia, and Brazil, not to negotiate the different interests of like-minded countries."[8]

## ENGAGING WITH ACTA

Ironically, not only did ACTA not entice support from developing countries, in particular emerging economies; it actually antagonised them. However, this happened progressively. From the formal launch of the ACTA negotiations in 2007 to 2009, there were seldom, if any, official reactions or statements by developing countries concerning ACTA. The lack of publicly available information, at least in the early stages of negotiations, made it difficult to gauge the reach and implications of the agreement being discussed. The first consolidated draft of the ACTA text was made available only after the eighth round of negotiations, on 21 April 2010.

From around that time, developing countries became increasingly vocal in their criticism of ACTA. At the fourth summit of the India-Brazil-South Africa (IBSA) Dialogue Forum, held in Brasília on 15 April 2010, leaders of these countries addressed ACTA indirectly in the Summit's final declaration. In it they "warned against attempts at developing new international rules on enforcement of intellectual property rights outside the appropriate fora of WTO and WIPO that may give free rein to abuses in the protection of rights, the building of barriers against free trade and undermining fundamental civil rights."[9]

At the WTO TRIPS Council, the mobilisation of developing countries against ACTA took place mostly during the 2010–2012 period. It was led by countries such as India, China, Brazil, Egypt, Indonesia, Pakistan and South Africa and was

7 D. Gervais, Country clubs, empiricism, blogs and innovation: the future of international intellectual property law making in the wake of ACTA, in *Trade Governance in the Digital Age: World Trade Forum*, edited by Mira Burri and Thomas Cottier (eds.), Cambridge University Press, 2012.

8 M. Masnick, Leaked State Department Cables Confirm That ACTA Was Designed To Pressure Developing Nations, *Tech Dirt*, 4 February 2011.

9 *Brasilia Declaration*, India-Brazil-South Africa (IBSA) Dialogue Forum, Fourth Summit of the Heads of State and Government, 15 April 2010, Brasilia. The *Tshwane Declaration*, adopted on the occasion of the Fifth IBSA Summit held in South Africa, on 18 October 2011, contained a paragraph with similar wording.

broadly supported by many developing countries including African countries, Least Developed Countries (LDCs) and African Caribbean and Pacific Countries (ACP).

The specific concerns of developing countries regarding ACTA have been addressed in other chapters and will thus not be analysed here in depth. They include the expanded scope of civil enforcement measures, the effects of border measures, the enforcement of IPRs in the digital environment and the shift to criminal enforcement measures. This chapter focuses more on the concerns regarding the systemic implications of ACTA that make it an important milestone in the contestation of TRIPS-plus initiatives.

## BRINGING ACTA TO THE TRIPS COUNCIL

The TRIPS Council witnessed intense and often polarized debates about ACTA from its 8–9 June 2010 session to its 28–29 February 2012 session. Controversy extended to procedural aspects, with repeated wrangling between ACTA countries and developing countries over the appropriate agenda item under which the agreement should be discussed at each session. Table 25.1 lists the TRIPS Council sessions held during that period and the agenda items under which ACTA was discussed.

During this time period, developing countries repeatedly voiced their concerns about ACTA, criticised the lack of transparency in the negotiation process and asked for clarifications regarding the agreement's provisions.

At the 8–9 June 2010 session, China and India requested for the first time in the history of the TRIPS Council the inclusion of an agenda item on "TRIPS-Plus Enforcement Trends" invoking TRIPS Article 68, according to which the Council "shall monitor the operation of the Agreement and shall afford Members the opportunity of consulting on matters relating to trade-related aspects of intellectual property rights."[10] China indicated that the "publication of the draft Anti-Counterfeiting Trade Agreement (ACTA) in April 2010 had added a new element" and that it wished to express its views on this important event.[11]

However, several industrialised countries were initially reluctant and recalled that developing countries had opposed, in the past, attempts to discuss enforcement issues at the Council as they considered it a matter for domestic implementation. They further argued that the suggested agenda item seemed to go beyond Part III of the TRIPS Agreement and concentrated more on elements outside the TRIPS Agreement and the WTO.[12] The EU was adamant in opposing the inclusion of the agenda item unless it was renamed.[13]

[10] TRIPS Council, Minutes of 8–9 June 2010 Meeting, IP/C/M/63, paras. 1–3.
[11] Ibid., Statement by China, para. 6.
[12] Ibid., Statement by Switzerland, para. 9.
[13] Ibid., Statement by the European Union, para. 7.

TABLE 25.1. *Agenda Items under which ACTA was discussed at the TRIPS Council (2010–2012)*

| TRIPS Council Session | Agenda item under which ACTA was discussed |
|---|---|
| 8–9 June 2010 | M. Enforcements Trends |
| 26–27 October 2010 | P. Other Business, (iii) IP enforcement trends |
| 1 March 2011 | ACTA not discussed |
| 7 June 2011 | ACTA not discussed |
| 24–25 October 2011 | O. Enforcement Trends |
| 17 November 2011 | ACTA not discussed |
| 28–29 February 2012 | N. IP Enforcement Trends |

*Source*: Compiled by the author.

Developing countries defended the consistency of their proposal with their past positions on this topic. India indicated that it "did not wish to discuss general enforcement issues, but specifically the current trends in IPR enforcement that went well beyond the levels enshrined in the TRIPS Agreement."[14] Switzerland proposed a more general wording which would allow all WTO members to present their views on the broader topic enforcement,[15] and ultimately the agenda item was renamed "Enforcement Trends" and adopted.[16]

At the 26–27 October 2010 session of the TRIPS Council, India and Indonesia raised the issue of "enforcement trends" under the agenda item "other business" with a view to express their concerns about ACTA,[17] following the release of a new version of the ACTA text on 2 October 2010.

After ACTA's final text was opened for signature on 4 October 2011, it was the turn of a number of ACTA countries to request the addition of an item entitled "Enforcement of Intellectual Property Rights (Part III of the TRIPS Agreement)" to the agenda of the TRIPS Council 24–25 October 2011 session[18] with a view to discussing ACTA."[19]

This time, developing countries were the ones opposing the inclusion of the agenda item, recalling their past opposition to a standing agenda item on enforcement as the item's wording seemed to suggest. India pointed out that information about recent developments in this area could be provided under "other business," adding

14 Ibid., Statement by India, para. 12.
15 Ibid., Statement by Switzerland, para. 9.
16 Ibid., paras. 27–28.
17 TRIPS Council, Minutes of 26–27 October 2010 Meeting, IP/C/M/64, paras. 440–441.
18 TRIPS Council, Minutes of 24–25 October 2011 Meeting, IP/C/M/67, para. 1.
19 Ibid., para. 14. The ACTA text was circulated in advance of the Council's meeting as document IP/C/W/563 entitled "Enforcement of Intellectual Property Rights."

that it "might be appropriate to make a notification under Article 63 so that the compatibility of the measures with the rights and obligations under the TRIPS Agreement could be scrutinized."[20] ACTA countries clarified that their intention was not to put forward a "standing" agenda item but to provide an opportunity to answer questions raised about ACTA.[21] The agenda item was finally adopted but renamed "Enforcement Trends" instead of the original suggested title: Enforcement of Intellectual Property Rights (Part III of the TRIPS Agreement).[22]

At the following TRIPS Council session (28–29 February 2012), several ACTA countries requested the inclusion of an item on "IP Enforcement Trends" in the Council's agenda.[23] Once more, it met with opposition from developing countries, which indicated that the Council was not an appropriate forum to discuss ACTA.[24] They also pointed to what they considered was an "inconsistency" between the proposed agenda item and the supporting documentation, arguing that "while IP enforcement was a broad issue on which Members had various views, the document supporting the inclusion of the item was solely focused on ACTA which did not represent IP enforcement trends in general."[25] For Brazil, "there was no mandate to discuss TRIPS-plus measures in the Council."[26]

ACTA countries pointed out that "to call for transparency and yet to oppose the proposed agenda item was curious and internally inconsistent."[27] Ultimately, China manifested its readiness to adopt the agenda with the understanding that the item was a temporary one.[28] On this basis, the agenda for that TRIPS Council session was adopted.[29]

At the 5 June 2012 TRIPS Council session, an agenda item on "Exchange of Information on Securing Supply Chains against Counterfeit Goods" was proposed by the United States, and was adopted.[30] However, ACTA was not discussed in that context.

This overview of the procedural skirmishes concerning the appropriate agenda item under which to discuss ACTA at the TRIPS Council is revealing because it reflects the wider substantive divergence of views among WTO members regarding

20 IP/C/M/67, Statement by India, para. 5.
21 Ibid., Statement by Canada, para. 20 and by Switzerland, para. 22.
22 Ibid., para. 30.
23 TRIPS Council, Minutes of 28–29 February 2012 Meeting, IP/C/M/69, para. 4.
24 Ibid., Statement by India, para. 5.
25 Ibid., Statement by China, para. 6.
26 Ibid., Statement by Brazil, para. 12.
27 Ibid., Statement by the United States, para. 15.
28 Ibid., Statement by China, para. 25.
29 Ibid., paras. 28–29.
30 The wording of the agenda item was changed so as to refer to "counterfeit trademarks" instead of "goods," at the insistence of developing countries. *See* TRIPS Council, Minutes of 5 June 2012 Meeting, IP/C/M/70, paras. 1–16.

the status of ACTA and its relationship to the TRIPS Agreement. The wording of the agenda item under which ACTA will be most recurrently discussed – IP enforcement trends – ultimately represented a compromise between developing countries which wanted the inclusion of an agenda item on "TRIPS-Plus Enforcement Trends" and ACTA countries which wished to discuss ACTA under an agenda item that would make explicit reference to "Part III of the TRIPS Agreement on Enforcement."

## DEVELOPING COUNTRY CONCERNS ABOUT THE SYSTEMIC IMPLICATIONS OF ACTA AND THE TRIPS-PLUS ENFORCEMENT TREND

Although developing countries did not succeed in adding an item on the TRIPS Council's agenda that would make explicit reference to the "TRIPS-plus enforcement trend," they used the Council's deliberations as a platform to voice their concerns about the systemic implications of the TRIPS-plus enforcement trend in general and ACTA in particular. Yet, this was not the first occasion for developing countries to express concerns about TRIPS-plus enforcement measures at the Council.

In December 2008, a shipment of the generic drug Losartan, produced in India and destined for Brazil, was seized in transit in the Netherlands, and later returned to the country of origin, pursuant to European Communities (EC) Council Customs Regulation No 1383/2003. As a result, in 2009 and 2010, many developing countries voiced their concerns at the TRIPS Council that the implementation of such TRIPS-plus border measures could undermine access to medicines and questioned their consistency with the GATT, the TRIPS Agreement and the Doha Declaration on TRIPS and Public Health. However, such concerns were directed at a specific category of TRIPS-plus measures – border measures – and in many cases at the EC customs regulation more specifically.

In contrast, during discussions of ACTA, developing countries made the most comprehensive and far-reaching criticism of TRIPS-plus standards that the TRIPS Council had witnessed. They argued that "a systematic consideration of TRIPS-plus enforcement trends was needed as the Council was the ultimate custodian of the TRIPS Agreement."[31] Furthermore, they considered that "agreements such as ACTA had the potential to completely upset the balance of rights and obligations of the TRIPS Agreement," and thus the WTO "could not remain a silent observer to such a development."[32]

[31] IP/C/M/63, Statement by Egypt, para. 299.
[32] Ibid., Statement by India, para. 273.

Developing countries' concerns about ACTA's systemic implications focused on four key issues: transparency, limits to TRIPS-plus standards, the impact on the balance in the TRIPS Agreement and the impact on multilateral institutions.

### *Transparency*

Developing countries denounced at length the lack of transparency and inclusiveness of the ACTA negotiating process, pointing to "the lack of transparency and clarity in the process, even for some of the parties involved in the negotiations and their legislatures."[33] For Brazil, the ACTA negotiating process lacked the legitimacy of initiatives conducted in multilateral organizations and "had been conducted in a non-transparent atmosphere of secrecy that was not conducive to trust."[34] Developing countries also explained that concerns over the "poor" transparency record of ACTA were pertinent because of the possible negative spillover effects on countries which were not party to ACTA, particularly as the agreement could encroach on their rights and flexibilities or add to their WTO obligations.[35] Ecuador argued that ACTA violated the basic principles of the United Nations Declaration (1986) on the Right to Development insofar "as the Declaration clearly established the primacy of self-determination and the principle of inclusive participation in multilateral decision-making processes affecting people's economic and social development."[36]

On their part, ACTA countries pointed to some of their efforts with regard to the transparency of the ACTA process such as making publicly available drafts of the negotiating text (since April 2010), the organisation of stakeholder consultations and the regular issuance of press releases, fact sheets and joint statements.[37]

### *Limits to TRIPS-Plus Standards*

Developing countries extensively argued that there were important limitations set by GATT and TRIPS on the ability of WTO members to adopt TRIPS-plus standards. They highlighted that the TRIPS Agreement provided "ceilings, some of which were mandatory and clearly specified in it," in addition to laying certain minimum standards.[38] In this context, developing countries made repeated references to: TRIPS Article 1 (1) which stipulates that "Members may, but shall not be obliged to, implement in their law more extensive protection than is required by

[33] IP/C/M/64, Statement by Egypt, para. 475.
[34] IP/C/M/63, Statement by Brazil, para. 318.
[35] IP/C/M/64, Statement by China, para. 459.
[36] IP/C/M/69, Statement by Ecuador, para. 279.
[37] IP/C/M/67, Statement by the EU, para. 536.
[38] IP/C/M/63, Statement by India, para. 265.

this Agreement, provided that such protection does not contravene the provisions of this Agreement"; the TRIPS' Preamble in which Members express their desire to ensure "that measures and procedures to enforce intellectual property rights do not themselves become barriers to legitimate trade"; and TRIPS Article 41, according to which enforcement procedures "shall be applied in such a manner as to avoid the creation of barriers to legitimate trade and to provide for safeguards against their abuse."

Furthermore, they underlined that TRIPS-plus enforcement standards should not "inappropriately restrict the inbuilt flexibilities and exceptions in the TRIPS Agreement" or "violate other covered agreements under the WTO or be applied in a manner which would constitute a means of arbitrary or unjustifiable discrimination among Members."[39] They further argued that "TRIPS-plus enforcement initiatives, in general and ACTA in particular, could lead to serious trade distortions by creating barriers to legitimate trade in contravention of Article 41 of the TRIPS Agreement."[40]

Developing countries also pointed to the most favoured nation (MFN) clause, emphasising that the MFN provisions of the TRIPS Agreement meant that "any TRIPS-plus protection secured by one trading partner in a regional or a plurilateral trade agreement was *ipso facto* applicable to imports from all WTO Members."[41] India contended that "while GATT and GATS provided for bilateral and multilateral derogations under Articles XXIV and V respectively, there was only a limited derogation from MFN in the TRIPS Agreement that did not apply to new agreements."[42] From the Indian perspective, WTO members might not be allowed to agree on higher enforcement levels "since such levels would impinge on the rights and obligations of Members not party to the plurilateral negotiations."[43]

Beyond the legal limitations on TRIPS-plus standards, developing countries claimed that these standards "had made the international legal framework on IPRs extremely complicated and unpredictable, which might cause an adverse impact on international trade."[44]

Even developing countries which were party to numerous bilateral and regional trade agreements, such as Chile, stated that it was "essential that international intellectual property rules – whether they be bilateral, multilateral or plurilateral – be

39 IP/C/M/63, Statement by China, para. 252.
40 IP/C/M/64, Statement by India, para. 445.
41 Ibid., Statement by India, para. 444.
42 Ibid.
43 IP/C/M/64, Statement by India, para. 444.
44 IP/C/M/63, Statement by China, para. 254.

consistent with the principles and objectives of the TRIPS Agreement and maintain a proper balance."[45]

However, ACTA countries defended the adoption of TRIPS-plus standards, recalling that Article 1(1) of the TRIPS Agreement allowed WTO members to implement "in their law more extensive protection than is required by this Agreement, provided that such protection does not contravene the provisions of this Agreement." They also pointed out that "developing country members already implemented so-called 'TRIPS plus' measures, such as border measures for infringing goods destined for exportation, which showed that it was not appropriate to criticize 'TRIPS-plus' measures in general."[46] The EU emphasized that by combating trade in infringing products, "ACTA promoted legitimate trade."[47]

It is worth noting that most developing countries refrained from pronouncing their stance categorically on ACTA's conformity with TRIPS. In October 2010, India indicated that it "would reserve its final position on this question until the text of ACTA was finalized"[48] but did not ultimately pronounce its opinion on this matter. China affirmed that it was "worth examining the consistency and compatibility between ACTA and the WTO legal framework"[49] but did not pursue it further.

### *The Impact on the Balance in the TRIPS Agreement*

Developing countries expressed recurrent concerns over the impact of TRIPS-plus enforcement initiatives and ACTA on the "very careful balance of interests" established by the TRIPS Agreement between "right holders, on one hand, and societal interests including development oriented concerns, on the other hand."[50] They asserted that TRIPS-plus enforcement trends in regional trade agreements (RTAs), FTAs and ACTA would reduce such balance and make it easier to build "technological barriers, with potential conflict between IP and other institutional arrangements."[51] Such developments were also likely, from their viewpoint, to "disturb the TRIPS balance" and had the potential "to constrain the flexibilities and policy space provided by the Agreement to developing countries (...) particularly in areas like public health, transfer of technology, socio-economic development, promotion of in novation and access to knowledge."[52]

45 Ibid., Statement by Chile, para. 307.
46 IP/C/M/64, Statement by Japan, para. 464.
47 Ibid., Statement by the EU, para. 470.
48 Ibid., Statement by India, para. 441.
49 Ibid., Statement by China, para. 459.
50 IP/C/M/63, para. 265.
51 Ibid., Statement by China, para. 264.
52 Ibid., Statement by India, para. 296.

For Brazil, in addition to being TRIPS-plus, ACTA might "end up being TRIPS-minus to the extent that it contributed to narrowing down the scope for flexibilities."[53] LDCs also shared these concerns, indicating that if higher standards than those set by the TRIPS Agreement were put in place, LDCs would find it difficult to exert TRIPS flexibilities in order to create a level playing field for their infant industries.[54]

One example highlighted by developing countries was the fact that ACTA (Article 23) set to reinterpret the term "commercial scale" with respect to wilful trademark counterfeiting and copyright piracy so as to refer to "commercial activities for direct or indirect economic or commercial advantage." In contrast, the WTO dispute settlement panel in the China Enforcement case was more cautious and flexible, pointing to "counterfeiting or piracy carried on at the magnitude or extent of typical or usual commercial activity with respect to a given product in a given market."[55] The ACTA interpretation, according to developing countries, highlighted "the risk posed to WTO law by turning enforcement matters over to small groups of plurilateral negotiators operating outside the WTO legal framework."[56]

Responding to these apprehensions, ACTA countries underlined that ACTA was an "enforcement treaty, not a substantive treaty, and it would therefore never affect the balance achieved in the TRIPS Agreement between the rights of the right holders and the legitimate goal of disseminating innovations."[57]

They explained they had been "very careful to include language in ACTA that would ensure that the Agreement captured important elements of the balance struck in TRIPS between the use and protection of IP."[58] Australia specifically made references to the mention of TRIPS Articles 7 and 8 in ACTA article 2(3),[59] of TRIPS Articles 41 and 46 in article 6 and of the Doha Declaration on TRIPS and Public Health in the Preamble. Thus, from its viewpoint, "ACTA explicitly preserved and affirmed the important balance and flexibilities contained in the TRIPS Agreement."[60]

However, developing countries did not seem convinced by these explanations. For them, "while the ACTA's Preamble made reference to the Doha Declaration on the TRIPS Agreement and Public Health, the provisions in ACTA pointed to the

53 Ibid., Statement by Brazil, para. 318.
54 IP/C/M/69, Statement by Bangladesh, para. 283.
55 WTO Panel Report, 26 January 2009, *China – Measures affecting the protection and enforcement of Intellectual Property*, WT/DS362/R.(at 7.577). *See* Chapter 6 in this book.
56 IP/C/M/64, Statement by the India, para. 444.
57 IP/C/M/63, Statement by the EU, para. 327.
58 IP/C/M/67, Statement by Australia, para. 504.
59 Article 2(3) of the final ACTA text states that the objectives and principles in Part 1 of the TRIPS Agreement, in particular Articles 7 and 8, were applicable to ACTA.
60 IP/C/M/69, Statement by Australia, para. 254.

opposite direction."[61] They also contended that TRIPS enforcement provisions were themselves "substantive obligations," even if they were only "procedural provisions," and that therefore "elevating the enforcement level did create substantive obligations on Members and consequently had an impact on them.[62]

*The Impact on Multilateral Institutions*

Developing countries expressed strong concerns that ACTA bypassed existing multilateral processes, in particular those provided by the WTO and WIPO.[63] They also considered that ACTA potentially "negated decisions taken multilaterally, such as the Doha Declaration on the TRIPS Agreement and Public Health in the WTO and the Development Agenda in WIPO."[64]

Brazil dwelt on the fact that ACTA carried the potential of establishing a "new international framework" on IPRs enforcement.[65] It pointed to certain provisions in the ACTA text,[66] which might be interpreted as creating "the seeds of a new international unit or organization": chapter 4, which contained elements of international cooperation and capacity building that extended to other international organizations, as well as the private sector and prospective member countries; chapter 5, which created an ACTA Committee with far-reaching powers that could "help institutionalize ACTA as a freestanding, self-evolving forum"[67]; and chapter 6, which foresaw that any WTO member country would be allowed to negotiate its terms of accession and become a party to ACTA. For Brazil, these provisions taken together "contained the necessary ingredients that might convert ACTA into a truly international organization dealing with the enforcement of intellectual property rights, whose impact on WIPO and the WTO, especially on capacity building and technical assistance, was unpredictable at this stage."[68]

Ecuador voiced concern that while the "draft ACTA text stated that accession was voluntary, there was a danger that the TRIPS-plus provisions would be transferred to developing countries through bilateral and regional free trade agreements."[69]

[61] IP/C/M/64, Statement by India, para. 448.
[62] IP/C/M/63, Statement by China, para. 332.
[63] IP/C/M/64, Statement by India paras. 444–446. On this issue, *see* S. Bannerman. *WIPO and the ACTA Threat.* PIJIP Research Paper no. 4. American University Washington College of Law, 2010. Washington, DC.
[64] IP/C/M/64, Statement by India, para. 449.
[65] *See* Chapter 11 in this volume; *see also* A. Abdel-Latif, ACTA: Original Expectations and Future Implications, *Bridges*, Volume 14, Number 4, ICTSD, December 2010.
[66] ACTA Text of 2 October 2010.
[67] *See* Chapter 8 in this volume.
[68] IP/C/M/64, Statement by Brazil, para. 451.
[69] Ibid., Statement by Ecuador, para. 476.

ACTA countries refuted such criticisms, underlining that circumventing the WTO had not been the intention of ACTA negotiations.[70] They recalled their preference for dealing with enforcement at the WTO and WIPO. However, previous opposition by some developing countries had led them to pursue such discussions outside the WTO.[71] Australia believed that ACTA "complemented" existing intellectual property enforcement standards, including the TRIPS Agreement,[72] and pointed to ACTA's preamble which mentions the desire of parties that the agreement operates "in a manner mutually supportive of international enforcement work and co-operation conducted within relevant international organisations."[73]

## SOME REFLECTIONS ON DEVELOPING COUNTRY CONTESTATION OF ACTA

Was the contestation of ACTA by developing countries effective? As previously mentioned, it is unlikely that the concerns of developing countries about ACTA would have led, on its own, to ACTA's subsequent de facto demise, which resulted more directly from the stalemate faced by the ratification process in a number of countries. This was most noticeably the case in the EU where the European Parliament refused, on 4 July 2012, to give its consent, as a result of widespread political and civil society opposition across European countries.

Nevertheless, developing countries' contestation of ACTA at the WTO TRIPS Council proved to be a potent argument in the debate on the agreement in several signatory countries. The study commissioned by the European Parliament to assess ACTA amply echoed the concerns expressed by developing countries at the Council. It then concluded by stating:

> What the debate and discussion at the TRIPS Council shows is that there is not simply a lack of interest in the ACTA on the part of significant developing countries, but that there is active opposition to the perceived goals and the standards that ACTA aimed to achieve. This may present an insurmountable obstacle to their participation in ACTA, or in ACTA-related processes.[74]

Civil society groups also exposed the fallacy of the ACTA official narrative mentioned earlier. As described by one group, European Digital Rights (EDRi), "[T]he secrecy and exclusionary nature of the negotiations, as well as the rejection

70 IP/C/M/63, Statement by the EU, para. 326.
71 IP/C/M/64, Statement by the EU, 469.
72 Ibid., Statement by Australia, para. 467.
73 Ibid., Statement by Australia, para. 468.
74 A. Kamperman et al., op. cit., p. 17.

of agreed multilateral forums have served to alienate exactly those countries that were the ultimate target of ACTA."[75]

At the level of the ACTA text itself, it is interesting to note that the first ACTA text to be made publicly available, in April 2010, did not contain many of the public policy–related references that were later introduced.[76] Mention of TRIPS Articles 7 (objectives) and 8 (principles) as well as reference to the Doha Declaration on TRIPS and Public Health only began to appear in the October 2010 ACTA text,[77] after the 8–9 June 2010 session of the TRIPS Council where developing countries expressed, for the first time, numerous specific and systemic concerns about ACTA and its implications in terms of public policy objectives. Thus, there is reasonable ground to believe that some of the changes to the ACTA text were made in response to these concerns, in addition to those emanating from civil society groups.

Developing countries did not only content themselves with contesting ACTA and the TRIPS-plus enforcement trend; they also made specific proposals to address them. China, for example, suggested that the TRIPS Council adopt a number of principles, already enshrined in the TRIPS Agreement, with which any WTO member party to such agreements should comply. These principles were the following: (1) the IP chapter or provisions of an RTA, FTA or regional agreement to which a WTO member was party shall not be inconsistent with the TRIPS Agreement; (2) the enforcement of IPRs shall not create distortive effects on legitimate international trade; and (3) no WTO member shall be restrained from the autonomy for utilizing its public enforcement resources.[78]

It is worth noting that several policy and scholarly writings have sought to build and elaborate further on such proposals. It has been suggested, for instance, that the TRIPS Council should "have a say" on IPRs provisions in Preferential Trade Agreements (PTAs) as it would be "a legitimate undertaking to consider how new agreements are fully consistent with TRIPS in line with the prescriptions of Article 1 (1)."[79] This would contribute to "decrease tensions and make PTAs more palatable as an integral part of the system and a genuine spinoff of TRIPS."[80] More recently, a group of experts and academics has

[75] EDRI, ACTA Fact Sheet, February 2012.

[76] Anti-Counterfeiting Trade Agreement, Consolidated Text, April 2010.

[77] Anti-Counterfeiting Trade Agreement, Consolidated Text, 2nd October 2010.

[78] IP/C/M/63, Statement by China, para. 259.

[79] P. Roffe, Intellectual Property, Preferential Trade Agreements and the Multilateral System, in ICTSD (2012) *The Future and the WTO: Confronting the Challenges. A Collection of Short Essays*; ICTSD Programme on Global Economic Policy and Institutions, Geneva, Switzerland pp. 60–63.

[80] Ibid.

proposed a series of "Principles for Intellectual Property Provisions in Bilateral and Regional Agreements."[81] Several of these principles echo the ones suggested by China or arguments made by developing countries during the ACTA debate at the TRIPS Council.

Overall, it appears that the contestation of ACTA by developing countries has contributed to a heightened awareness that the WTO in general, and the TRIPS Council in particular, should not remain a "silent observer" in face of the proliferation of TRIPS-plus standards in bilateral and regional FTAs, and plurilaterals such as ACTA, and that the question of the conformity of such standards with the WTO and the TRIPS Agreement merited close examination.

Beyond what the mobilisation of developing countries contributed to achieve, it also brought into light some of the weaknesses that have characterised the involvement of developing countries in international IP debates. One such weakness is the gap between the positions taken by developing countries at the multilateral level and their implementation of IP standards at the domestic level. Several scholarly works have now well documented this gap,[82] which also manifested itself during the discussions on ACTA at the TRIPS Council.

Several ACTA countries pointed out, during these discussions, that some vocal critics among developing countries already implemented several ACTA provisions in their domestic legislations. For instance, the United States indicated that India's customs legislation – Notification No. 47/2007 – Customs (N.T.) – appeared to implement numerous ACTA provisions such as Article 16(1) (a) on ex officio authority for customs officials, mirrored by Article 7(1)(b) of the Notification and Article 15 on the provision of information from rights holders to customs officials, which could be found in Article 7(5). Furthermore, the Notification covered copyright, trademark, designs and patents.[83]

The United States also made reference to several areas where Chinese law closely followed ACTA provisions, mentioning in particular provisions on damages and statutory damages. According to the United States, Article 65 of China's Patent Law, Article 56 of China's Trademark Law and Article 49 of China's Copyright Law aligned closely with ACTA Article 9.[84]

81 Max Planck Institute for Intellectual Property and Competition, "Principles for Intellectual Property Provisions in Bilateral and Regional Agreements," 2013.

82 C. Deere, *The Implementation Game: The TRIPS Agreement and the Global Politics of Intellectual Property Reform in Developing Countries*, Oxford: Oxford University Press, 2008.

83 IP/C/M/63, Statement by the United States, para. 259.

84 IP/C/M/67, Statement by the United States, para. 535.

Ultimately, the United States found it "curious that Members opposed ACTA because it was TRIPS-plus on one hand, but implemented ACTA provisions in their law on the other."[85] However the presence of TRIPS-plus standards in domestic legislations of developing countries does not necessarily imply that these countries should accept them when included in an international agreement, such as ACTA, because they would then become subject to monitoring and dispute settlement. In addition, it would become more difficult for these countries to amend their national legislations if they wished to backtrack from these TRIPS-plus standards. Nevertheless, this shows that developing countries need to pay closer attention to ensuring greater coherence between their positions at the multilateral level and their domestic implementation of IPRs, a long-standing challenge faced by many of these countries.[86]

Another area that exposed some possible weakness in developing countries' positions concerned their overall approach to discussions on IPRs enforcement at the WTO. The United States, the EU, Japan and Switzerland had raised IPRs enforcement at the TRIPS Council's in eight successive meetings in 2005, 2006 and 2007. On these occasions, developing countries, particularly China, India and Brazil, were reluctant to include an agenda item on the topic and to engage substantively on the issues raised. They repeatedly stated that this "enforcement was essentially a matter of domestic policy making and priority setting that had no place on the agenda of the Council."[87] They further argued that its acceptance during those years of an agenda item on enforcement was not meant to signal approval as a "permanent agenda item for the Council."[88] India and Brazil suggested that the sharing of national experiences on enforcement could instead take place at WIPO's Advisory Committee on Enforcement, which had been specifically designed for that purpose.

Later on, developing countries sought to discuss ACTA and the TRIPS-plus trend at the June and October 2010 sessions of the TRIPS Council. However, they subsequently manifested their reservation, in 2011, to the wish of ACTA countries to present the final agreement at the Council. As put by China, "given that ACTA did not form part of the WTO legal framework, it was not appropriate for the Council to discuss it."[89]

Developing countries had several procedural and substantive grounds to justify their positions and they defended the consistency of their approach. Such grounds ranged from a refusal to see enforcement become a permanent item on the TRIPS

[85] Ibid., Statement by the United States, para. 533.

[86] A. Abdel-Latif, *Developing Country Developing Country Coordination in Intellectual Property Standard-Setting*, TRADE Working Paper 24, Geneva: South Centre, 2005.

[87] IP/C/M/63, Statement by Brazil, para. 316.

[88] Ibid., Statement by India, para. 333.

[89] IP/C/M/69, Statement by China, para. 293.

Council's agenda to a belief that the Council did not have any mandate to adopt recommendations or best practices on enforcement, which they saw as the ultimate goal of the move by industrialised countries to discuss enforcement in the years 2005–2007. When raising ACTA at the Council in 2010, China and India contrasted their initiative with the earlier attempts of industrialised countries by underlining that their move came "in the systemic context of the TRIPS Agreement and not in the context of experience sharing of best practices."[90]

Nevertheless, it remains that the logic of the positions adopted by developing countries are not always easy to follow or understand by outside observers.[91] At the same time, these positions fed to some extent into the argument advanced by industrialised countries that the stalemate on enforcement discussions, at the WTO and WIPO, led them to consider other venues such as ACTA. While this argument has some resonance, it should not be taken at face value as it "it oversimplifies the complex politics behind the formation of the new ACTA country club." [92] Nevertheless, the question begs to be asked about whether developing countries could have taken a different approach.

The comparison might be useful here with international discussions on IP and genetic resources, traditional knowledge and folklore. Though industrialised countries tend to have defensive interests in this area, they have nevertheless accepted to engage substantively in discussions on these issues at the WTO and WIPO. Yet, deliberations at these forums have not reached any normative outcome despite having begun more than a decade ago. In the case of enforcement, it is possible that industrialised countries would have, in any case, opted for an ACTA-type process if the TRIPS Council discussions had not moved quickly enough in the direction they wished for. However developing countries would have at least deprived ACTA countries from one of the arguments they used to justify the ACTA process.

Looking into the future, it remains to be seen whether developing countries will continue to raise the systemic implications of the TRIPS-plus trend, particularly as the Transpacific Partnership (TPP) Agreement currently under negotiation seems to include ambitious IP provisions which are even more far-reaching than the ACTA ones are. At the TRIPS Council deliberations of October 2011, some developing countries voiced their concerns about the TPP. India mentioned that the agreement

[90] IP/C/M/63, Statement by India, para. 333.

[91] It is also challenging to follow, in some cases, the consistency of positions taken by ACTA countries. For instance, when at the June 2010 TRIPS Council session, India and China, proposed to discuss ACTA and TRIPS-plus enforcement, they considered the agenda item suggested to go beyond Part III of the TRIPS Agreement concentrating on elements outside TRIPS and the WTO. However, when they sought to discuss ACTA at the October 2011 session of the Council, after the agreement was concluded, they requested the addition of an agenda item that made reference to Part III of the TRIPS Agreement.

[92] P. Yu, op. cit, p. 12.

could seriously hamper public health efforts in developing countries.[93] Ecuador requested clarification from one of the members that were taking part in the TPP negotiations "to inform the Council as to the extent IP matters that were being negotiated in that forum were more restrictive than the provisions that were set out in ACTA and in the free trade agreements that the participants in that process had agreed to amongst themselves."[94]

However, developing countries so far have not engaged at the TRIPS Council in a substantive discussion about the TPP in a similar manner as they have done with ACTA. This might be explained by the fact that there are many more developing countries taking part in the TPP negotiations compared to the few ones involved in the ACTA process.

## CONCLUSION

For several years, there has been speculation about whether the increasing use of IP in many developing countries, in particular emerging economies, would change their approach to IP issues at the international level and lead them to align themselves with the practices and positions of industrialised countries. In other words, would developing countries "lead" or "follow" in IP in the twenty-first century?[95] While it might still be premature to bring categorical answers to this question, in the case of ACTA developing countries chose not to follow.

Emerging economies in particular saw in ACTA a hostile move by industrialised countries seeking to amplify their competitive advantage in a changing world economy where their manufacturing base was being eroded to the benefit of these emerging countries. As India put it, "TRIPS-plus measures like ACTA sought to introduce a new set of non-tariff barriers to trade that would preponderantly hinder developing country exports" as "goods and services of developing countries were becoming competitive with those of developed country producers."[96]

Although the final text of ACTA was ultimately less ambitious and its provisions less far-reaching compared to the earlier versions, developing countries still considered that ACTA could have major "systemic" repercussions. In particular, this included the "destabilisation" of TRIPS, stripping it of some of "its authority,

[93] IP/C/M/67, Statement by India, para. 517.

[94] Ibid., para. 524.

[95] H. Reichmann, Intellectual Property in the Twenty First Century: Will the Developing Countries Lead or Follow?, *Houston Law Review* 2009 46(4): 1115–1185.

[96] IP/C/M/63, Statement by India, para. 273.

prestige and legitimacy"[97] and the creation of new international enforcement framework that could undermine both the WTO and WIPO.

In this context, developing countries seized the opportunity of ACTA to question more broadly, and in a rather unprecedented manner, the systemic implications resulting from the proliferation of TRIPS-plus standards in regional and bilateral agreements. The use of the TRIPS Council as a platform for such contestation is noteworthy. Emerging economies such as China, India and Brazil were at the forefront of this contestation. This certainly makes ACTA a landmark in efforts by emerging economies to challenge TRIPS-plus initiatives. The future will tell if developing countries will continue such efforts to address even more challenging developments, such as the TPP, or whether the mobilisation on ACTA was an exceptional, one-shot exercise. In any case, the contestation of ACTA will remain an important milestone in the growing assertiveness of developing countries, particularly emerging economies, in the global intellectual property landscape and in global economic governance more generally.

97 J. Atik, ACTA and the Destabilization of TRIPS, in Hans Henrik Lidgard, Jeffery Atik, and Tu Thahn Nguyen, eds., *Sustainable Technology Transfer, Guide to Global Aid & Trade Development*, Berlin: Kluwer, 2012.

# 26

# ACTA: What Lessons for Future Plurilateral Trade Agreements?

*Ricardo Meléndez-Ortiz and Ahmed Abdel-Latif*

## INTRODUCTION

The stalemate in the Doha round of multilateral trade negotiations has moved plurilateral agreements, as a means to advance trade liberalisation, to the centre stage of the trade policy agenda. Concrete proposals have been recently made, and initiatives launched, for the negotiation of plurilateral trade agreements in the areas of green goods[1] and services.[2] However, the reflection on plurilateral trade agreements seem to have been insufficiently informed by the experience of the Anti-Counterfeiting Trade Agreement (ACTA).

Yet, ACTA remains the only major plurilateral trade agreement which has been recently negotiated and concluded outside the WTO. It became the subject of a controversial debate. Ultimately, the refusal of the European Parliament, in June 2012, to give its consent compromised its future political viability.

At the WTO and WIPO, developing countries are sometimes perceived as standing in the way of reaching consensual outcomes and concluding new agreements. Yet the fatal blow to ACTA, an agreement mostly among industrialized countries, came primarily from domestic stakeholders in these countries. Against this background, ACTA negotiations offer valuable lessons for the design and negotiation of plurilateral trade agreements. The purpose of this chapter is to identify some of these lessons and to contribute to the broader discussion on plurilaterals in the WTO context.

[1] On 8 July 2014, fourteen WTO members (Australia, Canada, China, Costa Rica, Chinese Taipei, the European Union, Hong Kong China, Japan, Korea, New Zealand, Norway, Singapore, Switzerland and the United States) announced the launch of negotiations on the Environmental Goods Agreement (EGA), to achieve their shared goal of global free trade in environmental goods.

[2] Negotiations on a plurilateral agreement on trade in services, known as the Trade in Services Agreement (TISA) began in early 2012. As of September 2013, participants in the TISA reached twenty-three countries. *See* Services Talks Advance as TISA Members Prepare to Exchange Offers, *Bridges Weekly Trade News Digest*, Volume 17, Number 31, 26 September 2013.

In this regard, the lessons can be divided into two groups. A first set of lessons concerns the general principles that should guide the negotiation of plurilateral agreements such as the need for a persuasive narrative, transparency, consultations with a broad range of stakeholders and impartial evidence. The second set of lessons concerns how plurilateral agreements should relate to the multilateral framework, in particular whether they should be concluded within the WTO or outside of it and the relationship between substantive standards incorporated in these agreements and existing WTO norms and rules.

## LESSONS IN TERMS OF THE PRINCIPLES AND PROCESS FOR THE NEGOTIATION OF PLURILATERAL AGREEMENTS

### *The Narrative*

When a group of countries and stakeholders wishes to pursue a plurilateral agreement, a persuasive narrative is desirable. This narrative should clearly spell out the agreement's objectives and ensure consistency between these objectives and the actions taken to advance them. On this account, the narrative behind ACTA was problematic since the very beginning. ACTA's declared objective was to address more effectively piracy of intellectual property rights (IPRs) and counterfeiting at the global level. Industrialised countries expressed their wish to see emerging economies and developing countries join the agreement. For instance, the European Commission stated, in May 2010, that the objective was that "large emerging economies, where IPR enforcement could be improved, will sign up to the agreement. In light of the growing international consensus on IPR enforcement, the Commission is confident that more countries will join ACTA."[3]

If this was the case, why weren't emerging economies at any point, formally invited to be part of the ACTA process or were seriously engaged with? Ultimately, only Mexico, Morocco, Singapore and the United Arab Emirates (UAE) ever participated at any point in ACTA negotiations and signed the agreement (with the exception of the UAE). Most of these countries have in common that they have concluded bilateral trade agreements with the United States, which already contain strong provisions on IPRs that go beyond those agreed in TRIPS (often referred to as TRIPS-plus).

When it became clear that a great number of countries particularly emerging economies were openly hostile to ACTA and it would be unlikely for them to be

3 European Commission, Follow-up to the European Parliament Resolution on the transparency and state of play of the ACTA negotiations, adopted by the European Commission on 12 May 2010.

ever joining it, ACTA stood on even weaker grounds. Improving IPRs enforcement could also be achieved through other means such as capacity-building and awareness-raising activities. Why was an agreement needed to harmonise enforcement practices between industrialised countries which already had high levels of IPRs enforcement and robust cooperation in this area?[4]

Furthermore, the arguments in favour of ACTA were strikingly similar to those that had been made more than twenty years earlier for the conclusion of the TRIPS Agreement itself, which had its origin in a proposal for an "anti-counterfeiting code" first tabled during the Tokyo round.[5] The TRIPS Agreement was the first international IP agreement to incorporate an "enforcement pillar" and to be backed by the powerful WTO dispute settlement mechanism. So why didn't ACTA countries use more widely this mechanism if they considered that levels of IPRs enforcement in some countries, particularly emerging economies, were not satisfactory or not compliant with their TRIPS obligations in this area?[6] ACTA countries struggled in responding to these questions during the entire negotiating process.

As it has been argued elsewhere in this volume, the prospect of an agreement targeting some countries but negotiated without their participation could only mean that it was intended to be a fait accompli, a "country club" agreement that new members would join based on membership rules already established and difficult to change.[7] Noting that ACTA does not include the emerging economies that are perceived to be the main sources of counterfeit products, even the study requested by the European Parliament to asses ACTA considered that it was "not clear what incentive such emerging markets would have to accede to ACTA."[8]

In this regard, the ACTA experience shows that promoters of a plurilateral agreement need to build a solid and coherent narrative that spells out the problem this agreement intends to address, the specific objectives it seeks to achieve and why the proposed agreement is the most appropriate means for doing so.

4 *See* Introduction to the volume, which elaborates on this particular aspect of the agreement.

5 C. Wadlow, "'Including trade in counterfeit goods': The origins of TRIPs as a GATT anti-counterfeiting code", *Intellectual Property Quarterly* 3 (2007): 350–402.

6 With the notable exception of China – Measures affecting the protection and enforcement of Intellectual Property. WT/DS362/R, 2009.

7 *See* Chapter 25 in this volume. The term "country club" is from D. Gervais, Country clubs, empiricism, blogs and innovation: the future of international intellectual property law making in the wake of ACTA, in *Trade Governance in the Digital Age: World Trade Forum*, Mira Burri and Thomas Cottier (eds.), Cambridge University Press, 2012.

8 Kamperman et al., The Anti-Counterfeiting Trade Agreement (ACTA): An Assessment, European Parliament Directorate-General for External Policies, 2011, p. 15.

### *Transparency*

Transparency was one of the thorny issues raised in the context of the ACTA negotiation process.[9] Civil society groups and a number of academics contended that the ACTA process lacked transparency pointing to the fact that the first ACTA negotiating text was made publicly available only in May 2010, almost three years after the negotiations had formally started in 2008.[10] The European Parliament also expressed its "concern over the lack of a transparent process in the conduct of the ACTA negotiations" and called on the Commission and the Council "to grant public and parliamentary access to ACTA negotiation texts and summaries."[11]

ACTA countries defended themselves against such criticisms, underlining their keenness "to provide as much transparency as possible within the bounds imposed by a negotiating process among States."[12] They also pointed to the release of fact sheets, the holding of press briefings and consultations with domestic stakeholders as examples of efforts to ensure transparency.[13]

However, there were also differences of views among ACTA countries regarding some aspects of transparency, particularly the appropriate timing to release the ACTA negotiating text, a decision that was subject to the unanimous agreement of all negotiating parties. Some countries, such as the United States, withheld their agreement until a late stage in the negotiations.[14] The first ACTA text to be released was made publicly available in May 2010, only a few months before the final round of negotiations held in October of the same year in Tokyo.

The issue of transparency in international trade negotiations is a complex one and an ongoing challenge. It has been raised in the context of the WTO negotiations as well as regional and bilateral trade agreements, more recently the Transpacific Partnership (TPP) negotiations. One key challenge resides in how to achieve a balance between confidentiality and openness.

International negotiations sometimes require some level of confidentiality, at a certain point, to be effective. Full transparency is unlikely to be achieved in any negotiation, even at the multilateral level, at the WTO or WIPO. Informal consultations involving smaller groups of countries are often critical in reaching

9 See the discussion on transparency in the Introduction and Chapter 24 of this volume. *See also* P. Yu, Six Secret (and Now Open) Fears of ACTA (2011) 64 *SMU Law Review* 975: 998–1019.

10 D. Levine, "Transparency Soup: The ACTA Negotiating Process and 'Black Box' Lawmaking", *American University International Law Review* 26 no. 3 (2011): 811–837.

11 European Parliament, Resolution on the transparency and state of play of the ACTA negotiations, 10 March 2010.

12 USTR, ACTA Fact Sheet, March 2010.

13 *See*, for instance, European Commission, Transparency of ACTA negotiations, European Commission – MEMO/12/99, 13/02/2012.

14 *See* Chapter 24 in this volume.

agreements that would be later endorsed by the entire membership of both these multilateral organizations. Often little transpires about what happens at these informal consultations.

In its closing statement at the WIPO Diplomatic Conference to Conclude a Treaty to Facilitate Access to Published Works by Visually Impaired Persons and Persons with Print Disabilities held in Marrakech (17–28 June 2013), a certain nongovernmental organisation regretted that "nearly all negotiations on the text took place either off the record, or in secret." However, it also pointed out that the public had "access to negotiating text, sometimes on a daily or even twice daily basis" and thus was able to provide feedback. The agreement resulted from this process had "more legitimacy."[15] It is ultimately debatable whether the expectations about transparency should be the same in a multilateral setting as in a bilateral, regional or plurilateral setting[16] given the inherent differences between institutionalised forums with universal membership and specific rules governing transparency and those processes limited to a group of like-minded countries, which result in the conclusion of one specific agreement.

Ultimately, the "controversy" surrounding transparency contributed to derailing ACTA as it undermined trust, particularly among civil society and public opinion and fuelled speculation about the reach and implications of the provisions being negotiated. Efforts by ACTA parties to address these concerns, particularly in the last stages of the negotiations, were, rightly or wrongly, perceived as being too little, too late. As stated by the study requested by the European Parliament to assess ACTA,

> The decision to maintain secrecy until the release of draft text in mid-2010 was to prove a significant handicap to public understanding and support for the treaty. The secrecy allowed significant misapprehensions to develop, while making it difficult for negotiators to communicate the actual scale and content of what was being achieved.[17]

The ACTA experience shows the need to address transparency concerns from the start of the negotiating process rather than to adopt a "reactive" and "defensive" posture when the process is more advanced. The public release of the negotiating text, as soon as possible in the negotiation process, emerges as an important measure in responding to transparency demands.

[15] KEI, Closing statement, Marrakesh Treaty to Facilitate Access to Published Works for Persons who are Blind, Visually Impaired, or Otherwise Print Disabled, 23 June 2013.

[16] The argument is also made by Sean Flynn: S. Flynn, WIPO Treaty for the Blind Shows That Transparency Can Work (and Is Necessary), *Inside View, IP Watch*, 26 June 2013.

[17] Kamperman et al., op. cit., p. 6.

*Consultations with a broad range of domestic stakeholders*

One of the criticisms directed towards the ACTA process, in particular by civil society groups, was the lack of sufficient and appropriate consultations with a broad range of stakeholders and the late stage at which these consultations took place. On their part, ACTA countries pointed out that their negotiators "had invited, met and extensively debriefed NGOs, academia and representatives from political parties such as the Pirate Party during the last four rounds of negotiations."[18]

Public information sessions and briefings by parties negotiating plurilateral agreements are certainly useful and informative in terms of outreach and transparency. Promoters of plurilateral agreements seem increasingly aware of that. In April 2014, countries negotiating the "Trade in Services Agreement" (TiSA) participated in a public information session, held in Geneva, where they presented an overview of the objectives and main elements of the negotiations, the progress that has been made as well as perspectives on new approaches to services negotiations.

At the same time, such public information sessions and briefings often do not amount to the level of formal consultations through which stakeholders, and in particular civil society groups, can make written proposals and submissions regarding the issues being considered. In this regard, concerns were also expressed during ACTA negotiations that preferential access to the negotiations was given to industry groups to the detriment of other constituencies. In the US, members of the Industry Trade Advisory Committee on Intellectual Property Rights[19] were consulted on the content of the draft ACTA agreement, with a number of companies receiving copies of the draft agreement under a non-disclosure agreement.[20] On its part, the European Commission denied having provided "any kind of preferential access to information to any group of stakeholders, be it from industry, trade unions or from other stakeholders."[21]

In any case, the need for countries engaged in plurilateral and regional trade negotiations to undertake consultations with a broad range of domestic stakeholders on the substantive issues raised, and not just mere briefings, emerges as one of the important lessons from the ACTA process. Such consultations, coupled with greater transparency, have multiple advantages in terms of strengthening the legitimacy

[18] European Commission, op.cit, 2012.

[19] The Industry Trade Advisory Committees (ITACs) are jointly administered by the Department of Commerce and the United States Trade Representative (USTR). They provide a unique public-private forum to ensure industry has a voice in formulating the trade policy of the United States (*see* http://www.ustr.gov/about-us/advisory-committees/industry-trade-advisory-committees-itac).

[20] G. Hinze, EFF and PK to Congress: U.S. Trade Advisory Committee Needs Technology Users' Input, 6 August 2009.

[21] European Commission, Transparency of ACTA negotiations, op cit.

of the negotiating process, enriching the texts being negotiated, addressing public interest concerns and facilitating the implementation of the negotiated outcomes.

Some ACTA Parties seem to acknowledge this. In its revised strategy for the protection and enforcement of IPRs in third countries (2014), the European Commission recognizes that one of the reasons for ACTA's rejection was "a view that public concerns had not been sufficiently taken into account (…) and recommends improving interaction 'not only with right-holders, but also with public authorities, civil society and the European Parliament' (…)."[22]

In the context of negotiations on the Transatlantic Trade and Investment Partnership Agreement (TTIP), it is worthwhile noting that the European Commission has undertaken broad consultations at an early stage of the process. In March 2014, less than a year after the launch of these negotiations, the Commission carried out an online public consultation on investment protection and investor-to-state dispute settlement (ISDS). The key issue of the consultation was whether the EU's proposed approach for TTIP achieves the right balance between protecting investors and safeguarding the EU's ability to regulate in the public interest. According to the preliminary report on the consultations, a total of 149 399 online contributions were received with the vast majority (99.62%) by individuals. In addition, 569 organizations responded to the consultation (many of these being NGOs).[23]

In the same vein, the European Commission had launched public consultations on the TiSA negotiations (which were completed in September 2013) and it has most recently carried out public consultations on the Environmental Goods Agreement (EGA) negotiations, which were formally launched in July 2014.

### *Impartial Evidence*

Countries and stakeholders wishing to pursue a plurilateral agreement should advance solid, objective and impartial evidence if they want to be credible in making the case for this agreement.

In the case of ACTA, while many countries, agreed that piracy and counterfeiting were important challenges, they diverged on the real magnitude and scale of the problem.

ACTA countries relied mostly on data and evidence provided by the OECD, national enforcement agencies and industry groups to point to the severity of the global counterfeiting and piracy problem and the need to address it. For instance,

[22] European Commission, Trade, growth and intellectual property – Strategy for the protection and enforcement of intellectual property rights in third countries, Communication from the Commission to the European Parliament, the Council and the European Economic and Social Committee, 2014.

[23] European Commission, Preliminary Report, Online Public Consultation on Investment Protection and Investor-to State Dispute Settlement (ISDS), 2014, at http://trade.ec.europa.eu/consultations/index.cfm?consul_id=179.

recurrent references were made by these countries, during TRIPS Council deliberations, to an OECD study which estimated that annual trade in counterfeit and pirated products accounted for more than US$200 billion in recent years.[24] According to Canada, "numerous statistics existed, including from the OECD, demonstrating the growth of this illegal activity which undermined legitimate trade, threatened sustainable development of the global economy, and in some cases posed a risk to public health and safety."[25]

A number of developing countries contested the accuracy of such data and considered it as self-serving. In a discussion at the TRIPS Council concerning securing supply chains against counterfeit trademarks, China indicated it had "serious doubts" regarding the authenticity of the data provided by the United States and Japan.[26] Civil society groups also pointed out to studies that emphasized the economic value of "fair use" as well as exceptions and limitations more broadly, stressing that ACTA's possible detrimental effect on them could also have negative economic consequences for innovation and knowledge diffusion.[27]

Interestingly, during the same time period that ACTA was the subject of global attention, little attention was paid to deliberations at the WIPO Advisory Committee on Enforcement (ACE) which was discussing a number of matters, including the measurement and economic effects of piracy and counterfeiting. Several studies submitted to the Committee's different sessions on these issues tended to underline the challenges in seeking to measure piracy and counterfeiting accurately.[28] One of these studies, authored by a group of prominent academics and experts, including WIPO's Chief Economist, states that most existing studies seeking to quantify the extent of counterfeiting or piracy at the aggregate – sectoral or economy-wide – level have "serious shortcomings, both concerning the data employed and the adopted methodologies. More importantly, aggregate estimates of the incidence of piracy and counterfeiting by themselves offer policymakers little guidance about appropriate IP enforcement policies."[29]

[24] TRIPS Council, Minutes of 8–9 June 2010 Meeting, Statement by the United States, para. 280, IP/C/M/63. The OECD study in question is: OECD, The Economic Impact of Counterfeiting and Piracy, 2008.

[25] TRIPS Council, Minutes of 26–27 October 2010 Meeting, Statement by Canada, para. 465, IP/C/M/64.

[26] TRIPS Council, Minutes of 5 June 2012 Meeting, Statement by China, para. 179, IP/C/M/70.

[27] CCIA, Fair Use in the US economy, 2011.

[28] C. Fink, K. Maskus and Y. Qian, The Economic Effects of Counterfeiting and Piracy: A Literature Review, WIPO/ACE/6/7. L. Yager, Observations on Efforts to Quantify the Economic Effects of Counterfeited and Pirated Goods, WIPO WIPO/ACE/6/4. C. Clift. A Review of Statistical Information on Counterfeiting and Piracy, WIPO/ACE/7/5.

[29] Fink et al., op. cit., p. 24.

Grounding the drive for a plurilateral agreement in solid and impartial empirical data can help to build the case for such an agreement, even though it might require more time and efforts. To the contrary, relying on partial and contested data can undermine it. This seems one of the key lessons to be drawn from the ACTA process in this regard.

## LESSONS IN TERMS OF THE RELATIONSHIP WITH MULTILATERAL FRAMEWORKS AND RULES

The relationship with the multilateral trading system is one of the key issues facing the design and conduct of any plurilateral agreement. Should the plurilateral agreement be concluded within the WTO framework or outside of it? How would it relate to existing WTO rules?[30] These matters were raised in the ACTA context and are examined more closely in the following section.

### *Within or Outside the WTO?*

The possibility of concluding issue-specific plurilateral trade agreements under the WTO exists, as exemplified by the Information Technology Agreement (ITA), the Government Procurement Agreement (GPA) or the Agreement on Trade in Civil Aircraft. These last two agreements were made part of the WTO by adding them to Annex 4 of the WTO Marrakech agreement. Under Article II.3 of the WTO agreement, such agreements are part of the overall WTO regime "for those Members that have accepted them, and are binding on those Members." Under Article X.9 of the WTO agreement, "The Ministerial Conference, upon the request of the Members parties to a trade agreement, may decide by consensus to add that agreement to Annex 4."[31]

One of the main criticisms directed at ACTA was that it was concluded outside the established multilateral frameworks of the WTO and WIPO.

For some, making ACTA a plurilateral agreement under the WTO would be "a way to move forward within the WTO without the need for a consensus among all WTO Members."[32] It is premised on the argument that the consensus required for adding ACTA to Annex 4 should not be an obstacle: "[W]hy should some WTO Members object if other WTO Members wish to negotiate WTO-plus obligations

[30] *See* M. Kennedy, Legal Options for a Sustainable Energy Trade Agreement, ICTSD, 2012.

[31] There are currently only two "plurilateral" agreements included in this Annex: the Agreement on Government Procurement and the Agreement on Civil Aircraft.

[32] J. Baccus, A Way Forward for the WTO, in *ICTSD, The Future and the WTO: Confronting the Challenges*. A Collection of Short Essays, 2012, pp. 8–9.

that will not bind them unless they choose to be bound by them?"[33] However, this argument does not take sufficiently into consideration the fact that several non-ACTA countries have expressed misgivings about ACTA's conformity with WTO rules and apprehension that it could have effects on third parties, in particular countries which are not parties to it.

There are clear advantages in concluding a plurilateral trade agreement within the WTO, most notably that the WTO Dispute Settlement Understanding (DSU) would automatically apply.[34] Although it seems challenging, at the present moment, promoters of plurilateral agreements might consider starting off by making a serious effort in this direction. This would signal a desire of inclusiveness and help to diffuse criticisms regarding "forum shifting". Interestingly, the fourteen WTO members (Australia, Canada, China, Costa Rica, Chinese Taipei, the European Union, Hong Kong China, Japan, Korea, New Zealand, Norway, Singapore, Switzerland and the United States) that announced, on 8 July 2014 negotiations on an Environmental Goods Agreement (EGA) seem to have taken this direction drawing the lessons from having had the ACTA process outside the multilateral framework. In their statement announcing the launch of the negotiations which took place at WTO premises, they characterised their move as a "WTO initiative" that "will strengthen the rules-based multilateral trading system" and benefit all WTO Members, "including by involving all major traders and applying the principle of Most Favoured Nation, once a critical mass of Members agree to participate."[35]

### *The Relationship with Existing Multilateral Trade Rules*

Any plurilateral agreement to which a WTO member is a party "must be WTO consistent even it is negotiated and concluded outside the WTO."[36] Yet, the first public draft of ACTA, released in May 2010, did not include almost any language that would clarify the agreement's relationship with the most relevant existing multilateral rules, namely those of the TRIPS Agreement.[37] Article 1.1 of that text only included a general provision on relations to other agreements, which stated that "[n]othing in this Agreement shall derogate from any international obligation of a

[33] Ibid., p. 8.

[34] J. Pauwelyn, Presentation on Plurilateral Trade Agreements: In or Out of the WTO? MFN or Preferential? The Graduate Institute's Centre for Trade and Economic Integration, 9 May 2012.

[35] Joint Statement Regarding the Launch of the Negotiations on the Environmental Goods Agreement (EGA), 8 July 2014.

[36] M. Nakatomi, Plurilateral Agreements: A Viable Alternative to the World Trade Organization? ADBI Working Paper, October 2013, p. 13.

[37] Anti-Counterfeiting Trade Agreement, Consolidated Text, April 2010, http://trade.ec.europa.eu/doclib/docs/2010/april/tradoc_146029.pdf

Party with respect to any other Party under existing agreements to which both Parties are party."

However, subsequent versions of the ACTA agreement, including the final text of May 2011, incorporated references and wording that made more explicit the relationship with the WTO regime in general and the TRIPS agreement in particular.[38]

The preamble of the final ACTA text states the desire of ACTA parties to "provide effective and appropriate means, *complementing the TRIPS Agreement*, for the enforcement of intellectual property rights" and that ACTA operates "in a *manner mutually supportive of international enforcement work and cooperation conducted within relevant international organizations*". A reference was also included in the preamble to the fact that parties recognize the principles set forth in the Doha Declaration on TRIPS and Public Health. Article 1.1 on relations to other agreements was modified to include an explicit reference to TRIPS.[39]

In addition, references to TRIPS Articles 7 and 8 were introduced in article 2(3) which states that "the objectives and principles set forth in Part I of the TRIPS Agreement, in particular in Articles 7 and 8, shall apply, *mutatis mutandis*, to this Agreement." For ACTA countries, ACTA thus "explicitly preserved and affirmed the important balance and flexibilities contained in the TRIPS Agreement."[40]

However, non-signatory countries were not entirely persuaded that these additions would mitigate the effects of certain provisions and ambiguities in the scope and reach of the Agreement. They argued that "while the ACTA's Preamble made reference to the Doha Declaration on the TRIPS Agreement and Public Health, the provisions in ACTA pointed to the opposite direction."[41] They also noted, for instance, that ACTA (Article 23) reinterpreted the term "commercial scale" and broadened it with respect to wilful trademark counterfeiting and copyright piracy so as to refer to "commercial activities for direct or indirect economic or commercial advantage." In contrast, the WTO dispute settlement panel in the China Enforcement case was more cautious in pointing to commercial scale as referring to "counterfeiting or piracy" carried out "at the magnitude or extent of typical or usual commercial activity with respect to a given product in a given market."[42] The ACTA interpretation, according to some, highlighted "the risk posed to WTO law by turning enforcement

38 The Final Text of the Anti-Counterfeiting Trade Agreement, May 2011, http://www.mofa.go.jp/policy/economy/i_property/pdfs/acta1105_en.pdf

39 Article 1.1 now stipulates: "Nothing in this Agreement shall derogate from any obligation of a Party with respect to any other Party under existing agreements, including the TRIPS Agreement."

40 TRIPS Council, Minutes of 28–29 February 2012 Meeting, Statement by Australia, para. 254, IP/C/M/69.

41 TRIPS Council, Minutes of 26–27 October 2010 Meeting, Statement by India, para. 448, IP/C/M/64.

42 WTO Panel Report, 26 January 2009, China – Measures affecting the protection and enforcement of Intellectual Property, WT/DS362/R. (at 7.577).

matters over to small groups of plurilateral negotiators operating outside the WTO legal framework."[43]

Ultimately, it seems that the final ACTA text, with the modification of the conflict clause of Article 1.1 so as to include a reference to TRIPS, permits to sustain the prevalence of TRIPS in case any conflict between both treaties arose. As stated elsewhere in this volume, the "reference to the no supersession of TRIPS obligations in ACTA Article 1 can be read as a conflict clause of subordination legally enforcing the reading of TRIPS as an agreement establishing ceilings."[44] It has also been affirmed that "the safeguards contained in the TRIPS Agreement, to the extent that they are mandatory, are in no way modified by ACTA which might, however, still restrict the use of TRIPS safeguards that are optional."[45] A viewpoint on the applicability to ACTA of Article 41 of the Vienna Convention on the Law of Treaties (VCLT), which concerns inter se agreements that modify multilateral treaties between certain of the parties, reaches a similar conclusion.[46]

The need to clarify the relationship between its substantive standards and relevant WTO rules became one of the pressing issues facing ACTA negotiations and is likely to confront any plurilateral agreement proposal or initiative. It is only in the last few months of the ACTA negotiations that language was introduced to allay concerns that ACTA would undermine the balance of rights and obligations enshrined in the TRIPS Agreement, although the extent to which this was effectively achieved remains open to debate. It would thus be preferable to address this issue as early as possible in a negotiating process.

### *MFN and Effects on Third Parties*

The status of the most favoured nation (MFN) clause is one of the recurrent issues to be addressed in the context of plurilateral trade agreements. In the case of ACTA, the situation with regard to intellectual property differs from the one in goods and services. While GATT and GATS provide for bilateral and regional derogations under Articles XXIV and V, respectively, there was only a limited derogation from MFN in the TRIPS Agreement that did not apply to new agreements. As a result, in principle, any TRIPS-plus protection secured by one trading partner in a regional or a plurilateral trade agreement is ipso facto applicable to all WTO members. In other

43 TRIPS Council, Minutes of 26–27 October 2010 Meeting, Statement by India, para. 444, IP/C/M/64.

44 *See* Chapter 2 in this volume.

45 Kamperman et al., op. cit., p. 21.

46 H. Ruse-Khan, A Trade Agreement Creating Barriers to International Trade? ACTA Border Measures and Goods in Transit, *American University International Law Review* (Spring 2011): 722–724.

words, "regionalism in IP is automatically 'multilateralized.'"[47] This has raised concerns among third parties that higher enforcement levels included in ACTA would impinge on the rights and obligations of WTO members not party to plurilateral or bilateral agreements.[48] At the same time, it has also been mentioned that "non-ACTA parties would also benefit from the enforcement that ACTA parties would be obliged to provide for their citizens."[49]

Border measures remain certainly the area where the concerns that ACTA could have detrimental effects on third parties are most salient,[50] particularly in view of the precedent set by the seizures in 2008 by Dutch customs authorities of Indian generic medicines in transit, and the resulting initiation of dispute settlement proceedings by India and Brazil against both the EU and the Netherlands at the WTO. In this regard, a number of scholarly opinions consider that while "the final ACTA text does not mandate the extension of border measures against goods in transit, it certainly allows the detention of goods suspected of infringing trademarks and patents in the transit country. This can easily lead to the seizure of transiting generics."[51] Similarly, the study requested by the European Parliament to assess ACTA affirms:

> Goods passing through to ACTA countries will be subject to information sharing provisions in Article 29(b) ACTA. However, that article this is also only a permissive obligation and not mandatory. Nevertheless, ACTA may play a role in restricting the trade in such goods from third countries into ACTA territories.[52]

Beyond MFN and substantive provisions, ACTA Article 35.1 envisages capacity building and technical assistance to be provided not only to other parties but also prospective parties. This could give considerable leeway to ACTA parties to shape the IPR enforcement legislation and practices of prospective members, most likely emerging economies, in accordance with their own views and interpretations of what ACTA standards entail and how they are to be implemented.[53]

It is often assumed and stated that plurilateral agreements only entail obligations and have effects for countries that agree to be bound by them. The WTO Marrakesh Agreement clearly stipulates that "the Plurilateral Trade Agreements do not create

47 J. Pauwelyn, Legal Avenues to "Multilateralizing Regionalism": Beyond article XXIV, in *Multilateralizing Regionalism: Challenges for the Global Trading System*, P. Low and R. Baldwin (eds.). Cambridge University Press, 2009, p. 383.

48 *See* Chapter 25 in this volume.

49 Kamperman et al., op. cit., p. 16.

50 *See* Chapter 5 in this volume.

51 H. Ruse-Khan, op. cit., p. 724.

52 Kamperman et al., op.cit., p. 16

53 A. Abdel-Latif, ACTA: Original Expectations and Future Implications, Bridges, Volume 14, Number 4, ICTSD, December 2010, at: http://ictsd.org/i/news/bridges/98805/. *See also* Chapter 8 in this volume.

either obligations or rights for Members that have not accepted them." However, the experience of ACTA shows that the perceived effects of such agreements on third parties can be the subject of heated controversy and affect public perceptions. While ACTA Article 6.1 mandates parties to take "into account the interests of third parties," in practice some of the Agreement's provisions could potentially undermine such interests. Thus, effects on third parties constitute an issue that requires close attention when negotiating plurilateral trade agreements.

### *Institutional Issues*

Last but not least, the conclusion of plurilateral trade agreements, particularly outside of the WTO, entails the examination of a series of institutional matters regarding the operation of the future agreement. How will its implementation be monitored? Shall it have a permanent secretariat? In the case of ACTA, the agreement did not envisage the creation of a permanent secretariat, but rather a system of contact points in ACTA parties. Most importantly, it envisaged the creation of a powerful body, the ACTA committee, with far-reaching powers, in particular the review of the implementation and operation of the Agreement and the endorsement of best practices.[54] For Brazil, this institutional feature, combined with the technical assistance provisions in ACTA, contained the "necessary ingredients that might convert ACTA into a truly international organization dealing with the enforcement of intellectual property rights, whose impact on WIPO and the WTO, especially on capacity building and technical assistance, was unpredictable."[55] Thus, beyond the concerns about the substantive standards in ACTA, third parties also had concerns about the institutional set-up entailed by ACTA, which could result, from their viewpoint, in the creation of a "third pillar" in the global IP protection regime next to WTO and WIPO. Thus, institutional aspects relating to how a plurilateral trade agreement will be implemented can have far-reaching implications and also require careful thinking.

## CONCLUSION

Ultimately, the ACTA negotiating process showed that the ability of addressing effectively public interest concerns is critical for the successful completion of plurilateral and regional trade negotiations or their failure. This is even more so the case if such agreements deal with regulatory issues which extend deep into the domestic

[54] *See* Chapter 8 in this volume.

[55] TRIPS Council, Minutes of 26–27 October 2010 Meeting, Statement by Brazil, para. 451, IP/C/M/64.

legal regimes of the negotiating parties and, thus, raise concerns, in particular for domestic stakeholders, in terms of the ability of parties to pursue public policy objectives. Addressing in a comprehensive manner the lessons to be drawn from the ACTA negotiating process, in terms of ensuring transparency, undertaking consultations with a broad range of stakeholders, relying on sound and impartial evidence and clarifying the relationship with existing multilateral rules, will be essential in this context.

While many countries engaged in the negotiations of plurilateral agreements seem keen to avoid the fate of the ACTA negotiating process and appear, in some instances, to have learned some of the lessons above-mentioned, the balanced composition of the group of countries advancing these initiatives will remain critical in shaping how these issues are addressed in the context of each negotiating process.

# Annex I

## Anti-Counterfeiting Trade Agreement

*The Parties to this Agreement,*

*Noting* that effective enforcement of intellectual property rights is critical to sustaining economic growth across all industries and globally;

*Noting* further that the proliferation of counterfeit and pirated goods, as well as of services that distribute infringing material, undermines legitimate trade and sustainable development of the world economy, causes significant financial losses for right holders and for legitimate businesses, and, in some cases, provides a source of revenue for organized crime and otherwise poses risks to the public;

*Desiring* to combat such proliferation through enhanced international cooperation and more effective international enforcement;

*Intending* to provide effective and appropriate means, complementing the TRIPS Agreement, for the enforcement of intellectual property rights, taking into account differences in their respective legal systems and practices;

*Desiring* to ensure that measures and procedures to enforce intellectual property rights do not themselves become barriers to legitimate trade;

*Desiring* to address the problem of infringement of intellectual property rights, including infringement taking place in the digital environment, in particular with respect to copyright or related rights, in a manner that balances the rights and interests of the relevant right holders, service providers, and users;

*Desiring* to promote cooperation between service providers and right holders to address relevant infringements in the digital environment;

*Desiring* that this Agreement operates in a manner mutually supportive of international enforcement work and cooperation conducted within relevant international organizations;

*Recognizing* the principles set forth in the *Doha Declaration on the TRIPS Agreement and Public Health*, adopted on 14 November 2001, at the Fourth WTO Ministerial Conference;

*Hereby agree* as follows:

# Chapter I

## INITIAL PROVISIONS AND GENERAL DEFINITIONS

### *Section 1: Initial Provisions*

**Article 1: Relation to Other Agreements**
Nothing in this Agreement shall derogate from any obligation of a Party with respect to any other Party under existing agreements, including the TRIPS Agreement.

**Article 2: Nature and Scope of Obligations**

1. Each Party shall give effect to the provisions of this Agreement. A Party may implement in its law more extensive enforcement of intellectual property rights than is required by this Agreement, provided that such enforcement does not contravene the provisions of this Agreement. Each Party shall be free to determine the appropriate method of implementing the provisions of this Agreement within its own legal system and practice.
2. Nothing in this Agreement creates any obligation with respect to the distribution of resources as between enforcement of intellectual property rights and enforcement of law in general.
3. The objectives and principles set forth in Part I of the TRIPS Agreement, in particular in Articles 7 and 8, shall apply, *mutatis mutandis*, to this Agreement.

**Article 3: Relation to Standards Concerning the Availability and Scope of Intellectual Property Rights**

1. This Agreement shall be without prejudice to provisions in a Party's law governing the availability, acquisition, scope, and maintenance of intellectual property rights.
2. This Agreement does not create any obligation on a Party to apply measures where a right in intellectual property is not protected under its laws and regulations.

**Article 4: Privacy and Disclosure of Information**

1. Nothing in this Agreement shall require a Party to disclose:
   (a) information, the disclosure of which would be contrary to its law, including laws protecting privacy rights, or international agreements to which it is party;
   (b) confidential information, the disclosure of which would impede law enforcement or otherwise be contrary to the public interest; or
   (c) confidential information, the disclosure of which would prejudice the legitimate commercial interests of particular enterprises, public or private.
2. When a Party provides written information pursuant to the provisions of this Agreement, the Party receiving the information shall, subject to its law and practice, refrain from disclosing or using the information for a purpose other than that for which the information was provided, except with the prior consent of the Party providing the information.

*Section 2: General Definitions*

**Article 5: General Definitions**
For the purposes of this Agreement, unless otherwise specified:

(a) **ACTA** means the *Anti-Counterfeiting Trade Agreement*;
(b) **Committee** means the ACTA Committee established under Chapter V (Institutional Arrangements);
(c) **competent authorities** includes the appropriate judicial, administrative, or law enforcement authorities under a Party's law;
(d) **counterfeit trademark goods** means any goods, including packaging, bearing without authorization a trademark which is identical to the trademark validly registered in respect of such goods, or which cannot be distinguished in its essential aspects from such a trademark, and which thereby infringes the rights of the owner of the trademark in question under the law of the country in which the procedures set forth in Chapter II (Legal Framework for Enforcement of Intellectual Property Rights) are invoked;
(e) **country** is to be understood to have the same meaning as that set forth in the Explanatory Notes to the WTO Agreement;
(f) **customs transit** means the customs procedure under which goods are transported under customs control from one customs office to another;
(g) **days** means calendar days;
(h) **intellectual property** refers to all categories of intellectual property that are the subject of Sections 1 through 7 of Part II of the TRIPS Agreement;

(i) **in-transit goods** means goods under **customs transit** or **transhipment**; (j) **person** means a natural person or a legal person;
(k) **pirated copyright goods** means any goods which are copies made without the consent of the right holder or person duly authorized by the right holder in the country of production and which are made directly or indirectly from an article where the making of that copy would have constituted an infringement of a copyright or a related right under the law of the country in which the procedures set forth in Chapter II (Legal Framework for Enforcement of Intellectual Property Rights) are invoked;
(l) **right holder** includes a federation or an association having the legal standing to assert rights in intellectual property;
(m) **territory**, for the purposes of Section 3 (Border Measures) of Chapter II (Legal Framework for Enforcement of Intellectual Property Rights), means the customs territory and all free zones[1] of a Party;
(n) **transhipment** means the customs procedure under which goods are transferred under customs control from the importing means of transport to the exporting means of transport within the area of one customs office which is the office of both importation and exportation;
(o) **TRIPS Agreement** means the *Agreement on Trade-Related Aspects of Intellectual Property Rights*, contained in Annex 1C to the WTO Agreement;
(p) **WTO** means the World Trade Organization; and
(q) **WTO Agreement** means the *Marrakesh Agreement Establishing the World Trade Organization*, done on 15 April 1994.

## Chapter II

### LEGAL FRAMEWORK FOR ENFORCEMENT OF INTELLECTUAL PROPERTY RIGHTS

*Section 1: General Obligations*

### Article 6: General Obligations with Respect to Enforcement

1. Each Party shall ensure that enforcement procedures are available under its law so as to permit effective action against any act of infringement of intellectual property rights covered by this Agreement, including expeditious remedies to prevent infringements and remedies which constitute a deterrent to

[1] For greater certainty, the Parties acknowledge that **free zone** means a part of the territory of a Party where any goods introduced are generally regarded, insofar as import duties and taxes are concerned, as being outside the customs territory.

further infringements. These procedures shall be applied in such a manner as to avoid the creation of barriers to legitimate trade and to provide for safeguards against their abuse.

2. Procedures adopted, maintained, or applied to implement the provisions of this Chapter shall be fair and equitable, and shall provide for the rights of all participants subject to such procedures to be appropriately protected. These procedures shall not be unnecessarily complicated or costly, or entail unreasonable time-limits or unwarranted delays.
3. In implementing the provisions of this Chapter, each Party shall take into account the need for proportionality between the seriousness of the infringement, the interests of third parties, and the applicable measures, remedies and penalties.
4. No provision of this Chapter shall be construed to require a Party to make its officials subject to liability for acts undertaken in the performance of their official duties.

### *Section 2: Civil Enforcement*[2]

**Article 7: Availability of Civil Procedures**

1. Each Party shall make available to right holders civil judicial procedures concerning the enforcement of any intellectual property right as specified in this Section.
2. To the extent that any civil remedy can be ordered as a result of administrative procedures on the merits of a case, each Party shall provide that such procedures shall conform to principles equivalent in substance to those set forth in this Section.

**Article 8: Injunctions**

1. Each Party shall provide that, in civil judicial proceedings concerning the enforcement of intellectual property rights, its judicial authorities have the authority to issue an order against a party to desist from an infringement, and *inter alia*, an order to that party or, where appropriate, to a third party over whom the relevant judicial authority exercises jurisdiction, to prevent goods that involve the infringement of an intellectual property right from entering into the channels of commerce.

[2] A Party may exclude patents and protection of undisclosed information from the scope of this section.

2. Notwithstanding the other provisions of this Section, a Party may limit the remedies available against use by governments, or by third parties authorized by a government, without the authorization of the right holder, to the payment of remuneration, provided that the Party complies with the provisions of Part II of the TRIPS Agreement specifically addressing such use. In other cases, the remedies under this Section shall apply or, where these remedies are inconsistent with a Party's law, declaratory judgments and adequate compensation shall be available.

**Article 9: Damages**

1. Each Party shall provide that, in civil judicial proceedings concerning the enforcement of intellectual property rights, its judicial authorities have the authority to order the infringer who, knowingly or with reasonable grounds to know, engaged in infringing activity to pay the right holder damages adequate to compensate for the injury the right holder has suffered as a result of the infringement. In determining the amount of damages for infringement of intellectual property rights, a Party's judicial authorities shall have the authority to consider, *inter alia*, any legitimate measure of value the right holder submits, which may include lost profits, the value of the infringed goods or services measured by the market price, or the suggested retail price.
2. At least in cases of copyright or related rights infringement and trademark counterfeiting, each Party shall provide that, in civil judicial proceedings, its judicial authorities have the authority to order the infringer to pay the right holder the infringer's profits that are attributable to the infringement. A Party may presume those profits to be the amount of damages referred to in paragraph 1.
3. At least with respect to infringement of copyright or related rights protecting works, phonograms, and performances, and in cases of trademark counterfeiting, each Party shall also establish or maintain a system that provides for one or more of the following:
   (a) pre-established damages; or
   (b) presumptions[3] for determining the amount of damages sufficient to compensate the right holder for the harm caused by the infringement; or
   (c) at least for copyright, additional damages.

[3] The presumptions referred to in subparagraph 3(b) may include a presumption that the amount of damages is: (i) the quantity of the goods infringing the right holder's intellectual property right in question and actually assigned to third persons, multiplied by the amount of profit per unit of goods which would have been sold by the right holder if there had not been the act of infringement; or (ii) a reasonable royalty; or (iii) a lump sum on the basis of elements such as at least the amount of royalties or fees which would have been due if the infringer had requested authorization to use the intellectual property right in question.

4. Where a Party provides the remedy referred to in subparagraph 3(a) or the presumptions referred to in subparagraph 3(b), it shall ensure that either its judicial authorities or the right holder has the right to choose such a remedy or presumptions as an alternative to the remedies referred to in paragraphs 1 and 2.
5. Each Party shall provide that its judicial authorities, where appropriate, have the authority to order, at the conclusion of civil judicial proceedings concerning infringement of at least copyright or related rights, or trademarks, that the prevailing party be awarded payment by the losing party of court costs or fees and appropriate attorney's fees, or any other expenses as provided for under that Party's law.

**Article 10: Other Remedies**

1. At least with respect to pirated copyright goods and counterfeit trademark goods, each Party shall provide that, in civil judicial proceedings, at the right holder's request, its judicial authorities have the authority to order that such infringing goods be destroyed, except in exceptional circumstances, without compensation of any sort.
2. Each Party shall further provide that its judicial authorities have the authority to order that materials and implements, the predominant use of which has been in the manufacture or creation of such infringing goods, be, without undue delay and without compensation of any sort, destroyed or disposed of outside the channels of commerce in such a manner as to minimize the risks of further infringements.
3. A Party may provide for the remedies described in this Article to be carried out at the infringer's expense.

**Article 11: Information Related to Infringement**

Without prejudice to its law governing privilege, the protection of confidentiality of information sources, or the processing of personal data, each Party shall provide that, in civil judicial proceedings concerning the enforcement of intellectual property rights, its judicial authorities have the authority, upon a justified request of the right holder, to order the infringer or, in the alternative, the alleged infringer, to provide to the right holder or to the judicial authorities, at least for the purpose of collecting evidence, relevant information as provided for in its applicable laws and regulations that the infringer or alleged infringer possesses or controls. Such information may include information regarding any person involved in any aspect of the infringement or alleged infringement and regarding the means of production or the channels of distribution of the infringing or allegedly infringing goods or services, including the identification of third persons alleged to be involved in the production and distribution of such goods or services and of their channels of distribution.

**Article 12: Provisional Measures**

1. Each Party shall provide that its judicial authorities have the authority to order prompt and effective provisional measures:
   (a) against a party or, where appropriate, a third party over whom the relevant judicial authority exercises jurisdiction, to prevent an infringement of any intellectual property right from occurring, and in particular, to prevent goods that involve the infringement of an intellectual property right from entering into the channels of commerce;
   (b) to preserve relevant evidence in regard to the alleged infringement.
2. Each Party shall provide that its judicial authorities have the authority to adopt provisional measures *inaudita altera parte* where appropriate, in particular where any delay is likely to cause irreparable harm to the right holder, or where there is a demonstrable risk of evidence being destroyed. In proceedings conducted *inaudita altera parte*, each Party shall provide its judicial authorities with the authority to act expeditiously on requests for provisional measures and to make a decision without undue delay.
3. At least in cases of copyright or related rights infringement and trademark counterfeiting, each Party shall provide that, in civil judicial proceedings, its judicial authorities have the authority to order the seizure or other taking into custody of suspect goods, and of materials and implements relevant to the act of infringement, and, at least for trademark counterfeiting, documentary evidence, either originals or copies thereof, relevant to the infringement.
4. Each Party shall provide that its authorities have the authority to require the applicant, with respect to provisional measures, to provide any reasonably available evidence in order to satisfy themselves with a sufficient degree of certainty that the applicant's right is being infringed or that such infringement is imminent, and to order the applicant to provide a security or equivalent assurance sufficient to protect the defendant and to prevent abuse. Such security or equivalent assurance shall not unreasonably deter recourse to procedures for such provisional measures.
5. Where the provisional measures are revoked or where they lapse due to any act or omission by the applicant, or where it is subsequently found that there has been no infringement of an intellectual property right, the judicial authorities shall have the authority to order the applicant, upon request of the defendant, to provide the defendant appropriate compensation for any injury caused by these measures.

## *Section 3: Border Measures*[4,5]

**Article 13: Scope of the Border Measures**[6]
In providing, as appropriate, and consistent with its domestic system of intellectual property rights protection and without prejudice to the requirements of the TRIPS Agreement, for effective border enforcement of intellectual property rights, a Party should do so in a manner that does not discriminate unjustifiably between intellectual property rights and that avoids the creation of barriers to legitimate trade.

**Article 14: Small Consignments and Personal Luggage**

1. Each Party shall include in the application of this Section goods of a commercial nature sent in small consignments.
2. A Party may exclude from the application of this Section small quantities of goods of a non-commercial nature contained in travellers' personal luggage.

**Article 15: Provision of Information from the Right Holder**
Each Party shall permit its competent authorities to request a right holder to supply relevant information to assist the competent authorities in taking the border measures referred to in this Section. A Party may also allow a right holder to supply relevant information to its competent authorities.

**Article 16: Border Measures**

1. Each Party shall adopt or maintain procedures with respect to import and export shipments under which:
   (a) its customs authorities may act upon their own initiative to suspend the release of suspect goods; and
   (b) where appropriate, a right holder may request its competent authorities to suspend the release of suspect goods.
2. A Party may adopt or maintain procedures with respect to suspect in-transit goods or in other situations where the goods are under customs control under which:

4 Where a Party has dismantled substantially all controls over movement of goods across its border with another Party with which it forms part of a customs union, it shall not be required to apply the provisions of this Section at that border.

5 It is understood that there shall be no obligation to apply the procedures set forth in this Section to goods put on the market in another country by or with the consent of the right holder.

6 The Parties agree that patents and protection of undisclosed information do not fall within the scope of this Section.

(a) its customs authorities may act upon their own initiative to suspend the release of, or to detain, suspect goods; and
(b) where appropriate, a right holder may request its competent authorities to suspend the release of, or to detain, suspect goods.

**Article 17: Application by the Right Holder**

1. Each Party shall provide that its competent authorities require a right holder that requests the procedures described in subparagraphs 1(b) and 2(b) of Article 16 (Border Measures) to provide adequate evidence to satisfy the competent authorities that, under the law of the Party providing the procedures, there is *prima facie* an infringement of the right holder's intellectual property right, and to supply sufficient information that may reasonably be expected to be within the right holder's knowledge to make the suspect goods reasonably recognizable by the competent authorities. The requirement to provide sufficient information shall not unreasonably deter recourse to the procedures described in subparagraphs 1(b) and 2(b) of Article 16 (Border Measures).
2. Each Party shall provide for applications to suspend the release of, or to detain, any suspect goods[7] under customs control in its territory. A Party may provide for such applications to apply to multiple shipments. A Party may provide that, at the request of the right holder, the application to suspend the release of, or to detain, suspect goods may apply to selected points of entry and exit under customs control.
3. Each Party shall ensure that its competent authorities inform the applicant within a reasonable period whether they have accepted the application. Where its competent authorities have accepted the application, they shall also inform the applicant of the period of validity of the application.
4. A Party may provide that, where the applicant has abused the procedures described in subparagraphs 1(b) and 2(b) of Article 16 (Border Measures), or where there is due cause, its competent authorities have the authority to deny, suspend, or void an application.

**Article 18: Security or Equivalent Assurance**

Each Party shall provide that its competent authorities have the authority to require a right holder that requests the procedures described in subparagraphs 1(b) and 2(b) of Article 16 (Border Measures) to provide a reasonable security or equivalent assurance sufficient to protect the defendant and the competent authorities and to prevent abuse.

7 The requirement to provide for such applications is subject to the obligations to provide procedures referred to in subparagraphs 1(b) and 2(b) of Article 16 (Border Measures).

Each Party shall provide that such security or equivalent assurance shall not unreasonably deter recourse to these procedures. A Party may provide that such security may be in the form of a bond conditioned to hold the defendant harmless from any loss or damage resulting from any suspension of the release of, or detention of, the goods in the event the competent authorities determine that the goods are not infringing. A Party may, only in exceptional circumstances or pursuant to a judicial order, permit the defendant to obtain possession of suspect goods by posting a bond or other security.

**Article 19: Determination as to Infringement**
Each Party shall adopt or maintain procedures by which its competent authorities may determine, within a reasonable period after the initiation of the procedures described in Article 16 (Border Measures), whether the suspect goods infringe an intellectual property right.

**Article 20: Remedies**

1. Each Party shall provide that its competent authorities have the authority to order the destruction of goods following a determination referred to in Article 19 (Determination as to Infringement) that the goods are infringing. In cases where such goods are not destroyed, each Party shall ensure that, except in exceptional circumstances, such goods are disposed of outside the channels of commerce in such a manner as to avoid any harm to the right holder.
2. In regard to counterfeit trademark goods, the simple removal of the trademark unlawfully affixed shall not be sufficient, other than in exceptional cases, to permit release of the goods into the channels of commerce.
3. A Party may provide that its competent authorities have the authority to impose administrative penalties following a determination referred to in Article 19 (Determination as to Infringement) that the goods are infringing.

**Article 21: Fees**
Each Party shall provide that any application fee, storage fee, or destruction fee to be assessed by its competent authorities in connection with the procedures described in this Section shall not be used to unreasonably deter recourse to these procedures.

**Article 22: Disclosure of Information**
Without prejudice to a Party's laws pertaining to the privacy or confidentiality of information:

(a) a Party may authorize its competent authorities to provide a right holder with information about specific shipments of goods, including the description and quantity of the goods, to assist in the detection of infringing goods;

(b) a Party may authorize its competent authorities to provide a right holder with information about goods, including, but not limited to, the description and quantity of the goods, the name and address of the consignor, importer, exporter, or consignee, and, if known, the country of origin of the goods, and the name and address of the manufacturer of the goods, to assist in the determination referred to in Article 19 (Determination as to Infringement);

(c) unless a Party has provided its competent authorities with the authority described in subparagraph (b), at least in cases of imported goods, where its competent authorities have seized suspect goods or, in the alternative, made a determination referred to in Article 19 (Determination as to Infringement) that the goods are infringing, the Party shall authorize its competent authorities to provide a right holder, within thirty days[8] of the seizure or determination, with information about such goods, including, but not limited to, the description and quantity of the goods, the name and address of the consignor, importer, exporter, or consignee, and, if known, the country of origin of the goods, and the name and address of the manufacturer of the goods.

*Section 4: Criminal Enforcement*

**Article 23: Criminal Offences**

1. Each Party shall provide for criminal procedures and penalties to be applied at least in cases of wilful trademark counterfeiting or copyright or related rights piracy on a commercial scale.[9] For the purposes of this Section, acts carried out on a commercial scale include at least those carried out as commercial activities for direct or indirect economic or commercial advantage.
2. Each Party shall provide for criminal procedures and penalties to be applied in cases of wilful importation[10] and domestic use, in the course of trade and on a commercial scale, of labels or packaging[11]:

[8] For the purposes of this Article, days means business days.

[9] Each Party shall treat wilful importation or exportation of counterfeit trademark goods or pirated copyright goods on a commercial scale as unlawful activities subject to criminal penalties under this Article. A Party may comply with its obligation relating to importation and exportation of counterfeit trademark goods or pirated copyright goods by providing for distribution, sale or offer for sale of such goods on a commercial scale as unlawful activities subject to criminal penalties.

[10] A Party may comply with its obligation relating to importation of labels or packaging through its measures concerning distribution.

[11] A Party may comply with its obligations under this paragraph by providing for criminal procedures and penalties to be applied to attempts to commit a trademark offence.

(a) to which a mark has been applied without authorization which is identical to, or cannot be distinguished from, a trademark registered in its territory; and
(b) which are intended to be used in the course of trade on goods or in relation to services which are identical to goods or services for which such trademark is registered.

3. A Party may provide criminal procedures and penalties in appropriate cases for the unauthorized copying of cinematographic works from a performance in a motion picture exhibition facility generally open to the public.
4. With respect to the offences specified in this Article for which a Party provides criminal procedures and penalties, that Party shall ensure that criminal liability for aiding and abetting is available under its law.
5. Each Party shall adopt such measures as may be necessary, consistent with its legal principles, to establish the liability, which may be criminal, of legal persons for the offences specified in this Article for which the Party provides criminal procedures and penalties. Such liability shall be without prejudice to the criminal liability of the natural persons who have committed the criminal offences.

**Article 24: Penalties**

For offences specified in paragraphs 1, 2, and 4 of Article 23 (Criminal Offences), each Party shall provide penalties that include imprisonment as well as monetary fines[12] sufficiently high to provide a deterrent to future acts of infringement, consistently with the level of penalties applied for crimes of a corresponding gravity.

**Article 25: Seizure, Forfeiture, and Destruction**

1. With respect to the offences specified in paragraphs 1, 2, 3, and 4 of Article 23 (Criminal Offences) for which a Party provides criminal procedures and penalties, that Party shall provide that its competent authorities have the authority to order the seizure of suspected counterfeit trademark goods or pirated copyright goods, any related materials and implements used in the commission of the alleged offence, documentary evidence relevant to the alleged offence, and the assets derived from, or obtained directly or indirectly through, the alleged infringing activity.
2. Where a Party requires the identification of items subject to seizure as a prerequisite for issuing an order referred to in paragraph 1, that Party shall not

[12] It is understood that there is no obligation for a Party to provide for the possibility of imprisonment and monetary fines to be imposed in parallel.

require the items to be described in greater detail than necessary to identify them for the purpose of seizure.

3. With respect to the offences specified in paragraphs 1, 2, 3, and 4 of Article 23 (Criminal Offences) for which a Party provides criminal procedures and penalties, that Party shall provide that its competent authorities have the authority to order the forfeiture or destruction of all counterfeit trademark goods or pirated copyright goods. In cases where counterfeit trademark goods and pirated copyright goods are not destroyed, the competent authorities shall ensure that, except in exceptional circumstances, such goods shall be disposed of outside the channels of commerce in such a manner as to avoid causing any harm to the right holder. Each Party shall ensure that the forfeiture or destruction of such goods shall occur without compensation of any sort to the infringer.
4. With respect to the offences specified in paragraphs 1, 2, 3, and 4 of Article 23 (Criminal Offences) for which a Party provides criminal procedures and penalties, that Party shall provide that its competent authorities have the authority to order the forfeiture or destruction of materials and implements predominantly used in the creation of counterfeit trademark goods or pirated copyright goods and, at least for serious offences, of the assets derived from, or obtained directly or indirectly through, the infringing activity. Each Party shall ensure that the forfeiture or destruction of such materials, implements, or assets shall occur without compensation of any sort to the infringer.
5. With respect to the offences specified in paragraphs 1, 2, 3, and 4 of Article 23 (Criminal Offences) for which a Party provides criminal procedures and penalties, that Party may provide that its judicial authorities have the authority to order:
   (a) the seizure of assets the value of which corresponds to that of the assets derived from, or obtained directly or indirectly through, the allegedly infringing activity; and
   (b) the forfeiture of assets the value of which corresponds to that of the assets derived from, or obtained directly or indirectly through, the infringing activity.

**Article 26: *EX OFFICIO* Criminal Enforcement**

Each Party shall provide that, in appropriate cases, its competent authorities may act upon their own initiative to initiate investigation or legal action with respect to the criminal offences specified in paragraphs 1, 2, 3, and 4 of Article 23 (Criminal Offences) for which that Party provides criminal procedures and penalties.

## *Section 5: Enforcement of Intellectual Property Rights in the Digital Environment*

### Article 27: Enforcement in the Digital Environment

1. Each Party shall ensure that enforcement procedures, to the extent set forth in Sections 2 (Civil Enforcement) and 4 (Criminal Enforcement), are available under its law so as to permit effective action against an act of infringement of intellectual property rights which takes place in the digital environment, including expeditious remedies to prevent infringement and remedies which constitute a deterrent to further infringements.
2. Further to paragraph 1, each Party's enforcement procedures shall apply to infringement of copyright or related rights over digital networks, which may include the unlawful use of means of widespread distribution for infringing purposes. These procedures shall be implemented in a manner that avoids the creation of barriers to legitimate activity, including electronic commerce, and, consistent with that Party's law, preserves fundamental principles such as freedom of expression, fair process, and privacy.[13]
3. Each Party shall endeavour to promote cooperative efforts within the business community to effectively address trademark and copyright or related rights infringement while preserving legitimate competition and, consistent with that Party's law, preserving fundamental principles such as freedom of expression, fair process, and privacy.
4. A Party may provide, in accordance with its laws and regulations, its competent authorities with the authority to order an online service provider to disclose expeditiously to a right holder information sufficient to identify a subscriber whose account was allegedly used for infringement, where that right holder has filed a legally sufficient claim of trademark or copyright or related rights infringement, and where such information is being sought for the purpose of protecting or enforcing those rights. These procedures shall be implemented in a manner that avoids the creation of barriers to legitimate activity, including electronic commerce, and, consistent with that Party's law, preserves fundamental principles such as freedom of expression, fair process, and privacy.
5. Each Party shall provide adequate legal protection and effective legal remedies against the circumvention of effective technological measures[14] that are

[13] For instance, without prejudice to a Party's law, adopting or maintaining a regime providing for limitations on the liability of, or on the remedies available against, online service providers while preserving the legitimate interests of right holder.

[14] For the purposes of this Article, **technological measures** means any technology, device, or component that, in the normal course of its operation, is designed to prevent or restrict acts, in respect of

used by authors, performers or producers of phonograms in connection with the exercise of their rights in, and that restrict acts in respect of, their works, performances, and phonograms, which are not authorized by the authors, the performers or the producers of phonograms concerned or permitted by law.

6. In order to provide the adequate legal protection and effective legal remedies referred to in paragraph 5, each Party shall provide protection at least against:
   (a) to the extent provided by its law:
      (i) the unauthorized circumvention of an effective technological measure carried out knowingly or with reasonable grounds to know; and
      (ii) the offering to the public by marketing of a device or product, including computer programs, or a service, as a means of circumventing an effective technological measure; and
   (b) the manufacture, importation, or distribution of a device or product, including computer programs, or provision of a service that:
      (i) is primarily designed or produced for the purpose of circumventing an effective technological measure; or
      (ii) has only a limited commercially significant purpose other than circumventing an effective technological measure.[15]
7. To protect electronic rights management information,[16] each Party shall provide adequate legal protection and effective legal remedies against any person knowingly performing without authority any of the following acts knowing,

works, performances, or phonograms, which are not authorized by authors, performers or producers of phonograms, as provided for by a Party's law. Without prejudice to the scope of copyright or related rights contained in a Party's law, technological measures shall be deemed effective where the use of protected works, performances, or phonograms is controlled by authors, performers or producers of phonograms through the application of a relevant access control or protection process, such as encryption or scrambling, or a copy control mechanism, which achieves the objective of protection.

[15] In implementing paragraphs 5 and 6, no Party shall be obligated to require that the design of, or the design and selection of parts and components for, a consumer electronics, telecommunications, or computing product provide for a response to any particular technological measure, so long as the product does not otherwise contravene its measures implementing these paragraphs.

[16] For the purposes of this Article, rights management information means:

(a) information that identifies the work, the performance, or the phonogram; the author of the work, the performer of the performance, or the producer of the phonogram; or the owner of any right in the work, performance, or phonogram;
(b) information about the terms and conditions of use of the work, performance, or phonogram; or
(c) any numbers or codes that represent the information described in (a) and (b) above;

when any of these items of information is attached to a copy of a work, performance, or phonogram, or appears in connection with the communication or making available of a work, performance, or phonogram to the public.

or with respect to civil remedies, having reasonable grounds to know, that it will induce, enable, facilitate, or conceal an infringement of any copyright or related rights:

(a) to remove or alter any electronic rights management information;

(b) to distribute, import for distribution, broadcast, communicate, or make available to the public copies of works, performances, or phonograms, knowing that electronic rights management information has been removed or altered without authority.

8. In providing adequate legal protection and effective legal remedies pursuant to the provisions of paragraphs 5 and 7, a Party may adopt or maintain appropriate limitations or exceptions to measures implementing the provisions of paragraphs 5, 6, and 7. The obligations set forth in paragraphs 5, 6, and 7 are without prejudice to the rights, limitations, exceptions, or defences to copyright or related rights infringement under a Party's law.

# Chapter III

## ENFORCEMENT PRACTICES

### Article 28: Enforcement Expertise, Information, and Domestic Coordination

1. Each Party shall encourage the development of specialized expertise within its competent authorities responsible for the enforcement of intellectual property rights.
2. Each Party shall promote the collection and analysis of statistical data and other relevant information concerning intellectual property rights infringements as well as the collection of information on best practices to prevent and combat infringements.
3. Each Party shall, as appropriate, promote internal coordination among, and facilitate joint actions by, its competent authorities responsible for the enforcement of intellectual property rights.
4. Each Party shall endeavour to promote, where appropriate, the establishment and maintenance of formal or informal mechanisms, such as advisory groups, whereby its competent authorities may receive the views of right holders and other relevant stakeholders.

### Article 29: Management of Risk at Border

1. In order to enhance the effectiveness of border enforcement of intellectual property rights, the competent authorities of a Party may:

(a) consult with the relevant stakeholders, and the competent authorities of other Parties responsible for the enforcement of intellectual property rights to identify and address significant risks, and promote actions to mitigate those risks; and
(b) share information with the competent authorities of other Parties on border enforcement of intellectual property rights, including relevant information to better identify and target for inspection shipments suspected of containing infringing goods.

2. Where a Party seizes imported goods infringing an intellectual property right, its competent authorities may provide the Party of export with information necessary for identification of the parties and goods involved in the exportation of the seized goods. The competent authorities of the Party of export may take action against those parties and future shipments in accordance with that Party's law.

**Article 30: Transparency**
To promote transparency in the administration of its intellectual property rights enforcement system, each Party shall take appropriate measures, pursuant to its law and policies, to publish or otherwise make available to the public information on:

(a) procedures available under its law for enforcing intellectual property rights, its competent authorities responsible for such enforcement, and contact points available for assistance;
(b) relevant laws, regulations, final judicial decisions, and administrative rulings of general application pertaining to the enforcement of intellectual property rights; and
(c) its efforts to ensure an effective system of enforcement and protection of intellectual property rights.

**Article 31: Public Awareness**
Each Party shall, as appropriate, promote the adoption of measures to enhance public awareness of the importance of respecting intellectual property rights and the detrimental effects of intellectual property rights infringement.

**Article 32: Environmental Considerations in Destruction of Infringing Goods**
The destruction of goods infringing intellectual property rights shall be done consistently with the laws and regulations on environmental matters of the Party in which the destruction takes place.

# Chapter IV

## INTERNATIONAL COOPERATION

### Article 33: International Cooperation

1. Each Party recognizes that international cooperation is vital to realizing effective protection of intellectual property rights and that it should be encouraged regardless of the origin of the goods infringing intellectual property rights, or the location or nationality of the right holder.
2. In order to combat intellectual property rights infringement, in particular trademark counterfeiting and copyright or related rights piracy, the Parties shall promote cooperation, where appropriate, among their competent authorities responsible for the enforcement of intellectual property rights. Such cooperation may include law enforcement cooperation with respect to criminal enforcement and border measures covered by this Agreement.
3. Cooperation under this Chapter shall be conducted consistent with relevant international agreements, and subject to the laws, policies, resource allocation, and law enforcement priorities of each Party.

### Article 34: Information Sharing

Without prejudice to the provisions of Article 29 (Management of Risk at Border), each Party shall endeavour to exchange with other Parties:

(a) information the Party collects under the provisions of Chapter III (Enforcement Practices), including statistical data and information on best practices;
(b) information on its legislative and regulatory measures related to the protection and enforcement of intellectual property rights; and
(c) other information as appropriate and mutually agreed.

### Article 35: Capacity Building and Technical Assistance

1. Each Party shall endeavour to provide, upon request and on mutually agreed terms and conditions, assistance in capacity building and technical assistance in improving the enforcement of intellectual property rights to other Parties to this Agreement and, where appropriate, to prospective Parties. The capacity building and technical assistance may cover such areas as:
   (a) enhancement of public awareness on intellectual property rights;
   (b) development and implementation of national legislation related to the enforcement of intellectual property rights;

(c) training of officials on the enforcement of intellectual property rights; and
(d) coordinated operations conducted at the regional and multilateral levels.

2. Each Party shall endeavour to work closely with other Parties and, where appropriate, non-Parties to this Agreement for the purpose of implementing the provisions of paragraph 1.
3. A Party may undertake the activities described in this Article in conjunction with relevant private sector or international organizations. Each Party shall strive to avoid unnecessary duplication between the activities described in this Article and other international cooperation activities.

# Chapter V

## INSTITUTIONAL ARRANGEMENTS

### Article 36: The ACTA Committee

1. The Parties hereby establish the ACTA Committee. Each Party shall be represented on the Committee.
2. The Committee shall:
   (a) review the implementation and operation of this Agreement;
   (b) consider matters concerning the development of this Agreement;
   (c) consider any proposed amendments to this Agreement in accordance with Article 42 (Amendments);
   (d) decide, in accordance with paragraph 2 of Article 43 (Accession), upon the terms of accession to this Agreement of any Member of the WTO; and
   (e) consider any other matter that may affect the implementation and operation of this Agreement.
3. The Committee may decide to:
   (a) establish *ad hoc* committees or working groups to assist the Committee in carrying out its responsibilities under paragraph 2, or to assist a prospective Party upon its request in acceding to this Agreement in accordance with Article 43 (Accession);
   (b) seek the advice of non-governmental persons or groups;
   (c) make recommendations regarding the implementation and operation of this Agreement, including by endorsing best practice guidelines related thereto;
   (d) share information and best practices with third parties on reducing intellectual property rights infringements, including techniques for identifying and monitoring piracy and counterfeiting; and
   (e) take other actions in the exercise of its functions.

4. All decisions of the Committee shall be taken by consensus, except as the Committee may otherwise decide by consensus. The Committee shall be deemed to have acted by consensus on a matter submitted for its consideration, if no Party present at the meeting when the decision is taken formally objects to the proposed decision. English shall be the working language of the Committee and the documents supporting its work shall be in the English language.
5. The Committee shall adopt its rules and procedures within a reasonable period after the entry into force of this Agreement, and shall invite those Signatories not Parties to this Agreement to participate in the Committee's deliberations on those rules and procedures. The rules and procedures:
   (a) shall address such matters as chairing and hosting meetings, and the performance of organizational duties relevant to this Agreement and its operation; and
   (b) may also address such matters as granting observer status, and any other matter the Committee decides necessary for its proper operation.
6. The Committee may amend the rules and procedures.
7. Notwithstanding the provisions of paragraph 4, during the first five years following the entry into force of this Agreement, the Committee's decisions to adopt or amend the rules and procedures shall be taken by consensus of the Parties and those Signatories not Parties to this Agreement.
8. After the period specified in paragraph 7, the Committee may adopt or amend the rules and procedures upon the consensus of the Parties to this Agreement.
9. Notwithstanding the provisions of paragraph 8, the Committee may decide that the adoption or amendment of a particular rule or procedure requires the consensus of the Parties and those Signatories not Parties to this Agreement.
10. The Committee shall convene at least once every year unless the Committee decides otherwise. The first meeting of the Committee shall be held within a reasonable period after the entry into force of this Agreement.
11. For greater certainty, the Committee shall not oversee or supervise domestic or international enforcement or criminal investigations of specific intellectual property cases.
12. The Committee shall strive to avoid unnecessary duplication between its activities and other international efforts regarding the enforcement of intellectual property rights.

**Article 37: Contact Points**

1. Each Party shall designate a contact point to facilitate communications between the Parties on any matter covered by this Agreement.

2. On the request of another Party, a Party's contact point shall identify an appropriate office or official to whom the requesting Party's inquiry may be addressed, and assist, as necessary, in facilitating communications between the office or official concerned and the requesting Party.

### Article 38: Consultations

1. A Party may request in writing consultations with another Party with respect to any matter affecting the implementation of this Agreement. The requested Party shall accord sympathetic consideration to such a request, provide a response, and afford adequate opportunity to consult.
2. The consultations, including particular positions taken by consulting Parties, shall be kept confidential and be without prejudice to the rights or positions of either Party in any other proceeding, including a proceeding under the auspices of the *Understanding on Rules and Procedures Governing the Settlement of Disputes* contained in Annex 2 to the WTO Agreement.
3. The consulting Parties may, by mutual consent, notify the Committee of the result of their consultations under this Article.

## Chapter VI

**FINAL PROVISIONS**

### Article 39: Signature

This Agreement shall remain open for signature by participants in its negotiation,[17] and by any other WTO Members the participants may agree to by consensus, from 1 May 2011 until 1 May 2013.

### Article 40: Entry Into Force

1. This Agreement shall enter into force thirty days after the date of deposit of the sixth instrument of ratification, acceptance, or approval as between those

[17] Australia, the Republic of Austria, the Kingdom of Belgium, the Republic of Bulgaria, Canada, the Republic of Cyprus, the Czech Republic, the Kingdom of Denmark, the Republic of Estonia, the European Union, the Republic of Finland, the French Republic, the Federal Republic of Germany, the Hellenic Republic, the Republic of Hungary, Ireland, the Italian Republic, Japan, the Republic of Korea, the Republic of Latvia, the Republic of Lithuania, the Grand Duchy of Luxembourg, the Republic of Malta, the United Mexican States, the Kingdom of Morocco, the Kingdom of the Netherlands, New Zealand, the Republic of Poland, the Portuguese Republic, Romania, the Republic of Singapore, the Slovak Republic, the Republic of Slovenia, the Kingdom of Spain, the Kingdom of Sweden, the Swiss Confederation, the United Kingdom of Great Britain and Northern Ireland, and the United States of America.

Signatories that have deposited their respective instruments of ratification, acceptance, or approval.

2. This Agreement shall enter into force for each Signatory that deposits its instrument of ratification, acceptance, or approval after the deposit of the sixth instrument of ratification, acceptance, or approval, thirty days after the date of deposit by such Signatory of its instrument of ratification, acceptance, or approval.

**Article 41: Withdrawal**

A Party may withdraw from this Agreement by means of a written notification to the Depositary. The withdrawal shall take effect 180 days after the Depositary receives the notification.

**Article 42: Amendments**

1. A Party may propose amendments to this Agreement to the Committee. The Committee shall decide whether to present a proposed amendment to the Parties for ratification, acceptance, or approval.
2. Any amendment shall enter into force ninety days after the date that all the Parties have deposited their respective instruments of ratification, acceptance, or approval with the Depositary.

**Article 43: Accession**

1. After the expiration of the period provided in Article 39 (Signature), any

Member of the WTO may apply to accede to this Agreement.

2. The Committee shall decide upon the terms of accession for each applicant.
3. This Agreement shall enter into force for the applicant thirty days after the date of deposit of its instrument of accession based upon the terms of accession referred to in paragraph 2.

**Article 44: Texts of the Agreement**

This Agreement shall be signed in a single original in the English, French, and Spanish languages, each version being equally authentic.

**Article 45: Depositary**

The Government of Japan shall be the Depositary of this Agreement.

# References

## BOOKS, ARTICLES, BOOK CHAPTERS AND REPORTS

Abbott, Frederick. 'Intellectual Property Provisions of Bilateral and Regional Trade Agreements in Light of U.S. Federal Law', *ICTSD Programme on Intellectual Property Rights and Sustainable Development*, Issue paper 12. Geneva: International Centre for Trade and Sustainable Development, 2006.

'Worst Fears Realised: The Dutch Confiscation of Medicines Bound from India to Brazil', *Bridges Monthly* no. 1, February–March 2009.

Abdel-Latif, Ahmed, 'Developing Country Coordination in Intellectual Property Standard-Setting', *Trade-Related Agenda, Development and Equity*, Working Paper 24. Geneva: South Centre, 2005.

'ACTA: Original Expectations and Future Implications', *Bridges Weekly* vol 14 no. 4 (December 2010 ). Available at: http://ictsd.org/i/news/bridges/98805/.

'Change and Continuity in the International Intellectual Property System: A Turbulent Decade in Perspective', *The WIPO Journal* vol. 3 no. 1 (2011): 36.

Adam, Ainee. 'What Is "Commercial Scale"? A Critical Analysis of the WTO Panel Decision in WT/DS362/R', *European Intellectual Property Review* vol. 33 no. 6 (2011): 342–348.

Akester, Patrícia. 'The Impact of Digital Rights Management on Freedom of Expression – the First Empirical Assessment', *IIC – International Review of Intellectual Property and Competition Law* vol. 41 no. 1 (2010): 31–58.

American University Washington College of Law. 'ACTA Section Analysis', *Program on Information Justice and Intellectual Property series*. Available at: https://sites.google.com/site/iipenforcement/acta-section-analysis.

Arezzo, Emanuela. 'Videogames and Consoles between Copyright and Technical Protection Measures', *IIC – International Review of Intellectual Property and Competition Law* vol. 40 no. 1 (2009): 82–95.

Arhel, Pierre. 'L'accord commercial anticontrefaçon: version finale', *Propriété industrielle* no. 3 (2011): 13.

Arlt, Christian. 'Marktabschottend wirkender Einsatz von DRM-Technik – Eine Untersuchung aus wettbewerbsrechtlichem Blickwinkel', *Gewerblicher Rechtsschutz und Urheberrecht* (2005): 1003–1011.

Assange, Julian. *The Unauthorised Autobiography*. Edinburgh: Canongate, 2012.

Atik, Jeffrey. 'ACTA and the Destabilization of TRIPS', in Lidgard, Hans Henrik, Jeffery Atik and Tu Thanh Nguyen (eds.), *Sustainable Technology Transfer: A Guide to Global Aid & Trade Development*. Alphen aan den Rijn: Kluwer Law International, 2012.

Ayoob, Emily. 'Recent Development: The Anti-Counterfeiting Trade Agreement', *Cardozo Arts and Entertainment Law Journal* vol. 28 (2010): 175–193.

Baccus, James. 'A Way Forward for the WTO', in Meléndez-Ortiz, Ricardo, Christoph Bellmann and Miguel Rodriguez (eds.), *The Future and the WTO: Confronting the Challenges*. A Collection of Short Essays, 2012.

Baker, Brook. 'ACTA – Risks of Third-Party Enforcement for Access to Medicines', *American University International Law Review* vol. 26 no. 3 (2011): 579–599.

'Settlement of India/EU WTO Dispute re Seizures of In-Transit Medicines: Why the Proposed EU Border Regulation Isn't Good Enough', *School of Law Faculty Publications*, Paper 37 (2012).

Band, Jonathan. 'The SOPA/TPP Nexus', *PIJIP Research Paper no. 6*. Washington, DC: American University Washington College of Law, 2012.

Bannerman, Sara. 'WIPO and the ACTA Threat', *PIJIP Research Paper no. 4*. Washington, DC: American University Washington College of Law, 2010.

Barbosa, Denis Borges. 'BRIIC: Laying a New Patent System', *IIC – International Review of Intellectual Property and Competition Law* vol. 43 no. 4 (2012): 369–498.

'Counting Ten for TRIPS: Author Rights and Access to Information – A Cockroach's View of Encroachment', in Kors, Jorge, and Bernard Remiche (eds.), *L'Accord ADPIC: dix ans après: regards croisés Europe-Amérique latine: actes du séminaire de Buenos Aires organisé par l'Association internationale de Droit économique*. Bruxelles: Larcier, 2007.

'Minimum Standards vs. Harmonization in the TRIPS Context: The Nature of Obligations under TRIPS and Modes of Implementation at the National Level in Monist and Dualist Systems', in Correa, Carlos (ed.), *Research Handbook on the Interpretation and Enforcement of Intellectual Property under WTO Rules*. Cheltenham–Northampton: Edward Elgar, 2010.

'Untoward Restrictions to Trade and Abuses of Intellectual Property Rights: A Brazilian Perspective to the ACTA Exercise', *Pontifícia Universidade Católica do Rio de Janeiro working paper series*. Rio de Janeiro: Pontifícia Universidade Católica do Rio de Janeiro, 2010.

Barbosa, Denis Borges, Margaret Chon and Andrès Moncayo von Hase. 'Slouching Towards Development in International Intellectual Property', *Michigan State Law Review* vol. 2007 no. 1 (2008): 71–143.

Bently, Lionel, Jennifer Davis and Jane Ginsburg (eds.). *Trade Marks and Brands: An Interdisciplinary Critique*. Cambridge: Cambridge University Press, 2008.

Benvenisti, Eyal and George W. Downs. 'The Empire's New Clothes: Political Economy and the Fragmentation of International Law', *Stanford Law Review* vol. 60 no. 2 (2007): 595–631.

Bitton, Miriam. 'Rethinking the Anti-Counterfeiting Trade Agreement's Criminal Copyright Enforcement Measures', *Journal of Criminal Law and Criminology* vol. 102 no. 1 (2012): 67.

Blakeney, Michael. *Intellectual Property Enforcement. A Commentary on the Anti-Counterfeiting Trade Agreement (ACTA)*. Cheltenham–Northampton: Edward Elgar, 2012.

'International Proposals for the Criminal Enforcement of Intellectual Property Rights: International Concern with Counterfeiting and Piracy', *Intellectual Property Quarterly* Issue 1 (2009): 1–26.

Bradley, Curtis and Martin, Flaherty. 'Executive Power Essentialism and Foreign Affairs', *Michigan Law Review* vol. 102 no. 4 (2004): 545–688.

Braithwaite, John and Peter Drahos. *Global Business Regulation*. Cambridge: Cambridge University Press, 2000.

Bridy, Annemarie. 'ACTA and the Specter of Graduated Response', *PIJIP Research Paper no. 2*. Washington, DC: American University Washington College of Law, 2010.

'Graduated Response American Style: "Six Strikes" Measured against Five Norms', *Fordham Intellectual Property, Media & Entertainment Law Journal* vol. 23 no. 1 (2012): 1–66.

Carrier, Michael. 'SOPA, PIPA, ACTA, TPP: An Alphabet Soup of Innovation-Stifling Copyright Legislation and Agreements', *Northwestern Journal of Technology and Intellectual Property* vol. 11 no. 2 (2013): 21–31.

Charlesworth, Hilary, Madelaine Chiam, Devika Hovell and George Williams. *No Country Is an Island: Australia and International Law*. Sydney: UNSW Press, 2006.

Chaudhry, Peggy and Alan Zimmerman. *The Economics of Counterfeit Trade – Governments, Consumers, Pirates and Intellectual Property Rights*. Heidelberg: Springer, 2009.

Cheng, Jacqui. 'Germany Says "Nein" to Three-Strikes Infringement Plan', *Ars Technica*, 6 February 2009. Available at: http://arstechnica.com/tech-policy/news/2009/02/germany-walks-away-from-three-strikes-internet-policy.ars.

Chow, Daniel. 'Counterfeiting as an Externality Imposed by Multinational Companies on Developing Countries', *Virginia Journal of International Law* vol. 51 no. 4 (2011): 785–823.

'Counterfeiting in the People's Republic of China', *Washington University Law Quarterly* vol. 78 no. 1 (2000): 1–57.

'Why China Does Not Take Commercial Piracy Seriously', *Ohio Northern University Law Review* vol. 32 no. 2 (2006): 203–225.

Clark, Bradford. 'Domesticating Sole Executive Agreements', *Virginia Law Review* vol. 93 no. 7 (2007): 1573–1661.

Clift, Charles. A *Review of Statistical Information on Counterfeiting and Piracy*, WIPO/ACE/7/5, 2011.

Coombe, Rosemary. *The Cultural Life of Intellectual Properties*. Durham, NC: Duke University Press, 1998.

Correa, Carlos. 'Anti-counterfeiting: A Trojan Horse for Expanding Intellectual Property Protection in Developing Countries?', in Geiger, Christophe (ed.), *Criminal Enforcement of Intellectual Property: A Handbook of Contemporary Research*. Cheltenham-Northampton: Edward Elgar, 2012.

'Bilateral Investment Agreements: Agents of New Global Standards for the Protection of Intellectual Property Rights?' Report commissioned by GRAIN, 2004.

'The Push for Stronger Enforcement Rules: Implications for Developing Countries', *ICTSD Programme on Intellectual Property Rights and Sustainable Development*, Issue Paper 22. Geneva: International Centre for Trade and Sustainable Development, 2009.

*Trade Related Aspects of Intellectual Property Rights*. Oxford: Oxford University Press, 2007.

Creemers, Rogier. 'The Effects of WTO Case DS362 on Audiovisual Media Piracy in China', *European Intellectual Property Review* vol. 31 no. 11 (2009): 568–590.

'Explaining Audiovisual Media Piracy in China', Doctoral Dissertation, University of Maastricht, February 2012.

Curran, Clare. 'ACTA, Secrecy, Copyright and Delays', *Labour blog (New Zealand)*, 16 December 2009. Available at: http://blog.labour.org.nz/2009/12/16/acta-secrecy-copyright-and-delays/?utm_source=wordtwit&utm_medium=social&utm_campaign=wordtwit.

Cutler, Claire, Virginia Haufler, and Tony Porter (eds.). *Private Authority and International Affairs*. Albany: State University of New York Press, 1999.

De Gucht, Karel. 'Speaking Points: State of play of negotiations on the Anti-Counterfeiting Trade Agreement (ACTA)', speech at the European Parliament, Committee for International Trade, Strasbourg, 8 September 2010. Available at: http://trade.ec.europa.eu/doclib/docs/2010/september/tradoc_146465.pdf.

Deere, Carolyn. *The Implementation Game: The TRIPS Agreement and the Global Politics of Intellectual Property Reform in Developing Countries*. Oxford: Oxford University Press, 2009.

DeLaurell, Roxane. 'The Anti-Counterfeiting Trade Agreement of 2010: Two Problems and one unanswered question', *The Global Business Law Review* no. 2 (2011): 175–192.

Devigne, Luc Pierre and Pedro Velasco-Martins. 'Where Is ACTA Taking Us? Policies and Politics', in Stamatoudi, Irini (ed.), *Copyright Enforcement and the Internet*. Alphen aan den Rijn: Kluwer Law International, 2010.

Dinwoodie, Graeme and Mark Janis (eds.). *Trademark Law and Theory: A Handbook of Contemporary Research*. Cheltenham-Northampton: Edward Elgar, 2008.

Dogan, Stacy and Mark Lemley. 'Parody as Brand', *Stanford Public Law Working Paper No. 2170498*. Stanford, CA: Stanford Law School, 2012.

Drahos, Peter. *The Global Governance of Knowledge: Patent Offices and Their Clients*. Cambridge: Cambridge University Press, 2010.

Drahos, Peter and John Braithwaite. *Information Feudalism: Who Owns the Knowledge Economy?* London: Earthscan, 2002.

Dreier, Thomas and Gernot Schulze. *Urheberrechtsgesetz: UrhG*. Munich: Beck, 2008.

Drexl, Josef. 'The Evolution of TRIPS: Towards Flexible Multilateralism', in Kors, Jorge and Bernard Remiche (eds.), *L'Accord ADPIC: dix ans après: regards croisés Europe-Amérique latine: actes du séminaire de Buenos Aires organisé par l'Association internationale de Droit économique*. Bruxelles: Larcier, 2007.

Dreyfuss, Rochelle. 'TRIPS-Round II: Should Users Strike Back?', *University of Chicago Law Review* vol. 71 no. 1 (2004): 21–35.

Eckes, Christina, Elaine Fahey, and Machiko Kanetake. 'International, European and US Perspectives on the Negotiation and Adoption of the Anti-Counterfeiting Trade Agreement (ACTA)', *Currents, International Trade Law Journal* vol. 20 no. 2 (2013): 20–44.

Edström, Jerker and Henrik Nilsson. 'The Pirate Bay Verdict – Predictable, and Yet…', *European Intellectual Property Review* vol. 31 no. 9 (2009): 483–487.

Eibauer, Josef. 'Blessing or curse? The effects of transparency on the European Commission's success at the international ACTA negotiations', *PIPE Working Paper no 14/2012*. Berlin: Centre for International Political Economy, 2012.

Ermert, Monika. 'ACTA Negotiators: Maximal Protection Proposals Unlikely in Final Text', *Intellectual Property Watch*, 18 February 2010. Available at: http://www.ip-watch.org/2010/02/18/acta-negotiators-maximal-protection-proposals-unlikely-in-final-text/

'ACTA Negotiators Vow to Mesh with National-Level Rights; Withhold New Text', *Intellectual Property Watch*, 2 July 2010. Available at: http://www.ip-watch.org/weblog/2010/07/02/acta-negotiators-vow-to-mesh-with-national-level-rights-withhold-new-text/.

European Academics. 'Opinion of European Academics on Anti-Counterfeiting Trade Agreement', *Journal of Intellectual Property, Information Technology and E-Commerce Law* vol. 2 (2011): 65–72.

European Digital Rights (EDRI), 'ACTA Fact Sheet', 2 February 2012, Available at: http://www.edri.org/ACTAfactsheet.

Ewing, Tom and Robin Feldman. 'The Giants among Us', *Stanford Technology Law Review* vol. 1 (2012). Available at: http://stlr.stanford.edu/pdf/feldman-giants-among-us.pdf.

Fink, Carsten. 'Enforcing Intellectual Property Rights: An Economic Prospective', *ICTSD Programme on Intellectual Property Rights and Sustainable Development*, Issue Paper 22. Geneva: International Centre for Trade and Sustainable Development, 2009.

Fink, Carsten, Keith Maskus, and Yi Qian, *The Economic Effects of Counterfeiting and Piracy: A Literature Review*, WIPO/ACE/6/7, 2010.

Floridi, Luciano. 'ACTA – The Ethical Analysis of A Failure, and Its Lessons', *ECIPE Occasional Paper no. 4/2012*. Brussels: ECIPE, 2012.

Flynn, Sean. 'ACTA's Constitutional Problem: This Treaty Is Not a Treaty', *American University Journal of International Law* vol. 26 no. 3 (2011): 903–926.

'USTR's precedents do not justify ACTA as sole executive agreement', *Infojustice*, 3 October 2011. *Available at:* http://infojustice.org/archives/5731.

Flynn, Sean and Bijan Madhani. 'ACTA and Access to Medicines', *PIJIP Research Paper no.22*. Washington, DC: American University Washington College of Law, 2011.

Flynn, Sean, Brook Baker, Margot Kaminski, and Jimmy Koo. 'Public Interest Analysis of the US TPP Proposal for an IP Chapter', *PIJIP Research Paper no. 21*. Washington, DC: American University Washington College of Law, 2011.

'The U.S. Proposal for an Intellectual Property Chapter in the Trans-Pacific Partnership Agreement', *American University International Law Review* vol. 28 no. 1 (2013): 105–202.

Frontier Economics. 'Estimating the global economic and social impacts of counterfeiting and piracy', report commissioned by the International Chamber of Commerce's BASCAP initiative, 2011.

Garretson, Heather. 'Federal Criminal Forfeiture: A Royal Pain in the Assets', *Review of Law and Social Justice* vol. 18 no. 1 (2008): 45–77.

Geiger, Christophe. 'Of ACTA, "Pirates" and Organized Criminality – How "Criminal" Should the Enforcement of Intellectual Property Be?', *IIC – International Review of Intellectual Property and Competition Law* vol. 41 no. 6 (2010): 629–631.

'The Anti-Counterfeiting Trade Agreement (ACTA): A Comprehensive Assessment from a European Perspective', *paper for the Committee on International Trade, Directorate-General for External Policies of the European Parliament.* Brussels: European Union, 2012.

'The Anti-Counterfeiting Trade Agreement and Criminal Enforcement of Intellectual Property: What Consequences for the European Union?', in Rosén, Jan (ed.), *Intellectual Property at the Crossroads of Trade*. Cheltenham–Northampton: Edward Elgar, 2012.

'Counterfeiting and the Music Industry: Towards a Criminalization of End Users? The French "HADOPI" Example', in Geiger, Christophe (ed.), *Criminal Enforcement of Intellectual Property: A Handbook of Contemporary Research*. Cheltenham-Northampton: Edward Elgar, 2012.

*Criminal Enforcement of Intellectual Property: A Handbook of Contemporary Research*. Cheltenham-Northampton: Edward Elgar, 2012.

'Exploring the Flexibilities of the TRIPs Agreement Provisions on Limitations and Exceptions', in Kur, Annette and Vytautas Mizaras (eds.), *The Structure of Intellectual*

*Property Law – Can One Size Fit All?* Cheltenham – Northampton: Edward Elgar, 2011.

'The Future of Copyright in Europe – Striking a Fair Balance between Protection and Access to Information', *Intellectual Property Quarterly* vol. 14 no. 1 (2010): 1–14.

'Intellectual Property Shall Be Protected!? Article 17.2 of the Charter of Fundamental Rights of the European Union: A Mysterious Provision with an Unclear Scope', *European Intellectual Property Review* vol. 31 no. 3 (2009): 113–117.

'Quelle mise en œuvre des droits de propriété intellectuelle au niveau international ? Retour sur l'Accord commercial anti-contrefaçon (ACTA)', *Propriété intellectuelle* no. 43 (2012): 201.

'Weakening Multilateralism in Intellectual Property Lawmaking: A European Perspective on ACTA', *The WIPO Journal* vol. 3 no. 2 (2012): 166.

Geiger, Christophe (with Michel Vivant). 'Comment of the Decision of the WTO Panel of 26 January 2009', *Propriété intellectuelle* no. 35 (2010): 747.

Geiger, Christophe, Jacques Raynard, and Caroline Rodà. 'What Developments for the European Framework on Enforcement of Intellectual Property Rights? – A Comment on the Evaluation Report of the European Commission dated 22 December 2010', *European Intellectual Property Review* vol. 33 (2011): 543–550.

Geist, Michael. 'ACTA's State of Play: Looking Beyond Transparency', *American University International Law Review* vol. 26 no. 3 (2011): 543–558.

'The ACTA Threat to the Future of WIPO', *Intellectual Property Watch*, 14 April 2009. Available at http://www.ip-watch.org/2009/04/14/the-acta-threat-to-the-future-of-wipo/.

'The Case for Flexibility in Implementing the WIPO Internet Treaties: An Examination of the Anti-Circumvention Requirements', in Geist, Michael (ed.), *From 'Radical Extremism' to 'Balanced Copyright': Canadian Copyright and the Digital Agenda*. Toronto: Irwin Law, 2010.

'The Trouble with ACTA: an Analysis of the Anti-Counterfeiting Trade Agreement', *report for the Committee on International Trade, Directorate-General for External Policies of the European Parliament*. Brussels: European Union, 2012.

Gerhardsen, Tove Iren. 'Japan Proposes New IP Enforcement Treaty', *Intellectual Property Watch*, 15 November 2005. Available at: www.ip-watch.org/weblog/index.php?p=135.

Gervais, D. 'Country clubs, empiricism, blogs and innovation: the future of international intellectual property law making in the wake of ACTA', in Burri, M and Cottier, T (eds.), *Trade Governance in the Digital Age: World Trade Forum*. Cambridge: Cambridge University Press, 2012.

Gervais, Daniel. 'China-Measures Affecting the Protection and Enforcement of Intellectual Property Rights', *American Journal of International Law* vol. 103 no. 3 (2009): 549–555.

'Criminal Enforcement in the US and Canada', in Geiger, Christophe (ed.), *Criminal Enforcement of Intellectual Property: A Handbook of Contemporary Research*. Cheltenham-Northampton: Edward Elgar, 2012.

'The TRIPS Agreement and the Doha Round: History and Impact on Economic Development', in Yu, Peter (ed.), *Intellectual Property and Information Wealth: Issues and Practices in the Digital Age*. Greenwood: Praeger Publishers, 2007.

GfK. 'Consumo de Contenidos Digitales en España', study for the Spanish Right Holders Coalition, February 2013. Available at: http://lacoalicion.es/wp-content/uploads/Observatorio_Pirateria-2012_Final.pdf.

Gibbons, Llewellyn Joseph. 'Do as I Say (Not as I Did): Putative Intellectual Property Lessons for Emerging Economies from the Not So Long Past of the Developed Nations', *SMU Law Review* vol. 64 (2011): 923.

Gibson, Johanna. 'The Directive Proposal on Criminal Sanctions', in Geiger, Christophe (ed.), *Criminal Enforcement of Intellectual Property: A Handbook of Contemporary Research*. Cheltenham-Northampton: Edward Elgar, 2012.

Gowers, Andrew. 'Gowers Review of Intellectual Property', *independent report to the UK Chancellor of the Exchequer*. London: UK Government, 2006.

Green, Stuart. 'Plagiarism, Norms, and the Limits of Theft Law: Some Observations on the Use of Criminal Sanctions in Enforcing Intellectual Property Rights', *Hastings Law Journal* vol. 54 no. 1 (2002): 167–241.

Griffiths, Jonathan. 'Criminal Liability for Intellectual Property Infringement in Europe: The Role of Fundamental Rights', in Geiger, Christophe (ed.), *Criminal Enforcement of Intellectual Property: A Handbook of Contemporary Research*. Cheltenham-Northampton: Edward Elgar, 2012.

Griffiths, Jonathan and Luke McDonagh. 'Fundamental Rights and European IP Law – The Case of Art. 17.2 of the EU Charter', in Geiger, Christopher (ed.), *Constructing European Intellectual Property: Achievements and New Perspectives*. Cheltenham-Northampton: Edward Elgar, 2013.

Groom, Nick. *The Forger's Shadow: How Forgery Changed the Course of Literature*. London: Picador, 2003.

Gross, Robin. 'IP Justice White Paper on the Proposed Anti-Counterfeiting Trade Agreement (ACTA)', 25 March 2008. Available at http://ipjustice.org/wp/wp-content/uploads/IPJustice_ACTA-white-paper-mar2008.pdf.

Grosse Ruse-Khan, Henning. 'A Comparative Analysis of Policy Space in WTO Law', *Max Planck Institute for Intellectual Property, Competition & Tax Law Research Paper Series No. 08-02*. Munich: Max Planck Institute, 2008.

'Criminal enforcement and international IP law', in Geiger, Christophe (ed.), *Criminal Enforcement of Intellectual Property: A Handbook of Contemporary Research*. Cheltenham-Northampton: Edward Elgar, 2012.

'The (Non) Use of Treaty Object and Purpose in Intellectual Property Disputes in the WTO', *Max Planck Institute for Intellectual Property, Competition & Tax Law Research Paper Series No. 11–15*. Munich: Max Planck Institute, 2011.

'A Trade Agreement Creating Barriers to International trade?: ACTA Border Measures and Goods in Transit', *American University International Law Review* vol. 26 no. 3 (2011): 645–726.

'From TRIPS to ACTA: Towards a New "Gold Standard" in Criminal IP Enforcement?', in Geiger, Christophe (ed.), *Criminal Enforcement of Intellectual Property: A Blessing or a Curse?* Cheltenham-Northampton: Edward Elgar, 2011.

Grosse Ruse-Khan, Henning et al. 'The Impact of the Anti-Counterfeiting Trade Agreement on the Legal Framework for IP Enforcement in the European Union', in Geiger, Christopher (ed.), *Constructing European Intellectual Property: Achievements and New Perspectives*. Cheltenham – Northampton: Edward Elgar, 2013.

Guibault, Lucie et al. 'Study on the Implementation And Effect in Member States' Laws of Directive 2001/29/EC on the Harmonisation of Certain Aspects of Copyright and Related Rights in The Information Society', report to the European Commission,

DG Internal Market. Amsterdam: Institute for Information Law at the University of Amsterdam, 2007.
Haas, Peter. 'Introduction: Epistemic Communities and International Policy Coordination', *International Organization* vol. 46 no. 1 (1992): 1–35.
Hardy, Trotter. 'Criminal Copyright Infringement', *William & Mary Bill of Rights Journal*, vol. 11 (2002): 305–341.
Hargreaves, Ian. 'Digital Opportunity, A review of Intellectual Property and Growth', independent report commissioned by the UK Government, 2011. Available at: http://www.ipo.gov.uk/ipreview-finalreport.pdf.
Harris, Donald. 'The Honeymoon Is Over: The U.S.-China WTO Intellectual Property Complaint', *Fordham International Law Journal* vol. 32 no. 1 (2008): 96–187.
Hathaway, Oona. Presidential Power over International Law: Restoring the Balance', *Yale Law Journal* vol. 119 no. 2 (2009): 140–268.
Hathaway, Oona and Amy Kapczynski. 'Going It Alone: The Anti-Counterfeiting Trade Agreement as a Sole Executive Agreement', *American Society of International Law Insights* vol. 15 no. 23 (2011).
Health Action International. 'ACTA and Access to Medicines: A Flawed Process, Flawed Rationale and Flawed Agreement', Policy Brief, February 2012. Available at: http://haieurope.org/wp-content/uploads/2012/02/27-Feb-2012-HAI-Europe-Policy-Brief-ACTA-and-Access-to-Medicines.pdf.
Health Action International Africa. 'A briefing paper on the utilization of TRIPS flexibilities in the EAC Region', Briefing Paper, July 2012. Available at: http://www.haiafrica.org/index.php?option=com_content&view=article&id=273:a-briefing-paper-on-the-utilization-of-trips-flexibilities-in-the-eac-region&catid=78:news.
Heide, Thomas. 'Copyright in the E.U. and United States: What "Access Right'", *European Intellectual Property Review* vol. 23 no. 10 (2001): 469–477.
Helfer, Lawrence. 'Regime Shifting: The TRIPs Agreement and New Dynamics of International Intellectual Property Lawmaking', *Yale Journal of International Law* vol. 29 no. 1 (2004): 1–83.
Henderson, David. *L'accord multilatéral sur l'investissement – Leçons d'un échec*. Paris: GEM, 1999.
Heyman, Laura. 'The Public's Domain in Trademark Law: A First Amendment Theory of the Consumer', *Georgia Law Review* vol. 43 (2009): 651–715.
Hilty, Reto. 'Economic, Legal and Social Impacts of Counterfeiting', in Geiger, Christopher (ed.), *Constructing European Intellectual Property: Achievements and New Perspectives*. Cheltenham – Northampton: Edward Elgar, 2013.
Hilty, Reto, Annette Kur, and Alexander Peukert. 'Statement of the Max Planck Institute for Intellectual Property, Competition and Tax Law on the Proposal for a Directive of the European Parliament and the Council on Criminal Measures Aimed at Ensuring the Enforcement of Intellectual Property Rights', *IIC – International Review of Intellectual Property and Competition Law* vol. 37 no. 8 (2006): 970–977.
Hoeren, Thomas. 'ACTA ad acta? Überlegunqen zum urheberrechtlichen "Shitstorm"', *MMR* vol. 3 (2012): 137–138.
Honsakasalo, Pessi. 'Criminal Proceedings against the Administrators of a BitTorrent Tracker: Finreactor KKO:2010:47', *European Intellectual Property Review* vol. 32 no. 11 (2010): 591–592.

Hugenholtz, Bernt and Ruth Okediji. 'Conceiving an International Instrument on Limitations and Exceptions to Copyright: Final Report', *Open Society Institute's Information Program*, March 2008. Available at: http://www.opensocietyfoundations.org/sites/default/files/copyright_20080506.pdf.

Ibáñez, Josep. 'Transnational Private Authorities and the Erosion of Democracy', in Cornago, Noé, Igor Filibi, and Justin Frosini (eds.), *Democracy With(out) Nations? Old and New Foundations for Political Communities in a Changing World*. Bilbao: Universidad del País Vasco, 2011.

Idris, Kamil. *Intellectual Property: A Power Tool for Economic Growth*. Geneva: World Intellectual Property Organization, 2002.

International Centre for Trade and Sustainable Development. 'Brazil, India Challenge Generic Drug Detentions', *Bridges Weekly Trade News Digest* vol. 14 no. 17, 12 May 2010. Available at: http://ictsd.org/i/news/bridgesweekly/75730/.

International Centre for Trade and Sustainable Development, *Fostering Low Carbon Growth: The Case for a Sustainable Energy Trade Agreement, ICTSD Global Platform on Climate Change, Trade and Sustainable Energy*. Geneva: ICTSD, 2011. Available at: http://ictsd.org/downloads/2012/05/fostering-low-carbon-growth-the-case-for-a-sustainable-energy-trade-agreement1.pdf

International Centre for Trade and Sustainable Development. 'EU Parliament Criticises Secrecy of ACTA Negotiations in Landslide Vote', *Bridges Weekly Trade News Digest* vol. 14 no. 10,17 March 2010. Available at: http://ictsd.org/i/news/bridgesweekly/72497/.

International Centre for Trade and Sustainable Development, 'European Generic Drug Seizures Take Centre Stage at TRIPS Council Meeting', *Bridges Weekly Trade News Digest* vol. 13 no. 21, 10 June 2009. Available at: http://ictsd.org/i/news/bridgesweekly/48330/.

International Centre for Trade and Sustainable Development. 'New Zealand Confirms Plans for Introducing Cigarette Packaging Law', *Bridges Weekly Trade News Digest* vol. 17 no. 7, 27 February 2013. Available at: http://ictsd.org/i/news/bridgesweekly/156105/.

International Centre for Trade and Sustainable Development – United Nations Conference on Trade and Development. 'Development Dimensions of Intellectual Property in Uganda: Transfer of Technology, Access to Medicines and Textbooks', *UNCTAD-ICTSD Project on Intellectual Property Rights and Sustainable Development*. Geneva: UNCTAD, 2010.

*Resource Book on TRIPS and Development*. New York: Cambridge University Press, 2005.

International Federation of the Phonographic Industry. 'Digital Music Report 2012 – Expanding Choice. Going Global', IFPI annual report, 2012. Available at: http://www.ifpi.org/content/library/DMR2012.pdf.

'Digital Music Report 2013 – Engine of a digital world', IFPI annual report, 2013. Available at: http://www.ifpi.org/content/library/DMR2013.pdf.

'IFPI Digital Music Report 2011 – Music at the touch of a button', IFPI annual report, 2011. Available at: http://www.ifpi.org/content/library/dmr2011.pdf.

International Intellectual Property Alliance. '2012 Special 301 Report on Copyright Protection and Enforcement', February 2012. Available at: http://www.iipa.com/2012_SPEC301_TOC.htm.

IP Australia. *Implementing the TRIPS Protocol*. Canberra: IP Australia, 2010.

IQsensato. 'The Proposed Anti-Counterfeiting Trade Agreement (ACTA): Global Policy Implications', *In Focus*, 2 June 2008.

Jaffe, Adam and Josh Lerner. *Innovation and Its Discontents: How Our Broken Patent System Is Endangering Innovation and Progress, and What to Do About It*. Princeton: Princeton University Press, 2004.

Jingzhou, Tao. 'Problems and New Developments in the Enforcement of Intellectual Property Rights in China', in Torremans, Paul, Hailing Shan and Johan Erauw (eds.), *Intellectual Property and TRIPS Compliance in China: Chinese and European Perspectives*. Cheltenham-Northampton: Edward Elgar, 2007.

Johns, Adrian. *Piracy: The Intellectual Property Wars from Gutenberg to Gates*. Chicago and London: University of Chicago Press, 2011.

Kahn-Freund, Otto. 'On Uses and Misuses of Comparative Law', *Modern Law Review* vol. 37 no. 1 (1974): 1–27.

Kaminski, Margot. 'The Origins and Potential Impact of the Anti-Counterfeiting Trade Agreement (ACTA)', *Yale Journal of International Law* vol. 34 (2009): 247.

'An Overview and the Evolution of the Anti-Counterfeiting Trade Agreement', *Albany Law Journal of Science and Technology* vol. 21 no. 3 (2011): 385–444.

'Recent Development: The Origins and Potential Impact of the Anti-Counterfeiting Trade Agreement (ACTA)', *Yale Journal of International Law* vol. 34 (2009): 247–256.

Kamperman Sanders, Anselm, Dalindyebo Shabalala, Anke Moerland, Meir Pugatch, and Paolo Vergano. 'The Anti-Counterfeiting Trade Agreement (ACTA): An Assessment', *study for the Committee on International Trade, Directorate-General for External Policies of the European Parliament*. Brussels: European Union, 2011.

Karaganis, Joe (ed.). *Media Piracy in Emerging Economies*. New York: Social Science Research Council, 2011.

Katz, Eddan and Gwen Hinze. 'The Impact of the Anti-Counterfeiting Trade Agreement on the Knowledge Economy: The Accountability of the Office of the U.S. Trade Representative for the Creation of IP Enforcement Norms Through Executive Trade Agreements', *Yale Journal of International Law Online* vol. 35 (2009): 24.

KEA European Affairs. 'The impact of culture on creativity', study commissioned by the European Commission, 2009. Available at: http://ec.europa.eu/culture/documents/study_impact_cult_creativity_06_09.pdf.

Keck, Margaret and Kathryn Sikkink. *Activists Beyond Borders: Advocacy Networks in International Politics*. Ithaca: Cornell University Press, 1998.

Kelsey, Jane and Lori Wallach. '"Investor-State" Disputes in Trade Pacts Threaten Fundamental Principles of National Judicial Systems', working paper, April 2012. Available at: http://tpplegal.files.wordpress.com/2012/05/isds-domestic-legal-process-background-brief.pdf.

Kennedy, M., Legal Options for a Sustainable Energy Trade Agreement, ICTSD, 2012.

Koelman, Kamiel. 'A Hard Nut to Crack: The Protection of Technological Measures', *European Intellectual Property Review* vol. 22 no. 6 (2010): 272–288.

Korff, Douwe and Ian Brown. 'Opinion on the compatibility of the Anti-Counterfeiting Trade Agreement (ACTA) with the European Convention on Human Rights & the EU Charter of Fundamental Rights', opinion commissioned by the Greens/European Free Alliance group in the European Parliament, 2011.

Kumar, Shashank. 'Border Enforcement of Intellectual Property Rights against In-Transit Generic Pharmaceuticals', *European Intellectual Property Review* vol. 32 no. 10 (2010): 506–519.

Kur, Annette and Henning Grosse Ruse-Khan. 'Enough Is Enough: The Notion of Binding Ceilings in International Intellectual Property Protection', *Max Planck Institute for*

*Intellectual Property, Competition & Tax Law Research Paper Series* No. 09-01. Munich: Max Planck Institute, 2008.

La Quadrature du Net. 'Three Core Reasons for Rejecting ACTA', *La Quadrature du Net*, 29 March 2010. Available at: http://www.laquadrature.net/en/three-core-reasons-for-rejecting-acta.

LaFrance, Mary. 'Graduated Response by Industry Compact', *Cardozo Arts & Entertainment Law Journal* vol. 30 no. 2: 165–186.

Lamy, Pascal. 'The Rise of Regional Trade Agreements could lead to "Policy Fragmentation"', speech at the University of International Business and Economics, Beijing, 20 September 2012. Available at: http://www.wto.org/english/news_e/sppl_e/sppl246_e.htm.

Lee, Timothy. 'As Curiosity Touches Down on Mars, Video Is Taken Down from YouTube', *Ars Technica*, 7 August 2012. Available at: http://arstechnica.com/tech-policy/2012/08/as-curiosity-touches-down-on-mars-video-is-taken-down-from-youtube/.

'Music Publisher Uses DMCA to Take Down Romney Ad of Obama Crooning', *Ars Technica*, 17 July 2012. Available at: http://arstechnica.com/tech-policy/2012/07/major-label-uses-dmca-to-take-down-romney-ad-of-obama-crooning/.

'New Zealand Prime Minister Apologizes For Illegal Dotcom Spying', *Ars Technica*, 28 September 2012. Available at: http://arstechnica.com/Tech-Policy/2012/09/New-Zealand-Prime-Minister-Apologizes-For-Illegal-Dotcom-Spying/.

Lefranc, David. 'Historical Perspective on Criminal Enforcement', in Geiger, Christophe (ed.), *Criminal Enforcement of Intellectual Property: A Handbook of Contemporary Research*. Cheltenham-Northampton: Edward Elgar, 2012.

Legrand, Pierre. 'The Impossibility of "Legal Transplants"', *Maastricht Journal of European and Comparative Law* vol. 4 (1997): 111–124.

Levine, David. 'Bring in the Nerds: Secrecy, National Security and the Creation of International Intellectual Property Law', *Cardozo Arts & Entertainment Law Journal* vol. 30 no. 2 (2012): 105–151.

'Transparency Soup: The ACTA Negotiating Process and "Black Box" Lawmaking', *American University International Law Review*, vol. 26 no. 3 (2011): 811–837.

Lewis, Meredith. 'The Trans-Pacific Partnership: New Paradigm or Wolf in Sheep's Clothing?', *Boston College International and Comparative Law Review* vol. 34 (2011): 27–52.

Liberman, Jonathan. 'Plainly Constitutional: The Upholding of Plain Tobacco Packaging by the High Court of Australia', *American Journal of Law and Medicine* vol. 39 no. 2 (2013): 361–381.

Lindsay, David. *International Domain Name Law: ICANN and the UDRP*. Oxford and Portland: Hart Publishing, 2007.

Lipton, Jacqueline. *Internet Domain Names, Trademarks and Free Speech*. Cheltenham-Northampton: Edward Elgar, 2010.

Loughlan, Patricia. '"You Wouldn't Steal a Car": Intellectual Property and the Language of Theft', *European Intellectual Property Review* vol. 29 no. 10 (2007): 401–405.

Malkawi, Bashar. 'A Long "TRIP" Home: How the Berne Convention, TRIPS Agreement, and Other Instruments Complement the International Copyright System', *European Intellectual Property Review* vol. 35 no. 2 (2013): 93–107.

Manta, Irina. 'The Puzzle of Criminal Sanctions for Intellectual Property Infringement', *Harvard Journal of Law and Technology* vol. 24 no. 2 (2011): 469–518.

Maskus, Keith. 'The Role of Intellectual Property Rights in Encouraging Foreign Direct Investment and Technology Transfer', *Duke Journal of Comparative and International Law* vol. 9 no. 1 (1998): 109–161.

'The Role of Intellectual Property Rights in Encouraging Foreign Direct Investment and Technology Transfer', in Fink, Carsten and Keith Maskus (eds.), *Intellectual Property and Development: Lessons from Recent Economic Research*. New York: World Bank-Oxford University Press, 2005.

Maskus, Keith and Jerome Reichman. 'The Globalization of Private Knowledge Goods and the Privatization of Global Public Goods', in Maskus, Keith and Jerome Reichman (eds.), *International Public Goods and Transfer of Technology under a Globalized Intellectual Property Regime*. Cambridge: Cambridge University Press, 2005.

Massey, Joseph. 'The Emperor Is Far Away: China's Enforcement of Intellectual Property Rights Protection, 1986–2006', *Chicago Journal of International Law* vol. 7 no. 1 (2006): 231–237.

Matthews, Duncan. 'Counterfeiting and Public Health', in Geiger, Christophe (ed.), *Criminal Enforcement of Intellectual Property: A Handbook of Contemporary Research*. Cheltenham-Northampton: Edward Elgar, 2012.

'The Rise and Fall of the Anti-Counterfeiting Trade Agreement (ACTA): Lessons for the European Union', *Queen Mary School of Law Legal Studies Research Paper No. 127/2012*. London: Queen Mary University, 2012.

Matulionyte, Rita. 'ACTA's Digital Chapter: remaining concerns and what can be done', *Queen Mary Journal of Intellectual Property* vol. 1 no. 3 (2011): 248–271.

Max Planck Institute for Intellectual Property and Competition. 'A Balanced Interpretation of the "Three-Step Test" in Copyright Law', declaration on the 'Three-Step Test'. Munich: Max Planck Institute for Intellectual Property and Competition, 2012.

'Principles for Intellectual Property Provisions in Bilateral and Regional Agreements', Munich: Max Plank Institute for Intellectual Property and Competition, 2013.

May, Christopher. *The World Intellectual Property Organization: Resurgence and the Development Agenda*. London: Routledge, 2007.

McGeveran, William. 'Four Free Speech Goals for Trademark Law', *Fordham Intellectual Property, Media & Entertainment Law Journal* vol. 18 (2008): 1205–1227.

McManis, Charles. 'The Proposed Anti-Counterfeiting Trade Agreement (ACTA): Two Tales of a Treaty', *Houston Law Review* vol. 46 no. 4 (2009): 1235–1256.

McManis, Charles and John Pelletier. 'Two Tales of a Treaty Revisited: The Proposed Anti-Counterfeiting Trade Agreement (ACTA)', *Legal Studies Research Paper no. 12-04-10*. St. Louis: Washington University in St. Louis, 2012.

Médecins Sans Frontières. 'A Blank Cheque for Abuse: The Anti-Counterfeiting Trade Agreement and its Impact on Access to Medicines', MSF Briefing document, February 2012. Available at: http://www.msfaccess.org/sites/default/files/MSF_assets/Access/Docs/Access_Briefing_ACTABlankCheque_ENG_2012.pdf.

Mercedes Frabboni, Maria. 'File-Sharing and the Role of Intermediaries in the Marketplace: National, European Union and International Developments', in Stamatoudi, Irini (ed.), *Copyright Enforcement and the Internet*. Alphen aan den Rijn: Kluwer Law International, 2010.

Mercurio, Bryan. 'Beyond the Text: The Significance of the Anti-Counterfeiting Trade Agreement (ACTA)', *Journal of International Economic Law* vol. 15 no. 2 (2012): 361–390.

'Drugs Seized in Transit: The Case that Wasn't', *International and Comparative Law Quarterly* vol. 61 no. 2 (2012): 389–426.

'"Seizing" Pharmaceuticals in Transit: Analysing the WTO Dispute that Wasn't', *International and Comparative Law Quarterly* vol. 61 no. 2 (2012): 389–426.

'TRIPS-Plus Provisions in FTAs: Recent Trends', in Bartels, Lorand and Federico Ortino (eds.), *Regional Trade Agreements and the WTO Legal System*. Oxford: Oxford University Press, 2006.

Mertha, Andrew. *The Politics of Piracy: Intellectual Property in Contemporary China*. Ithaca: Cornell University Press, 2005.

Metzger, Axel. 'A Primer on ACTA, What Europeans Should Fear about the Anti-Counterfeiting Trade Agreement', *Journal of Intellectual Property, Information Technology and E-Commerce Law* vol. 1 (2010): 109–116.

Metzger, Axel and Till Kreutzer. 'Richtlinie zum Urheberrecht in der "Informationsgesellschaft" Privatkopie trotz technischer Schutzmaßnahmen?', *MMR* (2002): 139–142.

Moore, Jeffrey, John Spink, and Markus Lipp. 'Development and Application of a Database of Food Ingredient Fraud and Economically Motivated Adulteration from 1980 to 2010', *Journal of Food Science* vol. 77 no. 4 (2012): 118–126.

Morris, Michael. 'ACTA's Abandoned Third-Party Liability Provisions and What They Mean for the Future', *PIJIP Research Paper no. 10*. Washington, DC: American University Washington College of Law, 2010.

Muchlinski, Peter. 'The Rise and Fall of the Multilateral Agreement on Investment: Where Now?', *The International Lawyer* vol. 34 no. 3 (2000): 1033–1053.

Muñoz Tellez, Viviana. 'The Changing Global Governance of Intellectual Property Enforcement: A New Challenge for Developing Countries', in Li, Xuan and Carlos Correa (eds.), *Intellectual Property Enforcement: International Perspectives*. Cheltenham-Northampton: Edward Elgar, 2009.

Musungu, Sisule. 'Sections of the Kenya Anti Counterfeiting Act Struck Down as a Threat to Fundamental Human Rights', IQsensato Ideas in Development Blog, 23 April 2012.

Mylly, Tuomas. 'Criminal enforcement and European Union law', in Geiger, Christophe (ed.), *Criminal Enforcement of Intellectual Property: A Handbook of Contemporary Research*. Cheltenham-Northampton: Edward Elgar, 2012.

Nakatomi, Michitaka, Plurilateral Agreements: A Viable Alternative to the World Trade Organization?, *ADBI Working Paper*, Number 439, October 2013, at: http://www.adbi.org/files/2013.10.24.wp439.plurilateral.agreements.alternative.wto.pdf

Ncube, Caroline. 'Enforcing Patent Rights Against Goods in Transit: a New Threat to Transborder Trade in Generic Medicines', *SA Mercantile Law Journal* vol. 21 no. 5 (2009): 680–694.

New, William and Kaitlin Mara. 'Near-Finished Anti-Counterfeiting Trade Pact Could Have Broad Reach', *Intellectual Property Watch*, 12 October 2010. Available at: http://www.ip-watch.org/2010/10/12/rights-holders%E2%80%99-anti-counterfeiting-trade-pact-could-have-broad-reach/?utm_source=weekly&utm_medium=email&utm_campaign=alerts.

Nguyên, Quôc Dinh. *Droit International Public*, 5th Edition. Paris: L.G.D.J, 1995.

Nunes, Ana Beatriz, Denis Borges Barbosa, and Karin Grau-Kuntz. *A Propriedade Intelectual na Construção dos Tribunais Constitucionais*. Rio de Janeiro: Lumen Juris, 2009.

O'Brien, Danny. 'Blogging ACTA Across the Globe: Lessons from Korea', *Electronic Frontier Foundation*, 29 January 2010. Available at: https://www.eff.org/deeplinks/2010/01/acta-and-korea.

Ohly, Ansgar. 'Counterfeiting and Consumer Protection', in Geiger, Christophe (ed.), *Criminal Enforcement of Intellectual Property: A Handbook of Contemporary Research*. Cheltenham-Northampton: Edward Elgar, 2012.

Outterson, Kevin. 'Import Safety Rules Should Not Hinder Legitimate Generic Drug Markets: The Anti-Counterfeiting Trade Agreement (ACTA)', in Coglianese, Cary, Adam Finkel, and David Zaring (eds.), *Import Safety: Regulatory Governance in the Global Economy*. Philadelphia: University of Pennsylvania Press, 2009.

Oxfam. 'Statement Regarding ACTA and Public Health', Oxfam position paper, October 2011. Available at: http://www.oxfamsol.be/fr/IMG/pdf/Oxfam_ACTA_analysis_FINAL.pdf.

Papadopoulou, Maria Daphne. 'ACTA and Copyright in the EU: a Love or Hate Relationship', paper presented at the *4th International Conference on Information Law and Ethics*, Thessaloniki, 2011.

Patry, William. *Moral Panics and the Copyright War*. Oxford: Oxford University Press, 2009.

Pauwelyn, Joost. 'Legal Avenues to "Multilateralizing Regionalism": Beyond article XXIV', in Baldwin, R. and P. Low (eds.), *Multilateralizing Regionalism: Challenges for the Global Trading System*, Cambridge University Press, 2009.

Peers, Steeve. 'EU criminal Law and the Treaty of Lisbon', *European Law Review* vol. 33 no. 4 (2008): 507.

Penalver, Eduardo and Sonia Katyal. *Property Outlaws: How Squatters, Pirates, and Protestors Improve the Law of Ownership*. New Haven: Yale University Press, 2010.

Peukert, Alexander. 'Why Do "Good" People Disregard Copyright on the Internet?', in Geiger, Christophe (ed.), *Criminal Enforcement of Intellectual Property: A Handbook of Contemporary Research*. Cheltenham-Northampton: Edward Elgar, 2012.

PharmaAfrica. 'EAC Pushes Towards Drug Registration Harmonisation and Integration', *AfriPharma Focus* vol. 1 no. 1 (2012).

Pires de Carvalho, Nuno. *The TRIPS Regime of Patent Rights*. The Hague: Kluwer Law International, 2002.

Pogge, Thomas Matthew Rimmer and Kim Rubenstein (eds.). *Incentives for Global Public Health: Patent Law and Access to Medicines*. Cambridge: Cambridge University Press, 2010.

Port, Kenneth. 'A Case Against the ACTA', *William Mitchell Legal Studies Research Paper No.* 2011-04. St. Paul: William Mitchell College of Law, 2011.

Porto, Patrícia. 'O interesse público brasileiro na adesão ao Anti-Counterfeiting Agreement (ACTA)', *Revista Eletrônica do Instituto Brasileiro de Propriedade Intelectual* vol. 1 (2011): 148–156.

Prakash, Saikrishna and Micheal Ramsey. 'The Executive Power over Foreign Affairs', *Yale Law Journal* vol. 111 (2001): 231–356.

Quinn, David. 'A Critical Look at the Anti-Counterfeiting Trade Agreement', *Richmond Journal of Law and Technology* vol. 17 no. 4 (2011): 1–25.

Ramalho, Ana. 'The European Union and ACTA – Or Making Omelettes without Eggs (Again)', *IIC – International Review of Intellectual Property and Competition Law* (2011): 97–101.

RAND Corporation. 'Film Piracy, Organized Crime, and Terrorism', *Safety and Justice Program*. Santa Monica: RAND, 2009.

Raustiala, Kal. 'Density and Conflict in International Intellectual Property Law', *University of California at Davis Law Review* vol. 40 no. 3 (2007): 1021–1038.

Reichman, Jerome. 'Intellectual Property in the Twenty First Century: Will the Developing Countries Lead or Follow?', *Houst Law Review* vol. 46 (2009): 1115–1185.

'The TRIPS Agreement Comes of Age: Conflict or Cooperation with the Developing Countries?', *Case Western Reserve Journal of international Law* vol. 32 (2000): 441–470.

Reichman, Jerome and David Lange. 'Bargaining Around the TRIPS Agreement: The Case for Ongoing Public-Private Initiatives to Facilitate Worldwide Intellectual Property Transactions', *Duke Journal of Comparative and International Law* vol. 9 no. 1 (1998): 11–68.

Rens, Andrew. 'Collateral Damage: The Impact of ACTA and the Enforcement Agenda on the World's Poorest People', *American University International Law Review* vol. 26 no. 3 (2011): 783–809.

'Enforcement Theater, the Enforcement Agenda and the Institutionalization of Enforcement Theater in the Anti-Counterfeiting Trade Agreement', *Suffolk Transnational Law Review* vol. 35 (2012): 553–574.

Rice, Nathaniel. 'Head-in-the-Clouds: The Public's Failure to Recognize How the Anti-Counterfeiting Trade Agreement Protects the Global Intellectual Property Marketplace in the Digital Age', *Suffolk Transnational Law Review* vol. 35 (2012): 631–650.

Rimmer, Matthew. 'Appearance before the Inquiry into the Anti-Counterfeiting Trade Agreement 2011', Australian Joint Standing Committee on Treaties, March 2012.

'Big Tobacco and the Trans-Pacific Partnership', *Tobacco Control* vol. 21 no. 6 (2012) 526–527.

'"Breakfast at Tiffany's": eBay Inc., Trademark Law, and Counterfeiting', *Journal of Law, Information and Science* vol. 21 no. 1 (2011): 128–166.

'Cigarettes Will Kill You: The High Court of Australia and Plain Packaging of Tobacco Products', *WIPO Magazine* no. 1 (2013): 20–23. Available at: http://www.wipo.int/wipo_magazine/en/2013/01/article_0005.html.

'A Dangerous Investment: Australia, New Zealand, and the Trans-Pacific Partnership', *The Conversation*, 2 July 2012. Available at: http://theconversation.edu.au/a-dangerous-investment-australia-new-zealand-and-the-trans-pacific-partnership-7440.

'A Fair Use Project for Australia: Copyright Law and Creative Freedom', *Copyright Reporter* vol. 28 no. 3 (2010): 165–212.

'Race Against Time: The Export of Essential Medicines to Rwanda', *Public Health Ethics* vol. 1 no. 2 (2008): 89–103.

'A Submission to the Joint Standing Committee on Treaties on the Anti-Counterfeiting Trade Agreement 2011', February 2012. Available at: http://works.bepress.com/matthew_rimmer/109.

Rodà, Caroline. *Les conséquences civiles de la contrefaçon des droits de propriété industrielle : droits français, belge, luxembourgeois, allemand, anglais*. Paris: Litec CEIPI Series, 2011.

Roffe, Pedro. 'Intellectual Property, Preferential Trade Agreements and the Multilateral System', in ICTSD, *The Future and the WTO: Confronting the Challenges. A Collection of Short Essays*; ICTSD Programme on Global Economic Policy and Institutions, Geneva, Switzerland, 2012. Available at: http://ictsd.org/downloads/2012/07/the-future-and-the-wto-confronting-the-challenges.pdf.

Roffe, Pedro and Luis Mariano Genovesi. 'Propuesta de estrategia y plan de acción: implementación del Acuerdo de Promoción Comercial con los EEUU en el área de propiedad intelectual', *Inter-American Development Bank*. Washington DC: IADB, 2009.

Roudaut, Mickaël. 'From Sweatshops to Organized Crime: The New Face of Counterfeiting', in Geiger, Christophe (ed.), *Criminal Enforcement of Intellectual Property: A Handbook of Contemporary Research*. Cheltenham-Northampton: Edward Elgar, 2012.

Ryan, Michael. *Knowledge Diplomacy: Global Competition and the Politics of Intellectual Property*. Washington, DC: The Brookings Institutions, 1988.

Saez, Catherine. 'ACTA a Sign of Weakness in Multilateral System, WIPO Head Says', *Intellectual Property Watch*, 30 June 2010. Available at: http://www.ip-watch.org/2010/06/30/acta-a-sign-of-weakness-in-multilateral-system-wipo-head-says/.

'WIPO Slowly Advances Industrial Design Treaty, Eyes ISP Liability for Trademarks', *Intellectual Property Watch*, 30 June 2010. Available at: http://www.ip-watch.org/2011/04/04/wipo-slowly-advances-industrial-design-treaty-eyes-isp-liability-for-trademarks/.

Salzman, James. 'Labor Rights, Globalization and Institutions: The Role and Influence of the Organization for Economic Cooperation and Development', *Michigan Journal of International Law* vol. 21 no.4 (2000): 769–848.

Sauvé, P. 'A Plurilateral Agenda for Services? Assessing the case for a Trade in Services Agreement (TISA)', Working Paper No 2013/29, May 2013.

Schiappacasse, Mikhaelle. 'Intellectual Property Rights in China: Technology Transfers and Economic Development', *Buffalo Intellectual Property Law Journal* vol. 2 (2004): 164–185.

Schmidt-Szalewski, Joanna. 'The French Case: Comparison of the Past, Present and Future of Criminal Law', in Geiger, Christophe (ed.), *Criminal Enforcement of Intellectual Property: A Handbook of Contemporary Research*. Cheltenham-Northampton: Edward Elgar, 2012.

Sell, Susan. 'Everything Old Is New Again: The Development Agenda Then and Now', *The WIPO Journal* vol. 3 (2011): 20.

'From Forum-Shifters to Shape-Shifters: Rulemaking and Enforcement in Intellectual Property', *International Studies Association Conference*, New York City, February 2009.

'The Global IP Upward Ratchet, Anti-Counterfeiting and Piracy Enforcement Efforts: The State of Play', PIJIP Research Paper no. 15. Washington, DC: American University Washington College of Law, 2010.

'Multinational Corporations as Agents of Change: The Globalization of Intellectual Property Rights', in Cutler, Claire, Virginia Haufler, and Tony Porter (eds.), *Private Authority and International Affairs*. Albany: State University of New York Press, 1999.

*Private Power, Public Law: The Globalization of Intellectual Property Rights*. Cambridge: Cambridge University Press, 2003.

'TRIPS Was Never Enough: Vertical Forum Shifting, FTAS, ACTA, and TPP', *Journal of Intellectual Property Law* vol. 18 no. 2 (2011): 447–478.

Seuba, Xavier. 'Checks and Balances in the Intellectual Property Enforcement Field: Reconstructing EU Trade Agreements', in Geiger, Christopher (ed.), *Constructing European Intellectual Property: Achievements and New Perspectives*. Cheltenham-Northampton: Edward Elgar, 2013.

'Free Trade of Pharmaceutical Products: the Limits of Intellectual Property Enforcement at the Border', *ICTSD Programme on Intellectual Property Rights and Sustainable Development*, Issue Paper 27. Geneva: International Centre for Trade and Sustainable Development, 2010.

Seuba, Xavier, Joan Rovira and Sophie Bloemen. 'Welfare Implications of Intellectual Property Rights Enforcement Measures', PIJIP Research Paper no. 5. Washington, DC: American University Washington College of Law, 2010.

Shams, Heba. '"Club Multilateralism" and Global Supranationalism: The Case of FATF', in Attanasio, John B. and Joseph J. Norton (eds.), *Multilateralism v Unilateralism: Policy Choices in a Global Society*. London: British Institute of International and Comparative Law, 2004.

Silva, Alberto Cerda. 'Enforcing Intellectual Property Rights by Diminishing Privacy: How the Anti-Counterfeiting Trade Agreement Jeopardizes the Right to Privacy', PIJIP Research Paper no. 11. Washington, DC: American University Washington College of Law, 2010.

Spindler, Gerald and Fabian Schuster (eds.). *Recht der Neuen Medien. Kommentar*. Munich: Beck, 2008.

Stamatoudi, Irini. 'ACTA, Internet Service Provider and the Acquis Communautaire', in Rosén, Jan (ed.), *Intellectual Property at the Crossroads of Trade*. Cheltenham-Northampton: Edward Elgar, 2012.

Stieper, Malte. 'Das Anti-Counterfeiting Trade Agreement (ACTA)', *GRUR International* (2011): 124.

Stopford, John and Susan Strange. *Rival States, Rival Firms: Competition for World Market Shares*. Cambridge: Cambridge University Press, 1991.

Strange, Susan. 'Big Business and the State', *Millennium Journal of International Studies* vol. 20 no. 2 (1991): 245–250.

*The Retreat of the State*. Cambridge: Cambridge University Press, 1996.

'States, Firms and Diplomacy', *International Affairs* vol. 68 no. 1 (1992): 1–15.

'Territory, State, Authority and Economy: A New Realist Ontology of Global Political Economy', in Cox, Robert (ed.), *The New Realism: Perspectives on Multilateralism and World Order*. Tokyo, New York, and Paris: Macmillan, 1997.

Szott Moohr, Geraldine. 'The Crime of Copyright Infringement: An Inquiry Based on Morality, Harm and Criminal Theory', *Boston University Law Review* vol. 83 no. 4 (2003): 731–783.

Tera Consultants. 'Building a Digital Economy: The Importance of Saving Jobs in the EU's Creative Industries', study commissioned by the International Chamber of Commerce's BASCAP initiative, 2010. Available at: http://www.iccwbo.org/Advocacy-Codes-and-Rules/BASCAP/BASCAP-Research/Economic-impact/Building-a-Digital-Economy-TERA-study/.

Thompson, William. *Bootleg Billions: The Impact of Counterfeit Goods Trade on New York City*, report by the City of New York's Office of the Comptroller, 2004. Available at: www.comptroller.nyc.gov/bureaus/bud/04reports/Bootleg-Billions.pdf.

Timm, Trevor. 'How PIPA and SOPA Violate White House Principles Supporting Free Speech and Innovation', *Electronic Frontier Foundation*, 16 January 2012. Available at: https://www.eff.org/deeplinks/2012/01/how-pipa-and-sopa-violate-white-house-principles-supporting-free-speech.

Tribe, Laurence. 'Taking Text and Structure Seriously: Reflections on Free-Form Method in Constitutional Interpretation', *Harvard Law Review* vol. 108 no. 6 (1995): 1221–1303.

Turana, Tariana. 'Government Moves Forward with Plain Packaging of Tobacco Products', *New Zealand Government*, 19 February 2013. Available at: http://www.beehive.govt.nz/release/government-moves-forward-plain-packaging-tobacco-products.

Van Alstine, Michael. 'Executive Aggrandizement in Foreign Affairs Lawmaking', *UCLA Law Review* vol. 54 (2006): 309.

van 't Klooster, Kelvin. 'Downloading … soon to be Illegal in the Netherlands?', *IRIS – Legal Observations of the European Audiovisual Observator*, May 2011. Available at: http://merlin.obs.coe.int/newsletter.php?year=2011&issue=5&iris_ref=2011+5+34.

Von Braun, Johanna and Peter Munyi. 'New Enforcement Mechanisms Challenge the Legality of Generics in the Name of Public Health: The Emergence of Anti-Counterfeiting

Legislation in East Africa', *African Journal of International and Comparative Law* vol. 18 (2010): 238–253.

von Lewinski, Silke. *International Copyright Law and Policy*. Oxford: Oxford University Press, 2008.

Voon, Tania, Andrew Mitchell, Jonathan Liberman, and Glyn Ayres (eds.). *Public Health and Plain Packaging of Cigarettes: Legal Issues*. Cheltenham-Northampton: Edward Elgar, 2012.

Voorhoof, Dirk and Inger Høedt-Rasmussen. 'ECHR: Copyright vs. Freedom of Expression', *Kluwer Copyright Blog*, 25 January 2013. Available at: http://kluwercopyrightblog.com/2013/01/25/echr-copyright-vs-freedom-of-expression/.

Vrins, Olivier. 'The impact of ACTA on the EU acquis and civil liberties', *paper for the Committee on International Trade, Directorate-General for External Policies of the European Parliament*. Brussels: European Union, 2012.

Wadlow, W. '"Including Trade in Counterfeit Goods": The Origins of TRIPs as a GATT Anti-Counterfeiting Code', *Intellectual Property Quarterly* 3 (2007): 350–402.

Walter, Michael and Silke von Lewinski (eds.). *European Copyright Law: A Commentary*. Oxford: Oxford University Press, 2010.

Walterscheid, Edward. 'To Promote the Progress of Science and the Useful Arts: The Background and Origin of the Intellectual Property Clause of the United States Constitution', *Journal of Intellectual Property Law* vol. 2 no. 1 (1994): 37–38.

Wambi, Michael. 'East Africa: Global Players Behind Anti-Counterfeit Law Campaign', *Inter Press Service News Agency*, 21 May 2010. Available at: http://www.ipsnews.net/2010/05/east-africa-global-players-behind-anti-counterfeit-law-campaign/.

'HEALTH UGANDA: EU Supports Law Threatening Access to Medicines', *Inter Press Service News Agency*, 15 March 2010. Available at: http://www.ipsnews.net/2010/03/health-uganda-eu-supports-law-threatening-access-to-medicines/.

Wan, Charn Wing. 'Three Strikes Law: A Least Cost Solution to Rampant Online Piracy', *Journal of Intellectual Property Law & Practice* vol. 5 no. 4 (2010): 232–244.

Watson, Alan. *Legal Transplants: An Approach to Comparative Law*. Edinburgh: Scottish Academic Press, 1974.

Wattal, Jayashree. 'Intellectual Property Rights and Agriculture: Interests of Developing Countries', paper presented at *The Conference on Agriculture and the New Trade Agenda*, World Bank, Geneva, 1999.

Weatherall, Kimberlee. 'ACTA – Australian Section by Section Analysis', paper draft, available online at: http://works.bepress.com/cgi/viewcontent.cgi?article=1020&context=kimweatherall.

'ACTA as a New Kind of International IP Law-Making', PIJIP Research Paper no. 12. Washington, DC: American University Washington College of Law, 2010.

'Politics, Compromise, Text and the Failures of the Anti-Counterfeiting Trade Agreement', *Sydney Law Review* vol. 33 no. 2 (2011): 229–263.

'Submission to the Joint Standing Committee on Treaties on the Anti-Counterfeiting Trade Agreement 2011', February 2012. Available at: http://www.aph.gov.au/Parliamentary_Business/Committees/House_of_Representatives_Committees?url=jsct/21november2011/subs/sub3.pdf.

Wechsler, Andrea. 'Criminal Enforcement of Intellectual Property Law: An Economic Approach', in Geiger, Christophe (ed.), *Criminal Enforcement of Intellectual Property: A Handbook of Contemporary Research*. Cheltenham-Northampton: Edward Elgar, 2012.

Westkamp, Guido. 'Criminalizing IP Use in the UK: From Trademark Use to Illicit Downloads', in Geiger, Christophe (ed.), *Criminal Enforcement of Intellectual Property: A Handbook of Contemporary Research*. Cheltenham-Northampton: Edward Elgar, 2012.

Wollgast, Heike. 'Intellectual Property Litigation Costs – An Introduction', *WIPO Magazine* no. 1 (2010). Available online at: http://www.wipo.int/wipo_magazine/en/2010/01/Article_0001.html.

Woolcock, Stephen. 'The Treaty of Lisbon and the European Union as an Actor in International Trade', European Centre for International Political Economy Working Paper no. 1/2010. Brussels: ECIPE, 2010.

Xue, Hong. 'An Anatomical Study of the United States versus China at the World Trade Organisation on Intellectual Property Enforcement', *European Intellectual Property Review* vol. 31 no. 6 (2009): 292–299.

'Enforcement for Development: Why Not an Agenda for the Developing World?', in Li, Xuan and Carlos Correa (eds.), *Intellectual Property Enforcement: International Perspectives*. Cheltenham-Northampton: Edward Elgar, 2009.

Yager, L., Observations on Efforts to Quantify the Economic Effects of Counterfeited and Pirated Goods, WIPO WIPO/ACE/6/4. 2010.

Yoo, John. 'Laws as Treaties? The Constitutionality of the Congressional-Executive Agreement', *Michigan Law Review* vol. 99 (2001): 757–852.

Yu, Peter. 'The ACTA Committee', *Drake University Legal Studies Research Paper* no. 12–34. Des Moines: Drake University Law School, 2012.

'ACTA and Its Complex Politics', *The WIPO Journal* vol. 3 no. 1 (2011): 1–16.

'The Alphabet Soup of Transborder Intellectual Property Enforcement', *Drake University Legal Studies Research Paper* no. 12–13. Des Moines: Drake University Law School, 2012.

'Currents and Crosscurrents in the International Intellectual Property Regime', *Loyola of Los Angeles Law Review* vol. 38 no. 1 (2004): 323–443.

'Enforcement, Enforcement, What Enforcement? IDEA', *The Journal of Law and Technology* vol. 52 (2012): 239–284.

'Intellectual Property and Human Rights in the Nonmultilateral Era', *Florida Law Review* vol. 64 (2011): 1045–1100.

'International Enclosure, the Regime Complex, and Intellectual Property Schizophrenia', *Michigan State Law Review* vol. 1 (2007): 1–33.

'The Middle Intellectual Property Powers', in Randall Peerenboom and Tom Ginsburg (eds.), *Law and Development in Middle-Income Countries: Avoiding the Middle-Income Trap*. Cambridge: Cambridge University Press, 2013.

'The objectives and principles of the TRIPS Agreement', *Houston Law Review* vol. 46 no. 4 (2009): 979–1046.

'From Pirates to Partners (Episode II): Protecting Intellectual Property in Post-WTO China', *American University Law Review* vol. 55 (2006): 901–1000.

'Shaping Chinese Criminal Enforcement Norms through the TRIPS Agreement', in Geiger, Christophe (ed.), *Criminal Enforcement of Intellectual Property: A Handbook of Contemporary Research*. Cheltenham-Northampton: Edward Elgar, 2012.

'Six Secret (and Now Open) Fears of ACTA', *SMU Law Review* vol. 64 no. 3 (2011): 975–1094.

'A Tale of Two Development Agendas', *Ohio Northern University Law Review* vol. 35 no. 2 (2009): 465–573.

'TRIPS Enforcement and Developing Countries', *American University International Law Review* vol. 26 no. 3 (2011): 727–782.
'The TRIPS Enforcement Dispute', *Nebraska Law Review* vol. 89 no. 4 (2011):1046–1131.
'TRIPS and Its Achilles' Heel', *Journal of Intellectual Property Law* vol. 18 no.2 (2011): 479–531.
'TRIPS and Its Discontents', *Marquette University Intellectual Property Law Review* vol. 10 (2006): 369–410.
'The U.S.-China Dispute over TRIPS Enforcement', *Drake University Law School Occasional Papers in Intellectual Property Law* no. 5. Des Moines: Drake University Law School, 2010.
Zilkha, Genan. 'The RIAA's Troubling Solution to File-Sharing', *Fordham Intellectual Property, Media and Entertainment Law Journal* vol. 20 no. 2 (2009): 667–713.

## OFFICIAL DOCUMENTS

ACTA negotiating parties. 'The Anti-Counterfeiting Trade Agreement – Summary of Key Elements Under Discussion', press release, 6 November 2009. Available at: http://www.ustr.gov/webfm_send/1479.
Anti-Counterfeiting Trade Agreement, *Consolidated Text: Prepared for Public Release*, April 2010, Available at: http://trade.ec.europa.eu/doclib/docs/2010/april/tradoc_146029.pdf
*Consolidated Text: Reflects Changes Made During the September 2010 Tokyo Round*, 2nd October 2010: Available at: http://trade.ec.europa.eu/doclib/docs/2010/october/tradoc_146699.pdf
Australian Advisory Council on Intellectual Property. *Review of Trade Mark Enforcement*. Canberra: IP Australia, 2004.
Australia, Department of Foreign Affairs and Trade. 'Discussion Paper: An International Proposal for a Plurilateral Anti-Counterfeiting Trade Agreement (ACTA)', 13 November 2007
Australian Joint Standing Committee on Treaties. *Protocol Amending the TRIPS Agreement*. Canberra: Australian Parliament, 2007.
*Report 126 – Treaty Tabled on 21 November 2011: Anti-Counterfeiting Trade Agreement 2011*. Canberra: Australian Parliament, 2012.
Australian Law Reform Commission. *Copyright and the Digital Economy: Issues Paper*. Sydney: Australian Law Reform Commission, 2012.
Brasilia Declaration, India-Brazil-South Africa (IBSA) Dialogue Forum, Fourth Summit of the Heads of State/Government, Brasília Declaration, 15 April 2010, Brasilia. Available at: http://www.ibsa-trilateral.org/index.php?option=com_content&task=view&id=102&Itemid=46
European Commission. '10 Myths About ACTA', position paper, January 2012. Available at: http://trade.ec.europa.eu/doclib/docs/2012/january/tradoc_148964.pdf.
'A Single Market for Intellectual Property Rights Boosting creativity and innovation to provide economic growth, high quality jobs and first class products and services in Europe', *Communication from the European Commission to the European Parliament, the Council, the European Economic and Social Committee and the Committee of the Regions*, 2011.

'Comments on the "Opinion of European Academics on Anti-Counterfeiting Trade Agreement"', *Journal of Intellectual Property, Information Technology and E-Commerce Law* vol. 2 (2011): 171–183.

'Enhancing the enforcement of intellectual property rights in the internal market', *Communication from the European Commission to the European Parliament, the Council, the European Economic and Social Committee and the Committee of the Regions*, 2009.

European Commission, 'Follow-up to the European Parliament Resolution on the transparency and state of play of the ACTA negotiations, adopted by the Commission on 12 May 2010' Available at: www.europarl.europa.eu/oeil/spdoc.do?i=18136&j=0&l=en, 2010.

'What ACTA is about', 2012, Available at: http://trade.ec.europa.eu/doclib/docs/2012/january/tradoc_149003.pdf.

European Data Protection Survey. 'Opinion of the European Data Protection Supervisor on the current negotiations by the European Union of an Anti-Counterfeiting Trade Agreement', 2010. Available at: https://secure.edps.europa.eu/EDPSWEB/webdav/shared/Documents/Consultation/Opinions/2010/10-02-22_ACTA_EN.pdf.

'Opinion of the European Data Protection Supervisor on the proposal for a Council Decision on the Conclusion of the Anti-Counterfeiting Trade Agreement between the European Union and its Member States, Australia, Canada, Japan, the Republic of Korea, the United Mexican States, the Kingdom of Morocco, New Zealand, the Republic of Singapore, the Swiss Confederation and the United States of America', 2012. Available at: https://secure.edps.europa.eu/EDPSWEB/webdav/shared/Documents/Consultation/Opinions/2012/12-04-24_ACTA_EN.pdf.

European Parliament, Directorate-General for External Policies. *The Anti-Counterfeiting Trade Agreement (ACTA): An Assessment*. Brussels: European Union, 2011. Available at: http://www.europarl.europa.eu/committees/en/studiesdownload.html?languageDocument=EN&file=43731.

Office of the United States Trade Representative. *2005 National Trade Estimate Report on Foreign Trade Barriers*. Washington, DC: United States Government, 2005.

Organisation for Economic Co-Operation and Development. *OECD Council Recommendation on Principles for Internet Policy Making*. Paris: OECD Publishing, 2011.

*The Economic Impact of Counterfeiting and Piracy*. Paris: OECD Publishing, 2008.

*Magnitude of counterfeiting and piracy of tangible products: an update*. Paris: OECD Publishing, 2009.

United Nations International Law Commission. 'Fragmentation of International Law: Difficulties arising from the Diversification and Expansion of International Law', *report of the Study Group of the International Law Commission*. Geneva: United Nations, 2006.

United Nations Office of the High Commissioner for Human Rights. 'Generic Drugs: UN Expert on Health Hails European Parliament's Rejection of Anti-Counterfeiting Trade Agreement', 9 July 2012. Available at: http://www.ohchr.org/en/NewsEvents/Pages/DisplayNews.aspx?NewsID=12332&LangID=E.

United Nations Educational, Scientific and Cultural Organization. 'Culture: a driver and an enabler of sustainable development', *Thematic think piece, UN System Task Team on the post-2015 UN Development Agenda*. Paris: UNESCO, 2012. Available at: http://www.un.org/en/development/desa/policy/untaskteam_undf/thinkpieces/2_culture.pdf.

United Nations International Law Commission. 'Fragmentation of International Law: Difficulties arising from the Diversification and Expansion of International Law', *report of the Study Group of the International Law Commission*. Geneva: United Nations, 2006.

United Nations Office of the High Commissioner for Human Rights. 'Generic Drugs: UN Expert on Health Hails European Parliament's Rejection of Anti-Counterfeiting Trade Agreement', 9 July 2012. Available at: http://www.ohchr.org/en/NewsEvents/Pages/DisplayNews.aspx?NewsID=12332&LangID=E.

United States Committee on Armed Services. *Inquiry into the Counterfeit Electronic Parts in the Department of Defense Supply Chain*. Washington, DC: U.S. Senate, 2012. Available at: http://www.armed-services.senate.gov/Publications/Counterfeit%20Electronic%20Parts.pdf.

United States Customs and Border Protection and United States Immigration and Customs Enforcement. *Intellectual Property Rights – Fiscal Year 2011 Seizure Statistics*, report prepared by CBP Office of International Trade. Washington, DC: Department of Homeland Security, 2012. Available at: http://www.ice.gov/doclib/iprcenter/pdf/ipr-fy-2011-seizure-report.pdf.

United States Economics and Statistics Administration and United States Patent and Trademark Office. *Intellectual Property and the US Economy: Industries in Focus*. Washington, DC: Department of Commerce, 2012.

United States Intellectual Property Enforcement Coordinator. *U.S. 2011 Intellectual Property Enforcement Coordinator Annual Report on Intellectual Property Enforcement*. Washington, DC: Executive Office of the President of the United States, 2012.

World Intellectual Property Organization. 'Counterfeiting and Piracy Endangers Global Economic Recovery Say Global Congress Leaders', WIPO Press Release PR/2009/621, 2009.

World Summit on the Information Society. *Tunis Agenda for the Information Society*. United Nations, Tunis, 2005.

World Trade Organization, TRIPS Council, Minutes of 8–9 June 2010 Meeting, IP/C/M/63, 4 October 2010.

TRIPS Council, Minutes of 26–27 October 2010 Meeting, IP/C/M/64.

TRIPS Council, Minutes of 26–27 October 2010 Meeting, IP/C/M/64, 17 February 2011.

TRIPS Council, Minutes of 24–25 October 2011 Meeting, IP/C/M/67, 15 February 2012.

TRIPS Council, Minutes of 28–29 February 2012 Meeting, IP/C/M/69, 15 May 2012.

TRIPS Council, Minutes of 5th June 2012 Meeting, IP/C/M/70, October 2012.

## NEWSPAPERS, BLOGS

ABC News. 'Julian Assange to Run for the Senate', *ABC News*, 19 March 2012. Available at: http://www.abc.net.au/news/2012-03-17/julian-assange-to-run-for-senate/3895958

Amnesty International. 'EU urged to reject international anti-counterfeiting pact', AI News, 10 February 2012. Available at: http://www.amnesty.org/en/news/eu-urged-reject-international-anti-counterfeiting-pact-2012-02-10

Anderson, Nate. 'Son of ACTA: meet the *next* secret copyright treaty', *Ars Technica*, 11 March 2011. Available at: arstechnica.com/tech-policy/news/2011/03/son-of-acta-meet-the-next-secret-copyright-treaty.ars?utm_source=twitterfeed&utm_medium=twitter&utm_campaign=rss

Bason, Tamlin. 'Wyden, Issa Say Digital Bill of Rights Needed to Prevent New Versions of SOPA', *Bloomberg BNA*, 12 June 2012. Available at: http://www.bna.com/wyden-issa-say-n12884909994/

Bloomberg Businessweek Magazine. 'Fakes!', 6 February 2005. Available at: http://www.businessweek.com/stories/2005-02-06/fakes

Cahir, John. 'High Court Approves File Sharing Settlement – ISP Addresses not Personal Data', *Ireland's IP & Technology Law Blog*, 8 May 2010. Available at: http://www.irelandip.com/2010/05/articles/privacy-1/high-court-approves-file-sharing-settlement-isp-addresses-not-personal-data/

Carter, Zach. 'Obama Trade Document Leaked, Revealing New Corporate Powers and Broken Campaign Promises', *The Huffington Post*, 13 June 2012. Available at: http://www.huffingtonpost.com/2012/06/13/obama-trade-document-leak_n_1592593.html

De Winter, Brenno. 'Dutch internal ACTA-documents', *Bigwobber*, 25 February 2010. Available at: http://www.bigwobber.nl/2010/02/25/dutch-internal-acta-documents/

Dean, Owen. 'ACTA – a sting in the tail for IP rights enforcement', The Anton Moster Chair of Intellectual Property Blog, 7 October 2011. Available at: http://blogs.sun.ac.za/iplaw/2011/10/07/acta-%E2%80%93-a-sting-in-the-tail-for-ip-rights-enforcement/

Engström, Christian. 'Introducing CETA, the ACTA Zombie', article from the author's blog (2012): http://christianengstrom.wordpress.com/2012/07/12/introducing-ceta-the-acta-zombie/

EurActiv. 'ACTA activates European civil society', *EurActiv News*, 2 February 2012. Available at: http://www.euractiv.com/infosociety/acta-activates-european-civil-so-news-510533

'Lawmakers call for halt to ACTA deal', *EurActiv News*, 5 October 2010. Available at: http://www.euractiv.com/infosociety/lawmakers-call-halt-acta-deal-news-498442

Foundation for a Free Information Infrastructure. 'Copyright Criminal measures in ACTA', *ACTA Blog*, 8 October 2010. Available at http://acta.ffii.org/wordpress/?p=34

'EU Commission propaganda on ACTA', *ACTA Blog*, 26 January 2012. Available at: http://acta.ffii.org/?p=1082

Geist, Michael. 'ACTA Ultra-Lite: The U.S. Cave on the Internet Chapter Complete', article from the author's blog (2010): http://www.michaelgeist.ca/content/view/5352/125/

'Here Comes ACTA: Canadian Government Introduces Anti-Counterfeiting Trade Agreement', article from author's blog (2013): http://www.michaelgeist.ca/content/view/6796/125/

'Toward an ACTA Super-Structure: How ACTA May Replace WIPO', article from author's blog (2010): http://www.michaelgeist.ca/content/view/4910/125/

'U.S. Intellectual Property Demands for TPP Leak: Everything it Wanted in ACTA But Didn't Get', article from author's blog (2011): www.michaelgeist.ca/content/view/5686/125/

Goldsmith, Jack and Lawrence Lessig. 'Anti-counterfeiting agreement raises constitutional concerns', The Washington Post, 26 March 2010. Available at: http://www.washingtonpost.com/wp-dyn/content/article/2010/03/25/AR2010032502403.html

Graeber, Charles. 'Inside the Mansion – and Mind – of Kim Dotcom, the Most Wanted Man on the Net', *Wired Magazine*, 18 October 2012. Available at: http://www.wired.com/threatlevel/2012/10/Ff-Kim-Dotcom/

Hilvert, John. 'Government Eyes Cost-Benefit Analyses for ACTA, TPP', *IT News*, 14 August 2012. Available at: http://www.itnews.com.au/News/311619,government-eyes-cost-benefit-analyses-for-acta-tpp.aspx

Inside U.S. Trade. 'Consumer Groups Fear ACTA Could Encourage Generic Drug Seizures', *Inside U.S. Trade's NewsStand*, 30 April 2010.

'De Gucht Lashes Out at US over ACTA, Geographical Indications', *Inside U.S. Trade's NewsStand*, 16 July 2010.exercises?', joint letter to U.S. Trade Representative, 21 July 2009. Available at: http://www.keionline.org/misc-docs/4/attachment1_transparency_ustr.pdf

Knowledge Ecology International. 'ACTA is secret. How transparent are other global norm setting exercises?', joint letter to U.S. Trade Representative, 21 July 2009. Available at: http://www.keionline.org/misc-docs/4/attachment1_transparency_ustr.pdf

Kuhn, Mart. 'ACTA means trouble, but don't take our word for it', *Public Knowledge Policy Blog*, 10 June 2010. Available at: http://www.publicknowledge.org/node/3155

Lee, David. 'European Parliament rapporteur quits in Acta protest', *BBC News Technology*, 27 January 2012. Available at: http://www.bbc.co.uk/news/technology-16757142

'Acta protests: Thousands take to streets across Europe', *BBC News Technology*, 11 February 2012. Available at: http://www.bbc.co.uk/news/technology-16999497

Llewellyn, Howell. '"Three-Strikes" Off Anti-Piracy Agenda In Spain', *Billboard*, 22 June 2009. Available at: http://www.billboard.com/biz/articles/news/1269047/three-strikes-off-anti-piracy-agenda-in-spain

Love, James. 'KEI comment on US signing of ACTA', *Knowledge Ecology International*, 3 October 2011. Available at: http://keionline.org/node/1291

'What's Still Wrong with ACTA, and Why Governments Should Reject the Illegitimate Treaty', *Knowledge Ecology International*, 26 February 2012. Available at: http://keionline.org/node/1369

Macpherson, Andrew. 'EU crossed wires over ACTA', *Iptegrity.com*, 11 July 2010. Available at: http://www.iptegrity.com/index.php/acta/545-eu-gets-wires-crossed-over-acta-transparency

MarkMonitor. 'Traffic Report: Online Piracy and Counterfeiting' report January 2011. Available at: https://www.markmonitor.com/download/report/MarkMonitor_-_Traffic_Report_110111.pdf

'Seven Best Practices for Fighting Counterfeit Sales Online', report September 2010. Available at: https://www.markmonitor.com/download/wp/wp-Fighting_Counterfeit_Sales.pdf

Martin, Peter. 'Emerson Chasing Deals That Look Like Sellouts', *The Sydney Morning Herald*, 7 August 2012. Available at: http://www.smh.com.au/business/emerson-chasing-deals-that-look-like-sellouts-20120806-23q6h.html

'Plain Packs: The New Kines of Attack. Big Tobacco Tries the WTO and TPPA', *The Age and the Sydney Morning Herald*, 20 August 2012. Available at: http://www.petermartin.com.au/2012/08/plain-packs-new-lines-of-attack-cancer.html

'What's Our Trade Minister Up To? What's He Signing in Our Name?', *The Sydney Morning Herald*, 7 August 2012. Available at: http://www.petermartin.com.au/2012/08/whats-our-trade-minister-up-to-whats-he.html

'Why Do We Negotiate Free Trade Agreements in Secret?', *The Sydney Morning Herald*, 22 May 2012. Available at: http://www.petermartin.com.au/2012/05/why-do-we-negotiate-free-trade.html

Masnick, Mike. 'Leaked State Department Cables Confirm That ACTA Was Designed to Pressure Developing Nations', *Tech Dirt*, 4 February 2011. Available at: http://www.techdirt.com/articles/20110203/16214712957/leaked-state-department-cables-confirm-that-acta-was-designed-to-pressure-developing-nations.shtml

'USTR Refuses to Release Congressional Research Service Study on Legality of ACTA', *TechDirt*, 28 March 2011. Available at: www.techdirt.com/articles/20110325/04480513628/ustr-refuses-to-release-congressional-research-service-study-legality-acta.shtml

Mannheim, Markus. 'Top Customs Executives to Bear the Brunt of Cuts', *The Canberra Times*, 27 February 2012. Available at: http://www.canberratimes.com.au/national/top-customs-executives-to-bear-brunt-of-cuts-20120227-1txnf.html

Mbatiah, Suleiman. '*Kenya: Pharmaceutical Companies Pushing Anti-Counterfeit Law*', *Inter Press Service News Agency*, 14 June 2010. Available at: http://www.ipsnews.net/2010/06/kenya-pharmaceutical-companies-pushing-anti-counterfeit-law/

McCullagh, Declan. 'Copyright Treaty is Classified for "National Security"', *CNET NEWS*, 12 March 2009. Available at: news.cnet.com/8301-13578_3-10195547-38.htm

Oberti, Charlotte. 'Hadopi: La police du Web Fliquée par Aurélie Filippetti', France24, 3 August 2012. Available at: http://www.france24.com/fr/20120803-france-hadopi-police-web-fliquee-aurelie-filippetti-internet-telechargement-illegal-politique-culture-musique-cinema

Pirate Party Australia. 'Government Should Follow EU in Rejecting ACTA, says Pirate Party', *Pirate Party Website*, 21 June 2012. Available at: http://pirateparty.org.au/2012/06/21/government-should-follow-eu-in-rejecting-acta-says-pirate-party/

Rimmer, Matthew. 'A Mercurial Treaty: The Trans-Pacific Partnership and the United States', *The Conversation*, 15 June 2012. Available at: https://theconversation.edu.au/a-mercurial-treaty-the-trans-pacific-partnership-and-the-united-states-7471

'Opening Pandora's Box: Secret Treaty Threatens Human Rights', *The Conversation*, 4 April 2012. Available at: https://theconversation.edu.au/opening-pandoras-box-secret-treaty-threatens-human-rights-6092

'The High Court and the Marlboro Man: The Plain Packaging Decision', *The Conversation*, 18 October 2012. Available at: https://theconversation.edu.au/the-high-court-and-the-marlboro-man-the-plain-packaging-decision-10014

'The Two Treaties: Obama, Trade, and the State of the Union', *The Conversation*, 14 February 2013. Available at: https://theconversation.edu.au/the-two-treaties-obama-trade-and-the-state-of-the-union-12197

Schaake, Marietje. 'FAQ: Transatlantic Trade and Investment Partnership (TTIP)', Marietje Schaake official website, http://www.marietjeschaake.eu/2013/06/faq-transatlantic-trade-and-investment-partnership-ttip/

'We Need Copyright Reform, Not ACTA!', *TorrentFreak*, 4 February 2012. Available at: https://torrentfreak.com/we-need-copyright-reform-not-acta-120204/

Schaffarczyk, Karl. 'Can Kim Dotcom's Mega Beat the Law Where Megaupload Failed?', *The Conversation*, 29 January 2013. Available at: http://theconversation.edu.au/Can-Kim-Dotcoms-Mega-Beat-The-Law-Where-Megaupload-Failed-11826

Schusterman, Michelle. (2011). 'How ACTA will take down the Internet, healthcare, and farming', *Matador Network*, 27 February 2012. Available at: http://matadornetwork.com/change/how-acta-will-take-down-the-internet-healthcare-and-farming-infographic/

Souppouris, Aaron. 'ACTA Unlikely to Happen, Says European Commissioner', *The Verge*, May 7, 2012. Available at: http://www.theverge.com/2012/5/7/3004275/european-commissioner-digital-agenda-acta-unlikely-to-happen

Sutton, Maira. 'Secretive Copyright Negotiations Continue at the 16th Round of TPP Talks', *Electronic Frontier Foundation*, 4 March 2013. Available at: https://www.eff.org/deeplinks/2013/03/secretive-copyright-negotiations-continue-16th-round-tpp-talks

The Guardian. 'US embassy cables: Italy, the EU and the Anti-Counterfeit Trading Agreement', *US embassy cables: the document series*, 22 December 2010. Available at: http://www.guardian.co.uk/world/us-embassy-cables-documents/176810

'US embassy cables: Sweden's concerns about Anti-Counterfeit Trading Agreement negotiations', *US embassy cables: the document series*,22 December 2010. Available at: http://www.guardian.co.uk/world/us-embassy-cables-documents/236363

Ulanoff, Lance. 'ACTA is more dangerous than SOPA', *Mashable Social Media*, 26 January 2012. Available at: http://mashable.com/2012/01/26/acta-more-dangerous-than-sopa/

Wallach, Lori. 'Can a "Dracula Strategy" Bring the Trans-Pacific Partnership into the Sunlight?', *Yes Magazine!*, 21 November 2012. Available at: http://www.yesmagazine.org/new-economy/can-dracula-strategy-bring-trans-pacific-partnership-into-sunlight

Wortham, Jenna. 'A Political Coming of Age for the Tech Industry', *New York Times*, 17 January 2012. Available at: http://www.nytimes.com/2012/01/18/technology/web-wide-protest-over-two-antipiracy-bills.html?_r=0

# Index

*A Metronome v. Altibox*, 131
ACTA Committee, 20–21, 43–44, 61, 122, 143–154, 171, 194–196, 321, 355, 368, 389, 410–412
Administrative
  enforcement/ procedures, 14, 25–26, 35, 39, 66, 71, 73, 79, 81, 132, 326, 393, 395, 401, 408
  penalties, 39, 106, 401
Agreement on Trade-Related Aspects of Intellectual Property Rights (TRIPS Agreement)
  Article 1, 63, 387
  Articles 7, 11, 35, 55, 81, 94, 98, 147, 233, 392
  Article 8, 14, 19, 35, 53, 82, 94, 98, 179, 331, 350, 392
  Article 9.1, 67, 83
  Article 41, 26, 34–35, 52–53, 67–68, 70, 95–96, 365
  Article 45, 82
  Article 46, 14, 70–71, 340
  Article 48, 73
  Article 50, 36, 81, 86–87, 340
  TRIPS Council, 8, 34, 53, 57, 59, 69, 98, 212, 215, 264, 267–268, 269, 357–375, 383, 386–387, 389, 423, 436
  TRIPS-plus, 8, 22–23, 47, 88–90, 114, 130, 141, 143, 149–150, 152, 154, 169, 191, 205, 209, 244, 331, 342, 357, 360, 362, 363–375, 377, 387, 427
Ambiguity, 17, 19, 28, 52, 72, 73–76, 77, 79, 92, 108, 111, 170, 234, 248
Amnesty International, 176, 195, 436
Arif, Kader, 197, 265
Asia-Pacific Economic Co-operation – APEC, 146
Australia
  Australian Constitution, 176, 190
Advisory Council on Intellectual Property, 185, 434
  Australian Digital Alliance, 171
  Copyright Act 1968, 140, 181, 192
  Department of Foreign Affairs and Trade – DFAT, 54, 170, 175, 197, 200
  Federation Against Copyright Theft, 171, 194
  High Court of Australia, 176, 178–189, 190, 425, 429
  Intellectual Property Laws Amendment Bill 2012, 188
  Joint Standing Committee on Treaties – JSCOT, 173–175, 180, 187–188, 198, 429
  Law Reform Commission, 172, 174, 177, 180, 434
  Parliament, 170–175, 177–178, 180, 184, 186–188, 191–193, 195–201, 434
  Patents Act 1990, 187
  Pirate Party Australia, 171–172, 175, 439
  Register of Therapeutic Goods, 188
  Tobacco Plain Packaging Act 2011, 171, 184, 191
  Trade Marks Act 1995, 183–184, 192
Austria, 100, 131, 264, 316, 412

Bahrain, 151, 232
Balance, i, xvi, 11, 14–17, 19, 23, 25, 28, 31–34, 38, 44–46, 48, 52, 54, 56–57, 71–72, 73–76, 78–79, 98, 133, 141, 147, 158–159, 163, 169, 171, 176–177, 180, 204–206, 208–210, 225, 227–230, 233–235, 257–258, 285, 293, 301, 307, 322–323, 326, 344, 351, 354, 363–364, 366–368, 382, 386–387, 391, 420, 422, 426
Berne Convention, 33, 51, 67, 137, 148, 226, 230–231, 233, 320, 425
*Betamax case – Sony Corp. of America v. Universal City Studios, Inc*, 122

*Bill Graham Archives v. Doring Kindersley Publishing, Inc*, 233
Birmingham, Simon, 173, 199
*Bonnier Amigo Music Norway AS v Telenor Telecom Solutions AS*, 123
Border measures
  detention, 72, 91, 92, 95, 98, 187, 192, 206, 251, 253, 254, 332–334, 351, 353, 388, 401, 423
  transhipment, 34, 64, 253, 394
  transit, 13, 20, 25, 27, 33–34, 38, 56, 58–59, 62, 64, 68–69, 88–93, 95, 96–98, 102, 117, 189, 206–207, 213–215, 220, 244, 251, 252–255, 268, 332–334, 338–339, 352–354, 363, 387, 388, 393–394, 399, 416, 421, 424, 426–427
Brazil, iv, 17, 21, 69, 88, 116–117, 151, 187, 202–210, 251, 261, 264, 268, 289, 303, 319, 320, 333, 343, 358, 359, 362–364, 367–368, 372, 375, 388–389, 415, 416, 423, 434
*British American Tobacco Australasia Limited v. The Commonwealth*, 183, 189–190
Brown, Widney, 176, 195
Business Action to Stop Counterfeiting and Piracy – BASCAP, 283–284, 419, 431

*Campomar Sociedad, Limitada v Nike International Ltd*, 183
Canada, 27, 31, 37–38, 54, 56–57, 69, 70, 95–96, 100, 108–109, 114–115, 145, 148, 150, 191, 196, 203, 213, 264, 269, 281, 297–298, 300, 314, 316, 330, 345, 349, 354–355, 362, 376, 383, 385, 412, 420, 435
Caribbean Community – CARICOM, 259
*Cartoon Network, LP v. CSC Holdings, Inc*, 233
Censor / censorship, 67–68, 176, 262, 263, 279, 286, 294
*Chamberlain Group v Skylink Technologies*, 140
China, 17, 21, 23, 40, 49, 52, 67–68, 70, 103–104, 109, 110, 117, 120, 148–192, 261, 262–264, 267–289, 295, 317, 319–320, 343, 358–360, 362, 364–368, 370–373, 375–376, 378, 383, 385–386, 417, 420–422, 424, 426–427, 430, 433–434
Civil
  Civil society/NGO, xiii–xiv, xvi, 4–10, 24, 28, 43–44, 146, 185, 191, 195–196, 198, 203–206, 209, 218, 227–230, 245, 255, 262, 265, 281, 292, 294, 303, 338, 341, 343–344, 346, 369, 370, 379–383, 437
  damages, 20, 35–36, 39, 78, 83–84, 87, 112, 162, 179, 184, 304–306, 331–332, 340, 352–354, 371, 396
  injunctions, 14, 19, 35, 68, 78, 80–82, 98, 119, 179, 186–187, 268, 304–308, 331, 334, 350, 395
  liability, 253
  liberties, 49, 78, 171, 175–176, 281, 300, 334–335, 432
  provisional measures, 26, 36, 68, 75, 80–81, 85–87, 186, 209, 251, 350–351, 398
  seizure, 19, 24, 26, 41, 56, 69, 73, 85–86, 88, 92, 95, 102, 166, 192, 206, 213, 215, 236–237, 241–243, 275, 332–334, 339, 341, 354, 388, 398, 402–404, 436
Club, country, xiv, 8, 22, 49, 150–151, 153–154, 193, 197, 287, 320, 325, 359, 373, 378, 420, 430
Commercial
  advantage, 26, 40, 104, 121, 268, 325, 339, 351, 367, 386, 402
  scale, 26, 40, 54, 62, 74, 102–104, 108, 110, 113, 120–122, 133, 141, 173, 180, 268, 317–318, 323–325, 351, 367, 386, 402, 415
*Commission v Council*, 260
Competition
  authority, 80
  generic, 187, 245, 256, 258
  policy / law / rules, 17, 56, 261, 343
Computer & Communications Industry Association – CCIA, 229–230, 233
Computer programmes, 42
Conflict clause, 27, 47, 49–50, 387
Congress on Public Interest Analysis of the Intellectual Property Enforcement Agenda, 7
Copyright
  author, 205, 284, 302–303, 305, 406, 416
  Copyright Alert System (CAS), 238
  online copyright enforcement, 26, 236, 240
  owners, 31, 36, 38, 88, 109, 169, 177, 192, 202, 232, 236–241, 269, 332
  performers, 40–41, 134, 406
  private copyright enforcement, 128, 141, 239
  producers of phonograms, 41, 51, 134, 406
  related rights, 36, 40–42, 66–67, 83–86, 118, 120, 122–125, 129, 132, 135–136, 138, 183, 225–226, 234, 241, 248, 285–286, 322, 325, 331, 335, 339, 350–351, 391, 396–398, 402, 405–407, 409, 421
Counterfeit
  Medicines, 111–112, 212–213, 253
  trademark goods, 20, 32, 41, 62, 84–85, 89–90, 182, 215, 245, 253, 393, 397, 401–404
Criminal
  enforcement agencies, 42–43, 219, 241, 276, 382
  imprisonment, 41, 111–112, 250, 252–254, 340, 403

infringement, 26, 152, 236, 242
liability, 33, 40–41, 108–109, 112, 117, 120–121, 242, 248, 403, 421
offences, 40, 76, 102, 105, 169, 171, 178–180, 350, 353, 402–404
Cross, Martin, 186, 191
Customs authorities, 27, 34, 36, 38–40, 45, 60, 69, 88, 90–91, 192, 207, 215, 251–252, 333–354, 371, 388–400

*De minimis*, 40
Designs, 3, 84, 190, 314, 339, 371
Destruction
of the goods, 14, 36, 39, 41, 43, 68, 78, 84–85, 95, 102, 192, 215, 401, 403–404, 408
or disposal outside channels of commerce, 14, 36, 68, 85
Developing countries, xvi, 1–2, 8, 33, 52, 56, 68–69, 74, 112, 117, 143, 147–154, 188, 205, 211–217, 221, 261, 267, 276, 286–288, 317–319, 328, 332, 357–377, 383, 417–418, 427–428, 432, 434
Digital
circumvention of effective technological/ technical measures – TPM, 41–42, 58, 134–140, 181, 335, 354–355, 405–406, 420
economy, 123, 126, 131, 170–172, 173, 177, 180, 182–183, 283, 431, 434
environment, 9, 16, 25–26, 32–33, 41–42, 66, 77, 88, 102, 117–118, 129, 147, 169, 179, 203, 207, 226, 228, 231, 233–234, 236, 285, 299, 301, 303, 308, 321, 324, 330, 334–336, 353, 360, 391, 405
rights management information – RMI, 42, 134–136, 138, 179, 181, 207, 226, 335, 406–407
Disclosure of information, 59, 132, 203, 353, 393, 401
Doha Declaration on the TRIPS Agreement and Public Health, 33, 82, 93, 94, 96, 152, 186–187, 201, 205, 262, 363, 367–368, 370, 386, 392
*Dudgeon v. the United Kingdom*, 111
Due process, 16, 20, 25–26, 33, 66, 70, 75, 78–79, 109, 127–128, 132, 170, 176, 194, 196, 206, 209, 219, 236, 242–243

East African Community – EAC, 244–245, 247–250, 254, 255–257
East African enforcement legislation, 244–257
*eBay Inc. v. MercExchange, L.L.C*, 80, 123, 182, 192, 429
Economic advantage, 105, 121
Economic Partnership Agreement, 48, 247, 264, 319
*Edonkey-Armata case*, 131
*EDÖB v Logistep AG.*, 130–132
Electronic commerce, 122, 124, 129, 183, 285, 334–335, 405
Electronic Frontier Foundation – EFF, 195, 229, 381
Emerging economies / BRICS, 289, 374–375
Emerson, Craig, 174, 188
*EMI Records & Ors v Eircom Ltd*, 131
EU law
Charter of Fundamental Rights of the European Union, 72, 109, 284, 299–300, 420
E-Commerce Directive, 122, 131
Information Society Directive, 13, 136–140
IPR Enforcement Directive, 18, 22, 84–86
Lisbon Treaty, 105, 297
Telecom Package, 126–127
Treaty for the Functioning of the European Union – TFEU, 105–106, 260, 291, 316
European
*Aquis*, 49, 61, 78, 85–86, 116, 120, 264–265, 281, 287, 289, 295, 300, 320, 322, 324, 326–328, 431–432
Commission, 2, 7, 10, 34, 54, 82, 84, 105–107, 113, 116–117, 120, 126–128, 131, 136, 204, 260, 264–266, 287–289, 292, 295, 297, 298–300, 313–314, 316, 319–321, 324, 326, 328, 348–349, 358, 377, 379, 381–382, 420–421, 424, 434–435, 437
Committee on International Trade of the European Parliament, 46, 49, 74, 80, 107, 265–266, 313, 327
Convention on Human Rights – ECHR, 111, 305–306, 326, 432
Court of Justice, 10, 33, 38, 69, 71, 72, 105–106, 131, 204, 260, 265, 281, 289, 299, 309, 326, 332
Data Protection Supervisor, 60–61, 116, 125–128, 300, 435
Digital Rights – EDRI, 349, 369–370, 419
Observatory on Infringements, 3, 282, 314
Parliament, 2, 9, 10, 12, 18, 27, 50, 75, 80, 82–83, 100–102, 105–109, 113–115, 120–122, 125–127, 130, 136–138, 157, 165, 170, 196–197, 204, 211, 217–218, 228, 265, 273, 279, 281, 284, 286, 289, 291–292, 294–300, 313–317, 320–324, 326–327, 330, 345, 347, 349–350, 352, 358, 369, 376–380, 382, 388, 418–420, 422–424, 432, 434–435, 438
People's Party – EPP, 292–293
*Ex officio*, 404

Exceptions / limitations, xv, 6, 23–24, 42, 49, 56, 75, 87, 95, 135–136, 138–139, 141, 171, 177–178, 180–181, 183, 184, 200–201, 225–235, 241, 258, 269, 286, 322, 324, 328, 341, 343–344, 365, 383, 407, 419, 423
Exportation of the law / legal transplantation, 12–15, 17, 62, 329–330
Exhaustion / parallel importations, 33, 37, 40, 53, 231

Fair
  process / trial, 25–26, 41, 60, 66, 70, 72, 75, 78, 86, 119, 122, 124, 128–130, 133, 141, 176, 183, 285, 308, 323, 335, 340, 395, 405
  use, 108, 176, 178, 180, 184, 227, 229–230, 233, 235, 240, 324, 383, 429
*FAPAV v Italia Telecom*, 131
*Flava Works, Inc. v. Gunter*, 243
Flexibilities – flexibility, 256, 322, 352–354, 419–420
Foreign direct investment, 261, 425–426
Forfeiture, 41, 237, 241–243, 256, 403–404, 419
Forum shifting, xvi, 21–22, 24, 114, 151, 202, 205, 212, 264, 319, 385, 430
Foundation for a Free Information Infrastructure – FFII, 203, 265, 300, 352, 437
Free Trade Agreements / Preferential Trade Agreements
  Australia-US FTA (AUSFTA), 169, 181, 226, 232
  Bahrain-US FTA, 232
  Canada-EU (Comprehensive Economic and Trade Agreement – CETA), 114, 170, 213, 221, 355, 437
  CARICOM-EU, 259
  Cariforum-EU, 48, 56, 63
  Central America and the Dominican Republic-US FTA, 232
  Central America and EU, 63
  Chile-US FTA, 227, 231, 233
  Colombia-EU, 48, 56, 63, 259
  Free Trade Area of the Americas – FTAA, 204
  India-EU, 10, 259, 262
  Japan-EU, 259
  Korea, Republic of -EU, 63, 259
  Korea, Republic of -US FTA, 124, 232, 234
  Morocco-US FTA, 205, 232, 358
  Singapore-US FTA, 232, 358
  Transatlantic Trade and Investment Partnership – TTIP, 11, 259, 269, 288, 298, 382, 439
  Trans-pacific Partnership Agreement – TPP, 7, 23, 27, 28, 114, 157, 170, 175, 191, 200, 201, 205, 212, 213, 221, 225–235, 239, 259, 263, 267, 309, 319, 336, 373, 374, 375, 379, 416, 417, 419, 424, 430, 437, 438, 439
  Trans-Pacific Strategic Economic Partnership Agreement-TPSEP/P4Vietnam-EU, 264
Freedom of
  association, 72
  expression, 25, 41, 60, 66, 72, 76, 96, 109, 117, 122, 124, 128, 129, 133, 139, 141, 176, 183, 204, 220, 281, 284–287, 299, 305, 306, 308, 323, 335, 405, 415, 432
Fundamental
  principles, xvi, 41, 60, 66, 77, 79, 122, 124, 125, 128–130, 183
  rights, 4, 9, 11, 12, 15, 16, 24–27, 66, 72, 76, 108, 109, 127, 128, 141, 176, 204, 207, 214, 217, 265, 281, 284–287, 293, 298–300, 305, 307–309, 315, 323, 326, 334, 335, 355, 359, 405, 420, 421, 424, 427

G-8, 146, 151
General Agreement on Tariffs and Trade – GATT, 65, 88, 151, 205, 363–365, 368, 387, 432
Geographical indication, 3, 32, 64, 84, 92, 333, 334, 339, 342, 438
George, Anna, 171, 191
Germany
  German Copyright Act, 120, 131–134
  German International Cooperation Agency – GIZ, 256
GlaxoSmithKline, 215, 247
Google, 131, 172, 177
Graduated response – 'three strikes', 17, 117, 124–127, 237–240, 266, 321, 334, 417, 425, 432, 438
Gulf Cooperation Council, 151

Hadopi, 13, 126, 237, 238, 419, 433
Health Action International, 187, 249, 251, 422
Hong Kong, 113, 151, 190, 376, 385
Hosting, 131, 144, 239, 411
Human Rights, 14, 24–27, 66, 69, 71, 109, 111, 127, 171–177, 189, 197, 201, 207, 214, 217, 284–289, 299–309, 326, 424, 427, 433, 435, 436, 439
Hungary, 100, 160, 264, 316, 412

*Inaudita parte*, 36, 75, 85, 86, 209, 351, 398
India, 10, 17, 21, 51, 52, 56, 69, 88, 95, 113, 117, 151, 187, 206, 213, 250, 251, 259, 261–269, 289, 295, 319, 320, 333, 343, 358, 359, 360–368, 371–375, 386–388, 415, 416, 423
*INS v. Chadha*, 158
Intellectual Property Enforcement Coordinator, 164
International Covenant on Economic, Social, and Cultural Rights (UN) – ICESCR, 56, 284, 299, 301–305, 307, 308
International Federation of the Phonographic Industry – IFPI, 3, 125, 282–284, 423
International Intellectual Property Alliance – IIPA, 203, 282, 353, 354, 423
International Law Commission, 47, 354, 435, 436
International non-proprietary name – INN, 91, 92, 215, 249
International Trademark Association – INTA, 46, 49, 74, 80, 107, 182, 265, 266, 273, 274, 278, 284, 313, 327
Internet
  Internet Corporation for Assigned Names and Numbers – ICANN, 196
  Internet Governance Forum, 152
  Internet Service Providers – ISPs, 5, 32, 33, 102, 117, 122, 234, 237, 239, 240, 279, 292, 322, 326, 335, 353, 391, 405
INTERPOL, 275, 276, 286
*INTERTANKO & Others v. Secretary of State for Transport*, 105
IP Justice White Paper, 149, 150, 421
Israel, 131
Issa, Darrell, 198

*James and Others v. The United Kingdom*, 72
Japan, 27, 31, 41, 54, 55, 63, 100, 114, 115, 137, 139, 145, 196, 203, 259, 263, 264, 273, 278, 281, 297, 300, 314, 316, 317, 341, 345, 359, 366, 372, 376, 383, 385, 412, 413, 420, 435
Joint Recommendation Concerning Provisions on the Protection of Marks and Other Industrial Property Rights in Signs on the Internet, 119
Jordan, 205, 358
*JT International SA v. Commonwealth*, 183

Kenya, 214, 244–257
Kirk, Ron, 27, 158, 161, 229, 232, 346
Knowledge Ecology International – KEI, 179, 194, 226, 239, 266, 267, 347, 380, 438
Koh, Harold, 162
Kuwait, 151
Kyoto Convention on the Simplification and Harmonization of Customs Procedures, 62

*Lenz v Universal Music Corp*, 133
*Lexmark International v Static Control Components*, 140
Library Copyright Alliance – LCA, 229, 230, 233
*LSG v Tele2*, 131
Ludlam, Scott, 175, 200

*Made in the USA Foundation v. United States* , 176
Max Planck Institute, 50, 56, 93, 94, 106, 110, 111, 227, 322, 343, 371, 421, 422, 424–426
Megaupload, 194, 439
Mexico, 31, 54, 57, 115, 145, 196, 203, 205, 264, 266, 273, 278, 281, 354, 358, 377
*Monis* v. *The Queen*, 176
Morocco, 31, 100, 114, 145, 151, 203, 211, 264, 278, 281, 300, 314, 316, 341, 358, 377, 415
*Murray v. Schooner Charming Betsy*, 168

NASA, 240
National Council to Combat Counterfeiting and Piracy, 206
*Network Ten Pty Ltd* v. *Ten Channel Nine*, 178
New Zealand, 31, 54, 57, 100, 114, 115, 126, 136, 137, 145, 191, 194, 196, 200, 201, 203, 225, 226, 237, 263, 264, 267, 278, 281, 300, 314, 316, 342, 349, 376, 385, 412, 418, 423, 425, 429, 431, 435
Norway, 123, 131, 371, 385

Obama, Barack, 160, 182, 201, 202, 240, 267, 292, 425, 437, 439
*Ochieng v Attorney General* , 214
Oman, 151
Online service provider – OSP, 41, 67, 117, 122–125, 129–133, 141, 142, 183, 240, 285, 335, 353, 405
Opinion of European Academics on Anti-Counterfeiting Trade Agreement, 7, 46, 51, 55, 82, 116, 204, 265, 300, 322, 324, 419
Organised crime, 2, 32, 111, 169, 182, 286
Oxfam, 187, 428

Packaging / plain packaging, 33, 40, 45, 170, 171, 182, 184, 189–191, 201, 214, 246, 248, 249, 275, 277, 393, 402, 423, 425, 429, 431, 432, 439
Paris Convention, 33, 51, 64, 148

Parke, Melissa , 173
Patent Cooperation Treaty, 148
*Patricia Asero Ochieng, Maurine Atieno and Joseph Munyi v The Republic*, 245
Peer-to-peer (P2P) / file sharing, 17, 42, 65, 77, 112, 113, 119, 121, 126, 127, 219, 237, 239, 241, 274, 284, 315, 321, 324, 326, 339, 350, 372, 373, 388, 426, 428, 433, 434, 437
Pharmaceutical products – medicines, 20, 25, 33, 36–38, 40, 51, 52, 56, 69, 70, 88–98, 102, 116, 123, 171, 185–189, 203, 206, 214, 215, 220, 235, 244–258, 262, 269, 275, 276, 279, 295, 332, 333, 350, 363, 388, 423, 424, 426–431, 435, 436, 438, 439
Pharmaceutical Research and Manufacturers of America – PhRMA, 185, 203
Philip Morris, 190
*Philips-Nokia*, 38, 332
Poland, 7, 100, 107, 203, 264, 296, 316, 412
Privacy, 25, 34, 40, 41, 59, 60, 61, 66, 67, 72, 76, 85, 109, 117, 119, 122, 124–134, 141, 171, 176, 177, 180, 183, 207, 220, 279, 281, 284, 285, 287, 299, 308, 323, 335, 341, 393, 401, 405, 431, 437
*Promusicae v. Telefonica* , 72, 131
Proportionality principle, 14, 16, 60, 66, 71, 72, 74, 76, 77, 79, 87, 94, 106, 109, 119, 130, 133, 178–180, 208, 323, 340, 351, 395
Public
  domain, 201, 240
  goods, 15, 31, 45, 109, 150, 426
  health, 4, 33, 56, 82, 92–97, 111, 152, 186, 189, 191, 201, 205, 206, 214, 215, 244, 245, 255–258, 262, 286, 329, 332, 333, 363, 366, 367, 368, 370, 374, 383, 386, 392, 426, 428, 429, 431, 432
  interest, 374, 383, 386, 392, 426, 428, 429, 431, 432

Qatar, 94, 151

*R (on application of) BT PLC and Talk Talk PLC -v- Secretary of State for Business, Innovation and Skills and others*, 123, 151
Rapidshare, 123
*Real Networks vs. Apple*, 140
Republic of Korea, 31, 63, 100, 115, 124, 126, 145, 150, 196, 203, 205, 232, 233, 237, 259, 263, 264, 281, 300, 314, 316, 341, 349, 376, 385, 412, 427, 435
Retail price, 18, 35, 83, 179, 396
Right to
  health, 188
  human dignity, 214, 245, 248
  information, 26, 76, 78, 118, 120, 127, 129, 130, 132, 236, 376
  life, 214, 248, 257
*Roadshow Films Pty Ltd v iiNet Ltd*, 123
Rome Convention, 230
Russia, 103, 151, 289, 303, 320, 359
Rwanda, 187, 245, 429

*Saadi c. Italia*, 72
*SABAM v Netlog*, 72, 326
Saudi Arabia, 151
*Scarlet Extended SA v SABAM*, 71, 72
Secondary liability, 58, 59, 68, 182, 252, 326, 350, 351
Seizure
  of assets, 41, 351, 403
  of goods, 85, 88, 95, 206, 215, 339
Senate Finance Committee, 160, 164
Singapore, 31, 57, 100, 103, 114, 115, 151, 196, 200, 205, 227, 259, 264, 267, 281, 298, 300, 308, 314, 316, 341, 358, 376, 377, 385, 415, 439
Small consignments / quantities, 37, 76, 352, 399
Small and medium enterprises – SMEs, 36, 280, 282
*Sophie in 't Veld v Commission*, 288
Spain, 100, 126, 136, 264, 282, 283, 285, 316, 354, 412, 438
*Stevens v. Sony*, 181
*Stichting BREIN NL v Euroaccess Enterprises LTD*, 131
Suspect goods, 38, 39, 73, 85, 93, 215, 351, 398–402
Sweden, 100, 264, 316, 347, 348, 412, 440
Switzerland, 31, 101, 115, 131, 137, 196, 203, 264, 278, 330, 333, 341, 353, 360–362, 370, 372, 376, 385, 429

Taiwan, 126
Technical assistance, 43, 149, 164, 368, 388, 389, 409
Technological/technical protection measures – TPM , 13, 118, 178, 179, 181, 207, 226, 338, 354
Technology transfer, 31, 45, 153, 259, 261, 262, 332, 375, 416, 425, 426, 430
*The Pirate Bay*, 112, 113, 123, 418
Three-Step Test, 225–235, 426
Trademark
  owners, 36, 182, 183, 275
  trademarked goods, 20, 34, 36, 37, 40, 245
Transparency, 8, 9, 11, 42, 44, 76, 101, 115, 116, 143, 146, 157, 170, 182, 195, 196, 198–200, 202, 211, 225, 261, 265, 266, 278, 281, 282, 287, 295, 298, 315, 316, 321, 323, 346–349, 356, 358, 360, 362, 364, 377, 379–381, 390, 408, 418, 420, 425, 435, 438

Ukraine, 190
UNESCO, 205, 286, 287, 435
United Arab Emirates, 151, 205, 358, 377
United States – US
Digital Millennium Copyright Act (DMCA), 117, 122, 136–138, 227, 240, 425
executive agreements, 158–159, 163–164, 166, 417
Freedom of Information Act – FOIA, 202, 203, 267, 349
Protect Intellectual Property Act – PIPA, 3, 6, 7, 220, 228, 235, 279, 294
Stop Online Piracy Act – SOPA, 6, 220, 225, 279, 294
*United States v. Dotcom*, 194
*United States v. HQ-Streams.com*, 242
*United States v. Pink*, 159
*United States v. Rojadirecta.org*, 243
United States Trade Representative, 148, 158, 170, 185, 190, 191, 200, 288, 381, 435
US Constitution, 207, 432
US Copyright Act, 229, 230, 233, 237
Uruguay Round, 103, 209

Vagueness, 15, 24, 173
Vienna Convention on the Law of Treaties, 8, 47, 49, 50, 55, 57, 77, 167, 210, 279, 300, 387

Washington Declaration on Intellectual Property and the Public Interest, 201
Washington Treaty on Intellectual Property in Respect of Integrated Circuits, 148
WikiLeaks, 266, 294, 347
World Conference on International Telecommunications – WCIT, 298
World Customs Organization – WCO, 21, 205, 247, 319
World Health Organization – WHO, 189, 247, 276, 347
World Intellectual Property Organization – WIPO, 2, 6, 8, 10, 21, 23, 33, 42, 55, 56, 57, 101, 116, 118, 119, 124, 136, 137, 141, 147, 151, 153, 154, 193–197, 205, 212, 227, 231, 264, 266, 288, 317, 319, 323, 327–329, 343, 347, 348, 369, 372, 373, 375, 376, 379, 380, 383, 384, 389, 415–417, 419, 420, 423, 426, 429, 430, 433, 436, 437
World Intellectual Property Organization Internet treaties, 23, 42, 118, 136, 137, 148, 231–233, 352, 354, 355, 420
World Summit on the Information Society, 152, 436
World Trade Organisation – WTO
Appellate Body, 51–54, 94, 95, 263
*Canada – Patent Protection of Pharmaceutical Products*, 37, 56, 69, 70, 96
*China – Measures Affecting the Protection and Enforcement of Intellectual Property Rights*, 21, 40, 49, 52, 67, 104, 110, 120, 150, 268, 317, 367, 378, 386, 420
*European Union and a Member State – Seizure of Generic Drugs in Transit*, 56, 69, 88, 95, 206, 215
General Council Decision on Implementation of Paragraph 6 of the Doha Declaration on the TRIPS Agreement and Public Health, 186
*Havana Club*, 64
*Japan – Taxes on Alcoholic Beverages*, 55
*United States – Section 211 Omnibus Appropriations Act of 1998*, 55
*United States – Standards for Reformulated and Conventional Gasoline*, 55
Wyden, Ron, 161